The Seed Catalog

BAKER-CHICAGO

The Seed Catalog

A Guide to Teaching/Learning Materials

by Jeffrey Schrank

Beacon Press Boston

For those sowing the seeds of learning for future generations

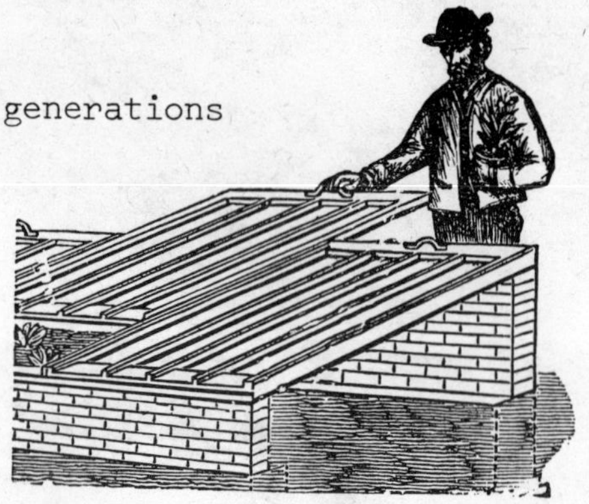

Beacon Press books are published under the auspices
of the Unitarian Universalist Association

Simultaneous publication in Canada by Saunders of Toronto, Ltd.

Published in simultaneous hardcover and paperback editions

9 8 7 6 5 4 3 2

Library of Congress Cataloging in Publication Data

Schrank, Jeffrey.
The seed catalog; a guide to teaching/learning materials.

1. Teaching--Aids and devices. 2. Educational innovations. I. Title.
LB1027.S36628 371.3'078 73-16888
ISBN 0-8070-3164-X
ISBN 0-8070-3165-8

Contents

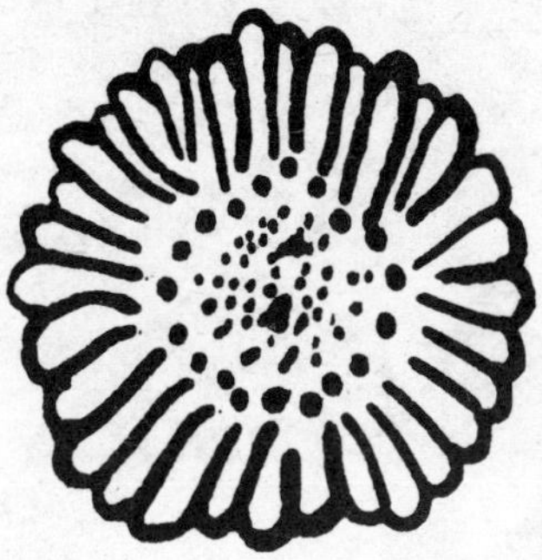

Introduction

The Seed Catalog: A Guide to Teaching/Learning Materials is a compendium of idea seeds. In these pages can be found access information to thousands of people, groups, books, films, tapes and records, publications, games, videotapes, and devices to provoke and educate.

The catalog is not written just for people living in country communes or working in free schools, but also for those in any situation who believe that learning takes place through involvement with a great variety of viewpoints and opinions. It is for professional educators as well as people who know that they can learn outside of school.

The Seed Catalog is by all means biased and opinionated. The materials included are more likely to be comparatively inexpensive rather than a $300 learning package. The materials are biased toward high school and adult learners, since they have been more neglected in educational reform than younger children. The catalog is prejudiced in favor of the humanities and the communication arts with special emphasis on media education.

It is biased in favor of provocative, creative, and controversial material and tends to neglect the standard and schoolish.

It is my hope that some of the learning seeds in this book will fall upon good ground and take root.

Jeffrey Schrank

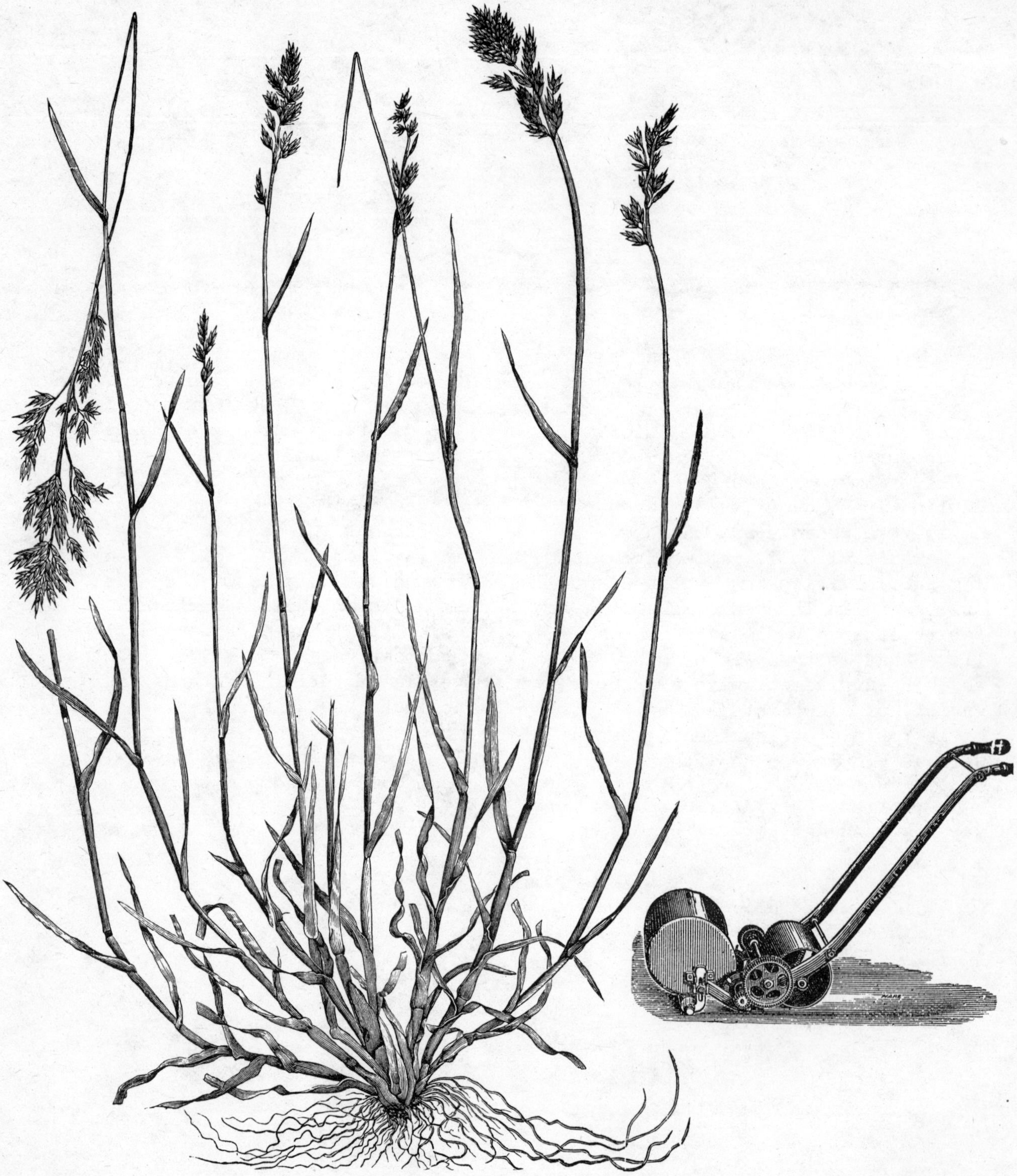

Publications

STUDENTS NONVIOLENT ACTION

TRAINING FOR NONVIOLENT ACTION FOR HIGH SCHOOL STUDENTS is a handbook prepared by the Friends Peace Committee based on much field work with students. $1 from Friends Peace Committee, 1515 Cherry St., Philadelphia, Pa. 19102.

CONTENTS

2 Publications

"We've tried nonviolence and it didn't work."

A friend of mine drew this, based on a comment by Martin Luther King: It was to the effect that when you throw water on a fire and the fire doesn't go out, you don't conclude that water doesn't put out fire, you get more water!

For those who make, or have heard, comments like this, I have some questions. Have you really tried enough? Are you well organized? Are you pursuing truth, not just your own interests? Are you really being nonviolent? Or are you passive and subordinate? Have you suffered any consequences as a result of your efforts?

"You're wasting your time! I tried water and it didn't put out the fire!"

PUBLIC AFFAIRS PAMPHLETS

Public Affairs Pamphlets are available on a wide range of topics and cost only 18¢ - 35¢ each, depending on quantity. A complete catalog is free from:

PUBLIC AFFAIRS PAMPHLETS
381 Park Avenue South
New York, N.Y. 10016

The Public Affairs Committee, a nonpartisan, nonprofit organization, was founded in 1935 "to develop new techniques to educate the American public on vital economic and social problems and to issue concise and interesting pamphlets dealing with such problems."

Public Affairs Pamphlets were the outgrowth of this action. During more than three decades they have gained a unique reputation for timeliness, accuracy, and readability. Keeping pace with changing needs and interests, today Public Affairs Pamphlets deal with family relationships and child development, health and science, and race relations as well as with social and economic issues.

pamphlet prices—how to order

quantity	same title	mixed titles
1 to 3 copies	35¢ each	35¢ each
4 to 9 copies	30¢ each	31¢ each
10 to 99 copies	23¢ each	24¢ each
100 to 249 copies	21¢ each	22¢ each
250 to 499 copies	20¢ each	21¢ each
500 to 999 copies	18¢ each	19¢ each
1000 to 4999 copies	17¢ each	18¢ each

Rates for larger quantities are available upon request. We pay postage on prepaid orders. All orders under $5 must be prepaid, by check or money order, please; no cash or stamps. On orders for $1.00 or less, please include 10 cents for handling.

493. WHEN PEOPLE NEED HELP, by Maxwell S. Stewart

492. SECURING THE LEGAL RIGHTS OF RETARDED PERSONS, by Elizabeth Ogg

489. THE BILL OF RIGHTS TODAY, by Thomas I. Emerson

487. A NEW LOOK AT COOPERATIVES, by Philip J. Dodge

484. HOMOSEXUALITY IN OUR SOCIETY, by Elizabeth Ogg

481. PUBLIC SERVICE EMPLOYMENT: JOBS FOR ALL, by Robert Lekachman

477. PORNOGRAPHY: THE ISSUES AND THE LAW, by Kenneth P. Norwick

474. SENSITIVITY TRAINING AND ENCOUNTER GROUPS, by Elizabeth Ogg

471. CAN WE AVOID ECONOMIC CRISES? by Maxwell S. Stewart

470. DAY CARE FOR AMERICA'S CHILDREN, by E. Robert LaCrosse

469. WOMEN'S RIGHTS — UNFINISHED BUSINESS, by Eleanor Flexner

461. MONEY FOR OUR CITIES: IS REVENUE SHARING THE ANSWER? by Maxwell S. Stewart

458. UNLOCKING HUMAN RESOURCES: A CAREER IN SOCIAL WORK, by Patricia W. Soyka

457. HUNGER IN AMERICA, by Maxwell S. Stewart

455. SOCIAL POLICY—IMPROVING THE HUMAN CONDITION, by John H. McMahon

453. **THE RESPONSIBLE CONSUMER, by Sidney Margolius**

450. **VIOLENCE IN AMERICA, by Irvin Block**

444. **A CHANCE FOR EVERY CHILD: THE CASE FOR CHILDREN'S ALLOWANCES, by Maxwell S. Stewart**

440. **THE UNMARRIED MOTHER, by Alice Shiller**

436. **WHAT ABOUT MARIJUANA? by Jules Saltman**

434. **WANTED: A WORLD LANGUAGE, by Mario Pei**

433. **LAW AND JUSTICE, by Joseph L. Sax**

431. **THE ECUMENICAL MOVEMENT, by Lee E. Dirks**

429. **WHEN SHOULD ABORTION BE LEGAL? by Harriet F. Pilpel and Kenneth P. Norwick**

428. **TELL ME WHERE TO TURN, by Elizabeth Ogg**

subscriptions

Keep up to date on many important public issues and family concerns by subscribing to the Public Affairs Pamphlet series. About 15 new titles are published each year. To receive each pamphlet upon publication, subscribe at these low rates: 15 issues, $4.50; 30 issues, $7.50; 45 issues, $10.00. Foreign rates on request.

public affairs pamphlet library

You can have a library of all Public Affairs Pamphlets now in print (about 200), plus a subscription to the next 15 issues, at the special rate of $27.50.

special packets

Selected Public Affairs Pamphlets come in packets useful for parents, teachers, doctors, therapists, ministers, and group discussion leaders.

Family Relations Packet—60 booklets—**$10.80**
Social Problems Packet—32 booklets— **$6.00**
Guidance Counselor's Packet—22 booklets—**$4.50**
Doctor's Packet—30 booklets—**$5.95**
Write for brochure describing each packet.

film program

The Public Affairs Committee also produces films on health and mental health topics, each with a companion pamphlet. Five films are currently available for purchase or rental: **Tell Me Where to Turn, Nine Months to Get Ready, Right From the Start, Headed for Trouble, Diabetics Unknown.** For details, write Public Affairs Committee, Film Dept.

reading for an age of change

Write for a descriptive folder on this series of ten reading guides on the arts and sciences today. Published jointly with the American Library Association.

HUMAN RIGHTS ORGANIZATIONS AND PERIODICALS DIRECTORY

The Human Rights Organizations and Periodicals Directory is published by the Meiklejohn Civil Liberties Institute.

This Directory lists organizations and periodicals concerned with human rights, with particular emphasis on those providing information or assistance on legal questions and engaging in litigation. We intend this list as a referral list for people seeking legal information or assistance in human rights cases; as a guide for students and researchers seeking hard-to-find sources of information; and as a resource for attorneys concerned with human rights cases. It may prove particularly useful to librarians as a guide in ordering periodicals to broaden the scope of their periodical holdings and to refer patrons for further communication with the organizations.

The literature published and distributed by some of these groups is not well-publicized, but is a vital source of information, as it is written by the participants in the struggle for justice, rather than by the observers of this struggle. Their point of view and investigative reporting differ from that usually found in the mass media.

The Directory is arranged both in alphabetical order and by areas of concern. $4.00 from:

LEGAL PUBLICATIONS
Box 673
Berkeley, Calif. 94701

California Rural Legal Assistance: NOTICIERO. Quarterly. 1212 Market St, San Francisco, Calif 94102.
CRLA is a federally-funded litigation service for the rural poor. NOTICIERO reports poverty law developments affecting rural minority families.

Center for Constitutional Rights: DOCKET REPORT. Twice a year. 588 Ninth Ave, New York, NY 10036. Free to donors.
Non-profit legal center dedicated to creative use of law as a positive force for social change; attorneys conduct litigation on discrimination, repression and social injustice. DOCKET covers the nature and current status of the Center's litigation and educational work.

4 Publications

Center for New Corporate Priorities: NEWSLETTER and REPORTS. Irregular. 304 S Ardmore, Suite 101, Los Angeles, Calif 90020. Subscription with membership: $10/yr.
Prepares research materials on corporate social policy; corporations' impact on society and politics (minority and women's rights, imperialism, ecology, etc.); provides research.

Center for Responsive Psychology: SOCIAL ACTION AND THE LAW. Bimonthly. Brooklyn College, Brooklyn, NY 11210. $5/yr.
Presents findings and ongoing research in social sciences to aid lawyers and others in legal, judicial and correctional disciplines.

Center for the Study of Legal Authority and Mental Patient Status (LAMP). c/o Bob Roth, 2014 Channing Way, Berkeley, Calif 94704.
Research center and clearinghouse for information on mental patients' civil rights; presently in transition to a litigation/advocacy agency with Bay Area focus.

National Senior Citizens Law Center: SENIORS IN SACRAMENTO. Twice a month. 1003 Forum Bldg, Sacramento, Calif 95814. $6/yr; free to Legal Service lawyers and those with incomes below OEO level.
Established by OEO, Center is the central national resource for legal problems of the low-income elderly; works with Legal Services programs. SENIORS IN SACRAMENTO reports on legislation affecting senior citizens: health, income, transportation, consumer, taxation, etc.

National Tenants Information Service: TENANTS OUTLOOK. Monthly. 425 13th St NW, Washington, DC 20004. $12/yr.
Information unit of National Tenants' Organization; concerned with tenants' rights, housing policy, landlord-tenant relations, urban environmental issues.

National Welfare Rights Organization: THE WELFARE FIGHTER. Monthly. 1424 16th St NW, Washington, DC 20036. Mailed to members and supporters who contribute $10/yr. This includes $2 for subscription to WELARE FIGHTER.
NWRO is an organization of welfare recipients and poor people with many local groups promoting goals of adequate income, rights and dignity of poor. WELFARE FIGHTER reports legislation and administrative decisions affecting poor, NWRO actions, conditions of poor.

National Women's Political Caucus: NEWSLETTER. 1302 18th St NW #603, Washington, DC 20036. $10/yr.
Promotes woman candidates; lobbies for action on women's issues.

National Women's Political Caucus of Northern California: NEWSLETTER. 1717 Berkeley Way, Berkeley, Calif 94703.

Native American Rights Fund: ANNOUNCEMENTS. Monthly. 1506 Broadway, Boulder, Colo 80302. Free to individuals; libraries $10/yr.
Reports history and litigation progress of matters involving Native Americans in which the Fund is involved; recent acquisitions of the National Indian Law Library of the Native American Rights Fund.

NORTH AMERICAN CONGRESS ON LATIN AMERICA LITERATURE

Yanqui Dollar: The contribution of U.S. Private Investment to Underdevelopment in Latin America (1971, 64 pages). A pamphlet on U.S. private investments in Latin America -- how they got there, what are their newest forms, how they have been modified in response to nationalism, and their effects and contributions to underdevelopment in Latin America. Well illustrated with graphics and charts. Single copies: $1.00 plus 25¢ postage; bulk orders (postage extra): 10-49 copies, 75¢ each; 50 or more copies, 60¢ each.

The NACLA Research Methodology Guide (1970, 76 pages). A comprehensive guide to research the U.S. Establishment and its overseas empire. Over 20,000 copies of this "how to do it" manual have already been sold. Includes chapters on Corporations, Labor, Political Parties, Personalities and Elites, the Military-Industrial Complex and the Universities, the Church, the Police, Imperialism and the Third World. Single copies: $1.00 plus 25¢ postage; bulk orders (postage extra): 10-49 copies, 75¢ each; 50 or more copies, 60¢ each.

NACLA Handbook: The U.S. Military Apparatus (1972, 108 pages). A comprehensive introductory guide to America's worldwide military apparatus, with extensive documentation and analysis on Department of Defense organization, the U.S. intelligence apparatus, U.S. military force structure, military police aid programs, arms sales, U.S. bases and forces abroad, etc. Includes a research guide on the military apparatus, maps, charts and tables. Single copies: $1.25 plus 25¢ postage; bulk orders (postage extra): 10-49 copies, $1.00 each; 50 or more copies, 75¢ each.

Subliminal Warfare -- The Role of Latin American Studies (1970, 68 pages). An analysis of how agencies of cultural imperialism service U.S. corporate and military domination of the Third World. Includes charts, tables and graphs on U.S. foundations, government organizations and universities active in Latin American affairs, plus a study of social science research and counterinsurgency, and one on the politics of cultural exchange (the Institute for International Education). Single copies: 75¢ plus 25¢ postage; bulk orders (postage extra): 10-49 copies, 60¢ each; 50 or more copies, 40¢ each.

Who Rules Columbia? (1968, 44 pages plus fold-out chart of Columbia's Ruling Elite). Originally published in June 1968 following the historic Columbia University strike, this analysis of the Columbia power structure has served as the model for dozens of institutional studies. Describe the nature of Columbia's ties with the CIA, the Institure of Defense Analyses, the Department of Defense, etc., and presents a documented analysis of the corporate, financial and real estate interests which govern the university. New edition includes original text plus additional documents, and fold-out chart. Single copies: 75¢ plus 25¢ postage; bulk orders (postage extra): 10-49 copies, 60¢ each; 40 or more copies, 40¢ each.

The Rockefeller Empire/Latin America (1969, 32 pages). A special reprint of two NACLA Newsletters cataloging the Rockefeller family's holdings and operations in Latin America -- including oil companies, estates, banks, resorts, "non profit" front organizations, etc. Also includes a description of Nelson Rockefeller's entourage during his 1969 fact-finding mission in Latin America. Single copies: 50¢ plus 15¢ postage; bulk orders (postage extra): 10-49 copies, 35¢ each; 50 or more copies, 30¢ each.

The University-Military-Police Complex (1970, 92 pages). The most comprehensive tabulation in print of military and police research on U.S. campuses. Contains an introductory essay, descriptions of some 40 military research organizations, and inventories of campus-based research on chemical and biological warfare, foreign affairs, and law enforcement. All documents are cross-indexed to expedite the correlation of data. Single copies: $1.00 plus 25¢ postage; bulk orders (postage extra); 10-49 copies, 75¢ each; 50 or more copies, 60¢ each.

U.S. Military and Police Operations in the Third World (1971, 32 pages). A basic compendium of data on U.S. forces stationed abroad, the Military Assistance Program, AID's police assistance programs, military and police training activities in the U.S., etc. Includes two articles from the NACLA Newsletter, "U.S. Military Operations/Latin America" and "U.S. Police Assistance Programs in Latin America," plus a list of U.S. bases in the Third World and an inventory of all U.S. military interventions abroad from 1789 to 1945. Single copies: 50¢ plus 15¢ postage; bulk orders (postage extra): 10-49 copies, 35¢ each; 50 or more copies, 30¢ each.

6 Publications

Please send the following:

SUBSCRIPTION TO NACLA'S LATIN AMERICA & EMPIRE REPORT
(check subscription category and number of years)

1 year	2 years	Subscription category
$6	$11	Individuals
$12	$22	Non-profit institutions
$20	$40	Profit making & military

[ ] Airmail -- add $8 per year.

NACLA PUBLICATIONS

____ copies of NEW CHILE
____ copies of YANQUI DOLLAR
____ copies of THE NACLA RESEARCH METHODOLOGY GUIDE
____ copies of NACLA HANDBOOK: U.S. MILITARY APPARATUS
____ copies of SUBLIMINAL WARFARE
____ copies of WHO RULES COLUMBIA?
____ copies of THE ROCKEFELLER EMPIRE/LATIN AMERICA
____ copies of THE UNIVERSITY-MILITARY-POLICE COMPLEX
____ copies of U.S. MILITARY & POLICE OPERATIONS
____ copies of THE GREAT SOUTH ASIAN WAR
____ copies of SPECIAL REPORT: ELECTION 1972

Enclosed find $_________ (NOTE: payment must accompany all individual orders; add 10% for postage on bulk orders)

Mail this form to:
NACLA-EAST, Box 57, Cathedral Station, New York, N.Y. 10025 or
NACLA-WEST, Box 226, Berkeley, Cal. 94701

NAME:______________________________

ADDRESS:______________________________

______________________ ____zip________

The Great South Asian War: U.S. Imperial Strategy in Asia (1970, 16 pages). A reprint of two articles by Mike Klare on U.S. military policy in the Pacific-Indian Ocean area: "The Great South Asian War," from The NATION; and "U.S. 'Basing Arrangements' in Asia," from COMMONWEAL. An analysis of the role of Vietnam in U.S. global strategy. Single copies: 35¢ plus 10¢ postage; bulk orders (postage extra): 10-49 copies, 25¢; 50-99 copies, 20¢; 100 or more copies, 15¢.

Special Report: Election 1972 (1972, 32 pages). Two articles which tell the story of Nixon administration corruption and political spying, concentrating on relationships to Organized Crime and the Watergate Affair. Single copies: 75¢ plus 25¢ postage; bulk orders (postage extra): 10-49 copies, 60¢ each; 50 or more copies, 40¢ each.

NACLA's Latin America & Empire Report (Formerly *NACLA Newsletter*). Each month the NACLA REPORT contains another chapter in the story of U.S. domination of Latin America -- naming names, corporations, foundations, lobbies, government agencies, universities, etc. These feature articles are accompanied by reprints and translation of important articles, book reviews, and significant research documents. Minimum contribution for one-year subscription (ten issues): individuals, $6.00 ($11.00 for two years); libraries and non-profit institutions, $12.00 ($22.00 for two years); profit making and military, $20.00 ($40.00 for two years). Air mail abroad: add $8.00 per year. Back issues: $1.00 per issue or $10.00 per volume.

Kalondi in PRIMERA PLANA, Buenos Aires

TIMES CHANGE PRESS

TIMES CHANGE PRESS
PENWELL RD. WASHINGTON, N.J. 07882
(201) 689-6659

Times Change Press is a not-for-profit, alternative press publishing books, pamphlets and posters on personal/political liberation. Our material covers a wide range of subjects including women's liberation and history, alternate culture, third world struggles, gay liberation, men's consciousness-raising, revolutionary poetry, youth liberation, ecology, etc.

With Winter '72/'73 publication, we've decided to publish some longer works, making hard cover editions of these available, especially for library use. In addition to bookstore distribution, we fill pre-paid orders sent directly to us by individuals. TCP publications are also widely used as course material in high schools and colleges.

HIP CULTURE: 6 ESSAYS ON ITS REVOLUTIONARY POTENTIAL

These are views of hip culture from people who are intimately involved (yippie, high school student, feminist, third world), with two short theoretical views (anarchist and marxist).

Hopefully, these disparate views will all add up to a comprehensive picture that we can use to make our own decisions about where, in a complex and changing "alternate culture", we see ourselves fitting.

SBN 87810-010-5; 64 pgs; $1.25

FREE OURSELVES
FORGOTTEN GOALS OF THE REVOLUTION

ARTHUR ARON **Illustrations by Elaine N. Blesi**

Free Ourselves is a book that sees social change and individual change as two aspects of the same struggle. Art discusses both these aspects as part of a more wholistic approach to revolution, an approach that many of us are now involved in developing.

We do need to remember the forgotten goals of the revolution. We need to remember that although liberation struggles have different realities, different needs—they all share the same aspiration: personal and political freedom. *Illustrated.*

SBN 87810-018-0; 64 pgs; NEW SQUARE BINDING; $1.35

THE TUPAMAROS
URBAN GUERRILLAS OF URUGUAY

CARLOS NÚÑEZ

This pamphlet tells the story, historically set by Tom Wodetzki, of the Tupamaros: their origin, popular support, political goals and tactics. The Tupas have combined guerrilla theatre and carefully-used violence in an assault on the government of the most western of Latin American countries. Certainly no blue-print for us—but a good source for developing our own way of bringing guerrilla warfare to the city.

SBN 87810-008-3; 48 pgs; $1.00

UNBECOMING MEN
A MEN'S CONSCIOUSNESS-RAISING GROUP WRITES ON OPPRESSION AND THEMSELVES

This pamphlet was written by a group of men who've come together because of their increasingly unavoidable awareness of sexism—how it operates against the people they most care for and ultimately, how it eats away at their own humanity.

These writings reflect their struggle, once the superficial layers of male competency and coolness were stripped away, to face the rigidity, emptiness and self-doubt that each individual found they all shared.

The response to *Unbecoming Men*, by men and women, straight and gay, has been so good that we've made a second printing. *Illustrated.*

SBN 87810-015-6; 64 pgs; NEW SQUARE BINDING; $1.35

GENERATIONS OF DENIAL
75 SHORT BIOGRAPHIES OF WOMEN IN HISTORY

KATHRYN TAYLOR

It feels good to read about all these women—they were whole people under the worst of circumstances, especially for those who, in addition to being female, were gay. Each one had to fight to participate in her society. Male supremist history continued the battle by ignoring their achievements or by falsely crediting them to men. These biographies are a pioneering collection with which to supplement history books and, if one is a woman, one's pride. *Illustrated.*

SBN 87810-014-8; 64 pgs; $1.35

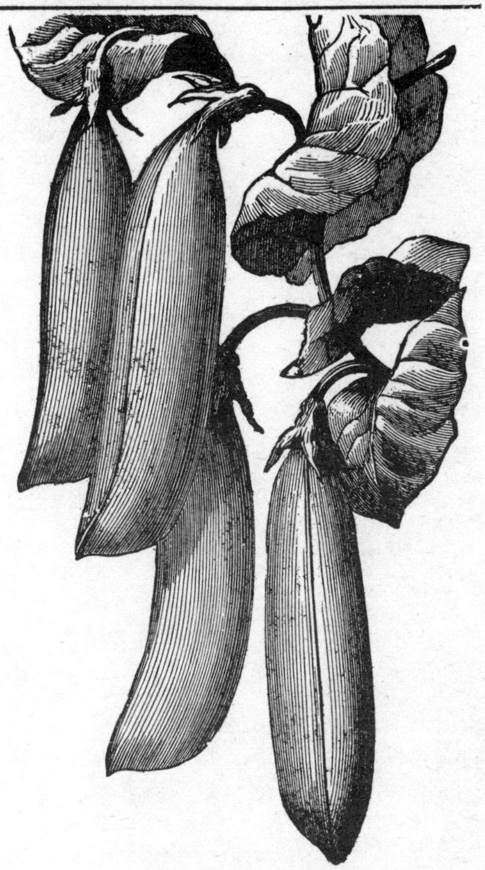

YOUTH LIBERATION
NEWS, POLITICS AND SURVIVAL INFORMATION

YOUTH LIBERATION OF ANN ARBOR

"We want power." The authors describe the oppression of being young in an adult chauvinist society: imprisonment in families and schools, economic dependence, denial of legal rights, and more. They see youth as encompassing many oppressed groups, and so their politics are broadly based.

They say *"We are the future"* because they know they are inheriting an ecologically and politically doomed world; they know that if there's to be any future at all, it's up to the youth of the world to bring it into being. *Illustrated.*

SBN 87810-019-9; 64 pgs; NEW SQUARE BINDING; $1.35

KID POWER!

Slowly surfacing now is the next big thrust for freedom (after Blacks, Women, and Gays)–the Children's Liberation Movement. Call it Kid Power if you must give it a media-type name. Many children and some adults are tired of children being told they can't go to this movie or that, tired of teachers and principals dictating what is and isn't appropriate dress, and even fed up with the way children are exploited in advertising.

As columnist Carroll Carroll commented in *Variety* this spring, children are used as "cute objects" by Madison Avenue, "forced, apparently by their parents need for residuals, to mouth platitudes and inanities that are inimical to any child's intellectual dignity." So we have a whole string of commercials exploiting freckles, tousled hair, lisps, lack of two front teeth, cuteness, cudliness–all exploited and commercialized for the sale of products. Carroll calls for an end to children as Cute Objects, as well as an end to such "denigrating descriptions" as moppet, tots, kiddies, and tykes.

If youngsters are exploited in TV commercials, consider how they're treated by the movie industry which has set up code ratings for movies–X, R, GP, etc. While these symbols are not law and are only guidelines, they are observed throughout the country. And what determines an "X" rating? Murder, gang warfare, blood, horror? No, just nudity. Let the youngsters watch double-feature violence, but God forbid they should see a nipple or two people making love to one another!

In Sweden it's just the opposite; the killings and mayhem may be regarded as unsuitable for children. Only in America could "The Vampire Strikes Again" be rated acceptable for children of all ages and "The Body," an instructive film on the functioning of the human body, rated as X, not to be viewed by anyone under age of 18, even if accompanied by Parent or Guardian, or the family doctor.

In a supposed democracy where everyone in theory has the right to life, liberty, and the pursuit of happiness, can the State order a child to attend school? In other words, are compulsory attendance laws constitutional? The free school movement has been all but obsequious toward these laws, but fortunately a growing number of homestead and commune parents are defying these laws. Schools just won't be in the picture at all.

The coming liberation of children is inevitable because deep down underneath all the loud protests to the contrary, Americans don't really appreciate their children. Oh, they live vicariously through their children's *accomplishments*, but seldom through their *joy*. They send children to school (protesting school taxes), gloat over their marks, their acceptance at college, their budding "careers," but during all those growing-up years how much do the parents groove on childhood joy?

Children's Liberation Movement is inevitable. Recent awareness of civil rights by high school students and pressing demands to assert these rights will filter down to the lower age-groups, and then the Children's Liberation Movement will be on full force. I can hardly wait.

FPS/Quicksilver Times

"I was told of a boy who, until he was almost four years old, thought that his name was 'Shut-up.' "–Shulamith Firestone, in *The Dialectics of Sex*

SANE STUDY PACKETS

Sane has a series of study packets available. Each packet includes leaflets and magazine reprints, resources, bibliography, and action ideas. Topics include:

Budget	$1.50
Disarmament	2.25
Dialogue With Middle America	2.50
Arms Conversion	1.00
Military-Industrial Complex	1.00
Peace and the News Media	.75

from:

SANE
318 Massachusetts Avenue, N.E.
Washington, D.C. 20002
(202) 546-4868

The Sane Taxpayer's Guide to the US Budget . . . *Sane*'s new information kit on the Federal Budget, the Military Budget, and National Priorities. The packet provides a basic understanding of the budget and thus the basis for the longer-range task of changing its priorities, and it includes:

"Do You Know What Your Tax Dollar Buys?" by *Sane* (discussion of the Federal Budget and its support of the military establishment, priorities within the budget -- military versus social)
"What Could Your Tax Dollars Buy?" by *Sane* (over 100 trade-offs between military and social expenditures)
"Every Gun a Theft . . ." by *Sane* (President Eisenhower's discussion of military versus social priorities)
"We're Number 1" by *Sane* (comparing America's rank among the nations in military power and the quality of life)
"Nixon's Priorities" by *Sane* (comparing Nixon's cuts in social expenditures with increases and requests for military and para-military programs)
"Bibliography" by *Sane* (resources for research on the Federal Budget, Defense Budget, and National Priorities)
"Functional Breakdown of US Government Outlays on the Federal Funds Basis for Fiscal Years 1972-1974" by *Sane* (where have all the taxes gone?)
"The Federal Budget and the Cities" by National League of Cities, US Conference of Mayors (report on Nixon's Fiscal Year 1974 budget as it affects the cities)
"A Counterbudget" by Senator William Proxmire (proposals for re-directing budgetary priorities in Fiscal Year 1974)
"New Look at the Military" by Senator George McGovern (proposals for defense budget cuts)
"How Michigan Pays for War" by Michigan Council of Churches (prototype for a study of a state's tax support of the military establishment)

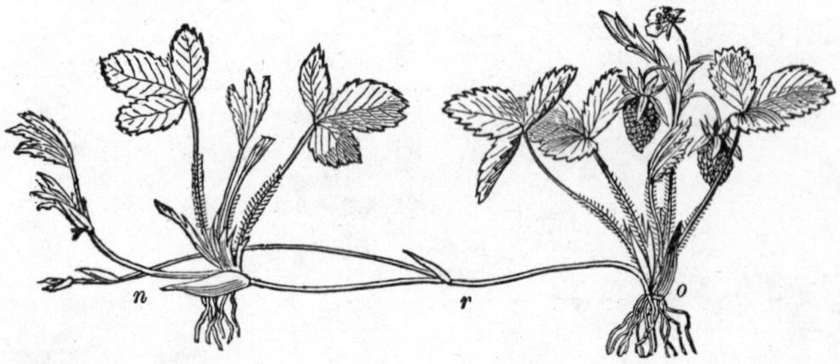

PLUS

"Translate the Words into Action" by *Sane* (citizen action proposals)

(NOTE: Periodically *Sane* revises its issue packets, deleting dated literature, adding new topical material. This will explain any possible inconsistency between the above listing of contents and the actual contents of the packet.) $1.50 prepaid
(NOTE: Each piece of literature contained in this packet is available separately from *Sane* at nominal cost.)

communities/housing

SOURCE CATALOG . . . an organizing tool . . . a resource encyclopedia of: exposes, counter institutional services, community control projects, and organizing strategies for institutional revolution. Each 150-250 page issue will contain over 800 group descriptions, plus thousands of annotated books, films, periodicals, tapes and pamphlets for consciousness raising and technical information.

14 ISSUES DEALING WITH: COMMUNITY PLANNING, COMMUNITY CONTROL, RURAL ORGANIZING, ECONOMICS, JUSTICE/REPRESSION . . .

COMMUNICATIONS CATALOG (Source No. 1) is ready for your use—$1.75—listener-controlled radio, video groups, boycotts, guerrilla theater . . .

HOUSING CATALOG (Source No. 2) $2.95 just released—tenants rights, community housing development, suburban economic and racial equality, citywide land and law battles, property tax redistributions, block busting, neighborhood control, public housing & tenant management, self help and co-op housing, peoples construction . . .

WRITE TO: SOURCE, PO BOX 21066, WASHINGTON, DC 20009, (202) 387-1145

12 Publications

Communications Catalog (Source No. 1) was put together by a group of people who traveled over 20,000 miles in a bus visiting fifty campuses during 1969-70. The plans for a resource listing quickly turned into a 13-volume resource encyclopedia. Volume I, on communications, is now available. The 118-page oversized paperback lists over 1500 organizations, films, books, pamphlets, and service groups in the categories of mass media, art, music, theater, film, TV-radio-tapes, periodicals, printing, language, libraries, and community communications. At $1.75 the book is practically a steal and an extremely valuable resource tool.

Just a tiny sample of the listings includes a service that does research on films for $3 an hour and 10¢ a xeroxed page, a videotape format magazine, access listings to underground and political films, books like Learning Through Movement and Children Make Murals and Sculpture, free publications, and much, much more. The catalog's accuracy is only fair and its film listing is weak, but still a good buy.

$1.75 postpaid from Source, Post Office Box 21066, Washington, D.C. 20009. The paperback is published by Swallow Press in Chicago and is available in some bookstores.

From
Communications Catalog (Source No. 1)

NEW YORK FREE THEATER . . . is a community theater for school kids, which, through workshops and street theater, brings community problems to focus while channelling the natural theatrics of children through self-expression and group creativity. Teachers are encouraged to incorporate these techniques into their classes and to prepare, through winter workshops, for a summer community-oriented street theater. A major project right now is to help build relations with the Cooper Union Project on the Lower East Side to induce a better job market for the residents. Other projects include two dance pieces and a rock musical about police/community relations. Contact NEW YORK FREE THEATER, 11 2nd Avenue, New York, NY 10003, (212) 477-0400.

"GUIDELINES FOR ESTABLISHMENT OF A HOTLINE SERVICE" . . . provides a basic outline of procedures, ethics, goals, etc. in setting up a hotline or crisis communication center. Available from Children's Hospital, Los Angeles, CA.

Truth and the Dragon, Elsa Bailey, 75 cents. American Friends Service Committee, 1965. BF637 .P4B28.
A basic primer in simple words and good natured allegorical graphics about propaganda, understanding it and how to fight it.

Creative Crafts for Today, John Prtchmouth. Viking, 1969. TT157 .P72.
"A source book of materials and activities," this gives concise (perhaps too much so) information on the use of household craft materials such as sawdust, balloons, bark, beads, bottles, bottlecaps, bricks, etc. for creative purposes. This reference book also contains a guide to the use of crafts tools and a table of which adhesives to use on the materials mentioned in the book.

SOUTHERN MEDIA . . . sprang from the realization that semi-literate rural Blacks, dependent on television, were receiving a stereotyped image of themselves packaged by white people. Black operated Southern Media is attempting to change these circumstances through the use of film by providing equipment and technical facilities and training to Black people so that they can record their own experiences. They are slowly workinc to attain their goal, but have very little money. A library of tapes from the movement in the South is available for rap sessions. Contact SOUTHERN MEDIA, 828 Lynch St., Jackson, MS 39203.

TOY LENDING LIBRARY . . . is based on the philosophy that it is healthy for children to play with someone, even just one hour a day. The library becomes the stage and the toy becomes the medium for developing interaction between parents and children. The atmosphere is completely unstructured; toys can be borrowed or children can come in and play. A parent can borrow two toys and one book a week. Toy Lending Library has existed for almost three years as a project of the National Institute of Mental Health, attempting to encourage mothers to play with children to prepare them for school. Contact TOY LENDING LIBRARY, 2311 - 18th St. NW, Washington, DC 20018, (202) 387-2467.

FILM INFORMATION SERVICE . . . is a non-profit group which exists primarily to give work to hungry students and filmmakers. Research on film and half-inch video is done by request, at $3.00 per hour and 10 cents per xerox page, with information gathered from books and magazines. People must list their specific needs in their requests . . . how much they are willing to pay and where they've looked already. Contact FILM INFORMATION SERVICE, 3601 Rue Ste. Famille, Suite 601, Montreal,

Future catalogs to be published by the *Source Collective* include: Justice/Repression, Rural, Health/Medibiz, Intra Communalism/Imperialism, Self Determination/Government, Education, Peace/Militarism, Economics, Food/Agribiz, Cultural Liberation, and Environment.

NEW ENGLAND FREE PRESS

New England Free Press is a clearinghouse for radical literature. They offer pamphlets, usually printed in mimeo, at very low prices. Scholarship and quality of writing varies considerably. A complete listing is free. Here is a selection of their offerings:

"Living Conditions in the US" by Joe Eyer (10¢)

"Life in the Factory" by Paul Romano (30¢)

"Literature on the American Working Class" by Evansohn/Foner/Naison/ et al. (15¢)

"Black Monday: How Business and Government Are Using Civil Rights to Make Other People Pay for Inflation" (10¢)

"On the Job Oppression of Working Women: A Collection of Articles" (20¢)

"Where It's At: A Research Guide to Community Organizing (1968)" by Jill Hamberg (75¢)

"Corporations and the Cold War" by David Horowitz (10¢)

"Use of US Armed Forces" (from the *Congressional Record* entered by Everett Dirksen) (5¢)

"Capital's Last Frontier: the US Role in the Pacific" by Jules Henry (5¢)

"Consumption: Domestic Imperialism" by David Gilbert (15¢)

"Exploitation or aid?: US -- Brazil Economic Relations: The Facts and Mechanisms of Imperialism, a Case Study" by Andre Gunder Frank (15¢)

"Notes on Inflation and the Dollar" by Paul Sweezy and Harry Magdoff (10¢)

"Taxation and Inequality" by Gabriel Kolko (15¢)

"GE: Profile of a Corporation" by Jerry DeMuth (10¢)

"Propaganda: a Worksheet" (10¢)

"On Aging" by Simone de Beauvoir (5¢)

"Ambush at Kamikaze Pass: Racism in the Media" by Tom Engelhardt (25¢)

"Radical's Guide to Grand Juries" by Alicia Kaplow and Ann Garfinkle (5¢)

"The Political Economy of Male Chauvinism" by Katherine Kaufer & Tom Christoffel (10¢)

Add to order postage based on: 20% on orders $2 and under, 5% on orders over $2 (Mass. residents add 3% sales tax) to:

NEW ENGLAND FREE PRESS
60 Union Square
Somerville, Mass. 02143
(617) 628-2450

PACKET OF SMALL ITEMS

Up Against the Law: the Legal Rights of People Under 21. . . by Joan Struuse (New American Library, 270 pp., 95¢) concerns students' rights to receive draft counseling, to invite controversial speakers to the school, to publish a censorship-free paper, to have due process before suspension or expulsion from school. The book's general approach is to outline recent court decisions and to remind students that these rights have to be won rather than merely received.

Student Legal Rights by Michael Nussbaum (Perennial Library, $1.25) is a similar book that discusses rules for students' conduct, the legal limits of student protest, unfair grades, privacy, etc.

Student Rights Handbook is a publication of the ACLU that tells students what to do if they are suspended, transferred, or stopped in the hall for an interview by the police. It also answers questions about pregnancy, draft counseling, and parents' rights to review school records. I believe this one is free from Student Rights Project, N.Y. Civil Liberties Union, 84 Fifth Ave., New York 10011.

A fine book published back in 1969 that never really caught on is **Language in America** edited by Neil Postman, Charles Weingartner and Terence Moran. The 230-page hard cover contains about 30 articles on various kinds of language in America. Chapter titles include "The Language of Politics," "The Language of Bureaucracy," "The Language of Censorship," "Language of Racism," "Language of Advertising," "Language of Love" and more. Well worth reading for any English teacher. *Published by Pegasus (850 Third Avenue, N.Y. 10022)*

Montage: Investigations in Language by William Sparke and Clark McKowen must be the snazziest textbook around as well as one of the most creative. Aside from its 500-page length there's not much in *Investigations* to make it look like a textbook—no chapters or questions or homework assignments. Contents include linguistics, film, McLuhan, comics, advertising, critical thinking, inventiveness, writing and lots of color. The book was published in 1970 by the Macmillan Company, but doesn't seem to have received the attention it deserves.

The Portola Institute (the money behind *Whole Earth Catalog* and *Big Rock Candy Mountain*) has published a new book—**Deschooling, De-Conditioning** edited by Cliff Trolin and Johanna Putnoi. The 64-page newspaper size publication contains a short article by Ivan Illich on deschooling and descriptions of learning exchanges such as Pacific High School's Apprenticeship Program, Evanston's Learning Exchange, Baltimore's Openings Networks, Philadelphia's Parkway School, the Wilderness School, and The Learning Resources Exchange of St. Louis. Also included are first person accounts of deschooling projects and a collection of miscellaneous philosophy-community raps.

$2.75 from *Whole Earth Truck Store, 558 Santa Cruz Ave., Menlo Park, Ca. 94025.*

A series of paperbacks of less than 100 pages called *The Opposing Viewpoints Series* is published by a small Minnesota publishing company, Greenhaven Press. So far there are four volumes in the series, aimed at high school social studies classes: *The Radical Left and the Far Right, Liberals and Conservatives, The Ecology Controversy, and Constructing a Life Philosophy*. Each book contains about a dozen readings that are 2-5 pages in length. There are discussion questions and some suggestions for group activities. Each book costs $1.55, even for an examination copy. A series definitely worth checking if you're in need of print material. Greenhaven Press, Box 831, Anoka, Minn. 55303.

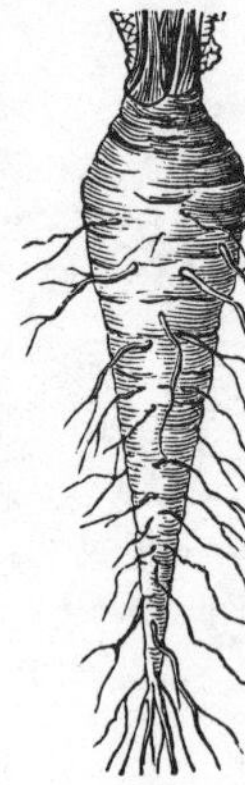

OPPOSING VIEWPOINTS is a series of paperbacks useful for social studies or moral problems classes. Each booklet is a well chosen collection of readings along with questions and teaching suggestions. CONSTRUCTING A LIFE PHILOSOPHY has readings from the Bible, Machiavelli, Billy Graham, Chardin, Joseph Fletcher and others. Each book is about 80-pages. Other titles in the series include LIBERALS & CONSERVATIVES, THE RADICAL LEFT AND THE FAR RIGHT, and THE ECOLOGY CONTROVERSY. Books sell for $1.55 each (even for an examination copy) from Greenhaven Press, Box 831, Anoka, Minn. 55303.

Alternative High Schools: Some Pioneer Programs. . .details already existing experimental programs within public school systems. There are adequate descriptions of nearly fifty high school programs, mainly of the school-within-a-school type. The book is very valuable to administrators considering setting up an experimental program. In addition to describing the programs the booklet deals with how colleges react to applications from students in such alternative schools, reactions of state departments of education and problems with accrediting agencies.

Available from Educational Research Service, Box 5 NEA Building, 1201 Sixteenth Street, N.W., Washington, D.C. 20036. $3.00 prepaid.

Future Planning Maps. . . . are designed as a series of learning activities for small groups. Each "map" is a single sheet of paper that folds out to poster size and has about four activities for a small group. For example, the one on "Tomorrow's Society?" outlines the basic features of a capitalist society, a welfare society and a socialist society and asks the group to make a majority decision on which they would want to live in. Another activity asks each student to redistribute the federal budget money for the second half of the decade and an another suggests that students "design an improved society."

Maps are available on the topics of "Constructing a Life Philosophy," "Ecology," "Constructing a Political Philosophy," "Prisons" and "Foreign Policy. Each costs 95¢ from Greenhaven Press, Box 831, Anoka, MN 55303.

Yesterday/Today is a new program developed by the Microphoto division of Bell & Howell and distributed through B&H's Charles E. Merrill Publishing Co.

The heart of the program is facsimile reproductions of four-page sections from old newspapers. Currently there are three units available: Westward Expansion 1841-1849; Progressive Era 1901-1917; and Great Depression & New Deal 1933-1939. Each unit contains fifty different newspaper segments grouped by important events within the era under study. The unit I saw had nine different front page reports on the sinking of the Lusitania, five on the Pure Food & Drug Act, five on the Panama Canal, etc.

Also included in each unit are transparencies from the papers which challenge most anyone's eyesight and a teacher's guide which seems little more than an index to the newspaper headlines.

The basic idea of making old newspapers available is excellent, but surely there has to be a more practical and less expensive way. *Each unit sells for $39.50 and is available on a 30-day examination plan from Charles E. Merrill Publishing Co., 1300 Alum Creek Drive, Columbus, O. 43216.*

Multimedia Materials for Afro-American Studies... an annotated bibliography of 1400 multimedia titles. Compiled by Harry Johnson. Sells for $15.95 from R. R. Bowker Co., 1180 Avenue of the Americas, New York, N.Y. 10036.

JUXTAPOSITION

Juxtaposition. . . Rarely do we recommend a book written as a textbook for use in school. **Juxtaposition** is an exception. The SRA text is intended for college literature courses but is well suited to high school. The anthology is a creative and provocative selection of graphics, ads, exercises, humor, literature, music, slanted language and definitions arranged according to eight themes: hot issues, feminism, ecology, student life, work, leisure, the arts, and "cold continuing causes." The 313-page oversized paperback contains excerpts from hundreds of writers including Alan Watts, William Buckley, I. Ching, Bertrand Russell, Richard Brautigan, Peter Max, James Joyce, G. B. Shaw and even The Whole Earth Catalog.

16 Publications

CONCERN AND MIXED BAG

Concern is a series of 14 small paperbacks for high school or adult discussion groups or social studies classes. Each book is a collection of twenty excerpts from people such as Arthur Clark, Marshall McLuhan, Frost and Sandburg, Loudon Wainwright, Jerome Frank, underground papers, James Herndon, G. B. Shaw, Norman Mailer, Dick Gregory, George Leonard and hundreds of others. Each book has illustrations that are as powerful as the printed words inside, if not more. The illustrations and convenient size of the booklets make them popular with students. Each booklet costs about 60¢. Titles in the series are *Poverty, Race, Violence, Revolution, Freedom, Generation Gap, Communication, Destiny, Drugs, Authority, World Religions, Extremists, Community* and *Youth Culture.* Information from *Silver Burdett Co., Morristown, N.J. 07960.*

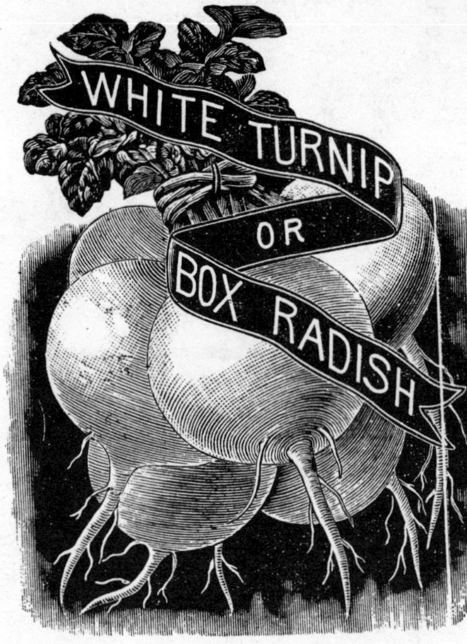

Twentieth-century time capsule. . . **Mixed Bag: Artifacts from the Contemporary Culture** is an anthology from Scott Foresman that's hard to describe. I'd suggest you get an examination copy – you might find it one of the better books you've read this year. Author Helene Hutchinson describes the book's purpose as "to excite interest and elicit emotional response by bringing into the classroom the colors and forms of the outside world." Included are ads, buttons, cartoons, photos, paintings, graffiti, song lyrics, poems, stories, and essays. Artifacts are arranged under such themes as family, violence, race, death, and religion. Selections are excellent, suitable for many kinds of high school classes. A copy of the 317-page hardback can be obtaine from Scott Foresman, price $5.95.

XEROX BOOKLETS

Xerox Education Publications has a series of 32 - 64-page pamphlets in English and the social studies selling for 40 - 45¢ each. The books sometimes "talk down" to students, but are generally well written, contain interesting student activities, and are about both crucial and naturally intriguing topics. Complete catalog available free. Minimum order is 10 books from:

XEROX EDUCATION PUBLICATIONS
Education Center
Columbus, Ohio 43216

NOW POETRY

Written especially for the disenchanted poetry students in your classroom, this unique Unit Book shows students that poetry isn't all flowers and birds and deeDum-deeDum rhythm—rather there is poetry that can speak simply and naturally about teenage life, its emotions, and feelings. Students discover that they not only can enjoy poetry, but they can even write poems of their own—and have fun doing it! The book gives students instructions and examples for writing different forms of poetry like Haiku, Tanka, Terse Verse, and many more. 64 pages. Grades 7-12. **No. 393—45¢**

NEWSMEN AND THE NEWS

This Unit examines press freedom and responsibility. What is the relationship between the press and the government? What is objectivity? Do journalists observe it? An exclusive interview with CBS correspondent Daniel Schorr details his harassment by the government. Vice-President Agnew and CBS president Stanton comment on TV news control. 32 pages. Grades 9-12. 40¢.

Book No. 511

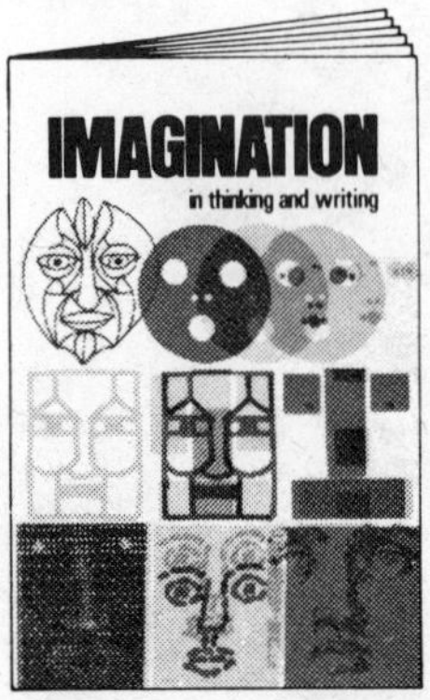

IMAGINATION

Imagination—the ability to come up with original ideas—this is what this Unit Book is all about! Students see designs come alive, colors take on feelings, and paintings become stories. They discover that their own minds become more aware of the imaginary world that exists beyond the real world around them. Imaginative thinking then leads to more creative writing. Each article and story ends with an interesting writing assignment. 32 pages. Grades 7-12. **No. 394—40¢**

HOW WORDS USE YOU

enables your students to explore the dangers of confusing a word (the symbol) with the thing it stands for. It also discusses euphemism, taboo words, advertising, and propaganda. **No. 389**

THE IMPACT OF WORDS

examines the connotations that words acquire in everyday use and shows your students how to avoid confusion by seeing the reality behind the word itself. **No. 390**

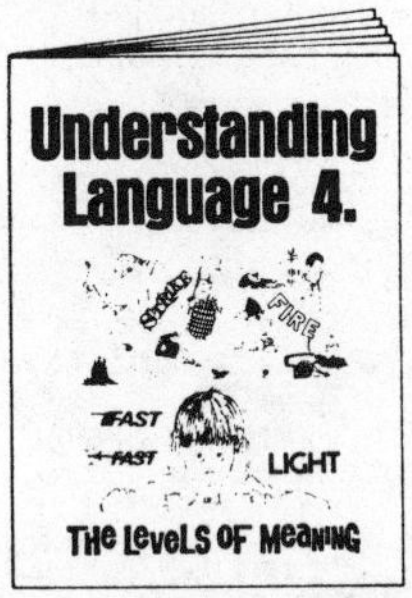

LEVELS OF MEANING

ties together the preceding three books and shows your students why words must be kept in context—and how a word's dictionary meaning differs from its connotative meaning. **No. 391**

CREATING DRAMATICS IN MOVEMENT AND WRITING

This new Unit Book combines the advantages of books for your students and a special free *record* and *Teacher's Guide* for you!

Creating Dramatics in Movement and Writing begins with some direct, uncomplicated fun exercises for your students to perform in groups or as individuals. As your students increase in skill and confidence, the book leads them into creating characters and improvising. By the end, your students will be writing their own skits and scenes—and, perhaps, even a complete play!

Side 1 of the record describes a chain of graphic scenes and events—such as being lost in a desert. Students are asked to act out their own interpretations of these situations. Side 2 leads students further into improvisations by supplying strange musical sounds and vibrations. Both sides of the record encourage students to respond creatively in physical movement as well as in writing. 48 pages. Grades 7-12. **No. 585—45¢**

CREATIVITY

Creativity — "the ability to invent, to design, to produce through imaginative skills." This is Webster's definition — and this is precisely what READ's Unit Book, CREATIVITY, is all about! This exciting book is designed to stir your students' minds — to make them more aware of their own creative potential. And the Editors of READ use every fun device to do exactly that — unfinished stories and plays, word games, ink blots, unusual puzzles using shapes and letters. An exciting, colorful vehicle for teaching composition, poetry, and drama. 32 pages. Grades 7-12. **No. 580—40¢**

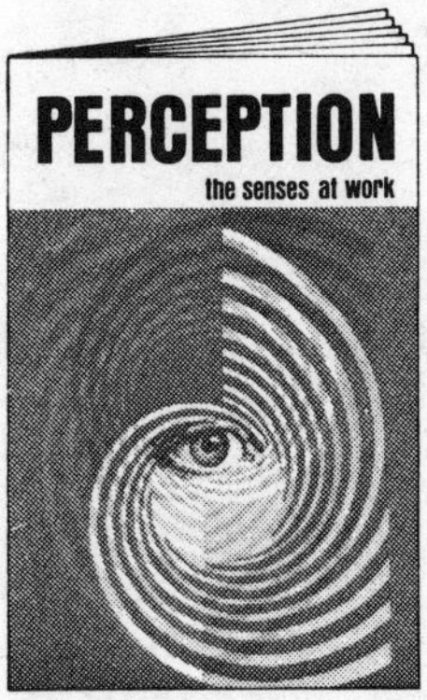

PERCEPTION

Seeing is believing. Right? Not according to READ's Unit Book, PERCEPTION. This book delves into the mysteries of awareness — the sensitivity that lies beyond the familiar, the accepted. Fascinating perception puzzles and optical illusions reveal familiar objects in unfamiliar ways! Then this book encourages students to apply their newly found senses. Through a variety of fun-exercises, photographs, and paintings, your students are shown how to use their "new awareness" in writing not only prose, but poetry too! 32 pgs. Gr. 7-12. **No. 581—40¢**

THEMES IN LITERATURE: PREJUDICE and STUDY GUIDE

Prejudice is a subject that rouses students' interest and concern. So we've organized a collection of short stories, poems, plays, and essays around the theme of prejudice. Students can use this 48-page "mini-anthology" alone—or in combination with the separate Study Guide (also 48 pages).

The Study Guide covers a wide range of literary elements, including word recognition, context clues, main ideas, connotation, tone, and symbolism. It has a side-by-side correspondence with the anthology, so students can read the selections without interruption. The anthology and guide are an excellent way to give your students practice and reinforcement in the many aspects of reading and evaluating literature. Grades 7-12.

No. 592 Prejudice (anthology)—40¢
No. 593 Study Guide—40¢
No. 594 (both books)—75¢

18 Publications

PEACEMAKING AND POWER POLITICS

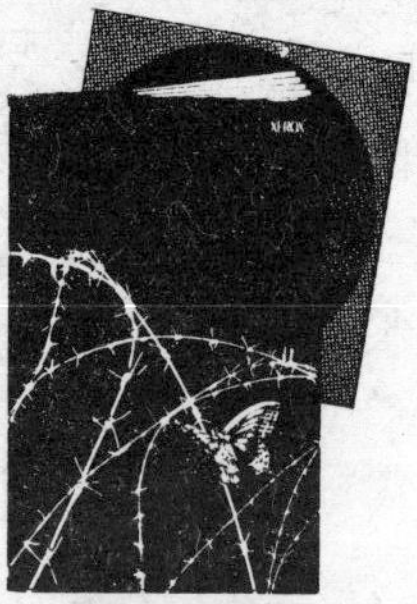

Why do men fight even though everyone wants peace? A moving excerpt from the film *The Americanization of Emily* suggests one answer to this question. How can we avoid war? Are summitry and super-power politics the answer? Students hear promises of peace by U.S. Presidents and other world leaders with actual sounds of war. 32 pages. Grades 9–12. 40¢ *Book No. 512*

DEMOCRACY AND DISSENT

What is dissent? Is it part of the democratic process? Here is a study of dissent from *within* the established institutions of our society (Supreme Court, Congress); dissent from *outside* the established institutions (anti-war movements, student movements, women's lib, consumerism). Exclusive interviews with Attorney William Kunstler, Senator Mike Gravel, Shirley Chisholm, Daniel Ellsberg, John Schmitz, and others. 32 pages. Grades 9–12. 40¢ *Book No. 513*

POVERTY AND WELFARE

How do the problems of the poor fit into our affluent, technological society? Where does the work ethic tradition belong in our society? Is a guaranteed minimum income the answer to problems of poverty? On whom does the tax burden of welfare fall? Where does private charity fit into modern social thinking? The record presents the voices of people involved in the welfare issue: welfare recipients, taxpayers, social workers, and others. 32 pages. Grades 9–12. 40¢

Book No. 514

THE AMERICAN WOMAN: Her Image and Her Roles

This new Unit Book focuses on the role of women in today's society. Is the "image" of the American woman based on reality or is it contrived? Do women try to conform to this image? Are women discriminated against? What will happen to the institutions of society if the woman's role is changed? 64 pages. Grades 9-12. 45¢.

Book No. 369

THE PENAL SYSTEM: Crime, Punishment, and Reform

In the wake of the Attica prison riot, the American penal system is under close scrutiny. What is the penal system's real purpose? Punishment? Reform? Or both? Does the penal system deter crime — or foster it? Case studies open up these and other questions for discussion. 64 pages. Grades 9-12. 45¢.

Book No. 378

WORK AND CAREER

This new Unit Book takes a broad view of our economy, where over 80 million people work at more than 20,000 kinds of jobs. It was written to help young people plan careers—instead of falling into work that might not be rewarding. Included are discussions of schooling and work . . . why some people feel trapped by their jobs . . . how some people combine interests and aptitudes for successful careers. Grades 7–12. 64 pages. 45¢

Book No. 565

NEW! PROPAGANDA AND PUBLIC OPINION

This is a close look at the way professional opinion-shapers persuade—and sometimes manipulate—their audiences. How they use contrived arguments, selected data, press releases, edited film clips, and other devices to bring about preconceived results. Through case studies, both past and present, the book reveals how propaganda devices have influenced elections and national policy. 64 pages. Grades 7–12. 45¢

Book No. 572

Book No. 503

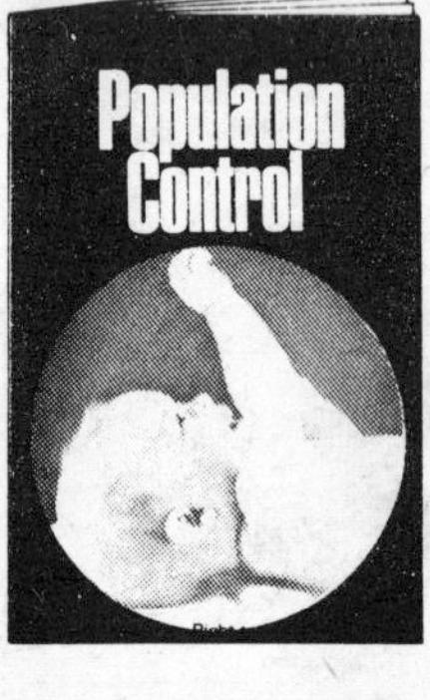

Book No. 501

POPULATION CONTROL: Whose Right to Live?

This Unit Book gives students a broad view of the population growth problem. Case studies probe such topics as abortion, management of the birth and death rates, and genetic engineering. Basic questions arise: What public policies (if any) should be considered in making decisions that directly cause some people to live and others to die? Should some people have the right to higher population growth than others? 64 pages. Grades 9-12. 45¢.

PRIVACY: The Control of Personal Information

The case studies in this book come to grips with issues such as: What rights should individuals and institutions have to gather and disclose personal information? What rights should an individual have to inspect, correct, or withdraw information so gathered? Under what conditions should the Government require individuals to give personal information? 64 pages. Grades 9-12. 45¢.

STRANGE & FAMILIAR

Strange & Familiar is a workbook on creative thinking. The workbook uses a system of thought called Synectics, developed by one of the authors, William J.J. Gordon.

In thirty-six units *Strange & Familiar* asks students to look at the familiar world in a new way. It invites students to make connections between the familiar and the strange in science, social studies, and creative expression.

The workbook is a bit expensive at $5 in lots of 1 - 4 copies, $3 in lots of 5 - 29 copies, and $2 in lots of 30 - 100 copies plus postage.

SYNECTICS EDUCATION SYSTEMS
121 Brattle Street
Cambridge, Mass. 02138
(617) UN 8-5747

INVENT-O-RAMA

Parts of this Unit may seem a little wild to you. For instance, you are asked to guess what animal might have given an African chief the idea for a vacuum cleaner. You could point out nastily that no African chief invented the vacuum cleaner — that it was invented by an American named Vack Hume Kleenah.

However, there are no right or wrong responses in this Unit. The next few pages are designed to start you making connections — some crazy ones and some sane ones, depending on how you feel. Making connections is the key to getting ideas and the best way to understand how ideas are born is to experience the process yourself!

What might have given the inventor of the vacuum cleaner his first idea? a Sneeze

Explain: When he sucked in air before he sneezed, he sucked in a fly!

20 Publications

Now you are on your own. From what ANIMAL could an Australai bushman have borrowed the concept of the KNAPSACK?

____

What are your connections? ______________________________

From what ANIMAL might the American Indian have LEARNED TO FISH? ______________________________

What did the American Indian learn about fishing from this animal?

____

What INSECT could a black hunter in South Africa have watched just before inventing an ANIMAL TRAP?

____

What did the trap look like? ______________________________

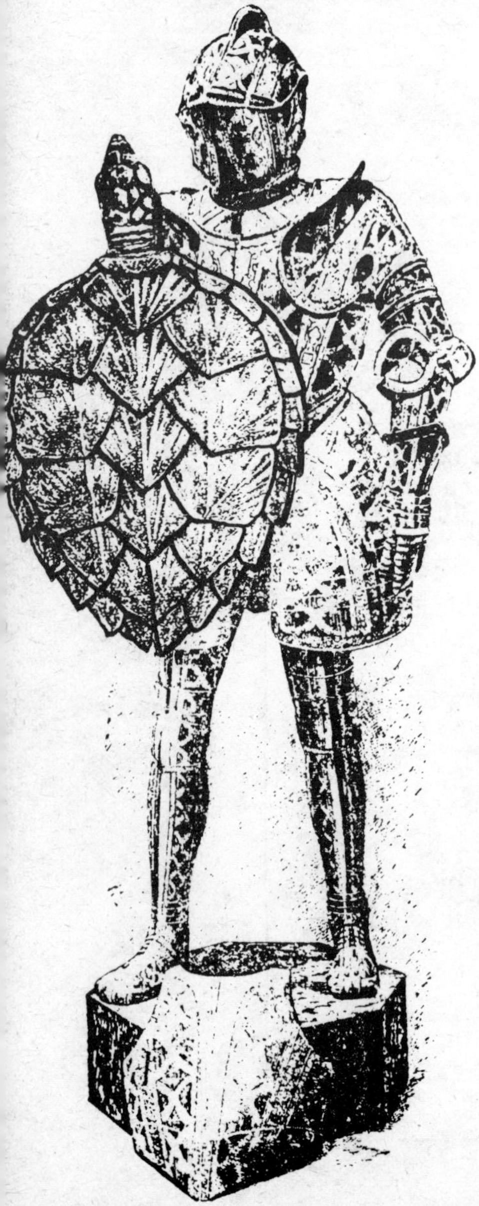

Until the time of the American Civil War almost all non-sailing ships were moved along by giant paddlewheels. When propellers were introduced into the United States Navy, ships were able to move much faster on the open ocean. From what NON-LIVING OBJECT might the PROPELLER concept have been developed? ______________________________

And, from what LIVING OBJECT? ______________________________

Which of the two do you think was the more likely model for the original invention? ______________________________

SAFE SAFETY PIN-O-RAMA

Safety pins work pretty well, but there are a couple of things wron with them. In the first place, they are not always safe. The points can slip out and stick into you. Maybe when you were a baby a safety pin slipped out of your diaper and stuck you.

In the second place, if you are trying to pin together two thick blankets, for instance, the safety pin won't work. The blankets are too fa and the safety pin can't be forced into its catch without bending it. When i is bent, the point slips out very easily.

INVENTION PROBLEM: Invent a safety pin that can hold things togethe but will never stick anyone. This must be your own invention, something that never existed before.

WHAT IS AIR POLLUTION?

General Motors offers a free booklet titled *What Is Air Pollution?* available in classroom quantities. The booklet is aimed at grade school students but is excellent for any level as an example of propaganda, persuasion, or corporate public relations.

Ralph Nader reviewed the booklet in the March 3, 1973, issue of *The New Republic*, pointing out that the booklet omits any mention of what air pollution does to human health. The various pollutants from autos are pictured as pixie "demons" that are very often harmless, sometimes annoying, but generally going away fast.

The booklet does not present carbon monoxide as a poison. Children are told that CO is blown away by the wind except where lots of cars are crowded together where too much of "Charlie Carbon Monoxide is not a good thing to have." The booklet does not talk at all about rubber and asbestos pollution from cars. Finally, the book concludes by saying that "Air pollution from cars has become less and less in the last few years."

The booklet might not be the best way to teach about air pollution, but it certainly could be used for other purposes in a high school or even college class. Free from:

PUBLIC RELATIONS
GENERAL MOTORS
Detroit, Mich. 48202

YOU'VE BEEN ARRESTED

You've Been Arrested is a 48-page paperback available for 75¢ from:

SCOTT, FORESMAN AND COMPANY
The School Department
1900 East Lake Avenue
Glenview, Ill. 60025

You've Been Arrested

This booklet begins with two questions directed to students: Do you know what to do if you are arrested? Do you know what your rights are if you are accused of a crime? The answers are provided in three sections — Constitutional Rights, Changing Court Views, and Juvenile Courts.

The story of a young gang member who was forced by police to confess to crimes he didn't commit is the first reading. It leads into a discussion of the Constitutional amendments that protect a person's rights when he or she is suspected or accused of a crime.

Changing Court Views examines three Supreme Court cases of recent years that relate to the rights of persons accused of crimes.

Injustices in the juvenile court system are discussed in the third part of the booklet.

Paperback 48 pages
03855-6 72 $0.75

FRAGMENTS

Fragments is a set of 158 cards, each giving an idea useful in teaching people about looking and seeing. The activities grew out of a course in "Visual Education" taught by Lowry Burgess to high school students.

The cards are color coded and grouped according to activities relating to Mapping and Representing, Enduring Activities, Sensory Awareness, Inner Landscape, and Building and Making.

Fragments comes boxed for $7.00 from:

WORKSHOP FOR LEARNING THINGS
5 Bridge Street
Watertown, Mass. 02172

MAPPING
REPRESENTING #3 Direction Giving

Tell or show (drawing) someone the way to your house. Examine each other's directions for different kinds of cues. Is there sight, sound, touch, smell, taste, color, number, direction, time, etc.? Can you create a map with just one set of cues? . . . with two? Give directions by smell. What about larger cues (rhythms, light, weather, etc.)? Watch yourself on your way home. Talk about it the next day. How would your cues change given different times of the year, the day, the night?

SENSORY AWARENESS #6 Putting Sounds Together

materials
tape recorder, tape

Record some sounds in juxtaposition. Edit the tape until you have something you think is interesting. Combine collected sounds with vocal or electronic sounds. Make compositions that have some meaning to you. Play them for a group. Make a group composition. Combine a tape with a live performance.

ENDURING ACTIVITIES #5 Discovering an Unkown or Forgotten Painter, Poet, Architect, Musician

Make at least a half-year, perhaps a whole-year project out of discovering some unknown or forgotten person in a field of particular interest. What can you find out from people, from archives and libraries, museums and buildings? It would be good to get into really first-hand research. Put together a notebook, essay collection on the person and his work. Organize and exhibit or perform his work.

BUILDING AND MAKING #15
Silly Machines

materials
any kind of junk you can find: motors, cranks, gears, glue, paper, wood, plaster, etc.

Design and make a fantastic machine (either individualy or as a group). Something that moves and does something, no matter how ridiculous or strange. It should be colorful and noisy, perhaps very elegant. Have an exhibit or fair.

You could make a human machine out of everybody in the class.

LOOKING AND LISTENING

Looking and Listening is a set of 168 cards similar to *Fragments*. This set of ideas is about the deepening of visual and aural perception and response. Developer Lowry Burgess has used these exercises from second grade through graduate school and in teacher training workshops. The exercises are divided into three categories: the first explores questions of the relationship of images to self, the second poses problems and perceptions caused by change, and the third deals with perception through more or less formal concepts. Some of the *Fragments* exercises are repeated here.

$7.00 (This set and *Fragments* when ordered together cost $13) from:

WORKSHOP FOR LEARNING THINGS
5 Bridge Street
Watertown, Mass. 02172

22 Looking for Something Without Looking for It

Can you tell your eye to look for a specific thing and let it? (circular things or certain colors, even definite things.) i.e. you might say for the next two hours I am going to notice everything red. (You should not look for red things, but allow your eye to notice them -- to take you to them.) Open yourself up to them, feel yourself being dragged about by your eyes!

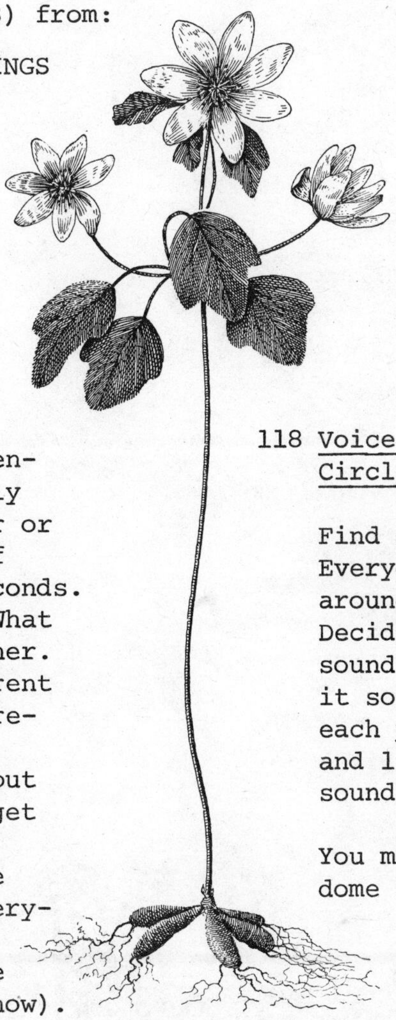

1 Responses of the Eye

In a very dark room stare without blinking at the center of either a brilliantly lit piece of colored paper or a colored slide. Turn off the projector after 25 seconds. Look into the darkness. What do you see? Tell each other. Do it again using a different color. The image can be renewed by blinking. Guess what you'll see when you put up another color. Don't get into explanations, just descriptions. Concentrate on sharing. Make sure everybody sees the phenomenon (some won't the first time but when they do you'll know). Any observation is valid.

118 Voice and Humming in a Large Circle

Find a large, quiet space. Everyone stand in a ring around the edge of the space. Decide on some sequence of sound and then hum or chant it softly. One at a time each person go to the center and listen to the ring of sound around him.

You might do this in a large dome if you have the chance.

54 Short Glance
Looking at an Image for a Flash

Select an unfamiliar work (preferably with little immediately recognizable images) and flash it on the screen or show it for the shortest time possible. Then ask what did you see? What was in the corners? (There will be arguments.) What is important is to allow disagreement to develop and allow separate views to develop as far as possible. After some time at trying to nail down the work as explicitly as possible, show it. What was there and what wasn't? (Now I can't warn you enough that there is no right or wrong to this -- that is not the point. I am far more interested in the developments beyond the image because they begin to reveal the evocative power of very small and short exposures. The question that comes out of this is how much is me and how much it. And this takes some very careful and precise thinking. It can open whole new areas within the work and yourself.)

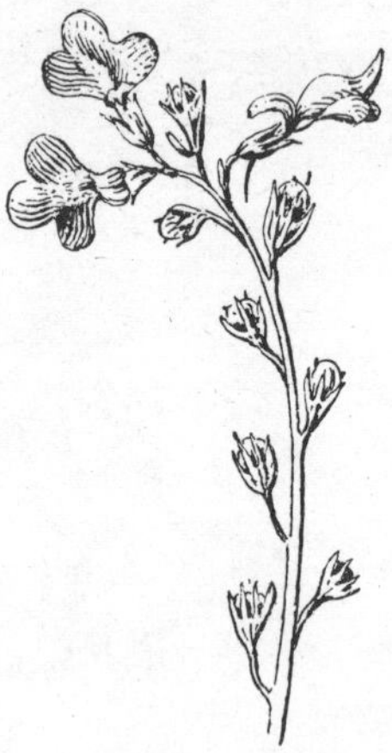

158 What Are the Largest, Loudest Sounds You Have Heard?

What are the largest rhythms, sounds, or complexes of sounds you have heard or experienced? (It is important to distinguish between sounds that are naturally large or loud and those experiences of rather normal sounds that suddenly seem very loud or important.) What relation do these very loud, large or important sounds have to the establishment of meaning? Do different groups or societies hear different kinds of sounds as large or important?

121 Sound Self-portrait

Can you develop a self-portrait in sound? What sounds are important to you? What sounds are deep or emotional? Can you put them together? Then describe them. This is a deep question and may be difficult, but try it.

PEOPLE AND POPULATION BOOKS

People! is $1.50 each, *This Crowded World* is $1.50 each, and *World Population Dilemma* is $2.00 all from:

COLUMBIA BOOKS
734 15th Street N.W., Suite 601
Washington, D.C. 20005

The world is clearly in the grip of a population dilemma. The scale of the dilemma has been detailed in earlier chapters; the causes of it—the Great Transformation in society that brought about a decrease in death rates first in the West and then in the underdeveloped world—have been described. The fact that birth rates have also declined somewhat in industrialized countries was also brought out, as well as the important point that this demographic transition has not yet taken place in the rest of the world.

There seems to be wide agreement that population growth should be slowed. But what if everyone accepted the need to limit childbearing, and was willing to translate that need into his own personal terms? If each family decided to have no more than two children—enough to replace the parents—would population growth stop?

The answer to that question is: No, not for many years.

Population would continue to grow for decades because of the momentum built up by the rapid growth of the present generation. The momentum comes from the large number of young people who are present in a rapidly growing population. It is an illustration of *how age structure affects population growth.*

The age structure of a population is usually represented in a diagram called an "age pyramid," in which the number of people in each 5-year age group—called a cohort—is represented by a horizontal bar. In underdeveloped countries with high fertility, there are a great many young children relative to the total population. In rapidly growing countries, young people under 15 years of age account for 40 – 45 percent of the total population.

As these children grow up, they move into their reproductive years. At the same time, the age group or cohort that has been having babies grows too old to have more. But because the younger cohort is more numerous than the older one, there will be more of them to have babies. Even if they are less fertile than their parents, they probably will produce more babies altogether.

India is an example of the continuing effect of age structure on population growth. Even if Indian parents were to decide by 1985 to have mostly two-child families, the country's population would continue to grow until the year 2035. By that time, unless death rates increased, there would be about 1.2 billion Indians. That is more than twice the present population of that overcrowded country.

The momentum of population growth can also be seen in the aftereffects of the post-World War II baby boom of the United States. Here the rapid growth was caused not by a sharp drop in mortality, as in the case of the underdeveloped world, but by a sharp increase in fertility.

Here again, as in India, population growth would continue even if U.S. parents had no more than enough children to replace themselves. Because of the great bulge of the population now entering the reproductive age—those who were born during the baby boom—growth would not be halted unless families had an average of 1.2 children each. Such a pronounced reduction in fertility could occur, of course, but it is unlikely.

Beyond Family Planning

Even though some family planning techniques are still controversial, the principle of deliberately limiting family size and thus avoiding unwanted births is almost universally approved. Sterilization has yet to win public favor, but its use is growing. Abortion is openly used in some cultures but opposed in others. If recent trends continue, potential parents will be able to use an increasingly wide range of methods to control their family size.

The key question, about which there is a growing amount of discussion, is whether the population problem would be solved if all these methods of birth limitation were universally available. The answer to this question hinges on how many children parents *want* to have. Obviously, if parents had a perfect way to have only those children they wanted, and if they actually wanted and produced three children on the average, the world or U.S. population would continue to grow rapidly. It would increase by about 50 percent each generation. This rate of increase could not long continue. And so the solution to the population dilemma requires still other approaches.

In a nation with strong democratic traditions, the idea of setting legal limits on family size runs contrary to what we think of as a cherished human freedom. It would face the strongest kind of opposition. Such limits have been proposed by some people, but no one has suggested how they could be enforced in the unlikely event that they were enacted.

Can effective steps be taken between the extremes of doing nothing about the population problem and seeking to apply coercive remedies? There *are* such steps. But the first question to be asked and answered is whether it is any of the government's business how many children people have. Is this not an exclusively private decision for parents to make?

What separates public concerns from private ones is whether people's

actions significantly affect other people. If one family decides to spend its income on a fancy car and another on expensive clothes and rare steak dinners, these are private decisions. If one person wants to read radical literature and another conservative journals and newspapers, this too is a private matter. If a family has been brought up in a particular religion, it is free to continue that religion, adopt another, or follow no religion at all. If a person decides he doesn't like his region of the country, he has the right to move wherever he wants. These decisions and actions do not injure or unduly constrain other people or society as a whole.

But when a person in a congested city burns an enormous pile of trash, he creates a nuisance for his neighbors. When a factory dumps chemical wastes into a river that is the source of a metropolitan water supply or a recreational resource, it impairs the freedom of many other people. Obviously such actions cannot be sanctioned by law.

Parents have long thought of children as their private property, even though laws have been enacted to protect children from parental abuse. Similarly, most people consider the procreation of children to be a wholly private right, like deciding how many cars to buy.

But circumstances have changed. Burning trash and fouling the water were of no social consequence when people were spread far apart, but they destroy rights when people are jammed together. Procreation was a purely private affair in agrarian societies when there was plenty of good land and children might be economic assets. But when a society urbanizes and agrees to build schools and educate children at public expense, when it creates parks and playgrounds, pays for health and welfare costs of people whose income is insufficient and provides public services of all kinds, children represent social costs which must be borne by society as a whole.

When children grow up, moreover, the costs continue to mount.

Income and Population Growth Compared

Since 1945, underdeveloped countries have made considerable efforts to industrialize and increase their income. These efforts have been somewhat successful—the total gross product of underdeveloped countries has increased from something like $150 billion in 1950 to a little more than 500 billion in 1968. Meanwhile, however, the developed countries have increased their income from a little more than $700 billion in 1950 to more than $1,500 billion in 1968.

More dramatically, population in underdeveloped countries more than doubled from a figure of 1.2 billion in 1950 to 2.5 billion in 1968. In the developed countries, population increased from 500 million in 1950 to about 750 million in 1968.

One way of measuring a country's prosperity is by per capita income—the amount of income divided by the population. In these terms, underdeveloped countries increased their per capita income from $125 per person per year to $200. At the same time, however, the developed countries increased their per capita income from $1,400 to $2,000. Thus the underdevelopment gap, as measured by per capita income, has increased rather than decreased.

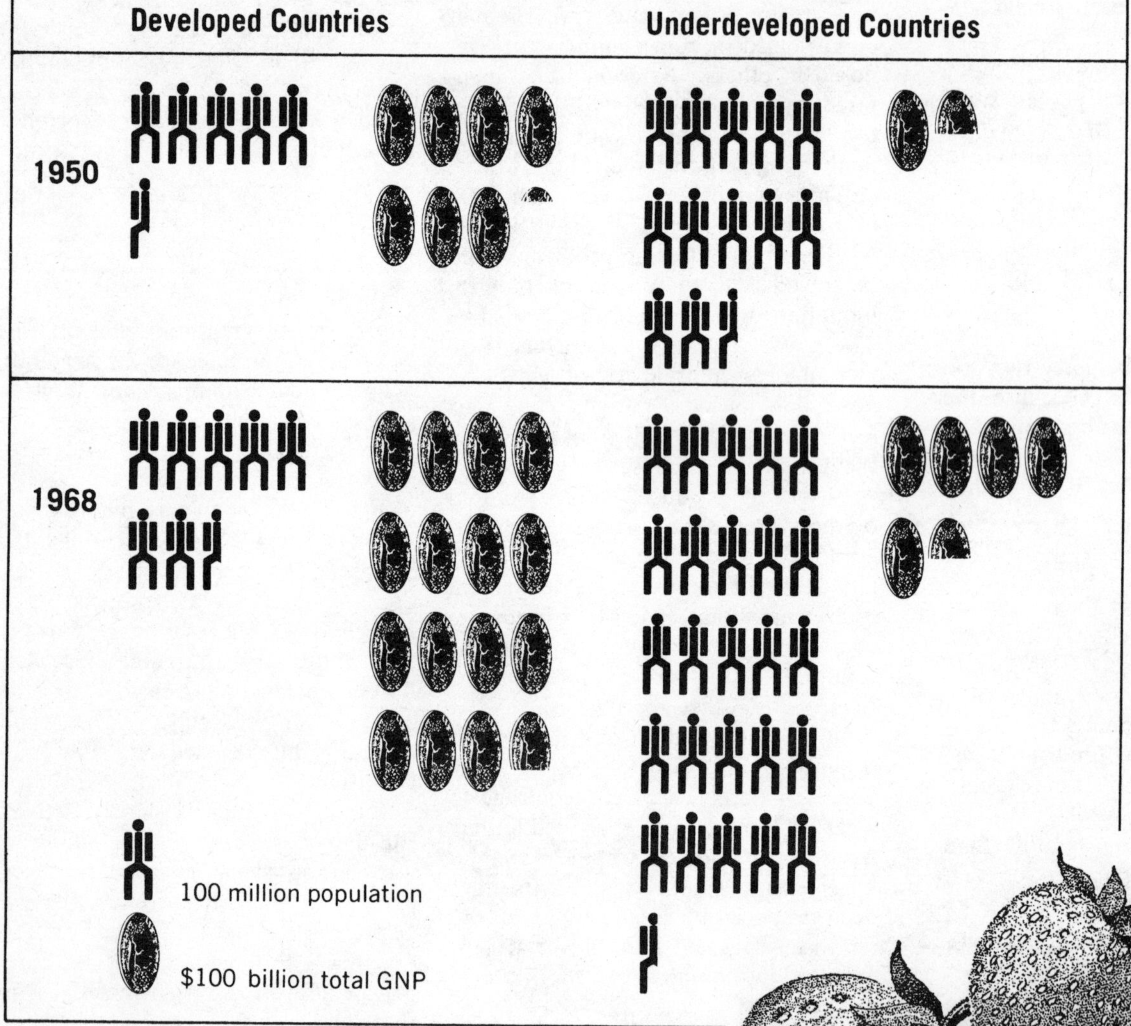

If each family decided to have no more than two children—enough to replace the parents—would population growth stop? No; not for many years.

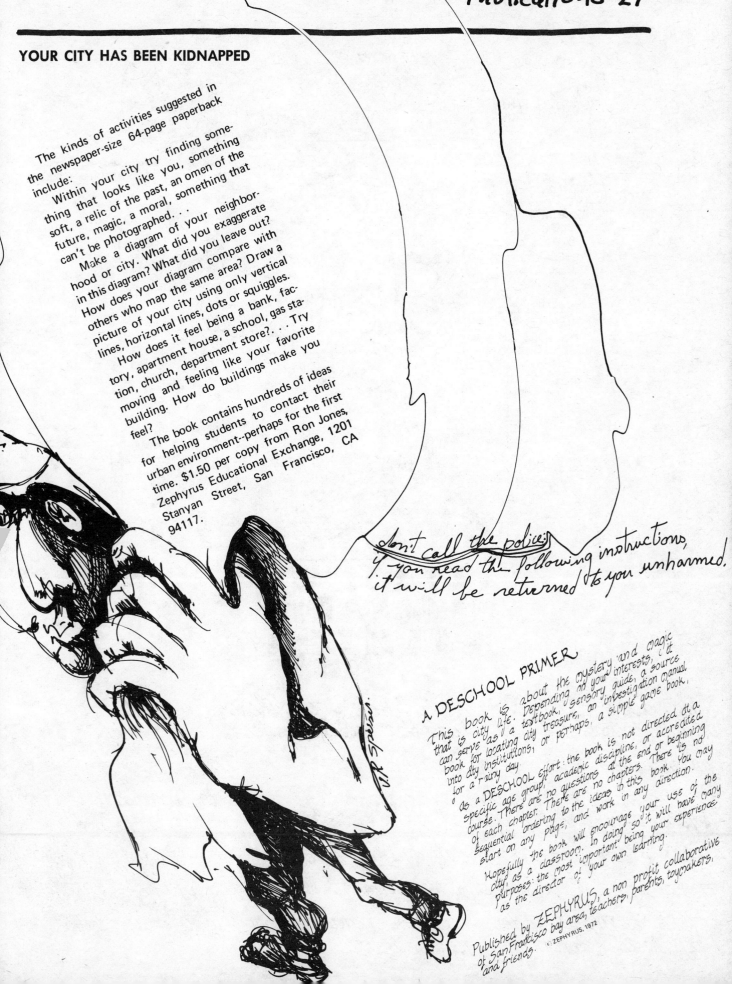

YOUR CITY HAS BEEN KIDNAPPED

The kinds of activities suggested in the newspaper-size 64-page paperback include:

Within your city try finding something that looks like you, something soft, a relic of the past, an omen of the future, magic, a moral, something that can't be photographed. . .

Make a diagram of your neighborhood or city. What did you leave out? What did you exaggerate in this diagram? How does your diagram compare with others who map the same area? Draw a picture of your city using only vertical lines, horizontal lines, dots or squiggles.

How does it feel being a bank, factory, apartment house, a school, gas station, church, department store?. . . Try moving and feeling like your favorite building. How do buildings make you feel?

The book contains hundreds of ideas for helping students to contact their urban environment--perhaps for the first time. $1.50 per copy from Ron Jones, Zephyrus Educational Exchange, 1201 Stanyan Street, San Francisco, CA 94117.

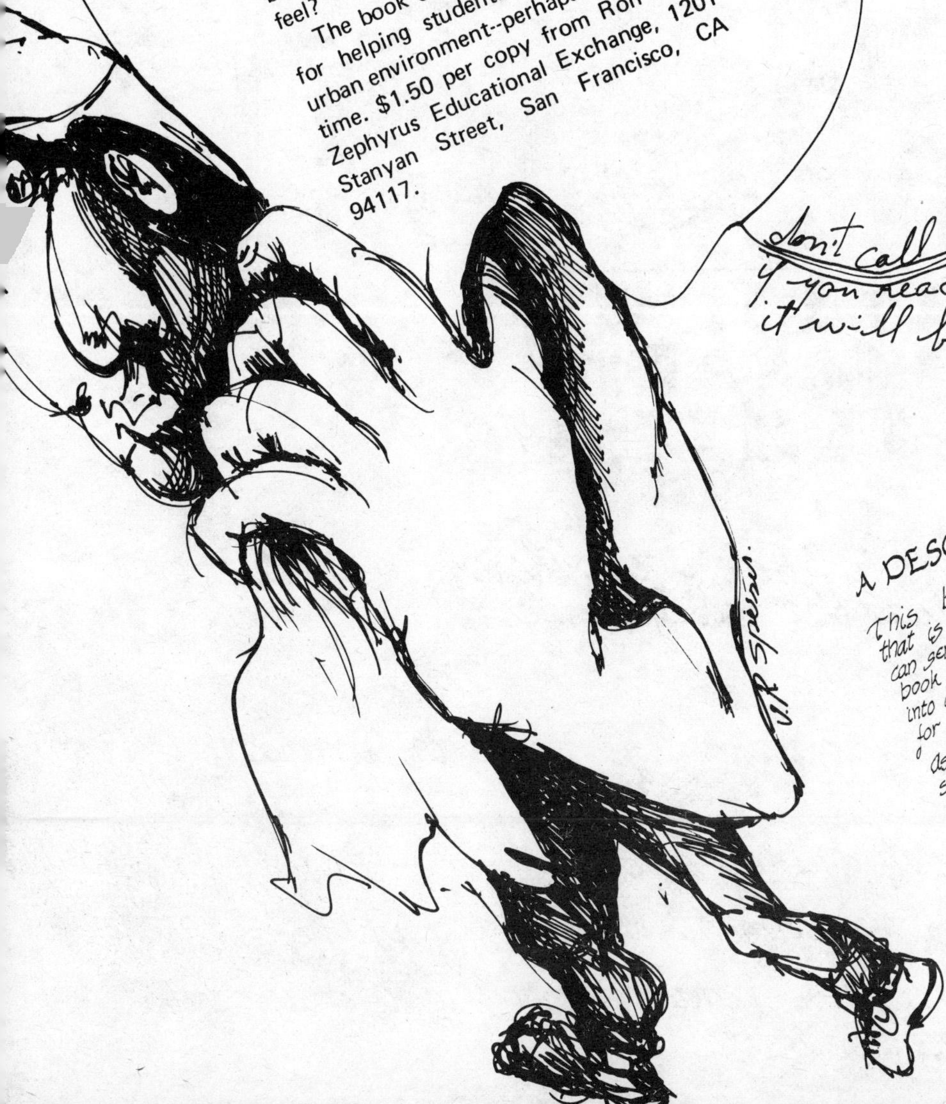

Don't call the police:
if you read the following instructions,
it will be returned to you unharmed.

A DESCHOOL PRIMER

This book is about the mystery and magic that is city life. Depending on your interests, it can serve as a textbook, sensory guide, a source book for locating city treasure, an investigation manual into city institutions, or perhaps, a simple game book, for a rainy day.

As a DESCHOOL effort: the book is not directed at a specific age group, academic discipline, or accredited course. There are no questions at the end or beginning of each chapter. There are no chapters. There is no sequential ordering to the ideas in this book. You may start on any page, and work in any direction.

Hopefully the book will encourage your use of the city, as a classroom. In doing so it will have many purposes: the most important being your experience as the director of your own learning.

Published by ZEPHYRUS, a non profit collaborative of San Francisco bay area, teachers, parents, toymakers, and friends.

what does garbage collected from one building, institution, or neighborhood tell you about that specific place?

what does your school discard?

is there such a thing as human garbage, people thrown away, left without hope or reason.

what ideas are thrown out and classified as unuseful at your school?

revive an old idea and experiment with its usefulness.

make a garbage index indicating valuable merchandise, discarded by local merchants and industry.

TRY COUNTING THE THINGS IN YOUR NEIGHBORHOOD THAT ARE NORMALLY NOT COUNTED.

for example, try counting the number of:
swings
garbage cans
bus stops.
beer cans sold on Friday night
people attending local government sesions
abandoned cars
legal suits against poor health or housing conditions
broken windows
trees
kids in school
kids out side school
vacant warehouses
prostitutes
pushers
landmarks
places you can't get into
ghosts
jobs
divorces
rats
bees
tournaments
tennants
public telephones
fire alarm boxes
stop signs
crack in the side walk
health inspectors
child care centers
things lost
things found
people called for jury duty
locks,
wire fences
promises
churchs
renovated buildings
people over 65

~how does the quantity of things you count compare to the number of similar things in different neighborhoods of the city?
~how are the things you counted, related?
are the things you counted, increasing, decreasing, remaining stable? part of a cycle?
~what might you do with this information once it is collected?

FINDING COMMUNITY ACTION

A strong recommendation for **Finding Community: A Guide To Community Research and Action** . . . by W. Ron Jones. It's a book for teachers who are concerned about relevant urban education. There are 11 sections in the 217-page paperback: Food Costs and Food Quality, Selling Practices and Credit Abuse, Experiencing the Welfare System, Corporate Medicine, The Condition of American Housing, Police, American School System, The Draft, The Warfare Economy. Corporate America and Curing the Environment.

Each chapter contains "indictments" which describe the problem, readings ranging from the **N. Y. Times** to the underground press which document the situation, community research and action projects for students to check out the local scene themselves, and a section giving possible alternatives. The guide is a **must** for any teacher of American Problems, social concern, ethics or morality, sociology or urban affairs. Copies can be obtained from J. Freel and Associates, 577 College Avenue, Palo Alto, Ca. Sorry, I can't find the price but order a copy anyway.

COMMUNITY RESEARCH AND ACTION:

LIVING IN POVERTY

This three week exercise will allow you and your family, or others who will join with you, to experience the reality of living on welfare. During the first week you will collect information on the operation of local welfare agencies. In the second and third week of the exercise you will use this information to simulate the conditions of local poverty by restricting your income to a hypothetical subsistence level.

Week Number One: Preparing for Poverty

1: During this first week, restrict your *food purchases* to the following budgetary amount.

YOUR FAMILY FOOD BUDGET DURING WEEK ONE OF THIS EXERCISE

NUMBER OF FAMILY MEMBERS

Number of wage earners	**1**	**2**	**3**	**4**	**5**	**6**	**7**
1 Wage earner	$7.20	$8.60	$11.00	$13.00	$15.00	$16.40	$17.60
2 Wage earners	$8.20	$9.60	$11.80	$14.00	$15.80	$17.40	$18.60

(Over seven members add $.60; each diabetic add $.05)

The scale down in your family's buying power is intended to reduce any surplus stock of food commodities in your home.

2: Find out the name, address and telephone number of local welfare agencies and list them below:

CITY: Agency: ____________________
Address: ____________________
Telephone: ____________________

COUNTY: Agency: ____________________
Address: ____________________
Telephone: ____________________

STATE: Agency: ____________________
Address: ____________________
Telephone: ____________________

3: To calculate your "buying power" in the simulation, inquire from these agencies the degree of aid you would receive given a hypothetical situation in which your family income was reduced from $700.00 a month to $120.00 a month.

				HOW LONG WILL IT TAKE AFTER DATE OF APPLICATION TO RECEIVE AID?
Federal unemployment		$______	a month	______Days
Dependent Children.	$______ per child	$______	(total) a month	______Days
Food Stamp Program	$______ stamp price			
	$______ bonus	$______	buying power per month	______Days
Commodity (Surplus food) Program.		$______	(retail value of goods available under program)	______Days
(free) School Lunch Program	$______ per child per month	$______	(total) a month	______Days
Private assistance program.		$______	per month	______Days
Other agency aid not listed above.		$______	per month	______Days
Add the $120.00 monthly income (listed above)		$120.00		
TOTAL (hypothetical) "Restricted" family income.		$______	per month	
Divide the total "Restricted" income in half—how much money would you and your family have to live on during a two week period?		$______	total (hypothetical) "Restricted" income for a two week period.	

4: Obtain a copy of the necessary forms used by the various federal and local agencies to determine "eligibility" for aid.

5: Obtain a copy of the monthly *Low Cost Food Plan* issued by the Department of Agriculture as a guide describing which nutritious foods can be bought at low prices for the two-week simulation, and how these foods might be used to plan a varied and well-balanced diet.

6: Record where you spend your normal family income by tabulating your family budget in percentages.

FAMILY EXPENDITURES

______% of the normal family income budgeted for the purchase *of food*

______% of the normal family income budgeted for *transportation*

______% of the normal family income budgeted for *rent*

______% of the normal family income budgeted for *public utilities*

______% of the normal family income budgeted for *entertainment*

______% of the normal family income budgeted for *clothing*

______% of the normal family income budgeted for *insurance* (savings)

______% of the normal family income budgeted for *other*.

Weeks Two and Three: Living on Welfare

1: Construct a "restricted" budget for the next two weeks by completing the table below:

RESTRICTED FAMILY BUDGET
FOR WEEK TWO - THREE

______% the purchase of food	$______	
______% transportation	$______	
______% rent	$______	
______% public utilities	$______	
______% entertainment	$______	
______% clothing	$______	
______% insurance (savings)	$______	
______% other	$______	
	$______	"Total restricted income" for the next two week period.

To construct your restricted budget, copy in the same percentage figures you recorded in your normal family budget (Week One, Step 6) for transportation, public utilities, clothing, and rent. For the remaining items (food, entertainment, insurance and other) distribute your remaining income as you chose.

Using these percentage figures and the total figure for your "restricted income" determine your actual monetary allotment for specifics such as food, transportation, etc.

2: During the next two weeks restrict family purchases of each item to the budget listed in the table above.

3: Keep a "family diary" recording your feelings and questions during this exercise.

4: Inquire from a local public medical facility the amount of medical aid available to a family stricken by financial hardship. Obtain a copy of the means test used to verify the release of Medicaid assistance to an impoverished family.

5: Spend an afternoon sitting in a local welfare agency and record your feelings and observations about its policy and practice.

PLACES AND THINGS FOR EXPERIMENTAL SCHOOLS

.Want to know how to lay down a floor that changes into an ice rink when a special conditioner is applied? Interested in converting an abandoned girdle factory or old mansion into an alternative school? Want to know the location of the nearest school experimenting with an "open space" plan? Or how about details on sharing a school with joint occupants, constructing prefabricated space frames, geodesic domes or urethane foam structures to enclose pools or recreational facilities? Home based schools, resource center design, reachout schools, and even non-school schools are treated in this fascinating collection of ideas.

This book is for the many schools who are in the process of planning changes for next year (or later) keyed around the concepts of alternatives and/or flexibility. A major problem is that older school buildings tend to restrict options. Remodeling a curriculum often involves remodeling a school building or at least a few classrooms. Reforms that neglect to change the physical structure are often stymied by the preconceptions built into physical space.

In **Places and Things. . .**each idea presented includes the name and address of an experienced resource person to contact for further information. No single idea is treated in depth so the book becomes a printed brainstorming session. But enough references and resource people are listed to make in-depth exploration of any of the ideas possible.

A valuable book, expecially to the reform-minded administrator. The 136-page book costs $2 from Educational Facilities Laboratories, 477 Madison Avenue, New York, N.Y. 10022.

TEACHING HUMAN BEINGS

Teaching Human Beings: 101 Subversive Activities for the Classroom
by Jeffrey Schrank (Cloth $7.95; Paper, $3.45)

Experienced teachers know that the most formidable obstacle to learning is not that students are ignorant but rather that they have been subject to institutional learning and parental training for so many years. What they do know is more limiting to their potential development than what they don't. Most books written for teachers are concerned with learning, Teaching Human Beings deals with unlearning. It is a book of ideas for group or classroom use to help teachers and students examine what they take for granted.

The book's 200 pages are packed with practical and usable teaching ideas for any course in the general humanities field-from social studies to religion, English or psychology. The basic theme of unlearning is divided into five main areas:

Sense Education--Schools are one of the institutions driving us sense-less. Here are some exploratory experiments to conduct to create awareness of the potential of the senses and to rediscover their power.

Hidden Assumptions--"The most important thing we can know about a man is what he takes for granted, and the most basic facts about a society are those that are seldom debated and generally regarded as settled or else are totally invisible."

Violence--A resource guide to the study of personal and social violence.

Death--Living fully and deeply is impossible unless one has come to grips with the problem of death and studied the art of dying.

Chemicals and the Body--A broad-based approach to drug education that concentrates on legal drugs especially food and its additives, coffee, nicotine, prescription drugs and alcohol.

Subversive Activities--A collection of group activities to promote unlearning in the area of human relations.

Each chapter contains teaching ideas, resources, filmographies with annotation and multiple sources, and research leads.

If you have even occasionally found good ideas in Media Mix or my other writings you should find Teaching Human Beings a storehouse of creative ideas.

Available now through any bookstore or from Beacon Press, 25 Beacon Street, Boston, Mass. 02108.

DESCHOOL PRIMER NUMBER FOUR

DESIGN A PACKAGE THAT WILL PROTECT AN EGG FROM BREAKING WHEN DROPPED FROM THE ROOF OF YOUR SCHOOL.
HOLD A CONTEST TO DETERMINE SUCCESSFUL DESIGNS!!!

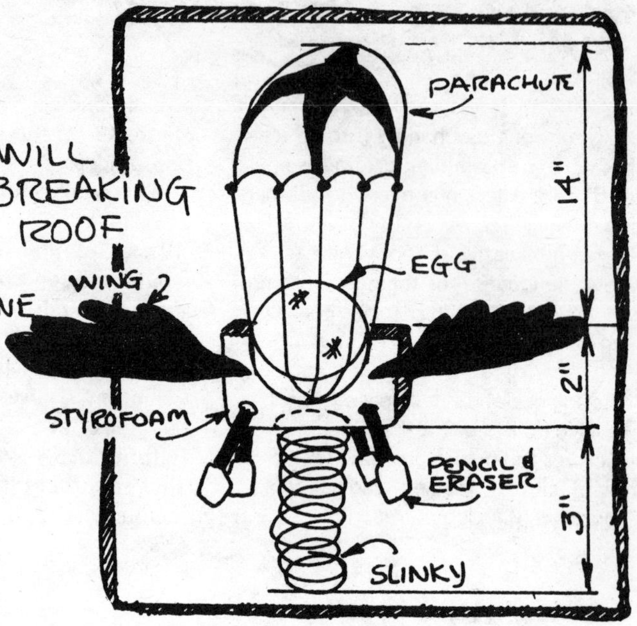

Ron Jones and the Zephyrus Exchange have done it again. **Deschool Primer No. 4** is an outlandishly oversized 24-page newspaper packed with wonderful ideas for creative teacher and learning. Some ideas are best for elementary school level but most are usable with a variety of age groups. The **Primer** costs $1.50 from Zephyus, 1201 Stanyan St., San Francisco, CA 94117.

What sort of subversive activities do Ran Jones and friends suggest? Here are a few samples:

CONSTRUCT A CONSUMER GUIDE FOR YOUR COMMUNITY.

1. Buy or bring from home different brands of the same food item.
2. Read the labels or ads for these items. What is the same or different in each product. How many additives are in each and what are they? Research everything on the labels.
3. Do a taste survey. Use blindfolds or hide the brand identification. Keep track of responses.
4. Do a "truth in advertising survey." Test your products against their advertising claims.
5. Do a cost analysis. Find the cost per ounce or pound, Which is most expensive. Which food do you think is the most expensive in the whole store? (clue: try the spice rack, some cost nearly $100 a pound).
6. Report your findings to the class and community. Rank order the brands. Publish the guide with an explanation of your methods.

INTRO TO FIGURATIVE LANGUAGE, POETRY. . .

1. Have each person make a list of their 20 favorite words. Four letter words, foreign words, made up words, words you don't know meaning of or can't spell are all o.k. No need for words to be related. No paragrpah writing with the words.
2. Once everyone has 20 have them cross out five. While this is being done sketch on the board a series of 15 blanks such as. . .

______ ______
______ ______ ______
______ ______
______
______ ______ ______ ______

Have each student fill in the blanks using the 15 words. Put them in any order. Try different combinations.

3. Depending on the group have them read results to each other, read some aloud, post them, print some on ditto sheets. The following samples are from Serramonee High School in Daly City, Calif: marshmellow comfy, wild russle jiggle o, sleek jitters, lith florescent blubber, burgandy claustrophobia.

FOCUS OR DO WITHOUT

Sometimes the only way to learn about something is to live without it; and sometimes we can appreciate something only when we draw attention or focus on it. . .

Try spending a day without: numbers, or books, or rules, or words, or winning, nouns, money, anger, machines, the color green, sugar, co-operation, freedom to assemble. Try spending a day with: someone new, or gratitude, or an old idea, a schedule, the color blue. . .

PEOPLE TELLING

(1) Place before students the contents of an individual's purse or wallet. (2) Invite the students to use this information in constructing a profile or description of the person who owns the item. (3) Discuss the problem solving strategies used by students during their investigation. (4) Invite the owner of the mystery items into class to determine the accuracy of the students' predictions.

PROVERB TELLING

(1) Obtain a book of proverbs and read one to your class -- but leave off the moral. (2) Instruct the class to write a moral that each person feels matches the fable. Read them one at a time. How close are they? Read the moral in the book. What does this all demonstrate?

FREE TEACHING MATERIALS

Catalog of Free Teaching Materials by Gordon Salisbury is a 364-page paperback listing over 8,500 free handouts supplied to teachers from kindergarten through college level. Much of the material is propaganda from government and industry, and much of very limited educational value. But amid the junk are some genuine finds.

Available for $3.25 (includes 25¢ postage) from:

CATALOG OF FREE TEACHING MATERIALS
P.O. Box 1075
Ventura, Calif. 93001

Civil Defense (Continued)

Statement of Understanding Between the American Hospital Asoc. & the American National Red Cross with Respect to Responsibility for Disaster Planning & Disaster Relief—4730 (12 pp.) (9-A)
Dew Line Photos (set of 8 x 10 photos of equipment & men on the Distant Early Warning System) (6-A)

See Also: SCIENCE, Atomic

AUDIO - VISUAL

A Treasure Chest of Audio Visual Ideas (teaching with film, use of A-V equipment, etc., 32 pp.) (A)
Timely Topics—For Media's Sake (use of media in classroom, 2 pp.) (A)
Atoms at the Science Fair—WAS-001 (how to prepare a project, 52 pp.) (10-A)
*How to Create Classroom Bulletin Boards—F-26 (planning and producing for teachers of all grades, 16 pp.) (A)
Graflex Audio-Visual Digest (suggestions on instruction with overhead projector, films, etc., 48 pp.) (A)
So You're Going On TV (9-A)
Large Screen Television Projection in Schools (4 pp. reprint, semi-technical) (A)
Shell Films (films available, 1967, 20 pp.) (A)
Released Textbooks, Films & Other Teaching Materials (gives publications, prices and where to purchase them, 1968, 72 pp.) (A)

See Also: TELEVISION: PHOTOGRAPHY

CIVIL LIBERTIES and RIGHTS

International Year for Human Rights—Vol. 49, No. 1 (civil rights and liberties, freedom and democratic responsibility, 4 pp., 1968) (9-A) 3
Our Freedoms (explanation of, booklet) (7-A)
Your "Bill of Rights" (sheet 8½x11 listing the first 10 amendments) (6-A)
A Survey of the Progress of Freedom in 1969 and th Legacy of the 1960's (in U.S. and in the world, 27 pp.) (10-A)
Not Every Battle is Armageddon (an address giving optimistic viewpoint on current problems, 11pp.) (6-A)
U.S. Immigration Policy (reprint from American Jewish Yearbook, 12 pp.) (10-A)
Human Background of the Civil Rights Issue (4 pp.) (10-A)
Policy Statement on Racial Discrimination (issued by Nat'l. Assembly for Social Policy and Development, Inc., 1968, pamphlet, 1 p.) (11-A)
Racial Equality: The Myth and the Realty—Reprint 26 (a speech by John Howard griffin, author of Black Like Me, 28pp.) (10-A)
Minority Access to College—A Ford Foundation report (the problem and effort made, good statistics, 48 pp.) (A)
A Survey of Black America Doctorates (statistics and trends, 11 pp.)
The Negro and the American Economy—Reprint No. 338 (unemployment, wages, discrimination and other factors, 60 pp.) (A)
Apprentice Training Programs and Racial Discrimination—Reprint No. 16 (nature of problem, unions, state action & 1964 Civil Rights Act, 24 pp.) (12-A
Minorities and Apprenticeship—Reprint No. 355 (history of discrimination and progress made, 14 pp.) (A)
How Management Views Its Race Relations Responsibilities—Reprint No. 336 (a study of trends, 28 pp.) (A)
The Courts, The Public, and The Law Explosion (recommendation of a group of Americans, 14 pp., 1965) (12-A)
Respect for the Law—Vol. 50, No. 3 (need for and part police play, 4 pp., 1969) (10-A) 3
State Legislatures In American Politics (recommendations are made, 14 pp., 1966) (12-A)
The Social and Economic Status of Negroes in the United States, 1969—BLS No. 375 (statistical info. from Bureau of Labor Statistics, 96 pp.) (A)
The Anxious Majority—Chicago's Working Class (series of conversations with white working class families—unrest, dissatisfaction, fears, 15 pp.) (12-A)
The Peace Corps: Black Pride, Black Action (an address encouraging black people to contribute to the building of a strong cultural, economic & political community—advantage of Peace Corps, 12 pp.) (9-A) 20

FARALLONES SCRAPBOOK

FARALLONES SCRAPBOOK is brimming over with creative ideas for changing classroom boxes into living spaces. The first part of the book presents poetically the theory of shaping environments:

"learning to shape
the spaces that enclose
your experiences
opens a door
to a consciousness
necessary to understand
the balance of man
and his natural environment..."

The book presents strong arguments for the fact that the class environment is itself a learning structure that has to meet certain needs--privacy, energy discharge, gathering, choice, ritual, freedom and creativity. The book encourages questioning of the "messages" given by a classroom's shape, the kind of lighting, the teacher's desk, the arrangement of working space, and the normal strait jacket desks. There are plenty of practical ideas for changing classroom space.

Some of the ideas? Ready made murals from billboard companies, painted walls, do-it-yourself library shelving for next to nothing, frame partitions, small rooms, bean bag chairs for under $20, cardboard construction, folded cardboard igloos, gigantic tinker toys, zones, inflatables, a trash list of free things, and an introduction to geodesic dome building. All the above ideas are treated in almost blueprint detail in the book.

Even if many of the ideas are not usable in your classroom the ideas can be used for festivals, celebrations, outdoor events, temporary structures, dances, displays, or student lounges.

The 142-page hand crafted book was put together by a group actively engaged in "returning architecture to its roots in each person...so that each of us can rediscover the innate pleasure and usefulness of participating in making a place." $4.25 postpaid from Farallones Designs, Star Route, Point Reyes Station, Calif. 94956. Orders must be prepaid. Calif. residents add 5% tax.

The only reason you never did it before is because you never did it before!

Help yourself to a new awareness:
Change your environment and
you change yourself

CONTENTS

OUR TRIPS

- 4 journeys into making schools better places
- the classroom box

WAYS TO CHANGE CLASSROOMS

- what to do with halls, walls, doors
- basic tools and how to use them
- building bargain goodies with kids
- painting
- building space dividers, quiet places
- cardboard carpentry
- classroom case histories

GEOMETRY & DOMES

- beyond the box: geometry for builders
- cardboard and stick domes
- plywood domes made easy
- building models

PLAYGROUND BUILDING

- building good stuff out of old tires and scrap lumber
- rope yoga
- inflatables
- surface materials

TRASH CAN DO IT

- personal ecology
- free materials: where to get them; what to do with them
- musical instruments

GRAB BAG

- a couple of letters
- family Spring Equinox
- an old Indian Game

FLAMEPROOFING PAPER AND PAPERBOARD

To flameproof paper and paper products in which afterglow may be a problem, the National Bureau of Standards suggests formulas containing ammonium phosphate, a chemical which has superior glow-inhibiting qualities. Here is a suitable formula devised by the Army Quartermaster Corps:

Borax	7 lb or 7 parts by weight
Boric acid	3 lb or 3 parts by weight
Diammonium phosphate	5 lb or 5 parts by weight
Water	13.2 gal or 110 parts by weight

Heat the water and dissolve the chemicals in it by stirring continuously as they are added. Cool it to lukewarm temperature before application. The addition of about 1/10 part of a wetting agent (liquid dishwashing detergent will do) will help it penetrate the paper. Application may be made by immersion, brush, or spray methods. Enough should be applied, however, so that the weight of the material when dry will have increased about 15 percent. Colors are not ordinarily affected by this solution more than they are by wetting with water, but it is best to test for color fastness before applying it.

The following formula is also effective for paper products:

Diammonium phosphate	10 lb or 10 parts by weight
Ammonium sulfate	5 lb or 5 parts by weight
Water	12 gal or 100 parts by weight

Mix, cool, add wetting agent, and apply as suggested for the formula above. In humid locations, it may be advisable to include 4 or 5 parts of a soluble mildew inhibitor, such as sodium benzoate, sodium propionate, or one of the proprietary fungicides.

FIRE-RESISTING PAINT

No paint can make a surface absolutely fireproof, but this one has proved useful in retarding fire:

Powdered asbestos	2 lb
Sodium aluminate	½ lb
Hydrated lime	½ lb
Sodium silicate, granular	1½ lb

The sodium silicate should be in the form of the granular metasilicate. Dissolve this, along with the aluminate and the lime, by stirring in the smallest possible amount of water. Then stir in the asbestos and add enough more water to make the paint easy to apply. Dry color may be added if desired. Apply at least 2 coats.

FIRE-RETARDING COATINGS FOR WOOD

Many coating materials protect wood against fire in varying degree. The amount of protection provided depends on the amount and thoroughness of the application and the severity of fire exposure. Most preparations are of value primarily for interior use and are not durable when exposed to weather.

Here is a water-base paint that blisters under fire to produce a nonburning insulating coating:

	Parts by weight
Sodium silicate solution (40-42° Baumé)	11
Kaolin	15
Water	10

Again, 3 or 4 thick coats are necessary with 4 coats covering about 100 square feet.

NIELSEN MATERIAL

Speaking of the Nielsens . . . free publications ideal for a teacher of TV are available from Nielsen -- the ratings people. They have an 18-page booklet which clearly and colorfully presents statistics about the growth of television in the past dozen years. In spite of utterly unreal artwork reminiscent of neo-first grade Dick and Jane the booklet is a nice discussion aid and available free in classroom quantities.

There is also a free-loan film, The Nielsen Ratings, which shows how an audometer records TV viewing and explains how sample testing gives an accurate estimate of who watches what. For either item write Larry Fergus, A.C. Nielsen Company, 2101 W. Howard St., Evanston, Ill. 60645.

DOING THE MEDIA

Doing the Media: A Portfolio of Activities and Resources is a compilation of articles, photos, sketches, resource listings, equipment guides, and bibliographies for people interested in doing media. The book is a result of a year-long media pilot study to teach various media activities to elementary school children. The contents cover a broad range of media projects -- from how to make your own still camera to suggestions for evaluating programming on network television; from guidelines for instituting and administrating a media program to teaching animation to little kids. There are sections on photography, filmmaking, audio- and videotaping as well as some bargain basement media programs for teachers with skinny budgets.

Although intended for teachers of elementary grades the book has direct use in junior high and for beginning media teachers at any level.

220 pages, $5.00, orders must be prepaid.

CENTER FOR UNDERSTANDING MEDIA, INC.
267 West 25th Street
New York, N.Y. 10001
(212) 691-2260

The underlying objective in all ten activities is to establish a process. I am trying to help my students isolate important pieces of behavior (both good and bad) determine why this is happening, discuss what might be done to make it work better, experiment with new kinds of behavior and, finally, study the effects of these new ways of interrelating with more videotaping.

Dramatic Modes

A common kind of videotape making involves acting out a story. Our immediate affinity to this kind of activity is natural. The predominant programming on broadcast TV is dramatic. The immediate playback ability of vt, plus its sound-synchronous capability, and ease of production (portable, no lighting, etc.) suggest classroom utilization on two levels: first, helping kids develop their skills as actors (or, more generally, developing their awareness of all their body's modes of communicating); second, allowing students to produce, write, direct, tape, evaluate) various sorts of dramatic material.

11. An Improvisation Becomes a Teleplay: This activity begins with an ordinary improvisational situation that the kids act out with very little planning. After a "situation" has been chosen, students quickly assign themselves the various "characters" that the scene calls for. (Two examples: the scene is a movie theater. The action consists of the interaction of various comic stereotypes - the lady with the hat, the man who always gives away the plot, the popcorn eater, etc. The scene is a locker room. The action develops between members and the coach of a team that has just lost a national championship because two of the stars broke training the evening before). The first run-through of the improvisation your students choose should be done fast and then played back immediately. During a viewing of the tape, kids naturally come up with ways to improve the presentation and this, of course, is the way in which they learn an important thing about the medium as well as their dramatic scene. For a second time, the class does the improvisation, studies the tape and, in the process, begins to "fix" both action and charac-

terization. Sometimes it is helpful to outline the developing "teleplay" on the blackboard. Usually, a director is appointed at this time. When everyone feels they are ready, the drama is taped for a final time in its more formal and scripted form. This means that the director and the camera man can interrupt a straight run-through in order to change angles, get a close-up and the like. This places new demands on the actors. If the students feel their teleplay is pretty good, they might ask another class to see it and give their responses.

12. Dramatic Readings and Plays: Whether in a classroom, on a stage, or "on-location" outdoors and elsewhere, the portable vtr equipment can be used to tape almost any sort of student drama. On a more informal basis, students can make effective tapes of dramatic readings. In this activity, the video image constantly remains close-in on the faces of the students reading parts in a play. The camera can be stopped between each reader to avoid panning movements. Because one never really sees background, costume, movement or the spatial relationships between characters, and because the "headshots" of students delivering their lines follow each other immediately, this format is very easy to do and requires little preparation. Taping of dramatic readings focuses on the verbal and facial expression of those participating and somehow asks the viewer to use his imagination in a highly participatory and effective way. Once students have rehearsed a play, it is easy and fun to videorecord it. If a production is being conducted on a school stage, the portable equipment can record the drama in different ways and usually without any additional lighting. Naturally, the simplest way to do this is by repositioning the camera on a tripod at the front center of the stage and then shooting the play continuously. A somewhat more complicated (and more effective) technique is to have the camera move around on the stage to cover different positions. Taping a play in this way, the actors will have to stop the action from time to time as the cameraman and sound-man choose a good location for the next scene or piece of stage "business". It will help if a student video director works with the players to develop a "shooting script" that delineates camera coverage. If you decide, as suggested above, to break up the shooting of a play in "real time", remember that you can also break up the locations of the shooting. Leave the stage and its sets for more realistic and varied sets. Also remember that with a single camera you cannot edit your tapes. Hence things have to be shot in their final order with as little discontinuity joining the various shots as possible. Always have your students try a sample scene first. They will soon discover both the difficulties and the rewards of this kind of videotaping.

Bio-Documentary Modes

For me there seems to be a kind of middle-ground between dramatic and documentary vtr production modes. It is a twilight zone that focuses on students' videorecording their own world and their own selves. For lack of a better term, I lump activities of this kind into a category labled Bio-Documentary. Here are two projects of this kind that students find rewarding. Note that both activities require that students use equipment on their own. In addition, bio-documentary videotaping often requires that a single student operate the portapak by himself. If your children are too little or if security problems are too acute, both activities will need major modification or may not be possible at all.

13. Portraits: The class divides into pairs. The idea is for each student to collect no more than five minutes of material on his partner. The visual material should be "unrehearsed" -- that is, the students should videorecord each other in what they feel are "natural" situations. The tape is not edited. The videomaker next creates a sound track. This audio material is dubbed in over the visual material (an easy process that the directions for your portable vtr will explain). The audio track can be made by having the videomaker "interview" his subject or by having the subject simply do an extemporaneous monologue about himself or herself. The audio track can be transferred to the videotape from an audio tape recorder or "dubbed live" by the pairs during playback. When the completed tapes are played for the class, the "subject" or a friend might be asked to comment on how close the portrait came to "real" life. When I have used this approach, I find that children get a lot out of reflecting on the demands placed on them as both the videomaker and the subject of the videotape portrait.

14. Self Portraits: In this activity an individual video maker creates an indirect portrait of himself or herself by collecting images and sounds of people, places and events that subjectively seem to capture that videomaker's own and very personal world. This kind of production might require a student to have access to the vtr while at home (optimal but often impractical). Or it might require a student's use of the vtr in unstructured parts of the school day (interviews with friends in other classes, taping of favorite recreational spots and times within the school day.) A class trip can provide an easier situation in which a youngster can collect self-portrait materials. The basic thrust behind this activity is to have students try to amplify their own interests and fascinations so that others can experience and know more about them.

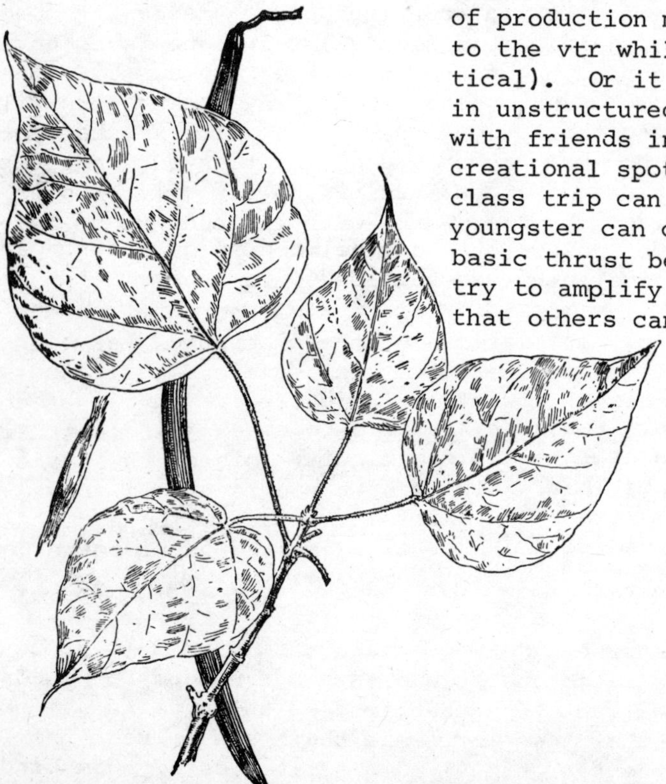

Video

MASS MEDIA (LOYOLA)

Mass Media. . . is a student text from Loyola Press by Ann Christine Heintz, Lawrence Reuter and Elizabeth Conley. The 240-page 8 1/2" x 11" workbook contains readings that rarely extend beyond one page. There are hundreds of scattered quotes, questions to discuss and/or research, descriptions of role playing situations, assignments, charts to fill in, and pictures. The book provides relatively little in the way of hard information preferring to have students go out and do their own research.

Mass Media deals with audience measurement, advertising, ratings, news reporting, the gatekeeper process, freedom of the press, popular magazines, and newspapers.

The student book ($3.20) and the teaching guide ($2.40) are both excellent idea sources for media teachers. Available from Loyola University Press, 3441 North Ashland Ave., Chicago, IL 60657. Prices given are for either single or multiple copies.

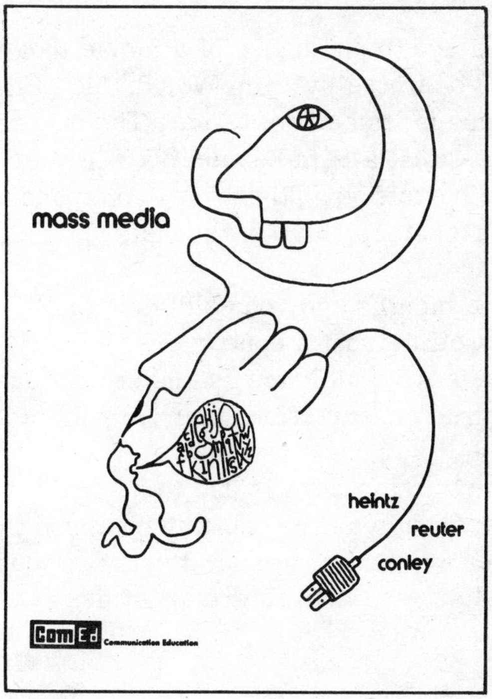

INVESTIGATE

1 INVESTIGATE the growing number of newspaper companies that also own radio and television stations. What is the possibility of single-control news presentations in a community?

2 INVESTIGATE the emerging cable TV industry to find out whether ownership will be more diversified than the present major media, or will it be under much the same control.

3 COMPARE the British government owned-and-operated broadcasting network with the privately owned networks in the United States.

Where I Stand -

Based on your experience with the units in this section, which of the following positions seems better to you?

a) The news process has become so complex today that it's impossible to say who's responsible for the finished product. It is not clear who to praise when it's good, or who to blame when it's bad.	b) The areas of influence in professional news reporting are still clear enough that people can evaluate the performance and assign responsibility for its strengths and weaknesses.

SIMULATE

Using the insights and conclusions you arrived at above, role play the following Media Man Simulation.

You are the manager of a movie theater, one of forty in a four-state area owned and operated by Film World, Inc. Film World makes the bookings for all the theaters in its central office. The only thing you do with regard to booking is to request that a film be held over in your theater if it has been especially successful at the box office. Otherwise, you manage the building, arrange publicity, manage the concessions, hire personnel, and deal with complaints.

Two months ago you exhibited an "X" rated movie that did remarkably well at the box office, but a controversy ensued because the PTA charged the movie contained "excessive violence and nudity." You received ten angry phone calls and several church organizations planned public censures and boycotts.

Now another film is due to be shown in your theater that has many of the same characteristics as the one which caused the controversy. You have previewed the film, advance publicity is on display in your lobby, and now representatives of the PTA and several church groups want to see you this afternoon. How will you deal with them?

contents

PERSUASION

Persuasion.....is the title of a textbook on how the media are used to persuade. The 225-page student workbook is accompanied by an excellent teacher's guide. Suitable for journalism, English or communications classes. From Loyola Press, 3441 N. Ashland Ave., Chicago, Ill. 60657.

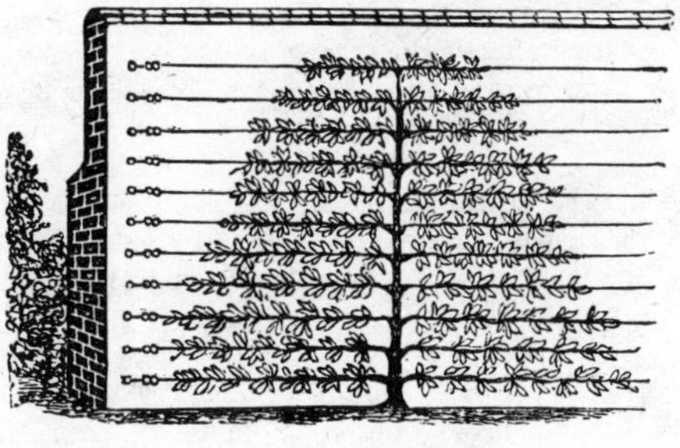

Somebody Ought To Do Something!

We students outnumber the faculty 20 to 1. It seems to us that we should have something to say about the things that affect us. Everybody feels that Mrs. Kilgallen is one teacher who really takes time to know her students. Even if she has only been here since September, she knows us better than some of the people who have been here for years. But *they* have to cut the budget, so Mrs. Kilgallen goes. That doesn't make sense. Somebody ought to do something. Here's a game that will tell you what you can do.

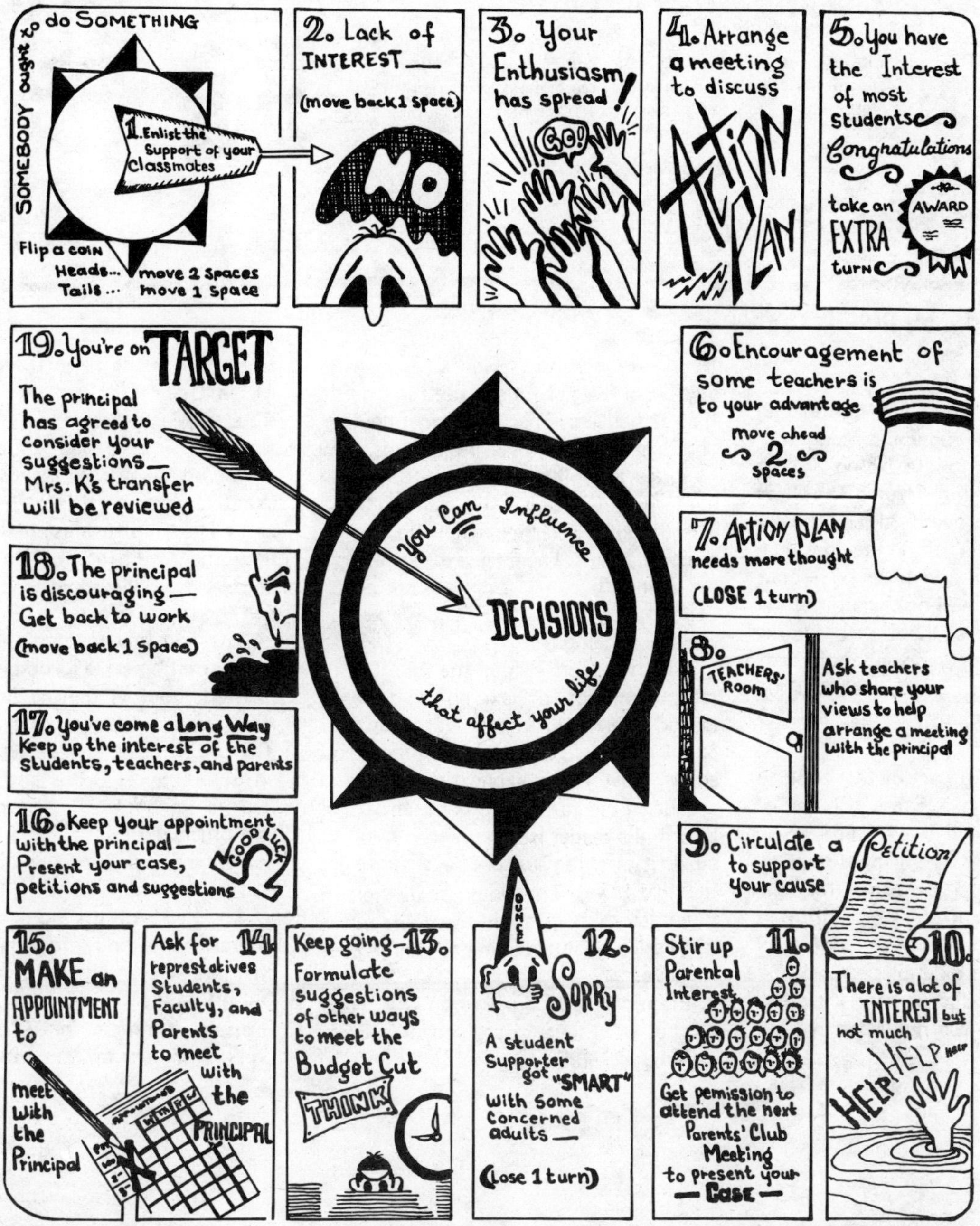

discover

Involvement is another technique a persuader can use to attract his audience and influence them. Oil company games, sing-alongs, audience participation shows and effective teachers all use involvement techniques. They stimulate interest, make people participate in a cause or project, make an audience a part of the show.

The Foster Parent ad makes a direct appeal to the reader and seeks a definite response from him. The headline "hooks" the audience into reading the copy and those who are moved by the appeal and want to help can get involved by mailing in the coupon.

Did you ever send in a box top? Write a letter to a newspaper? Phone in to a radio show? Vote in an opinion or political poll? This is audience involvement.

Some appeals seek help for the needy, for a worthy cause or program. They appeal to the generosity of the audience. Other involvement appeals offer benefits to the participant himself: an opportunity to influence decisions that affect him, a way to save money, a chance to win a trip to Hawaii.

The basic approach to involvement is through personal questions, opportunities that call for audience participation, or a message so constructed that the audience must help work it out like a puzzle or a game.

INTER FACE

Flip through a current magazine and cut out every involvement appeal you can find. What does each one ask you to do? What motive does each one propose to attract your involvement?

Appeal:	Request:	Motive:

BOOKS ON THE MEDIA

The News Twisters. . . After reading **Don't Blame the People** and being convinced the networks are biased against liberals pick up Edith Efron's **The News Twisters.** She "proves" in an equally convincing manner that the national newscasts are biased in favor of liberals and Democrats. The book examines the national newscasts of the three networks during the election campaign months of 1968. Much of her material is now dated but her methodology is adaptable to bias-searching on any topic.

The most useful part of the book to **Media Mix** readers is Efron's listing of thirty-three sneaky ways newscasters bias their reports. From mind-reading, to glamorization, fake neutrality, the poison sandwich, and one-word editorials she catalogs the crimes of pseudo-objectivity and provides examples of each.

Manor Books, 355 pages, $1.25. The hard cover edition was published in 1971 by Nash.

News: A Consumer's Guide. . . by Ivan and Carol Doig promises more in its title than it delivers. The "consumer advice" about how to spot bias and hoaxes, how to judge reliability in news and how to consume news selectively seems to be an afterthought, attached near the end of some chapters. The advice is vague ranging from "become a discerning critic" and (don't) "rely too heavily on the statement being true."

Afterthoughts aside, the book contains hundreds of examples of bias, loaded words, examples of deception, gobbledegook, slanted headlines and editing distortions from the press and broadcast media. The book has plenty of info if the reader is organized enough to pluck it out; the authors never quite get the fire going. The book reads well in some places, bogs down in others but is still basically entertaining as well as provocative.

Prentice-Hall, Englewood Cliffs, N. J. is the publisher. Hard cover $6.95, paperback $3.95.

Don't Blame the People: How the News Media Use Bias, Distortion and Censorship to Manipulate Public Opinion. . . Robert Cirino is a high school journalism teacher seemingly obsessed with showing exactly what the title of his book indicates. He demonstrates in over 300 pages how the media are biased in favor of conservative viewpoints, big business and the status quo.

The first few chapters have an identical format -- (a) a problem, (b) documented proof of the media's neglect of this crucial problem during the 1960's. The problems he approaches are hunger, auto safety, cigarettes and cancer, and later in the book VD, prison conditions, and organized crime. These chapters are convincing but hardly exciting to read and are definitely dated.

The heart of the book and its most interesting reading is found in the middle chapters -- "Prostitution: A Problem in Definition" (title derived from Theodore Dreiser's comment that "The Ameircan press, with very few exceptions is a kept press. Kept by big corporations the way a whore is kept by a rich man."), "How to Become Newsworthy," and "A Catalog of Hidden Bias." Any one of these chapters is well worth the cost of the entire book.

Don't Blame the People is not the kind of book that could be used as a text. Cirino himself has plenty of bias in his research, but any teacher should be able to mine it for a few dozen teaching ideas for a media course.

Paperback is $2.45, Vintage books V-788, from Random House.

Readings in the Mass Media . . . . is a series of three paperbound books on Journalism, Radio & Television and Film. All three are edited by Allen and Linda Kirschner and each contains about 300 pages of well selected readings. Definitely a series to consider for college and junior college media courses and perhaps a high powered high school class. The books also make fine teacher background readers and reference sources.

$4.35 each from Odyssey Press, 4300 W. 62nd Street, Indianapolis, Ind. 46268.

The Mass Media Book. . .edited by Rod Holmgren and William Norton (Prentice-Hall, $3.95, paperback, 421 pages) is another excellent anthology of readings for high school media classes. The book is marketed for the college and junior college level but its reasonable price places it well within the range of many high schools. There are 31 readings grouped into sections on news media, entertainment media, television and popular art. It is certainly a good library addition if not a textbook. For purchase or examination copies contact Prentice-Hall, Englewood Cliffs, N.J.

BOOKS: MEDIA

Mass Media: Forces in Our Society. . . . is an excellent anthology of readings in media usable in courses from senior high through college. The 395-page paperback has sections on general theories of mass communication, print, TV, radio, newscasting, censorship, periodicals, ads, politics, entertainment and even pop music. Each of the selections is brief. There is an occasional page of study questions but the book considerately leaves teaching ideas up to the teacher instead of suggesting dozens of "activities."

Among the most interesting features of the book are some comparative media case studies. One presents six versions of the story of Janis Joplin's death to reveal how the different print media treated the story. Another prints a Stewart Alsop column from **Newsweek** and then the **Reader's Digest** edited version showing how condensation can influence the effect of an article.

The anthology is cleanly designed, spiced with frequent cartoons and graphic displays. There is even an **Esquire** parody of the **Saturday Evening Post** titled "The Great Speckled Post."

The anthology is a well edited selection of readings that would make an excellent resource book for any media teacher and a textbook for others. It currently stands as one of the best readers available and is reasonably priced at $4.50 in paperback from Harcourt, Brace, Jovanovich, 757 Third Avenue, New York, N. Y. 10017. Edited by Francis and Ludmila Voelker.

The Information Machines: Their Impact on Men and the Media. . . by Ben Bagdikian is now available in paperback (Harper Colophon Books CN 258, $2.95). If a teacher preparing a high school media class could read only one book as preparation, **Information Machines** would have to rank among the most highly recommended. The book would make a fine student text on the college level or even in advanced high school classes in journalism or media.

Information Machines deals almost exclusively with the news gathering process. Bagdikian is an experienced news manager and among the best known and most hard-nosed news critics in the country.

One theme he dwells on is the importance of the gatekeeper in the news process -- that person who controls the valve and rejects four out of five news items that cross his desk. He also explores centralization of news sources, the effect of advertising on news and the near disappearance of competing newspapers in local areas.

Information Machines is one of those rare "must read" books for the teacher or consumer of news.

Mass Media & Society . . . . by Alan Wells is an excellent college level anthology of readings in mass media. It is also a fine teacher resource book for the high school level. All that keeps the paperback from an unqualified high-school recommendation is its $6.95 price, 400+ page length and absence of items on film and comics. A few of the 51 articles in the book are Raymond Nixon on "Trends in U.S. Newspaper Ownership: Concentration With Competition," "Can Mass Magazines Survive?" Sir William Haley on "Where TV News Fails," Nicholas Johnson on the FCC, David White on "The Gate Keeper: A Case Study in the Selection of News," "Behavioral Support For Opinion Change," "Mass Communication Among the Urban Poor," Herbert Schiller on "Mind Management: Mass Media in the Advanced Industrial State," and the obligatory McLuhan on "The Medium is the Message."

Unfortunately no index but still a fine reader with plenty of solid material. The National Press, 850 Hansen Way, Palo Alto, Calif.

New from Nicholas Johnson. . . Test Pattern For Living (Bantam paperback $1.25) by Nicholas Johnson makes nice lightweight diversionary reading for a media course. The slight paperback is Johnson's interpretation of how to move from CON II to CON III (or at least II 1/2) while still surviving in the Corporate State. The book is not notable for new ideas or poetic images but does sometimes stick to the mind and force readers to examine their own life style. Television plays only a supporting role in this drama of the villains of the Corporate State. The role is one of educator who teaches willing students that happiness and life is found in the Corporate products it pushes.

Media Violence. . . by Howard Muson is part of a **New York Times** "Issues and Perspectives" series. The nicely illustrated 64-page booklet provides a clearly-written survey of the problem of the romance between media and violence. The booklet touches upon scientific research, violence in the news, the effect of violence on children, the battle about human aggression. The book is written as a student discussion aid and serves this purpose nicely. List price is $1.32 and school price an attractive 99¢ from Harper & Row.

Readings in Mass Communication . . . . edited by Michael Emery and Ted Smythe is another fine anthology for a general media course. This 500-page paperback is a bit much for most high school situations but would be suitable for college or for teacher background on any level. Selections are grouped according to the topics of increasing access to the mass media, control of media, news sources and relevant reporting, change in the traditional media, alternatives for minorities, TV news, treatment of minorities and the changing content of stories and photos.

$6.50 from Wm. C. Brown Company, 135 S. Locust St., Dubuque, Iowa 52001.

About Television. . .by Martin Mayer (Harper & Row, hardcover, $10) is certainly one of the most readable books available about television. Mayer plays the role of the guide taking readers behind the scenes and screens of televisionland. He plays his role with fitting objectivity leaving criticism of TV for others.

In readable terms he explains which programs draw which kinds of viewers, the differences between American and European TV, how advertisers buy TV time, the contrasting view of networks and Public Television, how a TV show is put together, Monday Night Football, Fairness Doctrine and on and on. Reading level is suitable for high school but not as a text. **About Television** will be released as a paperback later this year.

COPING WITH MASS MEDIA
By Joseph Littell (ed.)
McDougal, Littell Co.

Textbook publishers used to model their offerings on the TV dinner--well balanced meals of knowledge requiring little preparation and almost totally lacking in taste and color. But now teachers and students are tired of the bland the publishers are taking the smorgasbord approach. They offer a wide variety of material attractively displayed to tempt even the unwilling consumer (student). The smorgasbord usually takes the form of a series of paperbacks from which the teacher can select for each semester.

COPING WITH THE MASS MEDIA is part of a smorgasbord from McDougal, Littell & Company. The 157-page paperback is extremely attractive and might well lure the non-reader to taste its wisely chosen offering of articles on media. The menu includes two selections by Stuart Chase on Mass Media, an excerpt from Nicholas Johnson's HOW TO TALK BACK TO YOUR TV SET, Pauline Kael on "Trash, Art and the Movies," an article on putting out a newspaper, excerpts from McLuhan and Carpenter, and passages from Tom Wolfe and Howard Gossage writing about McLuhan. The book is fun to read and teach.

In spite of its excellence, COPING... has the same problem all paperback texts share--cost. The book costs $2.67 (school price) or 1.7¢ per page. The average mass circulation paperback costs five times less than the average trade paperback. For $2.67 teachers could purchase the entire original paperback version of UNDERSTANDING MEDIA and HOW TO TALK BACK.. plus perhaps another anthology or book or magazine subscription. This "grocery store" approach allows greater flexibility, more depth and greater possibility that a few students will read the complete books.

With small budgets and rising costs teachers should definitely weigh very carefully the advantages and disadvantages of the offerings of textbook publishers vs. adapting mass circulation books for class use. If the course is mass media and the decision is to stick with the textbook, start the search with COPING WITH THE MASS MEDIA.

A free examination copy is available from McDougal Littell & Co., Box 1667, Evanston, Ill. 60204. They also have books on HOW WORDS CHANGE OUR LIVES, DIALECTS & LEVELS OF LANGUAGE, and USING FIGURATIVE LANGUAGE.

A BROADCAST RESEARCH PRIMER is a 64-page book designed for small radio stations to help them conduct their own surveys to judge size and quality of listening audience. The booklet is non-technical yet surprising in depth. It can give a creative teacher ideas for a unit on data gathering, opinion polls and media surveys. $1 per copy from Research Department, National Association of Broadcasters, 1771 N Street, N.W., Washington 20036 D.C.

POPULAR MEDIA AND THE TEACHING OF ENGLISH

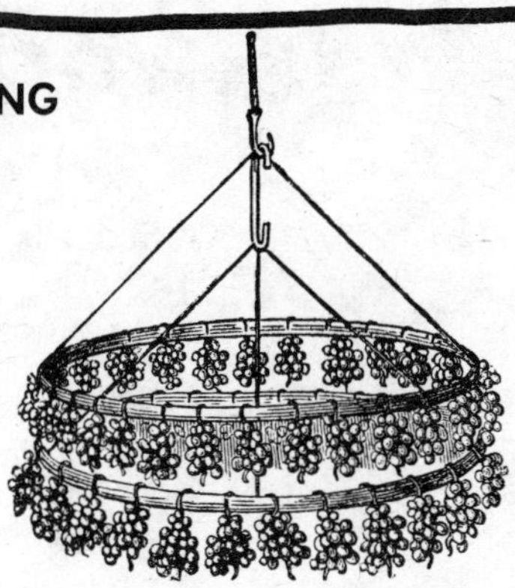

GIBLIN – Popular Media and the Teaching of English
Ed., by Thomas R. Giblin, Univ., of Colorado, Colorado Springs Center (276 pp., 1972)

Collection of articles dealing with the WHY and HOW of popular media study in the secondary English classroom: Why the high school English teacher needs to look more closely at the popular media, and how the teacher might act upon his perceptions. Unifying theme is that through popular media, both student and teacher learn more about themselves and society. CONTENTS: DEVELOPING A RATIONALE FOR POPULAR MEDIA STUDY: On Mediacy, *F. McLaughlin.* Popular Culture and Negro Education, *R. L. Beard.* Violence and the Mass Media, *C. M. Mance.* Mass Media Curriculum, *M. A. McCullough.* Image and Reality, *S. I. Hayakawa.* Film, Television, and Reality, *C. Solway.* AN ENGLISH TEACHER'S CHALLENGE: Wired for Sound, *W. Ong.* An Extension of Film and Television Study, *J. M. Culkin, S. J.* A Recipe for Triggering Relevance, *M. McLaughlin.* Tool, Weapon, Fine Instrument, *J. Schmittroth.* UNDERSTANDING McLUHAN: Gadfly and the Dinosaur, *T. Palmer.* Cooling Down the Classroom, *R. T. Sidwell.* Schoolman's Guide to Marshall McLuhan, *J. M. Culkin, S. J.* AN EXPANDING VIEW OF LITERATURE: Is Literature Dying? *S. Simonson.* Literature and the Resumption of Self, *E. J. Farrell.* The Lively Arts, *S. D. Wehr.* An Integrated Approach to the Teaching of Film and Literature, *J. S. Katz.* The Literate Adolescent in an Age of Mass Media, *J. Cameron* and *E. Plattor.* Rock Poetry, Relevance, and Revelation, *H. W. English.* Comics as Classics? *C. Suhor.* War in the Classroom, *L. Penfield.* PAPERBACKS: In Defense of Trash, *J. Rouse.* Slow Readers, *L. L. Hardman.* Here Come De Paperbacks, *R. Murdick* and *M. F. Kelly, Jr.* ". . . Think of the Kids, Too." NEWS, NEWSPAPERS, AND MAGAZINES: News Media and Social Science Teaching, *J. H. Langer.* The Newspaper, Part I & II, *L. S. Johnson.* Cartoons in the Classroom, *L. Brown* and *H. B. Wachs.* Five Dozen Ideas for Teaching the Newspaper Unit, *H. F. Decker.* Teaching Values in Magazine Reading, *T. N. Walters.* TELEVISION: What Is the High School Teacher of English Doing About Television? *S. Tengel.* A Chronicle of Television Use at Alhambra High School, *H. Lavern Coffey.* Get Smart, *R. Meadows.* A New Way to Evaluate Programs, *R. R. Monaghan.* FILM AND FILM-MAKING: Film Study is Here to Stay, *S. M. Grabowski.* I Was a Teen-Age Movie Teacher, *J. M. Culkin, S. J.* The Liveliest Art in the Classroom, *A. Franza.* To Look or To See, *F. Silva.* Animated Cinema, *F. D. Martarella.* Student Filmmaking, Why and How, *P. Carrico.* Sing Sweetly of My Many Bruises, *V. Tilford.* Can They Picture Themselves Better With Movies, *R. Bumstead.* Freaking Around With Films, *R. E. Sheratsky.*

Paperback, $3.95 from:

GOODYEAR PUBLISHING
Box 486
Pacific Palisades, Calif. 90272

THE POPULAR CULTURE EXPLOSION

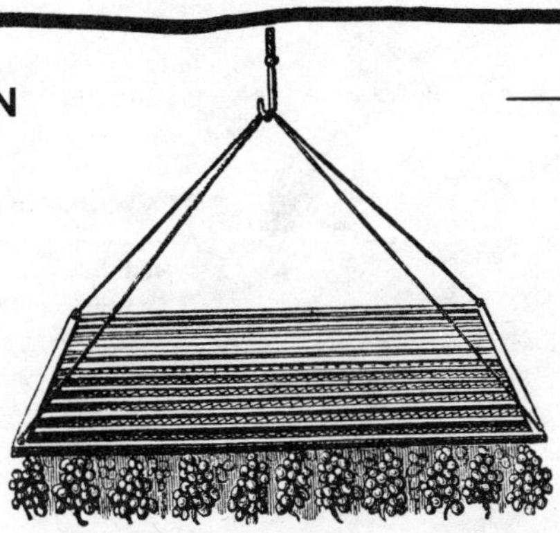

The Popular Culture Explosion. . . .by Ray B. Browne and David Madden is a 200+ page magazine-size "textbook" of pop culture. Designed for use in media courses the paperback text contains dozens of full page ads, articles like **McCall's** "Love Among the Rattlesnakes: Charles Manson," or **True** Readers Questions Column (where you can find out that the Average American adult male is 3.9 inches taller than his Japanese counterpart), or **Reader's Digest** on marijuana, the Boy Scout Handbook, **Mad**, song lyrics, Ron Cobb cartoons, short stories, a picture of Raquel Welsh, and more gems and jetsam of mass culture.

The book is a contemporary time capsule, a scrapbook for anyone over twelve and a provocative compendium highly useful to the creative teacher. Teachers will find no difficulty in getting students to read from this book, in fact they will have a hard time stopping them. **The Popular Culture Explosion** would be fine for a course in popular media. The $4.95 price tag however might limit its value to that of a teacher reference source. From Wm. C. Brown Publishers, 135 South Locust St., Dubuque, Ia. 53001.

A Scout is Trustworthy. . . . .

From the *Boy Scout Handbook*, published by the Boy Scouts of America.

from the BOY SCOUT HANDBOOK

A Scout Is **Trustworthy**

A Scout's honor is to be trusted. If he were to violate his honor by telling a lie or by cheating or by not doing exactly a given task, when trusted on his honor, he may be directed to hand over his Scout badge.

A Scout Is **Loyal**

He is loyal to all to whom loyalty is due, his Scout leader, his home and parents and country.

A Scout Is **Helpful**

He must be prepared at any time to save life, help injured persons, and share the home duties. He must do at least one Good Turn to somebody every day.

A Scout Is **Friendly**

He is a friend to all and a brother to every other Scout.

A Scout Is **Courteous**

He is polite to all, especially to women, children, old people, and the weak and helpless. He must not take pay for being helpful or courteous.

A Scout Is **Kind**

He is a friend to animals. He will not kill nor hurt any living creature needlessly, but will strive to save and protect all harmless life.

A Scout Is **Obedient**

He obeys his parents, Scoutmaster, patrol leader, and all other duly constituted authorities.

A Scout Is **Cheerful**

He smiles whenever he can. His obedience to orders is prompt and cheery. He never shirks nor grumbles at hardships.

A Scout Is **Thrifty**

He does not wantonly destroy property. He works faithfully, wastes nothing, and makes the best use of his opportunities. He saves his money so that he may pay his own way, be generous to those in need, and helpful to worthy objects. He may work for pay, but must not receive tips for courtesies or Good Turns.

A Scout Is **Brave**

He has the courage to face danger in spite of fear and to stand up for the right against the coaxings of friends or the jeers or threats of enemies, and defeat does not down him.

A Scout Is **Clean**

He keeps clean in body and thought; stands for clean speech, clean sport, clean habits; and travels with a clean crowd.

A Scout Is **Reverent**

He is reverent toward God. He is faithful in his religious duties and respects the convictions of others in matters of custom and religion.

HEROES OF POPULAR CULTURE

Heroes of Popular Culture. This review is taken from the free newsletter, *Popular Culture Methods.* The book is available from:

BOWLING GREEN POPULAR PRESS
Bowling Green University
Bowling Green, Ohio

Heroes of Popular Culture. Ed. Ray B. Browne, Marshall Fishwick, and Michael T. Marsden. Bowling Green, Ohio: Bowling Green Popular Press, 1972. 190 pp.

The popularly held view that there are no heroes anymore is consumately false. All th has happened is that the entire concept of the hero has diffused, scattered, exploded the twentiety century. Today, we retain the traditional concept of the hero in so aspects, but have added to it other types—the anti-hero, the comic book supe hero, "camp" heroes, and media super-stars. American society is so compartmentalized, so fragmented, that today almost anyone can become a hero, eve such diverse personalities as Spiro Agnew and Alice Cooper; both have the followings and each is a bonafide hero to a segment of our culture.

This is specifically the point of *The Heroes of Popular Culture*, an anthology of fifteen essays on the changing concept of the hero in Ame can culture. The selections are loosely chronological and deal with her ranging from "the Alger Hero" to "the Dog as Hero." Marshall Fishwi prologue and a follow up entitled "Heroic Style in America," and Fred MacFadden's "The Pop Panthenon" are fine, useful general introductio to the subject of the hero. Bruce Coad's "The Alger Hero," "Dick Whi tington and the Middle Class Dream of Success" by H. D. Piper, and "Hero of the Thirties—T Tenant Farmer" by Michael Mehlmann all explore the American Dream of material success in relation to heroism.

Other essays by Leverett T. Smith, Jr., Gerard O'Connor, and Ronald Cummings explo the changing image of the sports hero. Cummings' essay "The Superbowl Society" does an excellent job of placing sport in the context of ritual and its relation to society, and analyzes the roles of Arnold Palmer, Muhammad Ali, and Joe Namath in the current sport scene. Also interesting are David Stupple's "A Hero for the Times," which explores the rise of Mr. Belved a local Detroit businessman transformed into a camp hero by his humorously inept television commercials; and John Stevens' "The Dog as Hero," a history of canine greats in film, popula novels, and comic strips.

The Heroes of Popular Culture is a good source book for teachers of popular culture on any level. The book furnishes a plethora of ideas for further development and application to specific pedagogical situations. For example, Bruce Lohof in his essay, "The Bacharach Phenomenon" provides a test for determining whether a popular figure is truly a hero and applies this to the personality of Bert Bacharach. A teacher might employ this same method in testing the heroism of other popular figures. Any number of interpretive grids might be extracted from the essays and applied to discussions of the personalities of the American cultur The Alger Hero has his counterpart in Richard Nixon, for example. The creative teacher shou be able to make numerous connections between the theories of *Heroes of Popular Culture* an the actual heroes of our popular culture.

Dennis Bohnenkamp — Bowling Green University

POP CULTURE (BERGER)

Pop Culture . . . . by Arthur Asa Berger is Pflaum Publishing's first entry into the culture bag. The 191-page paperback is sometimes insightful, often superficial but usually entertaining in its romp through the surreal landscape that passes for ordinary life.

Berger compares TV football to **Last Year at Marienbad,** sees wrestling matches as an American morality play, finds football far more violent, urban and "sexy" than baseball which he considers boring, and observes that the Greeks had Euripides and we have the Associated Press. His section on toys, especially his explanation of why the "spider bike" has all but replaced the kind we rode on as kids, is excellent; but when he moves into the kitchen he betrays his lack of experience. He sees a blender as a way to turn everything into a "uniform slush" which symbolizes America's vaunted cultural pluralism in which "divergent strains are mixed until they become blobs in which all the uniqueness and every interesting variation is broken down, leading to a smooth, bland paste." Someone should send Arthur a blender cookbook.

The value of the book is that Berger can help readers see the ordinary in a new way, to see meaning where before there was only trivia. Other topics treated are comics, violence, heroes, ads, television, newspapers, soft drinks, corn flakes, pizza, the motel, gum, hippies and broadloom rugs. And what more could one ask from one book.

$3.65 each; study guide $2.00. Pflaum/Standard, 38 W. 5th Street, Dayton, Ohio 45402.

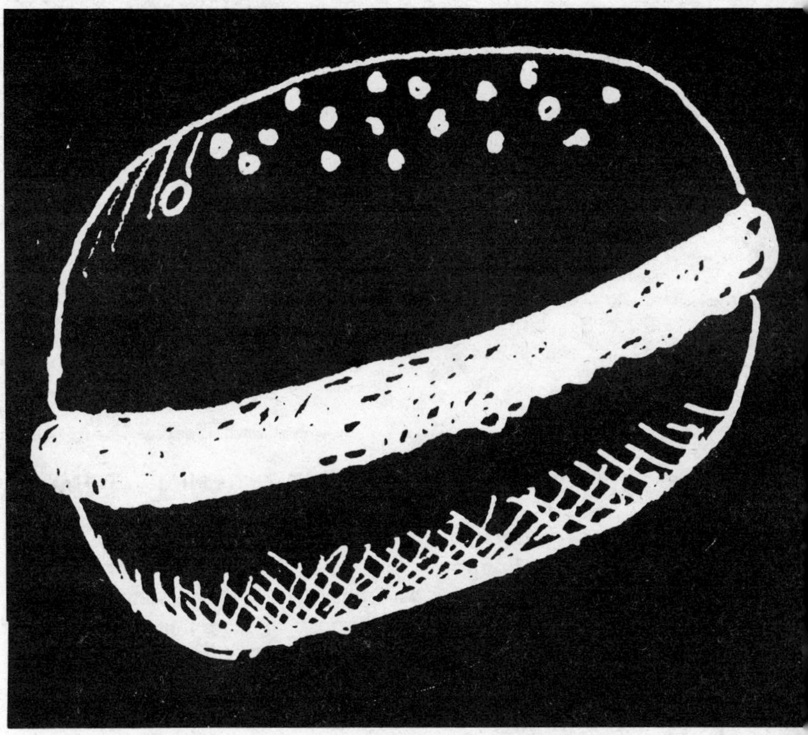

FILL IN THE NAME OF YOUR FAVORITE GREASY (PLASTIC) SPOON . . .

____________ offers the hamburger without qualities for the man without qualities. It must be seen as more than a gaudy, vulgar oasis of tasteless ground meat, a fountain of sweet, syrupy malted milks in a big parking lot, which caters to insolvent students, and snack seekers. ____________ is not just a hamburger joint—it is America, or rather, it is the supreme triumph of all that is insane in American life.

At ____________ there is no human touch . . . just little packets of hamburgers, sacks of fried potatoes. Everything is packed in bags to be thrown away. Is there any pleasure connected with eating a ____________ hamburger? Does one find it enjoyable? I think not! The only relief you have is that it didn't cost fifty cents or even forty-nine cents.

But we do purchase our ____________ hamburger at great cost. We cannot have it rare or well done, we cannot have it without "the works," for that would destroy its integrity. No! We get the great national hamburger—prepared to hamburgize the masses—which forces us to sacrifice our individuality, our gastronomic identity, for a few pennies. Instead of the hamburger being prepared for *our* tastes, we are forced to adapt ourselves to it; we must mold ourselves to *its* taste. The triumph of ____________ism is the death of individualism and the eating of a ____________ hamburger is the next thing to a death wish. (A ____________ hamburger reminds you how very mortal you are, how you too will be thrown away some day in the metal equivalent of a paper bag.)

ICONS AND SIDE-SADDLE

Icons of Popular Culture. . . by Marshall Fishwick and Ray B. Browne contains essays on the iconic importance of such, items of daily life as the Coke bottle, the Volkswagen, the Sears and Roebuck catalog, the match-book label, folk and popular artifacts, pop icons, icons and mass media. It includes an essay by Marshall McLuhan not previously published. 128 pp., paperback $1, hardcover $5 from The Center for the Study of Popular Culture, Bowling Green University, Bowling Green, O. 43403.

Side-Saddle on the Golden Calf: Social Structure and Popular Culture in America. . . .is edited by George H. Lewis and Published by Goodyear Publishing Co., 15115 Sunset Blvd., Pacific Palisades, Ca. 90272. 388 pages, paperback, $5.95.

The Popular Culture Explosion is a collection of print artifacts illustrating mass culture while **Side-Saddle. . . .** is an anthology of scholarly writings about mass culture. Lewis' selections include Tom Wolfe on Riverhead, William Martin on "The God-Hucksters of Radio," articles on "Love and Sex in the Romance Magazines," "The Social Stratification of Frozen TV Dinners," and even a piece on the 18¢ hamburger. There are also selections dealing with black culture, youth culture, rock culture and street theater.

After each selection a few discussion questions are presented. The book could work as a college text but is probably too specialized for the high school market. If your interpretation of mass media includes pop culture this book should prove highly useful and even fun to read.

IS TODAY TOMORROW? AND TEACHING TOMORROW

Is Today Tomorrow?: A Synergistic of Alternative Futures. . . . by Jerome Agel (Ballantine paperback, $1.95) is on one level a collection of suggestions for teaching a course in "future studies." On another level it is merely a nice collection of isolated quotes and pictures from Jerome Agel's files put together as a book. Agel did other non-books like **The Medium is the Massage, I Seem to be a Verb** and **War and Peace in the Global Village.** His layout in **Is Today Tomorrow?** is the sloppiest yet but there are some gems among the clunkers: "Computer devices already in use can cause all the phones in one area to ring simultaneously, and then play a recorded sales pitch. You ain't heard nothin' yet."

The book includes some "Astonishing Facts for Discussion" that could give some teaching ideas: "In 1965 an unmarried man in Oregon was granted the right to adopt a baby. Should he have been given this right? Should children be brought up in uni-sex households?" Or "More permits are being issued for construction of apartment dwellings than for private homes. Why?" Or "Prepare a film or a picture book on things that might shock people concerning the future." "Write a Laugh-In script featuring jokes, skits and songs dealing with change." There are about 100 other ideas on studying the future plus a list of organizations conducting research into the future.

If science fiction is part of your English curriculum pick up a copy of a slim paperback **Teaching Tomorrow: A Handbook of Science Fiction for Teachers** by Elizabeth Calkins and Barry McGhan. Part one of the book is a 25-page introduction to the how and why of using SF. Part two is a 60 page bibliography and list of magazines, book dealers, S-F for girls, S-F motion pictures, critical works and an annotated listing of 200 "recommended" novels. A nice reference book from which to explore Sci-fi. $2.20 from Pflaum/Standard, 38 West Fifth Street, Dayton, OH 45402.

SCIENCE FICTION THINGS

SCIENCE FICTION
The Future

Edited by *DICK ALLEN*, University of Bridgeport. The 28 selections in this anthology offer a stimulating introduction to the study of science fiction and its concepts of the future. Part I presents selections that treat the kinds of concerns that activate science fiction writers; Part II presents outstanding works of science fiction, chosen for their literary merit as well as for their interest as science fiction; and Part III contains theoretical discussions of and critical essays on science fiction. Each selection is followed by a series of questions. The editor also provides a general introduction, suggestions for short and long written assignments, and a selective bibliography.

OUTLINE OF CONTENTS

I. *First Perspectives*

Richard Wilbur, "Advice to a Prophet." *Time*, "No Way Out, No Way Back." David Lyle, "The Human Race Has, Maybe, Thirty-Five Years Left." George MacBeth, "Crab-Apple Crisis." Nathaniel Hawthorne, "Earth's Holocaust."

II. *Alternative Futures*

The Present as Future: Allen Ginsberg, "Poem Rocket." H. G. Wells, "The Country of the Blind." Isaac Bashevis Singer, "Jachid and Jachidah." Robert A. Heinlein, "They." Kenneth

ENGLISH: Introduction to Literature *Fiction*

Koch, "The Artist." Donald Barthelme, "The Balloon."

The Future: Ray Bradbury, "To the Chicago Abyss." Bob Shaw, "Light of Other Days." Kurt Vonnegut, Jr., "Harrison Bergeron." Robert A. Heinlein, "The Green Hills of Earth." D. M. Thomas, "Tithonus." E. M. Forster, "The Machine Stops." Roger Zelazny, "A Rose for Ecclesiastes." Harlan Ellison, "'Repent, Harlequin!' Said the Ticktockman." Frederik Pohl, "Day Million." Arthur C. Clarke, "History Lesson." H. G. Wells, from *The Time Machine*.

III. *Theories*

Kingsley Amis, "Starting Points." Isaac Asimov, "Social Science Fiction." Gerald Heard, "Science Fiction, Morals, and Religion." Arthur Koestler, "The Boredom of Fantasy." Susan Sontag, "The Imagination of Disaster." John P. Sisk, "The Future of Prediction."

Paperbound. 345 pages. $3.75
ISBN: 0-15-578650-4

Science Fiction: The Future by Dick Allen is a 345-page paperback available for $3.75 from:

HARCOURT BRACE JOVANOVICH
757 Third Avenue
New York, N.Y. 10017

MCNELLY/STOVER – Above the Human Landscape: An Anthology of Social Science Fiction
Ed. by Willis E. McNelly, Calif. State College, Fullerton, Leon E. Stover, Illinois Institute of Technology (387 pp., June 1972)

Collection of fascinating science fiction stories by such authors as Bradbury, Ellison, Sturgeon, Harrison and Heinlein, dealing with drugs, urban decay, race, ecology, generational conflict, sexual identity, individualism vs collectivism, the technological threat and other social problems.

CONTENTS: **Communities are for People.** The Highway, *Ray Bradbury*. The Waveries, *Frederic Brown*. Mother of Necessity, *Chad Oliver*. Black is Beautiful, *Robert Silverbergl*. Golden Acres, *Kit Reed*. **Systems are for People.** Adrift at the Policy Level, *Chandler Davis*. "Repent, Harlequin!" said the Ticktockman, *Harlan Ellison*. Balanced Ecology, *James H. Schmitz*. Positive Feedback, *Christopher Anvil*. Poppa Needs Shorts, *Walt* and *Leigh Richmond*. **Technology is for People.** The Great Radio Peril, *Eric Frank Russell*. Rescue Operation, *Harry Harrison*. Slow Tuesday Night, *R. A. Lafferty*. Light of Other Days, *Bob Shaw*. Who Can Replace a Man?, *Brian Aldiss*. **People Create Realities.** What We Have Here Is Too Much Communication, *Leon E. Stover*. The Handler, *Damon Knight*. They, *Robert Heinlein*. Carcinoma Angels, *Norman Spinrad*. Shattered Like a Glass Goblin, *Harlan Ellison*. The New Sound, *Charles Beaumont*. **Tomorrow Will Be Better (Bitter).** Rat Race, *Raymond F. Jones*. Coming of Age Day, *A. K. Jorgensson*. Ecce Femina!, *Bruce McAllister*. Seventh Victim, *Robert Sheckley*. Roommates, *Harry Harrison*. Mr. Costello, Hero, *Theodore Sturgeon*. **Afterword:** Science Fiction As Culture Criticism, *The Editors*. **Appendix:** 2001 Review, *Leon E. Stover*. Vonnegut's Slaughterhouse Five, *Willis E. McNelly*.

Hardcover $7.95, paperback $4.95 from:

GOODYEAR PUBLISHING CO.
Box 486
Pacific Palisades, Calif. 90272

THEMES IN SCIENCE FICTION *A Journey Into Wonder*

Edited by Leo P. Kelley

A collection of speculative fiction which explores inner as well as outer space, making it relevant to today's student. The use and appeal of this book is broad and equally exciting to new science fiction readers, to those already well-versed in the field, and to reluctant readers whose appetite is whetted by the relevancy and imagination of these stories.

PARTIAL LISTING OF CONTENTS

TOMORROW
The Last of the Romany — Norman Spinrad
The Total Experience Kick — Charles Platt

OUTER SPACE
Maelstrom II — Arthur C. Clarke
Founding Father — Isaac Asimov

HUMAN AND OTHER BEINGS
The Father-thing — Philip K. Dick
The Silk and the Song — Charles L. Fontenay

SOMEWHERE/SOMEWHEN
The Man Who Came Early — Poul Anderson
Soldier — Harlan Ellison

SPECIAL TALENTS
A Message From Charity — William M. Lee
Gomez — C.M. Kornbluth

MACHINERIES AND MECHANISMS
The World of Myron Flowers — Frederik Pohl & C.M. Kornbluth
EPICAC — Kurt Vonnegut, Jr.

THE DAY AFTER TOMORROW
The Survivor — Walter F. Moudy
The Travelin' Man — Leo P. Kelley

428 pp., 6x9, 1972
Code No. 07-033504-4
Price After Discount $2.58

A Science Fiction Reader, edited by Harry Harrison and Carol Pugner, is a collection of 15 short stories suitable for use in high school literature courses. It is also a fine collection of enjoyable and thought-provoking stories reasonably priced. A few questions are provided after each story, but other "classroom things" are kept in a separate teacher's manual.

"Heavyplanet" --- Milton A. Rothman
"Grandpa" -- James A. Schmitz
"Surface Tension" -- James Blish
"Traffic Problem" -- William Earls
"Nightfall" -- Isaac Asimov

276-page paperback available for $1.99 from:

CHARLES SCRIBNER'S SONS
597 Fifth Avenue
New York, N.Y. 10017

HUMAN REPRODUCTION AND FAMILY PLANNING

Human Reproduction and Family Planning: A Programmed Text, by Elizabeth Whelan and Michael Quadland, is a 150-page book designed for health and education professionals desiring to review and expand their knowledge of human reproduction and conception control. Single copies are $5.00, 50 or more copies are $2.25 each from:

HUMAN REPRODUCTION AND FAMILY PLANNING
350 Pacific Avenue
San Francisco, Calif. 94111

During Stage 4, that is after ovulation, the level of progesterone is *high/low*. During this stage, the cervical mucus changes and becomes hostile to sperm. Sperm mobility and survival in the woman's body at this time are poor. After ovulation, the mucous secretion in the area of the __________ changes. The secretions are hostile to ______________ .	high cervix sperm
Two important changes occur during Stage 4 of the menstrual cycle, that is during the ___________ weeks after ovulation. 1. Level of ____________________ becomes very high. 2. Mucous secretions in the area of the ____________ become hostile to _________ .	two progesterone cervix sperm
If pregnancy does occur, the corpus luteum does not degenerate and progesterone is continuously produced. This is necessary in order to maintain the lining of the uterus which will nourish the developing baby. If fertilization does not occur and there is no pregnancy, the corpus luteum deteriorates and estrogen and progesterone levels fall. This is the end of the menstrual cycle. If conception has not taken place, there *is/is not* a need for continued enrichment of the uterine lining. Therefore, levels of estrogen and progesterone will *rise/fall*. The fall in the levels of estrogen and progesterone causes menstruation to occur. Menstruation marks the beginning of the next cycle.	is not fall
In our discussion, we have divided the menstrual cycle into four stages. List what occurs during each stage of the cycle. Stage 1 ___ Stage 2 ___ Stage 3 ___ Stage 4 ___	1. Menstruation, FSH secreted. 2. Production of estrogen and build up of uterine lining. 3. LH surge causes ovulation. 4. Production of progesterone by corpus luteum. Cervical mucus becomes hostile to sperm.

FAMILY LIFE LITERATURE & FILMS

Family Life Literature and Films: An Annotated Bibliography is a 353-page listing of books and films on the subjects of: the family, sexuality, family planning, adolescence, looking toward marriage, marital interaction, family crises and disorganization, parenthood, middle and later years, self-growth, social issues and the family, and family life education. The listing is well organized and lengthy, but no evaluation is made of the materials listed. The book will acquaint readers with the existence of much material on the family but does not describe the material in detail or evaluate its contents.

Available for $6.50 from:

MINNESOTA COUNCIL ON FAMILY RELATIONS
1219 University Avenue S.E.
Minneapolis, Minn. 55414

THE HOW-NOT-TO-BOOK

Julius Schmid, Inc., distributes two free booklets for use in sex education classes. A six-page leaflet titled "Tell Me About IUD's Doctor" and a clever 16-page presentation called *The How-Not-To-Book* about birth control. Write:

THE HOW-NOT-TO BOOK

Julius Schmid's guide
to modern birth control methods

ED-U PRESS

760 Ostrom Avenue
Syracuse, N.Y. 13210
(315) 476-5541, ext. 4584

TEN HEAVY FACTS ABOUT SEX -- comic book. What kids want to know but no one will tell them. Single copy 25¢; 10-49 @ 22¢ each; 50-99 @ 20¢ each; 100-424 @ 18¢ each. (*Important:* Orders between 425-4250 available by box rate only. One box of 425 - $50; 2 boxes (850) $100, 4251+ @ 10¢ each.

VD CLAPTRAP -- Comic book. Straight info about syphilis and gonorrhea, including methods of prevention. Costs: same as above.

PROTECT YOURSELF FROM BECOMING AN UNWANTED PARENT -- Comic book. Concise info on birth control methods. For teenagers. Costs: same as above.

FACTS ABOUT SEX by Sol Gordon. Paperback. A clear, sensible little book with a more traditional approach. Good for parents as well as children. The revised edition will be available in May. Orders received before May will be filled with the old edition. Single copy $1.90. For bulk ordering, write the John Day Company, 257 Park Ave. So., NY, NY 10010.

THE SEXUAL ADOLESCENT by Sol Gordon. An expanded, updated version of Dr. Gordon's report to the National Commission on Population Growth and the American Future. Single copy $3.25. For bulk ordering, write Duxbury Press, 6 Bound Brook Court, North Scituate, Mass. 02060.

LOVE, SEX AND BIRTH CONTROL FOR THE MENTALLY RETARDED - A guide for Parents -- Booklet. "Don't assume the less the child knows, the better off he'll be." (Revised 1972 edition) Single copy 75¢. Bulk orders from Planned Parenthood-World Population, 810 Seventh Ave., NY, NY 10019.

A BASIC LIST OF SEX EDUCATION AND POPULATION IDEAS -- Typed. Lists of organizations, films, books, articles, slogans etc. Single copy 35¢.

LET'S BE SENSIBLE ABOUT SEX EDUCATION by Howard J. and Joy D. Osofsky and WHAT ADOLESCENTS WANT TO KNOW by Sol Gordon. Reprint from the American Journal of Nursing. Two excellent articles calling for mature, frank sex education. Single copy 25¢; 10 for $2.00; 100 for $15.

SAY IT SO IT MAKES SENSE (SISIMS) -- Newsletter. Subscription for two years. Individuals: $15; professional organizations and libraries: $25; public-spirited businesses: $50. Individuals may select Dr. Gordon's *The Sexual Adolescent* or *Facts About Sex* to accompany their subscription at no further cost. Professional organizations, libraries and businesses will receive all our current material as well as all new additions made to our publications list within the next two years.

WHY USE COMIC BOOKS AS TEACHING AIDS?

Current approaches to communicating the knowledge that adolescents need to protect themselves are being thwarted by several major barriers in adult thinking, including:

- The mistaken notion that the less an adolescent knows about sex, the less chance he will "get in trouble."
- The mistaken notion that the best way to keep kids in line is to "scare the pants off them."
- The strange idea that adolescents should only be presented with "tasteful" (teenage translation: syrupy) material.

And another barrier, of course, is that most people, teenagers included, don't much like to read.

On the first point, we comment: Keeping silent has never kept people "moral." The evidence strongly

suggests that the less youngsters know about sex, the *more* likely they will be sexually irresponsible.

Our response to the second point: Kids, like other people, resent overscare tactics. When they are fed a diet of scare and/or "moralistic" lectures they quickly learn to tune out. If we are truly interested in helping our youth and if we really believe we have some valid things to say, then we must first approach them in such a way that they would be willing to listen.

On the third point, we must understand that teenagers are particularly distrustful of the establishment's "tasteful" approaches to such things as sex and drugs. But no teenager loses status within his peer group for reading a comic book. What constitutes "good taste" for some adults is simply not read by most adolescents.

In this connection, it is interesting that when our first comic book, "Ten Heavy Facts About Sex," came out there were a number of reservations from professionals who ought to know better about its "tastefulness." Meanwhile, "Heavy Facts" has become enormously popular and gained wide acceptance and these complaints have petered out. However, we are starting to hear the same reservations about our newly released comic on birth control, "Protect Yourself From Becoming an Unwanted Parent." We expect that once it becomes accepted these murmurings will also die out.

It is also interesting that whenever an adult staff meets in advance to decide whether to use one of our comics, the decision is almost always negative. However, whenever an individual adult distributes copies on his own (the best way is to leave them lying around), his organization can't keep up with the demand. Again and again groups have begun by ordering a few and are soon ordering by the thousand.

Sometimes a professional educator will test it out on his own children and decide whether to use the comic on the basis of their response. First of all, very often teenagers will not acknowledge to their parents that they were interested because they don't want to give the impression that they don't already know everything. Secondly, such youngsters are often some of the brightest, most sophisticated of their age and are certainly not good reflectors of the needs and interests of the average adolescent.

Another important advantage of the "funnybook" technique: Humor helps reduce the anxiety that turns people away from reading about what they really need to know about.

Besides, comic books are the only things that a huge number of adolescents willingly read.

HOW YOU CATCH V.D.

Venereal diseases (V.D.) are spread by sexual contact. You can catch it any time you have sex with someone who has it. You can get V.D. through intercourse -- in the vagina or anus -- *and* from mouth-genital contact (oral sex). Whether a person "comes" or has pleasurable feelings has nothing to do with whether he or she catches V.D. You can get V.D. from a person of the same sex.

Many people believe you can catch V.D. from toilet seats. This is not true. V.D. germs can live only in warm, moist areas -- like the genitals (penis or vagina), mouth, and rectum (anus).

The two most dangerous types of V.D. are *gonorrhea* and *syphilis.*

It is possible to have both these diseases at the same time. If you've been cured, it is also possible to catch these diseases again.

From VD Claptrap

SYPHILIS (PART TWO)

Two to six months after the sore goes away other signs may appear. These signs include rashes and sores on other parts of the body, sore throat, hair falling out in patches, fevers and headaches. In general, these rashes and sores do not itch or sting. Some people think they have a heat rash or that they are allergic to something. These signs will also go away by themselves, but this does not mean the disease is not still there - doing serious damage inside.

After awhile a person with syphilis can't pass it on to other partners. This stage may come after two years but sometimes it can be catching up to five years. The person may feel healthy for a time. Between five and twenty years later, the disease will probably reach the heart, brain, and other organs and may result in death.

Pregnant women with syphilis risk causing serious harm to their babies. They may give it to their unborn babies even when they have passed the stage when they can give it to their lover. Brain damage, mental retardation and all sorts of problems may show up in the baby - if it lives at all. A pregnant woman should have a blood test done early in her pregnancy.

INCREDIBLE FACTS O' LIFE FUNNIES

Incredible Facts o' Life Sex Education Funnies is a regular size comic book giving sex education, especially about contraception. The comic also has a bibliography and a listing of centers which provide counseling and sex information.

75¢ each (quantity rates on request) from:

MULTI MEDIA RESOURCE CENTER
340 Jones Street #439
San Francisco, Calif. 94102

WILL THE REAL TEACHER STAND UP?

Will the Real Teacher Please Stand Up, edited by Mary Greer and Bonnie Rubinstein, is an excellent introduction to current thought on humanistic education. The 236-page paperback includes excerpts from the writings of George Isaac Brown, Robert Coles, Abraham Maslow, Gerald Leonard, Herbert Kohl, Sylvia Ashton Warner, Jules Henry, William Glasser, John Holt, Paul Goodman, George Dennison and more. The book also includes excerpts from literature about school, psychology, cartoons, and fine graphics. An excellent reader for future teachers. $4.95 as a paperback, $8.95 as a hard cover from:

GOODYEAR PUBLISHING COMPANY
15115 Sunset Blvd.
Pacific Palisades, Calif. 90272

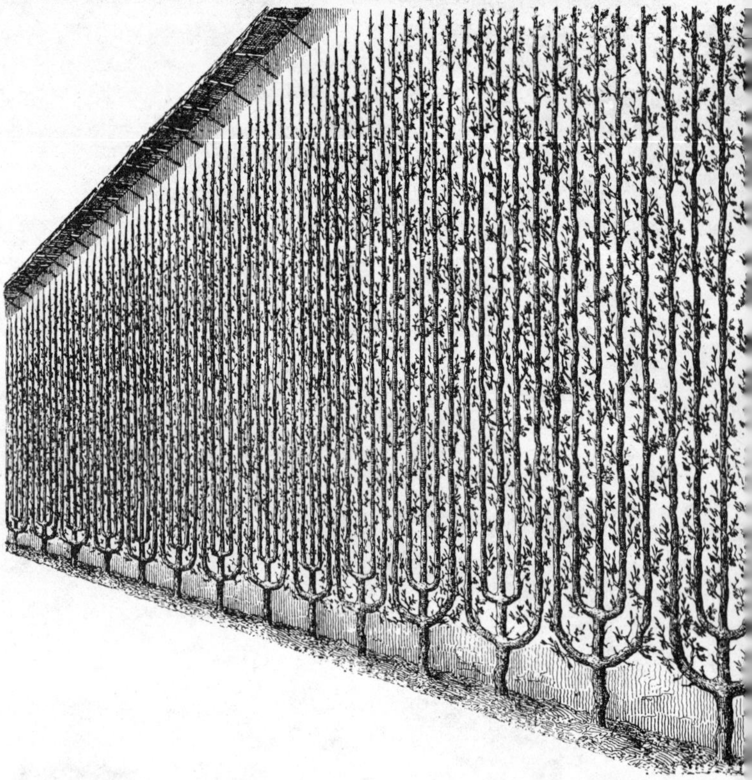

Games show human relationships.
Have you ever thought that some games are autocratic and some are democratic? Play some of these. Guess which are whic

Form a line
behind a leader.
Follow him wherever he goes,
doing whatever he does.
Take turns being leader.

One person begins a
mechanical movement.
Another person attaches
to him and adds a movement.
Continue to add yourselves
to the machine, using sounds
and moving through space.
If there are too many people
for one machine, make
several and let them meet
each other and interact.

Line up in front of the leader
or form a circle around him.
Do what the leader does
when he says "Simon says"
(or the leader's own name
can be used: "Freddie says")—
"Simon says put hands on head,"
"Simon says put hands on foot."
But if he says, "Put hands on nose"
and you do it, you're out because
Simon didn't say to do it.
The faster the pace
the funnier the game.

Make a mural together.
Fingerpaint a fresco.
Do tangrams together.
In small groups. (See page 223.)
See how many different
figures you can create
with the five shapes.

You are the leader.
Tell others to take a
specific number of steps forward.
They must ask, "May I?"
or they are penalized. The
first one to tag the leader wins.

One person goes to the
front and begins an
activity nonverbally.
Others enter once the
first person establishes what he's
doing. Form a scene
without words doing your
thing together and let
it play itself out.

One person stands up.
Another stands behind him
and plays on him as if he were
a musical instrument,
quietly humming a melody.
A third person makes the second
his musical instrument.
Continue until the line
is long enough to form a circle.
The first person then closes the circle
by playing on the back of the last person.
Enlarge the sounds, sing out loud.
Move the musical circle around the room
or stay in a line and navigate.

Use a ball or bean bag.
One person is the teacher, who
stands in the center.
Everyone else is a pupil and stands in
his numbered circle.
The teacher throws the ball
and if a pupil fails to
catch it, he goes to the
last circle and everyone
else moves up. If a pupil catches
the ball, he throws it back to
the teacher. If the teacher
misses the return throw, all the
pupils move up one circle and the
teacher takes the last circle.

Somebody is "It" and
leaves the room.
The rest of the group
stands in a circle.
Choose a leader who begins
and changes all movements.
Be aware of the leader
without looking directly
at him. Change movements
when he does.
Call back the person who is
"It." Tell him to stand
in the center and guess who
the leader is. If he
discovers the leader, the
leader becomes "It."

Lie down on the floor in
a wheel, faces up, heads toward th
center. One person begins a story
and, when ready, passes it
on to the next person.
Let the story travel around
the circle until it is finished.
What does it tell about the group?

Two partners begin a mirror.
Two more partners attach
themselves at some point to the
same part of the bodies of the
first set and begin their own mirror.
A third set attaches to the second s
until the entire group is involved
doing mirrors, still maintaining
contact with persons on both sides
Use sounds if they come naturally.

THE CONTROLLERS, THE HELPERS, THE FACADE

The Controllers, The Helpers, and *The Facade* by Jim Cole are books of simple line drawings dealing with human relations. The insights presented are profound, yet their expression very clear and deceptively simple. The line drawings make these books usable with almost any audience and age level. The books are now being made into filmstrips.

The Helpers is $2.50 and the others $2 each from:

SHIELDS PUBLISHING
855 Broadway
P.O. Box 1917
Boulder, Colo. 80302

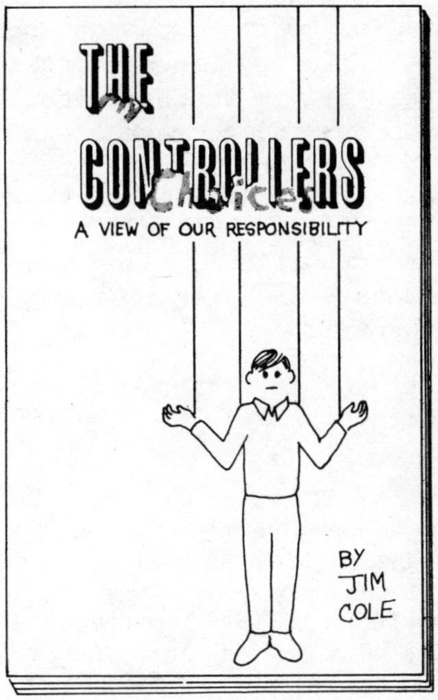

Sometimes being helped feels ok.

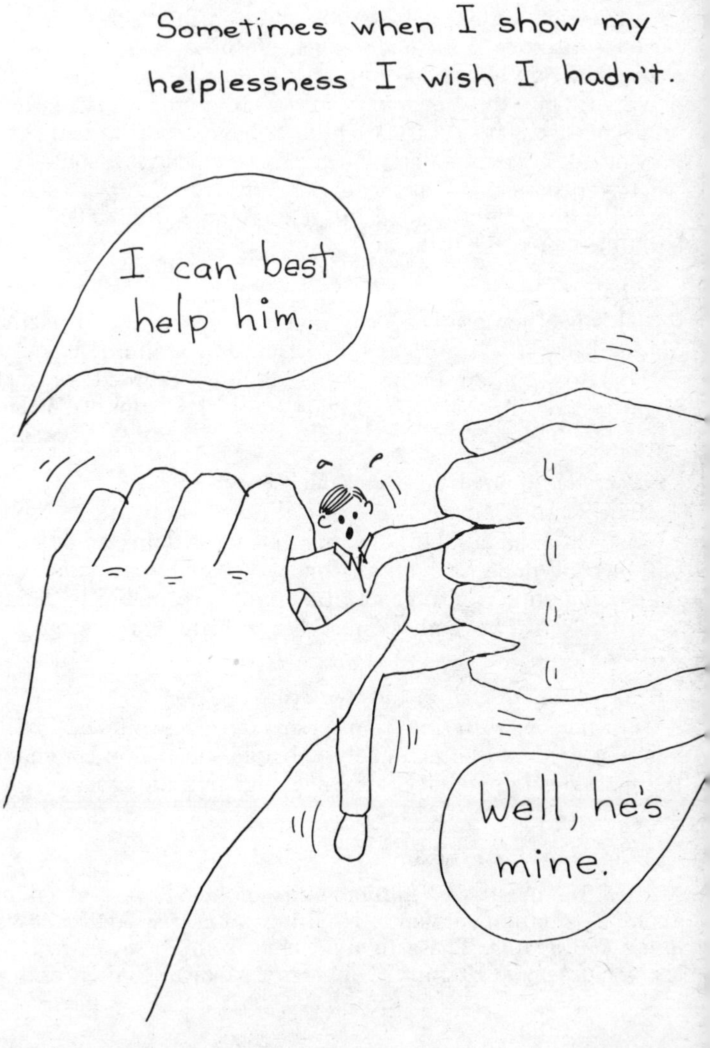
Sometimes when I show my helplessness I wish I hadn't.
I can best help him.
Well, he's mine.

A MANUAL OF DEATH EDUCATION

A Manual of Death Education and Simple Burial, edited by Ernest Morgan, is an excellent aid to teaching about death or for preparing to make one's own death a contribution to society. The 64-page booklet is only $1.00 from:

THE CELO PRESS
Route 5
Burnsville, N.C. 28714

UNIFORM DONOR CARD

OF ______________________________

Print or type name of donor

In the hope that I may help others, I hereby make this anatomical gift, if medically acceptable, to take effect upon my death. The words and marks below indicate my desires.

I give: (a) _____ any needed organs or parts
(b) _____ only the following organs or parts

____

Specify the organ(s) or part(s)

for the purposes of transplantation, therapy, medical research or education;

(c) _____ my body for anatomical study if needed.

Limitations or special wishes, if any: ______________________________

Radiation Research

There is important need for bodies of disease-free young adults (who have been killed in accidents) to permit the study of radiation normally present at various ages. Students and other idealistic young people are encouraged to ask their parents or spouses to sign a legal release that will let them bequeath their bodies (in case of accidental death) to this reserach. Suitable papers must be carried, with instructions to be followed in case of death. Inquiries may be directed to the Falconer Foundaton, 155 W. 68th St., New York City 10023, (212-877-7664).

Pituitary Glands

An estimated 5,000 to 10,000 children in the U.S. are suffering from serious pituitary difficiency. Each of these children needs the hormone extracted from about 300 pituitary glands to maintain normal growth for one year. Only three or four hundred children are getting it. An estimated additional 50,000 to 100,000 children have a partial deficiency and would be helped by growth hormones. Pituary glands should be "harvested" whenever possible. They can be kept frozen, or in acetone, and sent periodically to the National Pituitary Agency, Suite 503-7, 210 W. Fayette St., Baltimore, Md. 21202.

The Living Bank

This is a non-profit agency that coordinates the disposition and use of anatomical gifts. It supplies on request a Uniform Donor Card, plus a Donor Registration Form. Donor data is recorded for instant retrieval when needed. Address The Living Bank, P.O. Box 6725, Houston, Texas 77025. (713-528-2971)

The Naval Medical Research Center

The Tissue Bank, Naval Medical Research Institute, NNMC, Bethesda Md. 20014 (202-295-1121) is reported to be doing an outstanding job and will accept donations of anatomic material, particularly from persons under 35. Ordinarily transportation limits acceptance to donors near Washington, D.C. The bodies must be cremated or buried at the family's expense.

10. Skin for Dressing and Grafting

For persons suffering from serious burns, skin taken from a person who has just died can be extremely valuable. Such skin commonly constitutes the most desirable kind of dressing, and in some cases can be successfully grafted.

Blood for Transfusions

In 1971 about 6½ million units of blood were given in America to about 2¼ million patients, resulting in *nearly 70,000 cases of hepatitis and 8,000 deaths.* These figures come from Dr. J. Garrott Allen, Professor of Surgery at Stanford University Medical Center, and are backed by

XIP READINGS PROJECT

Xeroxography. . . The first shot in the battle against the textbook may have already been fired in Lexington, Massachusetts. The shot hasn't yet been heard around the world. In fact, it still hasn't been heard around the corner; but give it time.

Lexington is where Xerox College Publishing has set up headquarters for its **XIP Readings Project**. Xerox Individualized Publishing prints textbooks designed by teachers for their own classes. The program is aimed at those teachers who find anthologies of readings valuable but are not satisfied with any text on the market. These are the teachers who consider the duplicator an essential teaching tool and can often be found late at night running off their own reams of text material.

With the **XIP Readings Project** such teachers select the readings they want from the Xerox catalog of 1300 articles in their teaching field taken from scholarly journals as well as popular publications (**Psychology Today, Playboy, Time, New York Times**, etc.). They then add articles not included in the catalog or even their own manuscripts or charts and send the description off to Lexington. Two to three months later Xerox sends copies of the book they have designed at a price competitive with standard anthologies.

To keep the cost down teachers have to agree to order 300 books over a two year period but books are sold to the bookstore at a 20% discount. Approximate price for a 200 page anthology is $3.95 if 1000 copies are ordered or $6.95 each if only 300 are ordered. Articles included from sources other than the Xerox catalog raise the price about 20%.

Right now the program is available only in the field of psychology but plans call for catalogs in sociology and economics to be ready by the spring of 1973. The psychology catalog is aimed at college use but the diversity of the articles and the many popularized selections suggest wider possibilities.

More information from Xerox College Publishing, 191 Spring Street, Lexington, MA 02173.

The schedule for subject areas runs as follows:

1972- Psychology
1973- Sociology
Economics
1974- World History
American History
American Government
Anthropology

From XIP Readings in Psychology

JARVIK, M.E. The psychopharmacological expert revolution. ***Psychology Today*, 1967, 1, 51-59, May, 1967.**
Excellent discussion of pharmoceutical agents which have figured in psychologic research, past and present – alcohol, opium, marijuana, hashish, reserpine, chlorpromazine, LSD, etc. Also considers methods in psychopharmacological research and the future of that discipline. **0025**

KAMIYA, J. Conscious Control of Brain Waves. ***Psychology Today*, 1968, 1, 57-61, April, 1968.**
Reports research on voluntary control of alpha activity. **0026**

KRECH, D. The Chemistry of Learning. ***Saturday Review*, 1968, 51, 48-50, 68.**
Summarizes own work and that of Jarvik, Agranoff, and McGaugh which has centered on the biochemical bases of learning and memory. Implications for education are discussed. **0027**

LANG, P. J. Autonomic Control. ***Psychology Today*, 4, 37-41, 86, October, 1970.**
Surveys the fascinating recent research in conditioning of automatic functions and discusses the implications of these findings. **0028**

LUCE, G. G. and J. Segal. What Time is It? The Body Clock Knows. ***New York Times Magazine*. April 3, 1966.**
Excellent review of research with circadian rhythms in humans. **0029**

The Mind: From memory pills to electronic pleasures beyond sex. ***Time*, 1971, 97, 45-47, 19 April, 1971.**
Very readable summary of recent work in neuropsychology with particular emphasis on research with electrical and chemical stimulation of the brain and macromolecular transfer. Implications for control of human behavior and evolution are discussed. **0030**

OVERTON, D. "High" education. ***Psychology Today*, 3, 48-51, November, 1969.**
Describes experiments dealing with state-dependent learning. Suggests that students who take amphetamine during preparation for exams may forget what they have learned as soon as the drug wears off. **0031**

PALMER, J. D. The Many Clocks of Man. ***Natural History*, 1970, 79, 53-59, April, 1970.**
Surveys Studies of Rhythmicity in man's behavioral and physiological functioning. Specifically considered are (1) sleep-wakefulness cycles, (2) temperature rhythms, (3) rhythmic time perception, and (4) chemical rhythms. Also suggests particular directions for further research. **0032**

THE SPIRITUAL COMMUNITY

TAO BOOKS

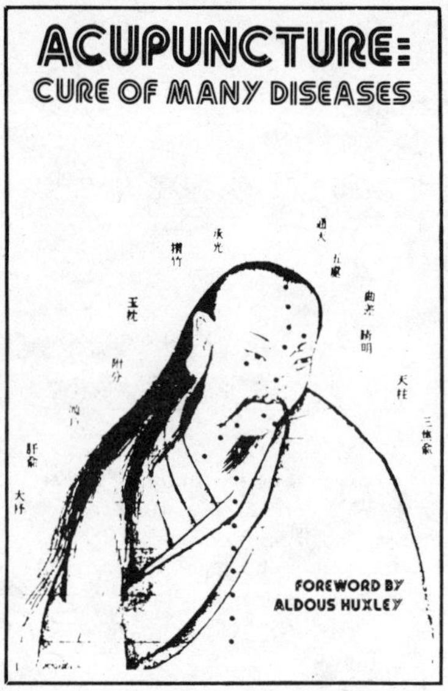

ACUPUNCTURE: CURE OF MANY DISEASES by Dr. Felix Mann.

This book has been written by an eminent practitioner of acupuncture, for the layman or non-medical reader who wants to grasp the subject in a few hours. This is the most complete, and at the same time simple, introduction to this ancient Chinese Art.

"Acupuncture consists of inserting a needle thiner than a pin into strategic nerve points on the skin. The nerve, along which an impulse travels to the diseased organ or part of the body, corrects the disfunction via the control exerted by the subconscious parts of the nervous system. The Chinese discovered acupuncture (Zhen Jui) in prehistoric times..."

80 pages, 52 illustrations, 6 x 9, perfectbound, paper $2.25.

THE TEACHINGS OF MICHIO KUSHI, The Order of the Universe, compiled edition, Volume One.

The uniqueness of Michio Kushi and his teaching is not easy to describe, but after experiencing the man, the world begins to change before your eyes, developing crystal clear lattice-works. The confused phenomenon of the world of appearances begins to congratulate each other, play together, and you find that this is the way it has always been.

"Every point of Infinity has infinite depth. Every individual within Infinity, has infinite depth. Because of this, everyone of us has the quality and image of Infinity itself. The purpose of life is to prove that we are Infinite through the expression of our ideas and our activity..."

"This is a changing world. You will disappear some day, the earth will disappear, the galaxy will disappear, this visible universe will change. But movement itself, change, is endless, constant, and immortal."

112 pages,6 x 9, perfectbound, paper $2.50.

FREEDOM THROUGH COOKING, The Macrobiotic Way, by Iona Teeguarden, Illustrations by Mary Purcell

There is some theory in this book, mostly it's a cook book to live with. Shopping guides, hints on saving money, add depth to a collection of recipes already rich. Foods gleaned from many cultures, both for day-to-day cooking and for special occassions, created to change what our bodies take in into the highest forms of energy.

128 pages, 6 x 9, perfectbound $2.50, second printing.

SPIRITUAL COMMUNITY GUIDE FOR NORTH AMERICA, A New Age Pilgrim's Handbook

The new revised edition of the *Spiritual Community Guide for North America* is the most comprehensive handbook available for the spiritual traveler. The new edition completely updates the state by state listings of spiritual-growth centers, natural foodstores, restaurants, new age centers, and metaphysical bookstores for the United States and Canada. There are articles on meditation, mantra, Sufi dancing, macrobiotics, massage, spiritual healing, breath, yoga therapy, astrology and more. Contributors include: Baba Ram Dass, Chogyam Trungpa, Gary Snyder, Yogi Bhajan, Pir Vilayat Khan and others.

208 pages, illustrated with many photographs and drawings, 5½ x 8½, perfectbound, $2.95, Revised Edition, April 1973.

EAST WEST SPIRITUAL COMMUNITY SUPPLEMENT, Handbook for a New Age

The *East West Spiritual Community Guide Supplement* is manifested through the combined energies of Spiritual Community and East West Journal (publisher of *Freedom Through Cooking* and *The Teachings of MIchio Kushi*). The *Supplement* both updates and expands the listings in the Spiritual Community Guide and stands independently as a unique "new consciousness" publication. Included are articles, charts, and photographs on macrobiotics, kundalini, yoga, Sufism, acupuncture, meditation, Do-In, spirituality in the ghetto, peyote, Mind Control, plus raps, book reviews, quotes, ads, and an international spiritual community directory. Also featured are koans, poems and prophecies from the minds of children.

112 pages, illustrated, contains advertisements, 8½ x 10¾, saddle-stitched, $1.00.

Order from:

THE SPIRITUAL COMMUNITY
Box 1080
San Rafael, Calif. 94902
(415) 453-9489

Forthcoming from Spiritual Community:

A PILGRIM'S GUIDE TO PLANET EARTH
A New Age Traveler's Handbook and Spiritual Directory compiled by the Spiritual Community

The *Pilgrim's Guide* will carry city by city listings of yoga, meditation and other spiritual centers; health food stores, macrobiotic, vegetarian and natural food restaurants; vegetarian hotels; occult, metaphysical and new age bookstores; ashrams and communes for Europe, the Middle East, Asia, Africa, etc.
The *Guide* will also feature cheap travel routes, currency exchange, food and dope hints, basics to take, on-the-road health care along with many articles on the where and how of Sacred Pilgrimages, astrology and travel, behavior in sacred places and more.

192 pages, illustrated with many drawings & photographs, 5½ x 9, perfectbound, $2.95, Summer 1973.

COMMUNICATION BOOKS

Most teachers in value education are familiar with the Rokeach Value Survey or can be by reading the September 1971 issue of PSYCH. TODAY. The two-part survey is available with gummed labels to facilitate changing rankings and to give the survey a more game-like atmosphere. The survey consists of ranking two sets of values, the first being states of being (exciting life, freedom, pleasure, salvation, wisdom, etc.) and the second modes of behavior (ambitious, capable, clean, honest, obedient, etc.). Each scale has 18 values to rank.

The three page survey is available to educators for 25¢ each in quantities of 50-499 (less in greater quantity) from Halgren Tests, 837 Persimmon Ave., Sunnyvale, Ca. 94087. Single sample is free. A definitely simple and versatile tool for value education.

Semantic stimulation. . . The International Society for General Semantics (P.O. Box 2469, San Francisco, Calif. 94126) has a catalog of books and teaching aids on semantics and communication. They also offer a copy of the **Uncritical Inference Test** ($.20) which is designed to test ability to reach logical conclusions. My sample didn't have answers with it – ask for that specifically.

PERSON-TO-PERSON

Interpersonal Speech-Communication . . . . is a rare creature, a traditional looking hardbound textbook on the subject of interpersonal communication.

The 420-page book is intended for college level courses and is a bit too textbookish for high school use. But as a teacher idea source or as a text in a teacher training course the book might serve nicely.

After each chapter is an annotated bibliography and a section called "Try This" giving experiments to try testing self-knowledge about communication. Some use awareness technique approaches while others are more traditional school assignments.

Topics include: feedback, non-verbal communication, decision-making, the many faces of you, communication breakdown, persuasion, conflict, small group interaction, public speaking and theater.

The text by John Keltner is published by Wadsworth Publishing Co., Belmont, California 94002. Hard cover only, price around $6.

Transactional Analysis . . . . is a school of psychology currently at fad proportions. It is, however, an excellent system to aid in self understanding and can be easily taught to others. Students find that it makes sense and in any class there will be some students whose parents are familiar with TA. As mentioned before in MM the best intros to TA are in Thomas Harris' book **I'm OK--You're OK** and in Jongeward and James', **Born to Win.**

The latter team of authors has now produced a TA "workbook" called **Winning With People** designed to teach TA to a group and to prove group exercises. I found the workbook fine for self teaching and feel it would work with a group of teens or adults. It certainly is better than the vast majority of "textbooks" aimed at high school group guidance classes. The 118 page magazine size book is priced at $3.95 from Addison-Wesley Publishing Co., Reading, MA.

Intercultural Communication: A Reader . . . . is a paperback textbook designed for those teachers who believe in the importance of teaching inter-racial and inter-cultural communication. The book is aimed at a college level but could work as a high school elective or at least as a teacher reference.

There are articles on how culture influences perception, on the differences in non-verbal communication between cultures, and on intercultural communication research. The book would be quite demanding for a high school level course but some articles would score well with students including "Time and Cool People" by John Horton, "Rapping in the Black Ghetto" by Thomas Kochman, "The Linguistics of White Supremacy" by James Sledd and most of the section on non-verbal language.

The 343 page book is edited by Larry Samovar and Richard Porter and published by Wadsworth Publishing Co., Belmont, CA 94002. Examination copies are available if text adoption is possible, write for single copy price.

VALUES CLARIFICATION

Values Clarification. . . . by Sidney Simon, Leland Howe and Howard Kirschenbaum is a follow-up to their popular **Values in Teaching.** The 390-page hard cover (Hart Publishing Co., 719 Broadway, N. Y. 10003 at $7.50) contains 79 classroom "strategies" useful in value education. By way of review and example here are three:

#55 Epitaph

Purpose: To gain a perspective on life by contemplating death.

Procedure: What would you want engraved on your own tombstone? What would be an accurate description of you and your life in a few short words?

To the teacher: Ask students to share their epitaphs. Extend to any student the right to pass in this exercise.

#57 Two Ideal Days

Purpose: To enable students to realize more clearly what they want from life.

Procedure: The teacher says, "Project yourself into the future, any time from tomorrow to several years from now, and imagine two days that would be ideal for you. Write about your perfect, ideal two days. Try to picture what you would be doing for the full 48 hours. Have student volunteers read their version aloud. A follow-up stragety is suggested to make the learning content more specific.

#60 How Would Your Life be Different?

Purpose: To help students think more deeply about some of their hopes and aspirations, and about what they are doing to achieve them.

Procedure: The teacher says, "You have just been informed by your doctor that you have only one year left to live. You believe that his diagnosis is absolutely accurate. Describe how your life during the next year would be different if you were to receive this news." Afterwards share ideas in small groups. After the discussion the teacher asks, "If you would change your life in some way, what's stopping you from moving in that direction now?" Other examples for this strategy include the gift of one million tax free dollars, the gift of the powers of Superman, a fairy godmother who could transform your appearance or your election as Dictator of the World.

To the teacher: Help the students see the values indicated behind their fantasies.

KNOW WHAT I MEAN?

Know What I Mean? . . . . is an anthology workbook in human communications ideal for high school English classes. The informal 83-page paperback contains short readings and many communication experiments and activities. The book deals with semantics, meaning, mind set, body language, programming, dealing with change, perception and the effect of the medium on the content of the message. The reading level and layout make the book well suited for a text. Some samples of the kinds of activities suggested in **Know What I Mean?**:

"The flicker of an eye, the raising of an eyebrow are the most important dramatic motions of the TV star. He seldom smiles, never laughs. This TV-inspired immobility of face accounts for the sullen appearance of most young people today." To test the above statement watch a TV drama turning off the sound. Concentrate on facial expression. If the first sentence in the statement is accurate, do you think the last sentence also is accurate?"

"To get an idea of the vast difference between speech and writing as media, try this with a tape recorder: Choose a passage from a famous speech but avoid something that most people would recognize. Without identifying the passage or its original speaker, have people of different ages, sexes or dialects record the speech. Ask a different group of people to read the same passage and make some guesses about the person who originally gave it. Play the tape for the latter group of people. What happened?"

"Print the word 'strike' on a card or on a blackboard. Show the word to ten people, and ask them to give you the first definition of the word that pops into their heads. Jot down their responses. Did people's responses tell you more about the word or about the people themselves? Other words that are good to use in this exercise are: 'soul,' 'hit,' 'block' or 'movement.'"

Besides the activities the book also contains short readings including: "The Road to Radicalism: a Semantic Aberration," "Brain Mold Seen Set at Age Twelve," "Rhythm Rules Your Daily Life," "On Communicating Across Cultural Lines," "The Un-Isness of Is," "Communication by Gesture in the Middle East." Most selections are from Newspaper articles and are aimed to stimulate thought rather than provide an exhaustive study of the subject.

Know What I Mean? by Victor Kryston and Portia Meares costs $1.95 a copy plus 20 cents for postage and handling from International Society for General Semantics, P.O. Box 2469, San Francisco, Calif. 94126.

How Is Your Radar System?

Since nonverbal messages can only be communicated nonverbally, we invite you to try the following.

With a group of people (class, gathering of friends, etc.), set aside a one-hour period in which the whole group is silent. Absolutely silent. No talking. No reading. No writing. Just the absence of sound. This is even more effective if the silence can be maintained throughout the entire day—even after the group separates.

In another exercise, the members of the group can try to communicate with one another without using words.

Can you create a special mood in a familiar setting—changing the environment, so to speak—by involving the senses of smell, sound, touch, and taste, as well as sight?

Experiments

Invade someone else's "private space." Stand closer to him than is normal.

What happened? ______________________________

____

Try rearranging space. For example, rearrange the furniture in the room to create a different pattern.* If the environment changes, do the people in that environment act differently?

What happened? ______________________________

____

Look someone straight in the eye for a longer time than is comfortable.

What happened? ______________________________

____

Reach out your hand to touch someone whom you normally would not touch.

What happened? ______________________________

____

***If your chairs are in rows, arrange them in a circle. How big is the circle? Do smaller circles have different effects? In a classroom, if the teacher did not have a desk in the room, would it make a difference?**

For information on the six-film series—Know What I Mean?—and a current catalogue of available publications on general semantics and on improving communication, write or call:

INTERNATIONAL SOCIETY FOR GENERAL SEMANTICS

P.O. Box 2469 | **509 Sansome Street**

San Francisco, California 94126 | **Phone (415) 392-9195**

AWARENESS

I've looked long and hard for good books on developing self-awareness. One of the best I've found is AWARENESS: EXPLORING, EXPERIMENTING, EXPERIENCING by John O. Stevens. The entire 275-page paperback is devoted to techniques for improving self-awareness grouped in sections such as communication within, communication with others, fantasy journeys, pairs, couples, group activities and art movement and sound.

The experiences are well constructed and Stevens' avoids the cookbook approach by giving brief but lucid explanations of the dynamics behind the techniques. An excellent resource book for yourself or for use with students from high school through adult. $3.50 from Real People Press, P.O. Box 542, Lafayette, Calif. 94549 and from larger bookstores.

Self-Awareness Through Group Dynamics. . . is a $1.95 paperback from Geo. A. Pflaum, Publisher, 38 W. Fifth Street, Dayton, O. 45402. The 120-page book by teacher Richard Reichert has brief discussions of topics like awareness, creativity, values, freedom and responsibility, respect, trust, prejudice, listening, male-female, generation gap, and hawk-dove. The discussion of each topic includes a classroom "game" used to stimulate discussion and provide a shared experience.

GROUP METHODS TO ACTUALIZE HUMAN POTENTIAL

An abundant source of ideas for improving self-awareness can be found in *Group Methods to Actualize Human Potential: A Handbook* by Herbert A. Otto, Ph.D. The handbook is especially suited for teachers who have had experience in small group work and in some form of human potential activity.

The book is a guide and "cookbook" to group work supplying detailed instructions for over 75 activities designed to help a group develop its own potential.

For example, one activity is titled the "Ideal-Self Utilization Method." The exercise is based on the idea that most of us at some time in childhood and during adolescence have a vision or dream of ourselves—what we want to be and what we want to contribute to the world in which we find ourselves. This vision is identified as the "ideal-self core" because it is usually very important at the time and still might be. The task is to recall this ideal-self core and to explore its meaning to us now. The group works to recall these early dreams and evaluate them in terms of the present. Most often they are looked upon as childish fantasies and are forgotten. In reality, they often contain clues to a person's basic goals and motives.

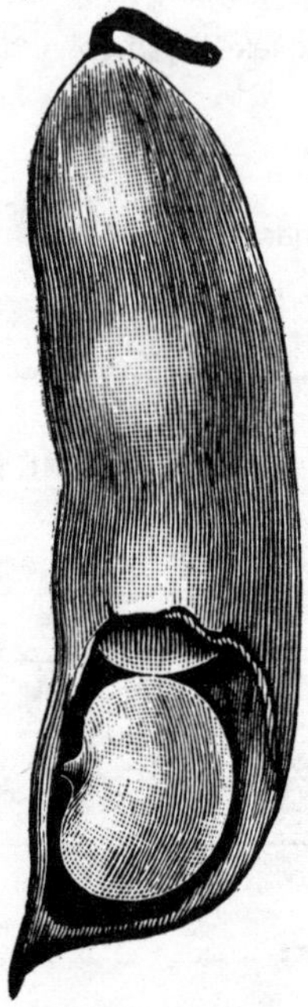

In this activity as in all the others, there is no attempt made by a group leader to analyze anyone else in the group. All the activities are for self-actualizing of one's own potential.

Group Methods to Actualize Human Potential: A Handbook costs $8.95 plus $1.00 postage and handling from:

HOLISTIC PRESS
160 S. Robertson Blvd.
Beverly Hills, Calif. 90211

The Donovan Fantasy -- A Nonverbal Experience . . . Although this can be a group fantasy or individual fantasy experience it seems to work best in a group environment.

The experience is based on the Donovan song, "A Legend of a Girl Child, Linda," found in the album

Sunshine Superman, EPIC, L.N. 24217. A good hi-fi or stereo sound system is essential for this experience. (Sound volume should be medium but high enough that everyone can clearly hear the words without straining. We have found that it is best to play the song twice for maximum fantasy effect.) The following can be read aloud:

"In order to get in the mood for this nonverbal experience, you may wish to proceed as follows (after everyone has settled down): Close your eyes (no talking) for three minutes -- let fantasies about children playing on the beach and fantasies of medieval times come in; try to have these fantasies in color. (Some one should call time after three minutes. Notice: Someone should be asked to volunteer to shut off the phonograph immediately after the song has ended.)

"Now let's start the record and close your eyes. Keep them closed. Let yourself go with the images of the song. Create the scenes and images of Donovan's song in your mind -- in color if you wish -- or you can become the experience. Follow your fantasy stream -- do what feels best and what you enjoy most.

"At the end of the song remain sitting or lying quietly, with eyes closed. When you leave the room, leave quietly so as not to disturb others. If you want to you can later share your feelings about this experience with someone."

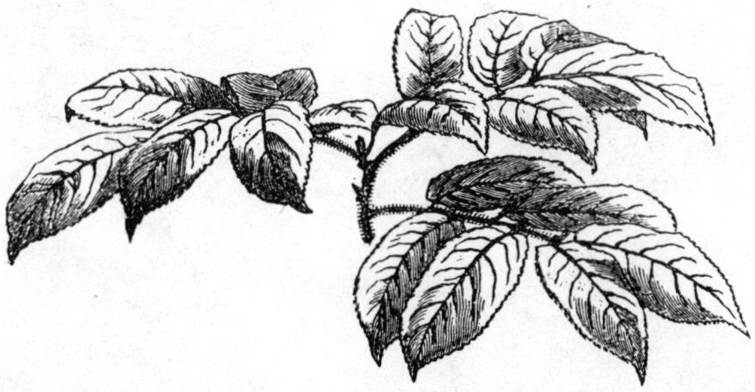

SOMEWHERE ELSE CATALOG

Somewhere Else: A Living-Learning Catalog, edited by the Center for Curriculum Design, is an annotated listing of places other than traditional schools to go for learning. There are listings for artisan and skills centers, media centers, gay liberation centers, outdoor living centers, social and political change co-ops, new-learning nets, and more. $3.95 from:

SWALLOW PRESS
1139 S. Wabash Ave.
Chicago, Ill. 60605

Tibetan Buddhism

PADMA-LING MONASTERY
c/o Tibetan Nyingmapa Meditation Center
2425 Hillside Avenue
Berkeley, Ca. 94704
(415) 549-1618

"Padma-Ling Monastery is the first Tibetan Center to be founded on the West Coast. In 1969, the Incarnate Lama Tarthang Tulku from Eastern Tibet founded the Tibetan Nyingmapa Meditation Center in Berkeley. He has since founded other branches throughout America and earlier in India. The transmission of the Tibetan Vajrayana teachings is available through the traditional methods of Dharma practice at the Center.

"Students can be either extensive or intensive, depending on the individual circumstances and Karmic vibrations. At present there are 100 students partaking in full practices and another eighty in basic practices. Seminars are held quarterly."

COUNTRY PHOTOGRAPHY WORKSHOP

Woodman, Wisconsin 53827 608·988·5492
c/o Peter Gold

"Country Photography Workshop is a year-round project for teaching photography to those who want to learn it. We approach photography as a language which depends on what you *feel* for its content and expression. We are on a 160-acre farm in southwest Wisconsin's hills, four hours' drive from Chicago.

"Six-day workshops are $150. Weekend sessions are $50. We provide instruction, darkroom facilities, equipment and chemicals, meals, and a place to sleep. "You bring a good attitude, camera, meter, film and paper and personal needs for the week." Instruction at Country Photography Workshop includes "Basic Seeing Workshop" for people "who have been working a little while. We also have Intermediate and Advanced workshops. . . . Our six-day and weekend workshops are very intensive and concentrated. Classes begin at sunrise." They also offer workshops and special rates for school groups.

"The backbone of our teaching is helping you connect with your intuition. Once you make this connection you will find your pictures inside yourself. Our goal is helping you become your own photographer."

WEAVING WORKSHOP
3300 North Halsted Street
Chicago, Ill. 60657
(312) 929-5776

A very friendly place where you can learn the whole business of weaving, beginning with wall hangings and progressing through a coverlet with the "Whig Rose" pattern.

Classes are six weeks long, and each class is three hours a week. Classes are limited to ten people.

Beginners work on wall hangings, while learning the basics of yarn, warp and woof, and eight or nine basic weaves. A beginners' class on the loom is $35, with a $5 fee for a small hand loom that's yours when the class is over. There are advanced classes in tapestry and rugs, also.

NATIONAL OUTDOOR LEADERSHIP SCHOOL
Box AA
Lander, Wyo. 82520
(307) 332-4381

NOLS believes that adventure is part of the growing up process, and encourages its incorporation in educational planning. Their courses are aimed towards, but by no means limited to, outdoor education leaders, and cover all phases of outdoor living and survival, plus practical conservation.

The format is backpacking expeditions, usually at 8,000-12,000 foot elevations, for two to five weeks. Expeditions include mountaineering in Wyoming, spelunking in Tennessee, folboting in Alaska, two weeks of ski touring and winter mountaineering in Wyoming, and a two-week Baja Mexico desert and marine course. All of these are for participants from 16-50 years, with special programs for 13-15 year-olds and 21-50 year-olds. The NOLS people seek a diversity of background in applicants. Rugged outdoor experience is not a requirement, but some experience is recommended.

The five-week courses cost about $550; winter mountaineering is $200, and the Baja expedition is $375, including transportation from the U. S. border. College credit can be arranged for some courses.

See also, Bridge Mountain Foundation; Hal Riegger Pottery Workshops; Jugtown Pottery; Mountain Institute for Man; Ontario College of Art; Questers Project; Sitka Center for Art and Ecology; Trout Fishing in America.

THE MACDOWELL COLONY

Peterborough, N.H. 03458
c/o Conrad Spohnholz
(603) 924-3886, 924-3563

This is a colony/retreat for painters, writers, sculptors, and composers in the "wilds" of New Hampshire. "To give painters, sculptors, and other artists an opportunity to pursue their projects under working conditions far better than they would normally find elsewhere is the simple function of the McDowell Colony.

"Established artists with projects requiring concentrated attention for one to four months will, in general, find acceptance whenever vacancies allow. Young artists who have done enough work to achieve reputations in a discriminating if limited circle are equally eligible. There is no 'community life' at the McDowell Colony beyond what an individual wishes to create for himself. Painters and sculptors may, if they wish, have breakfast and dinner in the central dining room with other artists; they are free not to. The midday meal is sent to the studios."

The Colony takes thirty painters, sculptors, writers, and composers during the summer and half this number at other times. Their fee is $35 per week, which covers room, studio, and meals. Some fellowships are available.

There are no accommodations for families at the Colony. Applications for the summer months have a February 15 deadline. An application at least 90 days in advance is required for other seasons. Each person accepted by the Colony has his own studio, a room in one of the residences, and in some cases he may be given a separate cottage equipped both as a residence and studio. Each artist has exclusive use of his studio while at the Colony.

DIRECTORY OF AMERICAN POETS

Is there a poet in the city? *A Directory of American Poets* is a 118-page listing of names, addresses, phone numbers, and teaching interests of published American poets. The primary purpose of the listing of 1200 poets is to assist in locating these writers for readings, workshops, and other assignments. The book also has an excellent bibliography on teaching poetry, films and videotapes on poets, and suggestions for workshops and class visits. $4.00 from:

POETS & WRITERS, INC.
201 West 54th Street
New York, N.Y. 10019
(212) 757-1766

THREE MORE GOOD BOOKS

BLAMING THE VICTIM (Vintage paperback, $1.95) by William Ryan is a book to read if you've even felt even a tinge of self-satisfaction at your liberal beliefs about social ills. If you believe in the sub-culture of poverty, in cultural deprivation, in compensatory education or the disadvantaged you are engaging to some extent in victim blaming.

The humanitarian is no Archie Bunker but he still concentrates his efforts in action designed to change the victim of society and not society. Examples of victim-blaming, well meaning reforms include the Peace Corps and VISTA, Head Start, compensatory education, the Coleman report, the report of the Kerner Commission and most any presidential commission in recent years.

The first chapter, "The Art of Savage Discovery" is itself worth the cost of the book. Ryan's book restores honor to the concept of being radical.

MYTH & MODERN MAN
By Raphael Patai
Prentice-Hall $9.95

MYTH AND MODERN MAN is a fascinating study showing that myth is very much alive in contemporary society. Patai finds myth-makers in Marxism, Nazism, religion, Che, SDS, the Black Messiah, comic books, Mickey Mouse, advertising, James Bond, Playboy and Teilhard de Chardin.

Patai compares soft drink ads with the Greek idea of ambrosia, nectar and honey as the food of the gods. With the Greeks, the consumption of honey was associated in their minds with imitating the Olympians, in partaking of their nature even if only to a tiny degree. In like manner, the modern-day consumer of Coke feels he imitates and associates himself with the quasi-mythological scenes of the television commercials. The health, beauty, youth, excitement and luxury shown in the commercials is the setting in which Coke is "enjoyed," and is far removed from everyday reality. In both cases, honey for the Greeks and Coke for us, there is the illusion of partaking of a world that one can never make, a world peopled by Divine Beings. Soft drinks use slogans which present the beverage as a bringer of youth (the now generation) or even of world harmony.

The media helps to present athletes as mythical beings who perform daring deeds on the battlefield of sport. To have an athlete endorse a product (drink, hair spray, etc.) is to invite the user to share in the mythical world in which the hero lives.

Patai claims that such commercials are not intended to sell products but to enhance their use by adding the mythic dimension.

Patai finds in communes parallels with mythical yearning for a return to a time before the fall, a Golden Era. In Chardin's cosmic vision he finds a utopia so similar to that of Marx "as to be almost interchangeable in their main features."

We still create heroes in the mold of Hercules. Hercules performed dangerous tasks against great odds, overcame all obstacles, was notorious as a ladies' man, had a male sidekick, conquered forces that threatened the common good, and served an inferior master. Our modern media-created heroes--John Wayne, Superman, James Bond, the FBI, Batman, Capt. Kirk, Bonnie & Clyde, Tarzan, the heroes on Saturday morning cartoon shows and coutless other examples--share most of the traits of Hercules. Man as myth maker is still very much alive.

The first three chapters of MYTH AND MODERN MAN are of interest mainly to scholars but as the book approaches modern life the insights into myth become increasingly interesting.

Printing It . . . . is a guide to printing and and graphic techniques for those with a severely limited budget. It serves as a highly practical beginner's manual on printing leaflets, posters, announcements, pamphlets and other matter mainly by offset duplication. Printing processes are explained, the selection and purchase of materials is detailed, as are procedures for printing and binding. Anyone who does printing could profit from **Printing It.** Written by Clifford Burke, published by Ballantine for $2.95. At book stores or from the publisher at 101 Fifth Avenue, New York, N.Y. 10003.

Organizations

DO IT NOW FOUNDATION

If you're a drug user who doesn't know much about drugs or if you think you know it all, contact the *Do It Now Foundation*. If you are at a school where drug education programs are either belittled or ignored, contact the *Do It Now Foundation*. *Do It Now* is a nonprofit, nonsponsored drug education foundation run by those who have had every conceivable type of prior drug experience. The average age of staff and directors is 23. The prevailing attitude among staff members is not one condemning or condoning drug use. *Do It Now* is respected by both counterculture people and fair-minded educators. Offices are located in Phoenix, Chicago, and Hollywood.

Their complete publication list and the pamphlet "Garbage: A Report on Street Psychedelics" are included here. Highly recommended for drug education.

DO IT NOW FOUNDATION
2515 E. Thomas Suite 25
Phoenix, Ariz. 85008
(602) 957-9617

Local Offices:

6136 Carlos Avenue
Hollywood, Calif. 90028
(213) 463-6851

407 S. Dearborn Suite 935
Chicago, Ill. 60605
(312) 922-4398

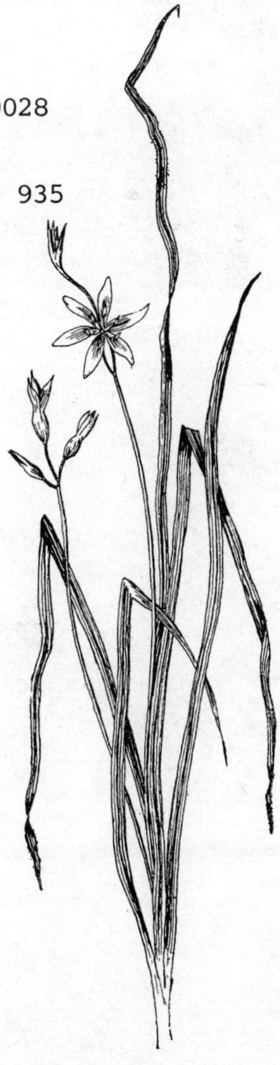

DO IT NOW Foundation

DRUG EDUCATION MATERIALS

PRICE LIST

REVISED FEBRUARY 1973

Pamphlets

* **101. A 19-Year Old Girl and Poet Allen Ginsberg Talk About Speed.** A basic true-to-life tool to understanding the amphetamine culture from the ground floor up. 10 cents single copy, 10/60 cents, 100/$4, 1000/$35.

Quantity desired:_____ Amount: $______

* **102. Amphetamine Abuse: Pattern and Effects of High Doses Taken Intravenously.** An accurate study of what happens when Speed is mainlined over medium to long periods of time. 10 cents each, 10/60 cents, 100/$4, 1000/$35.

Quantity desired:_____ Amount: $______

103. Drug IQ Test. For evaluation of basic street drug knowledge for students, parents and teachers. Contains 25 questions and answers with scoring guide. Set of two pamphlets (questions/answers) also includes a recommended reading list to expand your drug awareness. 15 cents per set, 10/$1, 100/$7, 1000/$60.

Quantity desired:_____ Amount: $______

(*: See 'Special Quantity Rates' for large orders)

* **104. The Facts About Downers.** A pamphlet containing straight information about barbiturates, aimed at upper grade school through high school levels. Illustrated and direct to the point. 10 cents each, 10/60 cents, 100/$4, 1000/$35.

Quantity desired:_____ Amount: $______

* **105. SMACK: The strongest thing you can buy without a prescription.** This is a matter-of-fact, hard hitting account of where the heroin scene is at in today's world of hard and soft dope. 10 cents each, 10/60 cents, 100/$4, 1000/$35.

Quantity desired:_____ Amount: $______

* **106. The Sniffing Spectrum.** An informative pamphlet aimed at educating young people about the dangers of vapor inhalation, from aerosol sprays to petroleum products to glue. 10 cents each, 10/60 cents, 100/$4, 1000/$35.

Quantity desired:_____ Amount: $______

* **107. Hard Drugs and the Movement.** A challenge to anyone involved with peaceful social change to rid their community of the hard drug menace. 10 cents each, 10/60 cents, 100/$4, 1000/$35.

Quantity desired:_____ Amount: $______

* **108. Barbiturates: Threat or Menace?** This is a pamphlet designed to help wake up the populace to the barbiturate problem, by far the most rapidly increasing hard drug manace today. 10 cents each, 10/60 cents, 100/$4, 1000/$35.

Quantity desired:_____ Amount: $______

* **109. GARBAGE: A report on Street Psychedelics.** One of the most menacing problems today is low quality and adulterated drugs, which may cause up to 80% of all bad trips. Latest factual information and analysis data was used to compile this pamphlet. 10 cents each, 10/60 cents, 100/$4, 1000/$35.

Quantity desired:_____ Amount: $______

* **110. Heroin: An In Depth Study on Abuse, Addiction and Withdrawal.** The title is accurate enough..Facts about street heroin, methadone, etc. 10 cents each, 10/60 cents, 100/$4, 1000/$35.

Quantity desired:______ Amount:$______

* **111. Barbiturates: Important Facts for Your Survival.** Another in-depth study on the present day use of Seconals, Tuinals, Nembutals, and other frequently occurring downers. 10 cents each, 10/60 cents, 100/$4, 1000/$35.

Quantity desired:______ Amount:$______

* **112. SPEED and WHITES are the SAME THING.** A much-needed pamphlet which points out the fact that pills can be just as harmful as injection of amphetamine in many cases. Basic factual information on whites, diet pills and pep pills. 10 cents each, 10/60 cents, 100/$4, 1000/$35.

Quantity desired:______ Amount:$______

* **113. The New Improved DRUG I.Q. TEST.** A new set of 25 questions and answers in one pamphlet, similar to the original Drug I.Q. Test but harder, and completely different. 10 cents each, 10/60 cents, 100/$4, 1000/$35.

Quantity desired:______ Amount:$______

* **114. GUNK.** A simple title, but full of impact on the problem of polluting yourself with paint, glue, aerosols and other vapors. Recommended for grades 3-6 especially. 10 cents each, 10/60 cents, 100/$4, 1000/$35.

Quantity desired:______ Amount:$______

* **115. LSD and the MARKET PLACE.** Reprint of a special report prepared by the University of the Pacific school of Pharmacy in Stockton, Calif. Predominant emphasis on impurities, low quality, misrepresentation and profit motives for street LSD. 10 cents each, 10/60 cents, 100/$4, 1000/$35.

Quantity desired:______ Amount:$______

* **116. Facts About P.C.P.** Maybe you have never heard of PCP, but it has quietly risen to being one of the greatest problems in the illegal drug world today, and is found in a great many street drugs. An excellent study from the Univ. of the Pacific, with bibliography. 10 cents ea., 10/60 cents, 100/$4, 1000/$35.

Quantity desired:______ Amount:$______

Other Important Publications

201. VIBRATIONS Newspaper. A 2-color, 8-page tabloid containing latest street survival news on drugs. Highly illustrated, Vibrations contains information that is up-to-the-minute and not otherwise available in a well-rounded, appealing format. Issued quarterly. Bulk quantities: 15 cents each, 10/$1, 100/$8, 1000/$65. (Current issue only).

Quantity desired:______ Amount:$______

201a. VIBRATIONS Subscriptions: Six issues $1 single subscription, 10 subscriptions to one address $6, 100 subscriptions $50.

Quantity desired:______ Amount:______

202. The Comic Book: Primary Supplement to Do It Now Educational Program. This is an 8-page, 7 x 8½ comic publication which was developed especially for ages 5 through 10. Illustrated by artist Mike Bedard, it is an effective approach to preventive drug education regarding pills in particular. 15 cents each, 10/$1, 100/$7.50, 1000/$60.

Quantity desired:______ Amount:$______

204. Drug Abuse: A realistic Primer for Parents. Or, "Things you should know about drugs after you've read the scare pamphlets." A 16-page guide written especially for parents who are worried about their kids experimenting with drugs. An explanatory, counter-hysteria booklet compiled by the combined Do It Now staff. 35 cents each, 10/$2.50, 100/$18, 1000/$150.

Quantity desired:______ Amount:$______

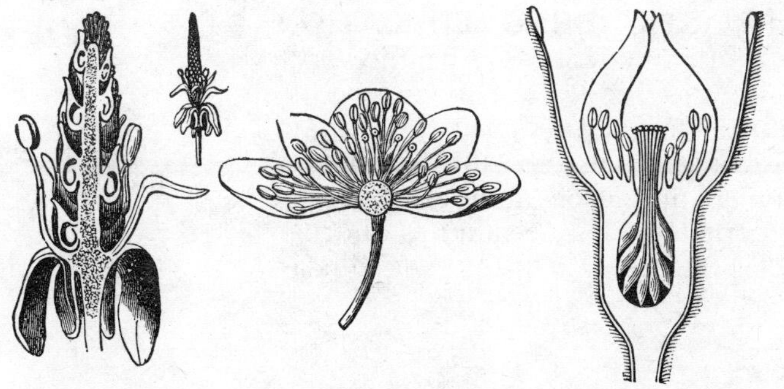

* **203. Conscientious Guide to Drug Abuse.** Now in its 4th printing, this 48-page, illustrated handbook takes a comprehensive look at street drugs as they actually exist. Conscientious Guide is immensely popular not only for personal information, but also is utilized extensively as a training manual and basic guide for staffs of hot lines, clinics, walk in centers, and other organizations involved with handling street drug traffic. $1 single copy, 10/$7.50, 100/$60.

Quantity desired:______ Amount: $______

* **205. FACTS ABOUT COMMONLY USED DRUGS,** by David P. Jenkins and Robert Brody, State Univ. of New York at Albany. This is a long-needed handbook covering the major drugs of abuse from a pharmacological as well as a non-medical standpoint. We recommend this as the best inexpensive handbook for all basics in drug education, and as an ideal companion to Conscientious Guide to Drug Abuse. 68 pages, paper. $1.25 each, 10/$9.50, 100/$75

Quantity desired:______ Amount: $______

206. Megavitamin Therapy and the Drug Wipe-out Syndrome, by Vic Pawlak. A 20-page primer, on megavitamin therapy in the treatment of schizophrenia in relation to previous drug usage. A long awaited work which contains additional lists of related books and organizations. 35 cents each, 10/$2.50, 100/$18, 1000/$150.

Quantity desired:______ Amount: $______

301. First Vibration LP Record Album. An educational peer-oriented record, built largely around the Speed and hard drug problem. The message is in the lyrics, as Psychology Today pointed out. Drug songs by Canned Heat, The Byrds, Hoyt Axton, Genesis. Other cuts by well-known musicians round out this educational – and entertaining – record album. $3 each ppd. in U.S., 10/$25.

Quantity desired:______ Amount: $______

302. A REALISTIC DRUG EDUCATION ALBUM. If you think you have heard everything in audio drug education, this 2-record set is for you. Especially designed for a 4-day classroom discussion and study, this 82-minute LP set contains approx. 67 minutes of verbal ideas and experiences, and 15 minutes of drug music. Can be one of your most vivid educational aids. Includes commentary by Richard Alpert, noted authority on psychedelics, as well as dozens of others. Meaningful dialogue on all major drugs and suitable for Jr. High School to College audiences. Comes with an instruction guide.
$6 per set, 3/$15, 10/$45.

Quantity desired:______ Amount: $______

401. "REDS" 2-color poster. This 20 x 25 2-color poster emphasizes the principal danger of reds (secobarbital), the fact that they are addicting, and can easily cause accidental over-dose. Used in clinics, schools, libraries, etc. $1.25 each, 3/$3, 10/$6, 50/$20.

Quantity desired:______ Amount: $______

Special Packets

501. SPECIAL PACKET FOR TEACHERS, COUNSELORS AND ADMINISTRATORS. Contains one each of 101-116, 104-106S, 201-206, 301, 401, (Total list price $9.45), plus assorted reprints and other materials. $8 each, 10/$60.

Quantity desired:______ Amount: $______

501-A. SPECIAL PACKET, as above, without 301. $5 each, 10/$38.

Quantity desired:______ Amount: $______

501-B. SPECIAL PACKET, as above, without 301 or 401. $3.75 each, 10/$28.50.

Quantity desired:______ Amount: $______

Pamphlets in Spanish

* **104S. La Verdad A Cerca De Los Barbituricos.** Same as "Facts About Downers." 10 cents each, 10/60 cents, 100/$4, 1000/$35.

Quantity desired:______ Amount: $______

* **105S. Pruebe Heroina.** Same as "Smack: Strongest thing you can buy without a prescription." 10 cents each, 10/60 cents, 100/$4, 1000/$35.

Quantity desired:______ Amount: ______

* **106S. El Olfateo Del Espectro.** Same as "Sniffing Spectrum." 10 cents each, 10/60 cents, 100/$4, 1000/$35.

Quantity desired:______ Amount: $______

SPECIAL QUANTITY RATES (*) : On all 10 cent pamphlets, 5000 of the same pamphlet $30 per 1000. On 10,000 orders for same title, $28 per 1000. On large orders for 203 Conscientious Guide, 500/45 cents each, on 1000 or more, 30 cents each. On 205 Facts About Commonly Used Drugs, 500/55 cents each, 1000 or more 40 cents each.

Please allow up to four weeks for delivery. All prices include shipping costs within U. S. (Canadian residents please add 10% to orders for the high cost of postage.) Foreign orders, please inquire or allow extra for postage also. No minimum cash order, however, billed orders & purchase orders must total $1 or more.

For prices on quantities greater than those listed, please write for quotes & discounts.

All profits made from sale of materials in this pricelist go towards free Do It Now street drug education programs in the U.S. & Canada.

THANK YOU FOR YOUR SUPPORT!

A "DO IT NOW" PUBLICATION

If you are a regular user of street psychedelics, or a layman who considers himself well informed on street dope, you may find it hard to believe the contents of this pamphlet. You may scoff, and go on making the same stupid mistakes everyone else is making, relying on the local dealers to give you the straight info on what is really going around. You may think that just because this pamphlet is being written on the West Coast in a particular city, that if you are in another place everything is different. Well, brothers and sisters, it's not different, no matter where you are or no matter where your dope is coming from. And if you can take it, here is our factual report which we entitle

GARBAGE:

A REPORT ON STREET PSYCHEDELICS

PLANNED PARENTHOOD (TRUE TO LIFE)

True to Life is a magazine about sex education written in the language and format of pulp magazines such as *Modern Romances* and *True*. The idea -- to teach sex education fundamentals to those who do not normally read books. A single copy is 50¢; 100 or more copies, 10¢ each; 1,000 or more, 8¢ each from:

PLANNED PARENTHOOD
810 Seventh Avenue
New York, N.Y. 10019

76 Organizations

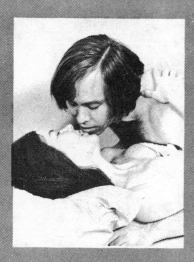

TRUE TO LIFE

November 1972

STORIES:

FEATURES:

ADVICE COLUMNS:

Editors: Marjorie Crow and Felicia Guest
Staff: Becky J. Cheek, William Darity Jr., Elizabeth Matthews, and John Tumlin
Medical Consultant: Robert Hatcher M.D.
Graphics: Susan Autry
Cover Photography: Gerald Jones

TRUE TO LIFE is a publication of Emory University School of Medicine, Department of Gynecology and Obstetrics, Family Planning Program, Box 26069, 80 Butler Street, Atlanta, Georgia 30303.

POPULATION REFERENCE BUREAU

The Population Reference Bureau was founded to provide information for educators, journalists, public officials, and others concerned with the facts and implications of world and national population trends. Members receive:

* *Population Bulletin* -- Authoritative comprehensive publications focusing on important aspects and consequences of population growth in the United States and abroad. Six times yearly.

* *PRB Selection*-Occasional short essays of special interest to PRB readers reprinted from existing articles or abridged from speeches.

* *Population Profile*-concise, illustrated analysis of significant, current population trends.

* *World Population Data Sheet*-An annual 11" x 17 1/2" chart, suitable for wall or desk use, providing detailed population information for 142 countries.

Annual membership is $8; $5 for teachers, libraries, or students.

PRB also publishes an excellent Population Education newsletter called *Interchange*. Subscriptions to this source-listing of teaching ideas and materials about population are $1 for members and $2 for nonmembers.

POPULATION REFERENCE BUREAU, INC.
1755 Massachusetts Avenue, N.W.
Washington, D.C. 20036

Sources and Resources

OPTIONS for Population and the American Future is a study guide to the written and film reports of the Commission on Population Growth and the American Future. Produced by the Population Reference Bureau, this 80-page guide is written for teachers and organization leaders to assist them in *involving* young people of junior high ages and above in the exploration of U.S. population issues. OPTIONS contains a condensed discussion of the Commission Report, a theme development of "Each of Us: A Population Actor," learning objectives, activities, references and the new PRB U.S. Population Data Sheet. Available soon for a $.50 mailing and handling charge from PRB, 1755 Mass. Ave. N.W., Wash. D. C. 20036.

The film, *Population and the American Future,* can now be purchased for $300 from Fisher Film Group, 216 E. 49th, New York, N.Y. 10017. It is also available on a free loan basis from Population Affairs Film Collection, National Audio-visual Center (GSA), Wash. D. C. 20409. Indicate preferred showing date with two alternates. Order at least two months in advance. One copy of *OPTIONS* will be sent with confirmation.

An Introduction to Population, Environment, and Society, by Lawrence Schaefer, is a 290-page manual offering class activities and background information for teachers at the secondary level. A student workbook, a collection of reprints, annotated film list and bibliography complete the manual. Available for $4.50 from E-P Education Services, Inc., 625 Orange St. #38, New Haven, Conn. 06511.

Environment and Population: A Sourcebook for Teachers, by Kathryn Horsley, et al, has just been published by the National Education Association. In manuscript form known as "Sourcebook for Teachers on Environment and Population," this material relates population variables to many different social and natural pressures. It includes discussion material, classroom activities, reference and audio-visual material recommendations. Concepts are written at two levels (jr. and sr. high school) for infusion into *Contemporary Issues, Family Life, Health, History/Social Studies, Science, and Sociology.* This 112-page sourcebook is available for $3.75 from NEA Publications, 1201 16th St., N.W., Wash. D. C. 20036.

PRB WALL CHARTS *

(A) PRESENT BIRTH AND DEATH RATES, BY AREA

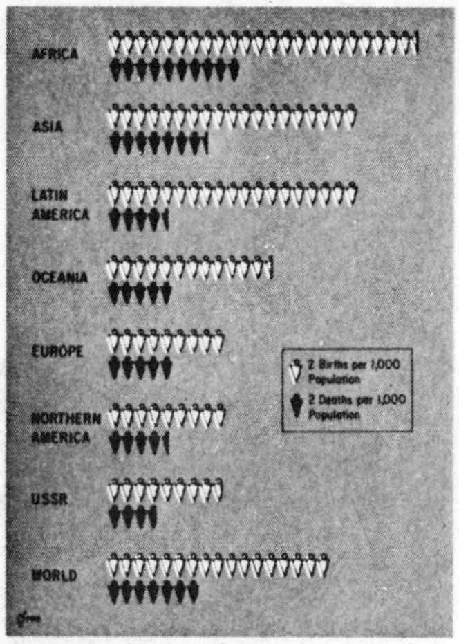

(B) ONE THOUSAND YEARS OF POPULATION GROWTH

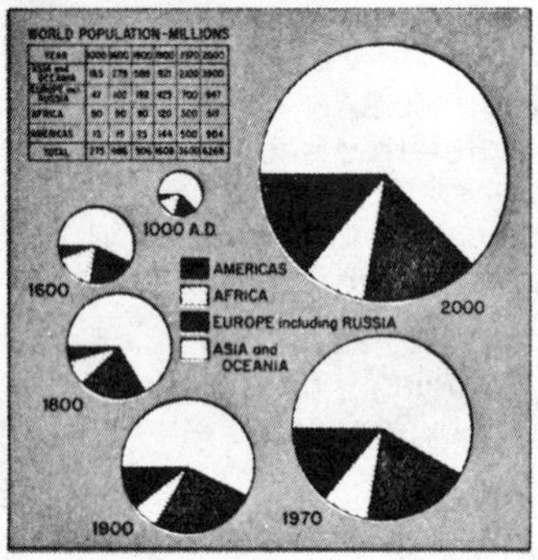

(C) ESTIMATED BIRTH AND DEATH RATES, 1770-1970

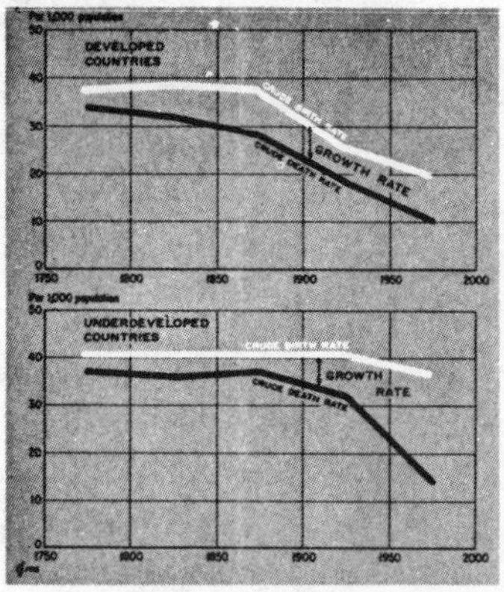

(D) POPULATION THROUGH HISTORY

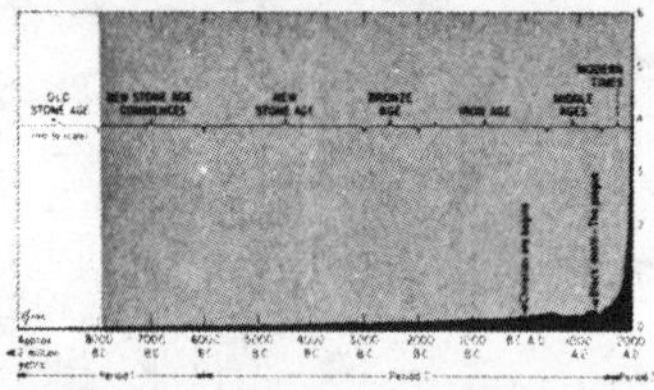

(E) INCOME AND POPULATION GROWTH COMPARED

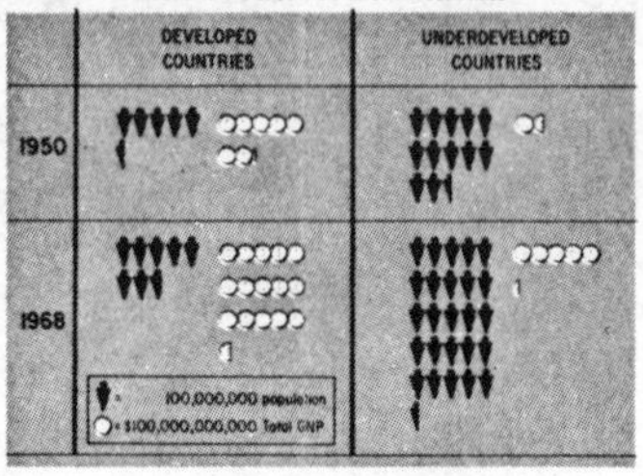

(F) THREE MODELS OF THE FUTURE
POSSIBILITY NO. 1. THE "POPULATION CRASH CURVE"

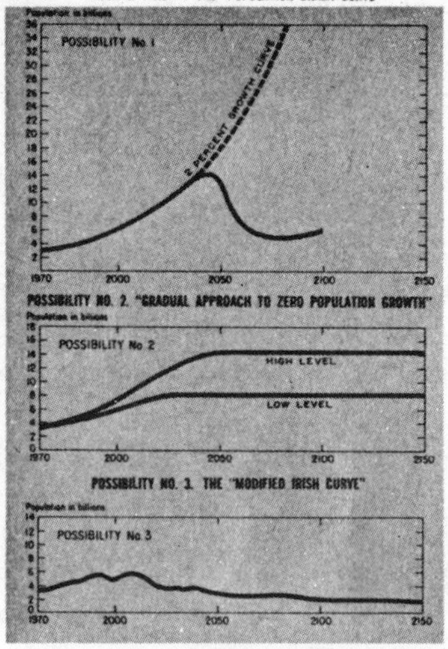

(G) WORLD POPULATION AND FOOD PRODUCTION, 1948-1968

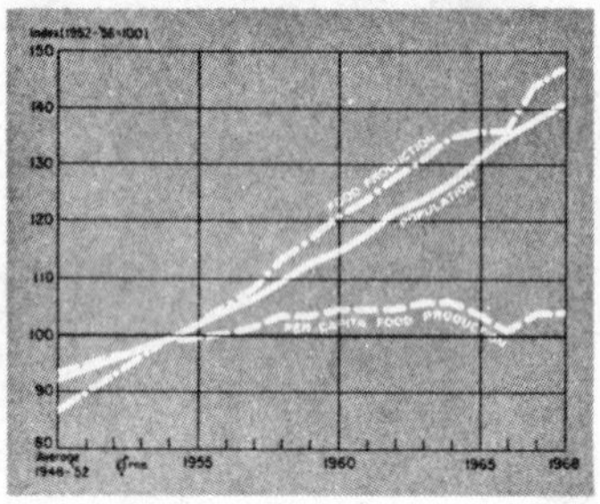

Each of the graphs shown above is now available from the Population Reference Bureau as an individual 17" x 22" wall chart in color. This wall chart series illustrates general population concepts on a global basis and can be a valuable classroom aid for the secondary or college-level teacher. The charts are designed to complement the popular *World Population Data Sheet*, issued annually by the PRB. A detailed discussion of the data presented in the charts is contained in the Population Bulletin, "Man's Population Predicament," Vol. 27, No. 3. A complimentary copy of that bulletin will be mailed with your purchase order.

If you would like to order the wall charts, please fill in the order coupon (on opposite side) and mail to Circulation Dept., Population Reference Bureau, 1755 Massachusetts Avenue, N.W., Washington, D. C. 20036.

** The wall charts are also part of a series of black and white 35mm slides from the Bulletin mentioned above. If you would like to order the entire series of 25 slides from that Bulletin, please indicate on the order form.*

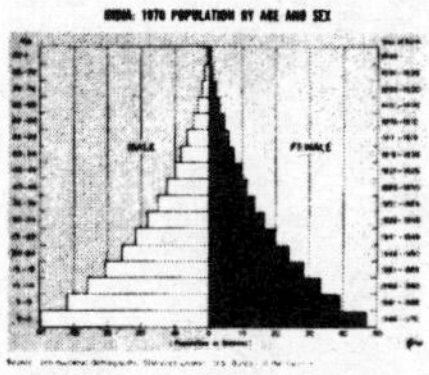

POPULATION CHALLENGE OF THE '70's, Vol. 26, No. 1, February 1970
Growth and Decline of County Populations, 1960-66 — $1.25 *(Series 1)*
Trends in U.S. Vital Rates, Natural Increase
Saga of the U.S. Passenger Car
U.S. Birth Rate: Impact of "Unwanted" Births
U.S. Share of World Consumption and Production, Selected Minerals, 1967

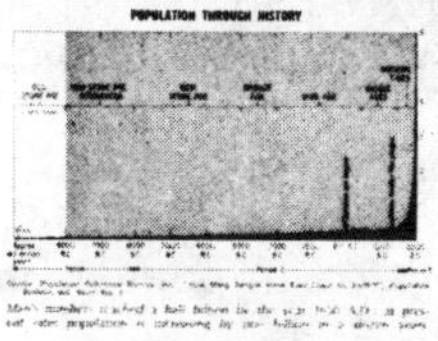

POPULATION AND RESOURCES: THE COMING COLLISION, Vol. 26, No. 2, June 1970
Water Required for Daily Per Capita Food Production, United States and India — $1.25 *(Series 2)*
Fertilizer Use, Consumption, Production, Selected Countries, 1965
Energy Consumption by Region, 1966
Possible Trends in Energy Consumption, 1950-2075
Estimated Growth of Nuclear Power in the United States, 1965-1980

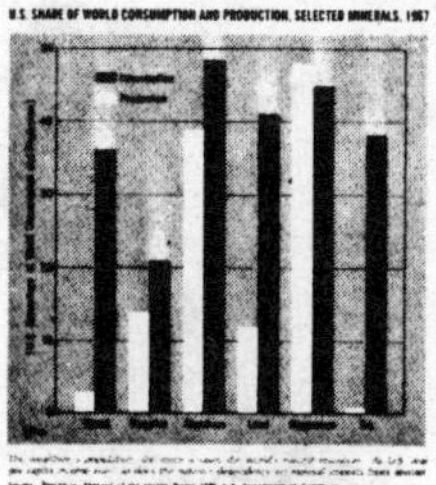

INDIA: READY OR NOT, HERE THEY COME, Vol. 26, No. 5, November 1970
India: 1970 Population by Age and Sex — $1.00 *(Series 3)*
Sweden: 1970 Age-Sex Pyramid
Four Projections of India's Population Growth
India's Contraception Performance

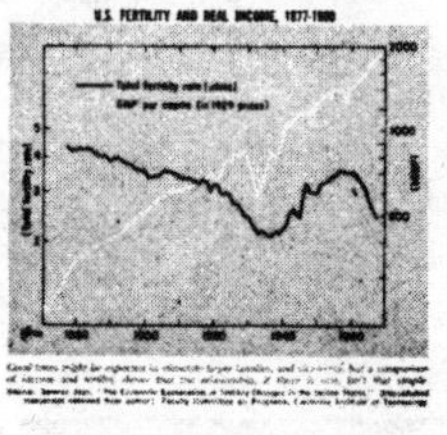

THE FUTURE POPULATION OF THE UNITED STATES, Vol. 27, No. 1, February 1971
Total Fertility Rates for the Total Population, 1925-1990 — $1.00 *(Series 4)*
Projected U.S. Population Distribution by Age and Sex, Year 2000 Compared to Year 1970, Series B
Projected U.S. Population Distribution by Age and Sex, Year 2000 Compared to Year 1970, Series C
U.S. Fertility and Real Income, 1877-1968

$6.25 *(Series 5)*

$ .50 *(Series 6)*

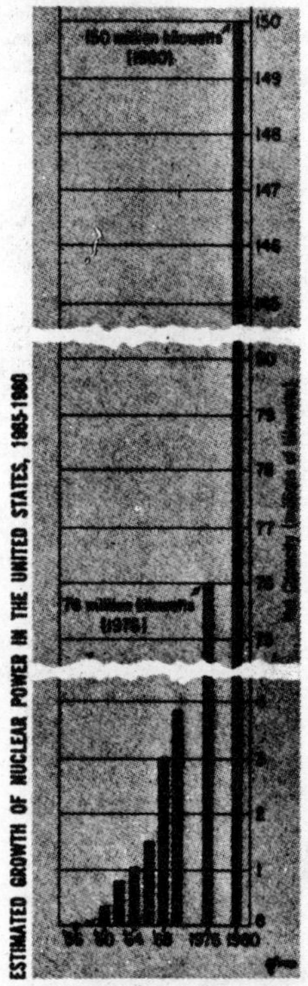

Sources: McHale, John. *The Future of the Futures.* New York: George Braziller, 1969. Projections for 1976 and 1980 given by Seaborg, Glenn T. Remarks at Financial Forum on Nuclear Energy, Waldorf Astoria Hotel, New York City, October 30, 1968.

The illustrations shown here are samples from six series of black and white 35mm slides now available from the Population Reference Bureau. Each series focuses on one aspect of worldwide population growth and its environmental, sociological and economic effects upon the world's people and resources. A detailed discussion for each series is contained in the *Population Bulletins* listed. A complimentary copy of the *Bulletins* corresponding to the slide series purchased will be mailed to you with your order.

If you would like to order one or more slide series, please fill out the order coupon (on back) and mail to Circulation Department, Population Reference Bureau, 1755 Massachusetts Avenue, N.W., Washington, D. C. 20036.

A forthcoming issue of *INTERCOM* is devoted to population and geared to the secondary school level. It includes an essay, teaching lessons, an annotated list of materials for teacher as well as student use, and a list of organizational resources. Available for $1.50 from *INTERCOM,* Center for War/Peace Studies, 218 E. 18th St., N.Y., N.Y. 10003.

The Scholastic Teacher, April 1973 issue, contains two departments focused on population education. One describes current school system pop ed programs in the U.S. The second is a select resource list of both student and teacher material for population education (material level selected separately for elementary and junior/senior teaching editions). Single copies (specify level) available for $1.00 from Scholastic Teacher, 902 Sylvan Ave., Englewood Cliffs, N.J. 07632.

Population Profiles (first six now available), are short, illustrated units for the study of demography in high school social studies. Written by Leon Bouvier and Everett Lee, these 8-page leaflets give clear explanations of various population processes. First six units are as follows: #1 Why Study Population?, #2 The United States Among the Nations, #3 The Vital Revolution, #4 The Health of Americans, #5 The Bearing of Children, #6 America as a Nation of Migrants. Available at $.50 per unit from Center for Information on America, Box C, Washington, Conn. 06793.

The December 1972 issue of AAAS *Science for Society: Education Review* (Vol. 2, No. 4) is devoted to population education. Statements of definition, needs, projects in progress, as well as descriptions of organizational activity are included.

SYNOPSIS, December 1972, devotes half of its articles to the question, "Population Control: Are There Too Many of Us?" A number of viewpoints (not information) are offered on a variety of controversial topics. Available from Curriculum Innovations, 501 Lake Forest Avenue, Highwood, Ill. 60040.

ASSOCIATION FOR THE STUDY OF ABORTION

The *Association for the Study of Abortion* has a large selection of free popular and technical article reprints about abortion. They also publish the *ASA Newsletter* and have a free-loan film on abortion available. Information from:

ASSOCIATION FOR THE STUDY OF ABORTION
120 West 57th Street
New York, N.Y. 10019
(212) CI 5-2360

The reprints listed are available free upon request:

M11. Dauber, Bonnie, *et al.,* "Abortion Counseling and Behavioral Change," *Family Planning Perspectives,* Vol. 4, No. 2, 1972, p. 23. Report on a San Francisco study which found that counseling just prior to, during, and following legal abortion can help prevent future unwanted pregnancies through contraceptive use.

M21. Hall, Robert E., M.D., "Induced Abortion in the United States, 1971," *The Journal of Reproductive Medicine,* Vol. 8, No. 6, June 1972, 345-347. A review of the legal and medical abortion picture in 1971.

M23. Hall, Robert E., M.D., "Time Limitation in Induced Abortion," *Abortion Techniques and Services,* Excerpta Medica, 1972. An analysis of the various legal time limits in light of the medical definition of abortion which is "the termination of pregnancy during the first 20 weeks."

M32. Kohl, Marvin, "Abortion and the Slippery Slope," *Dissent,* Fall 1972. The author considers and rejects the argument that if you permit the killing of fetuses it will be impossible to limit the killing to fetuses, and that killing will be extended to all who have not achieved or have lost their full potential as human beings.

M47. Pasnau, Robert O., M.D., "Psychiatric Complications of Therapeutic Abortion," *Obstetrics and Gynecology,* Vol. 40, No. 2, August 1972, 252-256. The author concludes that "there is no evidence to suggest that the risk of psychiatric complications in induced abortion constitutes a contraindication to the procedure in either normal or psychiatrically ill women."

M24. HARDIN, GARRETT, PH.D., "Abortion—or Compulsory Pregnancy?" *Journal of Marriage and the Family*, Vol. XXX, No. 2, May 1968. The proper question, the author argues, is not, "How can we justify an abortion?" but, "How can we justify compulsory pregnancy?"

M25. HARDIN, GARRETT, PH.D., "Semantic Aspects of Abortion," *ETC.*, Vol. XXIV, No. 3, September 1967. A penetrating examination of some typical abortion arguments.

M26. HARTING, DONALD, M.D., and HUNTER, HELEN J., "Abortion Techniques and Services: A Review and Critique," *American Journal of Public Health*, Vol. 61, No. 10, October 1971. Rapid changes in the abortion situation in the United States are reviewed, drawing primarily on papers presented at a national conference held in June 1971. Various aspects including the legal situation, the role of official health agencies, consequences of recent changes in legislation, and other matters discussed at the conference are included.

M29. KIMMEY, JIMMYE, "The Abortion Argument: What It's Not About," *Barnard Alumnae*, Vol. XIX, No. 1 (Fall 1969). An examination of some of the major arguments concerning the abortion problem.

M30. KNUTSON, ANDIE L., PH.D., F.A.P.H.A., "When Does Human Life Begin? Viewpoints of Public Health Professionals," *American Journal of Public Health*, Vol. 57, No. 12, December 1967. A study of the relationship between beliefs concerning the beginning of human life and the professional behavior of some graduate students of public health.

M33. KOHL, MARVIN, "The Term 'Human Being' and the Problem of Abortion," *Names*, September 1971. An analysis and refutation of the argument that the killing of a human fetus is the killing of a human being.

M37. MANNES, MARYA, "A Woman Views Abortion." A moving and perceptive look at this problem from the point of view of those most intimately involved.

M38. MARGOLIES, RABBI ISRAEL R., "Abortion and Religion." A thoughtful, penetrating examination of abortion as a religious problem.

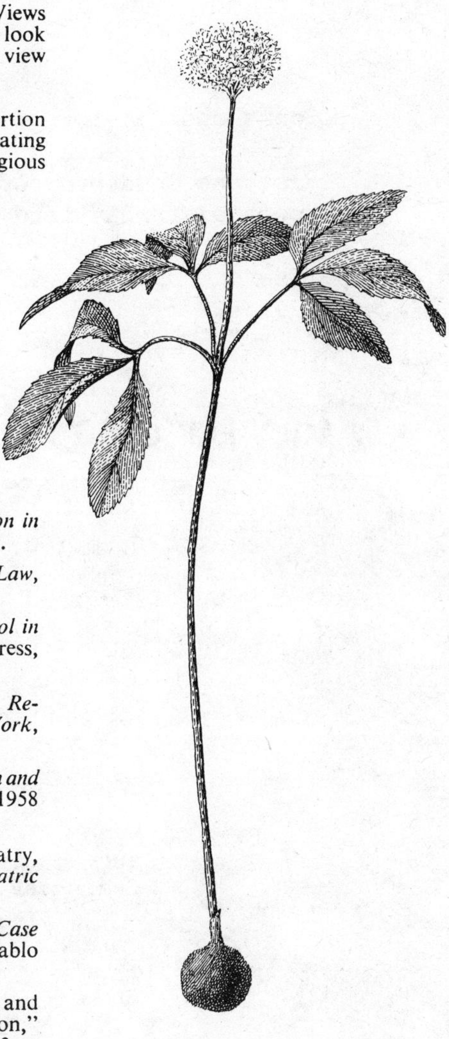

RECOMMENDED READING

(Not available from ASA)

"Abortion and Fertility Control." Special issue of *California School Health*, Vol. 6, October 1971.

Abortion: Classification and Techniques. International Planned Parenthood Federation, 1971. ($1.00, IPPF, 18–20 Lower Regent Street, London SW1Y 4PW, England.)

Abortion in Britain. Proceedings of a Conference held by the Family Planning Association at the University of London on April 22, 1966. London, Pitman Medical Publishing Co., Ltd.

Abortion Laws: A Survey of Current World Legislation, World Health Organization, 1971.

AF GEIJERSTAM, GUNNAR K., M.D., editor, *An Annotated Bibliography of Induced Abortion*, University of Michigan, 1969.

BERELSON, BERNARD, editor, *Family Planning and Population Programs*, University of Chicago Press, 1966.

"Birth Control—All the Methods that *Work* . . . and the Ones that *Don't*," Family Planning Resources Center, 44 Court Street, Brooklyn, N. Y. 11201 (single copy free).

BUCKLEY, WILLIAM F., JR., "The Catholic Church and Abortion," *National Review*, April 5, 1966.

CALDERONE, MARY, M.D., editor, *Abortion in the United States*, Hoeber-Harper, 1958.

CALLAHAN, DANIEL. *Abortion: Law, Choice and Mortality*, The Macmillan Company, 1970.

DEVEREAUX, GEORGE, *A Study of Abortion in Primitive Societies*, Julian Press, 1955.

DICKENS, BERNARD M., *Abortion and the Law*, MacGibbon and Kee, Ltd., 1966.

FELDMAN, RABBI DAVID M., *Birth Control in Jewish Law*, New York University Press, 1968.

FLETCHER, THE REV. JOSEPH, *Moral Responsibility—Situation Ethics at Work*, Westminster Press, 1967.

GEBHARD, PAUL H., *et al*, *Pregnancy, Birth and Abortion*, John Wiley & Sons, Inc., 1958 (paperback).

Group for the Advancement of Psychiatry, *The Right to Abortion: A Psychiatric View*, Scribners, New York, 1970.

GUTTMACHER, ALAN F., M.D., ed., *The Case for Legalized Abortion Now*, Diablo Press, 1967 (paperback).

GUTTMACHER, ALAN F., M.D., "The Legal and Moral Status of Therapeutic Abortion," *Progress in Gynecology*, Vol. IV, 1963.

HALL, ROBERT E., M.D., *A Doctor's Guide to Having an Abortion*, New American Library, 1971.

HALL, ROBERT E., M.D., ed., *Abortion in a Changing World*, 2 volumes, Columbia University Press, 1970.

HALL, ROBERT E., M.D., "Therapeutic Abortion and Sterilization," in S. L. Marcus,

E. C. BROWN FOUNDATION (FOCUS ON FAMILY)

A bimonthly publication, *Focus on the Family,* is produced by the E. C. Brown Foundation of Portland and Eugene Oregon, and is available upon individual written request to the Foundation's Eugene offices, 1802 Moss Street, Eugene, OR 97403.

Edited by Joyce Lang, the Foundation's coordinator of information and publications, each issue contains at least one in-depth report on some aspect of family life education, family research, or an innovative classroom application of family studies.

A regular feature of each 16-page issue is the annotation of some 40 new books, pamphlets, and reports concerning human sexuality, marriage, family research and study, designed to help the classroom teacher, curriculum developer, and other professionals keep abreast of new resource material.

E.C. BROWN FOUNDATION/CENTER FOR FAMILY STUDIES
1802 Moss Street
Eugene, Ore. 97403
(503) 686-4248

FOCUS on the family

FAMILY-FOCUSED FOUNDATION MATERIALS

ANY PUBLICATIONS ORDERED FROM THIS PAGE SHOULD BE PAID FOR BY CHECK OR MONEY ORDER MADE OUT TO: *E. C. Brown Foundation.* List prices are cash with order. A 10% library/professional discount is allowed. 50-cent handling fee charged on invoiced orders. *Payment must be in U.S. funds.* Include publication number and title. Send orders to: E. C. BROWN FOUNDATION, 1802 Moss St., Eugene, OR 97403.

PRICE	CODE	TITLE & DESCRIPTION
1.00	FP#10	New for 1973 -- *Supplement to Curriculum Guides for Family Life and Sex Education.* Companion publication to FP#4. Annotates several guides received after earlier publication; includes resource addresses and information from *Sex Education for the Handicapped & An Annotated Bibliography of Selected Resources* (CB-H) which is now out of print. Supplement is sent complimentary with orders for FP#4; substituted for orders for CB-H. Also sold separately. Paper.
$1.00	FP#5	*Course Synopsis: Professional Study of the Family* (rev. ed.). Describes course offerings at University of Oregon which focus on marriage, family, and human sexuality. Summarizes UO graduate programs with family emphasis. Paper. 24 pp.
2.00	FP#4	*Curriculum Guides for Family Life and Sex Education* (2nd printing). Annotated bibliography of public school curriculum guides in family life, sex education. Sample evaluation, check list, list of high school texts, readers. Paper. 56 pp.
1.00	FP#1	*Human Heredity.* Curriculum aid for teachers and students, senior high school level. Treatise on basic genetic facts by the late Curtis E. Avery. Paper. 32 pp.
.50	CR#1	*Children's Art and Human Beginnings.* Full color art reproduction of 80 drawings from primary classrooms; result of posing questions: "Where was I before I was born?" "What did I look like before I was born?" Summary of Foundation project. Paper. 16 pp.
2.00	CR#2	*Sex Education: Concepts and Challenges* (rev. ed.). Reprint of 10 articles by the late Curtis E. Avery, plus author's bibliography between 1948-70. Paper. 16 pp.

WOMEN'S HISTORY RESEARCH CENTER

WOMEN'S HISTORY RESEARCH CENTER, INC., 2325 OAK STREET, BERKELEY, CALIFORNIA 94708

The WOMEN'S HISTORY RESEARCH CENTER, INC., maintains the INTERNATIONAL WOMEN'S HISTORY ARCHIVE by and about the current women's movement and a TOPICAL RESEARCH LIBRARY of 2,000 files which documents the position of women past and present in all walks of life, in many countries and ethnic groups, in history, in women's organizations, in events, and in roles. The ARCHIVE and the LIBRARY constitute the WOMEN'S HISTORY LIBRARY which has been created by hundreds of women over the past four years. The LIBRARY is seeking money in the form of grants and memberships to continue its work.

AVAILABLE PUBLICATIONS:

THE CATALOG: a source index which includes the addresses from which the listed materials may be ordered. The complete CATALOG is available for $16.00 which includes postage and handling ($20.00 to institutions, organizations and groups). Parts of the CATALOG are also available separately TO INDIVIDUAL WOMEN ONLY; Index as of July, 1969, $1; Packet of Action Projects as of September, 1969, $5; Addenda to Index as of January, 1970, $2; Addenda to Index as of March, 1971, $7.

CATALOG SECTION UPDATES:

DIRECTORY OF WOMEN'S PERIODICALS (1971) $3 to individual women, $10 to institutions, groups and organizations.

INDEX by topic of WOMEN'S STUDIES COURSE OUTLINES and contacts for them, $3.00/$5.00.

INDEX by topic of BIBLIOGRAPHIES and contacts for them, $2.00/$2.00.

LIST of people doing RESEARCH PROJECTS (1971), $1.00/$2.00; Update will be $3.00/$4.00.

TAPE ARCHIVE INDEX (1971), $1.20/$2.00; Update will be $3.00/$4.00.

DIRECTORY of FILMS by and about WOMEN (75-Page Book, 1972) $3.00/$5.00.

FEMALE ARTISTS PAST AND PRESENT (1972), $3.00/$4.00.

NATIONAL ORGANIZATION FOR WOMEN NEWSLETTER DIRECTORY (1971) $3.00.

XEROX of our index cards on RAPE, $25.00.

XEROX of our index cards on ABORTION, $25.00.

ALSO AVAILABLE:

The WOMEN'S SONGBOOK, (pre-paid orders for a second printing), (1971), $2.50 including postage/$3.00.

The SYNOPSIS OF WOMEN IN WORLD HISTORY, (1969), $1.20/$2.00.

SPAZM, the Library's Newsletter, (April to Dec. 1969) 30 issues $15.00/$20.00, single issues 70¢ plus postage. Only national record of that period.

A DIRECTORY OF GAY WOMEN'S PERIODICALS (1972), 25¢ plus a self-addressed stamped envelope.

PLEASE MAKE CHECKS PAYABLE TO THE WOMEN'S HISTORY RESEARCH CENTER: ALL FUNDS SENT ARE TAX-DEDUCTIBLE DONATIONS, AS OUR PRICES DO NOT MEET OUR COSTS.

MICROFILM PUBLISHING PROJECT:

The INTERNATIONAL WOMEN'S HISTORY PERIODICAL ARCHIVE is available on microfilm through Bell & Howell, Wooster, Ohio. Your local library can now have this collection of women's liberation, and women's civic, religious, professional, peace newsletters, newspapers and journals from all over the world. URGE YOUR LIBRARY TO SUBSCRIBE by writing Bell & Howell ($550 for over 20 rolls). The Library is seeking funds to continue to archive and publicize the more than 300 titles on microfilm and also the new issues and titles published since October 1, 1971.

Because of lack of funds, we cannot be a library open to random visits from the public; however, we are open to donors of women's works, or of time, labor, supplies, equipment and money. Call for appointment.

Please include a donation and a self-addressed stamped business size envelope with all correspondence to:

WOMEN'S HISTORY RESEARCH CENTER, INC.
2325 OAK STREET
BERKELEY, CALIFORNIA 94708

(415) 524-7772

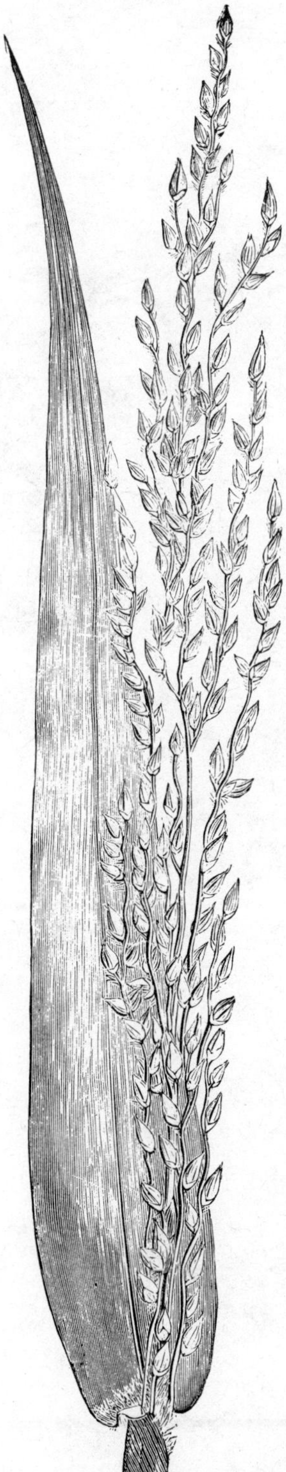

KNOW, INC.

KNOW, inc. P.O. Box 86031 / Pittsburgh, Penn. 15221

FREEDOM OF THE PRESS BELONGS
TO THOSE WHO OWN THE PRESS!

KNOW, INC. is a non-profit, tax-exempt corporation founded in the fall of 1969 by Pittsburgh NOW members who believed that you can't have a revolution without a press--and bought one. The original intention was to produce a newsletter, but several others began about that time and were successfully filling the need.

In the meantime, the press was being used to reprint feminist articles for free distribution at local NOW meetings. These articles were so hungrily sought after we decided we could support our press by reprinting and selling such articles at only slightly over the cost of the materials. KNOW, Inc., housed in a member's garage and later in a basement, began to flourish, supported by volunteer labor, donated supplies and money, good faith and growing sales. We quickly added many original articles, several longer works and books. Each step in our development brought us closer to the status of feminist publisher.

We now carry a wide range of topics, including our Female Studies Series--collections of course designs (I, II, III) and essays related to the Female Studies field (IV, V). We have published one full-length paperback book (American Women and American Studies I, by Betty E. Chmaj) with its sequel due mid-spring, and one hardback (I'm Running Away From Home But I'm Not Allowed To Cross The Street, by Gabrielle Burton) released with great pride on August 26, 1972.

While the publishing business grew, we had not given up the idea of an information network news service. We wanted a way to disseminate news to feminists, feminist publications and groups, without the rigid confines of a regular publication. Our increased volume of mail brought privileged information, announcements of job openings, conferences and feminist products and projects, which we felt should be communicated to persons involved in the women's movement. We began by printing single item news bulletins and enclosing them in all outgoing mail. On August 17, 1970, we announced KNOW NEWS, a bulletin issued approximately 10 times a year, going to feminist publications, reporters you can trust, and to subscribers who paid $4 per year. Another change in status for our bulletin was announced in January, 1973. KNOW NEWS is now free to members of KNOW, Inc. The yearly, tax-deductible membership fee is $4 per year for individuals, $8 for institutions, $6 for Canada and $8 for overseas.

There are others facets of KNOW: We publish a list of "Reporters You Can Trust," and a list of feminist periodicals and special publishing projects. For two years we have compiled a bibliography titled "Books of Interest To Feminists". All are periodically updated.

PRICE LIST OF AVAILABLE ARTICLES
[March 1973--210 items]

AUTHOR	TITLE	PRICE
Alice Rossi, Ph.D.	Discrimination and Demography Restrict Opportunities for Academic Women	10¢
Alice Rossi, Ph.D.	Job Discrimination and What Women Can Do About It	10¢
Alice Rossi, Ph.D.	Women in the 70's: Problems and Possibilities	20¢
Alta	Poems	50¢
Ann Scott	Feminism vs. the Feds: Woman's Place in the Work Force	20¢
Ann Scott	The Half-Eaten Apple	40¢
Ann S. Harris	Second Sex in Academe	35¢
Anselma Dell O'lio	Devisiveness and Self Destruction in the Women's Movement	5¢
Anne Grant West	The Black and White of Women's Liberation	20¢
Audrey Wells	On Dropouts	5¢
Beatrice Dinerman	Attitudes and Practices Toward Women in Architecture, Dentistry, Engineering and Law	35¢
Bernice Sandler	Testimony on Discrimination in Higher Education (5/6/70)	25¢
Dana Densmore	Chivalry: The Iron Hand in the Velvet Glove	10¢
Dana Densmore	Speech is the Form of Thought	10¢
Dana Densmore	Who Is Saying Men Are The Enemy?	10¢
Dana Densmore	Without You and Within You	20¢
Elizabeth Cady Stanton	Seneca Falls Resolution (1848)	5¢
Elizabeth Fisher	Children's Books: The Second Sex, Junior Division	5¢
George Washington University Women's Liberation	Position Paper on the Draft	5¢
Gerald H.F. Gardner	Discrimination in Help-Wanted Advertising	20¢
Gerald H.F. Gardner	Status of Women in the Field of Computing	5¢
Gunnar Myrdal	A Parallel to the Negro Problem	10¢
Herbert Barry	Cross-Cultural Perspectives	15¢
Inge and Don Broverman, Frank Clarkson, Paul Rosenkrantz, Susan Vogel, Helen Bee	Family Size and Sex-Role Stereotypes	5¢
Inge and Don Broverman, et al	Sex-Role Stereotypes and Clinical Judgments of Mental Health	20¢
Inge and Don Broverman, et al	Sex-Role Stereotypes and Self Concepts in College Students	25¢
Jack Sawyer	On Male Liberation	5¢
Jane Torrey	Psychoanalysis: A Feminist Revision	15¢
Jean Faust	Words That Oppress	5¢
Jo Freeman	Building The Gilded Cage	40¢
Jo Freeman	How To Discriminate Against Women Without Really Trying	40¢
Jo Freeman	The Legal Basis of the Sexual Caste System	45¢
Jo Freeman	The Social Construction of the Second Sex	25¢
Jo Freeman	Women on the Social Science Faculties Since 1892	45¢
Jo-Ann Evans Gardner	Autobiographical Notes	10¢
Jo-Ann Evans Gardner	On Sexism	5¢
Jo-Ann Evans Gardner	Sexist Counseling Must Stop	15¢
Jo-Ann Evans Gardner	What Effect Should the Feminist Movement Have on Higher Education	10¢
Jo-Ann Evans Gardner	Sesame Street and Sex-Role Stereotypes	5¢
Jo-Ann Evans Gardner, Inge Broverman, Susan Vogel	Sesame Street (updated)	10¢

KNOW PRICE LIST

Jo-Ann Evans Gardner and Phyllis Wetherby	Women: The World's Largest Oppressed Minority	5¢
Joreen	Bitch Manifesto	25¢
Joreen	51% Minority Group: A Statistical Essay	35¢
Joy Belle Conrad-Rice	Being Blonde and Hating It	5¢
Joy Belle Conrad-Rice	Letter To My Parents On Changing My Name	10¢
Joy-Belle Conrad-Rice	Poetry	50¢
Joy Belle Conrad-Rice	Religion, Language, Psychology: Women Left Out	5¢
Joy Belle Conrad-Rice	Women, Take Your Men Too	5¢
Judith Long Laws	Social Psychology of Women: Shibboleths and Lacunae	30¢
Juli Loesch	Poetry	50¢
Kathleen Shortridge	Woman as University Nigger	15¢
Kathryn F. Clarenback	Women Are People	25¢
Kingsley Widmer	Reflections of a Male Housewife	25¢
Leonard Swidler	Jesus Was a Feminist	20¢
Linda Gordon	Towards a Radical Feminist History	20¢
Lucinda Cisler	Abortion Law Repeal (Sort Of): A Warning to Women	15¢
Lucy Komisar	The Masculine Mystique	25¢
Lynn O'Conner	Male Supremacy	25¢
Marguerite Rawalt	Legal Arguments for the Equal Rights Amendment	10¢
Marilyn Goldberg	On Misandrism	5¢
Marion Bassett	Let's Call Their Bluff--And Take Courage	5¢
Marion Bassett	Property of Mothers	5¢
Martha S. White	Psychological and Social Barriers to Women in Science	15¢
Matina Horner	Why Bright Women Fail	10¢
Miriam Keiffer and Dallas Cullen	Discrimination Experienced by Academic Female Psychologists	25¢
Nancy	On Put-Downs	5¢
Nancy Henley	Facing Down the Man	10¢
Nancy Henley	Male Chauvinism--Attitudes and Practices	5¢
Nancy Henley	Politics of Touch	20¢
Nancy Henley	Psychology and the New Woman	20¢
Naomi Weisstein	Woman as Nigger	10¢
Natalie Shainess	Abortion Is No Man's Business	10¢
Natalie Shainess	Images of Women	35¢
Nicole Anthony	Letter to a Psychiatrist	5¢
Pat Mainardi	Politics of Housework	10¢
Patricia A. Graham	Women in Academe	20¢
Pauline Bart	Gilded Cage to Iron Cage: Sexism in Social Science	50¢
Pauline Bart	Portnoy's Mother's Complaint: Depression in Middle Aged Women	15¢
Pauline Bart	Social Structure and Vocabularies of Discomfort: What Happened to Female Hysteria?	15¢
Phyllis Chesler	Marriage and Psychotherapy	5¢
Phyllis Wetherby	Women: The Under-represented Majority	10¢
Robert Seidenberg	Drug Advertising and Perception of Mental Illness	30¢
Robert Seidenberg	Oedipus and Male Supremacy	5¢
Robin Morgan	Goodby To All That	15¢
Rona M. Fields	The Taxonomy of Sexism	15¢
Sally Wood	Questions I Should Have Answered Better	15¢
Sandra and Daryl Bem	Sex Segregated Want-Ads: Do They Discourage Female Job Applicants?	10¢
Sandra and Daryl Bem	Training the Woman to Know Her Place (revised)	35¢
Shirley Chisholm	The 51% Minority	10¢
Sonia Pressman	Job Discrimination and the Black Woman	15¢
Susan B. Anthony	The Revolution (January 22, 1848)	40¢
Susan Edmiston	The Psychology of Day Care	20¢
Sylvia Hartman	Princess Valium Meets Shrinkthink: Sexism in Psychiatry	10¢
Sylvia Hartman	Should Wives Work?	20¢

KNOW PRICE LIST

Una Stannard	The Male Maternal Instinct	25¢
--Unknown--	There Was A Young Woman (a poem with illustrations)	25¢
Vanuken	A Primer for the Last Revolution	45¢
Vivian Gornick	Women: The Next Great Moment in History Is Theirs	20¢
Wilma Scott Heide	New York Times Guest Editorial	5¢
Wilma Scott Heide	Reality and Challenge of the Double Standard in Mental Health and Society	25¢
Wilma Scott Heide	What's Wrong With Male-Dominated Society?	10¢
Women's Collective of Stratford, Connecticut	Consciousness-Raising	15¢

KNOW NEWS--a news bulletin issued approximately 10 times a year, containing announcements of of conferences and demonstrations, job openings, legislative actions, ads for feminist products--sharing the information we receive from sources all over the country. Each issue usually concentrates on a specific topic or event of current importance to feminists. KNOW NEWS comes to you FREE, as a KNOW MEMBER, when you make a TAX DEDUCTIBLE contribution of $4.00 or more per year (Canada $6.00, institutions and foreign $8.00).

KNOW'S MAJOR OFFERINGS

CORNELL CONFERENCE (Jan.'69) edited by Sheila Tobias [report of an early conference, now a classic] $2.50*

SIXTEEN REPORTS ON THE STATUS OF WOMEN IN THE PROFESSIONS (Apr.'70) $2.50*

FEMALE STUDIES I (Sept.'70) edited by Sheila Tobias [17 college level course syllabi] $2.00*

FEMALE STUDIES II (Dec.'70) edited by Florence Howe [65 course designs and reading lists. prepared for the MLA Commission on the Status of Women] $4.00*

FEMALE STUDIES III (Dec.'71) edited by Florence Howe and Carol Ahlum [for MLA Commission. 54 new course designs + 17 programs + GUIDE TO FEMALE STUDIES #1 (see below) included as first 30 pages] $4.50*

FEMALE STUDIES IV (Dec.'71) edited by Elaine Showalter and Carol Ohmann [for MLA Commission. 12 essays on teaching female studies] $2.00*

FEMALE STUDIES V (July '72) edited by Rae Lee Siporin Proceedings of the Conference Women and Education: A Feminist Perspective, co-sponsored by Univ. of Pittsburgh and MLA Commission [17 essays on women, education, sexism and female studies] $4.50*

GUIDE TO FEMALE STUDIES #1 (Oct.'71) edited by Florence Howe and Carol Ahlum [for MLA Commission. list of over 600 courses, giving course title, instructor, department, school and address] $0.75*

GUIDE TO FEMALE STUDIES #2 (Oct.72) edited by Carol Ahlum and Florence Howe [supplement to GUIDE #1, listing over 500 additional college, highschool, in-service, community and continuing education courses] $1.00*

AMERICAN WOMEN & AMERICAN STUDIES I (Oct.'71) Betty E. Chmaj [in 3 parts--Report of the ASA Commission on the status of Women; 25 course outlines; collage of previews, reviews and deja vus] $3.00*

*add 25¢ postage and handling

KNOW PRICE LIST MAJOR OFFERINGS

WOMEN'S WORK & WOMEN'S STUDIES 1971 (Oct.'72) Kirsten Drake, Dorothy Marks and Mary Wexford [bibliography of the year's scholarly research on women and directory of women's organizations, action projects, communications outlets] looseleaf $4.25*
hardbound library edition (**50¢ postage) $7.00**

I'M RUNNING AWAY FROM HOME BUT I'M NOT ALLOWED TO CROSS THE STREET: A PRIMER ON WOMEN'S LIBERATION (Aug.'72) Gabrielle Burton [hardbound] $3.50° [° requires $0.35 postage]

DISCRIMINATION AGAINST WOMEN AT THE UNIVERSITY OF PITTSBURGH (Nov.'70) University Committee for Women's Rights $2.00*

WOMEN & THE LAW: A COLLECTION OF READING LISTS Barbara Babcock, Ann Freedman, Eleanor Holmes Norton, Susan Deller Ross $0.75*

WOMEN'S LIBERATION: AN ANTHROPOLOGICAL VIEW (July'72) Minda Borun, Molly McLaughlin, Gina Oboler, Norma Perchonock, and Lorraine Sexton $1.00*

TIL DIVORCE DO YOU PART (Aug.'72) Roberta Greene [a handbook to help women confront the hassles from separation to final divorce decree] $1.50* [second edition]

WOMEN IN THE WASTELAND FIGHT BACK: A REPORT ON THE IMAGE OF WOMEN PORTRAYED IN TV PROGRAMMING--National Organization for Women, National Capitol Area Chapter $3.50#
[# requires $1.00 postage]

****

A POTPOURRI OF FEMINIST PRODUCTS CARRIED BY KNOW

Little Miss Muffet Fights Back: Recommended Non-Sexist Books About Girls for Young Readers compiled by Feminists on Children's Media $0.50
Dick & Jane As Victims: Sex Stereotyping in Children's Readers--Women on Words and Images $1.50
Let Them Aspire!--report on sexism and Ann Arbor public schools $2.00*
An Action Proposal--sequel to above $1.00
The Status of Women Faculty at Bowling Green State University $2.00*
Witches, Midwives and Nurses: A History of Women Healers--Barbara Ehrenreich and Deirdre English (Glass Mountain Pamphlets) $1.00
Women's Movement Newspapers--assorted back issues .... each $0.15

There's A Contradiction Inside--Linda April Raines (a marvelous collection of feminist poetry, with 4 paintings by the author, beautifully reproduced in color) .. hardbound $4.95*
Best Friends 2--women's poetry (116 pages) $1.00*
Woman Becoming--a journal of women's writings $1.00*

Children's Books--Feminist Press (FP) and Joyful World Press (JWP)
Challenge to Become a Doctor: The Story of Elizabeth Blackwell--Leah Luri Heyn, illustrated by Greta Handschuh (FP) [age 10-12] $1.50
The Dragon and the Doctor--written and illustrated by Barbara Danish (FP) [age to 8] $1.00
Firegirl--Gibson Rich, illustrated by Charlotte Purrington Farley (FP) [age 8-10] ... $1.95
Nothing But A Dog--Bobbi Katz, illustrated by Esther Gilman (FP) [age 5-8] $1.50
Penelope and the Mussels--written and illustrated by Shirley Boccaccio (JWP) [to 8].. $2.00
Feminist Press Biographies (B) and Reprint Series (R) [for adults]
Constance de Markievics--Jacqueline Van Voris (B).......... $1.50
Elizabeth Barrett Browning--Mary Jane Lupton (B) $1.50
Elizabeth Cady Stanton--Mary Ann B. Stanton (B) $1.50
Life in the Iron Mills--Rebecca Harding Davis (R) [With Biographical Interpretation by Tillie Olsen] $1.95

Equality Road and Other Songs--Phoebe Pfaehler and Lynne Leslie [5 feminist songs, with music, words, guitar cues and piano arrangements] single copies $2.50; 2 or more, each $1.50

Posters
FUCK HOUSEWORK, FUCK OFFICEWORK, WOMEN'S POEM and MOTHER LOVE--Virtue Hathaway . each $1.25
Golda Meir--BUT CAN SHE TYPE? $1.25
Mystical, astrological, colorful woman's art and poetry--designed, written and printed by Glene Sluiter [on heavy gold stock in green, orange and black] $3.00

*Items marked with an asterisk require a 25¢ postage and handling charge. See reverse side for ordering directions and other postage requirements!

KNOW PRICE LIST

1973 Women's Calendar--12 months of graphics and quotations [Diana Press] $2.00
Rising of the Women notecards (ivory) package of 25 .... $1.00
Bumper Stickers--plastic, gold colored, raised lettering SISTER or UPPITY WOMEN UNITE $0.75
Women's Symbol stickers, like above, 1 x 1 1/2", sheet of 20 .... $1.00
Buttons--assorted slogans for feminism $0.25

KNOW Lists
Recently Published Feminist Books--Ellen Stoll Isaly $0.10
Reporters You Can Trust--Anne Pride .... free!
Feminist Periodicals and Publications--Charlotte B. Warren $0.15

Packets

MODERN SWEATSHOPS
$1.00*
Could it be that colleges and universities are Modern Sweatshops????
--contents--
U.S. Dept. of Labor--The Earnings Gap
Ann Scott--Half Eaten Apple
Kathleen Shortridge--Woman As University Nigger
Bernice Sandler--Equal Rights for Women In Education

YOU'VE GOTTA MAKE NOISE IF YOU WANT TO BE HEARD
$1.00*
--contents--
Joreen--Bitch Manifesto
Robin Morgan--Goodby To All That
Vanuken--Primer for the Last Revolution
Vivian Gornick--Women: The Next Great Moment in History Is Theirs
Wilma Scott Heide--What's Wrong With Male-Dominated Society?

READ CAREFULLY BEFORE ORDERING

Some sad but trues: ALL ORDERS MUST BE PREPAID . . . MINIMUM ORDER IS 25¢!!!!!!!

TO ORDER: Please put an X in front of each article you wish to order (and a new price list will be included in your order). If you wish to list the articles you want on a purchase order or letter, please list them in the order which they appear on this list; this will expedite the filling of your order.

POSTAGE COSTS: You must add postage to your order; if you fail to do so YOUR ORDER WILL BE RETURNED UNFILLED! Items marked with an asterisk (*) require 25¢ postage and handling charge. To calculate postage on other items, add 15% of the total price of these items. This covers the cost of mailing material Third Class or Book Rate, which takes 2 to 3 weeks.

Example:				
	Female Studies V	$4.50*	($4.50 + .25)	4.75
	Assorted articles	5.00	(+15%)	5.75
	Total including postage			$10.50

FIRST CLASS postage: Add 30% of total cost (in example, 30% of $9.50 = $2.85; $9.50 + 2.85 = $12.35 total including postage)
FOREIGN POSTAGE: Air mail is 17¢ per half-ounce to Latin America, and 22¢ per half-ounce to Europe. Figure 5 sheets per ounce; articles are priced at 5¢ per sheet.

DATE________ AMT. FOR ARTICLES________ AMT. FOR POSTAGE________ KNOW NEWS________ [$4, $6 or $8 see page 4] TOTAL AMT. ENCLOSED________

NAME (print!)________________________ ADDRESS________________________

________________________________ ZIP____________

make checks payable to KNOW, Inc.
P.O. Box 86031
Pittsburgh, Pa. 15221
(412) 241-4844

KNOW has received its official non-profit status . . . all donations are welcome and TAX DEDUCTIBLE!

Bulk rates and consignment requirements available on request.

THE FEMINIST PRESS

The Feminist Press is a tax-exempt, non-profit educational and publishing corporation founded (in 1970) to produce some of the new literature needed most for educational change. From the beginning we set out to provide materials strategic in altering what women learn. We decided to publish high-quality, low-cost paperback books that would work well in evolving classrooms, sparking the imaginations of Americans interested in freeing children from sex role stereotypes. From the start we knew, too, that we would take part in the day-to-day process of educational change.

TO ORDER OUR BOOKS

Please order Feminist Press books directly from our distribution office:

10920 Battersea Lane
Columbia, Maryland 21044.

Orders for publications of the Clearinghouse on Women's Studies and all other correspondence should be directed to our editorial office:

Box 334
Old Westbury, New York 11568.

CONSCIOUSNESS RAZORS

Verne Moberg

1. Go to a playground in a park and watch some children. Pick one boy and imagine the rest of his life. Make a list of all the things people will tell him he shouldn't do because he's a boy. Then pick a girl and think about how she'll be spending her time from now on. Make a list of all the things everybody will tell her are illegal because she's a girl. Compare the lists. Get up and go over to the boy and girl and give them each their list; tell them it's all right to do all those things.

Walk home slowly, observing the adults who pass you by.

2. At 11 p.m. on the nineteenth day of every month think about what you've done all day. Next consider what you might have done that day if you had been a man (woman). By January 1 figure out what to do about this.

3. Ask the neighbor girl what she wants to be when she grows up. Then ask her what she would want to be *if she were a boy*. Find her brother and ask him what *he* wants to be when he grows up. Then ask him what he would want to be *if he were a girl*.

Later, mention to their parents what they said.

4. Force yourself to watch television for six hours. Write down every innuendo you see and hear that denigrates women. Translate all those into insults aimed at midgets. Ask yourself: Would midgets allow that? Would the FCC allow that? Would you allow that if *you* were a midget? If you weren't?

If these things offend you, telephone the TV station to let them know, since they say they are interested in public service.

5. Go to your nearest children's library and pick out twenty picture books at random. Page through them and count the number of aprons, checking to see who is wearing each one (males or females, both humans and animals?) Go home and count the number of aprons you own. Ask your neighbors how many they own.

Spend time wondering who is drawing all those aprons, and why?

—from Women's Studies Newsletter

FEMALE STUDIES VI: CLOSER TO THE GROUND—WOMEN'S CLASSES, CRITICISM, PROGRAMS, 1972. Eds. Nancy Hoffman, Cynthia Secor, Adrian Tinsley. Twenty-two essays about the *practice* of women's studies on campuses in 1972, all but one "close to the ground."

"They deal not with polemics justifying women's studies nor revelations of male images of women but with women at work with literature about women: teaching it in the classroom, writing criticism about specific authors, establishing a communal learning experience."

— Mary Anne Ferguson, *Women's Studies Newsletter*

235 pages

$2.50 (plus $.50 postage)

FEMINIST RESOURCES FOR SCHOOLS AND COLLEGES: A GUIDE TO CURRICULUM MATERIALS. Eds. Carol Ahlum and Jacqueline M. Fralley. An annotated bibliography for teachers who want to know where to begin, what to study and what's available for their students to read, see or hear: books, pamphlets, slide shows, films, tapes. All with prices and facts on how to order, where to write.

Late Spring — 16 pages (*Women's Studies Newsletter* format)

$1.00 (plus $.25 postage and handling)

HIGH SCHOOL FEMINIST STUDIES. Eds. Carol Ahlum and Jacqueline M. Fralley. The first published collection of high school course syllabi, bibliographies and materials, this volume communicates a sense of experimentation especially among teachers of English and social studies. The curriculum is problem-centered, interdisciplinary and directly related to the lives of students. The editors are in touch with 300 secondary school teachers, from whose work this material has been compiled. The introduction provides an overview and evaluation.

Summer — 150 pages

$2.50 (plus $.50 postage and handling)

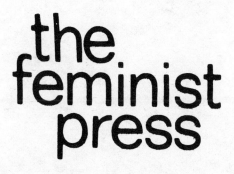

the feminist press

THE CLEARINGHOUSE ON WOMEN'S STUDIES

A unique service to college and public school teachers, the Clearinghouse has functioned, since 1970, as an information resource, spreading news about women's studies. To its files have come descriptions of some 1,800 courses and 62 programs underway on campuses across the country. In 1972 the Clearinghouse staff began collecting names of teachers of high school feminist courses and elementary school teachers creating nonsexist classrooms. To share its findings, the Clearinghouse issues a series of publications. It also serves as a source of information and advice to teachers, curriculum developers and program planners.

A CHILD'S RIGHT TO EQUAL READING: EXERCISES IN THE LIBERATION OF CHILDREN'S BOOKS FROM THE LIMITATIONS OF SEX ROLE STEREOTYPES
By Verne Moberg

Proceeding on the premise that "All girls and boys are created equal," this pamphlet outlines one possible introductory session for a community workshop on children's books. With affective steps of analysis in examining stereotype patterns in children's books, plus speculations on the hazards and benefits involved in recognizing—and changing—our roles.

10 pages
$.35 (plus $.08 postage)

THE GUIDE TO CURRENT FEMALE STUDIES I, II, III. Eds. Carol Ahlum, Florence Howe, Joanna Miller, Micheline Fitzmaurice. Separate bibliographies of women's studies teachers, courses and programs, published respectively in October 1971, October 1972 and April 1973.

$1.00 each (plus $.25 postage for one; $.40 for two or three)

WOMEN'S STUDIES NEWSLETTER. A quarterly publication, the *Newsletter* reports on women's studies in public schools and higher education. Issues offer news, close-ups of courses or programs, bibliographies, letters from teachers, students and curriculum writers, as well as brief listings of jobs, publications, conferences and projects in progress. Manuscripts (of no more than 1,200 words) should be sent to meet the following deadlines: May 20, August 20, November 20, February 20. A subscription ($5.00 for individuals; $10.00 for institutions) also includes the *Guides to Current Female Studies II* and *III* (see above).

EMMA WILLARD TASK FORCE ON EDUCATION

The *Emma Willard Task Force on Education* publishes a 90-page book, *Sexism in Education*, that is very useful and highly recommended for a high school or college course in women's studies. Cost is $3.50 for individuals; $5 for institutions from:

EMMA WILLARD TASK FORCE ON EDUCATION
Post Office Box 14229
University Station
Minneapolis, Minn. 55414
(612) 333-9076

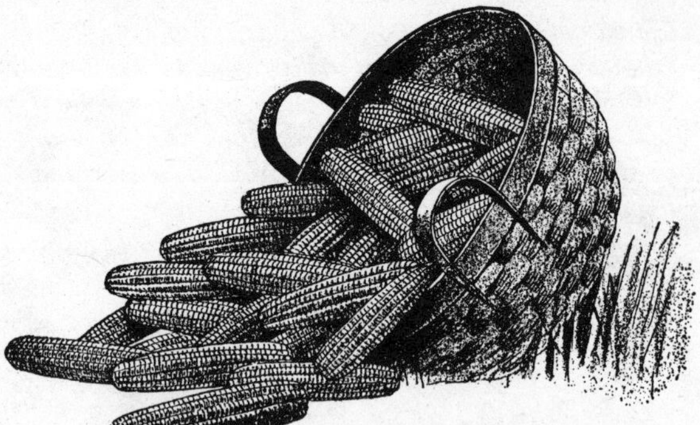

TABLE OF CONTENTS

CONSCIOUSNESS-RAISING IN THE CLASSROOM

Some Games, Projects, Discussion-Openers, etc.

Revised September 1972

1. Have the girls complete either or both "I would (would not) like to be a man because . . . " For the boys, substitute "woman". This should indicate what the students see as the privileges and burdens of each sex, and how they perceive the division of roles.
2. An alternate phrasing of the above – "If I were a boy (girl), I would (like to) . . ." Do the students feel that they can't do or become these things given their actual sex. For instance, if a girl says, "If I were a boy, I would climb trees and play baseball", she should be asked if she does climb trees and play baseball, why not if she doesn't, would she like to, what makes her think she can't.
3. Cut out pictures of people of various facial types and have students each describe one and speculate on what that person may be like. Do they react more favorably to women who fit the traditional concept of "feminine" and men who fit the traditional concept of "masculine"? How wide a range of fantasizing do they do about people of each sex? (E.g., in terms of occupations.) What aspects of personality and life-style do they concentrate on with each sex? (E.g., do they speculate on marital status and number of children more frequently with women than with men?)
4. Draw a series of stick figures (indistinguishable as to sex) holding objects or doing something (e.g., holding a broom, driving a van, holding a bat). Have the students make up stories about them.
5. Take the students on a discrimination trip, including a mock job interview, a men-only restaurant, a housecleaning, an application for credit at a department store, etc.
6. Keep a running list of "ways I have benefited by being a male (or female) today." Or keep two parallel lists, plus and minus.
7. To illustrate how selective generalization works, give some facts about men and have the students generalize from them. For example: FACT: Men have a much higher incidence of heart disease than women. GEN: Employer to male job applicant: "I'm sorry but we just can't afford to hire a man for this job. You might have a heart attack and die." FACT: The male hormone testosterone is considered by many endocrinologists to be the cause of aggression. GEN: Men are always fighting and getting violent. They can't be trusted in positions of power.
8. Word association games – Have the students sit in a circle and have each, in turn, say a word or phrase that is used negatively about women (shrill, hysterical, hag, old maid). Then do the same for men (cocky, bastard, henpecked). How many of the male words are actually anti-woman? (E.g., bastard and son-of-a-bitch reflect on his mother; henpecked reflects on his wife.)
9. Role-reversal games – Conduct a marriage ceremony in which the mother gives away the groom, they're pronounced woman and husband, and become Mrs. and Mr. Jane Smith. Have students conduct interviews with prominent men, asking them for their favorite home repair techniques, how they combine marriage and career, what size suit they wear, how they manage to stay young and handsome. This should illustrate the absurdity of some of our conventions that keep men's and women's roles strictly defined.
10. "Today is my 80th birthday" – Have students look back at their lives since leaving high school. This should show their aspirations and expectations.
11. Cut out questions from Ann Landers, Dear Abby, and Ellen Peck that relate to female and male behavior and sex-roles and relationships between the sexes. Have the students write their own answers.
12. Set up a display of cosmetics, beauty equipment, etc., with labels explaining how each is used. If you can get away with it, have the boys put on make-up and discuss how it affects their self-perception. If the girls are at the make-up wearing age, have them discuss how they feel with and without make-up.
13. Allow each student 10 minutes to make a list of characteristics of women (or men). If they have difficulty, tell them to try thinking of one woman (or man) they know. Then divide them into small groups (3-5) and have them first read their lists, then say which characteristics on the list are true of themselves, then which characteristics they like. Then have the small group, as a team, select 10 items from the combined lists that they think are most important. It is essential that they agree on the meaning of each characteristic. Then have them rank the items from 1 to 10. Who is the person they have created? The ideal woman (or man)? The typical woman (or man)? Are the characteristics positive or negative? Try several variations: girls working on female characteristics and boys on male, vice-versa, both sexes working on the same sex, all-female and all-male small groups, mixed small groups. Have the teams compare their results. **(cont'd)**

CONSCIOUSNESS-RAISING IN THE CLASSROOM (cont'd)

14. Have girls write on "What I like best about being a woman", "What I hate most about being a women", "What I like most in men", "What I hate most in men."

    Reverse for boys.

    Compare and discuss the male and female likes and dislikes. Are they complementary, similar, dissimilar, etc?

15. List words and phrases referring to unmarried women. To unmarried men.

16. Have females pretend they are male and plan their future. Reverse for males.

17. Have female students pretend that marriage is <u>not</u> an alternative and plan their future.

18. Have students monitor TV ads, TV programs and comic strip characters for examples of sexism.

19. Have class line up in a straight line and tell them to pick their position on the basis of their importance. (DO NOT try to tell them what to judge importance on.)

    What usually happens is that males are at the front of the line and the majority of females in the last half of the line.

20. Have males sit in a circle and the females sit in a circle around them.

    Each female picks a male to observe his verbal and non-verbal communication. (They may not say anything while the males are talking.)

    Pick one of the four for the males to discuss:
    - What they like about being male.
    - What they don't like about being male.
    - What they like about females.
    - What they don't like about females.

    When the males are finished, each female gives her observations of what the male she was watching said (verbally) and did (non-verbal motions, etc.). The males may not say anything while the females are discussing them.

    Reverse everything with the females in the center circle.

    When that is finished (males have finished saying what the females said and did), have general discussion of how everyone felt, their reactions, etc.

21. Make up a collage or montage or simply draw what society considers to be the "ideal women" and the "ideal man". Then students explain their ideal. (Include physical description, emotional characteristics, personality and mannerisms.)

    The same thing can be done using their peers – "popular girl" or "popular boy".

22. Students can analyze nursery rhymes or children's stories which include women alone or both women and men (boys and girls). What is the role played by each person? What do they think this implies or suggests as to the way girls and boys see themselves?

23. Students can watch television "situation" shows concerning or including women. Analyze the role of the woman in that particular segment. Present to class, either by skit or report.

24. Rewrite "Love Is" according to women's liberation.

25. Pick certain comic books and discuss the roles portrayed in them.

26. See "An Exercise in Logical Thinking" elsewhere in our book.

See "Example of Course Outline" for more activities.

FREEDOM OF INFORMATION CENTER

The *Freedom of Information Center* was founded in 1959 and now serves as the largest clearinghouse for information on the public's right to know. Its files include thousands of clippings, research reports, and other documents on hundreds of different subjects ranging from access to government data to the underground press.

The Center is located at the University of Missouri's School of Journalism and welcomes input from people involved in the area of freedom of information and will assist in providing information on questions that arise.

They also publish (for $7.50 yearly) two reports monthly, a Digest bimonthly, and occasional Opinion Papers.

Single copies of Digest and Reports cost 35¢. Sample of topics in past issues include:

FREEDOM OF INFORMATION CENTER
Box 858
Columbia, MO 65201

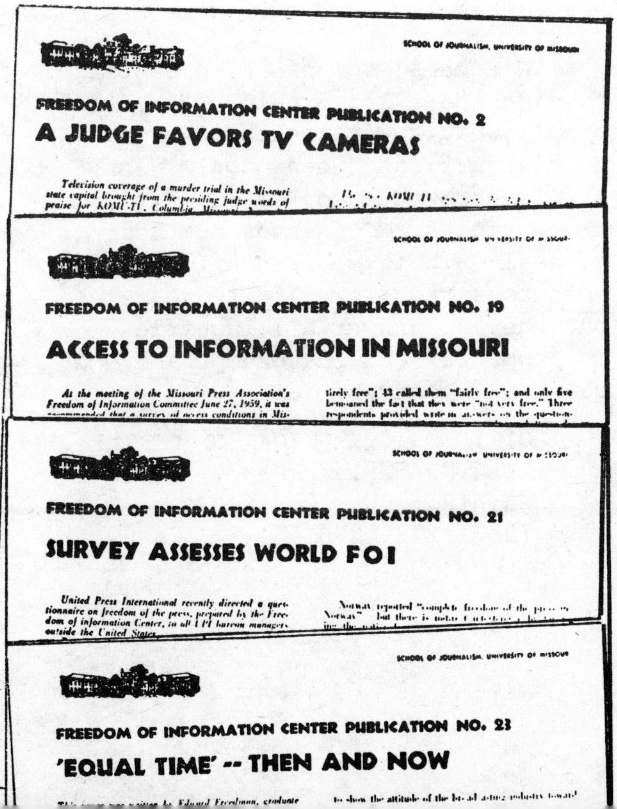
SCHOOL OF JOURNALISM, UNIVERSITY OF MISSOURI

FREEDOM OF INFORMATION CENTER PUBLICATION NO. 2

A JUDGE FAVORS TV CAMERAS

FREEDOM OF INFORMATION CENTER PUBLICATION NO. 19

ACCESS TO INFORMATION IN MISSOURI

FREEDOM OF INFORMATION CENTER PUBLICATION NO. 21

SURVEY ASSESSES WORLD FOI

SCHOOL OF JOURNALISM, UNIVERSITY OF MISSOURI

FREEDOM OF INFORMATION CENTER PUBLICATION NO. 23

'EQUAL TIME' -- THEN AND NOW

FOI REPORT NO. 298
REPORTS: AN ANNOTATED BIBLIOGRAPHY

234. Post Office Controls of Obscenity (George Tuck), 1-70.
Congressional laws limiting the mailing of pornographic materials are viewed by some constitutents as too lenient. This report discusses the possible implications of a conservative Supreme Court stance on the question which could mean easier convictions of mailers of pornographic material. (7 pp.)

235. Fairness in TV News (Bruce A. Kauffman), 1-70.
The Center's survey of television newsmen is reported. (5 pp.)

236. TV Violence: Apathy to Controversy (Richard L. Friedman), 2-70.
The extraordinarily pervasive force of television on American society is viewed in terms of the almost cyclical debate over the effects of violent programing. (5 pp.)

237. Letter Columns: Access for Whom? (Kenneth B. Stark Jr.), 2-70.
The role of the letter to editor in the coercive publishing controversy is discussed. (5 pp.)

238. TV Self-Regulation: Smothers Brothers (Jay L. Franz), 3 70.
A detailed study of the canceling of the Smothers Brothers Comedy Hour by CBS. (6 pp.)

247. FCC v. "Overcommercialization" II (Kathryn Kenyon), 9-70.
This report updates Center Report No. 115 and deals with the unresolved issue of overcommercialization in the broadcast media. (4 pp.)

248. Agnew's Criticisms: How Much Support? (Doran Levy), 9-70.
A nation-wide survey of college students reveals an interesting finding: students agree overwhelmingly with the vice-president's criticisms of the media but disdain any attempt to control the media's handling of the news. (4 pp.)

249. The Staging of the News (Edward M. Kimbrell), 10-70.
Congress is again concerned with alleged staging of the news by media, especially after recent hearings on the involvement of CBS News in a purported invasion of Haiti. (5 pp.)

250. Advocacy Comes to the Newsroom (Kathryn Keyon), 10-70.
A chronicle of the arguments that advocacy journalism has engendered within the media. (4 pp.)

251. Expansion of the Fairness Doctrine (Joe Lewels, Jr), 11-70.
Historically defined as a policy designed to insure airing of divergent opinions on controversial issues, the FCC's fairness doctrine has been broadened to include rebuttals of televised commercials and presidential claims. (4 pp.)

254. The Newspaper Preservation Act (Joe Lewels, Jr.), 1-71.
A lawsuit challenging the constitutionality of the Newspaper Preservation Act may settle the question of whether it preserves failing newspapers, thereby maintaining a multiplicity of editorial voices, or stifles new competition in cities with joint agreement newspapers. (5 pp.)

255. Criminal Law and the Press (Paul B. Parham), 1-71.
The author documents the legal and ethical restraints on reporting criminal acts.

256. Citizen Groups Challenge Radio-TV (David C. Loveland), 2-71.
This paper focuses on the citizen groups which have challenged the licenses of radio and television stations, outlining the methods and procedures they have used. (5 pp.)

0012. Why Network TV News is Criticized (Ralph L. Lowenstein), 5-71.
The author goes beyond Reuven Frank's speech (No. 0011) to explain why criticism of network television news is so intense, and why it is unlikely to cease. (3 pp.)

289. Liberating the Media: News (Muriel Akamatsu), 9-72.
Activities directed at securing fairer treatment for women in the news media's employment and reporting practices have escalated considerably in recent years. Despite its difficulties, the movement is becoming increasingly sophisticated, with progress that is likely soon to match. (6 pp.)

CITIZENS COMMUNICATION CENTER

Citizens Communications Center is a small (staff of 9) law firm offering free help to people who want to file complaints at the Federal Communications Commission about the kind of service they receive from their local broadcasters. The FCC regulates the broadcasting industry through a variety of procedures; some of these procedures are open for public participation.

For example, when a broadcaster asks the FCC to renew his license every three years, his audience can formally oppose the renewal if there is reason to believe that the broadcaster has not served his community well during the license term. Or, if a broadcaster presents only one side of an important controversial issue without balancing the viewpoint in his overall programming schedule, his audience can ask the FCC to force the broadcaster to provide free time for an appropriate spokesman to present the other side of the issue. There are other procedures by which people can participate in the regulation of the broadcasting industry. Unfortunately, the procedures are so complicated that a person generally needs a lawyer to help him know how to exercise his rights in broadcasting.

Citizens Communication Center provides that legal help. They tell people what their rights in broadcasting are; and when people want legal representation in exercising those rights, CCC serves as their counsel. Their small staff and limited resources require a limited caseload, but they do answer all inquiries. CCC is nonprofit and tax exempt and welcomes all contributions.

CITIZENS COMMUNICATION CENTER
1914 Sunderland Place, N.W.
Washington, D.C. 20036
(202) 296-4238

ACCURACY IN MEDIA, INC.

Accuracy in Media, Inc. . . . is a non-profit group with the self-proclaimed goal of making sure news consumers are getting the truth. The group functions as a watchdog to correct errors in TV documentaries and newspaper reports. So far their targets have been the proponents of "advocacy journalism" such as Tom Wicker, David Brinkley, an "unbalanced panel discussion of a Nixon speech on PBS, Jack Anderson, and WNET-TV in N. Y. for a onesided discussion of Vietnam highly critical of American policy.

AIM's executive secretary is Abraham Kalish, retired professor of communication at the Defense Intelligence School in Washington and feature writer for USIA. Kalish claims the group has neither liberal nor conservative bias and strives for objectivity. Their targets so far suggest a decided bias, but time will tell. To decide for yourself AIM has begun a monthly newsletter ($10 yearly) titled **Aim Report**.

Issue No. 1 of **Aim Report** made for fascinating reading with its charges of lack of media coverage and bias.

AIM takes on the big guns in media and has succeeded in forcing ABC to take time to correct errors in a documentary "Arms and security. . . How Much is Enough?"

Accuracy in Media, Inc., 425 13th St., N. W., Suite 1232, Washington, D. C. 20004. (202) 737-9357.

THE NETWORK PROJECT

The Network Project . . . . is a group of people at Columbia University working to improve the state of broadcasting in this country. To this effect they have produced a series of radio documentaries and a fine series of media studies in pamphlet form. They are involved in petitions to deny licensing and litigation aimed at decentralizing the control of public television.

The media studies issued so far include reports on "Domestic Communication Satellites," "Director of Networks," "Control of Information," "OTP," "Cable Television," and "Educational Television Programming." The series is available at a subscription rate of $10 to individuals or $25 to institutions from

THE NETWORK PROJECT
104 Earl Hall
Columbia University
New York, N.Y. 10027

SANE

SANE -- A Citizens' Organization for a Sane World - is a membership group and a source for materials about the demilitarization of America. Yearly membership is $19, $5 for senior citizens, $2 for students. Its newsletter, *Saneworld*, is published monthly and costs $3 for a year or $2 for students.

SANE
318 Massachusetts Ave., N.E.
Washington, D.C. 20002
(202) 546-4868

SANE's Strategy for Demilitarization

SANE has a two-part strategy for demilitarizing the country safely. First: Challenging the military-oriented assumptions of the cold war and replacing them with a new foreign policy based on disarmament agreements, international peacekeeping (and a rational level of deterrence in the meantime), and economic development. Second: Building a coalition of groups and individuals who seek to redirect federal spending to meet human needs and restore a sense of moral purpose to our nation.

If we mobilize an additional 15-25% of the public to work for the demilitarization of American society, we can convince Congress and the Executive Branch to adopt new policies by the mid-1970's.

What Can YOU Do?

The most effective work you can do is to help implement this strategy in your community.

Here's how: Commit yourself to maintaining contact with one specific group—the news media, clergymen, businessmen, labor leaders, minority groups, women's organizations, senior citizens, conservationists, city and county councilmen, etc. Provide them with information and ideas on a regular basis. SANE will suggest meaningful approaches and help you obtain the materials you will need: literature, films, radio tapes, and newspaper ads.

We call the local activists who perform this function *SANE Communicators*. You don't have to do it all yourself. We will give you the names of SANE members in your community, and you can recruit new people to share the work with you.

You can have a real impact in your community provided you pinpoint the people you want to influence and develop good working relations with them. If you and others work together as a team to reach most of the community groups named above, on a regular basis, your effectiveness will be multiplied far beyond your numbers.

If you don't have the time to devote to such an effort, you can help with contributions to finance SANE's production of audio-visual materials, appearances by prominent spokesmen on radio, TV, and other public forums, and lobbying activities in Washington.

SANE Stands For:

- Total withdrawal from Indo-China
- Negotiated settlement of international disputes
- Major cuts in arms spending
- An end to underground nuclear tests
- Repeal of the draft, and an all-volunteer army
- Transfer of resources to civilian programs at home and in underdeveloped countries
- Planning for conversion of arms industry and military bases
- Disarmament agreements
- Strengthened international agencies

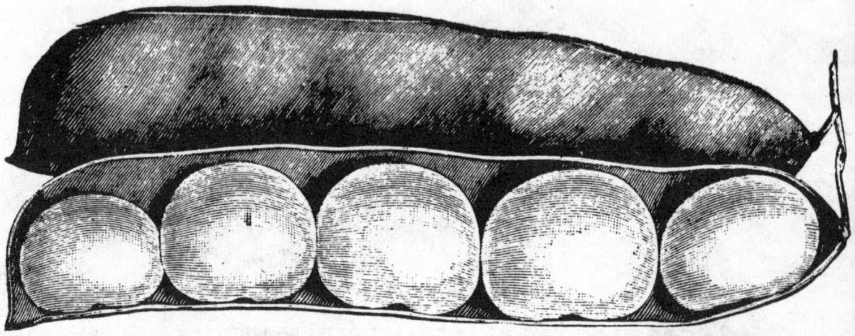

The Militarization of America

In the name of national security the United States has invested more than $1 trillion since the end of World War II to produce the most powerful military machine in history. Yet we can be destroyed in an hour in a nuclear war.

This trillion-dollar investment, which cannot buy us safety, created a new institution in American life—the military-industrial complex. In 1961 President Eisenhower warned against the "unwarranted influence" of the military-industrial complex, yet it is even more pervasive today. The influence of the Pentagon has mushroomed through defense contracts, research grants, and full-time public relations men and lobbyists—all paid for by our taxes.

By the end of the 1960's, half of each tax dollar levied by Congress went to the military, not including the costs of past wars. The budget proposed by President Nixon for fiscal 1973, a decade after Eisenhower's warning, allocated 60¢ out of every tax dollar for the costs of wars, past, present and future.

DO YOU KNOW WHAT YOUR TAX DOLLAR BUYS?

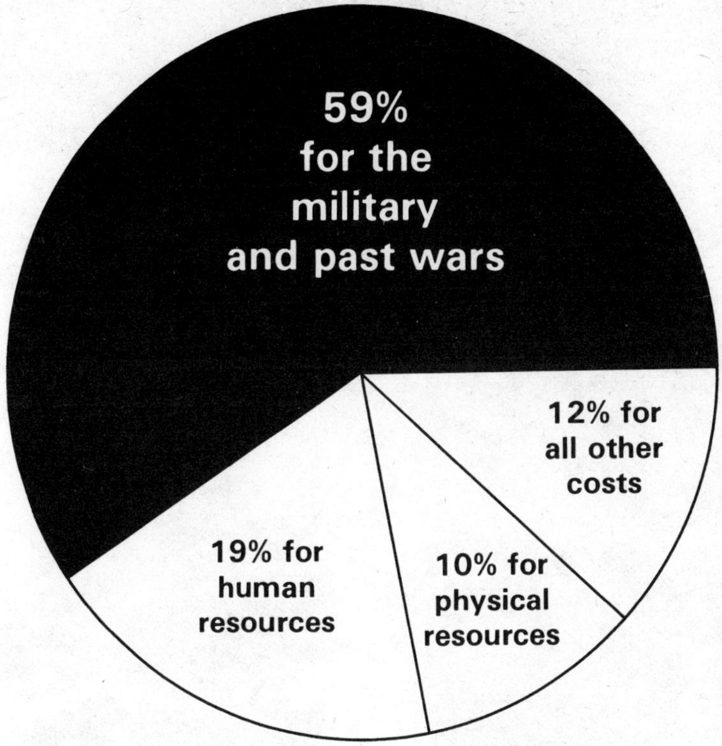

Where Do Your Taxes Go?

You work hard for your money. But most of your income tax dollar goes to pay for wars—past, present and future: 59% in the Fiscal Year 1974 budget proposed by President Nixon.

In fact, the U.S. has spent over $1 trillion—one thousand billion dollars—on the military since World War II.

The Nixon Administration is asking Congress for $199.1 billion in general funds for Fiscal 1974. Of this amount:

Military: 59%—41% is earmarked for current military expenditures and 18% for the cost of past wars—6% for veterans benefits (which the Administration includes in "human resources") and 12% for interest on the national debt (most of which is war-incurred).

Human Resources (education, manpower, health, income security): **19%**

Physical Resources (agriculture, rural development, natural resources, commerce, transportation, community development, housing): **10%**

All Other (international affairs and finance, space, general government, revenue-sharing, pay raises, contingencies): **12%**

The figures above have been compiled by the Office of Management and Budget and the Library of Congress Legislative Reference Service.

Nixon Budget

The Nixon Administration, however, presents a far different picture of federal spending priorities. It claims that the federal government will spend more money on "human resources" than on the military. This claim is based on a change in budget accounting, made in 1968, whereby tax revenues from income, inheritance and excise taxes are placed in the same pot as receipts from trust funds such as Social Security, Railroad Retirement and the Highway Trust Fund.

These trust funds were set up years ago to provide specific benefits. They are financed by separate taxes. For example, you pay social security taxes now and receive benefits when you retire. The federal government merely acts as caretaker for these funds. **Neither Congress nor the President can spend the money in the trust funds.** Therefore, if you want to know what happens to your tax dollars which the federal government can spend, the trust funds should be considered as separate cookie jars, not as part of the federal pie.

The accounting and the rhetoric have changed, but not the reality. Fifty-nine percent of the general funds that Congress and the President can control this coming year will go to pay for military-related programs.

Based on the budget figures from the Library of Congress and population figures from the Bureau of the Census, the average American family will spend $1486 in general taxes on military-related programs during Fiscal 1974. This compares with $126 for education and manpower, $63 for community development and housing, and $45 for natural resources (environmental programs).

Is this how you want YOUR taxes spent?

Are You More Secure?

At the end of World War II, no enemy could attack the United States. Today, after spending over $1 trillion on defense, the U.S. could be wiped out in less than an hour in nuclear war. On August 1, 1972, the State Department reported that the U.S. had 5900 long-range nuclear weapons, the Soviet Union, 2200. Just **200 to 400** of these weapons could destroy a third of the Soviet population and three quarters of its industrial capacity.

Are you more secure knowing we can "overkill" the Russians more times than they can "overkill" us? Are you more secure knowing that the U.S. has at least 48 military commitments to other countries and over 2000 bases and installations around the world? Are you more secure knowing the needs of the American people are being neglected while you pay for more "efficient" and sophisticated weapons—with cost overruns of more than three times the original estimates? Are you more likely to be attacked by Soviet missiles or by **other Americans**—violent, hopeless, desperate Americans?

Does spending over $80 billion a year on the military make you feel secure?

To see how the President wants to spend your tax dollars, turn to the other side.

sane **A CITIZENS' ORGANIZATION FOR A SANE WORLD**, 318 Massachusetts Ave., N.E., Washington, D.C. 20002

"WE'RE NUMBER 1"
Number 1 in military power[1]
but we're
Number 8 in doctor-patient ratio[2]
Number 14 in literacy[3]
Number 14 in infant mortality[3]
Number 25 in life expectancy[3]
Sources:
1. "Peace, National Security, and the SALT Agreements," Bureau of Public Affairs, Department of State, August 1, 1972.
2. *Statistical Yearbook*, Statistics Office of the United Nations.
3. *World Data Handbook*, "Issues in United States Foreign Policy," Department of State, 1972.
Photo of doctor and nurse provided by the National Institutes of Health
How strong are we?
sane
A CITIZENS' ORGANIZATION FOR A SANE WORLD
318 Massachusetts Avenue, N.E., Washington, D.C. 20002

ANTI-DEFAMATION LEAGUE

OBJECTIVES

. . . to preserve and translate into greater effectiveness the ideals of American democracy . . .

For more than fifty active years the Anti-Defamation League of B'nai B'rith has served as an educating force of American life. Anti-Defamation League programs have been directed, in particular, to combating discrimination against minorities, to fighting the threat of all forms of totalitarianism, and to promoting intercultural understanding and cooperation among all the religious faiths in America.

Through its 30 regional offices, the Anti-Defamation League offers consultant services to fraternal, civic, church, educational, labor and other organizations working on behalf of better intergroup relations. Each ADL regional office also maintains a human relations audio-visual library where films, filmstrips and recordings may be purchased or rented at nominal cost. Complete brochure sent on request, free of charge.

R 312/RESOURCE UNIT ON RACE, PREJUDICE AND DISCRIMINATION. Victor Leviatin. A comprehensive guide and study unit offering methods and materials for teaching about race, prejudice and discrimination. Provides basic information and a conceptual approach and gives complete, annotated listings of printed and audio-visual materials. For secondary school administrators, teachers and students. 31 pp. 75¢.

R 290/THE SCHOOLS AND PREJUDICE: Findings. M. Brewster Smith and Jane Allyn Piliavin. A preliminary study on the development of patterns of prejudice among teen-agers in junior and senior high schools. The authors believe that prejudice can crumble if educational institutions take steps to encourage communication and human encounter. 24 pp. 35¢.

G 496/SENSITIZING TEACHERS TO ETHNIC GROUPS. Gertrude Noar. Provides the teacher with basic historical and sociological information about Black, Jewish, American Indian, Spanish-speaking, and disadvantaged children with the aim of enlarging the teacher's own awareness of the traditions and contemporary experiences of her minority-group students. 23 pp. 35¢.

B 112/MINORITIES IN TEXTBOOKS: A Study of Their Treatment in Social Studies Texts. Michael Kane. A study of junior and senior high school social studies textbooks reveals that despite past criticism of publishers and authors, a significant number of texts continue to present a principally white, Protestant view of America with minority groups largely neglected. Quadrangle. 148 pp. $1.95.

R 294/MYTHS AND FACTS–1970. This supplement to the *Near East Report* for January, 1970, is made up of questions and answers concerning the conflict between Israel and the Arabs. Clearly and concisely states the case for Israel. The *Near East Report* is a newsletter published in Washington on American policy in the Near East. 39 pp. 25¢.

N 540/STEREOTYPES IN ENGLISH LITERATURE: Shylock and Fagin; The Jew in the Middle Ages: A Teachers' Study Guide. A combined guide to two films which present the social pathology of anti-Semitism as expressed in the form of literary stereotypes. Contents include suggested classroom activities, bibliographies and model instructional unit. 54 pp. 50¢.

B 45/FEIFFER ON CIVIL RIGHTS. Jules Feiffer. Foreword by Bayard Rustin. A collection of Feiffer's cartoons on reactions to the civil rights movement done with wit, irony and perception. For all Americans. Excellent discussion starter. 87 pp. $1.00.

G 480/TOWARD A CONTACT CURRICULUM. Mario Fantini and Gerald Weinstein. Study of curriculum concepts for the disadvantaged, embracing all the interacting forces at work in the learning experience of underprivileged pupils. Enlightened text for those whose concern is with educating the disadvantaged. The authors are educational staff members of the Ford Foundation. 55 pp. 90¢.

Reprint

R 174/GUIDELINES FOR TESTING MINORITY GROUP CHILDREN. Explains the conditions which prevent disadvantaged children, most of whom are from minority groups, from demonstrating their mental potentialities in school-administered I.Q. tests. (From *Journal of Social Issues.*) 18 pp. 35¢.

ANTI-DEFAMATION LEAGUE OF B'NAI B'RITH

315 LEXINGTON AVENUE, NEW YORK, N.Y. 10016, TEL. 689-7400

B 44s/THE TEACHER AND INTEGRATION. Gertrude Noar. Designed to help teachers deal with the special problems of the integrated school. Provides practical information on techniques and materials, as well as background in the theory and studies done on the subject of race and human relations. Includes articles by leading writers in the field of education, intended to be of use to the teacher in becoming familiar with the problems and nature of integrated education. National Education Association. Soft cover — $1.50.

B 67/RACE AND THE NEWS MEDIA. Paul Fisher and Ralph Lowenstein, editors. Papers presented at a conference sponsored by the Freedom of Information Center of the University of Missouri and the ADL. Included are: "Racial Coverage Planning and Logistics" by Claude Sitton: "The American Negro and Newspaper Myths" by Ted Poston; "An Overview" by George Hunt, and others. Praeger. 144 pp. $6.00. Soft cover edition — B 67s: $1.95.

B 97/CONCERNING DISSENT AND CIVIL DISOBEDIENCE. Abe Fortas. A vigorous, knowledgeable statement on dissent and how it may be expressed effectively within the law. Gives reasonings and conclusions on the limits of lawful civil disobedience. A Signet Special Broadside. 64 pp. Special ADL price 35¢.

F 106/ABC'S OF SCAPEGOATING. Fifth revised edition. Gordon W. Allport. Analyzes the motives, sources and forms of scapegoating and race prejudice. Recommends education to fight fear and frustration, and legislation to protect minorities. Professor Allport was the author of numerous publications, including the classic study, *The Nature of Prejudice*. 36 pp. 50¢.

FB 5/ANTI-SEMITISM: A Case Study in Prejudice and Discrimination. J. Milton Yinger. An analysis of the history of anti-Semitism since its inception, by the well-known sociologist and author of *Racial and Cultural Minorities in the United States*. A concise, lucid examination of the psychological, political and sociological aspects of prejudice in general and anti-Semitism in particular. 80 pp. $1.25.

G 349/INFORMATION IS NOT ENOUGH. Gertrude Noar. This handsome pamphlet illustrates that facts alone — about race, religion, social class and caste structure, distant lands and cultures — are not enough. An outline of how information plus self-understanding must be used to broaden one's outlook. 26 pp. 25¢.

G 376/THE TREATMENT OF MINORITIES IN SECONDARY SCHOOL TEXTBOOKS. Lloyd A. Marcus. A study of 48 leading secondary school history and social studies textbooks. In more than three-fourths of the books studied, the complex nature and problems of American minority groups are largely neglected or distorted, and Nazi persecution of Jews and other minorities is omitted or minimized. 64 pp. 50¢.

G 437/TEACHING THE BILL OF RIGHTS. William J. Brennan, Jr. The Supreme Court Justice discusses with deep awareness the problems of individual civil liberties within the framework of the Constitution. He presents teaching methods helpful in explaining the interdependence of our legal and educational systems. 23 pp. 25¢.

G 469/HOW TO LISTEN TO A JOHN BIRCH SOCIETY SPEAKER. Revised edition. Harvey B. Schechter. Designed to help community leaders deal with the most common gambits and half-truths employed by Birch Society spokesmen. Includes some of the most frequently asked questions about the society, the answers typically offered by their spokesmen, and penetrating comments. 135 pp. 35¢.

JF 100/PREJUDICED — HOW DO PEOPLE GET THAT WAY? William Van Til. Cogent explanation of how people become prejudiced and how prejudice can be prevented. Ample and humorous illustrations. Discusses such fallacious beliefs as the story of "superior" and "inferior" races, and others. 32 pp. 50¢.

N 307/KIT OF RELIGIOUS ARTICLES. Contains religious and ceremonial items (some in miniature) used in Jewish worship: tallit (prayer shawl); kippah (skull cap); menorah (candelabra); mezzuzah (parchment prayer scroll attached to doorways of Jewish homes); miniature Torah scroll; havdalah (Sabbath-end) candle; spice box; dreydel (toy top); matzot; and copies of the *Living Heritage of Passover with an Abridged Haggadah, Your Neighbor Celebrates* (pamphlet edition), *Your Neighbor Worships, The Sabbath* and a comprehensive, illustrated *Guide*. For Sunday schools and Christian study groups. $10.00.

PEOPLE AGAINST RACISM IN EDUCATION

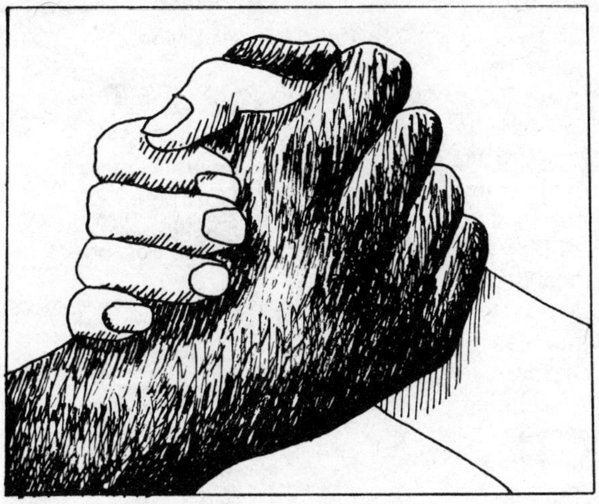

Ideas and Resources for Change

10600 PURITAN – DETROIT, MICH. 48238 – (313) 861-8820

People Against Racism in Education (PARE) is a national, non-profit, tax-exempt organization that will be sharing ideas and resources with members of educational communities and the general public. We are doing this so that an awareness and understanding of the causes and effects of racism will lead to action in eliminating racism from the education process.

We understand racism to be a white problem. We believe that racism is a systematic pattern of thought and action, based on color, that maintains and encourages attitudes and beliefs of white superiority. Briefly stated, racism is, "power plus prejudice."

We will actualize that purpose by:

A. Establishing an information referral service which will consist of a Resource Data Bank/Referral Library that will identify, evaluate, collect, compile, and disseminate, upon request, meaningful referrals to human, institutional, or material resources which are presently being used to combat racism in education. Subjects covered will include: testing, tracking, racism in textbooks, teacher preparation, hiring practices, state education codes, alternative curriculum designs and materials, etc. This service is <u>not</u> intended to provide copies of materials, books, etc. It <u>is</u> intended to <u>link</u> educators with people, programs, or printed references.

B. Publishing a newsletter that will: Provide information on materials available; let you know who's doing what, where, and when; look at alternatives to racism; identify gaps in materials and practices; and, serve as a linkage source with people and groups in order to maximize efforts to eradicate racism in education: The newsletter will be published bi-monthly. We anticipate that the first couple of issues will be distributed gratis. After that, we will ask for a nominal subscription fee.

We understand linkage and sharing to be a two-way interaction. In order for the linkage process to be effective we need <u>your</u> continued <u>participation and feedback</u> about the newsletter, your needs, articles, ideas, sources, or materials that you know. To that end, we have a recording service that will take your calls 24 hours a day. Our number is (313) 861-8820.

STUDENT RIGHTS

Teenagers' Rights and Responsibilities . . . . is a four-part course complete with student workbooks and teaching manuals. Part I deals with the concept of community, part two with "Why Communities Need Laws". Three is "How Laws are Made and Changed," and four is titled "How Disputes are Settled." There is one student book for each part; a set of the four student books costs $3.50.

The course does provide a basic introduction to the law making process and includes some interesting readings. The "learning activities" provided are very traditional things like filling in the blanks and learning new vocabulary words. A single set of student handbooks and a Teacher's Manual ($12) should give any social studies teachers usable ideas and enough information to decide about possible student use.

From Educational Facility Press, 2429 Linden Lane, Silver Spring, MD 20910

When dealing in a social studies class with the U.S. Constitution or the topic of justice little could be more relevant than the rights of high school students or of minors. The American Civil Liberties Union has a "Student Rights Handbook" available free on request from ACLU, 84 Fifth Avenue, New York, N. Y. 10003.

The "Civil Rights Test" below is taken from a prologue to a leaflet distributed to students by the Wisconsin Coalition for Educational Reform and the High School Students Union.

A CIVIL RIGHTS TEST

SCHOOL ADMINISTRATORS HAVE "IMPORTANT, DELICATE, AND HIGHLY DISCRETIONARY FUNCTIONS, BUT NONE THAT THEY MAY NOT PERFORM WITHIN THE LIMITS OF THE BILL OF RIGHTS."
—U. S. Supreme Court

1. Does your school carry out its job within the limits of the Bill of Rights?
2. Does your school administration treat you as a person under our Constitution?
3. Are you protected, at your school, from illegal search and seizure?
4. Are you accorded due process of law when you are accused of wrongdoing?
5. Does your school offer effective channels through which you can bring charges against school personnel who have unduly deprived you of your rights?
6. Can you challenge, or even see, any derogatory entries on your permanent record?
7. Does your school obtain your consent before it gives out confidential information about you to police, draft-boards, colleges, or employers?
8. Can you honestly state your views on controversial subjects without fear of harassment or retribution from school authorities?
9. Can you distribute your views in writing without prior censorship?
10. Can you "peaceably assemble" to hear any speaker or discuss any topic of your choice?

How does your school score?
What does that make you?
How do you like it?

"THE VIGILANT PROTECTION OF CONSTITUTIONAL FREEDOMS IS NOWHERE MORE VITAL THAN IN THE COMMUNITY OF AMERICAN SCHOOLS."
—U. S. Supreme Court Justice Brennan

SCIENCE FOR THE PEOPLE

Scientists and Engineers for Social and Political Action: Science for the People is a national group associated with the sciences who are critical of the present role of science in our society. It includes an active group concerned about the teaching of science. *SESPA/ Science for the People* publishes a magazine titled *Science for the People*.
Information from:

SESPA/SCIENCE FOR THE PEOPLE
9 Walden Street
Jamaica Plain, Mass. 02130
(617) 427-0642

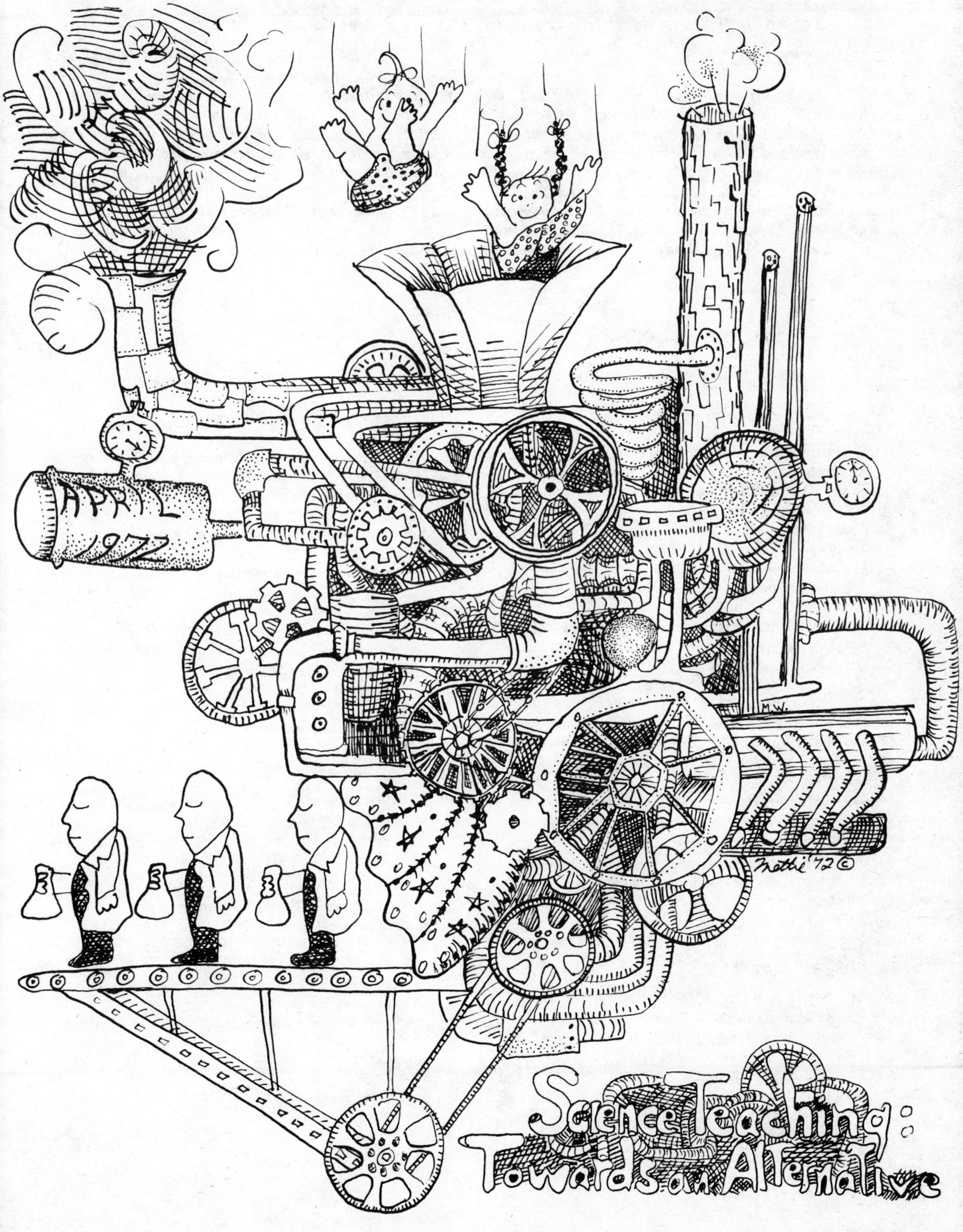
Science Teaching:
Towards an Alternative

106 Organizations

from "Science Teaching: Towards an Alternative"

STATEMENTS BY THE AUTHORS

For the last 10 years, I have been working as a research scientist. However, in the last couple of years, the questions of elitism in science, science to the service of the ruling class and the position of women in our society have made it very hard for me to keep my aloofness. Gradually I began to feel the need to expand my contacts and my consciousness. Thus my decision to switch to teaching science to undergraduate non-science majors. This course is an attempt to unite my knowledge with my political beliefs.

R.A.

It is a myth that scientists must be what no human can be–totally objective, free of prejudice, unfeeling. No human is capable of this objectivity. How could I admit to neutrality concerning life, death, starvation or illness? Should scientists be emotionless, like the 7 o'clock news; so stripped of feelings, so impartial that all horrors finally become acceptable as they parade before our senses in the numbing shrouds of objectivity? I will not deny my feelings, not when I find that the study of life itself is creating terrors for the living, not when I know that science has created the means to plunder our minds and steal our genes.

T.S.

TEACHING BIBLIOGRAPHY

Articles, Books, Laboratory Practices, Movies

A. ARTICLES

1. The Future of Asexual Reproduction, Watson, *Intellectual Digest,* Oct. 71
2. Reservations Concerning Gene Therapy, Fox and Littlefield, *Science,* 16 July 1971
3. From Hippocrates to Senate Resolution 75, Trotter, *Science News,* December 4, 1971
4. Ethnic Weapons, Larson, *Military Review,* Nov. 1970
5. Prenatal Diagnosis of Genetic Diseases, *Scientific American,*
6. Sickle Cell Anemia: An Interesting Pathology, Michaelson, *Ramparts,* October 1971
7. Off the Pill? Coburn, *Ramparts,* June 1970
8. Man and His Environment, Coale, *Science,* Vol. 170
9. Population Care and Control, Snow, *New Republic,* May 1, 1971
10. Population and Poverty, Hilton, *SSRS Review,* Sept. 1970
11. Overpopulated America, Davis, *New Republic,* January 10, 1971
12. My Answer to Genocide, Gregory, *Ebony,* October, 1971
13. Is Pregnancy Really Normal? Hern, *Perspectives (Family Planning),* January 1971
14. A Report on the Abortion Capital of the Country, Edmiston, *New York Sunday Times,* 1971
15. The Conquest of Syphilis, Horn, Chapter 9 of *Away With All Pests* (see books)
16. Experimental Pregnancy, Veatch, *Hastings Center Report, 1971 Institute for Society, Ethics and the Life Sciences*
17. The Myth of the Vaginal Orgasm, Koedt, New England Free Press pamphlet, 791 Tremont St., Boston
18. Psychology Constructs the Female, Weisstein, New England Free Press
19. Child-rearing and Women's Liberation, Wortis, Boston Area Child Care Action Group pamphlet, 12-14 Glenwood, Cambridge, Mass. 02139
20. On Killing Members of One's Own Species, Lorenz, *Bulletin of Atomic Scientists,* October 1970
21. The New American Militarism, Shoup, *Atlantic,* April 1969 1969
22. Science and Social Attitudes, Morison, *Science,* 11 July 1969
23. Where Are Our Women in Science? Kundsin, *Harvard Medical Alumni Bulletin,* Winter, 1965
24. Autopsy on Science, Roszak, *New Scientist and Science Journal,* 11 March 1971
25. Education of a Scientific Innocent, Galston, *Yale Review,* 1971
26. Margaret Sanger and Voluntary Motherhood, Sabaroff, *Women, A Journal of Liberation,* Spring 1970
27. The Case of Ritalin: Drugs for Hyperactive Children, Charles, *New Republic,* October 23, 1971
28. Brain Researcher Jose Delgado Asks, "What Kind of Humans Would We Like to Construct?", Scarf, *New York Times Magazine,* November 15, 1970
29. The Erich Fromm Theory of Aggression, Fromm, *New York Times Magazine,* February 27, 1972

B. LABORATORIES

For laboratory practice, we taught students how to do pregnancy tests, sickle-cell anemia testing, and blood typing. The equipment may be ordered from:

1. Carolina Biological Supply Company
   Burlington, N.C. 27215
   (for blood typing kits, basic, $6.95, Rh, $13.95, Chromosome, $6.95.)
2. Organon, Inc.
   West Orange, N.J. 07052
   (for Pregnosticon Dri-Dot Pregnancy Tests–100 for $110.00)
3. Orthodiagnostics
   c/o J.C. Poinier
   Buckboard Road
   Duxbury, Mass. 02332
   (for Pregnancy Test "Gravindex," 200 for $187.00 and Sickel Cell Test "Sickledex," 400 for $190.00)

C. BOOKS

The following were consulted for the preparation of the course

1. *Away With All Pests,* by Joshua S. Horn, Monthly Review Press, New York, 1969–$2.45 (A British surgeon writes about his 14 years in medical practice in China)
2. *The Earth Belongs to the People,* by Guiseppi Slater *et al.*, Peoples Press, San Francisco, 1970–$.75 for paperback booklet (Discusses ecology and resources)
3. *From Now to Zero–Fertility, Contraception and Abortion in America,* by L. Alderidge Westoff and Charles F. Westoff. Little, Brown & Co., Boston
4. *Who Shall Live? Man's Control Over Birth and Death*– a report prepared for the American Friends Service Committee. Hill and Wang, New York–$1.75
5. *Microbes and Morals–the Strange Story of Venereal Disease,* by Theodor Rosebury, Viking Press, New York, $7.95
6. *Marx and Engels on the Population Bomb,* edited by Ronald L. Meek, The Ramparts Press–$1.95
7. *The Closing Circle,* Barry Commoner, Alfred A. Knopf, New York, 1971 (Nature, Man and Technology)
8. *Women and Their Bodies, Our Bodies Our Selves,* New land Free Press 1971, Boston Women's Health Collective– $.35

<u>Science Teaching: An Alternative</u>: a pamphlet handed out at the National Science Teachers' Convention, reprinted in Sept.'72 issue of <u>Science for the People</u> magazine. Ideas for more "relevant" teaching.

15¢

<u>Towards a Science for the People</u>: (also known as <u>Censored</u>, <u>Counter-Science</u>, <u>A Strategy of Opposition</u>, and <u>Science for the People</u>, appearing in Liberation magazine, March 1972)

25¢

25¢

<u>Science for the People Magazine</u> (some major articles listed below)

50¢

March 1973: Preventive Genocide in Latin America, AAAS - Actions and Reactions, War Without End - a review, Army Math Research, Abortion experiments on Black Women.

January 1973: Remote Warfare, Workplace Politics, Stilberstrol, Midwifery, Runaway Electronics, Stopping War Research, ACS Actions, Ecology for the People.

November 1972: Occupational Health, Jason Confrontation, Questions from Argentina, Rat Control: People's Science in Philadelphia, The Tyranny of Structurelessness.

September 1972: (Science Teaching Issue): Science Teaching: Towards an Alternative, Up Against the NSTA, A Course in Biology, Resource Bibliography, Grading, Teaching Physics in Context, Computer Course Bibliography, Critique of the Project Physics Course.

SCIENTISTS AND ENGINEERS FOR SOCIAL AND POLITICAL ACTION · SESPA ·

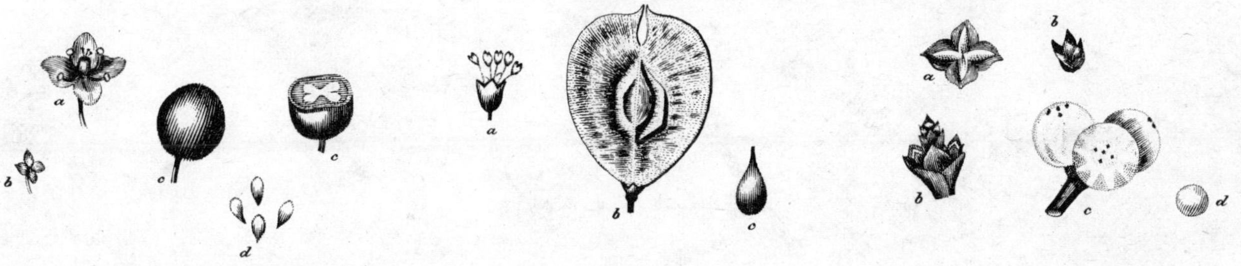

FOUNDATION FOR CHANGE

Foundation for Change is a nonprofit organization devoted to supplying educational materials for social change. They have the "Viewpoint" series (6 four-page brochures designed for classroom use and available free):

#1 Minorities & News Media
#2 Minorities & Police
#3 Minorities & Jobs
#4 Minorities & Courts
#5 Minorities & Prisons
#6 Minorities & Education

Other free brochures include:

Definitions of Racism
Racism Rating: Test Your Textbooks
Black Women Are Proud
Chicano and Proud (bilingual)
Indian and Proud
Puerto Rican and Proud (bilingual)
Black American Freedom Fighters

Write for single free copies and ask to be placed on the Foundation's mailing list:

FOUNDATION FOR CHANGE, INC.
1619 Broadway (Room 802)
New York, N.Y. 10019
(212) 765-2074

Are Your Textbooks Culturally Deprived?. . . asks a brochure available free in classroom quantities from the Foundation for Change. The student brochure, titled **Minorities and Education; Viewpoint #6,** explains how public schools can perpetuate racism with curriculum and texts that look at the world with white eyes and teachers who have low expectation levels for minority students.

The brochure points out common U. S. History textbook distortions in dealing with blacks, Indians, Puerto Ricans and Chicanos. Students can check their own texts to see if the distortions are taught at their school. The brochure also has a series of questions for students to use in evaluating their school. For example, "Do you learn how whites control many institutions and communities at the expense of minorities?", "Are all students assigned to read material that gives minorities' point of view?", "Does the school board have an organized program to overcome any racism in the school district?" and more.

Also available free is a one page "Racism Rating" evaluating a D.C. Heath text, **We the People** (revised 1971) and illustrating the errors it teaches and distortions introduced in treatment of minorities. .

Both items are excellent and solid for class use.

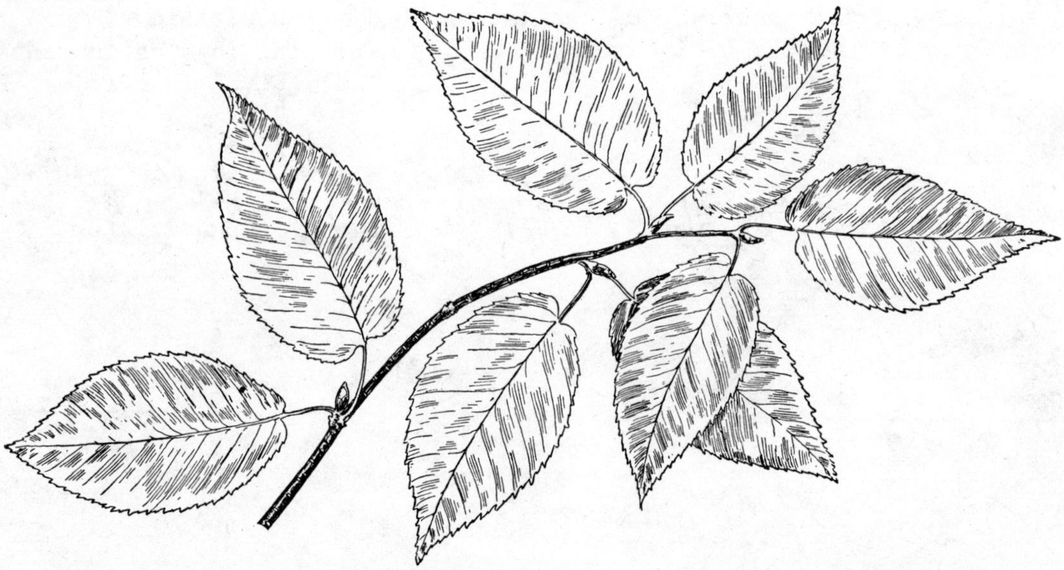

QUIZ: What's In A Word?

? ? ? Can you detect racial slights and slurs in these news items?

we-they words

New Haven Register editorial, 1967:

Declaration of a state of emergency was a bitter pill for Mayor Lee—as it was also for a community which has made every effort to give its Negro citizens the things they have asked.

New York Times movie review, 1969:

If we were Negroes rather than Americans, English and French, we would complain we were being stereotyped.

?? Is "we" a word written from a white viewpoint? And is "they" a word for people on the outside—the minority? Do you know that Blacks are almost one-third of the readers in some big cities; that Blacks are 21% of NYC's populationa and 32% of Chicago's, and are over 50% of the population in 16 cities?

well-dressed words

New York Times, reporting President Johnson's farewell talk before Black government officials, 1968:

The President spoke to the well-dressed Negro officials and their wives.

?? Is it news that professional Blacks dress like people in professional life?

first-last names

United Press International (UPI), reporting about Black Olympic champion Willie Davenport, 2/69:

Willie had to settle for a tie with Tom Von Ruden as the meet's outstanding athlete. Von Ruden, who managed only a ninth-place finish in the Olympic 1500 meters, set a record in winning 1000 yard run.

?? Do you know that a 1968 survey for the Columbia Journalism Review showed that Blacks are called by their first names in sports news more often that whites? Is this a harmless habit?

Sources: "They Still Write It White," Newsday reporter Robert E. Smith in Columbia Journalism Review, Spring 1969; U.S. Bureau of the Census Report, 1970.

What's In A Name—Negro, Black, Afro-American?

Ebony magazine asked 2000 of its readers in June/68 what they wanted to be called: 60% preferred African or Afro-American, 23.3% voted for Black. Only 8.1% preferred Negro. Most minority publications use the names Afro-American or black, some spelling black with a capital B.

?? Does the general press reflect the wish of the Black community to be called Afro-American or Black? Check your newspapers and see.

SCORECARD OF BIAS

who owns . . . . newspapers?

• Of 1748 dailies and 7610 weekly papers in the nation, 177 are Black owned. Blacks are over 12% of the population but only 1% of the newspaper owners. (1971)

who owns . . . . radio?

• Of roughly 8000 stations, about 30 are owned by non-whites. (1973)

who owns . . . . TV?

• Of 912 TV stations nationwide, not one is Black-owned and two are Black-managed. Yet 96% of Blacks have TV sets and depend on the medium for information and entertainment. (1971)

who controls . . . . newspapers?

• Less than 1/2 of 1% of news executive positions were held by non-whites in 1970. Non-white minorities still comprise less than 1% of the staffs of newspaper editors, writers, reporters and photographers (1972)

who controls . . . . radio and TV?

• The Federal Communications Commission (FCC) controls broadcasting on behalf of the public, granting licenses and monitoring programs. There is one Black on the FCC. All members are selected by the President of the U.S. for 7 year terms. Until 1972 all members in the 36-year FCC history have been white. The FCC, with more than 1,500 employees, does not have any Blacks in top grades. (1972)

who is employed . . . . . . on newspapers?

• *Nationwide,* in newspapers with more than 100 employees, 6.2% of the *entire* work force are non-white, while only 2.5% of the professional or professional-support group are non-white. (1972)

New York City's three major dailies reported that 22 out of 1,000 editorial employees are Black; only 1 of these is an editor. (1971)

who is employed . . . . .in TV?

• A 1972 study of 609 of the 728 *commercial* TV stations reveals that:

22.5% had *no* full-time non-white employees
77% had no non-whites in management jobs
50% had no non-whites in professional jobs
55% had no non-whites in technical jobs
81% had no non-whites in sales jobs

Of public television stations, 35% have no full-time minority-group employees and are run by governing boards "almost exclusively composed of whites." (1972)

COMMENT: Black on White Media

Out Of Sight: *"Think of a party at which one man does all the talking, including his telling of your stories on your behalf with you standing right there. If you can imagine it, you will begin to understand minority frustration."*
—Joseph Okpaku, editor, Third Press. *1971.*

---

from VIEWPOINT #1: MINORITIES & NEWS MEDIA

NATIONAL ADVISORY COMMISSION "The media report and write from the standpoint of a white man's world . . . The 'white press' . . . repeatedly, if unconsciously, reflects the biases, the paternalism, the indifference of white America."

CRISIS: IS THERE A DOUBLE STANDARD?

In Crime Reporting?

Jim Ingram, Black reporter for The Michigan Chronicle, witnessed the Attica Prison protest that ended in the death of 9 white guards and 32 inmates, mostly Blacks and Puerto Ricans. All were killed by. police officers. (Over 85% of Attica inmates were minorities.) Newspapers first reported that inmates slashed the throats of several white hostages. This was proved false by a medical examiner. Ingram wrote this comment to the N.Y. Times, 9/22/71:

The (white) reporters accepted everything prison officials said as fact. Anything imputed to the inmates by prison officials was usually reported as having actually occurred. "The inmates killed" or, "the rioters wounded" was common rather than the traditional reporting method: "according to prison officials," "prison authorities charge," etc.

In Headlines?

examples on Attica: The N.Y. *Daily News* had a by-line article headlined: I SAW SEVEN THROATS CUT—*9/13/71.* The N.Y. *Times* said in an editorial headlined MASSACRE AT ATTICA: "Prisoners slashed the throats of utterly helpless, unarmed guards."—*9/14/71.* This is how the *Times* corrected the error the next day: "The 9 hostages killed in the uprising in the Attica correctional facility died of bullet wounds, it was reported today after official autopsies."

In News Training?

Whitney M. Young, Jr., late director of the National Urban League, in his book, Beyond Racism, 1969:

A top newspaper would not think of sending a correspondent to Moscow without special training . . . Since Americans have made a foreign country out of the ghetto, our newspapers need to give reporters in Harlem and Hough the same preparation they give to reporters in Moscow and Paris.

In Racial News?

Ted Poston, a Black Newspaperman on New York City dailies for more than a quarter of a century, in Race and the News Media, 1967:

During the 1964 pre-Harlem-riot season, the New York *Post* got a telephone tip that a fight had broken out on a Harlem River excursion boat taking about a thousand high school pupils to Bear Mountain. The new-angle-seeking assistant city editor yelled excitedly to me, "Find out how many Negroes are on that boat and who started the race riot." It turned out that only ten Negroes were among the students and that the "race riot" was only a fist fight between two Italian youngsters.

PROJECT FOR CHANGE

????? Use the 5 basic questions of journalism—who, what, where, when and why—to analyze how your local press, radio and TV report the news.

WHO matters in reporting the news? In obituaries? In society and fashion news?
WHO reads and listens to the news? WHO advertises in the media?
WHO writes and edits the news?
WHO owns and controls the news media?
WHAT are the reporters' information sources for racial news?
WHERE does the white reporter get his training and understanding of the ghetto news beat?
WHEN is news about nonwhites "news"?
WHY is the news often written for, by and about the white world?

INSTITUTE FOR WORLD ORDER, INC.

Institute for World Order, Inc., is a nonprofit educational institution concerned with promoting peace studies in colleges and high schools. It publishes *Ways and Means of Teaching About World Order*, a free newsletter that provides teaching ideas about peace education. The Institute publishes other material and maintains a speakers bureau. When contacting the Institute tell them your interests and teaching level.

INSTITUTE FOR WORLD ORDER
11 West 42nd Street
New York, N.Y. 10036
(212) 947-2190

Peace Studies

)LLEGE COURSES ON PEACE AND WORLD ORDER

:ollection of 30 course outlines
d syllabi in the following areas:

onflict, revolution and peace
orld order
orld politics
he third world: perspectives on
 development and justice
ooking toward the future
ocial criticism and individual change
he United States context

152 pages

$2.00

Talking About Cartoons

One simple, effective, and inexpensive way to **start** classroom discussion on weaponry and technology issues is to use cartoons from newspapers and magazines. By projecting a series of cartoons for the class the teacher can quickly present a variety of opinions, encourage students to examine them, and let students explore their own positions on the issues depicted. If a projector is not available, the teacher can arrange a cartoon bulletin board reflecting the same variety of views.

A third simple technique (useful for written work because it relieves the teacher of the burden of reading nearly identical answers over and over again) is a grab bag of assorted cartoons. Each student can write about one cartoon drawn from the bag. His assignment might be to describe both the view of the cartoonist and his own view.

The cartoons reprinted here are two of the 1968 winners of the Grenville Clark Editorial Page Award sponsored by The Stanley Foundation. (Booklets containing all the award-winning cartoons and editorials are available from The Stanley Foundation, Stanley Building, Muscatine, Iowa 52761.)

Both these cartoons point out the disparity between the investment of resources — physical, financial, and intellectual—in the arts and sciences of peace and the investment in the technology of war.

To improve understanding of the issues involved, the teacher might lead a discussion by asking questions such as these:

1. What statements do the cartoons make about the use of technology?
2. Do you agree with these statements? What other information have you acquired that leads you to agree or disagree?
3. Have technological advances made the outbreak of international violence easier or harder to control?
4. Do you believe that technological advances should cause us to change the way we conduct international relations?
5. What do you think the technological achievements of the Apollo moon landings will mean for mankind? What do you hope they will mean? What can be done to make your hopes a reality?

For continuing discussions on science and technology both students and teachers might find these items interesting and useful:

The Andromeda Stain (fiction), by Michael Crichton, Knopf, 1969, 295 pp., $5.95.

The Biological Time Bomb, by Gordon Rattray Taylor, World, 1968, 240 pp., $5.50; Signet Books, 1969, $1.25 (paper).

The Cassiopeia Affair (fiction), by Chloe Zerwick and Harrison Brown, Doubleday, 1968, 235 pp., $4.50 (also available in paper).

The Future of the Strategic Arms Race: Options for the 1970's, by George W. Rathjens, Taplinger Publishing Co., Inc., 29 East 10th Street, New York, N. Y. 10003, 53 pp., 60¢; or 10-24 copies, 50¢ each; 25-99 copies, 40¢ each; 100-499 copies, 30¢ each.

Man . . . An Endangered Species?, U.S. Government Printing Office, Catalog No. I 1.954, 100 pp., $1.50.

The Ultimate Folly: War by Pestilence, Asphyxiation and Defoliation, by Cong. Richard D. McCarthy, Knopf, 1969, 176 pp., $5.95.

112 Organizations

BOOKS AND PAMPHLETS

Let Us Examine Our Attitude Toward Peace edited by Priscilla Griffith and Betty Reardon - a booklet of readings on the psychological and political barriers to world peace - discussion questions and activities suggestions.
For Grades 11-14 paperbound, 47 pp $1.00
SSSS order #WLF01

Peace Is Possible edited by Elizabeth Jay Hollins - a reader on world order focusing on the eradication of war as an accepted human institution.
For Grades 11-14 paperbound, 350 pp $3.75
ORDER FROM: GROSSMAN PUBLISHERS, INC., 625 Madison Avenue, New York, N. Y. 10022

Peace: The Control of National Power by Philip Van Slyck - core of a one-semester course on problems of world order - nine sessions, questions and a bibliography.
For Grades 11-14 paperbound, 186 pp $1.75
ORDER FROM: BEACON PRESS, 25 Beacon Street, Boston, Mass. 02128

Peacekeeping: Problems and Possibilities by Jack Fraenkel, Margaret Carter and Betty Reardon - examination of four models for peacekeeping and cases for studying the models. (Preliminary edition - revision to be published by Random House, 1973)
For Grades 8-10 paperbound, 77 pp $1.50
ORDER FROM: WORLD LAW FUND now INSTITUTE FOR WORLD ORDER, Inc

Preface to Disarmament: An Appraisal of Recent Proposals by Marion McVitty - discusses problems of general and complete disarmament with teacher's guide.
For Grades 11-14 $1.00
ORDER FROM: PUBLIC AFFAIRS PRESS, 419 New Jersey Avenue, S.E., Washington, D. C. 20003

"The Human Person and The War System", Intercom, Feb., 1971, Special Issue, edited by Betty Reardon - offers a framework of inquiry into issues related to war crimes - 7 articles each of which constitutes a lesson plan.
For Grades 9-12 $1.50
ORDER FROM: WORLD LAW FUND now INSTITUTE FOR WORLD ORDER, Inc.

COURSE OUTLINES

War and Peace: A World-Wide Problem by James Campbell & Donald Boyk - For Grades 9-10
The United Nations and Disarmament/Aggression by David L. Evans - For Grades 11-12
Learning About War and Peace by Gerald Hardcastle - For Grades 11-12
The Problems and Possibilities of the International System by A. Robert Lynch - For Grades 11-12
A Suggested Procedure for Teaching a Twelve Week Unit on Problems of Peace and War in the Modern World by Gerald L. Thorpe. For Grades 11-12
World Politics: The Search for World Order by Stephen Holman - For Grades 9-10
ORDER FROM: WORLD LAW FUND now INSTITUTE FOR WORLD ORDER, INC. .50¢ each

Ways and Means of Teaching About World Order - suggested resources, individual units, lesson plans sent regularly to teachers on our mailing list. Single copies free
Additional copies .10¢ each
ORDER FROM: WORLD LAW FUND Now INSTITUTE FOR WORLD ORDER, Inc.

Send us your name and address to receive Ways and Means regularly

VOCATIONS FOR SOCIAL CHANGE

WorkForce

One person can:
- organize a community school
- begin to strive for change at your job
- form a tenants' union
- collectivize and tackle large problems within the community.

WORKFORCE
5951 Canning Street
Oakland, Calif. 94609
(415) 653-6535

You can find out about how to do these and other things yourself, where they are being done already, and who to get advice from on problems and processes through *Vocations for Social Change.* We are a collective that functions as a national information clearinghouse for people and organizations working full-time for radical social change. Our magazine, *WorkForce,* contains job openings, articles on how to organize, create your own job or project, and a resource section of over 250 groups willing to answer questions and give advice on how to work in their fields. A $5 donation is asked for a six-month sub., since we are a non-profit corporation. Institutions are $10 for one year.

ALTERNATIVE FEATURES SERVICE, Box 2250, Berkeley, CA 94702, is a media collective which operates a non-profit press service for campus and community newspapers. Over 100 subscribing papers receive weekly packets of columns, cartoons, and illustrated feature news stories. AFS contributors include journalists, artists, cartoonists from around the world, and other media collectives and research groups. AFS is always looking for writing, art, and photos; payment is $40 for illustrated feature stories, and other rates are available on request. Free introductory packets are available to campus and community newspapers. Write AFS or call (415) 548-700 between 1:00 and 6:00 pm.

ALTERNATIVE RADIO EXCHANGE, Box 852, Felton, CA 95018, is a group of people and a publication who act as an information clearinghouse for other groups around the country into alternative radio. Subscriptions to their quarterly publication are $3 per year. Their information includes technical, financial, and procedural data.

★ AMERIKAN PRESS SYNDICATE, Box 5175, Beverly Hills, CA 90210, is a press and information service concerned mainly with independent alternative papers and high school free speech publications, presently nationwide.

APRIL VIDEO COOPERATIVE, Box AK, Downsville, NY 13755; (607) 363-7432, is a cooperative of groups and individuals working in community video and public access/local origination cable all around the country. Formed last April during a video conference at New Brunswick, NJ, the cooperative has been working at maintaining an open flow of public access information with the National Cable Television Association as well as other CATV interests. It hopes to serve video producers as a clearinghouse for access-oriented information including tape distribution, consultancies, etc., while allowing people to continue to work in a decentralized fashion. The Downsville collective is currently serving as a coordinating group while also relating to local cable and video activities. If you would like further information or would like to help, contact them. They also publish Dumping Place, an open access periodical for video, cable, and other media people. You can plug in by sending information, questions, tape catalogs, whatever, in camera-ready format, 8 1/2"x 11" or smaller, to the above address. Subscription donations are $5 per individual, $10 for institutional use.

LAW STUDENTS CIVIL RIGHTS RESEARCH COUNCIL, 22 East 40th St., New York, NY 10016, 212-689-2522, works with law students around the country to meet the legal needs of power-building civil rights and poor people's organizations, to support the legal defense of movement people singled out for attack because of their organizing work and to change the basic nature of the legal profession by recruiting poor and minority people into law school. In addition, the council has a limited capacity to help non-law students find volunteer work with community organizations.

LEGAL IN-SERVICE PROJECT, See: GI's AND VETERANS

MEIKLEJOHN CIVIL LIBERTIES LIBRARY, 1715 Francisco St., Berkeley, CA 94703, 415-848-0599, offers unique research services. The heart of the collection is not books, but files of recent cases which raise the central legal demands of the people: freedom, fair treatment and equality. The library collects complaints filed in state and federal courts plus briefs, motions, transcripts and other materials which can be used in the preparation of new cases. It acquires publications and reports on public law questions. The library also has an extensive collection of important unreported opinions on cases affecting individual rights, with large holdings on Selective Service law and student rights. Write for other services.

NATIONAL LAWYERS GUILD, 23 Cornelia St., New York, NY 10014, is a nationwide association of layers, law students and prisoner-lawyers who provide legal support for the movement for social change. Most of the work of the Guild is carried out by local and regional chapters, each of whom also develop their own programs. There are chapters in the following cities... contact the national office for more information: Boston, Chicago, Denver, Detroit, Fort Dix, Los Angeles, Philadelphia, Pittsburgh, Portland, New York, San Jose, San Francisco, Milwaukee, Seattle and Washington, DC.

WOMEN'S RIGHTS LAW REPORTER, See: WOMEN'S LIBERATION

S.F. BAY GUARDIAN

WORKERS DEFENSE LEAGUE, 112 East 19th St., New York, NY 10003, 212-254-4953, defends workers from job-related injustices, recruits and trains lawyers in employee protection helps household workers to upgrade their lives through forming unions and is concerned with the defense of GI rights. They distribute "American Servicemen Have Rights: Do You Know Yours?" free to servicepeople but ask 10¢ from others. The league also plans to train lawyers for GI counseling and set up a military justice institute.

ECOLOGY CENTER OF LOUISIANA, Box 15149, New Orleans, LA 70115 (street address: 932 Philip St.), (504) 522-4008, does research on issues of environmental concern and organizes ecology groups in Louisiana to take action on specific issues. It operates a general information desk, speaker's bureau, recycling center, research library and puts out "fact sheets" plus a newsletter on local activities. Currently, the center is selling paper made from 100% recycled papers for stationery, mimeo/offset printing and xerox to support its activities.

ENVIRONMENTAL ACTION, 1346 Connecticut Ave.,NW, Room 731, Washington,DC 20036, (202) 833-1845. This national organization is concerned with getting federal legislation passed that will be effective in cleaning up the environment and with seeing that this legislation is subsequently enforced. They mean mass transit, nuclear reactor safeguards and recyclable containers not just cleaner air. Environmental criminals and a wide range of ecological, social and political problems are discussed in their weekly newsletter (24 iisues for $7.50). Also available is Earth Toolkit, a manual for grassroots action on our environment ($1.25) and Ecotage, a collection of ideas from ecological saboteurs (1.25).

ECONOMIC ALTERNATIVES

★ BOSTON FOOD COOPERATIVE, 12 Babbitt St., Boston, MA 02215; (617) 267-9090, is a non-profit membership organization whose purpose is to buy high quality food and related consumer goods offered to its members at the lowest possible cost. They are now acting as food brokers for co-ops in New England, and have a complete listing of co-op literature, including all NASCO publications. They are happy to talk to co-ops all the time. (even at 3:00 am? -- typist.)

COOPERATIVE LEAGUE, 1828 "L" St., NW, Washington, DC 20036 (202) 872-0550, has literature available on starting and maintaining cooperatives. The league will supply literature lists and sample pamphlets to those who ask. Contact the league if you're interested in consumer co-ops, housing, group health or supply/marketing cooperatives. Family membership is ten dollars a year and includes subscriptions to all publications.

CORNUCOPIA, 2808 West Lake St., Chicago, IL 60612, (312)-722-5550, is a non-profit corporation which operates a warehouse and distribution center for food co-ops and buying clubs in the Chicago area and throughout the Midwest. It combines the huge economic power wielded by scores of co-ops and buying clubs to obtain even more savings and to give individual clubs more control over purchasing and distributing at the wholesale level. Cornucopia acts not only as a source of supply, it is also an organizational and information center; members receive a variety of printed materials dealing with such things as; food quality and availability; food preparation and storage, including recipes; and where to get items Cornucopia does not carry. In addition, the warehouse acts as a learning center to help with the organization of new buying clubs, and to help established groups with problems they have encountered.

NORTH AMERICAN STUDENT COOPERATIVE ORGANIZATION (NASCO), Box 1301, Ann Arbor, MI 48106; (313) 663-0889, is an organization serving people interested in consumer-owned and democratically controlled systems. NASCO publishes Monthly News of Co-op Communities ($2.00/year) and Journal of the New Harbinger ($6.00/year). Community Market Catalog and a Directory of Campus-based Cooperation are produced annually at a price of $1 each. NASCO is involved in campus-based management training programs and co-op education work. In addition to technical assistance on consumer-owned coops via correspondence and conferences, NASCO offers consulting services at cost.

TEACHER DROP-OUT CENTER

Teacher Drop-Out Center is a four-year-old national clearinghouse for information to help teachers find jobs in free, innovative public and alternative schools. If you're discontented with a rigid, inhuman style of education and want to share yourself in a freer, more humane environment join TDOC and they'll try to help.

The fee is $20 to register for their services. The $20 pays for: A nationwide directory of over 1,500 innovative and alternative schools, K - college, that is updated regularly (The directory is available to non-members for $5); descriptions of many of these schools written by administrators who like to hear from TDOC people; a monthly listing of job openings; and a newsletter on innovative education. TDOC is run by Len Solo and Stan Barondes. The March 1973 issue of the newsletter contained 11 pages of closely spaced job openings--at a time when jobs in schools are supposed to be all but nonexistent. Many listings were for traditional schools about which TDOC has no information.

TEACHER DROP-OUT CENTER
Box 521
Amherst, Mass. 01002

NATIONAL COMMISSION ON RESOURCES FOR YOUTH

36 West 44th Street, Room 1314
New York, N.Y. 10036
(212) 682-3339

National Commission on Resources for Youth, Inc., publishes a free quarterly newsletter describing outstanding projects in which young people perform significant and unusual tasks such as environmental protection, governance, day care work, producing *Foxfire*-type publications, etc.

CONTENTS

The newsletter and the book *40 Projects by Groups of Kids* offer seeds of ideas to give classes and "homework" a meaningful social function.

40 Projects is $2 from NCRY. Some of the projects explained in enough detail to allow adopting to your own needs include:

HOME ECONOMICS--FOR REAL*

American Friends Service Committee
Atlanta, Georgia 30304

In the summer of 1966, Bedford Pines Buttermilk Bottom's Buying Club, a cooperative project organized by youth and adults, devised a simple but effective strategy for consumer self-defense. They first surveyed their neighborhood and determined which foods are most frequently purchased. After compiling this list, they went to all the local stores and priced the goods. Their pricing showed variations in cost of as much as 150%. When made aware of these results, people in the neighborhood were happy to try another approach to buying groceries. Arrangements were made to purchase food in large quantities from a food wholesaler. This permitted substantial savings. The youth and adults went door to door getting orders for the food and collecting money. They then purchased and distributed the food.

One difficulty encountered by this group was the extensive footwork required to visit people for their orders and for distribution. Another group solved this problem when the student organizers had the orders brought to the school by the family teenager. The food was delivered by the same means.

MISSION MEDIARTS, INC.

Mission Mediarts, Inc.
27-73 23rd Street
San Francisco, California 94110

Youths from San Francisco's Mission District are making films and video-tapes for use by the public schools and TV stations in a program that provides skills training for the youth and a more positive image for the community. The educational TV station, KQED, and the local skills training center, Mission Mediarts, Inc., are co-sponsors of the project. Youth come from off the streets or are referred by community agencies and the courts. At any given time there may be 12 participants. During the summer, the number expands to 20 to include a Neighborhood Youth Corps component.

The workshop is contracted with KQED and National Educational Television to make 18 tapes about the varied lifestyles of the Mission community. A series of tapes made by the youths about drugs were used as part of a training program for teachers by the San Francisco public schools. Three other programs made by the youths were broadcast coast to coast by NET as part of its program, "San Francisco Mix".

The youths write and direct their own films and video-tapes with the technical assistance of professionals at the TV station and at the skills center. They also contact businesses and foundations to raise money for the program and elect their own officers to manage and allocate their budget.

THE CORONA EAST ELMHURST TRANSITION PRESS

The New York Times
229 West 43rd Street
New York, New York 10036

A cooperative effort by a newspaper giant, The New York Times, with a small group of teenagers has resulted in an exciting new community-based newspaper, staffed by the young people and published with the advice and assistance of the Times.

The Times searched among several poor communities for neighborhoods in need of a medium of constructive expression, but lacking in the resources to secure it. This Queens community qualified and the word went out that a staff would be assembled. With the help of local agencies, a group of mostly high school youth gathered. The Corona Elmhurst Transition Press was born.

The editors were quick to see that they play an important role in their community and have an advantage over outsiders in covering local news. The pages of The Transition Press abound with stories of interest to the community: the need for a frequent and efficient bus link with Manhattan, integrated housing projects, news about local talent groups. The paper, a monthly with some paid advertising, bases itself at the local library, an imaginative use of a community resource. The staff number between five and nine. Two Times reporters meet with the group on alternating Saturdays to discuss what goes into the paper. The staff decide who is to cover what, discuss story ideas and possible information sources, determine whether a story merits a picture, etc. The Times staffer listens to these exchanges and offers advice when asked. He may suggest that the youths read several newspapers to determine how a particular story might be handled. In doing so, the young reporters learn to examine their own work more critically. Moreover, the association with the Times staff gives the youths a tangible contact with the professional world and its concerns.

COMMISSION ON VOLUNTARY SERVICE & ACTION

The Commission on Voluntary Service and Action functions as a clearinghouse for groups needing people for social action and people looking for meaningful ways to spend a few weeks, a summer, or a lifetime. The Commission publishes an annual booklet, *Invest Yourself,* which serves as a catalog of service opportunities. It lists several hundred specific projects and placements with over 26,000 openings. Also included are many agencies and projects which offer alternate service placements for young men with 1-0 Selective Service classification.

The 1974 edition will cost $1.00 or slightly more from:

THE COMMISSION ON VOLUNTARY
SERVICE AND ACTION
475 Riverside Drive--Room 665
New York, N.Y. 10027

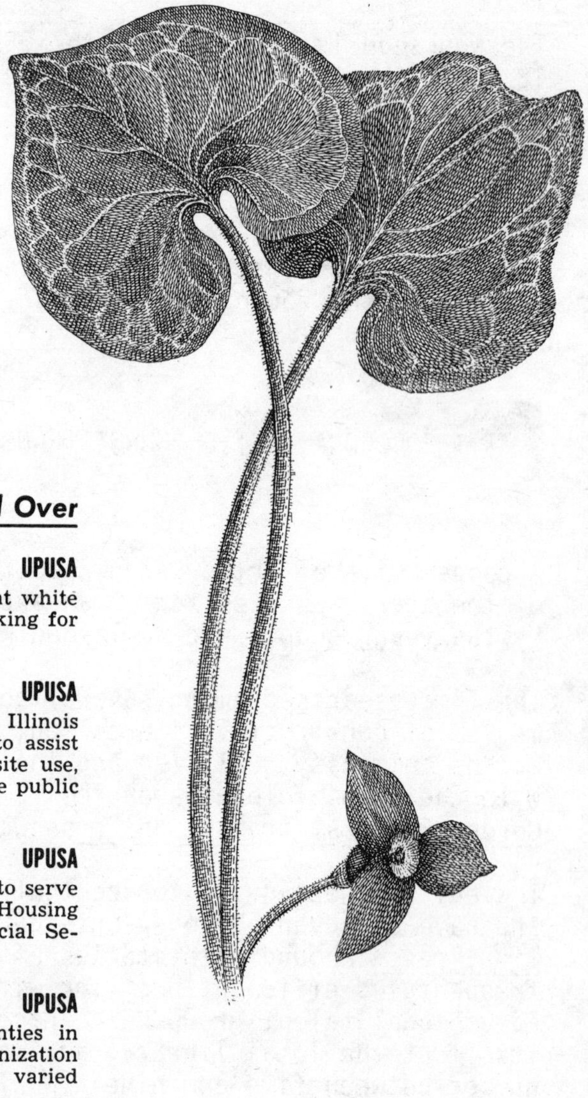

Canada and U.S. — ***18 and Over***

SYRACUSE, NEW YORK **1-2 Years** **UPUSA**

Project One of Greater Syracuse an advocate in the predominant white communities on behalf of racial and economic minorities, is looking for one man to manage their print shop and to handle its finances.

OREGON, ILLINOIS **1-2 Years** **UPUSA**

Stronghold, a renewal and study center serving four Northern Illinois Presbyteries, needs a man and a woman (or married couple) to assist director. The man will help on maintenance, coordinate campsite use, some public relations. The woman will help in the office do some public relations and assist on the program.

BLOOMINGDALE, INDIANA **8 Months** **UPUSA**

One man or a retired couple needed from April to November to serve as resident overseer of a camp owned by the Synod of Indiana. Housing in a mobile home. Salary to the maximum allowed under Social Security.

LAS VEGAS, NEW MEXICO **1-2 Years** **UPUSA**

A new regional mental health program serving several counties in Northern New Mexico needs a person with community organization experience to develop coordination and programming among varied mental health agencies in that part of the state.

ARRIVAL PROGRAM **YMCA**

Representatives meet foreign students at their ports of entry into the United States (primarily New York), help them with overnight living accommodations, give counsel on travel, deliver messages from their universities. Volunteer and salaried. Full-time during summer; part-time rest of year.

BERKELEY, CALIFORNIA **Year Around** **FI/IEU**

5 to 10 college students needed to aid in planning and doing work for the foundation of a degree-granting environmental university. Also needed to help in editing an ecological magazine. Some volunteers needed, some would receive subsistence salaries.

BIG STONE GAP, VIRGINIA **Summer** **FOCIS**

Two or three volunteers needed to work in arts and recreation program in mining communities in Central Appalachia. Prefer individuals with artistic abilities and/or experience with children. Volunteers are responsible for room and board & transp.

INDIANAPOLIS, INDIANA **1 yr. minimum** **FUM**

18 mature young people to live in white or black inner-city projects. Service jobs in first year. Pooled income covers living cost of Volunteer Service Mission community. Help write own job description second year.

WASHINGTON, D.C. **1 yr. minimum** **FUM**

6 mature people a year or more out of high school to be part of Quaker House. Pooled funds of first year work make it possible to write own job description in second year at coffee house, ghetto concerns, demonstrator nonviolent training, etc.

FORT WAYNE, INDIANA **Year Around** **GCMC**

Volunteers needed for one and two year assignments in a continuing program emphasizing housing reconstruction, day care centers, and work with mentally retarded. Room, board, travel and $25 a month are provided.

ELKHART, INDIANA **Year Around** **GCMC**

One and two year volunteers needed as part of a continuing service unit working in a small school for retarded and recreation programs, day care centers, and welfare related programs. Room, board, travel and $25 a month are provided.

BOSTON, MASSACHUSETTS **June 17-August 24** **UCC**

Six college students to work at Pilgrim Church in Dorchester area of rapid social and economic change. Vacation school, day and resident camp leadership, recreation leadership. Cost $15 plus travel.

KANSAS CITY, KANSAS **June 4-August 11** **UCC**

Four member team to share in total Cross-Lines summer program. Summer program. Summer activities extension of year round program. Workers serve as helpers on playground and in community centers. Usually has full responsibility for supervision. Summer volunteers assisted by Youth Corps workers. Wide variety of activities keyed to summer session. Cost $15 plus travel.

LINCOLN, MASSACHUSETTS **June 23-August 22** **UCC**

Two college girls to work with low income mothers and children from Boston and nearby areas. Equal distribution between black and white families. Many groups represented. Workers live in the Farrington Memorial Center. Cost $15 plus travel.

LOS ANGELES, CALIFORNIA **June 11-August 31** **UCC**

Summer volunteers will be assigned work with United Farm Workers. Most will work on boycott programs in California or other states, if desired. Some assignments on freedom schools for farm workers' children. Some clerical jobs open. Knowledge of Spanish very desirable although not required. Cost $15 plus travel.

PHILADELPHIA, PENNSYLVANIA **June 20-August 30** **UCC**

Four-six students to serve churches of five denominations called "Community Celebration," with basic responsibility for drop-in center, counseling, sports tournaments, remedial reading programs drug rehabilitation, creative arts. Need for positive social change. Cost $15 plus travel.

PHILADELPHIA, PENNSYLVANIA **June 25-August 4** **UCC**

Two male college students to work in continuing day camp at Bethel Lutheran Church, five day week, 10 AM-3 PM. Multi-racial group of children. 7-11 years old. Recreation, crafts, music, drama, trips. Cost $15 plus travel.

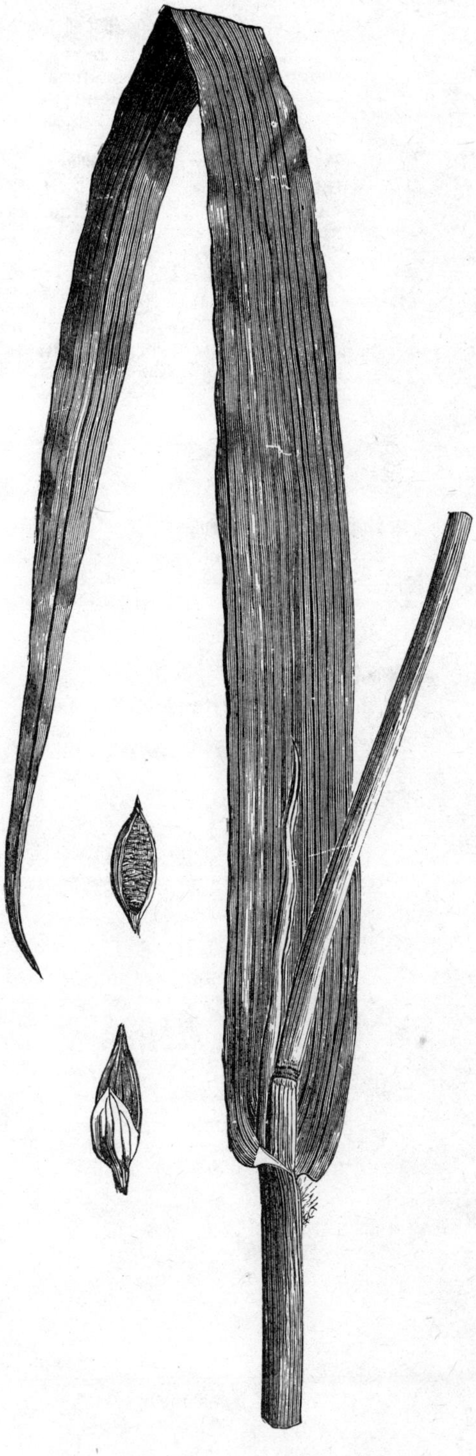

120 Organizations

Canada and U.S. — 18 and Under

COLORADO — **Year Around** — **CIA**

Volunteers needed to live in and work out of self-supporting and self-determining communal living arrangements in Denver and Colorado Springs. Individual "units" determine their own inner-city target areas, but work usually includes community and youth organizing, drug crisis work and Indian and ethnic problems. Cost: transportation.

HAYSVILLE, N.C. — **Summer, Special Sessions** — **HRLC**

Work/Study Projects for youth/counselors. Work Tasks defined by community leaders to meet definite needs, understand community processes, and experience cross cultural exchange. Application by groups only, not by individuals.

NEW HAVEN, CONN. — **Year Around** — **NN**

Interns of any age learn to help young people in Number Nine Crisis and Growth Center: hotline, drop-in counseling, workshops, seminars, alternate vocations counseling. Provide own room and board, no cost. (203) 787-2127.

UNITED STATES — **Year Around** — **WTR**

War Tax Resistance Centers all over the country need volunteers to help organize non-cooperation with federal taxes. Volunteers may distribute leaflets, become war tax resistance counselors, etc. Contact National Office to locate WTR Center nearest you.

MEXICO CITY — **Summer** — **CMP**

Counselors in a summer camp for poor Mexican children. Most other volunteers from Mexico and Europe. July and/or August. Very long hours. Short trips organized between groups. Pay own travel. Room, board, insurance provided.

GHANA — **Summer** — **EIL**

Following a three-week homestay, U.S. college students spend about 10 days helping Ghanaian students and villagers with a construction project. Brief travel period. Optional college credit. Fee, $1,275.

ISRAEL — **Summer** — **EIL**

U.S. college students work on agriculture projects during stays on a kibbutz and a moshav. Brief excursions with hosts during homestays. Travel period includes places of biblical and modern interest. Optional credit. Fee, $975.

KENYA — **Summer** — **EIL**

U.S. college students help Kenyan students and villagers with agriculture and construction projects during or following a three- or four-week homestay. Travel period includes visits to national game parks. Optional college credit. Fee, $1,375.

EUROPE — **July-August** — **EYS**

College age men and women. Four week projects in an international, interfaith community in several countries. Independent travel. Descriptions available February 1.

PACIFIC HIGH SCHOOL APPRENTICESHIP

12100 Skyline Blvd.
Los Gatos, Calif. 95030
408-867-2260

Pacific High School was established in the fall of 1961 as an alternative to conventional high schools. Since that time Pacific has acquired 40 acres of land in the mountains and has become a live-in learning community for teenagers. Recently we have become aware of two problems: (1) Since we have facilities that can handle 50 students at most, Pacific's impact on education and the lives of teenagers is extremely limited. (2) Schools and classrooms, no matter how relevant or free, are necessarily limited and abstract.

In September of 1970 we started PACIFIC HIGH SCHOOL'S APPRENTICESHIP SERVICE PROGRAM (ASP) as a partial answer to these problems. Informed and inspired by the writings of Paul Goodman and Ivan Illich among others, we concluded that the only truly rich educational environment is the on-going society itself. George Bernard Shaw said, "He who can does, he who can't teaches." We feel that teenage persons deserve as their teachers, not those who talk about it in classrooms, but those who can and <u>do</u> in the real world.

WHAT DOES ASP DO?

For high school age persons ASP provides:

a. Encouragement and support in having the courage to be responsible for one's own education in the real world outside of conventional educational frameworks.

b. Protection from the compulsory education laws. ASP students are fully enrolled students of Pacific High School, a high school listed and recognized by the State of California. ASP students are in no way truant.

c. High School credit leading to transcripts and a diploma. We require two reports a year from both teacher and student. Evaluations and transcripts are made on the basis of these reports.

d. Help in finding masters, teachers and mentors. ASP maintains a file of adults who are interested in working with the young. Occasionally we have been instrumental in getting adults and adolescents together. For the most part, however, we have found that it is more effective for persons to make the contact and find teachers for themselves. In fact, finding the teacher provides an initial educational experience for many ASP students. Apprenticeships can be set up anywhere in the world.

For adults ASP provides the opportunity to share one's skills and experience with young persons. In this age of rapid social change, often heralded by the young, ASP provides a priceless opportunity for adults to be in touch with and share with the young. Many of the adults who have been involved with ASP have indicated to us that they had learned as much from the experience as their students.

WHAT DOES ASP NEED?

Kids. Since its inception some 50 adolescents have been a part of ASP. The experience has been good. Without exception kids have reported back that they found their experience doing and being in the real world was more valuable, enjoyable and educational than their experiences in schools. Though few ASP students are interested in submitting themselves to the morass of higher education, those who have applied to college have been accepted. Colleges we have contacted have assured us that they will be able to fairly evaluate ASP students. Based on the past two year's experience, we feel ready to have a lot more students.

Adults. As more and more kids become aware of ASP, we need an increasing number of adults to help them. Since we have been working on this program, we have received many letters from teenagers. Some are full of wisdom and life; others full of determination and life. Many are touching pleas for help and life. We need persons to share their skills and knowledge. We need persons all over to open up their lives to the young and to encourage others around them to do it.

Money. ASP's financial base is tuition. Our full tuition is $200 for the academic year. (Students can enroll in ASP at any time. If a student is only enrolled for part of the academic year the tuition is correspondingly lower). We do not want anyone to be prevented from taking part in ASP for financial reasons. Tuition reductions are readily available for persons in financial need.

ASP's ability to get the word out to interested adolescents and adults has been limited by a lack of funds. Donations to ASP are tax deductible. Checks should be made out to the Pacific High School Giving Fund/ASP.

Publicity and Feedback. In one sense ASP has received a fair amount of publicity. John Holt has written about our program, "It is one of the most hopeful and constructive educational developments I've heard about for a very long time and could make a world of difference in the lives of very many young people." Information on ASP has appeared in publications as varied as THE WHOLE EARTH CATALOG and THE SATURDAY REVIEW. Yet surprisingly few adolescents have heard about ASP. Maybe we are doing something wrong - or at least not doing something right. Please help us get the word out, and please be in touch.

SOMEBODY SOMEWHERE WANTS TO LEARN EVERYTHING THERE IS TO KNOW ANYWHERE

VLTRA EFVTVENS

AHP EDUCATION NETWORK

The Association for Humanistic Psychology is presently nurturing the evolution of the Education Network. Its goals are to help fill both the emotional and practical needs of educators who are moving toward more humanistic teaching practices. The Education Network plans to offer the following services to the more than 500 world-wide members:

1. Organize Teacher Labs where several members live within reasonable traveling distance. These Labs provide an opportunity for educators to share their experiences, to economically utilize resource persons, and to find emotional support for the difficulty in humanizing education.

2. Develop regional weekend workshops directed toward the goals cited under Teacher Labs but involving more resource people.

3. Publish a free Education Network Newsletter to inform members of the activities of the various labs and to provide examples of successful teaching methods involving the affective domain. We welcome contributions.

4. Provide inexpensive reprints of materials selected to aid teachers and educators implement humanism in education. Now available are:

	Cost
A. Bill Bridges' paper describing the Education Network concept and presenting introductory exercises.	$0.50
B. Paper Dragon #1 Essays by teachers on how they have humanized their classrooms.	1.00
C. Paper Dragon #4 An annotated bibliography of books, tapes, and films relevent to humanistic education.	2.00

5. Developing and up-dating listings and program descriptions of colleges and universities which are humanistically oriented or are moving in that direction. The 1973 listing is available for $1.00. Please send a complete description of any that you know of.

6. Support humanistic education by providing validating information (studies, films, testimonials, or ?) and by gaining exposure in educational journals and conferences. Please send any information to help.

This summarizes the present stage of development of the AHP Education Network. It is an infant now; as it grows in scope and vitality it will lend increasing support and opportunity for growth to educators during this age of educational transition.

Membership in the Education Network is free; write the AHP office, 416 Hoffman Avenue, San Francisco, California 94114, to be put on the mailing list.

YOUTH LIBERATION

2007 Washtenaw Ave.
Ann Arbor, Mich. 48104
(313) 662-1867

CHIPS, the Cooperative High School Independent Press Syndicate, will be active again in 1973. The purpose of CHIPS is to help students who have started high school underground papers. Members can participate in the newspaper exchange which allows them to see copies of other papers from around the country. To do this, each month a paper sends 50 copies of its current issue, and in return, we will send copies of all the papers we received that month. Send papers and requests for more information to --
CHIPS, 2007 Washtenaw Ave.
Ann Arbor, Michigan 48104

School got you down?

Then bring it down. A group called Youth Liberation has a packet of pamphlets (incl. How to Start an Underground Paper and Student and Youth Organizing Manual), buttons, and 5 sample high school underground papers. All for only $2. Write to Youth Liberation, 2007 Washtenaw Ave., Ann Arbor, Michigan 48104.

DROPOUT PROPAGANDA A HOAX

(FPS) A study by the University of Michigan's Institute for Social Research challenges the widely held belief that dropping out of high school makes it harder for young people to find jobs. Most problems a dropout faces later in life, the study contends, are problems that exist at the time he leaves school, and "there's little proof that dropping out makes matters worse."

The study calls the media campaign to discourage dropping out "highly deceptive" and says the publicity may actually hurt the dropout. "One of the side effects of downgrading the status of dropouts may be to encourage employers to make the diploma a requirement when it need not be," the report says.

fps the high school news service

What is it?

FPS (the letters, contrary to popular opinion, do not stand for Fuck Publik Skool) is a tri-weekly news service published by Youth Liberation. Since its inception in September, 1970, twenty-six issues have gone to press.

The purpose of the news service is to provide news and graphics to high school papers, both official school newspapers and underground ones, and other articles of interest to students and young people. FPS also prints information to help high school organizers and articles discussing youth related and national issues.

How to Subscribe

A one year subscription to FPS, which is 13 issues, costs $5 for movement groups and youth, $8 for other people, and $12 for institutions. Sample copies may be obtained for 25 cents. Send to Youth Liberation/FPS
2007 Washtenaw Ave
Ann Arbor, Mich. 48104
Make checks to *Youth Liberation*

RED WAGON GANG IS NABBED

DETROIT (FPS) The Milk Chute Gang and its little red get-away wagon have been apprehended, according to police who say they arrested four young people who have allegedly broken into 37 Detroit homes - via milk chutes - since September.

The four boys, aged 10 to 13, would haul away their loot, including radios, rings, watches, and an electric saw, in a red wagon, juvenile officers said.

Only $200 of goods has been recovered of the $900 stolen, police said, including 52 cents in cash.

The boys would knock on a door, and if no one answered, one would crawl into the house through the milk chute and open the door for his comrades, police said.

Youth Liberation Materials

Pamphlets

Student and Youth Organizing (92 pages).........$.50
Major Court Decisions Regarding the Rights of Students and Youth (26 pages).........$.25
Teaching Rebellion at Union Springs (26 pages)..$.25
How to Start a High School Underground Paper (18 pages)...............................$.25
White House Conference on Youth (42 pages)......$.35

Directory

of high school/junior high school independent and underground papers, including information about how to get subscriptions and sample copies.......................................$.25

Sample Packet

of ten high school underground papers..........$1.00

Reprints

Booklet containing reprints of about 10 FPS articles from old issues, approximately 40 pages.......................................$.50

Subscription

One year subscriptions to FPS
for movement groups and youth.............$5.00
for other people..........................$8.00
for institutions.........................$12.00

Buttons

"Youth Liberation" (3 colors)...................$.25
"Power to Young People" (3 colors).............$.25

TEACHERS AND WRITERS COLLABORATIVE

Teachers and Writers Collaborative brings together writers, teachers and students for the purpose of creating a curriculum which is relevant to the lives of children today. We believe that writers and teachers working together can encourage children to create their own literature from their own language, experience and imagination. The Collaborative places professional writers in classrooms to work on a regular basis with interested teachers. The writers maintain detailed diaries of their work there, and these diaries, along with the works of the students, become the raw materials for the project's publications - newsletters, curriculum materials, anthologies. We particularly hope that other teachers may find in our materials some ideas that will be of use to them in classrooms. Toward that same end we have conducted formal and informal workshops for teachers since the inception of the program.

Anyone interested in writing poetry or in teaching others of any age to write poetry should joint *Teachers & Writers Collaborative*. They issue a quarterly "newletter" that is a 120-page

collection of highly original and creative ideas for teaching poetry. A subscription is $5.00 for four issues. Back issues of the newsletter are available at $1 each. Items on this page are taken from past issues of the newsletter.
Subscription from:

TEACHERS AND WRITERS COLLABORATIVE
C/O P.S. 3
490 Hudson Street
New York, N. Y. 10014
(212) 691-6590

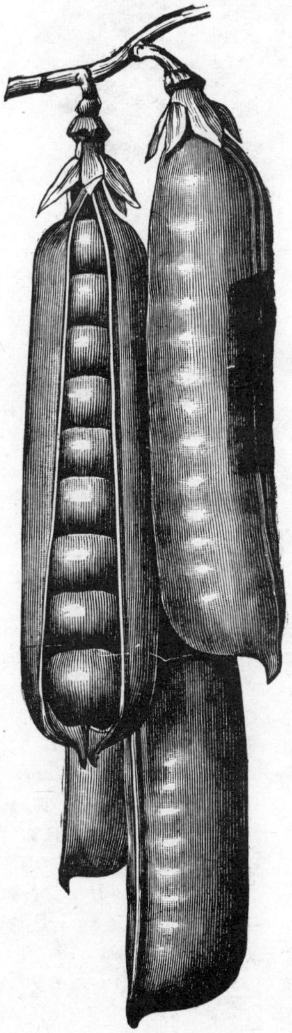

BLUES AND BLUELETS

The Blues are a great source for poetry, a poetry of intense, direct feelings. The best blues don't waste words. Much of popular music, movies and TV portrays the most vague and romanticized versions of love and suffering---at times, we need music like the blues to say those emotions explicitly, to confront our deepest feelings.

If you're using contemporary rock music as a source of poetry, or a stimulus to writing, with teenagers, mix in some timeless blues---records by Blind Lemon Jefferson, Billie Holliday, Bessie Smith, B.B. King, Albert King, Sonny Boy Williamson and Sonny Terry and Brownee McGee. Two of the best books on the blues are Samuel Charters' THE POETRY OF THE BLUES (Oak Publications) and Leroi Jones' BLUES PEOPLE.

Art Berger: "I developed a simple form for a mini-blues---three lines with a 4-4-6 beat called a <u>bluelet</u> and a four-liner with a 6-4-4-4 beat called a <u>rocku</u>. Using words with a jazz sound and a basic blues beat I asked the class to write their own personal message in this form."

Like most professional writers, children sometimes clutch when confronted with the blank page, and need something from outside to get their imaginations going. Many of the following ideas have long been standard creative writing procedures---others are fairly new---but all are addressed to the need, at times, for catalysts and surprises in the classroom.

SENTENCE EXPANSIONS and CONTRACTIONS

This and the other two games described on this page are half-quoted, half-paraphrased from an article by Tony Kallet, "Fun and Games with the English Language" (OUTLOOK, pub. Mountain View Center for Environmental Education, Univ. of Colorado, Boulder 80302). The games are difficult, but useful.

Begin with any sentence. Expand or contract that sentence by replacing words at the rate of, say, two words for every one. Thus "The dog ran quickly" could become "The pink tiger ran quickly;" and then "The pink tiger ate pancakes quickly" and so on until every word has been replaced by two. Here's a sample contraction from Kallet's article, which kidnaps words and sense in two's.

Six sad sheep sat
silently mourning
the midnight moon.

Slippery sheep sat
silently mourning
the midnight moon.

Slippery sheep sat
silently mourning
the dawn.

Rupert sat silently
mourning the dawn.

Stop mourning the dawn.

Behold the dawn!

Behold Jello!

Oops!

SUBSTITUTIONS

For any word in a sentence, anything may be substituted as long as the "sentenceness" is kept inviolate; i. e., as long as the parts of speech stay the same through the word changes. This is a good way to show how syntactical form is constant, no matter how the content changes. You can even use made-up words, as in "Twas brillig and the slithy toves" from ALICE IN WONDERLAND. (Kallet)

ARRANGING WORDS

Especially useful in suggesting some of the features of words which determine their positions in sentences. Write down a fairly straightforward sentence (no capital letters), cut it up into individual words, tell the player that there are six words, say, and give him one word. Ask him to write down what he thinks your sentence is. Give him a second and ask him to place it where he thinks it goes in relation to the first word. Give him all the words one at a time, having him revise his sentence as he goes. What he comes up with may make no sense at all, though he will have made it correct, grammatically. Or he might have a plausible sentence, but not yours. Or he might have yours. (Kallet)

WRITING TO MUSIC

Anything goes, depending on the teacher's individual tastes. It helps to choose a piece because you love it, rather than because it would seem to make good "program music," since kids pick up quickly on excitement or contempt. The writing might be anything—a dream, a memory, stream-of-consciousness, monster stories evoked by contemporary electronic music.

TOUCHING, SMELLING, TASTING

Set out on the desk a battery of things with interesting surfaces to be touched by a blindfolded child.

Make it clear that the point is not to try to identify the object, but to say what it feels like, what it makes him think of or remember.

Encourage him to search for many associations, unusual "synaesthetic" descriptions—crossings-over from one sense to another, such as "this grater feels like my dog barking."

The same can be done with tasting, by pushing words like sweet and sour into greater concreteness, or with a series of smells.

With all these the blindfold (or eyes shut) makes a difference: it prevents distraction and enforces concentration of the essences of the things at hand.

This can be viewed as an exercise in metaphor, complete in itself, or used as a jumping-off place for writing about memory.

(Rosellen Brown)

WRITING TO PICTURES

Using magazines such as Life, Ebony, National Geographic, etc., pick out interesting photos, minus captions, give them to the kids, and ask them to write a poem or story to accompany the picture (i.e., what's going on?).

Reproductions of modern art, and especially personal photographs—families, vacations, portraits, —might be useful too.

INTERNATIONAL SOCIETY FOR GENERAL SEMANTICS

International Society for General Semantics is an organization that provides materials for teachers about semantics and communication. A catalog of materials and membership information is free from:

> INTERNATIONAL SOCIETY FOR
> GENERAL SEMANTICS
> Post Office Box 2469
> San Francisco, Calif. 94126

When it's a

QUESTION OF SEMANTICS

this BOOKLET can help students find answers--

"What everyone should know ABOUT SEMANTICS" is an ideal introduction to the study of meaning in language. The study of semantics is so closely interwoven with every subject area that every student should have a knowledge of the subject.

16 pages, 8½" x 11"
2 COLORS

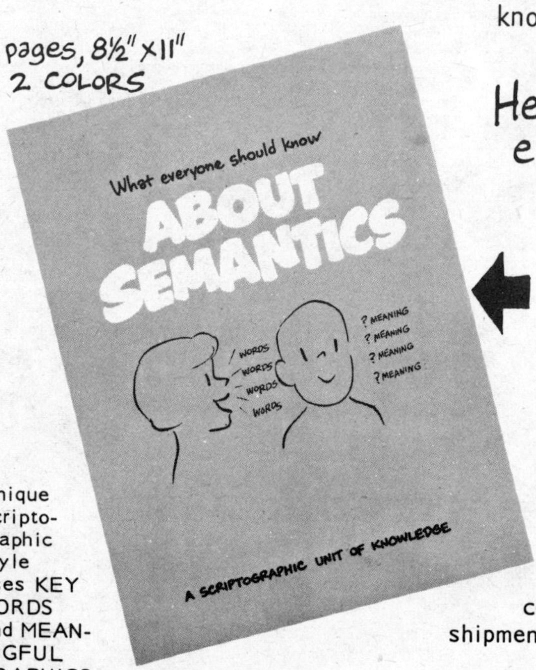

Unique scriptographic style uses KEY WORDS and MEANINGFUL GRAPHICS to make learning easier!

Here are the elements covered:

- verbal and non-verbal language
- levels of abstraction (why they are important)
- semantics and logic
- semantics and propaganda
- how grammar affects semantics
- comprehensive reading list

PLUS MUCH MORE!

This BEST SELLER can be used as part of every English course. Available for immediate shipment at these low quantity prices:

PRICES:

1 to 74	$1.00 ea.
75 to 199	.80 ea.
200 to 399	.60 ea.
400 to 1,199	.40 ea.

f.o.b. San Francisco, Calif.

COMMUNICATIONS, The Transfer of Meaning
by Don Fabun
Illustrated in color, this popular introduction to the principles of general semantics and effective communication is being used in hundreds of high schools, colleges and universities, business and professional organizations, both in the United States and abroad.
Members of ISGS $1.00 Non-members $1.25

SENSE AND NONSENSE A Study in Human Communication
by Alfred Fleishman
Published in April of 1971, this 80-page, illustrated booklet is already being used in communication improvement programs in many corporations, schools, and in city, state and federal agencies.
(See ad on back cover for prices.)

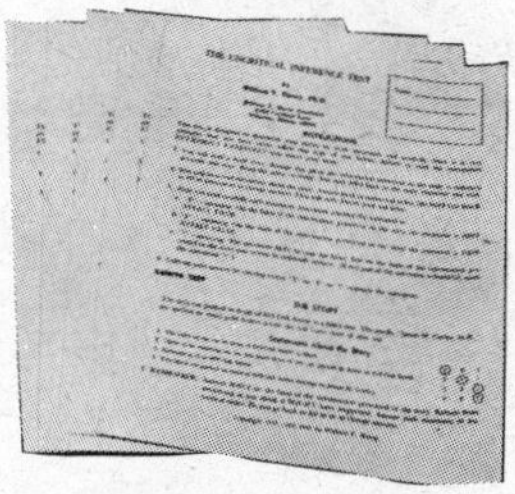

THE UNCRITICAL INFERENCE TEST by William V. Haney
Widely used in schools and business organizations, this test works as an effective *learning device.* It quickly makes students, employees and others taking it *aware* of their tendencies to jump to conclusions, to over-generalize and confuse inferences with factual information given. One answer sheet is furnished with each order of tests.
MINIMUM ORDER 5 TESTS. Price $ .25 per test.

HOW TO ATTEND A CONFERENCE by S. I. Hayakawa
First appearing in ETC., this 7-page article has been reprinted and over 100,000 copies distributed to conference-goers. Illustrated with drawings by William Schneider.
Members of ISGS $4.00 per hundred Non-members $5.00 per hundred

WHO IS SABOTAGING YOUR COMMUNICATION? by Alfred Fleishman
This five-page ETC. reprint, only recently made available, has already stimulated orders for thousands of additional copies. It is illustrated with drawings by William Schneider.
Members of ISGS $2.40 per hundred Non-members $3.00 per hundred

TEACHER'S GUIDE TO GENERAL SEMANTICS
by Catherine Minteer, Irene Kahn, J. Talbot Winchell
A general semantics guide to books, devices and materials for elementary, junior high, and senior high school teachers. Includes reports on the effects of teaching general semantics, basic lessons, and resource material.
Members of ISGS $1.60 Non-members $2.00

WORDS AND WHAT THEY DO TO YOU
by Catherine Minteer
A guide for presenting an introductory course in general semantics to junior and senior high school students. Recommended for teachers.
Members of ISGS $2.35 Non-members $2.95

THE LANGUAGES OF DISCOVERY
by Neil Postman and Howard Damon
A high school text suitable for either English or Speech courses. Considers language as a means of systematizing the world and focuses on the use of "different languages" for such purposes as scientific reports, fiction, news reports, fairy tales, prayers, etc.
Members of ISGS $4.80 Non-members $6.00

132 Organizations

Why Do We Jump to Conclusions?

by Sanford Berman

The instructional manual to help correct habits of over-generalizing and of making fact-inference confusions.

An excellent training follow-up for THE UNCRITICAL INFERENCE TEST (see page 3). This book gives exercises and presents in detail ways to distinguish between factual and inferential statements; it also includes sections on Assumptions of Certainty, Assumptions of Probability, and the Proper Use of Inferences.

Order this book, the test and answer sheet for **$1.50**

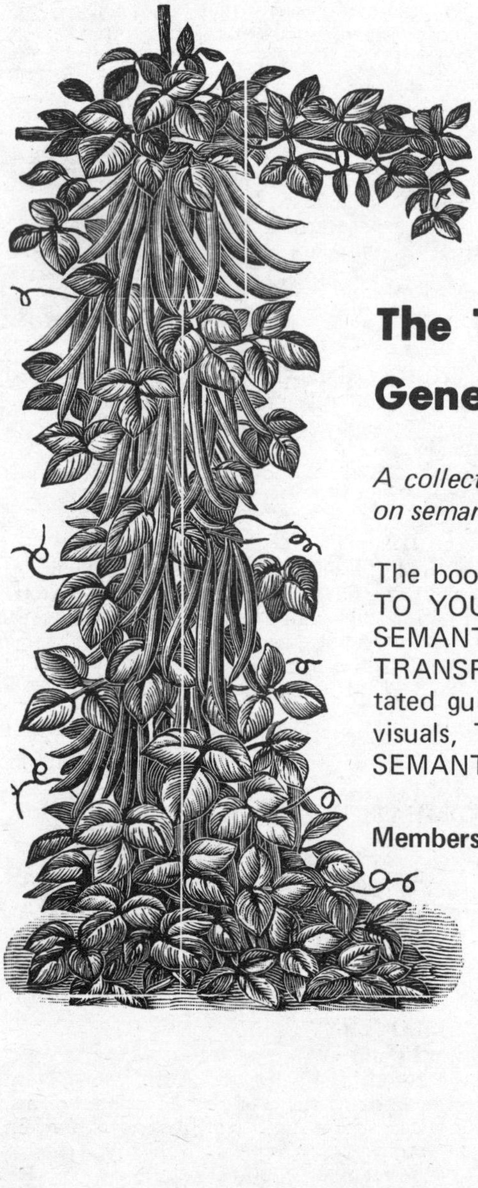

The Teacher's Kit on General Semantics

A collection of best-selling teaching materials on semantics which includes:

The book, WORDS AND WHAT THEY DO TO YOU; two illustrated booklets, ABOUT SEMANTICS and COMMUNICATIONS: THE TRANSFER OF MEANING; and an annotated guide to other publications and audio-visuals, TEACHERS GUIDE TO GENERAL SEMANTICS.

Members of ISGS $5.40 Non-members $6.75

WORKSHOP FOR LEARNING THINGS

The *Workshop for Learning Things* produces classroom materials especially for primary and elementary education. Their catalog is a must for those working with young children but is also useful to anyone in need of practical materials for working with groups on a limited budget. They have inexpensive photography kits, instructions for making cardboard furniture and storage units, dome kits, stream tables, playground things and tools.

40-page catalog is 50¢ from:

WORKSHOP FOR LEARNING THINGS, INC.
5 Bridge Street
Watertown, Mass. 02172
(617) 926-3491

The Workshop's interest in photography in the classroom goes back a number of years now...to the time when we discovered how exciting photography is for children and how useful an activity it is for integrating the development of programs in math, science, social studies, art and language development.

The materials we suggest have been chosen--after thousands of trials in classrooms all over the country--for their usefulness in making photography interesting, easy, manageable and inexpensive in a classroom setting. With these materials, children will be able to take their own photographs, develop their film and make prints by the dozens...in ordinary classroom conditions (or outdoors) without room-darkening curtains or elaborate plumbing. The procedures are exciting and yet simple; rich in new experiences yet quite down to earth. The Camera Cookbook gives a clear, running account of how it all works.

WHY PHOTOGRAPHY ?

Many teachers find life in the classroom full already--there never seems to be time for everything--so it seems fair enough to ask "why photography?"

Part of the answer is that, in our time, full literacy is a complex achievement...it requires a familiarity and interest in many literatures...the literature of books certainly...but also the literature of photographs and cinema, television and the arts. It involves getting to know and love The Little Prince...and Lartigue's photographs of his family and Houston's African Queen as well. In this context, photographs and the skills of the photographer have a place in the classroom analogous to that of books and reading skills.

Another part of the answer lies in photography's usefulness to the teacher and the child. Having cameras in a classroom is a catalytic activity...an activity, with a high interest of its own, that often makes other classroom activities (reading, social studies, science, etc.) more interesting as well. It usually begins as a group affair...the whole class learns to use cameras, develop film and make prints. After this first experience, it can become a highly individualized activity...children use the materials when they need to, with little supervision by the teacher. At that point, photography has become a real and useful tool for children in their work...as well as fun. It has also provided a structure for children's need to work by themselves.

THE CAMERA COOKBOOK BA003-3 $2.00

This is a basic recipe book for using photography in the classroom. The approach is "how-to-do-it-step-by-step." The book explains each of the materials in our photography kits and has, as well, many hints about classroom management of this lively activity. Complete instructions on mixing chemicals, developing and printing are also included.

IT'S SO SIMPLE: CLICK AND PRINT BA004-3 $1.25

This book was written for us by a sixth grade class in a nearby school. They got very excited by their work in photography and volunteered to write a book telling others how to do it. The writing, photographs, drawings, book design and layout were done entirely by the kids. They also supervised its printing and binding. Click and Print is a nice example of the sort of deep involvement of children that photography in the classroom can promote.

3 CAMERA KIT
PA100-3 10 lb. $27.50

3 cameras
6 rolls of film
1 developing tank
1 changing bag
1 can developer, to make 2 gallons
1 bag hypo-fixer, to make 2 gallons
3 glass sandwiches
1 pkg. Studio Proof paper (25 sheets 4 X 5")
1 The Camera Cookbook

6 CAMERA KIT
PA200-3 20 lb. $59.50

6 cameras
18 rolls of film
2 developing tanks
2 changing bags
1 can developer, to make 2 gallons
1 bag hypo-fixer, to make 2 gallons
6 glass sandwiches
1 pint peroxide
1 pkg. Blueprint paper (25 sheets 8 X 10")
1 pkg. Studio Proof paper (25 sheets 8 X 10")
1 pkg. Repro-negative paper (25 sheets 5 X 8")
1 The Camera Cookbook

35 CAMERA KIT
PA300-3 64 lb. $227.50

35 cameras
100 rolls of film
7 developing tanks
7 changing bags
2 cans developer, to make 4 gallons
2 bags hypo-fixer, to make 4 gallons
6 plastic pails
10 absorbent trays
50 clothespins
1 pkg. sponges
1 roll twine
15 glass sandwiches
1 roll masking tape
2 pints peroxide
1 pkg. Blueprint paper (25 sheets 8 X 10")
1 pkg. Studio Proof paper (25 sheets 8 X 10")
1 pkg. Repro-negative paper (25 sheets 5 X 8")
3 The Camera Cookbook

BOOKS ABOUT CARDBOARD CARPENTRY

CARDBOARD CARPENTRY WORKSHOP
BA001-3 $2.00

A few summers back, we had a chance to invite a group of school people to come to the Workshop and join in a several week session of designing and building with Tri-Wall. This book is the record of what we did and what we learned. Lots of drawings and photographs. 36 pages.

THE FURTHER ADVENTURES OF CARDBOARD CARPENTRY
BA002-3 $3.00

This is our most recent book on Cardboard Carpentry ...the best from all previous publications and lots of recent ideas as well. It's a combination of writings, drawings, plans and photographs ...detailed enough to be useful to those getting started and suggestive to experienced hands as well. 72 pages, approximately 300 drawings and photographs.

Dome!

If you want a bigger structure, use 6 panels in each tier. If it's an outdoor dome, and you want to weatherproof it, swathe it with thin polyethylene sheeting. Cut any window holes you like. Plastic screening could be used. Don't forget a smoke hole in the top if you want a campfire.

DOME KIT
CA900-3 10 lb. $22.00

35 threaded dowels
70 nuts
2 wrenches
1 corner folder
1 3/4" hole cutter

THREADED DOWELS CA055-3 5 lb. 35 for $5.25
3/4" X 4" threaded wooden dowel pieces: the bolts.

NUTS CA054-3 3 lb. 70 for $7.00
Threaded 3/4" nuts to fit the threaded dowels.

WRENCH CA053-3 2 lb. 2 for $1.60
Made of wood for tightening 3/4" nuts.

CORNER FOLDER CA052-3 5 lb. $4.50

3/4" HOLE CUTTER CA013-3 1 lb. $4.50

LEARNING EXCHANGE NETWORKS

Free Learning Exchange
c/o Paul Knatz
305 Riverside Drive, Apt. 7-E
New York, NY 10025

Peer Matching-Learning Experience
Catalogue
6421 Pitt Street
West Vancouver, B.C.
Canada

Campus-Free College
Central Office
466 Commonwealth Avenue
Boston, MA 02215
(617) 262-7226

Opening Networks
613 Winans Way
Baltimore, MD 21229

Peoples Resource Directory
University for Man
615 Fairchild Terrace
Manhattan, KS 66512

The Learning Exchange
Rob Schachter & others
303 Sunset Place, W. Apt. E
DeKalb, IL 601115

Learning Exchange
Project One
1380 Howard Street
San Francisco, CA 94103

To Learn.....To Teach
c/o Action Studies Program
303 Jefferson Building
Iowa City, IA 52240

Education Exploration Center
1304 16th Avenue South
Minneapolis, MN 55407

Evanston Learning Exchange
828 Davis Street
Evanston, IL 60201

Free Learning Exchange
c/o Dave Minkler
University of Virginia
Charlottesville, VA 22903

The Learning Network
c/o New School Movement
Earth Station 2
402 15th Avenue, E.
Seattle, WA 98105

Learning Resource Exchange
4552 McPherson
St. Louis, MO 63108

Chico Learning Exchange
PO Box 3305
Chico, CA 95926

Idea Exchange
Education Association, Inc.
Upward Bound
171 Massachussetts Avenue
Washington, DC 20002

Network for Better Education
c/o Ed Wynne, Box 4348
College of Education
University of Illinois
At Chicago Circle
Chicago, IL 60680

New Schools Switchboard
319 East 25th Street
Baltimore, MD 21218

Program for Study of the
Future in Education
School of Education
University of Massachusetts
Amherst, MA 01002

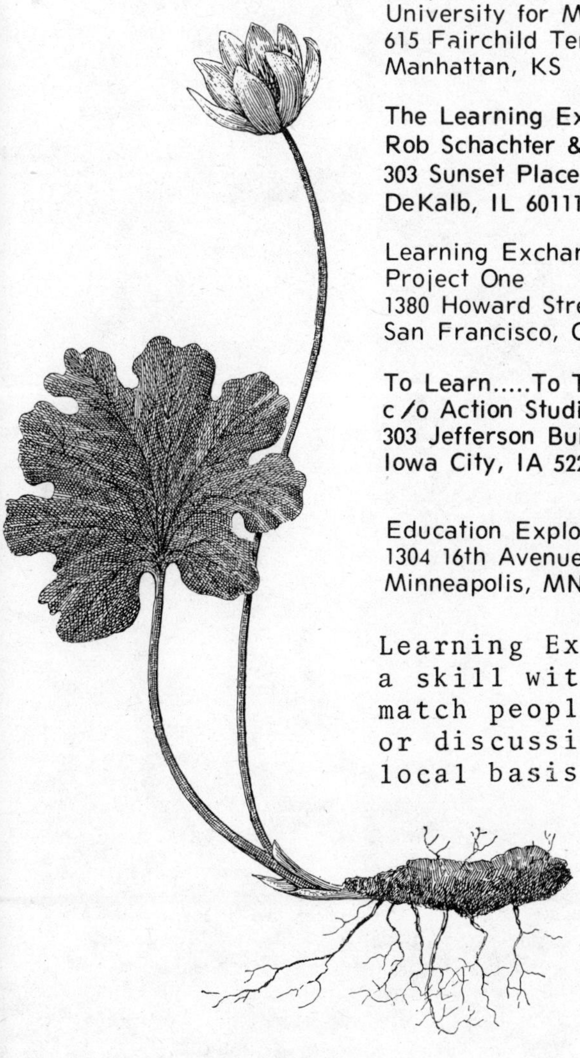

Learning Exchange Networks match people who want to learn a skill with those willing to teach that skill. They also match people of like interests and form groups for study or discussion on particular topics. They operate on a local basis only.

ZEPHYROS LEARNING EXCHANGE

The Zephyros Learning Exchange is a group of San Francisco teachers, parents, and artists who gather, create, publish, and distribute creative teaching ideas. Their aim is pre-high-school level, but many of the ideas are usable in high school and even college teaching. Ron Jones, a founder of Zephyros, sees the message of the exchange as the alternative system of distribution they have established. The following article explains a bit of the history of Zephyros and gives ideas so that others can start similar exchanges.

Zephyros makes materials available in huge newspaper-size publications called "Deschool Primers." The items on the following pages are taken from these "Deschool Primers" available from:

ZEPHROS MATERIAL EXCHANGE
1201 Stanyan Street
San Francisco, Calif. 94117

P.S. Please be patient they have a "new baby that loves to eat paper and crunch up letters."

How to write and publish your own "Dick and Jane"

Every year textbooks pop out of the publishers oven with new covers and new titles, but the content is always the same. They define learning in terms of divisible subject areas in which things like math and English never meet. They structure learning into steps and reading levels which insist upon a domino theory of knowledge. They encourage verbal skills and deductive paths of logic, yet avoid the use of intuition and imagination or contemplation and direct action as problem-solving tools.

Although these textbooks purport to be a universal guide to learning of great worth and importance—there is a single clue that points another direction. In the six years I taught in city and country schools—no one ever stole a textbook.

If textbooks don't respond to the questions you ask or the methods of learning you use, then it's up to you to commence writing your own histories, adventures, and inquiries into the world. Writing your own *Dick & Jane* can be a great deal of fun. It might even be informative.

The following is a true story about how a group of teachers, parents, kids, and friends wrote and distributed their own textbook. It all started a year ago in a San Francisco warehouse. Antioch West had established an urban campus along with Interaction Associates in a warehouse on 9th Street. This common meeting ground allowed teachers and students from every grade level to meet and share ideas. During one meeting, it became apparent that there was need for a workbook or guide that would use the city as a classroom. This workbook would have to include many disciplines, appeal to any age, and stress various methods of problem-solving as well as the answers. Such a text did not exist. We decided to make one.

We started by making a list of ideas that such a text might include. Our list eventually covered eight lengthy sheets of butcher paper. Every idea submitted was accepted and printed on the list. Once the list was complete to everyone's satisfaction, we lumped together ideas that seemed alike or supportive of each other. For example, ideas that used drawing or diagraming were placed in another category. As a result of this brainstorming and collecting process, we had the framework for our book and a title, *Your City Has Been Kidnapped.*

To test and extend our ideas we created 20 large posters. Each poster contained a specific theme for seeing and investigating the city. We took the posters to street corners, factories, and schools to encourage the passerby to comment on the ideas and add new ones. Within two months we had 43 posters, and more excitement than we could deal with. It was time to take one giant step forward and translate our posters into book form.

Printing a book starts by determining what words and images will appear on what size and number of pages in what order. In our case, we wanted to maintain the poster format so we settled on a large 11" x 15" page size. Once we decided the size of page it was a simple matter of filling the page with the ideas and images we had collected.

When we wanted to place words on the page we could type them out and paste them into place using rubber cement or write them directly onto the page using a black ink dispersed by a handy felt-tip pen or rapidograph or stamp them onto the page using a stencil or rubber stamp set.

When we wanted to place an illustration on a page we would create our own line drawing using black ink or cut an illustration from a newspaper or magazine and paste it into place or have a photograph halftoned (reduced to a dot pattern) and then glue the half-tone into position on the page.

By doing our own layout we experienced the enjoyment of translating ideas into visible forms. We learned to sparingly use rubber cement, keep a box of photographs and magazine illustrations, and use blue pencils to mark the boundaries of our pages. Most important of all, we learned that inexperienced individuals can design and prepare a book for printing.

Upon delivery of "camera ready copy" (our layout pages with all pictures, drawings, and words pasted in place), our printer invited us to watch the printing of our book. The printer made photographic plates from our copy, placed them on a WEB press, pushed a button and asked us for $1400. $1400 later we had five thousand copies of *Your City Has Been Kidnapped.* We had done it. Printed our own book. Now we had to sell some or move into a bigger house.

To our surprise the act of distributing our book became as exciting as its writing. Whereas textbook publishers rely on state adoptions, conventions, and a massive sales force, we decided to depend on our Volkswagen, postage stamps, and the classroom teacher.

Instead of filtering books down a funnel from the top, we planned to distribute our book from the bottom up. It was our hope that teachers would like our book, pass it around, and buy a copy. In June (quite late in the school year), we mailed out free to teachers two thousand copies of our city book. Our mailing list was a collection of friends, and local AFT, *Bartoc,* and Big Rock subscribers. We enclosed a letter saying

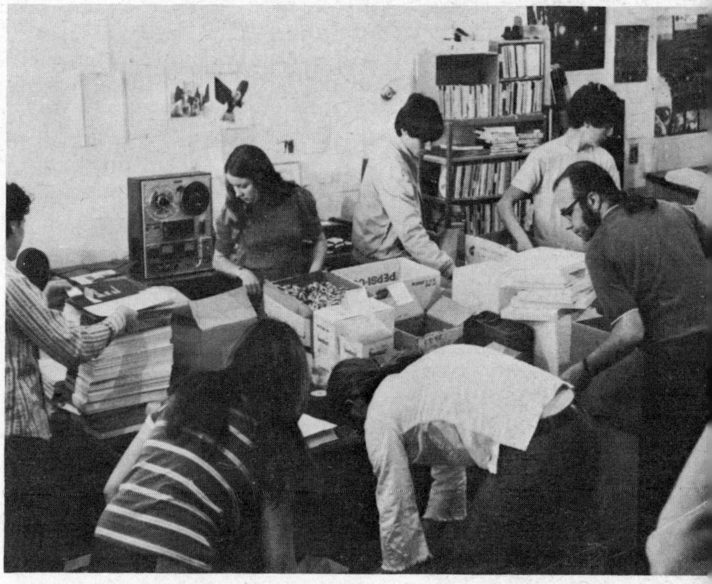

who we were and what we were doing. Within four months we sold the remaining three thousand copies of our book and prepared to complete another printing. The greatest sense of accomplishment, however, appeared in the thousands of letters people sent encouraging and thanking us for our effort. One letter particularly sticks in my mind. A brief note from an elementary school teacher in Chicago thanked us for the book and in closing mentioned that she needed another copy. Her children and then a parent and even a fellow teacher kept trying to steal her copy. At last a book worth stealing.

The Son of Dick and Jane
(or how to start your own materials exchange.)

The mail just keeps coming. Opening a daily tide of letters became an adventure in itself. Someone sent us a Wheaties box top and the local teachers association enrolled us in their tire buying club. Most of the letters were from parents, teachers, and kids describing how they used our book and what they thought about school. Sometimes we would get a delightful poem or love letter and always we would get encouragement. The letters came by the hundreds from every corner of the nation. Yes, there are good people in the biggest and smallest of places. And yes, they have ideas and experiences to share. We had sent our one hand crafted textbook and received enough material in return to compose 20 more.

To continue this exchange of ideas we decided to assemble a scrapbook of learning. Hopefully this scrapbook would be a convenient and inexpensive way for teachers to share their lesson plans with each other. It would be easy. We would assemble the various ideas sent to us into a scrapbook; have it printed on newsprint; and mail it to the contributors and others interested in its content. Like most scrapbooks it would contain memoribilia of classroom events, some photos of loved ones, and at least one vision of the future. It would be fun to look at and use. And like most scrapbooks, it would be for every age group. Most important of all, it would be incomplete. It could stretch in any direction and be used in a variety of ways.

Our first attempt at printing a scrapbook of learnings was called *De school Primer Number Four.* As a compendium of ideas it contained lessons in fantasy, comouflage, matrix games, plans for milk carton boats, recipes, rules for a capitalistic lunch and lots more. There were activities for theatre, photography, problem solving, art, magic, numbers, and even reading. When completed, this Primer looked like a supplement in the Sunday paper. The cost for printing such a paper was extremely low. In fact, to print ten thousand copies cost less than $800.

It was our intention to mail several thousand copies of the Primer free to teachers and hopefully sell the remainder to accrue enough money to print additional materials. To avoid the perils of becoming a big business we formed a non-profit collaborative managed by a teacher parent group called Zephyros. What had started as teachers writing their own text had merged with a larger group of parents and teachers organized to support each other in the formation of a materials exchange, people's computer center, kids teaching kids project, and store for open classroom materials. As a part of this non-profit education group, the materials exchange decided to tythe a percentage of any revenue to support other projects by local teachers. The exchange also determined to stay intentionally small. By remaining small, we could enjoy and personalize a service thereby avoiding the need for offices and purchase order mania. Most important of all, we wanted to demonstrate the feasibility of a small group of teachers actively exchanging and building their own learning tools.

On mailing our Primer we were stunned by the reaction. Through out the country, ad hoc groups of teachers and parents began to send us texts that they had assembled. One book from a parent group in New York was in the form of a report card evaluating their school. From *Teacher Works* in Portland, we received a box full of learning ideas. *Lollipop Power,* a womens collective in North Carolina sent us several books for pre-school children. The books that we received came in every size and format. They were about every conceivable topic. They often blended academic disciplines and were addressed to a variety of age groups. In viewing this collection of parent/teacher compositions I have a new fantasy about textbooks. It goes something like this. There is a group of people—Dick, Jane, Mother, Father and Spot. One day they come to life and decide to write their own guide to learning about the questions and needs they encounter in their local neighborhood. It's not a big book, and it's of little concern to schools of education, professional groups, or commercial publishers. But, it's an important book because it's the responsibility and creation of the people that will use it.

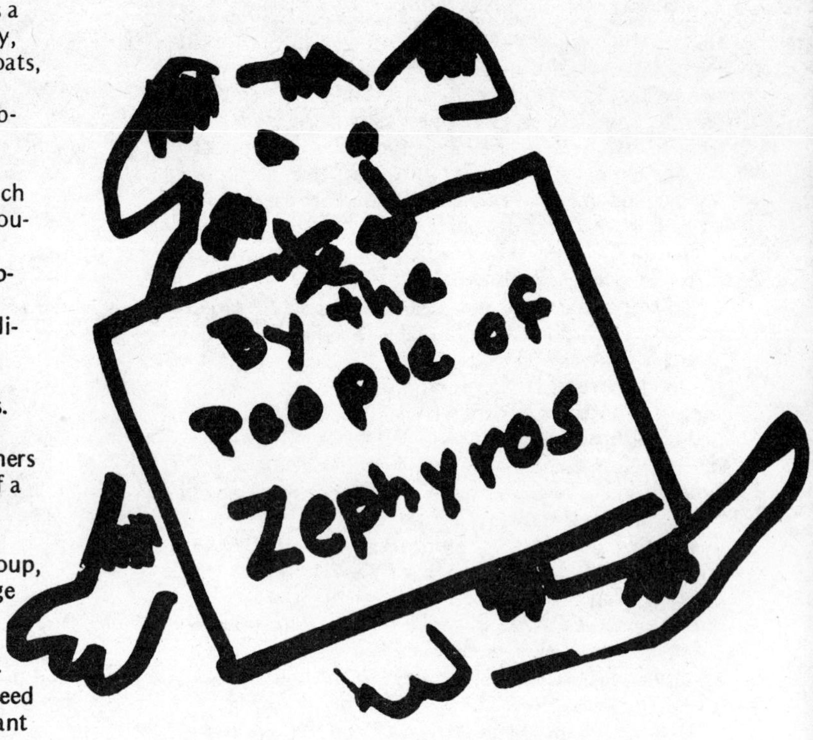

DESCHOOL PRIMER Nº2 FINDING COMMUNITY IS A GUIDE TO COMMUNITY RESEARCH & ACTION. THIS TEXT IS DESIGNED FOR USE AT THE HIGH SCHOOL OR UNIVERSITY LEVEL. ITS EXPENSIVE, SO YOU MIGHT WANT TO GET A COPY FROM A LOCAL LIBRARY. (217 PG.) COST $3.45 PER COPY.

DESCHOOL PRIMER Nº3 YOUR CITY HAS BEEN KIDNAPPED IS A COLLECTION OF TEACHING STRATEGIES THAT UTILIZE THE CITY AS A CLASSROOM. THESE IDEAS HAVE BEEN USED IN VARIOUS GRADE LEVELS FROM PRE-SCHOOL TO GRADUATE SCHOOL TO NO-SCHOOL. (64 PG) COST $1.50 PER COPY.

DESCHOOL PRIMER Nº4 [NO TITLE] IS A "NEWSBOOK" COLLECTION OF INVENTIVE GAMES, LESSON PLANS, & LEARNING EXPERIENCES FOR USE IN & OUT OF THE SCHOOL. (20 SUPER PGS.) COST $1.50 PER COPY.

DESCHOOL PRIMER Nº 5 A WHALE FOR SALE CONSISTS OF IDEAS FOR THE HOME LEARNER. CONTENTS OF THIS PRIMER INCLUDE HOW TO BUILD A FERRO CONCRETE PLAYGROUND, MASK MAKING, A BESTIARY, THE CREATIVE USE OF TRASH, AND MORE. THIS PRIMER IS DIRECTED AT THE HOME LEARNER. (40 PG.) COST $1.50 PER COPY.

DESCHOOL PRIMER Nº 6 A SCRAPBOOK OF LEARNINGS IS A COLLECTION OF COMMENTARIES & LESSON PLANS BY TEACHERS, PARENTS & ARTISTS. INCLUDED IN THIS PRIMER IS A 'TEST' TO EVALUATE "HOW YOU SOLVE PROBLEMS," IDEAS FOR A CHILD CARE CENTER, PLANS FOR CONDUCTING WOMEN'S THEATRE, A LOOK AT COMMUNIST CHINA BY TOURING BAY AREA TEACHERS, IMPRESSIONS OF A LEARNING FAIR A LESSON PLAN ON THE AMERICAN REVOLUTION, AND MORE. (128 PG) COST $3.50 PER COPY.

DESCHOOL PRIMER Nº 7 [NO TITLE] IS A "NEWSBOOK" COMPENDIUM OF IDEAS THAT TEACHERS HAVE SENT TO ZEPHYROS. (20 SUPER PGS) COST $1.50 PER COPY.

Making A Time Capsule

TO CONCLUDE A UNIT OF STUDY ON SOCIETY & CULTURE – I DIVIDED MY CLASS INTO 3 GROUPS & INSTRUCTED EACH GROUP TO MAKE UP A SOCIETY.

DAY 1-2 EACH GROUP MET FOR 2 DAYS TO DETERMINE THE COMPOSITION OF THEIR IMAGINED SOCIETY. ONCE EACH GROUP ESTABLISHED A WAY TO MAKE DECISIONS THEY WERE TO DESCRIBE THEIR SOCIETY IN TERMS OF WHEN IT EXISTED WHERE IT EXISTED ITS POPULATION, LANGUAGE, SOCIAL ARRANGEMENTS, RELIGIOUS BELIEFS, GOVERNMENT, ART FORMS, HISTORY, ETC.

DAY 3-5 EACH GROUP WAS THEN GIVEN THREE DAYS TO MAKE & PLACE ARTIFACTS OF THEIR IMAGINED SOCIETY INTO A TIME CAPSULE. THE TIME CAPSULE WAS THEN BURIED ALONG WITH OTHER "CLUES" DESCRIBING LIFE IN THEIR SOCIETY. CLUES MIGHT BE IN THE PLACEMENT OF THE CAPSULE BETWEEN STRATA OF DEBRIS OR IN NOTES/PRAYERS/WARNINGS/CHARMS/ETC. PLACED AROUND THE CAPSULE.

DAY 6-8 EACH GROUP CAREFULLY EXCAVATES A TIME CAPSULE (NOT THEIR OWN) GIVING SPECIAL ATTENTION TO THE STRATA IN WHICH THE CAPSULE IS FOUND & THE CLUES THAT EXIST IN & OUTSIDE THE CAPSULE. ON THE BASIS OF THESE CLUES THE "FINDERS" ATTEMPT TO ASSEMBLE A DEFINITION OF WHAT THE SOCIETY THAT MADE THE CAPSULE WAS LIKE."

DAY 9 EACH "FINDER GROUP" PRESENTS ITS CONCLUSIONS TO THE ENTIRE CLASS FOLLOWED BY A "PRESENTATION OF TRUTH" BY THE GROUP THAT MADE UP THE CAPSULE.

DAY 10 CLASS EXAMINATION OF THE PROCESS IT USED IN DESIGNING & INVESTIGATING IMAGINED SOCIETIES.

SOURCE: R. JONES

FOR A COMPLETE PROBLEM SOLVING UNIT ON CREATING SOCIETIES WRITE:
RICHARD F. HANALSHUL
FRANCIS W. PARKER SCHOOL
330 WEBSTER AVE.
CHICAGO, ILLINOIS 60614

HOW DO YOU FEEL ABOUT MONEY?

WANT TO FIND OUT?

MONEY$$

1. TAKE A GIVEN AMOUNT OF MONEY FROM EVERY STUDENT IN YOUR CLASS. (PENS, PURSES, SWEATERS ETC CAN BE USED IF STUDENTS ARE WITHOUT FUNDS) $
2. PLACE ALL THE MONEY INTO A HAT OR BOX. $
3. INFORM THE CLASS THAT THEY ARE TO DECIDE (WITHIN 1 HR.) WHO IN THE CLASS SHOULD RECEIVE ALL THE MONEY IN THE HAT. $
4. EVERYONE SHOULD HAVE A CHANCE TO EXPRESS WHY THEY WANT OR NEED THE MONEY. FOLLOWING THIS, A VOTE CAN BE TAKEN TO DECIDE WHO GETS THE MONEY. (IT HELPS TO GIVE EVERYONE TWO VOTES) $
5. ONCE A DECISION IS MADE THE MONEY SHOULD BE GIVEN TO THE PERSON CHOSEN BY THE CLASS. $
6. REVIEW THE INSIGHTS & VALUES EXPOSED BY THIS EXERCISE. $
   - THIS EXERCISE CAN ALSO BE DESIGNED TO GIVE CLASS FUNDS TO A CAUSE OR GROUP OUTSIDE THE CLASS.
   - THIS EXERCISE CAN ALSO BE USED TO DEMONSTRATE "TAXATION WITHOUT REPRESENTATION"

SOURCE: DAVID STEINBERG
R. JONES
AFSC

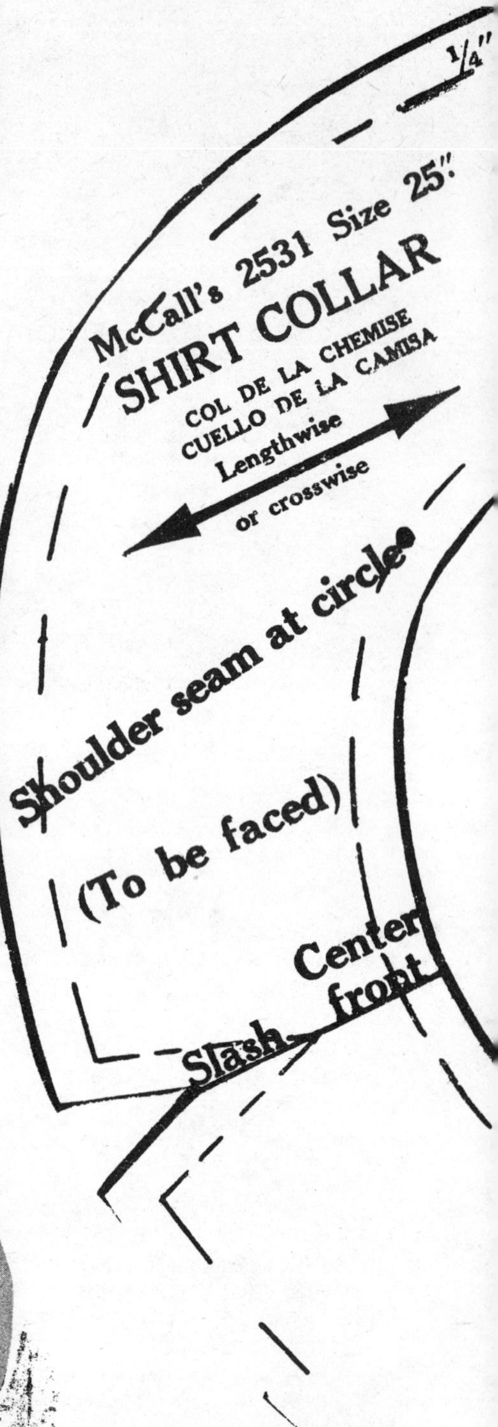

IF YOU HAD A PHONE IN YOUR CLASS, WHO WOULD YOU PHONE? WHO WOULD PHONE YOU?
HAVE YOU EVER CONDUCTED AN IDEA AUCTION? TRY IT!

SOME

PEOPLE GAMES

GIVE EACH STUDENT A PIECE OF A PUZZLE; THE TASK IS TO PUT THE PUZZLE TOGETHER. STUDENTS FIRST MUST MAKE UP THE COMMUNICATION RULES THEY WILL FOLLOW —(IE) "YOU CAN ONLY SPEAK TO THE PERSON SEATED ON YOUR RIGHT." ONCE THE COMMUNICATION RULE IS DETERMINED STUDENTS CAN TEST ITS EFFECTIVENESS BY TRYING TO SOLVE THE PUZZLE.

TRY THIS IN FORMING COMMUNITY IN THE CLASSROOM... STUDENTS ARE ASKED TO MAKE & WEAR A NAME TAG THAT IDENTIFIES SOMETHING THEY NEED. (IE) SECURITY, ATTENTION, SUCCESS, ETC. STUDENTS ARE THEN ASKED TO WALK AROUND THE ROOM & FIND SOMEONE WHO HAS A SIMILAR NEED. AFTER A WHILE THEY THEN ARE ASKED TO LIST THE RESOURCES THEY CAN OFFER AS PERSONS - THEY THEN HAD TO FIND OTHERS WHO MATCHED NEEDS & RESOURCES.... THIS BEGINNING OF IDENTIFICATION BECOMES THE BASIS FOR FURTHER GROUP/ COMMUNITY WORK.

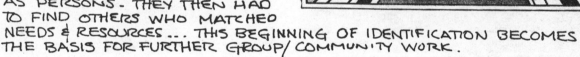

GIVE EACH PLAYER 2 CARDS. ASK EACH PLAYER TO WRITE ON THEIR CARD A FAVORITE SAYING, SLANG TERM, OR QUOTATION. COLLECT ALL OF THOSE CARDS, MIX THEM UP & PASS THEM OUT SO THAT NOBODY GETS THEIR OWN CARD BACK. ASK PLAYERS TO CUT PHOTOS FROM MAGAZINES THAT WILL MATCH THE SAYING. HAVE STUDENTS PASTE THAT PICTURE ON THEIR REMAINING 3"x5" CARD. WHEN THIS IS COMPLETE THEY HAVE TWO CHOICES TO MAKE AS A GROUP TO CHOOSE BETWEEN FINDING THE PERSON WHO WROTE THE SAYING & SHOW THEM THE PICTURE THEY CUT OUT OR COLLECT ALL THE CARDS & TRY TO MATCH THEM AS A GROUP. IF THEY PICK SEEKING OUT THE WRITER, THE GAME STOPS THERE, BUT IF THEY DECIDE TO COLLECT THE CARDS THEY HAVE THE SECOND CHOICE TO MAKE. THEY CAN EACH GET THEIR WRITTEN CARD & THEN TRY TO FIND THE MATCHING PICTURE OR THE CARDS ARE MIXED UP IN TWO SEPARATE DECKS & THEY GET A PICTURE CARD & A WRITTEN CARD. THEY THEN TRY TO BE THE FIRST ONE TO MATCH THEIR DELT CARDS. THE PLAYERS DECIDE BY VOTE IF THE CARDS MATCH.

(SOURCE: JOHN WASHBURN)

FOOT PRINTS

WHAT KIND OF FOOT PRINTS CAN YOU FIND?
CONSIDER ALL SURFACES AND MARKINGS. (IE FLOORS, CEILINGS, WALLS, LAND SURFACES, THE SKY, ETC.)

MAKE A SKETCH OR IMPRESSION OF THE MOST INTERESTING FOOTPRINT YOU CAN FIND.

HOW WOULD YOU CHARACTERIZE THE ANIMAL (OR THING) THAT MADE THIS FOOTPRINT.

DRAW A PICTURE OF IT.
RECONSTRUCT A THREE DIMENSIONAL IMAGE.
BRING IN OBJECTS THAT WOULD MAKE UP ITS HOME ENVIRONMENT.
DOES THIS SPECIES EXIST IN LARGE NUMBERS?
WHAT CIRCUMSTANCES WOULD INHIBIT THIS SPECIES GROWTH?
IN WHAT CONDITIONS WOULD THIS SPECIES MULTIPLY?
WHERE IS THE HOME OF THIS SPECIES?
IS THIS SPECIES A THREAT TO THE EXISTENCE OF HUMAN BEINGS?

CAN YOU FIND THE FOOTPRINT OF AN EXTINCT SPECIES?

TEACHER WORKS IN A BOX

Teacher Works, Inc., is a non-profit, tax-exempt corporation, established in May, 1971 by five Portland area teachers. The purpose of Teacher Works is to help teachers help themselves become better teachers by providing information and assistance in dealing with practical classroom problems. We want to put teachers in touch with each other, to share ideas, curricular materials, and various approaches to instruction. In a sense, Teacher Works is offering a continuing educational process for teachers; the major difference between Teacher Works and already established teacher training institutions is that in our programs the teacher is an active participant in his/her training and renewal, instead of having it "done" to him/her by someone removed from the realities of classroom teaching.

Teacher Works is not funded by lots of outside money. In order to maintain our teacher drop-in center and meeting place, a large house in northeast Portland, and to initiate a series of workshops and activities for teachers, we are soliciting memberships in Teacher Works.

We are offering the first in a series of boxes of teacher-designed and teacher-tested materials as an incentive for membership in Teacher Works. "Teacher Works in a Box" (disguised as a tube this first time) contains a Deschooling Primer from Zephyrus, full of practical classroom suggestions; the October, 1972 issue of the Teacher Paper; a five part series on problem-solving for kids; posters; group process materials; the Nacirema; geography lessons; elementary classroom lessons; culture; non-sexist lessons to raise everyone's consciousness level; and maybe even more . . .

Membership in Teacher Works, Inc. is $10.00 per year. Student and institutional rates are available upon request. This fee also entitles you to admission to Teacher Works parties during the year and access to other activities. It also helps us raise enough capital to do some exciting and educational things for and with teachers. To join Teacher Works, Inc. and to receive your very own "Teacher Works in a Box" send your name, address & school/position/other. Please make checks payable to: Teacher Works, Inc. 2136 NE 20th Ave. Portland, OR 97212.

CULTURAL ANTHROPOLOGY & INDIVIDUAL STUDY PROJECTS

1. Listen to a radio station consistently. Note the variation in cultural information, such as values, customs, tastes, kinds of ads. Describe the kinds of music, ads, news, talk shows, and community announcements.

2. Do the same as the above, but compare two stations.

3. Do the same as the above, but with TV stations.

4. Watch "Sesame Street." Do subcultures exist on this program? Do you feel there is an attempt to break down cultural differences on the program? Explain.

5. Do research in the library on 2 or 3 cultures that differ from ours. Write an essay describing in detail what confiicts you see in their value systems.

6. Investigate at least 3 ethnic groups or subcultures in the U.S. today (blacks, Indians, Chicanos, etc.) Write a detailed essay pointing out the differences in value systems, customs, traditions, taboos, rituals, etc., between the groups.

7. Interview five of your friends and report on what variations you find in how they and their families celebrate the same cultural event.

8. Report on the rituals, taboos, etc., associated with a sport such as baseball.

9. How many hours a week do you spend doing each of the following?
   a) watching TV
   b) listening to the radio
   c) reading
   d) talking on the phone
   e) sleeping
   f) eating
   g) socializing
   h) loafing

10. Create a visual representation of your understanding of our culture.

11. What rituals are you going through to reach full status in our culture?

12. What taboos exist in our culture? How are they enforced?

13. Do teenagers in the U.S. represent a subculture? Give reasons for your answer.

14. Discuss American dating habits as an anthropologist would. If there are differences for different groups, note them. Include the purposes and methods of dating.

15. Make up your own project.

FREEDOM

"...but before I'll be a slave,
I'll be buried in my grave..."

This is a line from an old spiritual. What would make a man say that he would prefer to die than be a slave? Would you say that yourself, if you were in the position of being made a slave? What does being a slave to another person do to your own personality? Is it possible to have only your body enslaved but not your mind? How could you keep your mind from being enslaved?

There are different kinds of slavery. Are you a slave right now?

--to what person?

--to which institution?

--can you see yourself ever being <u>completely</u> free?

If so, how do you get out of the kind of slavery you're in now in order to reach that freedom? If not, what or who will keep you enslaved, and why can't you become free?

"...we'd rather die on our feet
than be living on our knees."

--James Brown
"Say It Loud (I'm Black and I'm Proud)"

TIME CAPSULE EXERCISE

SETTING: You are a member of a committee of scholars who will be working to develop a list of items to be put in an American Time Capsule. These items are to reflect the American political and social system at this time -- 1973. The Capsule is approximately 2 feet in diameter and 10 feet long. It is to be opened 5000 years from now. What should be included in it?

DIRECTIONS:

1. Individually make your list of items to be put in the capsule. List your reason for including each item.
2. In small group, decide which ten items should be selected, IN ORDER OF IMPORTANCE!

YOUR LIST: REASON:

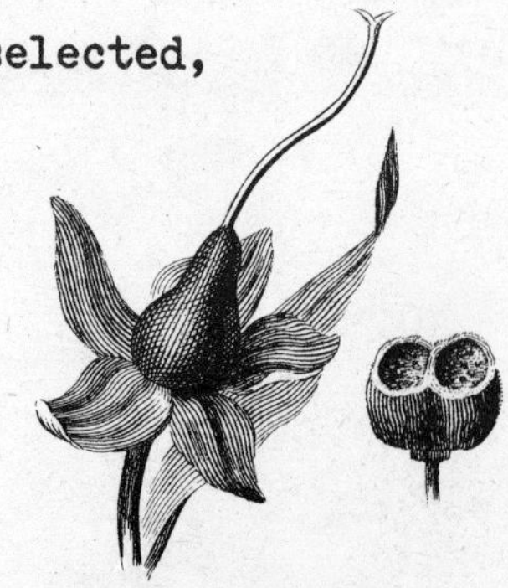

THE <u>CLASS</u> LIST (in order of importance):

SHOP THE OTHER AMERICA

Shop the Other America is a mail-order catalog of goods made by the poor engaged in self-help. Most of the products offered--jeans, toys, clothes, art supplies, handbags-- are made by Community Development Corporations. These CDC's are ghetto- and rural-based self-help organizations which provide community services and spawn economic development.

Shop the Other America is not a "buy a pencil from a blind man operation." STOA serves as a way to link education with action for a large, white, middle-class constituency. Through STOA consumers are made more aware of where their money is going. The act of giving money and getting a product becomes more than just the unconscious exchange of money for goods. It becomes a conscious act of supporting social justice. It lets people know there are alternative ways to buy--ways that are nonexploitative and beneficial to those who need support.

SHOP THE OTHER AMERICA
25¢ from:
New World Coalition
419 Boylston St., Room 209
Boston, Mass. 02116
(617) 266-6120

NO. 5 JAVA PRINT DASHIKI - Men's: S-M-L **$14.95**

NO. 1 AFRICAN PRINT DASHIKI - Men's: S-M-L. **$11.95**
NO. 2 AFRICAN PRINT SHORT DASHIKI DRESS - Women's: S-M-L **$11.95**

NO. 3 AFRICAN PRINT FLOOR LENGTH DASHIKI DRESS - Women's: S-M-L **$17.95**

On items No. 1 thru No. 3 please specify:
a) reddish-brown tones
b) olive green tones
c) no preference - I like every color.

NO. 4 JAVA PRINT FLOOR LENGTH DASHIKI DRESS - Women's: S-M-L **$21.95**
On items No 4 and No. 5, please specify:

a) black-green
b) beige-wine
c) orange-green
d) blue-red
e) no preference - I like every color.

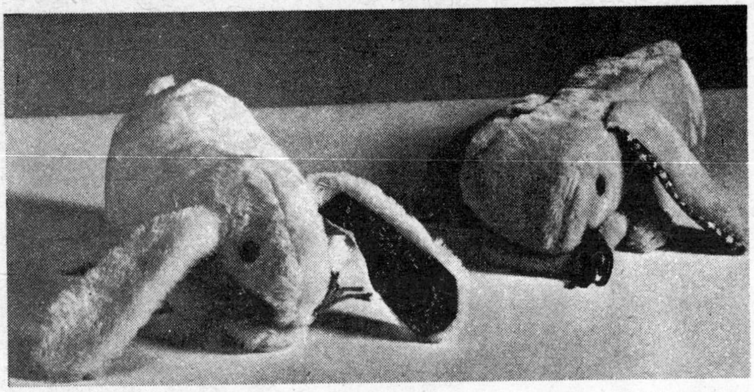

The mountain people who make these toys have a pride in themselves and in their craftsmanship which is amply exhibited in the quality of the entire Possum Trot Collection. They work together with imaginative designers who have adapted their creative genius to the requirements of this method of production.

006 RABBIT PUPPET - Gold plush-cotton print Dacron Polyester stuffing, hand washable - $10.00.

by Coburn Everdell.

POPULAR CULTURE LECTURES

AMERICAN DREAM, AMERICAN NIGHTMARE: THE EVOLUTION OF AN IDEA. A description of American arts and artifacts demonstrating the mutation of the idea that prompted the growth and development of its culture. Slides, tape. *—Sam Grogg, Jr.*

CULTURE IN THE SADDLE: THE WESTERN FORMULA AS AMERICAN MYTH. The archetypal n of the Western Experience in our most popular story form and its continued influence on our culture. S tape, film clips. *—Michael Marsden*

FROM THE BOSTON MASSACRE TO BULLMOOSE: A LOOK AT POLITICAL CARTOONS. Popu attitudes in the 19th century as evidenced in famous political cartoons. Slides, tape. *—Thomas Trou*

:OM HOWDY DOODY TO VIDEO BACKPACKS: DO IE PEOPLE REALLY OWN THE AIRWAVES? A capsule mer on telelvision history and an examination of the sent and future influence of TV on American culture. des, tape, film. —*Michael Marsden*

A LITTLE BIT OF HEAVEN FOR A NICKEL: OR, MOVIES REALLY HAVEN'T CHANGED VERY MUCH. How and why the early American film industry created movie conventions still present in most contemporary popular American films. Slides, tape, film clips, transparencies. —*John Nachbar*

: GOLDEN AGE OF RADIO. A nostalgic analysis of vork radio shows 1930-1946. Slides, tape. Especially ictive for non-academic groups. —*Thomas Trout*

PHILOSOPHY IN POPULAR LITERATURE: LEARNING TO FLY WITH *JONATHAN LIVINGSTON SEAGULL.* An explanation for the popularity of the "glorious No. 1 bestseller" with special attention given to the novel's ideological roots. Slides, tape. Suitable for university audiences. —*David Sowd*

THE LANGUAGE OF THE VISUAL. A basic, heavily illustrated correlation between verbal and visual media. Slides, transparencies, film clips. —*Sam Grogg, Jr.*

THE POLITICS OF FOOD. Present methods of food preparation and manufacturing and popular alternatives such as organic gardening and foraging. Slides and "objects." —*John K. Cornillon*

POPULAR CULTURE AND EDUCATION. The theoretical and practical use of popular artifacts in the classroom. Slides, tape, film clips. Suitable for groups of educators. —*Sam Grogg, Jr.*

:Y HAD FACES THEN: THE AMERICAN FILM INDUSTRY'S STAR SYSTEM. An examination of American public's need for secular gods and goddesses during Hollywood's halcyon days. Slides, tape. —*John Nachbar*

'HE WOMEN'S LIBERATION MOVEMENT: HISTORY ISSUES AND GOALS. The women's liberation novement from the civil rights movement of the 60's to various contemporary attitudes and philosophical ositions. Slides, tape. —*Susan K. Cornillon*

148 Organizations

POPULAR CULTURE LECTURES

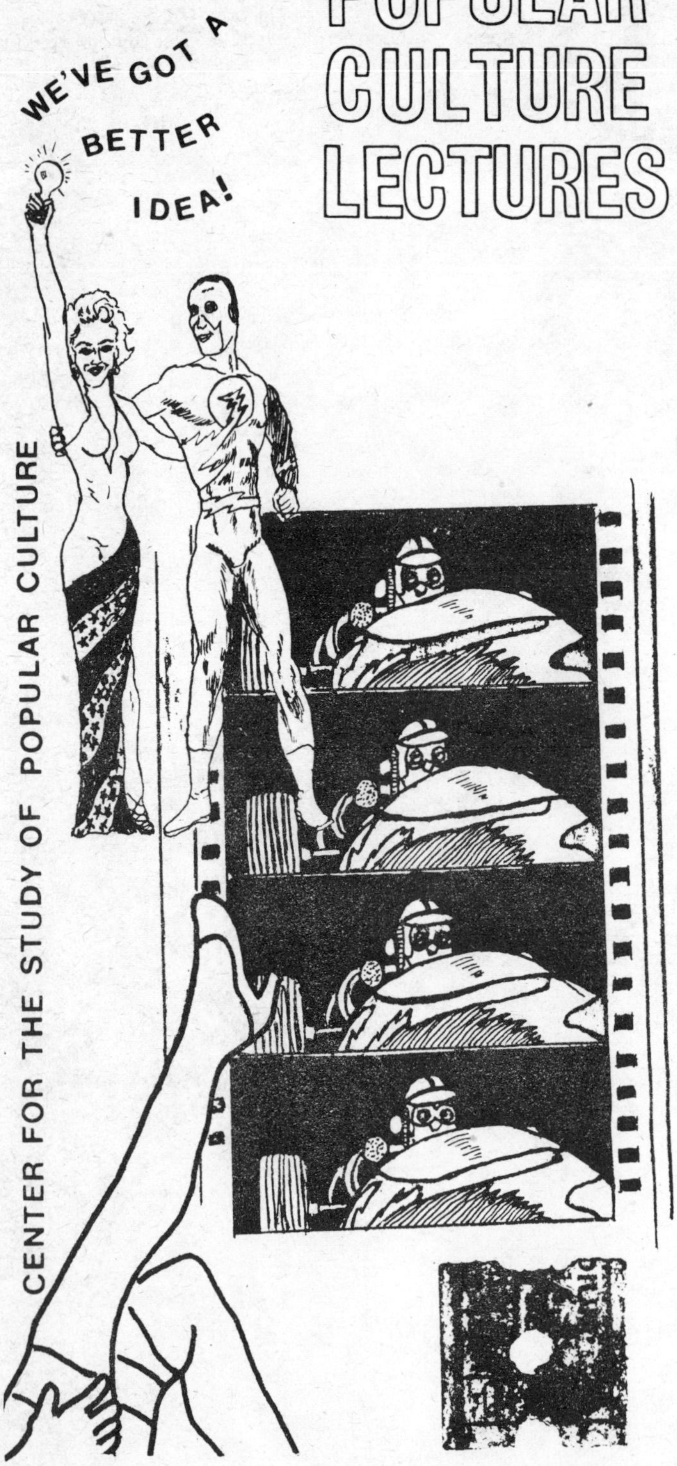

WE'VE GOT A BETTER IDEA!
CENTER FOR THE STUDY OF POPULAR CULTURE

CENTER FOR THE STUDY OF POPULAR CULTURE LECTURE SERIES

Gable and Leigh in *Gone With the Wind* . . . McDonald's Land . . . Fibber McGee's closet . . . Marlboro Country . . . Archie, Maud and Sanford . . . "Love means never having to say you're a Seagull. . . ." The materials of the American popular arts are very often vulgar and trite. But few would also deny that they are also rich, varied, and curiously fascinating.

The Popular Culture Lecture Series presents twelve lectures examining our best known arts and artifacts for the sources of their fascination and their influence on past, present and future American culture.

The presentations are both entertaining and informative. Each lecture is multi-media in format and is presented by a qualified associate of the Center for the Study of Popular Culture. The format of the lectures are adaptable and are, unless otherwise stated, appropriate for all types of audiences.

FEES: The stipend for each lecture is $50.00 plus expenses ($25.00 in Northwest Ohio). Included in this fee is the lecture itself plus the availability of the lecturer for several hours to discuss popular culture with small informal groups or with individuals.

For more detailed descriptions of the lectures or booking information write:

John Nachbar
Center for the Study of Popular Culture
101 University Hall
Bowling Green University
Bowling Green, Ohio 43403

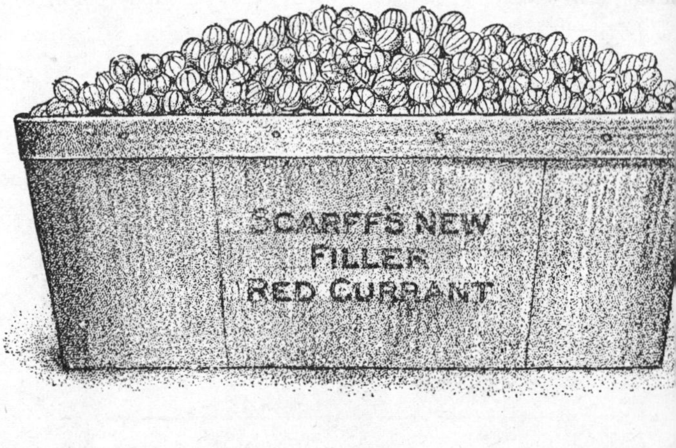

Periodicals

intercom

Intercom is concerned with global issues that affect war, peace, conflict, and change. It advances constructive alternatives to violence in seeking the changes needed to advance justice, democratic values, and human dignity. These involve goals in addition to peace -- goals such as economic development, protection of the natural environment, health, education, population control, and human rights.

Intercom is designed specially for the classroom teacher or community educator who understands the need for dealing with these issues from a global perspective, but lacks the time to research and prepare original material.

Each issue concentrates on a single subject (some recent issues are: Understanding U.S.-China Relations; Development -- New Approaches; Southern Africa -- Problems and U.S. Alternatives; and Teaching About Spaceship Earth). In preparation is an issue on the multinational corporation, dealing with its potentiality as a force for peace as well as a vehicle for ecomonimc exploitation of underdeveloped countries.

Each subject is introduced by a background essay by an expert in the field, setting the context and highlighting the special problems that need attention. This is followed by a complete and self-contained teaching unit, requiring no additional materials, which includes a discussion leader's guide, readings, and questions for discussion. This section serves as the basis for a number of sessions, depending on interest. For those who wish to continue beyond, each issue also includes annotations on: books, magazines, and audiovisual materials; teaching materials and aids; and organizations in the subject field and materials available from them.

Intercom is published from 3 to 5 times each year, depending on the availability of suitable material. Individual issues are $1.50 (bulk rates on request). Subscriptions, which may begin with any number, are available in units of 5 consecutive issues. Subscription rates are: 5 issues - $6.00; 10 issues - $11.00; 15 issues - $15.00. Published by the Center for War/Peace Studies of the New York Friends Group, Inc., 218 E. 18th St., New York, N.Y. 10003.

Back issues of *Intercom* are still available for $1.50 each. Some of the more interesting issues include:

#69 -- "Development: New Approaches, A Teaching Guide with Issues and Resources," April 1972. Comes to grips with the problems involved in Third World development, including the attitudes of the developing countries and peoples.

#71 -- "Teaching About Spaceship Earth: A Role-Playing Experience for the Middle Grades" (4 to 6), November 1972. A simulation involving a spaceship voyage, stressing interdependence. Complete in itself, usable for five or more classroom periods, with additional audiovisual, bibliographic, and organizational resources annotated.

#73 -- "Teaching Toward Global Perspectives," July 1973. A rationale for introducing the global perspective into the classroom, and some ideals and suggestions for direct classroom use.

#72 -- "Teaching About Population." Provides a wealth of data about the domestic and global aspects of population, including some proposed solutions. Most of the issue is devoted to original classroom lesson plans.

THE FUTURIST

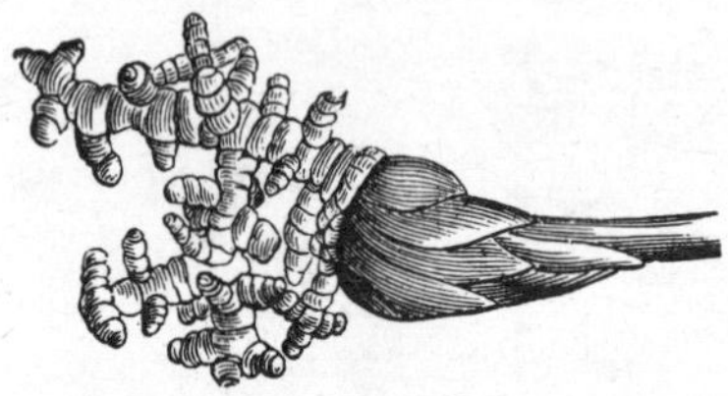

The Futurist is a bimonthly magazine of forecasts, trends and ideas about the future. The sample copy I saw looked very interesting, with articles on our changing values, the creation of technological man, the next 30 years of American history, the changes in the arts and fiction, and an article on anti-utopias. Subscription comes with membership ($7.50) in The World Future Society, 4916 St. Elmo Ave. (Bethesda), Washington, D.C. 20014. Write them for a more complete description and/or sample copy.

Winters Become Colder

Winters have been getting colder during the past few decades, causing a wide variety of changes.

Russian crop failures are increasing. The pack ice around Iceland in winter is growing and en dangering ships. Armadilloes that moved into the U.S. Midwest in the first half of the century now are re treating southward toward Oklahoma and Texas.

Throughout history, the climate has fluctuated dramatically. During the last great Ice Age, whic ended only 17,000 years ago, great glaciers covered North America as far south as Long Island.

Climatologists do not agree on how long the cooling trend may last nor what its causes are. I addition to the natural factors that have affected climate down through the years, human activities ma now be playing an important role. For example, industrial exhausts add huge amounts of dust to the atmo sphere, and the dust screens out the warming rays of the sun.

If the cooling trend continues, it will place further pressure on the world's dwindling fuel reserve

(See "The Ice Age Cometh" by James D. Hays of Columbia University's Lamont-Doherty Geological Observatory, *Saturday Review:* The Scienc April, 1973.)

Contents

Vol. VII, No. 2 April 1973

AKWESASNE NOTES

Akwesasne Notes is a newspaper published by Mohawks, designed to increase public awareness of the situation of native Americans as well as to communicate with members of other tribes. The paper is free, but donations are most appreciated by:

AKWESASNE NOTES
Mohawk Nation
c/o Rooseveltown, N.Y. 13683

THREE BOOKS: THE LAW, THE HISTORY, THE PROPHECY

THE LAW OF THE GREAT PEACE – the constitution of the League of the People of the Longhouse. 80 pages, illustrated by Kahonhes. $1.00

MIGRATION OF THE IROQUOIS – told in English and in pictographs, with illustrations by Kahonhes. 36 pp. 50 cents.

THE HOPI PROPHECY – as told by Dan Katchongva. A new booklet of spiritual directions published by White Roots of Peace. Illustrated. $1.00.

Posters published in the centerspread of each issue of AKWESASNE NOTES are available on heavy poster paper for fifty cents each, or three for $1. There are twelve now available:

SITTING BULL	THREE HORSEMEN
CHIEF JOSEPH	LONGHOUSE TO KIVA
ZUNI GOVERNOR	FAMILY PORTRAIT
GRANDMA HUNTER	SOUTH AMERICA
POUNDMAKER	WOUNDED KNEE
FIRE-CARRIER	THREE SISTERS

The posters are also available for resale for bookstores and for fund-raising by Indian groups for 25 cents each.

Even though it's April, the 1973 White Roots of Peace Calendar is still in demand – it makes a good set of posters when the year is over, with portraits by Kahonhes, and historical dates of interest and quotations to pass each day and month by. The calendar is 17x24, and has an attractive cover with an address list of some Indian organizations on the reverse side.

The current stock of calendars is all there is, and there will be no further reprinting for this year. It costs $2 postpaid, or $1 in quantities of 50 or more.

* * * * * * * * * * * *

All Kinds Of Terror

(This statement was made by Dave Long, vice-president of the Pine Ridge Tribal Council, on March 2. He spoke immediately after a government press conference, although many reporters left the room and few even bothered to listen.)

Our conditions here at Pine Ridge are bad, very bad. There is all kinds of terror here. There is little work. We live in very bad conditions. We are at the mercy of the Bureau of Indian Affairs.

The cattle you see here on this land is owned by whites. The Sioux have "unit grazing" which is in small parts of land. This is no good, and we can't make it like that. We had to give up grazing, and our horses and cattle.

. . . The BIA has never taken action to satisfy the needs of the people. Money is handled by the Bureau of Indian Affairs. They pass on responsibility for criticism to Aberdeen office, and from Aberdeen to Washington. People are tired of this kind of life.

At the hospital, we get doctors, newly learned only from books. They stay here a short time, leave, and go into practice. You can see for yourself the records at the Public Health Service.

Today, people want to be heard, and it seems they are not. We formed a Civil Rights Organization at Pine Ridge. The people were scared. We need change, and we thought this would help us and bring support. So far, we have no support.

I personally asked [Senator] Abourezk to come here. But we were not allowed to talk to Mr. Abourezk and Mr. McGovern. Yesterday, people were waiting in front of the Billy Mills House, our center in Pine Ridge. We wanted to talk to our two representatives in Congress. But tribal police came; drunks came; they started to make trouble. Then the police came and moved the people away. We never did get to talk to these congressmen. Looks like they want to keep us quiet, like always.

. . . I am not an AIM member. Now someplace we have to get help.

. . . Our medicine man, Pete Catches, was picked up by tribal police, and they are BIA police, and he has not returned. We don't know where he is. We had threats of bombing our homes against myself and another tribal council member. We called Mario Gonzales, a lawyer. Now I can't telephone out of Pine Ridge. . . . they put in something called "rumor control." This is maybe "people control."

The Tribal Council has not been called in session to do business since October, 1972. The people are intimidated.

I invite the press to go and take pictures of the housing, the streets and the community here — it's miserable. . .

We need help. We want the whole world to know what is going on here in Pine Ridge and how the people live. The AIM people are here because we asked them.

Where else are we going to get help?

BOOKS

A BOOKSHELF WE RECOMMEND

American Friends Service Committee: *Uncommon Controversy* $2.50. On Washington State Fishing problems.
Armstrong & Turner: *I Have Spoken: History Through Voices of Indians.* $2.95. A source book of quotations.
Borland: *When the Legends Die.* 75 cents. A novel.
Brandon: *American Heritage Book of Indians.* 75 cents. A historical/cultural summary.
Brandon: *Magic World.* $2.50. Translations of poetry.
Brown: *Bury My Heart at Wounded Knee.* $1.95. The true story of how the west was lost.
Brown: *The Sacred Pipe: The Seven Rites of the Oglala Sioux.* $1.45. A basic understanding of the spiritual perspective.
Cahn: *Our Brothers Keeper.* $3.95. A chronicle of contemporary wrongs and abuses.
Council on Interracial Books: *Chronicles of American Indian Protest.* $1.25. A survey of resistance and struggle.
Deloria: *Custer Died for Your Sins.* $1.25. Inside viewpoint.
Deloria: *We Talk, You Listen.* $2.45. Discussion of contemporary situation, philosophy, solutions.
Forbes: *The Indian in America's Past.* $1.95. Historical.
Josephy: *The Indian Heritage of America.* $1.65.
Jacobs: *Dispossessing the American Indian.* $3.95.
Jacobs: *To Serve the Devil: America's Racial History, vol. I.* $2.45. The roots of American racism.
Josephy: *Red Power: American Indians' Fight For Freedom.* $2.95. Documentation of the current struggles.
Neihardt: *Black Elk Speaks.* $1.50. The Oglala Way of Life.
Ortiz: *The Tewa World: Space, Time, Being and Becoming in Pueblo Society.* $2.45. Heavy but worthwhile.
Steiner: *The New Indians.* $2.75. A 1968 book of merit.
Steiner & Hill: *The Way: An Anthology of American Indian Literature.* $1.95.
Deloria: *Of the Utmost Good Faith.* $1.95. Treaties, history.
Wallace: *Death and Rebirth of the Seneca.* $2.45.
Bibeau, Gawboy & Lyons: *Everything You Ever Wanted to Ask About Indians But Were Afraid to Find Out.* $1.25. A cartoon book of laughs on ourselves and those about us.
Osborne: *Who Is Chairman of This Meeting?* $2.50. A collection of essays from Neewin Press.
Laubin: *The Indian Tipi.* $1.65.
Brown: *Spiritual Legacy of the American Indian.* 70 cents.
Fast: *The Lost Frontier.* 75 cents. A novel of freedom.
Abbott: *Paha Sapa (The Black Hills).* $2.25. A prophetic novel of 1970 pointing toward Wounded Knee.
Mooney: *Ghost Dance Religion and the Sioux Outbreak of 1890.* $2.95. A reprint, now useful for historical notes.
Landes: *Ojibwa Woman.* $2.25. Women's roles in society.
Lurie: *Mountain Wolf Woman.* $1.75. Winnebago biography.
Van Every: *Disinherited.* $1.25. The Trail of Tears.
Brant: *Jim Whitewolf: The Life of a Kiowa Apache.* $1.75.
Eastman: *Indian Boyhood.* $2.00. Autobiography.
Howard: *War Chief Joseph.* $2.65.
Jackson: *Black Hawk.* $1.75.

RECOMMENDED—HARDCOVER ONLY

Vogel: *American Indian Medicine.* $12.50. Definitive study.
Cohen: *Handbook of American Indian Law (1939 edition)* $20. A valuable reference for legal work.
Washburn: *Red Man's Land, White Man's Law.* $8.95.
Bird: *Tell Them They Lie: The Sequoyah Myth.* $7.95. Cherokee history — an important new perspective.
MacEwan: *Tatanga-Mani: Walking Buffalo of the Stonies.* $7.95. A biography of a Stony wiseman.
Burnette: *The Tortured American.* $7.95. A recent expose of tribal government with U.S. sanctions in South Dakota.
Ball: *In the Days of Victorio: Recollections of a Warm Springs Apache.* $6.50. A biography.
Stember: *Heroes of the American Indians.* $5.00. Good for junior high age and adults too.
Clutesi: *Potlatch.* $5.95.
Fenton: *Parker on the Iroquois. $8.95.*
Waters: *Man Who Killed the Deer.* $2.50. A novel.
Corle: *Fig Tree John* $2.45. A novel.

We carry in stock, as a service to our readers, most books in print on native peoples. This is a listing of only a few. Other books can be obtained by request. Specify publisher, and whether you wish paperback or hardcover.

TAPES

NOTES has a series of tapes available for school use, discussion groups, tape libraries. Prices below are for reel-to-reel (at 3 3/4 ips) or cassette.

SOUNDINGS from Akwesasne: $7.00. 30 minute documentary on the history of the Longhouse and occupation of islands in the St. Lawrence river in 1970.
MANIWAKI Indian Boy: $7.00 30 minutes. Story of the shooting of an Algonkin boy caught stealing a lightbulb.
THREE MESSAGES by Ray Fadden: $7.00. History of the Iroquois Confederacy, Contributions of Indians, Problems.
I AM A MOHAWK: by Ernie Benedict. 15 minutes $5.00. The Jay Treaty and a free border for native peoples.
CONCERNS OF James Bay Cree: $10.00 60 minutes. The price native people will pay for a hydroelectric project.
LOUIS RIEL ALIVE: $7.00. A half-hour debate on the hanging of a leader for nationhood of native peoples.

XTRA COPIES

Additional copies of this issue have been printed to make bulk distribution possible at a cost of 25 cents per copy in quantities of 20 or more. For $5, then, a person could give twenty copies to friends, members of clubs, to a social studies class for study. For $25, a reservation group could see that 100 homes each receive a copy. Funds can be raised to help participating groups by reselling this issue on campuses, on the street, any place, at the usual cover price of 50 cents. Churches with a genuine concern for Indian events could order copies for distribution within the parish.

By whatever means, we urge each person reading this to consider ways by which this message can reach the most possible people.

Prepaid orders may be sent to AKWESASNE NOTES, Mohawk Nation, via Rooseveltown, N.Y. 13683 for immediate shipment. Please send money with your order — we are glad to send single copies free, but we will need money even to cover postage. printing, etc.

MICROFILM

AKWESASNE NOTES is available on microfilm from Underground Press Package, Bell & Howell Co., Microphoto Division, Old Mansfield Road, Wooster, Ohio 44691. It is also available from Kraus-Thomson Organization Ltd, Route 100, Milwood, New York 10546.

Volume One (1969) is out of print but available on microfilm. There were ten issues that year. Vol. Two (1970) had seven issues. Two issues are still available. Volume Three (1971) had nine issues, and are available only on microfilm. Vol. Four had seven issues. Four are still in print. Vol. Five has one back issue for 1973, and this is number two. All back issues are available for $3.50, or 50 cents per copy.

HELP

This paper cannot exist without the support of you — the human being who reads these words now. There are many ways you can keep the paper strong:

take action on what you read. Write letters, think, give support, lend spiritual strength.

send clippings from your local papers. If there is a good photo, ask the photo dept. for the loan of a print. Make sure all clips are dated and source given.

send your own materials: photographs you have, or can take. Cover an event with your camera. All can be returned upon request.

send us articles, essays, editorials, letters-to-the editor, suggestions, cartoons. Cover an event in your area with interviews and on-the-scene report.

sell the paper at a powwow, meeting, church, on your reservation, at the Indian center, in bookstores in town and on campus. You send us 35 cents for each paper after and if they are sold.

send us mailing lists. We will send sample copies of the next issue. How about a list of all Indian schools? of every family on your reservation? of the members of your organization?

let us know of people we should send the paper to — Indians in institutions, friends, anyone who may want to see this paper.

check out your school or public library. If they don't subscribe, ask them to do so. If they can, encourage them to send a contribution. Most send $5.

support the paper financially, if you are able. we need money for stamps, printing, typewriter ribbons.

Everything in this paper came from someone who cared to send it in. And to you all, we are grateful.

AKWESASNE NOTES NEEDS:

- **empty tape cassettes**
- **a ditto machine**
- **a pair of binoculars**
- **sleeping bags, tents, camping gear**
- **loan of videotape gear**

SCHISM

A JOURNAL OF DIVERGENT AMERICAN OPINION

"The peculiar evil of silencing the expression of an opinion is that it is robbing the human race."—John Stuart Mill

WAR/PEACE REPORT

THE INTERCOLLEGIATE REVIEW

A Journal of Scholarship and Opinion

Dan Smoot Report

Freedomways

WESTERN SOCIALI

JOURNAL OF SCIENTIFIC SOCIALISM IN THE WESTERN HEMISPHE

White Power

the newspaper of White Revolution

THE CATHOLIC WORKER

American political and cultural trends are well reflected in hundreds of small and obscure publications long before they are noticed by mass publications. *Schism* is an excellent, nonpartisan quarterly that collects articles from such publications on the premise that meaningful debate should be open to all voices, not simply those that echo the editors' personal sympathies.

Each issue has about twenty reprints from all sorts of journals ranging from the quasi-hip to fascist. Single copies of *Schism* are $2. A yearly subscription is $7.50 from:

SCHISM
1109-A West Vine Street
Mount Vernon, Ohio 43050

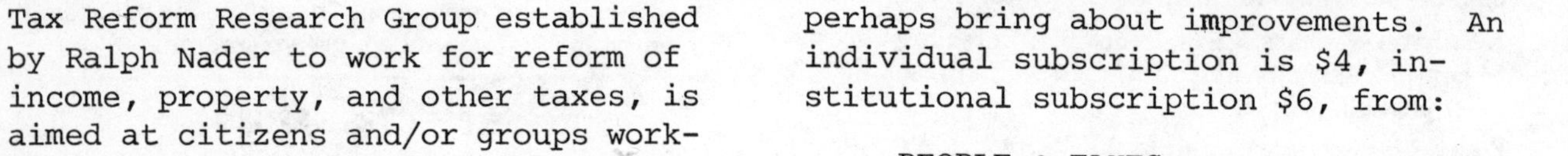

People & Taxes, a publication of the Tax Reform Research Group established by Ralph Nader to work for reform of income, property, and other taxes, is aimed at citizens and/or groups working on a local level for tax reform. The publication could easily serve as a guide to social studies teachers and students looking for relevant ways to study local communities and perhaps bring about improvements. An individual subscription is $4, institutional subscription $6, from:

PEOPLE & TAXES
P.O. Box 14198
Ben Franklin Station
Washington, D.C. 20044

WOMEN STUDIES ABSTRACTS

Abstracts of articles (200 in each issue) on education and socialization, sex characteristics and differences, employment, society and government, sexuality, the family, mental and physical health, and the Women's Liberation Movement. Bibliographic essays and lists of book reviews and additional articles of interest.

WOMEN STUDIES ABSTRACTS is published quarterly. Subscription is for the calendar year. Library edition (including annual index) is $10.00; individual subscription is $7.50 prepaid; and student subscription is $5.00 prepaid. Subscription on annual basis. The equivalent of $1.00 for additional postage should be added for foreign subscriptions outside the North American continent. Send all subscription requests and checks to WOMEN STUDIES ABSTRACTS; P. O. Box 1; Rush, New York 14543.

EDUCATION AND SOCIALIZATION

601. Angrist, Shirley S. **Variations in women's adult aspirations during college.** JOURNAL OF MARRIAGE AND THE FAMILY 34:465-8 Ag'72.

Intensive study over four years of one class in the women's college of a private coeducational university yields varied types of adult aspirations. Since all the women aspire to family life, career aspirations are defined as the desire to pursue one's chosen occupation in addition to familial roles. Five types of students are described: Careerists, Noncareerists, Converts, Defectors, and Shifters. Only the Careerist consistently plans her adult life around both family and occupation; the Convert comes to that plan by senior year. While some students develop career interests, some move away from them, and still others oscillate in uncertainty. Most striking is the large number of women whose adult aspirations remain unaffected by the college years. JOURNAL ABSTRACT.

602. Coates, Thomas J. and Mara L. Southern. **Differential educational aspiration levels of men and women undergraduate students.** THE JOURNAL OF PSYCHOLOGY 81:125-8 My'72.

Inside and outside the professional community definite negative attitudes exist toward the married professional woman in her dual role, perhaps because the successful woman deviates from traditional feminine expectations. One study found that when equally qualified applicants were considered, a man would be chosen, and this might generalize to graduate school selection. Another discriminatory factor may be the aspiration level of women or their mobility. This study of 364 undergraduates enrolled in an upper division course required for the B.A. in psychology reviewed answers to a questionnaire and the Concept Mastery Test (CMT) and the Wechsler Adult Intelligence Scale (WAIS). The results indicate that a larger proportion of females planned to terminate their education with a B.A. or M.A., while a larger proportion of males aspired to the doctorate. Differences in verbal facility and test marks in the course were not significant. These data provide empirical verification for the contention that underrepresentation of women in academia is accounted for not only by discrimination, but also by the fact that women set lower goals for themselves. It may not be enough to legislate versus discrimination or change the attitudes of those in decision making positions, but also to change the attitudes of women. S. WHALEY.

603. Cartwright, Lillian K. **The personality and family background of a sample of women medical students at the University of California.** JOURNAL OF THE AMERICAN WOMEN'S MEDICAL ASSOCIATION 27:260-6 My'72.

Internal and comparative studies with four other groups of women (students in college, graduate psychology, social work, and mathematicians) showed no significant variables which distinguished the medical students from all of the other groups. However, they did rank significantly higher on the Dominance and Self-acceptance scales and significantly lower on the Femininity scale of the California Personality Inventory than three of the four comparison groups. The self-descriptive adjective which they most preferred was "healthy." They are more likely to have highly educated parents than are their male counterparts. R. R. GUTZKE.

(MORE) AND COLUMBIA JOURNALISM REVIEW

(*More*) is a monthly 20-page paper that muckrakes the press and media, especially the New York newspapers. Recent articles included a story about ten newspapers across the country who refused to accept advertising from a company who told people how to buy cars for less (Car-Puter) for fear of offending their lucrative ad accounts with auto dealers. Another article examined critically the syndicated columns used on editorial pages, another gave a few editorial reasons for *Look's* demise, another examined a revised trend in advertising toward the "free-form" ads, one article looked at a ghetto news service that is being ignored and another covered the control of sports reporting. *One year (12 issues) for $7.50, two for $12 from: (More) Box 2971, Grand Central Station, New York, N.Y. 10017.*

The Chicago Journalism Review is a small magazine that tackles far more than Chicago media. Half of each monthly issue delves into failures in the national media, including recent examinations of "Attica: Where the Media Went Wrong"; and "Missing the Story in Northern Ireland"; another fine article on how race riots in the last fifty years have been treated by newspapers to exploit their white readership; an article on "What Do Doctors Recommend For Pain of Misleading TV Commercials?" plus more about the lack of coverage of the Pakistan-India crisis, censorship of movie ads, and the press's treatment of the Mafia. *One year (12 issues) for $5 from: Chicago Journalism Review, 11 E. Hubbard St., Chicago, Ill. 60611.*

The above two deal with the nitty gritty, the day to day problems of a newspaper and media while **Columbia Journalism Review** is more the scholarly granddaddy of the journalism reviews. It is more literate and has a broader scope and more well-known writers than the other two reviews. Students are more likely to pick up and read (*More*) or *CJR* before *Columbia JR*, but all three make for valuable tools for any media teacher. *Columbia Journalism Review is bi-monthly and costs $9 for one year or $16 for two from: 700 Journalism, Columbia University, New York, N.Y. 10027.*

MEDIA ECOLOGY REVIEW

Media Ecology Review. . . is a small magazine published 16 times yearly at the New York University School of Education by the students in the Media Ecology doctoral program. Contents include a bit of philosophizing and meandering around media and technology. Pick up a sample ($7 for a one-year subscription) from **Media Ecology Review,** School of Education, New York University, 23 Press Annex, Washington Square, New York 10003.

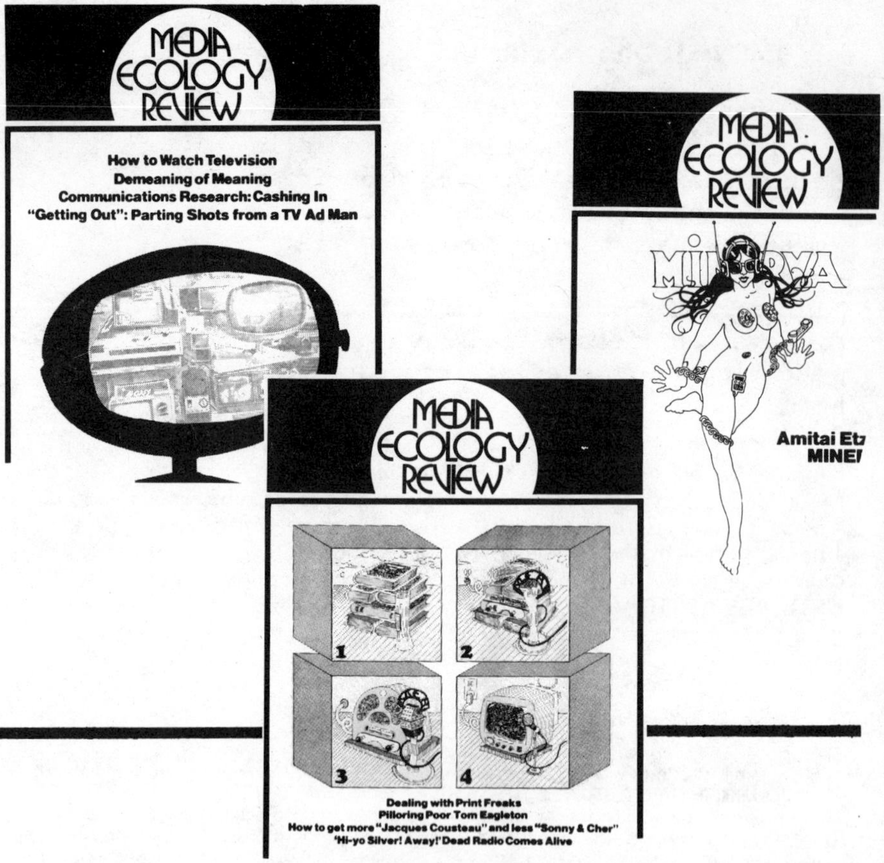

Dealing with Print Freaks:

A Guerrilla Guide by Frank Miceli

Everyone should learn the power of the typewriter and of the printed word. If you have a complaint about something, it is an utter waste of time to complain to your friends. Write letters. Letters upset people, and you can draw attention to your complaint by putting it in writing. The reverse is also true. Confusing? Let me give you an example of what I mean.

Whenever anyone asks you to defend yourself in writing against some charge or other, always ask him to put the charges in writing. In almost 90% of these cases, he will not. The secret to remember is that print freaks are really afraid of print. They think print is holy, not subject to challenge, and unassailable. When a person has spent his whole life reading the print produced by someone else, what he has learned besides "literature" is fear of the book. Remember: in the beginning was the word. You will find--and test it out if you don't believe it--that the more educationally conservative people are, the less they like to reproduce their ideas in print. The duplicating machine is the darling of the Left; the shredding machine is the love of the Right.

There is an additional point to be understood here. If print freaks are afraid of print, why is it that tons of printed material pour forth from all offices at all levels? And all the time? What you must keep in mind is that this print reproduction system doesn't mean anything. What is important is that it creates the illusion that something is going on. (Plus it keeps people employed. In our economy, that is no small consideration.) It is possible to take most of the mail most of us receive and throw it out without even looking at it. The result is that nothing happens. Nothing was intended to happen. The purpose of print flow is to keep things as they are.

If the first rule is never to answer anything in writing unless it is first put in writing, the second rule is never to write anything without sending copies to at least five different people. You will find that the letters you write will get "lost," and you will never receive a reply. By sending copies of your letter to five different people, you insure yourself of a reply. Also, if your letter is not answered within, say, two weeks, you can then write a follow-up letter, sending copies to the same five people. Print freaks always answer follow-up letters, especially when they see all the carbon copy names at the bottom.

It may be wise at this point to remind you of some basic rules in dealing with print freaks that have been used over the years with great success:

1. Always request far more than you really want. Bureaucrats are usually willing to give you anything just to keep you quiet. Remember that administrators were selected because they carry out the wishes of their superiors with dispatch. When things go wrong, their superiors will not like it, and will begin to perceive that something is wrong with them. This is increasingly true the higher up one goes on the administrative ladder.

2. Because print freaks are afraid of print, you have to use the very words they have written to bring about your own reform. Almost every school, for instance--on paper-- is delightful. The problem is that the paper never conforms to the practice. You have to read through the publications of each institution to find what it is they have written about themselves, examine those statements, and read them back to the same people who wrote them. What's on paper is always good. The problem is that it's usually not practiced. Hardly ever, in fact.

3. Print demands that people be alone. Groups cannot read together. Groups talk. A book forces you to demand silence in others so that you can be silent yourself. Perhaps it might be helpful to mention the obvious: you can only read a book in one way, that is, word by word (or, if you are a good reader, cluster by cluster), left to right, from the top of the page to the bottom. Then you turn the page and repeat the process. No matter how well-read you are, you can't do it any other way. Both the good reader and the poor reader read in the same manner.

Print freaks have spent an enormous part of their lives behaving in exactly the manner I have described: moving their heads from left to right, top to bottom. This is what has made them freaks.

Now, within this system of print reading, the best person is he who has read the most print with the greatest understanding. The most "informed" person begins naturally to rise to the top. This method worked well in the past, before the electric plug replaced print as a more efficient means of distributing information. Because print is well-ordered, it survives best in a well-ordered environment. No wonder it's having a difficult time in the electric age! Print freaks are usually obsessed by what they call "noise"--and noise means any kind of electronic communication. Electronic

music is also "noise," television is noisy, and the radio, most of all, is highly distracting to them.

It ought to tell you something that it is considered "good behavior" to take notes in school while someone is talking--providing you use a pencil or pen; but all kinds of problems will develop if you try to use a tape recorder.

Print freaks are downright hostile to electric freaks.

Notice, if you will, that to bring about reform you've got to do at least as much work as those intent upon preventing reform. Probably more. You're new at it--and they've turned preventing reform into an art form.

MASS MEDIA BOOKNOTES

Mass Media Booknotes is an essential resource for high school and college mass media teachers. The mimeo newsletter is a nearly comprehensive review of new books and periodicals about mass media and the popular arts. The MMB service is available only by subscription for the current volume year (subscribe at any time in the year and get all 12 issues for the September - August period). Cost is a reasonable $3.50 per year prepaid from:

TEMPLE UNIVERSITY
Department of Radio-TV-Film
Philadelphia, Pa. 19122
Attn: Christopher Sterling

MEDIA & METHODS

Media & Methods is one of the best publications available for teachers of English and social studies. Emphasis is on educational media, but the magazine carries articles on ecology, woman's studies, humanizing education, feature films, and social concerns. Published monthly, September through May, for $9.00 from:

MEDIA & METHODS
134 N. 13th Street
Philadelphia, Pa. 19107

media mix

Media Mix is the publication that most resembles *The Seed Catalog*, which might have something to do with the fact that Jeff Schrank edits both. *Media Mix* is a sort of continuing *Seed Catalog* with emphasis on high-quality short films and documentaries, critical reviews of learning materials for high school and college levels, and much material especially for media education. Many items in this catalog have appeared in past issues of *Media Mix*.

$7.00 for one year (8 issues) from 221 West Madison Street, Chicago, Ill. 60606

KEEPING UP, NEW SCHOOL OF EDUCATION JOURNAL, POP CULTURE METHODS

Keeping Up. . . .is a free social studies newsletter published by the Clearinghouse for Social Studies. The newsletter lists microfische or xerox abstracts, curriculum studies and books of interest to social studies teachers. ERIC/CHESS, 855 Broadway, Boulder, Col. 80302.

New School of Education Journal . . . has the format of any scholarly journal, replete with footnotes and occasional lapses into jargon like "techno-urban fascism." The Journal is published by the Berkeley New School of Education (U. of C.) and takes a radical stand toward organized education in America. The issue I saw had articles on "Education: Tool of an Emerging Fascist State?" "Corporate Involvement in Elementary and Secondary Education," and "A Critique of the 'Pathology' Model in Psychological Inquiry: Learning Disabilities and Cultural Deprivation." If you are seriously into school reform and need more depth than other educational reform magazines, check out the **New School of Education Journal**, 4304 Tolman Hall, University of California, Berkeley, Ca. 94720. Published quarterly; $5 for individuals and $6 for institutions.

Popular Culture Methods. . . . is a free newsletter aimed at teachers of popular culture or any teachers who can incorporate elements of pop culture in their teaching. From TV shows, to the Beatles and Bob Dylan, from Hoola hoops to **Easy Rider** pop culture has invaded the traditional curriculum. First issue had items about TV Commercials in the classroom, suggested readings for a "Course in the History of American Culture in the 20th Century," and an article on the "Study of Popular Culture in the Public School," among other items.

Subscription is free from Sam Grogg, Center for the Study of Popular Culture, 101 University Hall, Bowling Green State University, Bowling Green, OH 43403.

FREE SCHOOL PUBLICATIONS

Publications aimed at those people in free schools and alternative education include:

New Schools Exchange Newsletter is the "Bible" and central clearinghouse for free-school news. The twice-monthly newsletter is the most thoughtful and well written of the free-school publications. *NSEN* is famous for its listing of places (free schools) needing people and people looking for free schools in which to teach or even to attend. $10 yearly from Pettigrew, Ariz. 72752

Edcentric bills itself as a "radical education journal" and is the most substantial of the movement education publications. They feature special issues on such subjects as women in education, student power, free universities. If you can afford only one alternative education magazine, *Edcentric* would make sense as that one choice. Free sample to librarians, $1 for ordinary mortals, or $5 for a one-year (8 issues) subscription to: 2115 "S" St. N.W., Washington, D.C. 20008.

Why shouldn't you ignore a magazine that you've never even seen?

Because Edcentric publishes writers who are educators who are activists.
In addition to often-overlooked local organizers, Edcentric contributors include such prominent authors as John Holt, China expert Willian Hinton, child psychologist Robert Coles, Berkeley activist Michael Rossman and Jose Angel Gutierrez, founder of La Raza Unida Party.

Because Edcentric critically examines both the conventional schooling system and the movement for educational change.
Not only has Edcentric investigated such abuses as the drugging of unmanageable schoolchildren and the muzzling of anti-war college athletes; it has also explored the contradiction between Ivan Illich's deschooling philosophy and the traditional structure of his Center for Intercultural Documentation (CIDOC). Not only has Edcentric denounced the academic oppression of women, Blacks, gay people, Chicanos and prisoners; it has also criticized the cloistered elitism of certain free schools and cautioned against the reversal of victories won by student militants during the 60's.

Because Edcentric can keep you abreast of significant experiments both within and beyond U.S. borders.
For example, recent issues have featured in-depth reports about Communitas College (which offers an original program for training community organizers), five Chicano alternative schools, Cuba's new work-study program, Campus Free College (which grants low-cost diplomas for real life work experiences) and Los Angeles' Open Space Program (which was set up within the public school system by citizens committed to imaginative eco-education).

Because Edcentric is the only radical education journal that offers a new, extensive resource directory in each issue.
Edcentric's movement section regularly lists and describes as many as 150 organizations, projects, clearinghouses, bibliographies, conferences, pamphlets, periodicals, films, tapes and other useful tools.

Centerpeace Newsletter is a kind of East Coast *New Ways* . . . that has been around now for over two years. Previously a small newsletter, *Centerpeace* is attempting to survive as a full-size magazine. A cross between *Edcentric* and *NSEN* but concentrating on the East Coast. $4 for individuals, $8 for libraries, and $10 overseas to 57 Hayes Street, Cambridge, Mass. 02139.

Alternatives For Education Newsletter

The only voice that speaks for the alternative school movement in Southern California.

The only newsletter in California which "pictures" schools, with on the spot interviews.

A newsletter providing the schools themselves with a web of communication.

The newsletter exists: to be a vehicle, a printed organ, a cauterizer, a catalizer, an imaginizer, a focusizer, a target, a starting place, an arena, a loverletter.

Aternatives for Education Newsletter is similar to *New Ways* . . . and is again California oriented. Subscription to the monthly newsletter is $5 for parents, students, and alternative schools, $10 for libraries and institutions, and $12 outside the USA from P.O. Box 1028, San Pedro, Calif. 90733.

Outside the Net . . . is a newspaper-format magazine about alternative education. It comes out three or four times a year. The first issue contained articles questioning compulsory school attendance, tips on hitching, a reprint from the *Summerhill Society Bulletin* on child rearing, and two articles describing existing alternative schools. It also has underground comix, book reviews, and even a bit of poetry. Really worth looking into at $4 for a two-year (six issues and maybe two summer issues) subscription to P.O. Box 184, Lansing, Michigan 48901. The editors describe themselves as an alternative to the "mindless empiricism of the *AERA Journal*, the mid-west anti-intellectualism of *Phi Delta Kappan*, and the vacuous liberalism of *Saturday Review, Harvard Educational Review* and *Teachers College Record*."

New Ways in Education is a Southern California-based mimeo packet/clearinghouse. Each monthly issue contains news of California get-togethers, brochures about humanistic education events and schools, and reprints. Of prime interest to California residents but useful elsewhere. Sample copy $1, monthly for $5 from *New Ways in Education*, 1778 S. Holt Avenue, Los Angeles, Calif. 90035.

NEW WAYS

NEW WAYS IN EDUCATION*, a monthly newsletter, explores what is happening with the new schools movement in Southern California; issues of national interest directed toward humanizing education; book reviews; articles by radical thinkers in the field of education; events happening of interest in the way of courses, meetings, fund-raisers, schools opening, jobs available - in other words, whatever comes to my attention, I share with subscribers and listeners to the radio show "Alternatives" heard on KMET-FM(94.7) Sunday mornings at 9:30
(Editor: Gladys Falken)

NEW WAYS IN EDUCATION
1778 S. Holt Ave.
Los Angeles Ca 90035
(213)839-6994

Sample copy $1; one-year subscription(12) $5
Schools/resources list 50¢(free to subscribers)

*In cooperation with
CENTER FOR STUDIES OF
ALTERNATIVES IN EDUCATION

MONSTER TIMES

THE MONSTER TIMES is a bi-weekly newspaper devoted to science fiction and monsters in film, comics and literature. The first issue had features on the men behind King Kong, Nosferatu, the Golem legend, Buck Rogers, sci-fi versions of the end of the world, and a review of the 1936 version of H.G. Wells Things to Come. Issue #2 was devoted entirely to Star Trek. One copy free as a sample. 13 issue (6 month) sub is $6 or $10 for one year from THE MONSTER TIMES, P.O. Box 595, Old Chelsea Station, New York, N.Y. 10011.

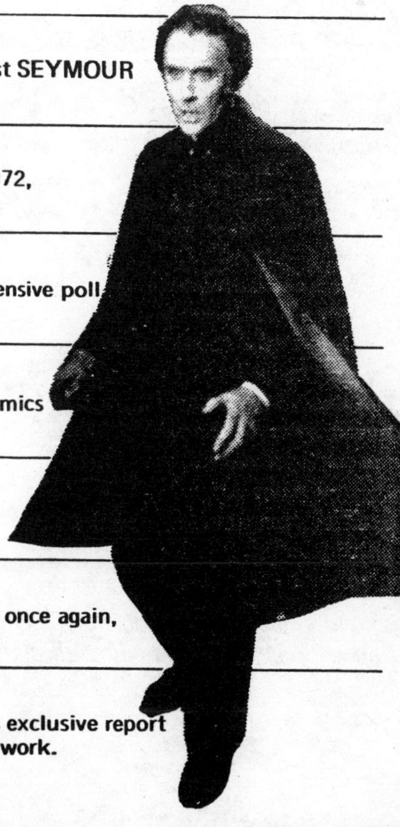

PERIODICALLY

Periodically is a free newsletter aimed at high school psychology teachers. Published monthly during the school year, *Periodically* reviews high school textbooks and resources in psychology and has a monthly "gimmick" for teaching some aspect of psychology. The newsletter is useful for any teacher interested in humanistic education. Free from APA Clearinghouse on Precollege Psychology and Behavioral Science, 1200 Seventeenth Street, N.W., Washington, D.C. 20036.

CULTURAL INFORMATION SERVICE

Cultural Information Service is a monthly survey of the contemporary arts aimed at "Christians" either in teaching or the ministry. Its scope goes far beyond the limited interests of religious education, however; *CIS* is a finely produced review of the newest in films, literature, art, theater, television, and rock music. Very up to date and well written. Each monthly issue is around 30 pages. A one-year subscription is $12 from:

CULTURAL INFORMATION SERVICE
P.O. Box 92
New York, N.Y. 10016
(212) 689-0039

Art

NEW SCULPTURE BY GEORGE SEGAL

The Sidney Janis Gallery, New York City

I deal primarily in mystery, and in the presentation of mystery. If I cast someone in plaster, it is the mystery of a human being that is presented. If I put this next to a real object, it also raises a question about the nature of the real object.

— George Segal

Picture the artist wrapping the model's hair in Saran Wrap and covering the body with plaster cloths. Only certain sections of the body are done at one time, usually taking twenty minutes or so. George Segal is interested in gesture: "People have attitudes locked up in their bodies, and you have to catch them." White plaster sculptures cast from life—so to speak—are his specialty. The figures are then set in an environment of commonplace objects.

In this exhibit of twenty-six new sculptures, Segal has caught a variety of characters in a potpourri of situations evoking a variety of moods. There is a girl, oblivious to the world, washing her hair at a sink—in touch only with her scalp; another girl in the shower caught in a moment of privacy; a lonely female at a window peering forlornly into the day or night; a woman on a swing poised to launch upward. In each case, the viewer can imagine the moment—transfixed in time by Segal. Several nude sculptures reveal the female form, in a chair, sleeping, embracing a man. The texture of the skin—the closeness of skin and wood—an ode to physicality and furniture. Other sculptures look like forms chiseled in stone.

In "Man Installing Pepsi Sign," Segal evokes a humorous image as the man on a ladder reaches for the pinnacle of pop culture. My two favorites: "Girl With Clock" and "Gertrude: Double Portrait." The former (right) reveals a Greek or Roman head juxtaposed with a large clock, making a moving comment on the evanescence of time. And in "Gertrude: Double Portrait," Segal creates a multi-media sculpture with a figure and a home-made film. A woman sits on her porch while a film, chronicling the movement of her days, is shown over her right shoulder.

These new sculpture pieces do fulfill Segal's intention to convey the mystery of people: their loneliness and moments of privacy, the comedy and transitoriness of the human situation, the intimate qualities of the body, gestures that express more than words can bear.

A Bulova clock juxtaposed with a woman's head brings many thoughts to mind about time. Has the woman turned away from the electronic measurement of her moments? Is she killing time in a dream reverie? Or is the clock here grafted onto her psyche dominating the rhythm of her days?

Sam Keen once noted: "If we become sensitive enough to our organic rhythms and needs, there is no reason why we must allow the character of modern life to be determined by the necessity of perpetual machine tending and consumption of what the machine produces. The time has come to talk back, to insist that clocks are made for men and not vice versa."

JOURNAL OF POPULAR CULTURE

The *Journal of Popular Culture* is a 300-page quarterly situated in format and approach in the mainstream of small academic publications. Articles in past issues have included "America's Manufactured Villain -- the Baseball Umpire," "Long Hari: Taboo in England," "The Agrarian Myth in *Midnight Cowboy*, *Alice's Restaurant*, *Easy Rider*, and *Medium Cool*," plus features on political cartoons, the Beatles, fairy tales, and Easter eggs. All the articles are done in a most scholarly fashion, complete with footnotes.

The journal is $15 for one year ($7.50 for students) or $4 for a single copy from:

JOURNAL OF POPULAR CULTURE
100 - 101 University Hall
Bowling Green State University
Bowling Green, Ohio 43403

Volume V Spring 1972

CONTENTS

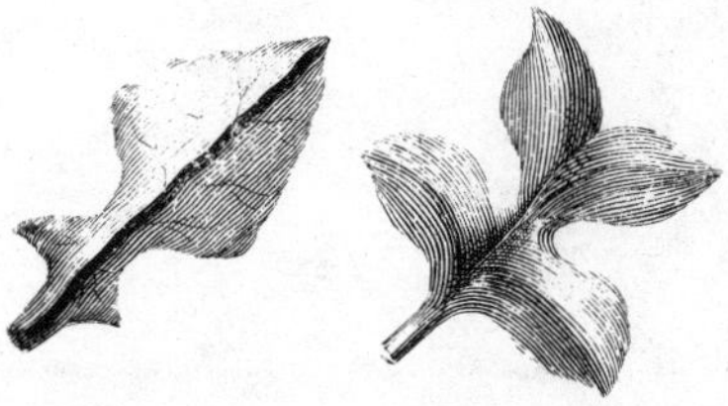

ROLLING STONE

Rolling Stone has been variously described as the rock lover's Bible and the *Time* of the counterculture. Whatever, it's much more than a music magazine. *RS* is not really a radical publication at all; it's more hip capitalist and even takes out full-page ads in trade journals looking for new advertisers by reminding potential customers that *RS* readers are really good consumers.

RS is the source of some excellent journalism, ecstatic record reviews, and lots of counterculture gossip. A free sample is available from *RS* at P.O. Box 12976, Oakland, Calif. 94604. Subscriptions are $10 for a year of 26 issues.

ROCK MARKETPLACE

Rock Marketplace is a semimonthly magazine for pop music record collectors. Besides usual articles on various pop groups the magazine has a classified section in which people list used records for sale and old and usually obscure records and memorabilia needed. $4.50 for a one-year (six-issue) subscription from:

THE ROCK MARKETPLACE
P.O. Box 253
Elmhurst, N.Y. 11373

POPULAR MUSIC AND SOCIETY

Popular Music and Society is another publication of the Center for the Study of Popular Culture at Ohio's Bowling Green University. Like the others, this quarterly treats a popular culture subject in a scholarly fashion.

$6 for one year of four issues, students for $4 a year, single issues are $2 from *PM&S*, Bowling Green State University, Bowling Green, Ohio 43403.

Volume II Fall 1972

CONTENTS

Taking the Roll Out of Rock 'n' Roll: Reverse Acculturation
Jonathan Kamin

Meaning in Rock Music: Notes Toward A Theory of Communication
James E. Harmon

Middle-Class Delinquents and Popular Music: A Pilot Study
Russell E. Shain and Kent Higgins

"Hot Jazz," The Jitterbug, and Misunderstanding: The Generation Gap In Swing 1935-1945
J. Frederick MacDonald

REVIEW ESSAY

Mr. Jones, The Professors, and the Freaks (or Every Man His Own Philosopher King): The Philosophical Implications of Rock
Robert A. Rosenstone

INTERVIEW

Mimi Fariña with Patrick Morrow

REVIEWS

Books

Records

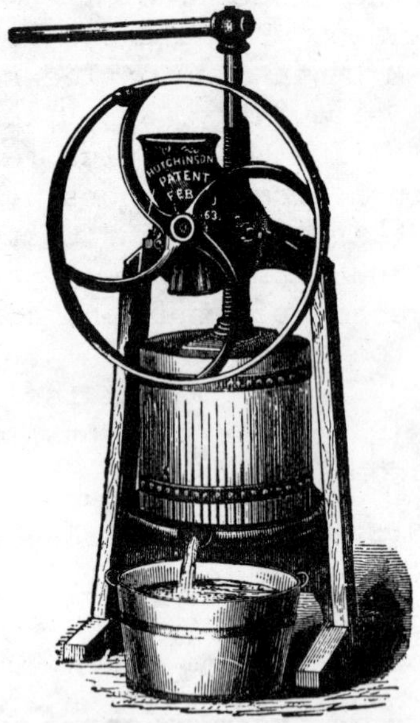

ADVERTISING AGE

Advertising Age is the weekly trade publication of the advertising industry. Since we live in a consumer-oriented society *AA* becomes the kind of publication suitable for burying in a time capsule to tell future generations about us. It is an honest publication yet very much pro advertising. *AA* gives a behind-the-scenes look at new product designs, ad campaigns, the economics of mass markets, and the ad campaigns of tomorrow. A fascinating trip into the creative, sometimes absurd, but always amazing world of human motivation. Only $10 for 52 issues from:

ADVERTISING AGE
740 Rush Street
Chicago, Ill. 60611

CAVEAT EMPTOR

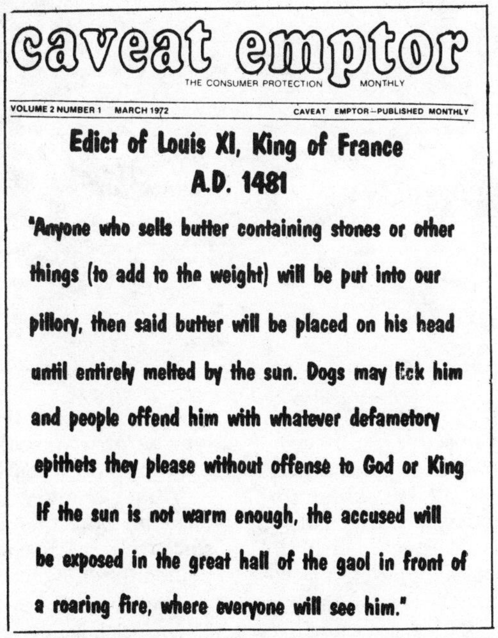
caveat emptor
THE CONSUMER PROTECTION MONTHLY
VOLUME 2 NUMBER 1 MARCH 1972 CAVEAT EMPTOR—PUBLISHED MONTHLY

Edict of Louis XI, King of France
A.D. 1481

"Anyone who sells butter containing stones or other things (to add to the weight) will be put into our pillory, then said butter will be placed on his head until entirely melted by the sun. Dogs may lick him and people offend him with whatever defametory epithets they please without offense to God or King If the sun is not warm enough, the accused will be exposed in the great hall of the gaol in front of a roaring fire, where everyone will see him."

Caveat Emptor is a promising consumer publication that has been around since 1971. Articles range from personal accounts of consumer frauds to exposés of the inner workings of large corporations and governmental agencies. They include explanations of fraudulent advertising used by major corporations as well as small-time operators, advice to consumers on food and clothing purchases, and personal interviews with prominent figures in the consumer movement. Published monthly, a introductory 6-month subscription is $3.95 and includes six free back issues. Twenty copies or more of a single issue available for 10¢ each.

CAVEAT EMPTOR
556 U.S. Highway 22
Hillside, N.J. 07205

CONSUMER NEWS

Consumer News . . . . if advertising is part of your curriculum you might consider at $1 a one-year subscription to **Consumer News** a publication of the Office of Consumer Affairs. The bi-monthly newsletter reports on the FTC's moves on false ad claims, product recalls and major consumer proposals that come before Federal agencies. Office of Consumer Affairs, New Executive Office Building, Washington, D.C. 20506.

book magazine

Book Magazine is an alternative book review publication. The magazine reviews books often neglected in more popular publications and carries provocative features about contemporary journalism, the book world, and contemporary culture. Published monthly except July and February at $6.50 per year from:

BOOK MAGAZINE
222 West 23rd Street
New York, N.Y.

Media & Consumer

Media and Consumer gives you food for thought... ideas for follow-ups... leads to stories in your own localities. Here are the kinds of stories you'll find in Media & Consumer:

- ☐ how a Boston butcher short-weighted, not in ounces but in pounds
- ☐ why consumers in Binghamton, N.Y. are now able to learn whether the kitchens in their favorite restaurants are clean or filthy
- ☐ how car repair men can pad your bill
- ☐ how an anti-consumer conspiracy in the Washington, D.C. area makes the cost of buying a house there among the most expensive in the nation
- ☐ how major food companies are responding positively to consumerism
- ☐ how one company used complex corporation laws to stay one step ahead of consumers who had won judgments against it
- ☐ how a hospital that engineered national publicity for itself when it announced rate cuts, quietly raised those rates beforehand
- ☐ how furniture bills often outlast the furniture
- ☐ how straightening your child's teeth can cost as much as $2,000 or as little as $100
- ☐ how one city's long-standing TV repairmen law is a joke among those it's designed to regulate

$12 for one year, published monthly by:

MEDIA & CONSUMER
P.O. Box 1225
Radio City Station
New York, N.Y. 10019

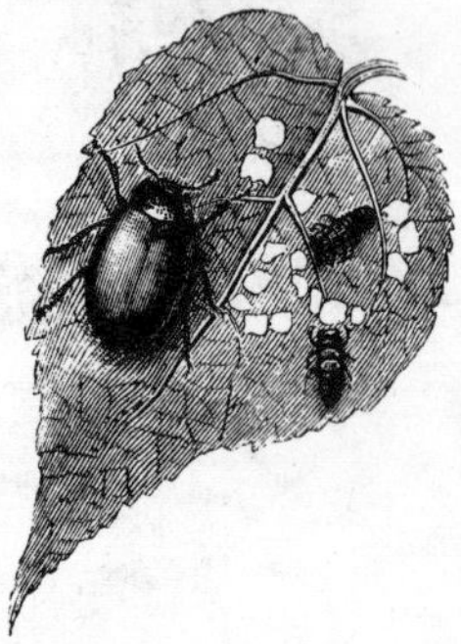

Hershey's Shrinking Bar

"That American staple, the 10-cent Hershey bar, which weighed a full two ounces in 1949, has shrunk to 1.26 ounces today. The chocolate bar began to grow smaller in 1951 and has since undergone eleven separate fractional weight reductions. A Hershey Foods Corporation executive gave us the information, but his superior later called back to say that additional weight and price data would be made public only if Hershey were given permission to clear the story first."
—*New York* (2/19/73)

But Most of All, Not My Employer

"I thought there was a law against notifying an employer (about an employee's debt), and if there isn't one, there definitely should be. . . . Calling an employer is like putting an ad about it in the newspaper. It's unfair.

"I'd probably be fired if my supervisor were told I was in financial trouble."

—Wayne Cash, Richmond manager of Financial Collection Agencies Inc., quoted in *The Richmond Times-Dispatch* (1/8/73).

Little Cigars: A Puff of What?

"These small cigars that are sold in drugstores . . . are just as dangerous to smoke as cigarettes.

"They also have the same inferio type of tobacco, stuff we usually refer to as floor shavings.

"About 21 different chemicals, including potassium nitrate and some from the arsenic family, are poured into these cheap small cigar and cigarettes so that the tobacco and paper burn evenly."

—Walter A. Rosenblum, Detroit tobacconist, quoted by Lou Mleczk in *The Detroit News*.

A Warning For Readers Only

"A commercial for one company's product showed a double-edged razor blade being flexed between two fingers. As might be expected, a child in Dallas tried doing just what he saw on TV and was cut seriously.

"(But) the Federal Trade Commission, which has jurisdiction, decided to do nothing. The Bureau of Product Safety within the Food and Drug Administration proudly announced it had prevailed upon the company to 'correct' the problem by including a printed message on the screen warning, 'Sharp edged—don try this at home.'

"Now I ask you, as mothers and fathers: What good is a printed warning for young children, who are good imitators but can't read?"
—Sen. Charles H. Percy (R-Ill.), in his keynote address before Consumer Assembly '73 in Washington, D.C. (1/26/73).

YOUTH PUBLICATIONS

Dobler World Directory of Youth Periodicals. . . lists publications that print student work (all ages). By Lavinia Dobler and Muriel Fuller, $4.25 from Citation Press, Professional Relations Division, Scholastic Magazines, 50 West 44th St., New York, N.Y. 10036.

Typog is a magazine which publishes only original work by high school students—writing, art, photography. The first issue came out last February and was a nicely done 112 pages with works by 80 students (available for 75¢). The work sent *Typog* should be accompanied by a statement that it is original; mimeographed or photo copies should not be submitted; only black and white art work is used; photographs should be glossy prints 5"x8" or larger; a $10 honorarium plus three complimentary copies is paid to any students whose work is used. *Typog*, Room 2301, Scott Foresman and Co., 1900 East Lake Ave., Glenview, Ill. 60025.

INFO JOURNAL

The INFO Journal is a publication of the International Fortean Organization. The organization is one of "skeptics; of individualists who are never afraid to vent a loud Bronx cheer in the direction of any pompous certitude, no matter where its point of origin." The journal carries collections of stories about crypto-scientific subjects -- falling objects, monsters, unrecognized civilizations in ancient America, UFOs, ghosts, people who appear and vanish inexplicably, etc.

Each mimeo copy of the quarterly journal costs $1 or $4 for a one-year subscription to:

THE INTERNATIONAL FORTEAN ORGANIZATION
P.O. Box 367
Arlington, Va. 22210
(703) 979-5179

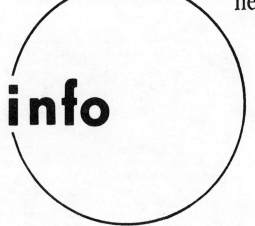

info

Leonardo advanced science in nearly every known field of his day.

And he worked alone.
What if he'd been able to work with 16,000 scientists and engineers?

May we suggest -- <u>nothing</u>.

HUMAN BEHAVIOR
The Newsmagazine of the Social Sciences

Human Behavior has a winning formula. They turn the results of technical research and articles in professional journals into easily readable accounts. Each issue contains a few feature articles plus nearly fifty of these concise summaries. Each summary has a footnote providing the original source of publication, making *Human Behavior* a useful research vehicle. Listed subscription price is $14 for the monthly publication, but reduced rates are often offered.

HUMAN BEHAVIOR
Subscription Department
P.O. Box 2810
Boulder, Colo. 80302

Radical Chic, High School Style

Sixteen-year-old Monty may march around with a sign disclaiming any allegiance to the way things are, but personally he is likely to have options on some of the more solid investments offered on the American Dream market. Apparently, that sweet sense of security is necessary as a safe base from which high school activists can protest about the rest of the world's ills.

Most high school activists are good little radicals, say Judith A. Lewis, education professor at Loyola University of Chicago, and Michael D. Lewis, human learning and development professor, Governers State University, Park Forest South, Illinois. The Lewises painted a picture of 30 pubescent activists and their more satisfied peers in a suburban, upper middle-class area. Activists were members of an organization seeking to increase student participation in school policy-making and to bring about social reform and "raise the level of consciousness" of other students by publishing an underground newspaper.

Solid Stock. The radicals came from the best families, were active in extracurricular activities, made good grades and were generally headed for the professions. The Lewises were off when they predicted activist students come from families where the parents' occupations were intellectual, social or artistic; in both groups, the fathers were "enterprising" businessmen and all the mothers but one were full-time homemakers.

As expected, the activists didn't participate in the same extracurricular activities as supporters of the status quo; the latter cornered the athletics-cheerleading department, but activists outnumbered the others in all other areas. This participation, comment the Lewises, demonstrates activists hadn't abdicated their role in the established student structures. Nor were they particularly alienated. Their numerous school activities indicate, according to the Lewises, that "they have not given up the hope of effectiveness through participation."

All of the students planned to continue their education, but more non-activists limited college plans to two years. Most of both groups intended to go into professional, technical or managerial occupations with an eye on the social aspects of those fields, emphasizing a "trend toward interest in aiding society so present in this age group without regard to the extent of political activism." Predictably, more activists were interested in unconventional or artistic careers.

Academic Go-getters. Activists had high grade averages and higher scores on IQ, aptitude and achievement tests. This was yet another mechanism, say the educators, to stay within the confines of accepted success; they had not only the ability, but the motivation, to succeed academically.

In every way—choice of occupation, participation in school activities, success in academic endeavors—young activists are laying groundwork for security and acceptance, which in turn lays the groundwork to defy those comforts.

Teen rebels are not about to saw any limbs off after them, at least not the ones they might want to light on again.

"High School Activists: They're Not Just Passing Through" by Judith A. Lewis and Michael D. Lewis in SCHOOL COUNSELOR. November 1972. Vol. 20, No. 2, pg. 122-125.

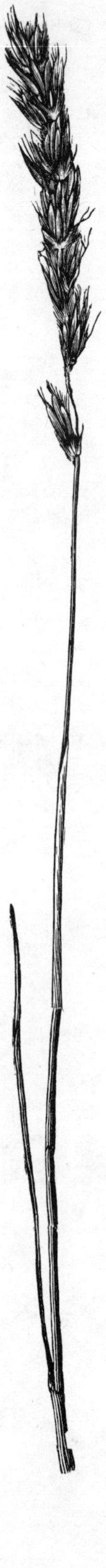

Audio

CBC TAPES

High quality tapes at reasonable prices mark the offerings of the *Canadian Broadcasting Corporation*. Tapes in either reel or cassette format are $7 per half hour. A complete catalog is free from:

> CBC LEARNING SYSTEMS
> P.O. Box 500, Terminal A
> Toronto 116, Ontario
> Canada

David Bakan, professor of Psychology, York University, in a series of five talks on child abuse (now called the "battered baby" syndrome) in which he relates this phenomenon to infanticide as a practice which has at different times carried sacrificial, pathological, and (at all times) deeply symbolic significance. (Text available in paperback in Canada only.)

Cat. Nos. 160 to 164: five talks, each 30 minutes

Ugly Teenaged Girls

What do plain girls do in a society that demands model proportions and beauty? The program presents interviews on the subject with a group of plain, teenaged girls in Montreal. (From Concern, Nov., 1970)

Cat. No. 525: 30 minutes

Children and Evil

Many of our ideas of evil are formed in early childhood. The program examines both fairy-tales and child-psychology to find out what some of the most important influences are in the development of one's first ideas about good and evil. A child-psychologist, Esther Greenglass, and a nursery-school teacher, Geraldine Lindquist, Lindquist, are interviewed by David Rapsey. (From Ideas, May, 1971)

Cat. No. 690: 30 minutes

Sane And Insane

Psychiatrists and patients who have undergone psychiatric treatment discuss their experiences and their reaction to the problem of mental health. Recorded at the Clarke Institute of Psychiatry, Toronto. (From Concern, Oct. 1970)

Cat. No. 486L: one hour

The Mafia

An interview with author Gay Talese *(Honor Thy Father)*. Mr. Talese talks about the Mafia and about the "family" problems of the underworld and the future of organized crime. (From Ideas, December, 1971)

Cat. No. 793: 30 minutes

Thinking For Alternatives

A conversation between Dr. Ivan Illich, director of the Centre for Intercultural Documentation in Cuernavaca, Mexico, and Robert Fugere of York University, Toronto. Dr. Illich's first-hand experience of the underdeveloped world gives him reason to reject the basic institutional patterns developed by the North Atlantic "rich" nations and exported everywhere. He systematically looks for alternatives to our present dilemmas, not in more of the same "value packages" we are already producing and institutionalizing at such great expense, but in letting elemental human needs speak for themselves *against* our institutions. (Paperback, *Balance and Biosphere,* available.)

Cat. No. 416L: one hour

The Language Of Now

Robert Fulford, editor of Saturday Night magazine, suggests some of the sources upon which North American English draws to make itself more colorful. Among other things, he shows how upper economic classes borrow language from lower classes and how Negro ghetto words can mean exactly the opposite to their use outside.

Cat. No. 210: 30 minutes

"... Therefore Choose Life"

Six lectures by Dr. George Wald, the winner of the 1967 Nobel Prize in medicine, a teacher of Biology at Harvard, and a critic of governments and corporations. As positively as he can, Dr. Wald endeavors to set out his belief in the "oneness" of nature and the efficacy of science to unravel the awe and beauty of our origins. He seeks to demonstrate what a wonderful achievement life is and thus to argue implicitly against uses of technology which are not life-enhancing. (The 1970 Massey Lectures, November, 1970)

Cat. Nos. 510 to 515: six lectures, each 30 minutes

The Power Of Symbols

A documentary that looks at the mysterious power bestowed upon images, idols, relics, figure-heads, witch doctors, medicine men, and heroes, by the communities of savage and civilized men who have given these objects and people the power of supernatural spirits. Besides the shaman, the program looks at such figures as the femme fatale, and even the car (or chariot), that symbol of divine freedom of movement. The participants include a science fiction writer, two anthropologists, a sculptress, and a Indian mask-maker. Also included are a talk on the movies and an interview on Japanese symbolism. (From Ideas, November, 1971)

Cat. No. 790L: one hour

Future Shock

Sociologist Alvin Toffler, author of the recent book, *Future Shock,* points out how technology is upsetting the natural cyclic patterns of human biology, ecology, economics, and history. The linear pattern of mechanics, and the time and space warp caused by modern scientific advances, threaten to make us less, not more, efficient. "Jet lag" is only one example. (From Ideas, November, 1970)

Cat. No. 585L: one hour

Death: Its Psychology

A documentary about the various aspects of death as determined by the research of the Swiss-born psychiatrist, Dr. Elisabeth Kubler-Ross of the University of Chicago. She found there were five stages through which a dying patient passed: denial, anger, bargaining, increasing depression, and finally, acceptance. A woman hopelessly ill with cancer tells how she learned to accept it. Her husband talks about his reactions and acceptance.

Cat. No. 316L: one hour

The Politics Of The Family

R.D. Laing, chairman of the Philadelphia Association, London, England, and a private psychiatric practitioner in that city, has made a special study of schizophrenia and has published several books on mental illness. In these lectures, he presents an overview of the interaction within the family, and of the family within society, that exposes a radical isolation of spoken and unspoken rules which govern individual socialization and help or hinder growth. (Text available in paperback in Canada only.)

Cat. Nos. 041 to 045: five lectures, each 30 minutes

My Two Eyes And The Cyclops

A documentary/discussion dealing with the confrontation between the individual and that great livingroom massifier, the TV set . Participants include Dr. Vivian Rakoff, psychiatrist, and director of post-graduate education, department of Psychiatry, University of Toronto; John David Hamilton, broadcaster and film-maker; and Susan Jersak, freelance newswoman. (From Ideas, May, 1970)

Cat. No. 437: 30 minutes

Eugene Hallman on Dramatization in The Mass Media

From his long experience in public affairs broadcasting, Eugene Hallman, Vice-President and General Manager of the CBC's English Services Division, speaks to an audience at the University of Victoria, B.C. He sees TV newscasts as actuality dramas having all teh dramatic requirements — heroes, villains, conflict, denouement. He talks about how the media use people and how people use the media. (From Ideas, February, 1971)

Cat. No. 594: 30 minutes

The Drama of Sports

An analysis of the dramatic appeal of sports. The hockey rink and the football field are variants of the theatre stage. The dramatic confrontation between sides, the tension of the spectator, the catharsis at the conclusion of the game, have their counterparts in the theatre. (From Ideas, February, 1971)

Cat. No. 599: 30 minutes

The Place Of The Child

Three talks by Dr. Robert Coles, research psychiatrist at Harvard University, author of *Children of Crisis and Teachers and The Children of Poverty.* Talk I deals with *The Child Within* — the gigantic, awesome, and often frightening struggles the awakening mind of the infant makes, as the child begins to appraise and interpret the world around him. II — *The Child in the Family* — the learning of boundaries to behavior, emotion safety. III — *New Limits* — the child of the backyard, the block, the schoolyard, and what part those new limits, rules, and faces play in the child's still-forming picture of himself. (From Ideas, December, 1971, and January, 1972)

Cat. Nos. 805L and 806L: three talks on two one-hour tapes

Glenn Gould On The Moog Synthesizer

Glenn Gould, Canadian concert pianist, musical commentator, and broadcaster, talks about the Moog synthesizer used in the production of the highly successful recording "Switched on Bach" containing some of J.S. Bach's most famous compositions, all rendered with electronic rather than conventional instrumental sound. Also included are interviews with Walter Carlos, whose feat the Moog recording was, and with Jean leMoyne, Canadian poet, essayist, and philosopher of culture, who talks about the human fact of musical automation, and its sociological and theological implications. The program is rounded out with reflections by Dean J. G. Parr of the University of Windsor, a writer-engineer.

Cat. No. 326L: one hour

Telling it Like It Ain't

An examination of the language of education, by Neil Postman, a professor of English Education, New York University, and author of *Linguistics: A Revolution in Teaching;* and *Education as a Subversive Activity.* (From Ideas, February, 1971)

Cat. No. 574L: one hour

Hollywood Masks

Bruce Martin, freelance writer, journalist, and movie critic, discusses how the motion picture industry, in its half century of life, seemed to repeat the stages of the 3,000-year-old theatre. The first movies used only long shots, the close-up was as yet unknown; thus, as in Greek theatre, the "mask" of the movie actor was used for identification. Then came the "type" – Buster Keaton, Chaplin; then the stock character; Boris Karloff, mask-roles such as Jekyll and Hyde. Finally the new art reached the modern stage, and we see real abstract characters, the masks behind the faces. (From Ideas, March, 1970)

Cat. No. 410L: one hour

Maidstone

American writer and film-maker Norman Mailer manages, through the flak from his audience, to describe his latest film and the new technique of film-making which he believes his method heralds. (From Ideas, March, 1971)

Cat. No. 608: 30 minutes

Political Film

A program concentrating on political film, which includes both propaganda and films dealing in either a straight or ironic fashion with political subjects. John Grierson, the noted documentary film-maker, author, founder of Canada's National Film Board, and teacher at McGill University, talks about his view of film and politics, outlining his theories, giving examples from practical

Utopias: Pro And Con

In four talks, George Woodcock, author, editor, and teacher, discusses nineteenth-century attempts to create practical utopias; the utopia conceived as the early city of God; the case against utopias – a survey of fictional anti-utopias (Huxley, Orwell); the influence of Utopian thinking in men such as Kropotkin, Lewis Mumford, and Buckminster Fuller on the politics and technology of the contemporary city; the practicability of utopian thought in planning for the future.

Cat. Nos. 366 to 369: four talks, each 30 minutes

Dreams And Dreamers

The dream is another language, having meaning only for the dreamer: for anyone else it is untranslatable. Information from the subconscious. Famous dream-interpreters from Joseph of Egypt to Dr. Sigmund Freud, on to the contemporary institutes of sleep. The REM (Rapid Eye Movement) period and its cyclical repetitions during sleep Dream-types: wish fulfillment, anxiety, guilt, memory, déjà-vu, recurring dreams. Archetypal and racial dreams. The dreamer as the producer, director, stage-manager, writer, actor, and audience of his dream. A talk by Chris Scott, illustrated with dreams re-enacted (From Ideas, October, 1971)

Cat. No. 720L: one hour

Ditto-People

Will there be a time when a Leonardo da Vinci could be doubled and given eternal time to think for mankind's sake? The answer lies in the nature of the cell and the chromosome which carries hereditary information through generations. The Russians succeeded in producing a double-headed dog. Some years ago in Cambridge, a duplicate frog was grown from the single cell of its "parent's" stomach lining: a process called cloning. A talk by Chris Scott. (From Ideas, October, 1971)

Cat. No. 722: 30 minutes

Marshall McLuhan Gets Processed

A conversation between Professor McLuhan and a group of bright and dissatisfied high school students who have better luck with the mandarin of the media than most professional interviewers. The taped happening says a lot about McLuhanism, students, curiosity – and process. (From Ideas, December, 1969)

Cat. No. 460L: one hour

Buckminster Fuller

In a discussion of the importance of cycles in his life, work, and thought, Buckminster Fuller talks about the constructive use of advanced technology and also about his experiments in architectural design. He has a very interesting view of ecology and natural process, which he says he tries to reflect in his work (the famous geodesic dome at Expo '67 was just one example). (From Ideas, October, 1970)

Cat. No. 475L: one hour

Art, Anarchy, And Education: Paul Goodman

Paul Goodman talks about ideas of chaos and anarchy as a creative source. He says formlessness is a much better structure for an artist to work from, and for, than is an authoritarian structure which stifles creativity. After his talk, a panel of thinkers from New York discuss Mr. Goodman's viewpoint. They include Nat Hentoff, Henry Aiken from Brandeis, and Sidney Morgenbesser from City College. (From Ideas, December, 1970)

Cat. No. 548L: one hour

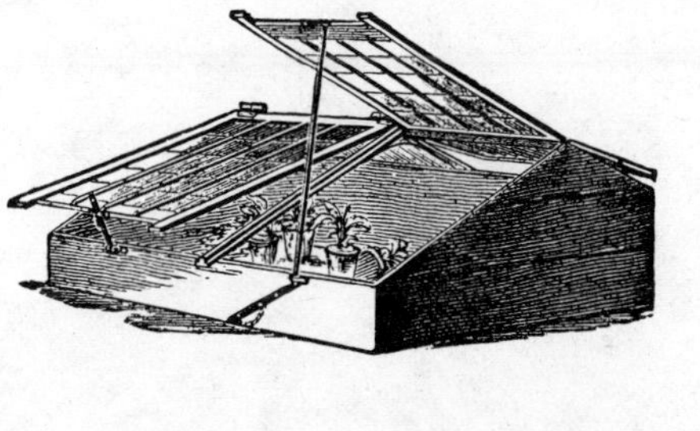

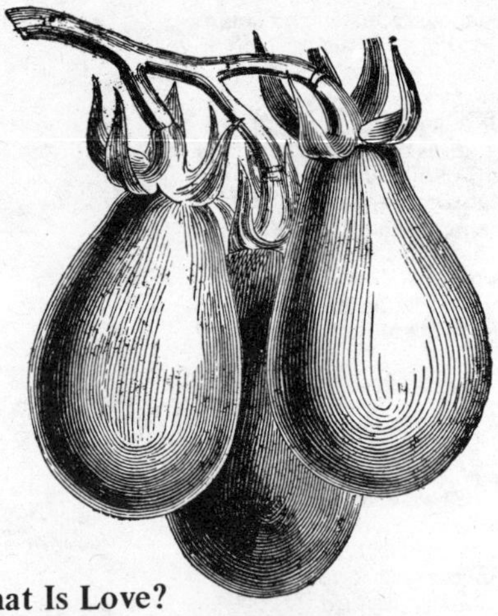

What Is Love?

The well-known anthropologist and author, Ashley Montagu, discusses the nature of love, its physical and psychological aspects. He offers a definition of what we mean by love, drawing on his extensive knowledge of scientific research on the subject.

Cat. No. 264: 30 minutes

Love: To Construe And Practise

Dr. Ashley Montagu describes some of the important ways in which love has been construed and recounts some of the ways in which it has been practised, particularly in nonliterate societies.

Cat. No. 265: 30 minutes

Kurt Vonnegut, Jr.

An interview with the American author in which he talks about his books, career, and philosophy. (From Concern, February, 1971)

Cat. No. 758L: one hour

Susan Sontag

An interview with Susan Sontag, author of *Against Interpretation* and *Styles of Radical Will*, concentrating on the power of style in art – its power to express, to impress, to form, to cover up, to disturb, to soothe, to crystallize, and to shatter. The discussion also deals with the wider range of her thought, and her recent novels and films, as well as her criticism. Miss Sontag currently lives in Paris, but she gave this interview to Ideas during a brief visit to New York. (From Ideas, December, 1971)

Cat. No. 798L: one hour

Consumerism And The Youth Market (Ages 15–up)

The youth market is big business. This program considers some of the mechanisms of business by showing how the youth market works – how businessmen pour immense amounts of money into getting to youth, creating a demand for goods that for the most part are non-essentials. Included are interviews with an economist, an advertiser who specializes in selling to young people, a writer for a magazine aimed at the young, and a consumer specialist who explores the quality and values of some of the items manufactured for the young. (Canadian School Broadcasts, October, 1972)

Cat. No. 881: 30 minutes

The Occult

A documentary about spirits, good and evil, and experiences and happenings that defy rational explanation. Included are interviews with those involved with the subject in various ways.

Cat. No. 310L: one hour

A Modern Magus: Aleister Crowley

An in-depth portrait of Aleister Crowley – self-styled "wickedest man in the world" and archetypal modern magician. A specialist in the black arts, Crowley has been described as "one of the most notorious men of the early part of the 20th century" and a "sex-obsessed voluptuary, irresistible to women", whose interests reputedly included drugs, poetry, mountain climbing, chess, yoga, and esoteric eastern philosphies (From Ideas, April, 1971)

Cat. No. 636L: one hour

White Magic And Alchemy

The enigma of alchemy: crude science or mystical discipline? Agrippa, Paracelsus, Fulcanelli; modern alchemists; Jung on alchemy; Bergier's interpretation of alchemy (alchemy and nuclear physics . . . !); alchemy and surrealism. Includes interview with Greg Simpson, Vancouver artist and alchemist. (From Ideas, April, 1971)

Cat. No. 635L: one hour

Satanism

A discussion of the origins of these cults, and interviews with some of the modern practitioners. Arthur Lyons and Peter Goddard, students of the Satanist phenomenon, are participants. The interviewer is John Disney. (From Ideas, May, 1971)

Cat. No. 678: 30 minutes

Skinner On Freedom

B. F. Skinner, the man behind the "operant conditioning box", the dean of strict behaviorists, is interviewed about his book *On Freedom and Human Dignity* and about what individual freedom might mean in an all-powerful environment. (From Ideas, April, 1970)

Cat. No. 424: 30 minutes

TECHNICAL DATA

Reels -- Are recorded full-track at 3.75 ips on 1.5 mil stock. They are provided boxed and labeled, one-hour items on seven-inch reels, half-hour items on five-inch reels.

Cassettes -- Are recorded full-track on one side only, and provided in labeled plastic boxes.

PRICES

One-hour items (reel or cassette)	$14.00
Half-hour items (reel or cassette)	7.00

These prices do not include shipping charges which will depend, of course, on the size of the order and will be billed extra. Prices are subject to change without notice.

HOW TO ORDER

Orders for audio tapes, preferably in the form of official purchase orders, should be mailed to the address below. Telephone orders are not accepted. To ensure that orders are filled promptly and accurately, be sure to give the catalog number and title of each item. Important: It is essential to indicate clearly on all orders whether reels or cassettes are desired. Orders not so marked will be returned for clarification.

Because our tape reproduction system depends upon high-speed duplication of individual tapes rather than on a large inventory, we regret that we cannot extend preview privileges to prospective purshasers.

THE CENTER FOR CASSETTE STUDIES

The Center for Cassette Studies distributes a mushrooming collection of tapes, now at nearly 3,000 programs. Schools and libraries who purchase the Center's cassettes are given the right to make as many copies as they wish. Of all the tape distributors listed in this section the Center has the largest collection as well as the highest prices ($11 - $19 per tape).

The complete Center for Cassette Studies' catalog comes in two boxes of booklets arranged by subject area. A complete catalog is free, or state your particular field of interest to:

THE CENTER FOR CASSETTE STUDIES, INC.
8110 Webb Avenue
North Hollywood, Calif. 91605

World of tomorrow

2000 A.D.

A documentary on life in the universe in the 21st century

Square tomatoes, low gravity hospitals floating in space, computers that can reproduce themselves, vacations at the bottom of the sea, a shuttle service to Mars, containerized travel for people—these are just some of the things foreseen by the experts interviewed on this program concerning life on the planet earth in the year 2,000. Predictions range from the resolute pessimism of architect Philip Johnson, who sees little hope for the cities, to the optimism of a computer expert who predicts a new morality based on leisure. Most believe that the pressing problems of population growth and urban overcrowding can be solved by the technology of the future. For the listener living in an era of enormous breakthrough in the physical sciences, this cassette is of particular value as a document of concern for the present and of hope for the future through man's inexhaustible inventive genius. □

How will people in the U.S. live in 2000 A.D.?

What will the main source of energy be in 2000 A.D.?

How will the electronics revolution affect life by 2000 A.D.?

What will people in the U.S. do with leisure time in 2000 A.D.?

How will man use the ocean in 2000 A.D.?

How will private enterprise be involved in education and government by 2000 A.D.?

Collateral Readings of Interest:
Bell, Daniel, ed. *Toward the Year 2000.* Boston: Houghton Mifflin, 1968. Gaddis, Vincent H. *Invisible Horizons.* Philadelphia: Chilton, 1965. Huxley, Aldous. *Brave New World and Brave New World Revisited.* New York: Harper & Row (Paperback). Spicer, Edward H. *Human Problems in Technological Changes.* New York: Wiley (Paperback). Wall Street Journal (eds.). *Here Comes Tomorrow.* New York: Dow Jones, 1967 (Paperback).

Order no. **3358** **Time: 51 min.**
$14.95

The American environment

The Transportation Mess

A survey of the hazards of U.S. mass transit

By auto, rail, plane, or even on foot, getting to where you want to go becomes more exasperating all the time. The complaints heard on this cassette all add up to a plea for survival. Scientists, executives, and politicians offer a variety of solutions, all with one common denominator — money. The automobile was hailed for years as a great blessing and now it is fast becoming one of our great burdens. This cassette provides you with a comprehensive, concise, vivid description of both the problem and ways out of the near chaos in our private and public transportation system. For the social historians it is a fascinating document of one of the great problems of the era. For students and teachers alike, it is a cogent summary of vital issues, realistic proposals and plausible solutions. □

Why is there no mass public transportation system in Los Angeles?

What is BART? The Metroliner? MTA?

Why is the Long Island Expressway known as the world's largest parking lot?

How much does the automobile contribute to air pollution?

Collateral Readings of Interest:
Commoner, Barry. *Science and Survival.* New York: Viking (Paperback) / Lansing, John B. *Transportation and Economic Policy.* New York: Macmillan / Lindsay, John Vliet. *The City.* New York: Norton, 1969 / Lyon, Peter. *The Hell in a Day Coach: An Exasperated Look at American Railroads.* Philadelphia: Lippincott, 1968 / Munby, D. L. (ed.). *Transport Economics.* Baltimore: Penguin (Paperback) / Serling, Robert. *Loud and Clear: Are Jets Really Safe?* New York: Doubleday.

Order no. **10995** **Time: 44 min.**
$12.95

Urban America

The Welfare Tangle

Experts discuss the urgency of immediate welfare reform

"Welfare reform must come. If it does not come through systematic planning, then it will come through further social disorder and chaos." In agreement with this sober thought, a panel led by sociologist Kenneth Clark and Mitchell Ginsberg, New York City Commissioner of Human Resources, discuss the problem of welfare. Although America prides itself on being a very advanced nation, it follows an archaic approach to treating matters of human welfare. About 16% of America's citizens live below the accepted level for economic well-being. Two-thirds of this figure is made up of whites. Contrary to public belief, most welfare recipients have nowhere else to turn. A negative income tax would, at this time, appear to be the only logical alternative. This informative cassette goes a long way toward dispelling several middle-class myths concerning welfare, and also offers a parcel of useful suggestions aimed at improving the system. □

What affect has the "frontier psychology" had on America's attitude to welfare and social security?

Are most welfare recipients lazy?

What is a "negative income tax?"

Why must there be poverty in a nation of such vast resources?

Collateral Readings of Interest:
Donovan, John C. *Politics of Poverty.* New York: Pegasus (Paperback) / Durbin, Elizabeth F. *Welfare Income and Employment.* New York: Praeger, 1969 / Kafoglis, Milton G. *Welfare Economics and Subsidy Programs.* Gainesville: University of Florida, 1962 (Paperback) / Moynihan, Daniel P. *Understanding Poverty.* New York: Basic Books, 1969 / Riessman, Frank. *Strategies Against Poverty.* New York: Random House, 1968 / Scheibla, Shirley. *Poverty Is Where the Money Is.* New Rochelle: Arlington, 1968.

Order no. **13697** **Time: 27 min.**
$12.95

Criminals at large

Crime, Calendars & Weather

An expert discusses second-hand antecedents of serious crime.

The folklore of crime reaches as far as the moon and sometimes rides the wind, according to Dr. Douglas M. Kelley, University of California professor of criminolgy and former consulting psychiatrist at the Nuremberg Trials. Summing up the mythology created by men trying to understand criminal behavior, Kelley weighs the evidence for a relationship between crime and time, weather, and the moon. He finds it without substance. Only in some cases—some crimes can be carried out effectively only in the dark—is there a second-hand relationship. There is no direct relation between crime and heredity, body type, race or culture, glands and appearance. Sometimes society's reaction to these conditions or characteristics stimulates criminal behavior among people who suffer from the reaction. □

How does climate affect criminality?

How does a full moon affect pyromaniacs?

Do wind directions have a bearing on types of crimes committed?

What is the best time for crime?

Collateral Readings of Interest:
Abrahamsen, David. *Psychology of Crime.* New York: Wiley (Paperback) / Glueck, Sheldon and E. Glueck. *Predicting Delinquency and Crime.* Cambridge: Harvard University, 1959 / Lindner, Robert M. *Rebel Without a Cause.* New York: Grove, 1956 (Paperback) / Roche, P. Q. *Criminal Mind.* New York: Wiley (Paperback) / Sloane, Eric. *Folklore of American Weather.* New York: Meredith, 1963 / Trasler, G. *Explanation of Criminality.* New York: Humanities, 1962.

Order no. **11979** **Time: 22 min.**
$14.95

LIVING LIBRARY CORPORATION

Living Library Corporation has a collection of over 100 tapes available either as cassettes or in reel-to-reel format. Tapes are about 50 minutes each and sell in the cassette format for $8.99 and in reel-to-reel for $9.99 from:

LIVING LIBRARY CORPORATION
P. O. Box 5405
Linden Hill Station
Flushing, N.Y. 11354

Ivan Illich, *An Educational Bill of Rights for Modern Man.* By exploring the myth of schooling, Illich forces us toward a reshaping of society's structures for learning and the awarding of credentials. An educational bill of rights is proposed for all humanity, and Illich contends that all revolutionary societies will hereafter be judged by their recognition of the individual's freedom to function without institutional credentials. (50 minutes)

Ivan Illich is a cofounder of the Center for Intercultural Documentation in Cuernavaca, Mexico, and is the author of *Deschooling Society*.

Jonathan Kozol, *Basic Training Begins in Kindergarten.* Rejecting the popular outcry that the schools are not working, Kozol insists that they have done their job all too well. While failing educationally, schools have succeeded as agencies of political socialization in producing a manageable, dependent citizenry whose ethical sense is homogenized under state control. Schools don't require corrective surgery -- political confrontation is prescribed. (56 minutes)

Jonathan Kozol is the author of *Free Schools*.

Jonathan Kozol, *White Schools, Black Revolution.* "Why don't Black children trust us?" Why has the school, the arena where the Black child meets the

White world, been filled with mutual hatred? Against the backdrop of the King assassination, this "unforgiving second look" at the basic problem of a divided society reveals the unstated assumptions and emotions behind the teaching of Blacks in America's public schools.

Jonathan Kozol, *The Open Classroom and the Open Society*. Jonathan Kozol boldly confronts the growing public euphoria over the potentially liberating effects of the open classroom, asserting that, in the name of freedom we are actually limiting children's access to knowledge crucial to understanding of their society. He warns that our open classrooms may become environments in which the child is deadened to passion and outrage by absorbing an anesthetized image of the world as strictly "a nice place."

Paul Goodman *Beyond Schools: The Rediscovery of the Wild*. Hoping to develop liberating lifestyles, Goodman dismantles society's equation of learning with schooling. The vital need is to recapture real, firsthand experience in education by de-institutionalizing the learning process. Goodman cites the vested economic interests in centralized public education as a critical obstacle. Characteristically, he offers freewheeling visionary and practical socioeducational alternatives. (50 minutes)

Paul Goodman's book include *Growing Up Absurd, Compulsory Mis-Education, The Community of Scholars*, and *People or Personnel*.

Paul Goodman, *Professionals vs. Professionalism*. What is the role of the professional in a highly technological society? The autonomous professional, free of corporate and bureaucratic restraints, has traditionally been a central ideal in Western society. Goodman discusses the necessity of attempting to realize this abandoned ideal as an instrument for radical change. (50 minutes)

Paul Goodman, *Use and Abuse*. In a penetrating analysis of the degeneration of the quality of everyday life, Goodman explores alternatives for two central problems: our measuring of social usefulness against the outmoded yardstick of an increasing Gross National Product dominated by three useless industries - education, automobiles, and the military; and the denial of access to socially useful, personally meaningful, activity. (50 minutes)

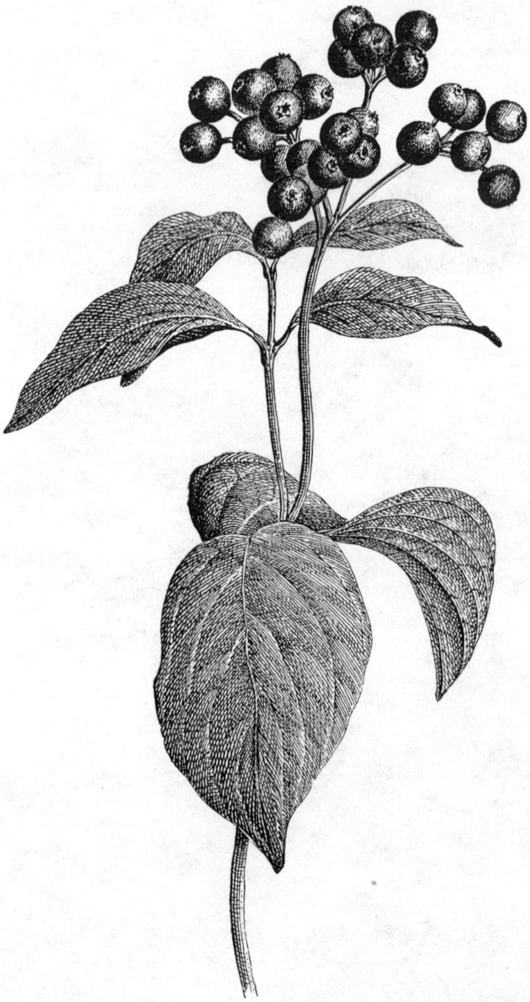

John Holt, *Within Schools Without Schools*. "Educational resources should be put into the hands of the learner, not the learning institutions." The destructive competition for scarce educational resources, institutionalized through outmoded conceptions of learning, can be replaced by turning our environment into the educational resource. Holt concretely illustrates how practical and experimental approaches, both in traditional and alternative schools, can yield abundant new learning resources. (54 minutes)

John Holt's books include *How Children Fail, How Children Learn,* and *What Do I Do Monday?*

John Holt, *Deschooling*. "If you could be anything you wanted, what would you like to be?" The widespread inability to answer this question reveals how much schools have starved our sense of possibilities and left many of us socially useless and personally unfulfilled. Developing Illich's deschooling thesis in an American context, Holt challenges us to disenthrall ourselves from schooling and engage in both school and credential resistance.

John Holt, *The Daily Life of an Autodidact*. Speaking as an autodidact and a "para-professional" in the field of education, Holt maintains, "You don't have to have schools in order to have education and you don't have to have school buildings in order to have schools."

In the place of conventional schooling, Holt suggests a number of ways to help children act intelligently and purposefully when coming to grips with the problems and needs of the world. Further, Holt provides concrete educational alternatives to replace the ineffective methods of our schools. The use of "reading guides" and mini-library centers are some of the practical alternatives explored to help children learn how to read as well as to help the society get what it likes, rather than like what it gets.

Nat Hentoff, *Inner City School Blues*. While Nat Hentoff sympathizes with those who go outside the System to create humanizing alternative models of learning, he nonetheless confronts the question, "Who's going to stay behind?" Without apologizing for public education, Hentoff believes teachers can still provide consistently humane - even joyous - learning environments within the system, provided they are fully committed to being real. Hentoff argues that only by transcending the narrow, authoritarian role in which many teachers now are caught can they even begin to earn the personal respect upon which a teacher's "natural authority" is based.

The demand for authenticity - that teacher and system be real - is explored both as part of an overall change in student/parent expectations, and as a means of eliminating that crippling inferiority felt by students and induced by schools. (55 minutes)

Nat Hentoff is the author of *Our Children Are Dying* and *In The Country of Ourselves*.

Ned O'Gorman, *The Wilderness and the Laurel Tree* O'Gorman combines the acute sensitivity and passion of the poet with the unique experience of simultaneously running a storefront school and a Head Start program in New York's ghetto. He delivers an eloquent, irreverent testimonial to the momentous drama of the learning encounter between child and adult. He brilliantly defines and explores the crucial problem of early education: how to love and preserve that primitive and mystical wilderness that is the child while presenting him with "the laurel tree" -- the gifts of civilization. O'Gorman denounces the traditional, overstructured classroom as a repressive "obstacle-course to the spirit" and urges teachers to develop learning environments where children can be "so free that they can roam, find bottlecaps, and rejoice." (55 minutes)

Ned O'Gorman is the author of *Storefront* and a volume of poetry, *The Harvester's Vase*.

Lillian Weber, *Creating an Open Classroom*. Weber gives a personal history of the development of the open classroom in the United States. From its beginnings as survival techniques within the traditional pedagogy and behind closed doors, open education has generated intense interest on the part of teacher, parent, and administrator.

Weber talks to teachers about support for each child's individual learning; related organizational problems; structuring of working relationships with administrators, other teachers, and the children; and establishing guidelines for the introduction of new materials, new techniques, and a new spatial and temporal understanding of the learning environment. (51 minutes)

Lillian Weber, an associate professor at City College of New York, is one of America's foremost spokeswomen for open education and its earliest pioneer. She is the author of numerous articles on the open classroom.

Florence Howe, *The Education of Willing Slaves*. In a probing analysis of the effect of schooling on women, Florence Howe debunks the myth that it has a positive effect on the character, work opportunities, and social mobility of women. Howe sees the primary function of schools vis-à-vis women as the reinforcement of a rigid sex-role differentiation inculcating conformity to a male-dominated world of subordinate social functions and passive acceptance of pre-defined career goals. Howe arrives at the harrowing conclusion that while it is essentially human to believe that one can change one's condition, the purpose of the education of women is to prevent such belief. It is "the education of willing slaves." (53 minutes)

Florence Howe is coauthor of *The Conspiracy of the Young* and has contributed to the *New York Review of Books*, *The Nation*, and other magazines.

Neil Postman, *2001: An Education Odyssey*. Neil Postman asserts that our schools face extinction if they continue to be based upon assumptions no longer viable in our rapidly changing culture. Five major assumptions are examined: that there is more reliable information inside the school building than outside; that knowledge is more or less stable; that intellectual competence is best measured by reading ability and the written expression of analytical thought; that older people are best suited to teach the young; and that past experience is necessarily relevant to future needs. In short, Postman calls for and suggests concrete means by which schools can orient themselves to a culture marked by radical changes in technological organization, esthetic sensibility, predominance of mass media, and the intensity and nature of change itself. (60 minutes)

Neil Postman is coauthor of *Teaching as a Subversive Activity* and *The Soft Revolution*.

Neil Postman, *The Conspiracy to Learn*. Neil Postman examines the crucial problem of change and strategy within our public school systems. As he sees it, the central problem is "to achieve revolutionary changes without using revolutionary means." While we know what is wrong with schools and are familiar with promising alternatives, Postman calls on us to focus upon the development and refinement of strategies to implement desired changes. He advances the "judo strategy", which is designed to use one's opponent's -- the Educational Establishment's -- strength against

himself. Such a strategy involves the mastery of our society's clichés, rituals, and symbols for use in attaining diverse ends such as the introduction of alternative classroom forms into the same school and the abolition of grades.

Participants in the discussion include Charles Weingartner, coauthor of *Teaching as a Subversive Activity;* Martin Engel, formerly with the U.S. Office of Education; and Ronald Gross, vice-president of the Academy for Educational Excellence. (50 minutes)

Charles Silberman, *Progress Report on the Crisis in the Classroom.* Charles Silberman presents a cogent statement of the origin, development, experience, and rationale behind the writing of his influential work. Arguing that "mindlessness" is the root cause of the admittedly "joyless, banal, trivial, and often brutal" experience of public school classrooms, Silberman insists upon "reformability from within," citing numerous examples of the responsiveness of "traditional" educators. Concluding that teachers and administrators, as well as students, are victims of this systematic, dehumanizing mindlessness, Silberman holds that it is both possible and probable for our schools to unite freedom with structure, personal growth and development with intellectual discipline, child-centered experiences with knowledge-centered curricula. (53 minutes)

Charles Silberman is the author of *Crisis in Black and White* and *Crisis in the Classroom.*

Judson Jerome, *The Living-Learning Community.* Judson Jerome gives eloquent testimony to his vision of an alternative mode of learning and living which rescues learning from its destructive institutionalization and living from its increasing entrapment in the over-structured, highly technological society. The living/learning or "intentional community" is advanced as a means of integrating education with life, thought with feeling and delight and satisfaction in production. The intentional community is an alternative to the over-structured "Buck Rogers technological future" and the randomly structured laissez-faire past; it is a community in which education functions to develop and reinforce values that prize humanity over technology. (53 minutes)

Judson Jerome is the author of *Culture out of Anarchy.*

Mario Fantini, *Schools Within a School.* Mario Fantini offers a realistic strategy for reforming the monolithic and failing school systems of America. Fantini rejects all reform proposals geared to provide only one particular set of objectives. In a highly diverse society the real need is to provide the maximum number of options within the public schools.

Fantini develops the notion that the individual is entitled to a choice in his children's education, provided that others are not deprived of their choices as a result. Only in this way can the schools hope to meet the needs of all the people. (52 minutes)

Mario Fantini coauthored *Community Control and the Urban School, Designing Education for Tomorrow's Cities, The Disadvantaged: Challenge to Education,* among other books.

Edgar Z. Friedenberg, *Traveling First Class on the Titanic.* A witty and personal testimony to both the real need for institutional reform and the severe limitations placed upon reform movements by an absurd universe.

Friedenberg advocates a free-flowing education; and yet, he sees school reform as pointless in a repressive society in which school is but a facet. (45 minutes)

Edgar Z. Friedenberg is the author of *Coming of Age in America*, *The Dignity of Youth and Other Atavisms*, and The Vanishing Adolescent.

Richard Grossman, *The Human Potential Movement*. Starting with William James's statement in 1903 that "all my researches lead me to believe that man never goes beyond achieving 10% of his strengths," the idea of studying human potential has come to be the center of modern humanism and humanistic psychology. Richard Grossman traces the psychological and philosphical basis of this movement toward self-actualization.

The role of sensory awareness, gestalt psychology, affective education, Esalen-type growth activities, and free learning are explained as techniques for developing healthy and responsible people. (55 minutes)

Richard Grossman, editor-in-chief of Grossman Publishers, has led seminars in the human potential movement at New York University.

Gloria Channon, *The Free Classroom*. How does a teacher begin to open his/her classroom? What are the first steps in the gradual introduction of freedom? What are the problems encountered in response to this new freedom? Ms. Channon explores in detail these among other concerns of all beginning teachers in the open classroom. She offers a wealth of practical suggestions which have proven successful in her own classroom year after year toward fulfilling the four goals she considers crucial: proficiency in reading, in math, the development of critical thinking, and enhancement of the youngster's self-esteem. (52 minutes)

Gloria Channon is a teacher and the author of *Homework*.

Gloria Channon, *The Teacher in the Open Classroom*. Ms. Channon offers practical "how-to advice" for those teachers who have tried to open their classroom only to discover that the newly created environment is not all it should be. She advises doing what is comfortable and natural, and learning to forgive one's own failures. She dispells some prevailing myths that an open classroom means no discipline problems, continuously excited students, and lack of "confrontations and conflicts." At the same time, she offers thoughtful remarks on the underlying goals of American education and the need for change. (50 minutes)

George Leonard, *Sense & Sensibility*. In the hope of realizing educational-cultural change, George Leonard presents a plan for an effective mode of learning which is, at once, joyous and productive. Leonard envisions a learning environment in which the educator becomes nonessential, if not superfluous, and in which students determine and direct their own education. The students' role entails and encourages intense commitment, patience, and inner discipline. Leonard demonstrates that effective learning is not only compatible with cognitive development, but is a pre-condition for compehensive learning. (58 minutes)

George Leonard is the author of *Transformations* and *Education and Ecstasy*.

Edward Carpenter, *The Harlem Prep Experience*. Edward Carpenter delivers an impassioned and inconoclastic portrait of the genesis and functioning of Harlem Prep and the moral vision which infuses it. While Harlem Prep was founded to service the Harlem community's crying need for a school "which the people could identify with, be proud of, and consider meaningful in the lives of their children," it has become a global community in miniature, consciously embracing the widest diversity of races, ideologies, classes, and nationalities in its student body and staff. Perceiving living and learning as an identical process, Carpenter sets forth a working vision of school as a community process to achieve sexual, racial, and economic equality both within the school and in the larger context of society. (55 minutes)

Edward Carpenter is the founder and former headmaster of the Harlem Prep School.

Rhody McCoy, *Schooling as a Community Process*. In a passionate yet practical critique of ghetto-based education, Rhody McCoy calls for community participation in the schooling of children, especially in the face of white America's failure to educate black children. McCoy decries teacher education, inadequate to meet the gap between the teacher's background and the experience of ghetto children. He asserts that the physical decay of the school environment prevents schooling from being more than baby-sitting, and he points to the punitive atmosphere in ghetto schools.

McCoy envisions and explores schooling as a community process where responsibility for the child's educational success or failure is based on collective accountability of teachers, parents, administrators, community persons, and students who jointly devise and fulfill criteria for real learning. (54 minutes)

Rhody McCoy was the unit administrator of the famed Ocean Hill - Brownsville experimental district in New York City.

Marilyn Gittel, *The Politics of Decentralization*. As one deeply involved in the struggle over community control of the New York City School System, Marilyn Gittel candidly analyzes the ideology and dynamics of power behind that struggle. She sees that none of the significant innovations proposed by education reformers can be adopted unless schools become environments open to change by giving parents, students, and educational professionals the chance to make significant inputs to the system.

Gittel offers an illuminating analysis of the struggle between middle-class professionals, who have monopolized decision-making under the subterfuge of expertise and merit, and an alliance of an upper-class power Establishment anxious to maintain its power through accommodation with local community elites hungry for a piece of the action. (53 minutes)

Marilyn Gittel is the author of *Participants and Participation* and co-author of the Ford Foundation's controversial *Bundy Report on Decentralization*.

Ronald Gross, *Lockstep, Hop, Skip, and Jump*. In a thorough survey and analysis of the last decade's promises and failures to change our schools, Ronald Gross recognizes three basic phases. The innovative phase, characterized by the introduction of team teaching, nongraded classes, programmed learning, and teaching machines, failed since it addressed only "the facade" of public education and neglected its core. The radical reform phase attempted to institute "a Copernican Revolution" in learning by shifting emphasis from "the teacher teaching to the learner learning," but failed to produce lasting institutional alternatives. Lastly, in a radical departure from the previous school-bound phases, Gross heralds the coming of the deschooling phase, which will attempt to liberate the learning process from its bureaucratized, institutional context. Recognizing that we have reached "the last generation of school children" that will obediently trudge through the lockstep of grade school to college, Gross explores the deschooling ideas of Ivan Illich with modifications of his own in the hope of creating nonschool learning environments characterized by autonomous, creative individuals rather than coercive institutions. (57 minutes)

Ronald Gross is coeditor of *Radical School Reform* and *High School*.

Thomas Szasz, M.D., *Psychiatry: Medicine or Politics?* In a scathing analysis of the myth of "mental illness," Dr. Szasz develops the idea of psychiatry as an ideology. Drawing an important distinction between voluntary and involuntary psychiatric treatment, he insists that the latter is a form of immoral social control. Embracing such libertarian issues as the individual's right to reject assistance and treatment, yet to remain socially free, Dr. Szasz argues that mental illness is a metaphorical disease. If a person seeks psychiatric treatment, he chooses one method of change. Involuntary psychiatric treatment, however, is an attempt to change that individual against his will and is therefore a moral and political enterprise. What television viewer, Dr. Szasz asks, would send for a television repairman because he doesn't like the program he sees on the screen? (50 minutes)

Thomas Szasz is a professor of psychiatry at the State University of New York Upstate Medical Center in Syracuse. His books include *Pain and Pleasure, The Myth of Mental Illness: Law, Liberty, and Psychiatry*, and *Ideology and Insanity*.

Dr. John Bardach, *Myth of the Endless Sea*. By exploding the myth that the oceans will someday solve man's acute food shortages, Dr. John Bardach attempts to clarify environmental and especially marine realities.

Describing two of the ocean's most important functions as supplying more than half of the atmosphere's oxygen and supplying human beings with essential animal proteins, Dr. Bardach explains why only a small percentage of the oceans will ever be harvested. Such issues as the future potential of aquaculture, the effect of pesticides on the photosynthesis of certain algae, the relationship of our rivers to the oceans, and the harmful effects of "technological fixes" in lieu of fundamental industrial reform are explored in this extremely informative talk.

Audio 183

On a planet where 71 percent of the surface is water, man had better learn to care for this crucial life-support system lest this primal bath deny its own creation. (58 minutes)

Dr. John Bardach is the author of *Down Stream, The Natural History of Rivers*, and other volumes on the natural resources of the oceans.

René Dubos, *The Limits of Growth: The Technological Steady State*. In a plea for major ecological reforms, one of the world's most distinguished scientists here issues an urgent message to the general public. Exploring the present state of the environmental crises, Dr. Dubos predicts that the quantity growth phase of modern society must and will end by the year 2000 and that a "technological steady state" must be maintained. Without exception, ecological equilibriums, regenerating both energy and materials, must be recognized globally as our first priority. If not, Dr. Dubos insists, disaster is inevitable.

Yet there are hopeful signs, and Dr. Dubos explores striking examples, including that of London, of success in retrieving a natural and healthy environment. Almost as an omen of better times, certain birds not heard in London since Shakespeare's day have once again begun to sing. (58 minutes)

Dr. René Dubos was awarded the Pulitzer Prize for *So Human an Animal*. His other books include *Man Adapting; Man, Medicine, and Environmental;* and, with Barbara Ward, *Only One Earth*.

Dom Hélder Câmara, *The Hour Has Come*. Dom Hélder issues an urgent and impassioned appeal to the citizens of the wealthy nations to recognize their role in keeping the majority of mankind in a subhuman situation. Seeking to lend his voice to the world of those without voice, Archbishop Câmara reveals the falsehoods, the degradations, the threats under which Third World peoples suffer. Focusing on multinational corporations, on the military, on foreign aid, Dom Hélder courageously forces a rethinking of basic Christian morality and clearly calls for the true revolution through peace. (60 minutes)

Dom Hélder Câmara, Archbishop of Recife and Olinda in the northeast of Brazil, has courageously fought government, military, and business intersts in the interest of the poor. A symbol of justice, religious, and intellectual freedom, Archbishop Câmara has not been silenced by the criticism of Church and State, nor by the extreme personal danger under which he has lived. Dom Hélder has been awarded the Martin Luther King International Peace Prize and was nominated for the Nobel Peace Prize in 1970.

Pete Hamill, *800 Rounds a Minute*. Recorded in September 1970, prior to the publication of the Pentagon Papers and the Watergate revelations, Pete Hamill delivers a stunning indictment of the Nixon administration. Hamill speaks of U.S. violations of international law and the Constitution, and of the coming repression at home. He describes the contradiction in U.S. priorities between the 30 billion dollars a year spent on destruction in Indochina and the dearth of money and of hope on the streets of American cities. He describes the great promise that drew throngs of immigrants to our land and the more than 50,000 children of these immigrants driven as exiles to Canada. Hamill warns that the choice must soon be made between "the victim and his oppressor, between the peasant and the landlord, between the student and the FBI agent, between those who have been jailed for their political beliefs and those who have jailed them." We cannot, Hamill pleads, choose silence. (10 minutes)

Pete Hamill is a columnist for the *New York Post*.

CENTER FOR THE STUDY OF DEMOCRATIC INSTITUTIONS

The Center for the Study of Democratic Institutions has 300 cassette and tape recordings for sale. The tapes are discussions among members of the Center, not lectures. All tapes and cassettes on this page are $7.50 each. Recordings are available on both cassettes and five-inch 3 3/4 ips, half-track, reel-to-reel tape. A complete catalog of tapes is free.

THE CENTER FOR THE STUDY OF
DEMOCRATIC INSTITUTIONS
P.O. Box 4446
Santa Barbara, Calif. 93103

#308 A Harvest of Thorns

"An army's harvest is a waste of thorns."—Lao-tzu. A moving program of readings with music about the many faces of war in the words of Euripides, Horace, Genghis Khan, Wilfred Owen, Shakespeare, Richard Lovelace, Stephen Crane, Lao-tzu, e. e. cummings, Thomas Merton, Yorifumi Yaguchi, and Mark Twain. 28:45

#482 "Suppose They Gave a War and No One Came?"

Japan, which has a constitutional prohibition against war, stands in a unique position to usher in the warless world. William O. Douglas, Associate Justice of the United States Supreme Court, interrupts a Conference on China Policy with an impatient plea that we break with our bankrupt political policies and seek innovative paths to peace under law. He is joined by Senators Fulbright and Hatfield and their Japanese opposite numbers in a moving montage that demands respect for all living things—including man. 29:46

Peace and War

#527 The Haunting Past

Sooner or later the United States will withdraw fron Vietnam, but Vietnam is only a small part of far thornie problems that lie ahead and which stem from tragic miscon ceptions, misinformation, and miscalculations. Nor are thes mistakes wholly ideological. The same misunderstandings the same misinformation, the same miscalculations can b laid also at the door of the Soviet Union as to *its* policy i Southeast Asia. George McT. Kahin, foremost among spe cialists on Indochina, here warns that unless we understan why or how these policies were initiated, and what their effec has been on the political landscape of Southeast Asia, w may, in Santayana's words, be condemned to repeat the his tory we have not learned. The case example here detailed i Cambodia. 27:4

#29 The Politics of Ecology

Aldous Huxley here says that the most pressing problem facing democracy in the next ten years are the populatio explosion, the arms race, and rising nationalism. He sugges that a shift in our attention from bad politics to enlightene ecological understanding may help prevent war. 44:0

#457 Creative Non-Violence

Cesar Chavez, charismatic, non-violent leader of far workers, here recorded before the grape strike was wo speaks informally with Center Fellows about his view things to come. Ranging from the future problems of aut mated picking to the diminishing sense of community th is already a result of union success, this tape makes clear, understatement, the force of Chavez' personality, appeal ar principles. 19:

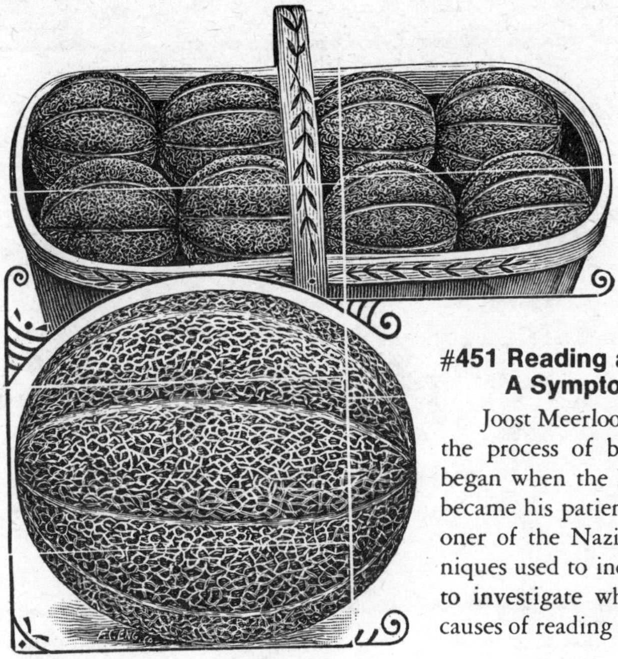

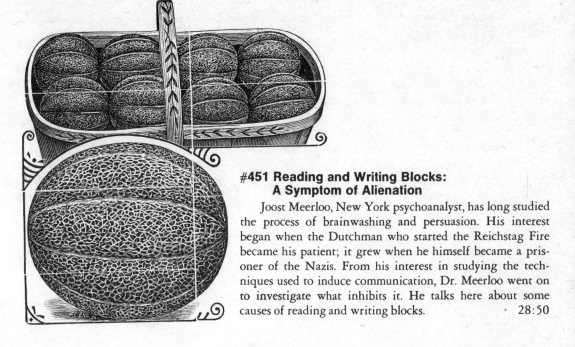

#451 Reading and Writing Blocks: A Symptom of Alienation

Joost Meerloo, New York psychoanalyst, has long studied the process of brainwashing and persuasion. His interest began when the Dutchman who started the Reichstag Fire became his patient; it grew when he himself became a prisoner of the Nazis. From his interest in studying the techniques used to induce communication, Dr. Meerloo went on to investigate what inhibits it. He talks here about some causes of reading and writing blocks. 28:50

#510 Adolescence Is No Time for School

The post-Freudian, post-industrial era may demand rethinking our past schedule of schooling. Perhaps students should not attend school during adolescence but be allowed to have experiences and opportunities for learning consistent with this period of psycho-sexual development. An animated conversation which is at the same time an example of good dialogue "when the conversation is allowed to follow the question wherever it leads." Participants include Kenneth Tollett, Professor of Education at Howard University, and Center Fellows. 28:58

#283R The Youth Culture

"We put kids in school today at age four or five—curious, intelligent, interested, prepared to be themselves—and by the time they've been there six years, we turn them into dull, normal kids with no curiosity, who hate the process of learning. Hippi-ism is a reaction, saying 'it doesn't have to be this way.' " A lively conversation involving sharp clashes in the views about the youth culture and some questions as to whether youth even represents a culture. Guest William Kiely, M.D., Associate Professor of Psychiatry at the University of Southern California, talks with Harry S. Ashmore, John R. Seeley and Hallock Hoffman of the Center. (Recut from an earlier program entitled *The Hippies: Forecast or Fad*) 42:01

Dissent

#542 What Can the Individual Do Against the Power of the State?

If law is the rampart of liberty, what about oppressive laws that limit liberty? What about evil laws which moral men ought not to obey? Some of the views heard in this lively symposium: "... dissent is the voice of powerless people...." "... the state is as tyrannical as it needs to be to preserve itself...." "... the courts are not a bargain counter that allows us to violate any law we choose...." "... the idea of community requires the renunciation of absolute liberty." Speakers include Ramsey Clark, Sander Vanocur and Milton Mayer, whose book, *Man Vs. the State,* is discussed. (Excellent for political science groups in high school or college.) 29:08

NOUMEDIA

Noumedia is a supplier of "New age educational tape recordings." They have a large number of tapes by Richard Alpert/Baba Ram Dass, a two and a half hour series of talks by Ronald Laing, and a ninety-minute talk/demonstration by Virginia Satir, and series by Fritz Kunz, Ivan Illich, and Margaret Mead. Tapes are reasonably priced. Write for a catalog to:

NOUMEDIA CO.
Box 750
Port Chester, N.Y. 10573

MEDITAPES

Meditapes is a cassette series produced by the Thomas More Association and intended primarily for a Catholic audience. Thomas More has a free catalog listing hundreds more titles; the ones described on this page are those of a less religious nature. Catalog or orders to:

THOMAS MORE ASSOCIATION
180 North Wabash
Chicago, Ill. 60601

Sex and Violence in the Film . . . . is a tape by Chicago film critic Roger Ebert. Ebert is a rarity among film critics - - - someone who can write and speak ordinary English clearly. His talk, read rather matter-of-factly into a studio mike, is filled with dry wit and opinionated insights. He says:

"Movie critics who would never dream to admit being aroused by a skin flick will admit readily to their respect for the artistry of violence."

Newsweek in a film review referred to violence as an "initiation into manhood." Ebert comments, "As if we belonged in short pants until we've killed."

"**Love Story** isn't really about love, but about death."

"Hard core porno flicks are to the cinema what the telephone book is to literature."

Ebert stresses that movies are becoming more explicit but less erotic.

"The extremes of violence are cinematic, but the extremes of sex are not. Violence can go further than sex. There are more stops to pull."

"Those who wonder if movie violence is really a metaphor for sex are advised to study that chase sequence (in **French Connection**) carefully. It is paced and edited to resemble sexual foreplay, intercourse and climax. It ends with a killing, of course."

31 minutes (#M67) for $5.95.

CONFRONTING DEATH (M46)
Input **No. 1**
The first "issue" of the unique new cassette magazine produced by the Thomas More Association under the editorship of Todd Brennan. This sixty-minute audio collage confronts the human and religious problems raised in our personal lives and in society by the fact of death—its acceptance and its non-acceptance. Conversations, dialogues and commentary are blended to create a stimulating yet informative perspective on a subject which everyone must think about but which few like to dwell on. Features interviews with Dr. Elizabeth Kubler-Ross, author of the best-seller *On Death and Dying,* Dr. Carl Nighswonger of the faculty of the Divinity School at the University of Chicago and head of the University's Chaplaincy Services and Sister Mary Peter McGinty, who teaches a unique course on death at Chicago's St. Mary of the Lake Seminary. The diversity and appeal of broadcast techniques make this audio magazine ideal for discussion groups and religion classes. (58 minutes)
Individual issue to non-subscribers: $8.95

MOVIES AND MORALS (M116)

a Todd Brennan Omnitape

What effect do movies have on the way people think and act? If we believe some commentators, many movies today are contributing to the moral deterioration of society. But others hold that the increased violence, sex and moral ambiguity which we see on the screen today is simply a reflection of the changes in social values which America is actually experiencing and thus should legitimately be explored by serious film-makers. To probe the relationship between movies and morals, Todd Brennan interviewed three nationally known film critics and a film historian (for *Input*, the cassette magazine) and you will hear: Andrew Sarris of New York's *Village Voice*, considered by many to be the most influential film critic in the U. S.; Roger Greenspun, the insightful young critic of the *New York Times*; John E. Fitzgerald, for sixteen years film critic for *Our Sunday Visitor* and one of the few film columnists in the Catholic press whose opinions are respected by fellow professionals; and Gene Phillips, a Jesuit priest on the faculty of Loyola University, whose articles on film history have appeared in a number of national periodicals. They explore such questions as: Whether violence on the screen desensitizes us to real violence? Does explicit sex in films encourage promiscuity? When is a film immoral?
(57 minutes) $8.95

THE VISION OF TEILHARD DE CHARDIN (M88)

by Hugh McElwain

While the name Teilhard de Chardin has become familiar to many, there is still widespread confusion and difficulty with what he thought, wrote and taught. In some real way Teilhard has helped open up for contemporary man a vision of himself in his world which has made the vital task of "building the earth" and continuing the dynamic progression of "the future of man" seem not only possible but challenging. This cassette summarizes in clear and bold terms the major theories and thought of Teilhard. Father Hugh McElwain, Professor of Doctrinal Studies at the Catholic Theological Union, Chicago, and author of *An Introduction to Teilhard de Chardin*, insists that his thought must be seen in terms of something akin to a vision. Having experienced in his own life and study the marvelous interpenetration and mutual enrichment between the scientific and the religious, Teilhard saw the clear convergence of cosmic, human, religious and Christian history. The point of that convergence was Love, incarnated in Christ and, through that incarnation, made operative at the very core of all reality as

THE RIGHT TO LIFE (M56)

by Daniel Callahan

How absolute is the basic right to life? Daniel Callahan, who is director of the Institute of Society, Ethics and the Life Sciences and author of such widely discussed books as *Abortion: Law, Choice and Morality* and *Honesty in the Church*, believes that the problem of the right to life rises today particularly in three areas: (1) In problems of death and the dying patient—particularly because of the prolongation of life of the sick and elderly; (2) the delivery of medical care—the disproportionate care that is available to the rich and well-to-do versus minority and poor peoples; (3) in the questions of contraception and abortion—particularly the latter. He explores the hard questions rising from these new problem areas: Is there a natural life span? Is there a right to die as well as to live? How do we balance the right to life with the consideration of the quality of life? Who is to make decisions concerning the right to life? And most importantly, the "protection of the weak and the deprived, those whose life will be in jeopardy unless others protect them." The organization which Dr. Callahan heads is dedicated to exploring just such questions as these which promise to become even more burning in the months and years ahead. A major cassette which will both provoke and illuminate debate and discussion in these vital areas.
(27 minutes) $6.95

THE OCCULT (M50)

by Richard Woods

After long repression the occult has surfaced again in the United States. Covens regularly hold Witches Sabbaths in every city and large town in the country; astrology columns are a popular feature in nearly every major newspaper; palmists, card-readers, crystal gazers and mediums are flourishing. Satanist churches have been founded throughout the U.S., South America and Europe; psychic research into levitation, telepathy, reincarnation is being undertaken in a number of universities. Even in the Christian churches pentecostalism, faith healing and mysticism have taken on new significance. According to Father Woods, author of *The Occult Revolution,* the return to the "magic" of these things rises out of the overwhelming mood of powerlessness which grips modern man in times of stress and danger. The scientists and theologians seem to have nothing new to say for the time being. The occult is always ready to emerge to meet these deep-seated needs for a way to control, predict or manipulate our destiny. Father Woods explores these manifestations in detail and concludes by saying that the occult may offer hope but it is false: "Only faith, confidence in God and brotherly love will enable us to put that hope into action for tomorrow's world, to make it happen."
(28 minutes) $6.95

RELIGIOUS THEMES IN CONTEMPORARY CINEMA (M79)

by Gene Phillips

Theologian William F. Lynch once called for a "sympathetic alliance between theologian and film-maker" to help to make it possible for motion pictures—which wield such enormous influence—to be instilled with a spirit that is both human and Christian. In this interesting and informative cassette, Father Phillips (who is a member of the executive board of the National Center for Film Study, has served on the juries of the Cannes and Chicago Film Festivals and is the author of many articles and two forthcoming books on the film) examines to what extent this alliance has been realized not only in films that have an overtly religious theme such as Fred Zinnemann's *The Nun's Story* and *A Man for All Seasons* but also in films that prod us to religious reflections in a more indirect and implicit way—Ingmar Bergman's *Through a Glass Darkly*, Federico Fellini's *La Dolce Vita*, Stanley Kubrick's *Dr. Strangelove*, Luis Bunuel's *Viridiana*, John Ford's *My Darling Clementine* and John Schlesinger's *Midnight Cowboy*.
(30 minutes) $4.95

MYSTICISM (M49)

by Richard Woods

With the advent of the Maharishi Mahesh Yogi, neo-Pentecostalism and the occult revolution, mysticism in a variety of new and old forms has forced itself into the awareness of many Christians. Everyone from students to housewives are dabbling at it while Gurus and Zen Masters are teaching it in colleges. Father Woods, who is the author of *The Occult Revolution* and a staff member of Loyola University's (Chicago) Pastoral Institute, presents a wide-ranging but helpful guide to the confusing, frequently bizarre, but always fascinating varieties of religious and pseudo religious experiences which shelter under the word mystical. Such manifestations as speaking in tongues, healing and prophecy are *not* specifically Christian, says Father Woods, since they are found in all religions, but when they appear among Christians we must evaluate them from a Christian perspective to measure their worth, with brotherly love as our yardstick. Do such things build up community or do they create distrust and dissension? Can they be counterfeited in purely emotional and hysterical ways or do they spring somehow from the Spirit? What is the place of genuine Christian mysticism in the overall picture? These and many other challenging questions are confronted in this fast-paced, richly informative cassette.
(33 minutes) $6.95

ARE YOU A RACIST? (M6)
by Albert Miller
The title question is one that most people ask more easily of others than themselves. Many who are concerned about the evils of racism have examined their own attitudes and motives and found themselves blameless. "Racist," most white Americans will insist, is a label reserved for those who have demonstrated by acts or attitudes an overt and vicious hatred for blacks and members of other minority groups. But Albert Miller, a black lecturer, writer and college professor, insists that there is far more to being a racist than overtly demonstrating active hatred. He probes the full meaning of racism from both a social-scientific and a personal viewpoint, showing how most American whites are knowingly or unknowingly involved in institutional racism which in spite of all the best intentions still represses the black man in this country. Mr. Miller does not insist that all whites are racists but speaking with great candor and documenting his case with compelling statistics and examples, makes it abundantly clear that this fact is of little help to blacks who are the victims of racist employment, educational, social and economic practices. You'll find this presentation highly effective and of compelling interest to students and all people who may not, up to now, have faced the personal challenge implicit in the question: "Are you a racist?"
(31 minutes) $5.95

VOICE OVER BOOKS

Voice Over Books provides carefully edited cassette versions of best-selling books. Read by actors and edited in such a way as to preserve as much of the integrity of the full work as possible, the cassette is ideal for the blind or the busy. Each condensation is about 90 minutes and sells for $6.95. Current titles include *I'm OK -- You're OK*, *My Name Is Asher Lev*, *The Best and the Brightest*, *Chimera*, *Bury My Heart at Wounded Knee*, *The Peter Prescription* and *The Peter Principle*, *Beyond Freedom and Dignity*, *A Nation of Strangers*, *August 1914*, and *Breakfast of Champions*. Complete list or orders from:

VOICE OVER BOOKS
P.O. Box 75
Old Chelsea Station
New York, N.Y. 10011
(212) 929-0950

PACIFICA FOUNDATION

The Pacifica Foundation operates a group of listener-supported radio stations. The tapes in the Pacifica Tape Library are programs aired on these stations. A complete catalog is free from:

PACIFICA TAPE LIBRARY
5316 Venice Boulevard
Los Angeles, Calif. 90019
(415) 848-3785

185 KEN KESEY TALKS TO ENGLISH TEACHERS—the brilliant American author in a free-wheeling talk sponsored by the National Defense Educator's Act, the same group that also heard William Saroyan. The purpose of the summer institute held in 1965 was to teach teachers to teach writing. 62 min.

AP 1249 SCHOOLS AGAINST CHILDREN—John Holt, author of "How Children Fail," and "The Underachieving School," talks at a conference on education held on the University of California campus in Berkeley. A good discussion of how the public schools in this nation have worked contrary to the needs of children. March 1970. 29 minutes.

AP 1250 HERB KOHL ON "EXAMINING THE CRISIS IN EDUCATION"—recorded at the Conference for Elementary and Secondary School Teachers held March 29, 1970 on the University of California campus in Berkeley. The program is an account of his experimental program in the Berkeley schools; Kohl and his kids give a delightful account of their life in the school. 26 minutes.

AP 1244 CAN CHANGE TAKE PLACE IN THE PUBLIC SCHOOL CONTEXT?—that's the question asked (and answered) by Herbert Kohl, author of "36 Children" and several other books on education and the child. It's a relaxed talk with topical examples from his own experiences in bringing new, and often radical, methods to the continuing problem of public schools and the child. Mr. Kohl tells what is wrong and what should be done about education, delivered informally yet coherently and much to the point. Recorded at the LeConte Elementary School in Berkeley April 1970. 35 minutes.

599 DR GEORGE WALD: "THEREFORE CHOOSE LIFE"—speaking at Grace Cathedral in San Francisco, Dr. Wald continues his discussion of war as international suicide. His speech at M.I.T. in March '69 evoked nationwide comment and was widely reprinted in many magazines and newspapers. Bishop C. Kilmer Myers delivers the welcoming remarks and Dr. Wald is introduced by Dr. Owen Chamberlain of the U.C. faculty. Dr. Wald's appearance was sponsored by KPFA and 22 other Bay Area groups. 65 minutes.

AP 0671 CREDIT AND THE MIDDLE CLASS—Attorney Bennie L. Cass, who is also a consumer consultant to several national groups, talks about the truth in lending law and how it assists consumers. He also speculates on the day when we will have a national data bank that will make cash buying obsolete. Other topics include what happens to your credit rating when you don't pay for goods charged up on a stolen or lost credit card, and the "holder is due course" law which makes it possible (except in Massachusetts), to collect both the goods and the money on unpaid debts. Bill Schechner of Pacifica's Washington Bureau is the interviewer. 30 minutes.

BC 0274.06 PEOPLE'S LAW SCHOOL: JUVENILE LAW For young people in the Bay Area, the Juvenile Law Forum of the People's Law School is presented in two segments: 1) High School Rights: dealing with the student's First Amendment Rights, Free Speech, the distribution of leaflets, grooming rights, rules of suspension by administrative officials, disciplinary procedures and what to do, how school principals deal with with students, how local judges relate to the high schools. 2) On the streets: curfews, what to do if you are arrested, shoplifting, dope, the California Youth Authority and Juvenile Court. Produced by Patric Mayers. 120 min.

BC 0869 FEMINIST FORUM: SELLING WOMEN SHORT An interview with Colette Nijhof of NOW's National Image committee about the image of women in the advertising media. Ms. Nijhof discusses the harmful, long-term effects that a continuous projection of a negative image has on women's self-esteem and sense of identity. She describes the selling techniques which are responsible for this image: the "sexual sell" which is used as a dumping ground for advertisers who are not creative; and, the "psychological sell" which is used to synthesize new problems that the advertising market can zero in on. This program clearly shows the relationship between the sexual exploitation of women in the advertising media and the systematic oppression of women in American society. Produced by WETA. 28 min.

P-4 MARGARET MEAD ON SEXUAL FREEDOM AND CULTURAL CHANGE — the noted author and anthropologist speaking at the San Francisco State College public forum on the subject of "The Pill and the Puritan Ethic." In this talk she attacks the "idiocy of modern marriage" and she's not afraid to laugh at the prudity and funnier sides of sex. 80 minutes.

BC 0335 BOYS ARE BOYS AND GIRLS ARE GIRLS Is it really true that sex roles begin at an early age? To find out, Sebern Fisher of WBAI assembled a group of children aged five to nine years old to talk about the subject. He posed some questions about boys and girls and the young people took it from there. A free-wheeling rap session, which you will find amusing and poignant, yet quite revealing. 43 min.

XX 0046 ON BEING GAY—a serious discussion with four "gay" people talking it out with four "straight" people. A straightforward rap session with homosexuals "Joe Lee" and "Dan," lesbians "Barbara" and "Lee" airing their side of life with the "straights"—Steve Kortemeier, Matt Walsh, Sarah Laidlaw and Rob Poleyn. Kortemeier handled the continuity chores. This program is from Pacifica Affiliate KUNM, Albuquerque, New Mexico. 64 minutes.

BC 0202 THE POLITICAL USES OF JUNK: SOL YURICK SPEAKS - the author of 'The Bag' talks about how the government, through the CIA, is using heroin as a tool of repression. His wanderings carrying him into pseudo-hippie land (a creation of the media), and back into American history to talk about rebellions and alcohol. As for 'junk', 85 percent of it is grown in Indochina, not in Iran and Asia Minor as we are led to believe. Most of the dealing is done on the Plaines of the Jarres in Laos where there are a lot of CIA camps. This interview was recorded in Hilly's Bar on New York's Bowery, March 1971. It was produced for WBAI by Wally Roberts. 55 minutes.

AP 1369 LIFE BEFORE DEATH IN THE CORPORATE STATE—Nicholas Johnson, FCC Commissioner, is a "liberal" member of that regulatory board and is secure in his job until 1973. From this unique situation he is free to "tell it like it is" concerning TV and radio in this country. In this talk delivered November 5 at the University of California in Berkeley, he talks about the unrest and dissent in America. A witty and enormously entertaining speaker, some of his statements include: "children are fair game and legitimate prey in commercial TV . . . encourages them to continue in infantile withdrawal and develop the hedonistic habits of their elders." "No force has demeaned women more than TV." "The same guys putting garbage in the air are putting garbage in our minds." "TV as presently run is the enemy." Needless to say, he is not popular with TV network execs, the present administration or the business world. He quotes many people from Mason Williams to Arnold Toynbee. 72 minutes.

ALW 620 JOHN GERASSI ON EDITING REALITY—a former staff member for both Time and Newsweek, and currently a faculty lecturer at San Francisco State, discusses the pressures which shape the political tone of each magazine. Paul Schaffer asks the questions. 53 min. 1-67

tm

Jonathan Kozol: *Political Indoctrination in the Public Schools* . . . BC1042.07, 73 Mins., $12.00. Mr. Kozol is a radical teacher and author of *Death at an Early Age*. In this program, Mr. Kozol explains why he feels that our educational system is outdated and essentially worthless. He gives a very personal account of his career in the field and very vivid examples of inhuman approaches to teaching, which he believes permeates current methods. Mr. Kozol was once fired for "curriculum deviation" and hired ten days later by another system for "curriculum development." A highly emotional appeal to all members of the teaching profession to examine their consciences. Sensitive Language. (Note: There are slight and brief off-speed sections throughout the speech.)

PRICE SCHEDULE

30 minutes or under	–	$ 8.50 reel or cassette
31 to 60 minutes	–	10.00 reel or cassette
61 to 90 minutes	–	12.00 reel or cassette
91 to 120 minutes	–	14.00 reel or cassette
121 to 150 minutes	–	16.00 reel or cassette

Over 150 minutes, add $2.00 for each 30 minutes.

Please specify reel or cassette.

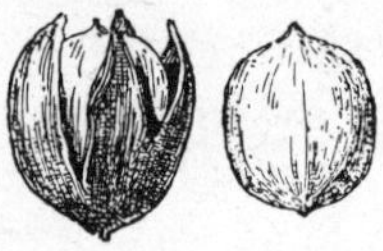

RADIO FREE PEOPLE

Radio Free People. . . is a source of "movement oriented" tapes. "Turn Off Turn On" is a tape of Nicholas Johnson in discussion after a recent FCC ruling against drug lyrics. On the tape songs under question are played and discussed. The FCC ruling is now dated but the tape is still good. "Who Programs the Computers" features a computer mathematician talking about computer research directed towards surveillance, manipulation and control of people. Other offerings are "Paul Goodman on Compulsory Mis-Education," and "News from Vietnam: What Happens vs. What you Hear." "Up Against the Mattress: Down in the Valley" is a collage of the most irritating put-down cliches women must face daily. The tape is a combination of music, raps and ads.

Tape prices range from $4 to $20. Catalog and orders to:

RADIO FREE PEOPLE
133 Mercer St.
New York, N.Y. 10012
(212) 966-6729

SOUNDS

Feedback Series . . . . is five tapes of radio documentaries produced by The Network Project. Network Project is a collective research and action group formed to investigate U.S. television and to get people to think seriously about the present system and how it affects their lives. The series was presented on Pacifica Foundation station WBAI-FM in New York City.

Feedback: Television as a Medium (35 min.) is an examination of TV as a communications and artistic medium. The concepts of image, myth, propaganda and feedback are central to the discussion. Participants include Rudolph Arnheim, Erik Barnouw and CBS producer Merrill Brockway.

Feedback II: Television as a Business (50 min.) won an Armstrong award for the best non-commercial radio news program produced in US. It examines the corporate structure of U.S. network broadcasting. Topics explored include: the networks' broadcast and non-broadcast holdings; ties with the banking, military and governmental establishments through inter-locking directorates and contracts; the role of the sponsor in program selection and production; the methods of advertising and their effects on programming and audience; ratings and their relation to the viewer-consumer. The show includes a dramatized tour of the networks. Heard on the program are Spiro Agnew, Les Brown, Jerry Della Femina, Nicholas Johnson, Evelyn Sarson (founder of ACT) and CBS Vice President Thomas Swafford.

Feedback III: The Fourth Network (55 min.) concerns the fate of public television.

Feedback IV: Broadcast Journalism (45 min.) takes a look at news, documentary and special events programming with particular attention to the processes by which news is managed and controlled in the mutual interests of the broadcaster, advertiser and Government. Subjects discussed include the mechanics and conventions of news gathering and presentation; the myth of objectivity, fairness and balance; the biases of the corporate journalist.

Feedback V: Entertainment Programming (60 min.) deals with that 90% of the broadcast schedule known as entertainment. It is a cultural critique of the programs: the processes involved in their production; the assumptions implicit in their presentation; and the imperatives of the consumer society they serve. The program includes dramatized anti- commercials. Heard are Dick Cavett, Ruby Dee, Paul Klein and Robert Lewis Shayon.

All programs are monaural recorded on both sides of the tape. Available on 7" or 5" reels or cassettes. $55 for the five tapes or $12 each from Radio Free People, 133 Mercer Street, New York, N. Y. 10012. Transcripts of the entire series are available for $2.50. Highly recommended material for any media teacher.

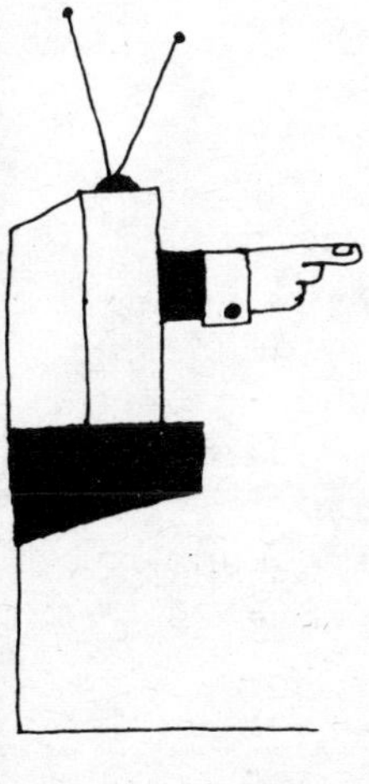

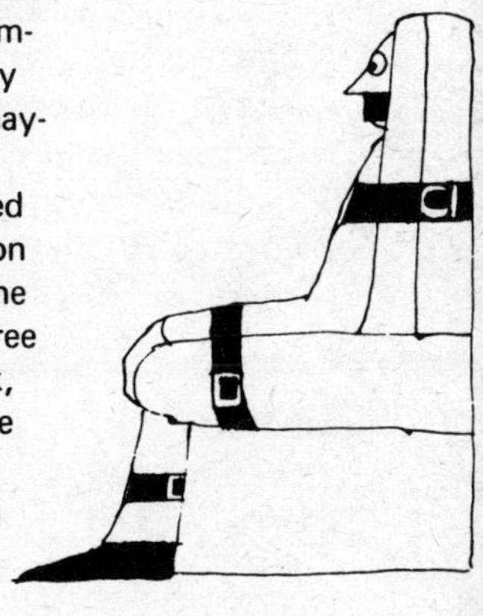

The People's Tape Guide. A concise summary of what you need to know to make good tape recordings with minimum equipment: minimizing extraneous noises, miking, tape storage and labeling, choice and care of equipment. Written by RFP. Send 25 cents to cover printing and mailing (stamps OK).

Supplementary catalogs of Music Tapes, Women's Programs, and other new tapes can be obtained by writing to us directly.

69-1 *Radical Perspectives, 1969*. The three speakers on this tape -- Carl Oglesby, Herbert Marcuse, and H. Rap Brown -- provide a window into the mind and heart of the growing movement for radical social change in America.

Oglesby and Marcuse state that the movement is the only hope for restoring human values to this society. H. Rap Brown tries to distinguish between militancy, radicalism, and revolution, but begins by criticizing the audience, who shout right back at him. Brown walks off stage, and the evening comes to an abrupt end. (Running time 59 minutes) Price $6

69-2 *Eldridge Cleaver's Affidavit*. Cleaver's statement of what happened on April 6, 1968, when Bobby Hutton was shot down after he and Cleaver were surrounded and attacked by the Oakland police. Sound quality poor due to recording conditions. (Running time 29 minutes) Price $6

69-12 *Paul Goodman On Compulsory Mis-Education*. Paul Goodman, author of *Growing Up Absurd* and *Compulsory Mis-Education*, argues that today's schools are not merely useless, but actually destructive of initiative and creativity. He suggests what students might do to break the stranglehold schools have on them. (Running time 28 minutes) Price $6

69-19 *Up Against the Mattress: Down in the Valley*. A collage of the most irritating put-down clichés women must face in their daily efforts to live like human beings -- on the job, with the family, in bed . . . put-downs so familiar we have almost come to accept them. A combination of music, raps, and advertisements. Easy to listen

to, good for starting meetings or consciousness raising. (Running time 10 minutes) Price $4

70-1 *Capitalism Plus Heroin Equals Genocide*. Michael Cetewayo Tabor, one of the Panther 21, recorded in jail this statement about drugs. Ghetto conditions plus the addictive nature of heroin create an insatiable demand for drugs, which keep oppressed people under control by killing them off and keeping them stoned. (Running time 28 minutes) Price $6

70-10 *I'm Female, I'm Proud*. This tape shows how business and advertising create a totally unrealistic picture of women and their needs, and then use the anxieties created by this image to sell products. Beulah Richardson's poem "A Black Woman Speaks of White Womanhood" is especially fine. (Running time 29 minutes) Price $6

71-11 *Interview with Angela Davis*. *Muhammad Speaks* canvassers walked the streets of Harlem and asked a wide variety of black people what they would ask Angela Davis if they could talk to her. This interview is Angela's answers to the most frequently asked questions. (Running time 25 minutes) Price $6

71-23 *The Soledad Brothers.* On January 13, 1969 three black convicts in Soledad Prison -- Fleeta Drumgo, John Cluchette, and George Jackson -- were accused of the murder of a prison guard, not because of any evidence but because they were considered "black militants" by the prison authorities. Fleeta and John now face mandatory death penalties; George Jackson has already been executed. Interviews with fellow inmates, prison guards, and relatives of the Soledad Brothers. Produced by the Committee to Defend the Soledad Brothers. Sound quality poor, due to recording conditions. (Running time 30 minutes) Price $6

72-1 *Laying Down the Tower.* "We shall all waken to be human . . . waking is the sharpest pain I have ever known." In this sequence of poems, a reading of the eleven Tarot cards, Marge Piercy leads us through the painful process of awakening, redefinition, revolution, and rebirth. Recorded by WBAI, New York. (Running time 36 minutes) Price $6

Prices listed are for individuals and movement groups. Please note INSTITUTIONAL RATE: $4 and $6 tapes, $10; $10 & $12.50 tapes, $20. Exception: the Feedback Series. All Feedback programs, $12; entire series, $55.

Don't forget to indicate on your order whether you want 3 3/4 or 7 1/2 ips reels or cassettes.

All prices include 4th Class postage. For 1st Class: add $1 per reel, 25¢ per cassette.

Check, money order, or purchase order must accompany order. No CODs, please.

72-3 *Poems of Love, Doubt, and Struggle.* Ten poems written and read by Todd Gitlin, including "Aliens," "On Power Structure Research," "New York, Last Look Around," "Prayer to the Laundromat God," and others, plus an untitled song. The poems grow out of his experience in the early student peace movement, in SDS, in the Chicago "JOIN" project, and various struggles since. They were recorded at KPFA, Berkeley. (Running time 29 minutes) Price $6

73-1 *Guatemala: Vamonos Patria.* A concise, moving introduction to the realities of Guatemala and its struggle for liberation, featuring the poetry of Otto Rene Castillo, with music; a brief history of Guatemala and its relations with the United Fruit Company and the U.S. government; and an overview of the Guatemalan guerrilla movement, by a man who lived with the guerrillas. Co-produced by the North American Congress on Latin America. (Running time 37 min.) Price $6

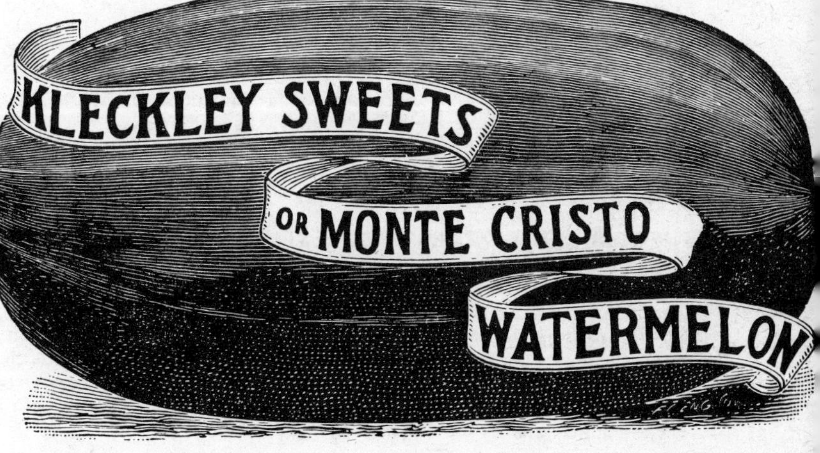

GREAT ATLANTIC RADIO CONSPIRACY

Each of the programs described on this page is about thirty minutes in length. For libraries and radio stations a tape sells for $10. For individuals an open reel copy (3.75 or 7.5 ips mono) is $7.50 and cassette copies are $2.50. Cassettes for institutions are $5.00 from:

THE GREAT ATLANTIC RADIO CONSPIRACY
2743 Maryland Avenue
Baltimore, Md. 21218
(301) 243-6987

POETRY OF THE MOVEMENT. "There is no atom that is not political and poetry can be quite dangerous propaganda, especially since all worthwhile propaganda ought to move its readers like a poem." — Robin Morgan

SEXISM. In America people are often treated in a particular way because they happen to be men or women — and women are particularly restricted by this process. The news media present distorted views of women, as do history textbooks — although both of these media purport to provide the truth. In high school, as in marriage manuals, women are channelled into only one occupation — housewife. And women who do enter professions such as the law have to deal with much discrimination. In this program we explore why all of these things occur.

POLITICS OF MENTAL HEALTH I. In this first of two programs, we focus on the ways in which the mental health establishment functions as a tool of repression. Dr. Peter Breggin and Dr. Nancy Henley discuss the problem from their role, as therapists, and three members of the Mental Patient's Liberation Front present the inside perspective on the consequences of being labe'ed mentally ill.

POLITICS OF MENTAL HEALTH II. During the past several years, there has been a vast increase in psychosurgery in this country. Dr. Peter Breggin discusses this type of operation which he calls "the mutilation of healthy brains." But psychosurgery is only one example of a general trend toward biochemical explanations of "undesirable behavior" and the dismissal of such behavior as diseased.

THE MUSIC OF WORKER'S PROTEST. This program presents the struggle songs of the people — the music of worker's protest. John Greenway in his history of folksongs of protest said of this music "these are the outbursts of bitterness, of hatred for the oppressor, of determination to endure hardships together, and to fight for a better life . . . They are imbued with the feeling of communality . . . they are songs of unity . . . To understand the area of protest out of which they grew, they should be read and sung with a history of organized labor open beside them, preferably a history which shows that American unionism was idealistic as well as practical, that it was class conscious as well as job conscious."

SEXIST PRACTICE IN AMERICA. Sexism, being defined in one's role by one's sex, pervades everything in life from birth to death. For this reason, it is difficult to choose what to talk about. As a start, the Great Atlantic Radio Conspiracy examines women's studies in schools, the media's distortion of women, the economic status of working women, and what men should and should not do vis-a-vis the women's movement.

CONTROL OF THE MEDIA. Beginning with a case study of the treatment of an event of political protest in the Baltimore and Washington, D.C. media, this program considers the implications of the concentration of the control of the mass media for the functioning of a democracy. "People are not free," the program concludes, "if the events of [their] society are systematically unreported or distorted . . . Most persons are imprisoned in a network of myths and lies, in an environment where the media have become a mass means for pacification."

Audio 195

ALTERNATIVES TO THE FAMILY – GROUP MARRIAGE. There are some alternatives to that seemingly indestructible social institution, the nuclear family. We talk with Larry and Joan Constantine about their three years of research on group marriages in America. And we talk briefly about other alternatives to the nuclear family – alternatives such as communes, extended families, single living, and homosexual groupings.

RACE AND ETHNIC CONFLICT. Intergroup conflict in the United States is increasing. The major conflicts of the 1960's were those of black and white, but the conflicts of the 1970's may well extend across all colors and ethnic groups. The Great Atlantic Radio Conspiracy explores some of the issues of conflict resulting in part from the development of a black and white ethnic underclass in a rigidifying class structure. Featured are interviews with Thomas Pettigrew, Lewis Killian, and Irving Levine.

"VOLUNTEERS FOR AMERICA" – THE POLITICS OF POPULAR MUSIC. Since the mid-1950's, there has been a decline in songs about love and an increase in lyrics dealing with poverty, war, racism, alienation, and liberation. The politicization of much popular music is the theme of this program. The program consists of music with just enough commentary to clearly make the point.

ECOLOGY AND THE ENVIRONMENT. Smog is increasing; rivers get filthier; the woods are full of plastic cups, non-returnable bottles, and soda cans. Our relationship with the environment is not good. This is largely a consequence of what companies produce and how they produce it. One example is the textile industry's shift from natural fibers to the synthetic. Featured is a seriocomic dialogue between a liberal and radical on how to solve the ecology problem.

THE CORPORATE REVIEW NO. 1. A brief look at four different corporations as a means of showing their commonalities as profit-oriented and anti-human enterprises. The program examines Polaroid, General Motors, The Bank of America, and Civic Progress, Inc. (of St. Louis).

DEATH OF PROFESSIONALISM. Professionalism at its best is a means of insuring a minimal level of competence in a job. Typically, however, professionalism is a means of maintaining the current social order and insuring that people can not have access to knowledge that would enable them to control their own lives. Interviews with Noam Chomsky, Robert Lifton, Fred Pincus, and Barbara Ehrenreich are featured.

CAPITALISM AND THE FOOD INDUSTRY. As long as corporations own half the cultivated land in America, as long as agribusiness puts profits above food quality, as long as food workers are alienated from their labor, as long as corporations have the economic power to control the government, we will all be unable to feed and adequately nourish the American people. Contamination by pesticides, food additives that are at least sometimes harmful, malnutrition, high food prices, the death of the family farm all come from the fact that food is grown, processed, and distributed for profit, not for people.

MA BELL. American Telephone and Telegraph Co. is the largest corporation in the world. As such it proves an excellent example of the abuses of power, common to all large corporations. The clever ways in which Ma Bell takes our money and manipulates our lives might be funny if they were not so serious.

HEALTH CARE IN AMERICA. Health care has a depressingly large number of side effects: high costs; inability to reach the poor; inability to abolish certain diseases, like tuberculosis; drug-induced diseases, like cancer and thrombosis from the birth control pill. These side effects arise from immediate causes such as the deliberate mystification of medicine, high salaries of hospital administrators, and the lies and distortions of drug company advertisements. And these causes go back to the fact that medicine is run for health care professionals and not for consumers.

A HISTORY OF THE AMERICAN WOMEN'S MOVEMENT. This program briefly traces the historical development of the movement for women's liberation. Some of the ideological differences and the strategies for societal change which current feminists advocate are presented in the context of an interview with Marlene Dixon. Musical background is drawn primarily from songs of the suffragists.

ELECTORAL POLITICS. There are problems working through electoral politics. The costs are so high that only the rich can win major office. When they get in, they naturally favor the rich. Third parties haven't worked. They serve to contain protest and rage within the electoral process. Looking at Chile where a divided electorate voted in a socialist president, you can see that it takes more than an election to make a socialist society.

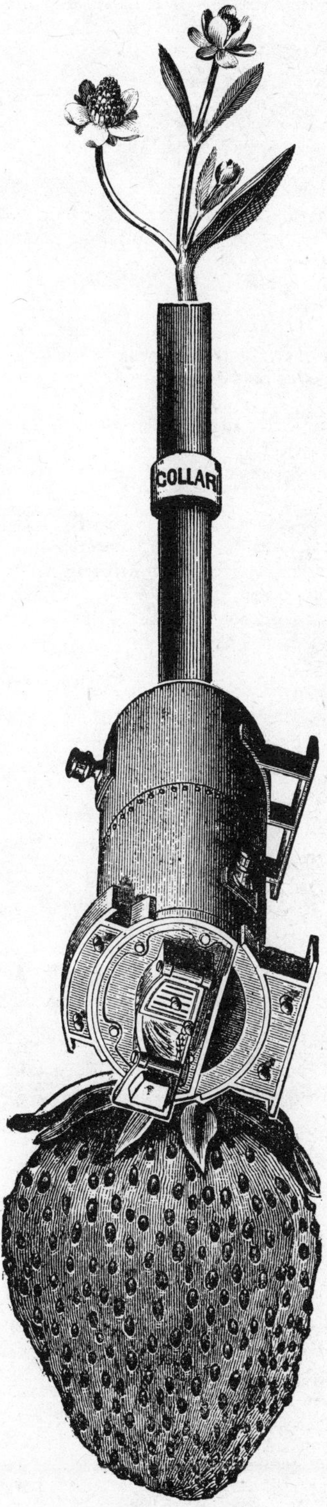

STOP THE ROAD. This program talks about that great symbol of progress and national development, the highway. We talk about the Great Highway Robbery — the agreement between Big Government and Big Business to build roads we don't need — roads that destroy our cities and add to the destruction of our environment — roads that cost billions of dollars which could be better employed in the service of people. We interview representatives of two action groups which have battled to stop the coming of the roads: Tom Collins of the Greater Boston Committee on the Transportation Crisis and Allan Marcus of MAD, the Movement Against Destruction which is based in Baltimore.

EATING FOR FUN AND ANTI-PROFIT. This is a program on organizing food-cooperatives. The emphasis is on how-to-do-it; and interviews are featured with persons running different kinds of co-ops. The perspective is on the food cooperative as an alternative institution — a politicized, worker-controlled structure providing cheap and nutritious foods in a context of struggle with the larger institutions of food production and distribution.

THE OBSOLETE PERSON — I. In America, if you live long enough you will become poor. Stripped of human dignity and worth, most older Americans face extreme poverty, ill health, and personal isolation. This program combines interviews and demographic materials in an in-depth look at the problems of America's aged.

THE OBSOLETE PERSON — II. A look at the aged in China; the militant aged in America; some proposals for short range reforms — or, what can be done for the elderly before the revolution.

THE GREAT UTILITIES RIP-OFF. Utilities keep asking for higher and higher rates. In the 1971 electric rate cases a total of $802 million in increases was granted across the country. In 1972, electric utility rate increases applications amounted to $1.3 billion. We look at one company's request for increased rates, and discuss some measures that would make these rate increases unnecessary. All power to the people.

FREE CLINICS -- The coordinator of the Waverly People's Free Medical Clinic, Shelley Bronson, discusses health care and the operational problems of free clinics. They aren't by themselves going to bring about the revolution, but they do get medicine to people, and they do give people the chance to run their own institutions.

ATTICA -- Several of the survivors of the Attica massacre and two Baltimore prison organizers -- Paul Coates, of the George Jackson Prison Movement, and Hank Smock -- talk about prison conditions and about the social implications that in America the powerless go to prison and the powerful remain free.

CONSPIRACY REVIEW, v. 6 -- A three-part feature: strip mining in Appalachia from the perspective of the local residents; our first pair of male chauvinist awards; and an interview with Terry Ann Knopf on racism and sexism in soap operas.

THE IQ FALLACY -- We explore the meanings of intelligence and the use of science to subordinate people by class, race, and sex. This program traces the history of elitist theories of intelligence from Galton through Jensen and Herrnstein.

ART HAS POLITICS, SOMETIMES -- Music, poetry, and provoking perspectives on politics and art by The Great Atlantic Radio Theater and by Lannes Kenfield and Tuli Kupferberg of The Revolting Theater.

SCIENCE FOR THE PEOPLE -- In a technological society, science is never politically neutral or value free. It is not necessarily of benefit to humanity. And if it is beneficial it may be available only to the rich and powerful. SESPA (Science for the People) is an organization of radical scientists who have come together to combat this misuse of science. This program is about their work.

Film

Rental rates for short films range from the cheap, to the merely expensive, to the extravagant. For the same film.

It all started when I sent off letters to two film distributors asking why one offered *Cool Hand Luke* for a rental fee of $65 and the other for $120. I never really found out why in spite of replies from both companies. Seemingly, both firms are serving the needs of those who rent *Cool Hand Luke.*

I was told that the added cost for rental was caused by extra careful handling of prints and high quality original print condition. True, the distributor does have a fine reputation for excellent quality and nearly flawless service, but does this have to double the cost of each rental print? The other distributor claimed that they too provided the same kind of service and that, except on rare occasions, prints all come from the same lab and are of identical quality. They suggested that the larger the company, the lower the rental charge. I later found that this wasn't always true either. I decided to find out why film rental rates vary by as much as 300%

and immediately narrowed the field down to my specialty, short films.

Rental prices for short films range from the tiny distributors whose high fees are tailored to the unlimited film budgets at Camelot High, to the university film libraries who charge less for rental than some companies ask for postage. I consulted the best-known commercial and non-profit university library film distributors anticipating a scathing exposé that would make *Unsafe At Any Speed* sound like a Corvair commercial. But after hundreds of pages of letters and hours of rather pleasant conversation there was no sign of scandal and so I settled for this report which will hopefully enlighten more than inflame.

I quickly found that the image of the university film library is changing. They still strongly emphasize the curriculum-oriented film *(The Mosquito and Its Control, Modern France: The Land and the People, Crayfish Anatomy)* but like schools in general they are moving toward acceptance of more creative film art.

The university libraries acquire their films from the commercial distributors and proceed to rent them for less than the distributor. Their rental rates are lower because they have no need to show a profit (although many university film libraries are self-supporting), have little need for expensive promotion, usually pay less for facilities and personnel and need not pay royalties to the filmmaker.

If lack of money is the guiding light in film planning, then there is little choice but to utilize free public library films and at least some university films. The film renter can save from 20-60% by so doing. He could rent *Chairy Tale* for under $3 instead of $5 or $6 or *Hangman* for $5 instead of $13. But he will often pay the difference in receiving films cut into small pieces ready for exciting visual displays when run through the projector, or films that are cancelled two days after they were to arrive, or films available only after June 15, 1984.

One class I know used to applaud every time a university rented film made it through the projector without shredding to bits. But other teachers have reported excellent and consistent service from certain university libraries. It is not that university libraries are careless operations (in fact they might be less susceptible to Parkinson's Law and the Peter Principle) but that their films seem to suffer a greater casualty rate. Seemingly, film renters tend to feel less responsible for a film they've shelled out only a few bucks for than one which has cost them three math classes.

If you can plan film usage months in advance (last minute orders are almost always better handled by the commercial distributors), if you have a 16mm splicer and splicing tape, time to preview all films before showing them to an audience, and a film budget that sounds more like a golf score, give the university libraries a try. It is not a question of choosing either the commercial distributors or the non-profit libraries since each has a great number of films the other does not. It is simply a matter of finding out who offers the most film for your time, money and effort. There are university libraries that compare favorably in every way with the best of the commercial distributors. Start the search with local university libraries and see what happens.

Some university film libraries rent only to state residents (Wisconsin, for example) and others only to regions (Arizona and Oregon now rent only to Western states). Film libraries which rent to any "qualified institution" in the country include:

INDIANA (their catalog is over 1100 pages, they distribute NET films, their prices are reasonable. Their catalog does not provide dates for the films and many are outdated)

ILLINOIS (600-page catalog is $3 to non-users, mostly curriculum films)

CALIFORNIA (most useful short film catalog in existence, varied collection, more expensive than average university library)

UNIVERSITY OF MICHIGAN-MICHIGAN STATE ($2 catalog of 570 pages, issues periodic supplements announcing new films)

KENT STATE ($2 catalog similar to Michigan)

FLORIDA STATE (400 page catalog, supplements)

TEXAS

MINNESOTA

MISSOURI

BOSTON UNIVERSITY

SOUTHERN CALIFORNIA

NEW YORK (small but unique collection, highest rates)

MOUNTAIN PLAINS (combines Brigham Young and the universities of Utah, Nevada, Colorado, and Wyoming)

GEORGIA

SOUTHERN FLORIDA

As a general rule those libraries with rock bottom rental rates have more trouble with damaged prints, heavy bookings and unreliable film users. The rule does have exceptions, however, but to list here libraries which provide the best service would be to attempt the impossible. Rental rates of the University of California and New York University are the highest of the libraries and Arizona and Minnesota rank near the lowest.

To check comparative film availability I ordered the same five often used short films from three university libraries and two commercial distributors. The commercial distributors replied first with confirmations, one being able to supply four of the five within three weeks and the other three of the five within seven weeks. Both confirmed all five films ordered in late January for use by mid-May. One university library with low rates had one film damaged beyond use and the other four unavailable during the remainder of the school year; the other low price library was able to supply three of the five, but at least one of the three arrived in poor condition. The third university library was able to confirm three out of the five within three weeks, one in May and one not available until June. This last library had rental rates higher than the other two but still about 30% lower than the commercial distributors.

So far the commercial film distributors have come off as people who provide excellent service and drive gold plated projectors. Actually, the film distributors are not in the film business primarily to rent films. They are far more interested in selling films. As high as the current rental rates might seem many distributors see film rental as more of a public service than a profit making venture. The real profit comes from the sale of films, a relatively simple process compared to the elaborate paperwork involved in rental. As one distributor-producer put it, "In spite of what many schools consider high rentals ($25 for a 15-minute film), the distributor is lucky to break even on rentals. This is particularly true on rentals by public schools which often hold prints long after the date for which the print was rented." A small film distributor echoed these sentiments, "As far as we are concerned, renting films is not a profitable venture from a strictly cash point of view, but we nevertheless are anxious to make our films available . . . because people who rent films frequently end up buying a print. We use our rental department as a way to advertise our films and solicit sales." One of the largest short film distributors quoted a cost of $6700 to prepare a film for the market and a cost of $10-12 just to service any order no matter how small. The same distributor called its film rental operation a losing proposition; a sort of advertising write-off.

In spite of the economic drawbacks the film distributors do an excellent job of servicing rental requests. When customer complaints arise they are handled in a manner that must be among the most considerate in any service industry. Many of the men and women who manage commercial film distribution are film afficianados and many have had teaching experience; they are more than sales people or desk riders.

What emerges from this consideration of the economics of short film rental is that no one is really satisfied with the existing situation. The basic problem is neither the distributor nor the customer; it is the medium itself. Film is still a rather primitive mode for presenting moving pictures. Today's films are expensive to make, easy to damage, difficult to repair, require a complicated machine to project, are difficult to store and ship, wear out rather quickly, are noisy and generally clumsy. What we need is a good five dollar film.

We need a medium that can be purchased as easily as a book and shown on some sort of projection system vastly improved from those existing today. The "film" should last practically forever and be foolproof to view. The videocassette people claim they have the answer but are faster with their projections into the future than they are with their projectors. CBS is the only company to have delivered an actual product to the market at this writing and their system allows the lucky viewer to view only CBS product. Sort of like having a record player that can only play the records on the Columbia label.

What is needed is some sort of system that will allow the user both to play commercially made cassettes and to make his own.

Manufacturers fear piracy with such a system and so are designing complex systems to eliminate this flexibility. Eventually such a cassette man will cometh but not before you have to list three alternate dates for that next film order and hope the film arrives on time and in one piece. There are hundreds of people sitting behind typewriters poised with invoices and six carbons ready to make sure you get the film. And as Aldous Huxley says at the end of his Foreword to *Brave New World,* "You pays your money and you takes your choice."

by Jeffrey Schrank

The films evaluated in this section have been very carefully selected from the thousands released during the past few years. All have been screened and critically evaluated with an eye toward a group of teenagers or adults as a viewing audience.

Criteria for inclusion in this listing include a creative approach, entertainment value, quality of the images, and educational impact. The films come from both amateurs and professionals around the world. With few exceptions, typical classroom films that instruct rather than educate have not been included in this list. Most of the films here were made out of conviction or simply for the love of creative filmmaking.

Purchase and rental sources are provided for all the films. The best policy to follow in ordering films from this section is first to request the catalog of the film distributors. Price changes always seem just around the corner. The catalog will also provide detailed ordering instructions.

The films are grouped here according to very general categories. Many of the films could easily find dozens of uses in a number of different subject areas. Addresses of distributors can be found on pp. 242-255.

ADVERTISING AND TELEVISION

Harold and Cynthia explores the impact of advertising on people. Like the rest of us, Harold and Cynthia are two people who live in a value-atmosphere conditioned by Madison Avenue. They meet at a bus stop and are attracted to each other. But their attempts to establish a relationship are distorted by their value systems created by corporations who insist that importance and value are measured by the use of the right products and the proper image.

The simple animation changes to live action to present actual commercials that Harold and Cynthia see: "Smoke this and win the girl of your dreams"; "Spray on a little of this and he'll follow you anywhere."

Harold and Cynthia have difficulty getting in touch with themselves or each other. The simple animation style conveys perfectly the emptiness of their world. Only when they go to a place of no advertising does the animation style become fuller and they are able to dance, to express joy and tenderness. The film's theme is that the false values proposed incessantly by ads is a factor contributing toward problems in personal relationships.

The sound track uses pop tunes unobtrusively—"Sounds of Silence" is done with a solo flute. The film has definite appeal to almost any audience and makes its point clearly and with visual interest.

10 min., color, animation, rental $15, sale $140 from The Eccentric Circle.

Good Goodies A parable about advertising. A truck selling "Goodies" opens for business across from a similar truck in the same business. The truck puts out a "New Goodies" sign to attract cutomers. The first truck responds with a "Newer Goodies" sign and the battle is on. One truck finally collapses under the weight of its own ads. The other now has a monopoly and serves a swarm of customers.

Bosustow Productions. 5 min., color, animation, sale $80, rental inquire.

Television and Politics is a 25-min. excerpt from Mike Wallace's CBS-TV show *60 Minutes*. The 1970 film has the high quality that was a *60 Minutes* trademark and a topic that is both timely and crucial.

The film could be named "How to Sell a Candidate" or "Buying Votes with Ads." Political spots are shown beginning with Harry Truman's in 1948, through the clever *March-of-Time* commercial for Eisenhower in 1952, Nixon's almost legendary "Checker's Speech," Kefauver's use of Eisenhower's own commercials in 1956, the 1960 debates and finally those of Barry Goldwater in 1964 that made the TV spot a lethal weapon. The film clips are damning, revealing, embarrassing and often humorous.

After tracing the recent history of the political ad the film switches to interviews with the people who market the candidates. Wallace asks the man who packaged Hubert Humphrey about the morality of a spot in which Agnew is shown on screen and the sound track consists simply of a man laughing. The media man claims to be concerned about politics, not government and views himself as a "gun for hire."

The economics and morality of TV campaigns is questioned. Agnew's media man says, "we want our candidate to be liked more than understood, we're reaching for the heart rather than the mind."

There are surprisingly frank interviews with political and communications industry people. The film is very much concerned with media-morality and even more basically with a Brave New Worldish use of the media in politics.

25 in., color, sale $325, rental $25 from BFA Educational Media, rental $11.40 from the University of Michigan.

A Special Report. . . . is a satire about the fascination of television news with violent death. In it Robert Rancor presents a special report for "Channel Three Moment News" on the brutal murder of Candy Parabola, a 22-year old topless go-go dancer.

Using all the cliche camera shots and narration of a TV documentary, the report tells how the murder happened as "the curvacious lady moved quietly in the privacy of her own home." There are the inevitable interviews with a neighbor who says "she was a nice girl," and the police inspector who casually says it was "probably just your typical irritations killing," and the reporter's comment that "she is a symptom of the disease of violence."

Each time a new character appears an identifying tag is superimposed on the screen. CANDY PARABOLA--VICTIM and NEGRO POLICE INSPECTOR are two that make viewers aware of the danger of these all-too-compact labels flashed so innocently on the screen.

Since Candy was shot with an arrow there is an interview with an arrow maker who explains how to obtain maximum kill capacity from an arrow. Since Candy was female there is the visit to a local Karate school where an instructor tells of an influx of women seeking training to protect themselves. One woman interviewed even claims "violence gets too much publicity." The reporter wraps up the special standing by a tombstone and quoting Shakespeare.

A Special Report is wacky yet incisive. It deals with the dangers involved in the media's handling of crime, its tendency to label and to sound profound while saying nothing. It captures perfectly the ability of a medium to use the guise of public service to play a titillating strip tease (will they show the corpse?) with a frightened and yet blood hungry public.

The film was made by USC students in 1970, 17 min., b&w. Sale: $130 from United World Films; rental: $5.50 from University of Southern California.

Smokescreen . . . is the first "scare film" about cigarettes I've seen. It is admittedly frightening, even gory. The history of the U.S. as seen through cigarette ads is flashed on the screen. There are glimpses of surgery with pulsing lungs bulging out of the patient's chest. The film is well done in a strange sort of way even though it is doubtful if it would induce smokers to quit. It should certainly provoke reaction from both smokers and non-smokers in a group.(Pyramid Films, Purchase for $90, rental for $10. Color, 5 min.)

Ashes of Doom. . .is an almost guaranteed show stopper from the National Film Board of Canada. This 90 second anti-smoking spot is set in a Gothic boudoir where a young woman lights up one cigarette after another. The clock strikes twelve, the candles blow out and a vampire appears. He approaches the sultry beauty slowly (giving her time for another cigarette) and pounces on her. His fangs approach the smoke filled throat and . . .

Lots of fun and an excellent example for students of how much can be done in only 90 seconds. Preview prints available, purchase price $25 from United World Films

AMERICA AND ITS LIFESTYLES

Blake Everyone at some time had admired the freedom of a bird gliding seemingly unbound by gravity, cities, and freeways. But how many people act on this passing feeling? Blake James does; he bases his life upon it.

Blake owns a yellow biplane small enough so he can push it around like a wheelbarrow yet large enough to give him the freedom of the skies.

Blake hates cities, lives in a log cabin in the country, and frequently takes off on cross-country air trips that can last as long as two years. When on the ground, he drives a barely living VW that starts with a screwdriver; his philosophy being that "what you don't spend you don't have to earn."

While the screen is filled with poetic images of Blake floating through the clouds, off-camera voices talk admiringly about the sense of child-like freedom he imparts to whomever he contacts. Blake flies along in fur coat and open cockpit, navigating by sight and flying until tired then landing and sleeping on the ground near the plane until the next morning.

To the voices Blake is a legend, a mythical possessor of that elusive quality freedom. Even though the reality of his freedom is debatable, there is no doubt his lifestyle and the film's viewpoint strike a responsive chord in any audience concerned with finding personal freedom.

The film is simply and beautifully directed by Bill Mason, was nominated for an Academy Award, and was produced in 1969 by the National Film Board of Canada.

19 min., color, rental $25, sale $260 from Contemporary Films/McGraw-Hill. Code number 408523.

The House That Jack Built is a National Film Board of Canada animation that is a modern version of two tales: "The House That Jack Built" and "Jack and the Beanstalk." This modern Jack builds a house that is just like the house that Jack built. There's a box in the house that tells his wife what to buy. There's a car that takes Jack through crowded expressways to the place where he works to pay the bills that come from the goods his wife is told by the box to buy. Jack is caught in the suburban rat race; his secret wish is to be unique.

One day Jack's car falls apart and someone gives Jack beans for it. His wife angrily throws the beans out the window

and a giant beanstalk grows. Jack climbs the beanstalk and meets a phony giant from whom he steals a magic mirror.

Looking into the mirror makes Jack feel like the most marvelous person in the world. With his new self-image he becomes a success. He buys a mansion a little different from the others in the neighborhood, works 12 hours a day, takes pills and has little time for his family. The film ends with Jack declaring that he's tired of being unique; he really wants to be different.

Discussion should center on questions such as: What does "being different" really mean? Are the rich and middle class caught in the same trap? How could the situation be changed? Do you identify in any way with Jack? Ideal for adult groups and high school.

9 minutes, color, rental $15, purchase $115 from Learning Corporation of America

Sisyfos . . . "Sisyphus is the absurd hero. . . . his passion for life won him that unspeakable penalty in which the whole being is exerted toward accomplishing nothing . . . The workman of today works every day in his life at the same tasks, and this fate is no less absurd." —Albert Camus. In Greek mythology Sisyphus was assigned the task of rolling a boulder up a hill. Whenever he neared the top the rock would roll back down and he began again. The tragedy in the myth was that the task prevented Sisyphus from using his creativity which earned him the reputation as one of the cleverest living things.

In **Sisyfos**, a Czechoslovakian animated version of the Greek myth, Sisyphus is a lumberman. At the beginning of the day his detailed instructions float down from above and he sets to work. He chops down a mammoth tree and begins further cutting, sawing and planing. He follows directions exactly and seems contented and competent.

Finally he is finished. The directions have been followed and a day's labor is done. His finished product? A toothpick. He tries the toothpick; it breaks. Another set of instructions floats down.

An excellent film for discussing work and its meaning, goals, the concept of the "absurd," the Greek myth itself, and the nine-to-five routine. (Contemporary/McGraw-Hill Films Code No. 408267. Animated, color, 8 minutes, sale $115, rental $12.50)

Order in the House. . . Society as seen through the eyes of a law-and-order garbage collector is the subject of this Hungarian animated gem. The anti-hero garbage collector believes people are like animals, good people are home by eleven and a strong hand is all people need to keep them in order. He has in mind to impose a system based on garbage usage. The "most garbage people" should live on the first floor, those who are born stinky should be dead, those who are sloppy with garbage will be put down in a book, those who are really rotten will be sent to a special house, and everyone should go to bed after TV and be up by six.

The garbage man's system is frightening and his respect for individual liberty non-existent. Because he's only a garbage man his views might easily be dismissed. But who is to say that judging people by their garbage is any less rational than categorizing them by I.Q., financial status, color, religion or any other division? And isn't every man's view of the world governed by his position -- each is affected by his contact with a limited reality. Each person, from a doctor to a garbag man, sees things as "he is," not like "they are."

The animation technique of **Order in the House** is supurb and communicates as much as does the monologue of the garbage man. The distributor claims the visual technique suggests Ernst Trova's "Falling Man," while I find it reminiscent of early animation by Peter Foldes.

Themes in the film include the formation of ones' image or world view, law and order, classification, the establishment of systems, and individual survival amid a system.

5 min., color, animated. Sale $75, rental $10 from Learning Corporation of America and $4.40 from Kent State University.

Hello Mustache is a boy-meets-girl story. She a child of the high rise, he a genuine freak. Sonny invites Alan over to her apartment for a visit. She never met Alan but heard about him from Latrisse, the girl with the wooden leg. Alan declines at first, being busy doing his nails. But he gives in and cycles over to meet Sonny who reacts with a few dozen "wow's." It seems she's never met a real hippy before.

The dialogue is brilliant, near absurd, and sharper than viewers have any right to expect from a student film. Sonny advises Alan to shave off his mustache, and Alan replies that it's a government-issue nose and mustache given him when the real one was lost in Vietnam.

The twists and turns of their conversation are as complex as they are entertaining. When shown to groups of high school girls they laughed and enjoyed the film yet found its ending touching and were sensitive to the meaning beneath the surface.

Ultimately the film is about self-hiding and self-revelation. Sonny is more a freak than Alan and has her own form of put-ons. *Hello Mustache* is about love and lifestyles, about the problem of being real in the city, about friendship and understanding.

The film defies brief description but is certainly one of the best and most useful student-made films currently available for high school use.

32 minutes, b&w, 1970, rental $25.00 from Films, Inc., 1144 Wilmette Ave., Wilmette, Ill. 60091.

Sean . . . Sean is a precocious 4-year-old growing up in a commune with parents leading an alternative lifestyle. In this straight interview he reveals the unique attitudes of a child of the new world. Sean knows "speed freaks are scarey" but claims he eats grass. About police he says, "When I see them I throw up." He also expresses feelings belonging to children of all time: big people are "creepy," darkness is scarey: "How should I know what's there and what isn't?" he asks. Some will find Sean a victim of hippy brainwashing, and others will see in him the new freedom of tomorrow. 15 min., b&w, sale $150, rental $15 from New Line Cinema.

The Sixties . . . Charles Braverman's films (*American Time Capsule*, *World of '68*, etc.) are popular with high school students, who often request repeat showings. This one is a look at the turbulent 1960s. CBS originally bought the film for around $15,000.00 to use on their January "60 Minutes" program. TV producer Don Hewitt claimed the film "just wasn't very good. It was neither stylish, witty, nor perceptive." Hence it was cut from the show.

The film is far from a masterpiece, but it is stylish and perceptive. The theme of *The Sixties* is polarization, especially as reflected through the influence of George Wallace and Stokely Carmichael. Braverman presents this decade as a time when "right" and "left" became more than marching orders of obscure political labels. Because of his point of focus, Braverman leaves out many significant events from this period -- thus sparing us scenes we've already witnessed many times over. The result is a sharply honed comment on the times.

Before watching the film, students (and teacher) could list what they thought to be the most significant trends of the 60s. Then view the film and compare results. (15 min., color, available from Pyramid Films -- rent $15, sale $185. Rent $13 from University of California.

Who Invited Us?. . . is a one-hour NET documentary that caused much controversy when shown on TV.

Many stations refused to carry the program, the educational channel in Washington included.

The documentary traces the history of American foreign policy from 1918 to the present, focusing on military intervention. The viewpoint of the film is that most of the intervention is based on a basic conflict between capitalism and socialism which dates back to 1918, when we sent 10,000 troops to aid the French in Siberia after the Russian Revolution. We failed and one-sixth of the world was closed to American economic interests. Since then we have intervened when it was to our "best interests" – Cuba, Dominican Republic, Iran (CIA), Greece, Guatemala, Mexico, Honduras, Haiti, Philippines, Columbia and Bolivia among others. In theory we do not support dictatorships; in practice this policy applies only to Cuba.

Considering that most high school history texts are a cautious mixture of fact and propaganda, this well researched but slanted documentary should prove most valuable.

60 min., b&w, sale $265, rental $13.50 from Indiana University. Rental $10 from University of Michigan and $18 from University of California.

America . . . . The Alistair Cooke TV series, *America,* attracted an unexpected amount of attention and viewers during its two thirteen-week runs on national TV. Time-Life Films now has the series available in two formats. Either thirteen 52-minute episodes, or twenty-six 26-minute episodes. The 52-minute episodes sell for $600 each and rent for $100 each. The 26-minute versions sell for $300 each and rent for $50 each. More info on the series from Time-Life Films.

Rental also from the University of California.

Visual Encyclopedia of American History . . . is a collection of nearly 200 film loops made from newsreel footage of 20th Century America. Little Egypt's Belly Dance, Teddy Roosevelt at the Panama Canal, Sacco-Vanzetti Case, riot at Rudolph Valentino's Funeral, soup lines and jitterbugs, Hitler, Gandhi, Castro, FDR, and Kennedy are all here. The idea is an excellent one. For more information write Bro-Dart, 1609 Memorial Avenue, Williamsport, Pa. 17701.

"BEYOND" THE NATURAL

Psychics, Saints, and Scientists . . . The leaf pictured below is fringed with a glow of energy photographed by a Russian device that is said to convert bioplasmic energy into electrical energy, thus permitting a photo to be made. *Psychics, Saints, and Scientists* includes a demonstration of the bioplasmic "camera" with the speculation that people give off radiation and that perhaps the artistic convention of depicting holy people with halos of light might in fact be based on a yet-to-be-discovered scientific truth.

The experiment with bioplasmic energy is only one of many parapsychological phenomena shown in the film which explores the science of consciousness.

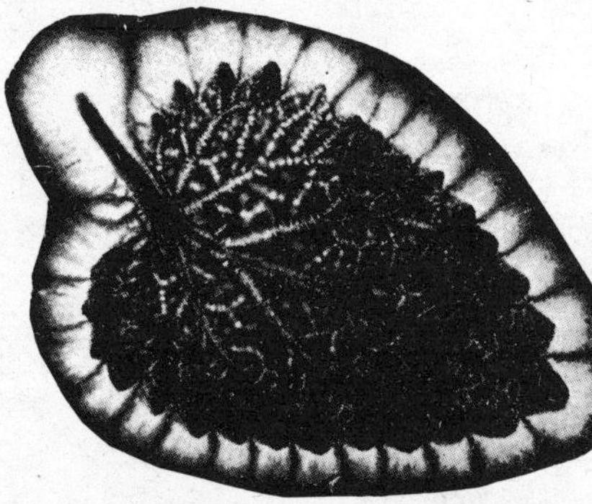

The film suggests that states of higher consciousness that have in the past been the domain of mystics and saints can be explored by science and even taught to anyone willing to journey into inner space.

Dr. Thelma Moss, of UCLA's Neuropsychiatric Institute, narrates this fast-paced glance at the joining of science and the inner life. Experiments in parapsychology, ESP, telepathy, control of matter by mind, biofeedback training, control of body temperature, telepathic dreams, electro sleep, and the photographing of body radiation are shown.

The treatment of each is extremely superficial and perhaps even scientifically misleading, but the film does suggest that the human potential is far more cosmic than ever imagined. The film will not convince the skeptics, but it will show that religious and mystical experience can be studied scientifically.

33 min., color, 1972, sale $350, rental $40 from Hartley Productions.

The Unexplained

Most schooling teaches about what scientists have been able to explain. Students often have the idea that man today knows everything about what already exists and that if a scientist can't prove something then it must not be true. Such thoughts sometimes are connected with a crisis of faith and a demand of scientific proof of whatever is to be believed. *The Unexplained* is a journey into the realm of what is not known, a revelation about what is before our eyes yet still remains unexplained.

This made-for-TV documentary explores the Devil's Triangle area of the Caribbean Ocean that has mysteriously swallowed ships and planes at an alarming rate without apparent cause. It shows New England's Mystery Hill, an American mystery as complex as Stonehenge.

Futurologist Arthur C. Clark predicts that we will soon know the answers to questions that have plagued men of many eras: how life originated, how the earth was formed, the whys of signals coming from space. Clark suggests that we may have intelligent life beginning to evolve on Jupiter and that intelligent life may indeed already exist in another solar system. Biologist Paul Weiss discusses genetic engineering, suggesting that evolution may be controlled so that man will naturally develop gills which will allow him to live under water as well as on land. Many of my students found this possibility a fascinating solution to the problem of overpopulation and crowding.

An interesting explanation of many of the scientific findings students of religion will be questioning in the future. 52 min., color, $500 sale, $25 rental from Films Incorporated.

HOLY GHOST PEOPLE

Peter Adair's cinema verite looks into the "holy roller" community at Scrabble Creek, West Virginia is a moving, perhaps even frightening, experience. This is a film that will never be forgotten, an experience which will challenge middle class worship and one's own preconceptions of religion.

The holiness churches follow a literal interpretation of the Gospels complete with healing, tongue speaking and snake handling. The film takes the viewer into a holiness way service. There is no appointed minister; who ever the spirit moves to say or do something takes over.

The emphasis is on the freedom to worship in whatever way one wishes — quiet thought, babbling, singing or playing music, shouting, or convulsions and dancing. "Just be yourself, obey the Lord, just be yourself, don't come to church and just sit down and depend on the other fellow to provide the preaching. I think that's wrong" says the self-appointed minister for the evening.

A request for prayers is made of the group and in response a number of people speak in tongues, a senior citizen dances gleefully, teenagers pray and go into convulsions, rattlesnakes are thrown about the room, a member makes a personal and public declaration of independence, and the viewer is overwhelmed by their honesty, fervor and power.

A woman who claims to have been practically dead tells of her cure and another asks for a healing of her ailing back. The group leader takes up a collection for one of the members and receives $50 for the needy family. He proclaims "if God does not want me to die by snake bite, he will not let me die." In the closing burst of prayer and snake handling he does get bit, the hand slowly swells, the viewer recalls the earlier comment that many have died because of this belief, the frame freezes, film ends.

53 min., b&w, sale $400, rental $35 from Contemporary Films. Rental $12.50 from University of Southern California, $10 from University of Michigan, and $24 from University of California.

Anastenaria was made in 1967 for college anthropology courses, but proves fascinating for almost any audience above grade school level. Anastenaria is a form of popular worship carried on even today among the peasants in some sections of Greece. The feast occurs May 21, the Greek Orthodox holy day of St. Constantine and his mother St. Helen. The ceremony includes a fire-walking ritual in which the dancers literally stomp on burning embers without pain or apparent harm, much to the mystification of impartial scientists. The ritual also includes a ceremonial slaughter of an unblemished animal which has lived an odd number of years, the distribution of the animal in the village, the use of holy water as protection, icons, ecstatic dances, incense, healing, and finally the fire-walking.

The film documents the ritual without frills. It is extremely effective to aid discussion of religious rituals, human potential, ecstasy, other cultures, or simply as a mind-expanding experience which some students will have a hard time believing or accepting. (17 min., b&w, from the University of California, rental $9, sale $100.

Meditation. . .is an audience participation film, a primer in the art of meditating. Alan Watts conducts the introductory lesson in meditation which he describes as "getting in touch with reality, the art of temporarily silencing the mind." Western Man thinks of meditation in terms of filling the mind with thoughts but the Eastern expert knows that a person who thinks all the time has nothing to think about except thoughts--mere chattering inside the skull. The mind cannot be forced into silence anymore than a person can force himself not to think of an elephant for two minutes. So in order to demonstrate how this silence of the mind is achieved Watts leads viewers on several experiments to be conducted while watching this film.

"Hear all that's around you," he instructs. "Don't try to identify sounds. Listen without asking what it means. Be concerned with what is -- not past or future, only now. Don't seek a result, simply be here, in the world of sound and the eternal now."

He goes on to demonstrate how a gong and mantra are aids to meditation and leads the audience in an OM chant. He describes OM as an audio rainbow encompassing the entire range of sound. He gives lessons on breathing techniques and proper posture for meditation. There is quiet time in the film for a bit of practice in meditation. But the film unexpectedly ends with a different kind of meditation -- "put your hands on your hips and just laugh."

An excellent film for a cooperative audience willing to take the lesson seriously. Watts' instructions will hardly lead to the instant creation of meditation experts but they will give insight into the difference between Eastern and Western approaches to reality.

The film is 28 minutes, color, sale at $300, rental $35 from the directors and producers, Harlety Productions,

Note from Above . . . In this two-minute Derek Phillips animation people's hands are seen through a stained glass window as they receive notes which come floating down from above

giving commands. The first note reads "I am the Lord," the hands are shown praying. The second note commands "Thou shalt have no other gods but me," and we see the hands throwing out statues and totem poles. Other notes float down and the people respond by loving their neighbors and by returning stolen property. The fifth note that comes down reads "Thou shalt kill." The sixth floats quietly down and states "Sorry, my mistake. That should have been: Thou shalt not kill." But there is no one left to receive the correction. (2 min., color, animated. Sale $100, rental $10. Mass Media Associates. $8, United Church.

THE CITY: TECHNOLOGY—ECOLOGY

The End of One

Screeching masses of seagulls fight for growing mounds of garbage while off to the side a single lone gull dies quietly. Such is the simple plot of **The End of One**, a seven minute masterpiece by Paul Kocela. Mr. Kocela grew up on a farm in Czechoslovakia and when asked to describe himself replied: "I love mother earth and hate oil companies. I love sunrises, women, Andrew Wyeth, clean brooks and spring time, furry kitty cats, and the smell of emulsion." He also has a feel for nature and cinematography which is lavishly displayed in **The End of One.**

Although the plot sounds simple, and perhaps far from interesting, the sensitive camera work makes the film an emotional experience. Some viewers will see the dead gull as abandoned by the other birds; others say he died from old age; still others surmise that it was the garbage itself which killed him. To me the film says we have converted flight from a thing of beauty to a thing of commerce and now have little use for birds except to leave them our garbage. Some viewers will say, with cause, that the film is a parable about life itself—civilization is a garbage heap that people fight over while others die.

The film is excellent for a discussion that can go to the root of the values of ecology. Seven minutes, color, purchase for $100 or rental for $15 from Learning Corporation of America.

Rental $3 from University of Michigan, $5 from Kent State University, and $15 from NEFC.

The Tragedy of the Commons is one film with more material for discussion than most any two or three other ecology films. It is part of the BSCS inquiry film series and is based on an article by biologist Garrett Hardin, which appeared in the December, 1968 issue of *Science* magazine. The film comes with a 31-page study guide (which includes Hardin's original article) that could serve as a model for any other short film guide in existence.

The film is divided into four parts, each a short film in itself. After each part a question mark appears on the screen as a signal to stop the film and hold a discussion before moving on to the next section.

The film begins in 18th Century England where there was common pasture ground which could belong to no one and be used by all. The "commons" is shown becoming overused and useless for grazing. After a discussion break part II presents Dr. Hardin's analysis of the situation and the role of the profit motive. His basic theme is that "In an uncrowded world you can do things you can't in a crowded world." At this point students accept this viewpoint as rather obvious and necessary, but by the end of the film its inescapable logic causes controversy. Dr. Hardin goes on to explain that in a crowded world individuals psychologically "wall out" large numbers of people because it is impossible to acknowledge all of them; thus contributing to urban alienation. He asks other questions which give rise to another discussion break.

Part III deals with crowding and stress as evaluated by different segments of the population—five girls sharing a Manhattan apartment, a black militant, an art lover. Visuals raise questions about the implications of overcrowding that are discussed before part IV.

In part IV Dr. Hardin returns to explore the population problem and its solution. Here is where the film becomes exceptional. Dr. Hardin claims that birth control is a must. After he does this, viewers are shown a film editor who slips into the film his own possibility. He claims that the people with a conscience who have only two-child families will not be competitive with people who have no conscience. In other words, if family planning is left to the individual, an evolutionary factor will be created wherein those with a global conscience will have a disadvantage to those who lack such a conscience. After the editor's insertion, Dr. Hardin gives his own opinion—unless we want disease and stress to control population size, we have to pass laws to restrict family size. Little prompting is needed for discussion after this section.

The final sequence in the film equates the planet earth with the 18th century commons which began the film. Dr. Hardin's idea of "mutual coercion mutually agreed upon" is controversial and sure to spark lively thought and debate.

The 23-minute color film is excellent for provoking discussion.

For purchase and rental inquire Holt, Rinehart & Winston, Inc. Rental $19 from the University of California.

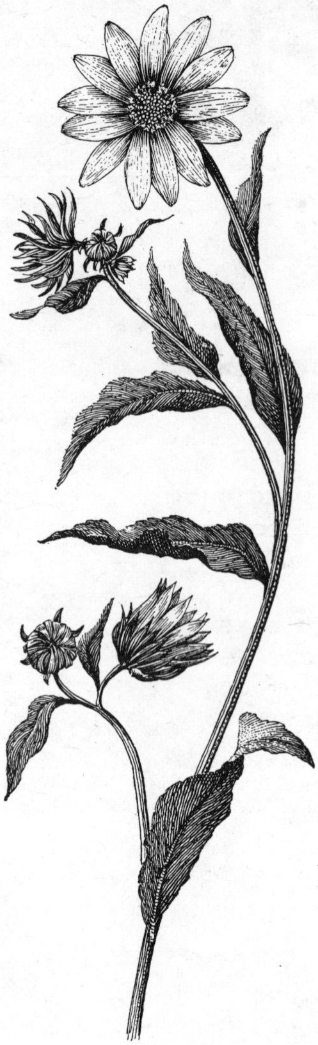

Junkdump

What's the difference between a grocery store and a pile of garbage? What keeps a parking lot from being seen as a junkyard? Simply a question of time and a few mental abstractions we all agree upon. **Junkdump** is a film that removes these differences and place a typical family in the middle of its own junk and garbage.

An alarm clock sounds and a man slowly awakes on his bed located outdoors. A wife, in curlers, still sleeps as the sound of a dump truck is heard unloading. The only difference between this family and any other is the fact that they live without walls (all the better to see them) and have a trash heap as a home. As breakfast is prepared and another day begins we see that the couple is a sort of King Midas in reverse. Everything they touch turns to trash—egg shells, an empty cereal box, toothpaste tubes are all casually thrown on the ground. But why not, since they live in a dump?

The family's situation at first seems outrageously absurd, but on second thought it is closer to reality. If walls could be taken down and time manipulated a bit the average family could be observed producing a trash pile of used goods every minute of the day. Trash and garbage collections hide this truth from urban families.

The husband goes off to work where he fills orders for junk replacement parts—once again seemingly absurd but little different from reality. Detroit ultimately produces nothing more than junk, factories turn out trash and stores sell garbage. All our valued material goods can be considered existing in a pre-dump state.

The husband returns home to soothe a crying baby. The baby turns out to be a plastic doll. Viewers who found the rest of the film believable will find the ending chilling; those not lucky enough to be so involved will find it laughable. No matter, the film has fantastic discussion possibilities and is excellent for pointing out the simple fact that without efficient solid waste disposal systems every consumer is merely a junkman in disguise.

Twenty minutes, color, 1970, directed by John Camie.

Rental $4.50 from the University of Michigan.

Go Faster . . . Peter Foldes is one of the most creative animators around today and one you'll be hearing more of. In *Go Faster* he satirizes the tendency for efficiency and speed coupled to the fact that no one seems to know where they're going with all this speedn. Excellent animation, but not his best. The same theme is handled by Jiri Trinka in his film *Passion*.

Color, animation, 9 min., rental $20, sale $125, from Learning Corporation of America.

That Time . . . Peter Fonda knows it; that's why he included the short scene at the beginning of Easy Rider in which a wristwatch is thrown away. Charlie Chaplin knew it in Modern Times. Lewis Mumford knew it when he wrote, "The clock is not merely a means of keeping track of the hours, but of synchronizing the actions of men." And Marshall McLuhan saw it too when he wrote, "Time measured not by the uniqueness of private experience but by abstract uniform units gradually pervades all sense life. Not only work, but also eating and sleeping come to accommodate themselves to the clock rather than to organic needs." What they all know is that the clock is far more than a servant obediently telling us "the time" when we ask. It is also a slave-master and the measure of a real commodity which can be "spent," "wasted," "bought," "lost," "gained," "saved," and even "killed."

That Time is about the clock as master controller. It presents a colorless world in which the clock's rule is taken to a surreal but logical extreme. Clocks reach out physically and force people to act, an alarm clock controls the length of an automat meal of spaghetti and nuts and bolts, even seduction has a time limit. Schooling is measured by a clock and calendar rather than by learning, music is in perfect time but lacking in soul. Finally the clock captures a human being and feeds it to its inner works where it grinds away slowly but exceeding small.

That Time is a 15 min., b&w, live-action film from Czechoslovakia that has nearly endless discussion possibilities. Code 408334, sale $220, rental $21 from Contemporary/McGraw-Hill Films.

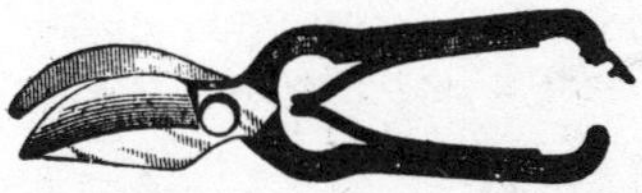

The Claw is a subtle film best appreciated by those with an eye for poetry and beauty. The film begins with a magnificent comparison of cliffs with the sides of old buildings with their carvings of stone faces which "gaze from granite palisades." Some of the narration sounds too much like reading, but the sound track gives way to snatches of live sound used in a college-like manner.

The "claw" of the film's title is the machine that reduces buildings to rubble; the monster that need only graze a wall and six stories fall. It is a claw that scratches out the stone faces on buildings, for new buildings are faceless. Perhaps better to mirror the anonymous urban man they protect. The old buildings slowly crumble to the almost Satanic sounding chant: "Must what is done be undone —done and undone—done and redone."

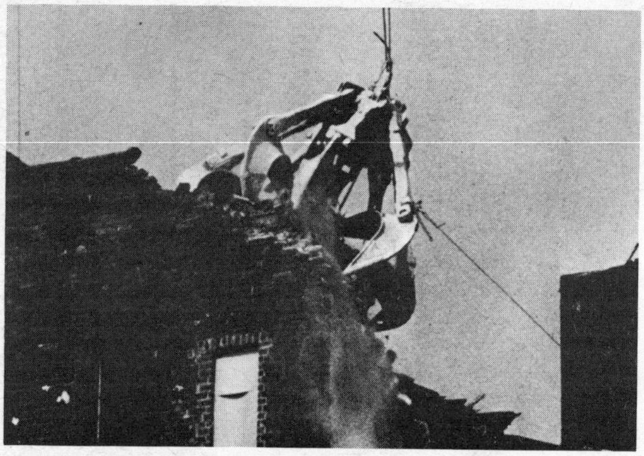

Every shot is poetic in a way that modern architecture is not. Men build while others tear down; reflections bounce off a glass box building; a boy and girl play; a woman leans out of a building next to a sign saying the entire building is being remodeled; a little girl backs slowly away from the "claw;" an artist works in ruins. Sounds drift in and out all the while the stone faces from a gentler age watch with disapproval.

The film is excellent for a study of the problem of urban renewal, cushioning against future shock, modern architecture, preserving what is of value from the old. The film is a fine example of how cinematic art can be used to make powerful emotional and intellectual statements.

Directed by Manfred Kircheimer, 1968, 30 min., b&w, rental $15, sale $250 from Pyramid Films.

The Crowd.....This is a fine visual study of man as a member of a crowd. Through skillful editing, most every crowd situation imaginable is presented and commented upon. Human crowds are juxtaposed with animal herds, so that the whole psychology of the crowd instinct comes to mind. Crowds at auto races, bull fights, carnivals and wrestling bring to mind thoughts of how violence is a spectator sport. The closing shot is of the ultimate crowd — human chromosomes. Available from Learning Corporation of America,

Hard Times in the Country. . . is a solid NET investigative report on the American food industry. Commentary and interviews with farmers quickly show that rising food prices are not caused by greedy farmers. In fact the small farmer is being driven into the city.

As is often the case, federal legislation disguised as a means of "helping" a nearly powerless segment of society is in reality a means of suppression. Farm subsidies have a regressive effect, with the 20 largest farmers receiving more money than the smallest 300,000. The top men have Congressional representation; in fact in 1969 Senator Eastland of Mississippi received a $117,000 farm subsidy. Since subsidies began, over 50% of small and medium sized farmers have been forced off their land. The U.S. is losing an average of 100,000 farmers per year.

Farming has given way to 100 billion dollar a year food industry. A few corporations control food; the top 50 food manufacturers make more profit than the next 30,000. A&P, Kroger, Safeway and Acme account for 50% of urban food sales. Kellog makes double the national average return on investment. Campbell sells 85% of all soup in the country.

The food processors pay low prices for natural farm food and turn it into high priced pseudo-food. A consumer group is shown squeezing a loaf of Wonder Bread that truly deserves the adjective "wonder" since without air it almost magically disappears into a lump of goo.

The film goes behind the story of rising food prices as superficially reported in the newspapers. In fact newspapers are dependent on the food industry for advertising income. **Hard Times in the Country** is a solid documentary with a point of view not often seen in the media.

58 min., color, purchase $550, rental $20.50 from Indiana University, $19.50 from the University of Michigan, and $18 from the University of California.

Footnote to Genesis . . . Here is a lyrical documentary about a couple who live practically alone in the wilderness of Western Canada. They live 45 miles from the nearest settlement and are devoted to saving the trumpeter swan from extinction. The appeal of the film is in its idyllic view of living in the woods, a view that is becoming more popular among those stuck in the city. Fine for discussing alternative life styles and inner resources and aloneness.

25 min., color, 1970, by Peter Flemington. Sale $300 from Carousel Films.

Rent $8 from the University of Michigan; $19 from the University of California.

Leaving Home Blues: An NBC White Paper on Rural Migration . . . A classic TV documentary by Martin Carr that is a must for rural high schools and a should for others. For the last 30 years 1 million people yearly have left the countryside for the city until now 75% of us live on 2% of the land. There is no end in sight. The film concentrates on young people in Nebraska, Houston and North Carolina and examines why they are part of this forced migration to the cities.

53 min., color; $15 from the University of Michigan; $30 from the University of California; $17 from Kent State University; and $25 from NBC.

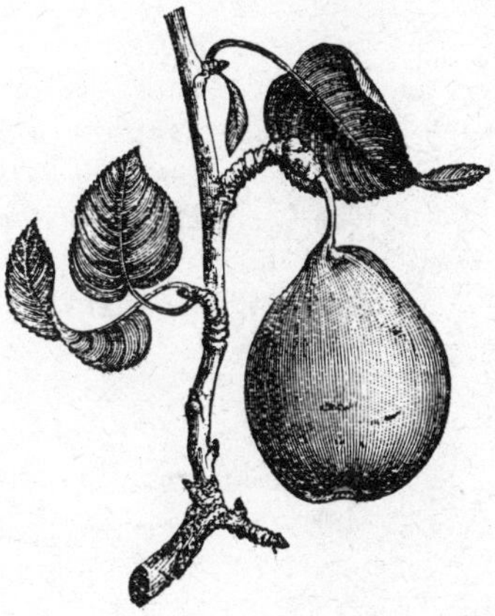

Tamer of Wild Horses . . . is an extremely well animated European short dealing with the power and effect of technology on man. It has the same theme as **#00173, Day After Day, Have I Told You Lately That I Love You** and others, but has a unique feature. It does not merely say that machines can control man and destroy him. It also points out the beauty of technology with man as master, and deals with the power and potential of machines as well as their dangers.

8 min., color, animated, sale $115 and rental $12.50 from Contemporary/McGraw-Hill Films.

TO DAZZLE THE EYE

The Persistent Seed. . . Hundreds of films tell of man's destruction of nature and warn against human folly. But only a handful use the poetry of film to compose a paean to the tenacity of life. The **Persistent Seed** is such a meditation.

The National Film Board of Canada presentation is about the creation of tomorrow as it quietly takes place today, about the tough but tiny seed of life that survives in spite of monstrous obstacles. It is a film about survival, about huge drop forges and delicate flowers, about children playing in lawn sprinklers so they are recreated along with the grass, about people in concrete canyons planting flowers on window sills to remind them of life.

The color and sepia cinematography overflows with the loving eye of the artist. No narration or dramatic musical score is needed to carry the film's power. **The Persistent Seed** is a hymn of praise that touches that spot in each viewer where there still remains a child-like love of nature.

A 1963 production, directed by Christopher Chapman. 14 min., color, rental $15 from Contemporary/McGraw Hill,

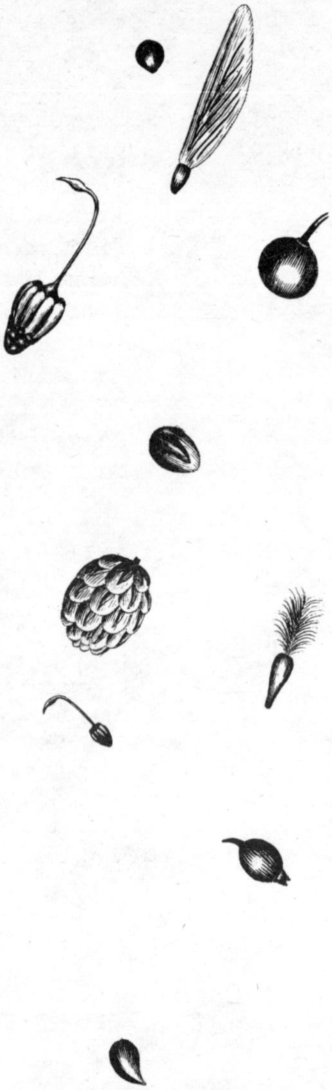

Omega.....This is the most visually magnificent short film I've ever seen — the *2001* of the short film. It should become a classic among film study groups and an inspiration for amateur filmmakers who have limited funds and equipment. Made by UCLA student, Donald Fox, this 12-minute color film is almost totally special effects — many of them done with little more than kitchen equipment. The end result is as professional as films made with enormous budgets.

Omega deals with the end of man in an evolutionary sense: his re-birth and liberation from the planet earth. By sending an "energy ray" to the sun and harnessing its solar power, man is transformed in an evolutionary leap. The film is more a "trip," or visual experience than a documentary or story film. It contains visual, audio and thematic references to Kubrick's *2001: A Space Odyssey*.

Like Kubrick's work, *Omega* should evoke an enthusiastic response more from young people than adults. If you get it, be sure to show it on as large a screen as possible, and make the room as dark as you can. A tiny image in a light-streaked room will reduce the total impact that this film can have.

Omega is available from Pyramid Films,

Seashore . . . Fred Hudson (*Leaf, Dunes, Gyser, etc.*) is one of the country's leading nature cinematographers, and *Seashore* is his most spectacular film yet. A reading from Loren Eiseley's *Immense Journey* sets the mood, but then Hudson's fluid camera and classical music takes over. The film works wonderfully to capture the mood and mystery of the meeting of land and sea.

Pyramid Films, 8 min., color, sale $125, rental $10. By Fred Hudson, 1971.

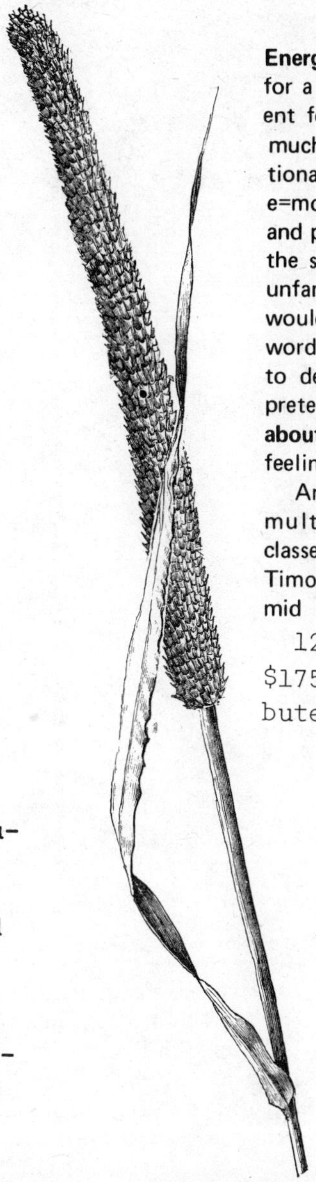

They Shall See . . . . is five minutes of visual beauty. Water, trees, seeds growing under ground, birds, leaves, plant cells, a spider, the human eye, sun, clouds are all superbly photographed by Steve Craig. **They Shall See** contains no narration and uses a single piano for musical background. Occasionally an ultra close-up of the human eye is shown. The film ends when the eye closes and the beauty disappears.

The film was made by the Franciscan Communication Center for religious education purposes but is a paen to the gift of sight and the beauty of nature for viewers in any group. The film would also be excellent for multi-media presentations.

Purchase is about $70, rental about $10 from your nearest office of Association Films, 600 Grand Ave., Ridgefield, N. J. 07657.

Energy . . . is really intended as a film for a science class to explain the different forms of energy. The film is not so much "instructional" as it is "educational." It does attempt to show what $e=mc^2$ means, how energy is converted and produced, how atoms and lasers and the sun provide energy. But to anyone unfamiliar with these concepts the film would offer little light. I'd probably use words like "meditation" or "revelation" to describe **Energy**, a beautiful, pretty, pretentious, and dazzling film. It tells **about** energy and it **is** energy; it gives a feeling of what energy is all about.

An excellent film for film study, multi-media presentations, science classes, or just plain delight. Directed by Timothy Huntely. (Distributed by Pyramid Films,

12 min., color, purchase $175, rental $15, distributed by Pyramid Films.

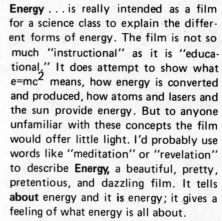

Rodeo . . . is a fantastic short documentary along the lines of Daunant's *Dream of Wild Horses* and *Corrida Interdite* but has greater texture and feeling. *Rodeo* is a drama of the battle of a man to ride a bull and survive. Contemporary/McGraw Hill has Carroll Balard's 20-minute masterpiece available for $275 or rental at $25.

Corrida Interdite.....This 10-minute, color film is composed entirely of slow motion shots from bull fights, set to concert organ music. The film was originally part of the Janus New Cinema collection which toured college campuses in concert form.

The classical music combined with the beauty and gore of the visual creates a powerful mood. Many of the shots are not for those with a queasy stomach, especially when the bull comes out on top.

One reaction I've found in using this film in high school is an identification with the bull. Cheering has greeted the bull's goring the fighter. Available from Pyramid Films (rental $15, purchase $130).

The Flat is a surrealist nightmare. As one teenager said, "It's about this guy who lives in a slum castle where weird things happen."

He stands on a chair but it descends into the floor, a light bulb flashes against the wall and breaks through it, a live rat scampers out from his bread, the soup spoon has holes in it, and the beer pitcher turns into a shot glass. An egg goes through the wall, rocks come out of the faucet, and dogs jump from the cupboard. In the most fantastic of the many special effects his entire bed simply decays into a mass of powder.

The film has no plot, coming instead from the tradition of *Un Chien Andalou*.

Excellent for film study, poetry courses, or art. The film is foreign made, but I have no information on who directed or produced it.

15 min., b&w, sale $120, rental $12 from Contemporary Films/McGraw-Hill.

DEATH AND AGING

When Angels Fall. . . an aged lady walks to work early in the morning through the streets of an even more ancient Polish town. Her work is in a basement men's room – ornate and baroque like none in America. She tends the room like a high priestess, occasionally receiving an offering in small coin. All classes and types visit her quiet cathedral.

In the ceiling is a skylight over which people walk on the sidewalk above She gazes upward, her lips moving, and reminisces of her youth. . . the wrinkled old lady was once a sensual woman who bore a child conceived in a moment of passion with a soldier-lover. The wars of the past have shaped her life. Her lover became a victim and her son died an absurd death.

It is evening now and she is alone, gazing upward again. Crashing through the skylight comes a figure dressed as an angel – her lover has returned.

When Angels Fall is another Roman Polanski masterpiece (my favorite) that defies written description. The film does have the power to move emotions deeply. (Contemporary Films, 21 min., color, sale $285, rental $25)

How Could I Not Be Among You. . . .is a film portrait of Ted Rosenthal, a poet told he has luekemia and will live for only six months. The mixture of stills and cinematography blends nicely with the narration consisting mainly of Rosenthal's own poetic thoughts on the approach of death. First shown two years ago on Great American Dream Machine, **How Could I Not Be Among You** possesses a grace and power rarely found in short films and a topic of ultimate relevance.

Some of Rosenthal's comments: "I was dying according to a pattern--the pattern of terminal cancer patients, they predicted how I would feel and they were right. I didn't have a self-image to worry about, nothing I had to be, and I felt free, I could leap out the window for the fun of it. At first I called people and told them 'guess what, I'm dying' this felt good, immediate and complete sympathy. Once you have nothing you can be anything. I think dying is not different than being born. I don't think people are afraid of death, they're afraid of the incompleteness of their life. I'm sick of dying, it's a drag, makes me depressed. I was a happier person when I became sick. Life is grim, but not necessarily serious. Never yearn for your past, your childhood is worthless, there is no escape in Christmas, no fantasy will soothe you, you must open your heart and expect nothing in return, return to your simple self."

The 30 year old Rosenthal's poetry is both tough and tender and often reminiscent of Ferlinghetti. As the film ends Rosenthal is still living as a man who knows death, perhaps cured perhaps soon doomed.

Directed by Thomas Reichman and distributed by Eccentric Circle Films. 28 min., color, sale $350, rental $35. Rental $12.15 from the University of Michigan and $22 from the University of California.

Tomorrow Again. . . Every day in any large city the obituary column is filled with the names of the old who were simply too tired to wake for another day. The death certificate will list some purely scientific cause for the end. But those who know are aware that these "causes" are mere excuses. Causes of death are rarely known. Diseases such as loneliness, isolation and feelings of uselessness never appear in medical reports no matter how much they are written on the faces of the old.

Grace is an old lady living with other "retired people" in a dreary San Francisco rooming house. In her one-room apartment she carries out the rituals that define the narrow boundaries of life. Her dream is to receive attention, praise, recognition. Her tragic flaw is that she is trapped not so much by tired blood and wrinkled skin as by her conception of how to gain affection and her belief in the destructive stereotype of the aged.

She wraps herself in a fur stole and imagines the attention the old men in the lobby will lavish upon her. But in the lobby she is ignored -- the old men are more interested in the newspaper and the football game on TV. She imagines herself carried out on a stretcher, thus gaining the attention she so desperately desires. But this is only fantasy, instead she returns to her room to await tomorrow again.

Director Roberth Heath (age 25) has come up with a cinematic and moving slice of life that invites an exploration of how to learn to age gracefully beginning as a teen-ager. The attitudes students have today about aging determine how they will act as old people. Although students will not immediately care to consider something as remote (and perhaps frightening) as aging there is common ground between the two age groups. For both the future can look black and unappealing and preoccupation with death and nothingness is frequent. Both can pass endless days in doing nothing and feeling there is nothing to do. Both groups are very likely to be self-absorbed and both alternate between battling for independence and leaning excessively on others.

Tomorrow Again is a simple film and an excellent starting place for a serious consideration of the art of aging.

1971, b&w, 16 min., rental $15, sale $140 from Pyramid,

EDUCATION

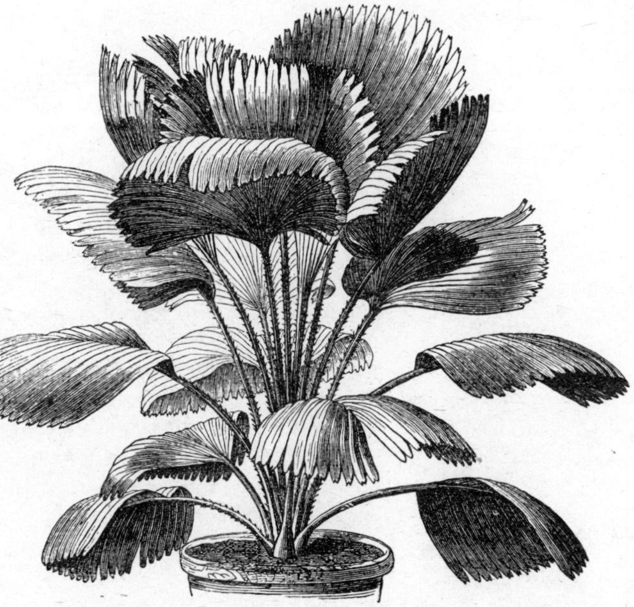

Replay tries to show that kids today aren't any wilder than their parents were as teens. One belligerent adult says of today, "I don't consider it dancing at all," while the screen is filled with scenes of bedraggled marathon dancers and flappers. Adults talk of way-out fashions and dirty movies while the screen proves that things in the 20's weren't much different.

The film ends with an encounter between a freak and an old lady; he called her "groovy" and she recognizing him as "wonderful." The film is sponsored by Arrow Shirts, no doubt in the hope that dressy shirts won't be one value the new generation will fail to replay.

A superficial but slick film with good discussion possibilities. Unless used carefully in a teen/adult group it will generate more heat than light.

8 min., color, rent $15, sale $125 Contemporary. Rental $10 from the University of California; $10 from United Church.

SIT DOWN, SHUT UP OR GET OUT is a one-hour TV drama shown one Sunday morning on NBC. The film is similar in theme to the popular NO REASON TO STAY. Both concern the dilemma of survival as an individual in a public school system, both feature a boy named Christopher who is a bright non-conformist.

In Allan Sloane's TV drama the creative rebel, Christopher Bright, is introduced as on trial by his teachers and administrators. Teacher-witnesses testify: a math teacher judges him "brilliant, but won't follow the rules," while viewers see in flashback that the teacher merely wants the boy to use his methods even though others are better. His English teacher also calls him brilliant but "a bad speller, can't capitalize, bad penmanship." The boy responds to the unfair charges and the audience sees the problem in oversimplified terms with the boy playing the role of the persecuted genius and the school serving as evil fall guy.

The boy's father is supportive telling him he must "do what you have to do." The father exemplifies a finding by Kenneth Keniston that the "young rebels" are not those reacting against strict parents but those carrying out the values taught them by their more liberal parents. The psychologist is also on Chris' side but the principal finds the boy a misfit and troublemaker.

Unlike his namesake in NO REASON TO STAY Christopher decides to remain at the school if only to "lose on my own terms rather than win on yours."

The drama is well-performed and its ability to provoke thought is attested by the more than 1,500 letters NBC received after its first showing.

55 min., purchase from NBC, rental for $30 from Broadcasting and Film Commission, National Council of Churches, 475 Riverside Drive, N.Y., N.Y. 10027.

55 min., purchase from NBC, rental $30 from Broadcasting and Film Commission, National Council of Churches, 475 Riverside Drive, New York, N.Y. 10027. Rental $31 from the University of California.

Higher Education: Who Needs It? . . . could be a rather frightening documentary for high school seniors. The CBS-TV film deals with the problems experienced in job placement by recent college graduates. Stories are told of college grads who are unemployed, sweeping floors, or delivering newspapers. The argument of the film is that colleges and universities are not facing reality and need some drastic changes. According to Hughes Rudd and the CBS team, the facts point to a system of higher education irreversibly locked in a sorry state of overproduction with no eye toward the needs of society.

High school teachers and parents of teens have for many years assumed college is the only way to obtain a satisfactory career in adulthood. *Higher Education: Who Needs It?* should help them face the fact that college is no longer such a panacea.

51 minutes, color or b&w. Sale price is $575 in color or $275 in b&w from Carousel Films. Rental, $19.65 from the University of Michigan and $18 from the University of California.

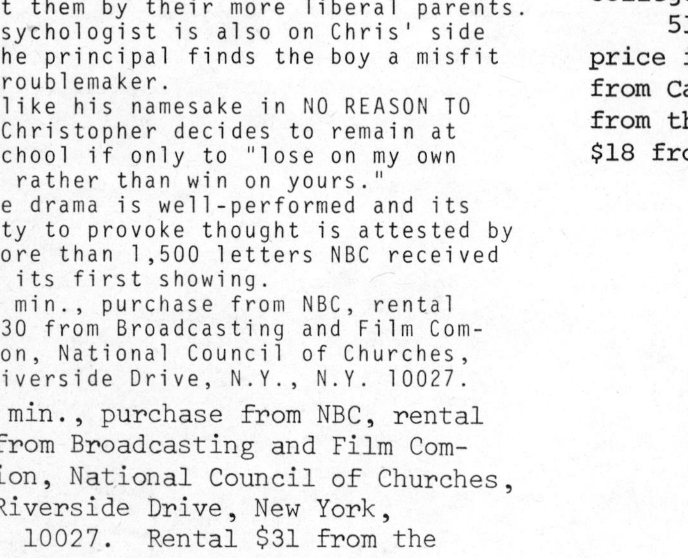

With Such as These. . . is an anti-school film, or rather a pro-children film. The visuals are all stills of children at play. The soundtrack is derived primarily from the writings of John Holt. The juxtaposition of the happy, smiling faces with the somber words about the harm school can cause is intended to incite viewers to "emote" or at least become defensive. It should then stimulate verbal interaction about school, children and freedom.

The film often works as a discussion stimulator and is a nice review of where John Holt was three or four years ago. Technically the film is rough with many of the black and white stills over exposed perhaps intentionally so the kids wouldn't look quite as happy and glowing.

17 min., b&w, rental $17.50, purchase $100 from Center for Curriculum Design, 823 Foster St., Evanston, Ill. 60204. No preview prints available, but rental is applicable to purchase price.

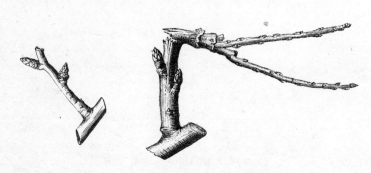

Play Mountain Place . . . Begun in 1950, *Play Mountain Place,* was one of the first American "free school" alternatives to public education. This film about the school is no slick PR trick; it is a film that captures the lively and open spirit of the school. Children take part in the actual filming and are the real stars of the film. For a taste of what a free school is like either visit one or watch this film.

28 min., color, sale $265, rental $30 from Cinema Kiva, 314 Marguerita Ave., Santa Monica, Ca. 90402. By Trevor Black. $9.25 rental from the University of Michigan.

Children as People . . . John Holt narrates this 1969 film about the Fayerweather Street School in Cambridge. Holt's comments are fine, "we put kids in school with others but ask them to sort of act as if they aren't there. A sort of training in indifference to others." Most of the film shows kids doing things kids in school rarely do, but nothing beyond the possibilities of a traditional school. The film gives some idea of what a free school is like. A gentle introduction.

(Polymorph Films.) About 30 min., b&w. Rental: $6 from the University of Michigan, $15 from United Church, and $27 from the University of California.

FILMS ON FILM

Synchromy . . . In Norman McLaren's *Synchromy* what you see is what you hear. What you see on the screen is something like the bars and stripes arrangement pictured on this page. What you hear resembles the kind of sound McLaren used twenty years ago in *Neighbors*. The visuals and sound match precisely because the visuals are the sound track transferred to the visible part of the film. McLaren photographed a set of white cards, each containing black stripes and each representing a semi-tone in a chromatic scale of six octaves. Pitch is produced according to the number of stripes -- the more stripes the higher the note. Volume is controlled during the shooting; when the camera's movable shutter is almost closed, the stripes emerge as a narrow band giving a pianissimo note, and with the shutter wide open the stripes are broad and the note loud.

The overall impression of the film is a sort of psychedelic, hypnotic sound-sight experience best viewed in a very dark room with the volume a bit louder than normal.

Rental $15 and sale $115 from Learning Corporation of America, and rental $10 from the University of California.

Arthur Penn . . . a superb documentary on Arthur Penn, director of *Bonnie & Clyde, Alice's Restaurant, Little Big Man,* and others. The NET-CBC-BBC-produced film uses extensive footage from Penn's films to illustrate aspects of his philosophy and theory of filmmaking. The film nicely balances elements of Penn's personal outlook on life, his biography, technical accomplishments, and personal lifestyle.

Drifting through the film to help explain Penn are Eugene Ionesco, William Gibson, Anne Bancroft, Warren Beatty (who seems either stoned or highly inarticulate), and Arlo Guthrie. Penn is shown, like Mick Jagger in *Gimme Shelter*, viewing takes from the film about himself on the editor. This 1970 Robert Hughes film should hold the interest of almost anyone with the least bit of curiosity about film. Fun, informative, and with surprising depth; the best film about a director I know of.

86 min., color, rental $65 minimum from MacMillan Films.

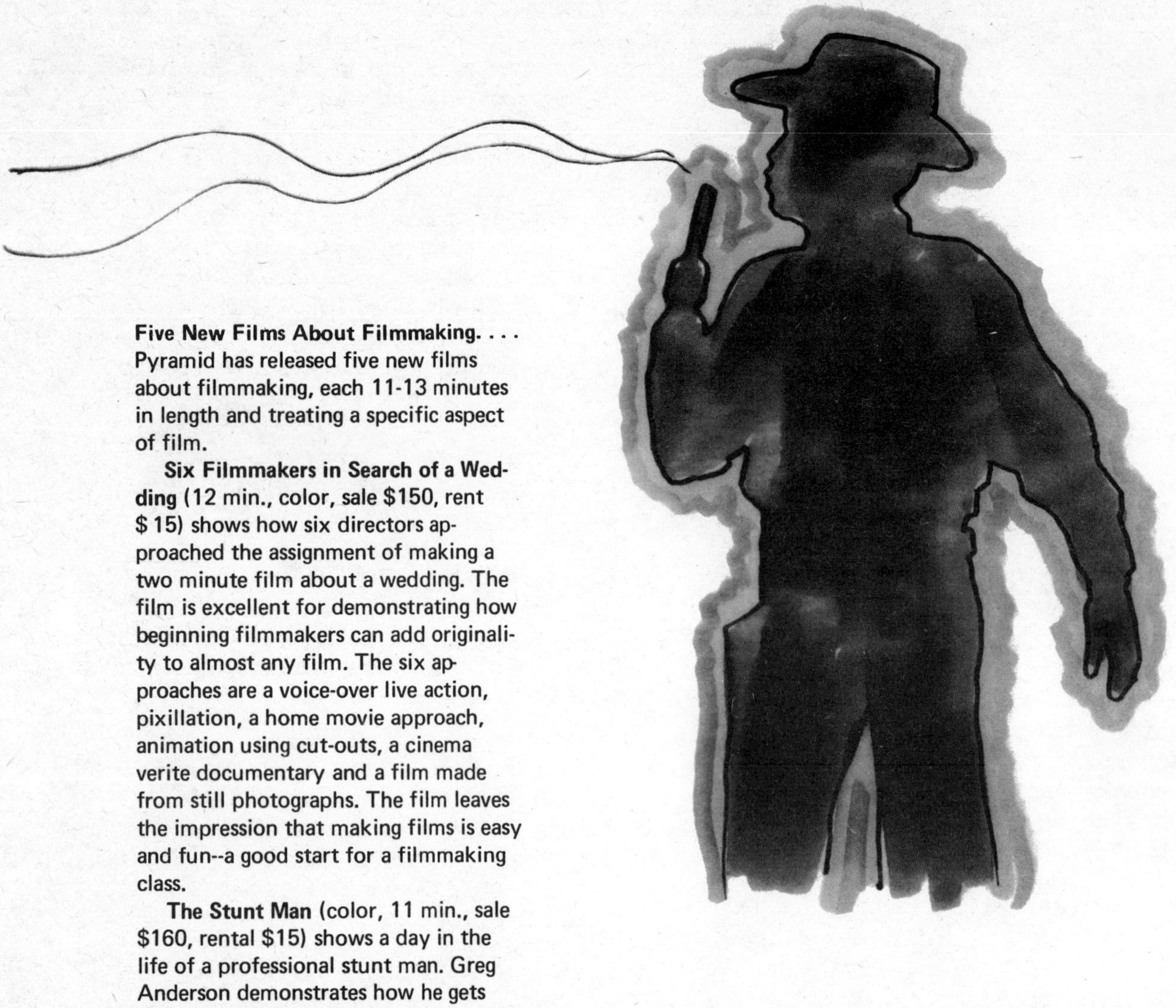

Five New Films About Filmmaking. . . . Pyramid has released five new films about filmmaking, each 11-13 minutes in length and treating a specific aspect of film.

Six Filmmakers in Search of a Wedding (12 min., color, sale $150, rent $ 15) shows how six directors approached the assignment of making a two minute film about a wedding. The film is excellent for demonstrating how beginning filmmakers can add originality to almost any film. The six approaches are a voice-over live action, pixillation, a home movie approach, animation using cut-outs, a cinema verite documentary and a film made from still photographs. The film leaves the impression that making films is easy and fun--a good start for a filmmaking class.

The Stunt Man (color, 11 min., sale $160, rental $15) shows a day in the life of a professional stunt man. Greg Anderson demonstrates how he gets shot in the back, falls off buildings, gets blown up and other routine jobs that are part of his daily work. No big secrets given away here but a nice film.

The Screenplay (color, 13 min., sale $175, rent $18) is the weakest of the new releases. Beginning with a short sequence from a drama, just to illustrate what a story is, it continues with advice about verb tenses and typing indentations.

Electric Flag (12 min., color, sale $160, rent $15) seems placed in this series as an afterthought. Supposedly the film gives "insights into the making of a feature film." In reality **Electric Flag** is little more than a glorified promotional trailer for the Robert Redford feature **The Candidate.** Not much insight and not much on media and politics either.

Frame By Frame (about 15 min., prices about the same as others) is the best of the series. The film illustrates how animation is done and demonstrates at least six different do-it-yourself techniques for making animated films. **Frame By Frame** has lead me to dust off my super 8 and start making an animation film. Highly recommended for film making classes.

Basic Film Terms: A Visual Dictionary . . . is a quick and light series of examples of cinema terms such as script, sequence, shot, scene, two shot, slow motion, pulled focus, telephoto, pan, tilt, dolly, boom, cut, dissolve, fade, freeze frame, etc. The film is simple but effective since many of the terms are difficult to describe verbally.

15 min., color, rental $18 and sale $175 from Pyramid Films and rental $5.75 from the University of Michigan and $13 from the University of California.

The Dove has captured an Academy Award and numerous film festival prizes. I have seen it twice theatrically, both times to packed houses that reacted with hilarity unlike that I've seen for any other short film.

The Dove opens with a serious tone and credits that indicate it is a Swedish Industries Production and has won the "Golden Escargot" of the Pan-European Film Festival. English subtitles are provided and the plot seems similar to other Swedish features, especially the films of Bergman. An aging professor is en route to receive a Nobel Prize and stops at his old house to relive memories.

After a few minutes a trace of snickers can be heard in the audience, while more serious viewers quietly puzzle out the exploration of existential anguish on screen. But the laughter spreads as the audience gradually realize they have been taken. *The Dove* turns out to be a slapstick lampoon of Bergman.

The scenes and situations are all taken from various Bergman classics, the language spoken is actually a comic hybrid of English and Swedish-sounding suffixes. Viewers are so busy reading subtitles that they rarely notice the film is in English until halfway through.

The fun of the film is in watching the truth slowly dawn on viewers. The more scholarly and accustomed to foreign films the audience the better the reaction. The audience should be unsuspecting and perhaps even prepared by a pompous introduction. A good audience laughs as much at its own gullibility as at the eventual slapstick humor of *The Dove*. A must for film societies, especially after a Bergman series.

Rental $20 from Pyramid Films. The film is about 15 min. , b&w.

THE FUTURE

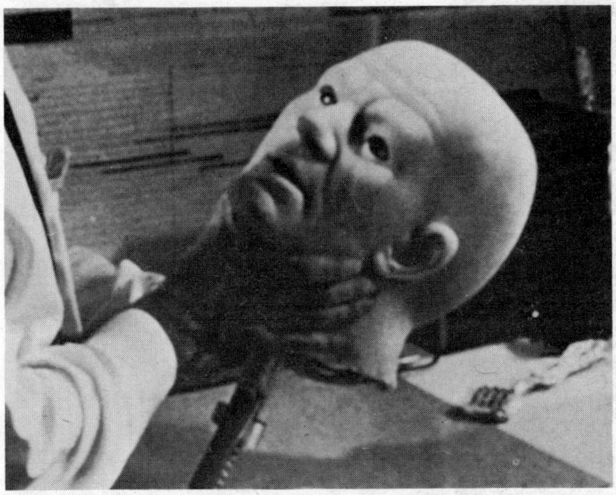

Future Shock was one of 1972's most discussed books and now promises to be an extremely popular educational film. McGraw-Hill Films has released a 42-minute documentary based on Toffler's book with narration by Orson Welles.

The film reveals that yesterday's science fiction is today's reality. Such rapid change, the film contends, leads to a kind of "sickness" which comes from too much change in too short a time. This sickness of future shock comes when the future arrives prematurely.

Rapid-fire film sequences dramatize man's loss of a sense of belonging in the new world of change. The camera follows scientists through a maze of staggering experiments -- organ transplants, computer art, rejuvenation surgery, test tube fertilization, intelligent machines, frozen bodies, and even "baby shopping" in a mock genetic supermarket. Superimposed are scenes of social change -- revolt, group marriage, riots, a homosexual wedding ceremony. The message is clear -- the only constant is change itself.

But *Future Shock* is neither pessimistic nor doom-saying. Toffler comments in the film, "If we can begin to think more imaginatively about the future, then we can prevent future shock and use technology itself to build a decent, democratic, and humane society." But that "if" at the beginning of Toffler's statement is what the film is all about. Wherever an "if" is considered, there also is ethics. The film gives no answers but poses ethical and moral questions that each individual must answer while the "if" still remains.

Future Shock is recommended as both engrossing entertainment and provocative mind bending. 42 min., color, produced by Metromedia Corporation. Sale price $575, rental $35 (code No. 103758-6) from McGraw-Hill Films, and rental $35 from NEFC and $33 from the University of California.

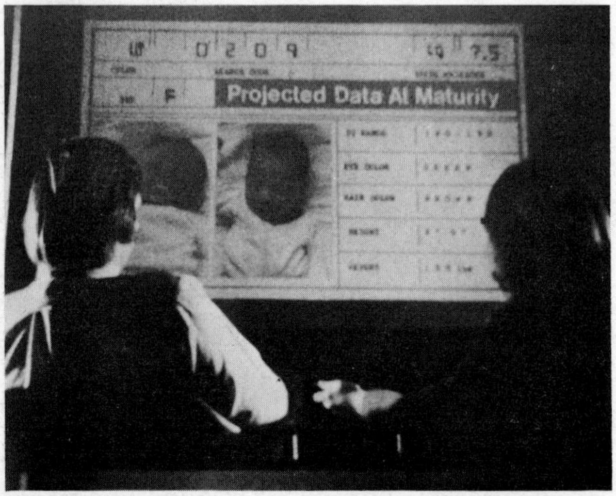

1985 is an hour-long TV special that was shown in Los Angeles, New York, Washington, and Kansas City and is now available in 16mm. The Metromedia Television special is set 11 years from now, as the announcer tells us, when "the worst of the prophecies have been fulfilled. The United States, and indeed the world, are locked deep in an environmental crisis -- the atmosphere, the earth, and the seas are perilously polluted. For the first time in human history the total extinction of man is possible -- even likely."

The president has just delivered an emergency speech to the nation. As the fictionalized news special unfolds, actual Metromedia newsmen are shown enlarging on the speech by describing crises in air and sea pollution, garbage collection, traffic, food contamination, population, and noise in several major cities. The program ends with the anchorman losing contact with each of his correspondents and finally the picture disappears completely.

There are good film clips of parched land, tire-strewn lakes, and starving children. The dialog is generally restrained and poignant. The Washington correspondent at one point reports that "our streets and lots are buried in one-way, no-return bottles and aluminum cans."

1985's producer Zev Putterman realized that most ecology presentations are highly intellectual and wanted something that would catch an audience at the gut level, the way Orson Wells' 1938 *War of the Worlds* did. His final 56-minute, color film can be rented from Kent State University for $18.70.

INDIVIDUALITY—CONFORMITY

New Harmony: An Example and a Beacon . . . With all the interest in alternative life styles and communal living, a unit on the history of American utopias from the New World through Walden II and after is fitting. NET has a 30-minute film about one of the most famous utopian attempts, New Harmony, Indiana. The Rappites of New Harmony held property in common, practiced celibacy, and prepared themselves for the coming of Christ. When they moved out in 1825 Robert Owen took over and attempted to recruit educators and establish a new socialist environment emphasizing intellectual freedom. Owen's experiment did not quite live up to his expectations, but its effects are still felt in midwest education.

29 min., color, #CSC-2180, sale $315, rental $11.50 from Indiana University.

Vonnegut Space Fantasy . . . . *Between Time and Timbuktu*, the film based on early Vonnegut writings, is available from New Line Cinema. The 90-minute film was shown on PBS last year; a print version has since been released in paperback. Rental for 1973-74 will be expensive, but the film will very likely become available in later years at a more reasonable cost. New Line Cinema.

Death of a Peasant. . .is based on a true story of the last minutes in the life of a Yugoslav peasant farmer in September of 1941. As the film opens a group of peasants faces a German firing squad. One by one they are slaughtered by the efficient squad lined up on an open field probably once farmed by the victims.

But one man, not willing to die at the hands of the Germans, makes a running escape through a corn patch. The firing squad quickly finishes off the other victims and takes off on horseback after the escapee. The chase sequence is very well constructed, using the cornfield as a dramatic setting much as Hitchcock did in **North by Northwest.**

The horizon presents no refuge, only open fields where a man running can hardly hope to evade a squad of soldiers on horseback. The peasant runs to where a few cows graze and snatches a rope from one and mysteriously places it around his own neck. Still running with the Germans in close pursuit, he approaches a horse-drawn wagon, ties the end of the rope to the wagon and yells at the horses. As the soldiers close in the horses leap forward strangling the peasant as they drag him behind.

Viewers think in terms of escape as they watch **Death of a Peasant** and find the ending a shock. The peasant has escaped death at the hands of the enemy and has taken control of his own death, perhaps the ultimate freedom. He has defeated the Germans and affirmed human dignity in a hopeless situation. Some viewers will find his approach "dumb," while others will begin to see the self-chosen death as a kind of final victory. An excellent film for discussion about choosing death as well as a finely made work for film study.

Directed by Predrag Golubovic, 10 minutes, color, rental $15, sale $150 from Mass Media Associates,

Solo is a lyrical look at a one-man mountain-climbing expedition. Mike Hoover's efforts and film direction leave audiences on the edge of their seats. In a school, visitors gather outside the door when *Solo* is shown and students sneak back for a second viewing. Some teen girls will fall in love with Mike totally taken with his self-portrait as a rugged, brave, but tender, independent individual.

Uses: enjoyment, discussion of the mystique of the rugged individual, daring and adventure, motivation, thrills, etc. Pyramid, color, 15 min., rent $15, sale $175.

The Trendsetter . . . This simple animated film yields surprising depth when carefully considered. The film deals with the frustrations of a compulsive nonconformist. He is a true trendsetter, everything he does is turned into a fad by his loyal followers. If he takes up a pogo stick soon everyone is hopping around; if he lives in tree tops not long after the trees will contain thriving colonies of followers. But the trendsetter's driving interest is to be different, so every success forces him to some other "far out" action. Finally, in an attempt to evade his followers he fakes a suicide; but his disciples imitate him without faking. Now he is without followers and can be truly unique; or so he thinks. He discovers that his individuality was phony and depended on the following of others. The trendsetter is as much enslaved by his need to be different as the masses are in their rush to be "in."

Excellent for a study of fads, conformity, mass culture, and individuality. 6 min., color, animation. Sale $100, rental $10 from Pyramid Films.

UP IS DOWN, winner of the peace prize at the Atlanta Film Festival, is about a little boy with a strange sort of defect—he's upside down. Since he walks on his hands, he sees things differently. To him, frowns look like smiles and life is one adventure after another.

But he makes people uncomfortable so a town meeting is held to decide how to solve the problem. A doctor reports a rare case of deficiency of tension and clear lungs. A psychiatrist diagnoses an obvious case of well being, the absence of paranoiac behavior and a repressed hate instinct. The sociologist reports

a lack of competitive drive, a naive trust of human nature and passivity toward the war. Clearly this will not do.

The decision is made; he must be corrected. So he is placed under therapeutic treatment— injections, hot and cold baths, centrifugal spinning, tractions, lobotomy— frontal and backward, brainwashing three times a day, saturation with TV commercials, and red and blue radiation. Finally, he is judged cured.

When the little boy stands up he sees that what he thought was love was really hate, individuality was conformity, plenty was poverty, concern was indifference and joy was despair. He was frightened.

And so he goes back to the wise adults and tells them, "If you want me to stand on my feet, you'll have to make some big changes first."

6 min., color, sale $100, rental $10 from Pyramid Films. Rental $3 from the University of Michigan and $9 from the University of California.

CAGES

Man's dependence on authority and the consequences when accepted rules are broken—these are the themes of the Polish animated short CAGES.

The story begins with a little everyman trapped in a prison cell. The warden tries to cheer him with some toy blocks. But the prisoner is too inventive; his construction is vastly superior to the warden's. The warden takes the blocks away and the prisoner is left to his own thoughts. The jailer sees the thoughts appearing in balloons and races after them with a butterfly net. A door in the background opens and we discover that the warden is being watched by other jailers and so on **ad infinitum.**

We are all prisoners—of ourselves, our ideas, our dreams and our place in the world. The theme is presented powerfully enough to make this short one of the most popular for religious education in 1971.

9 min., animation, sale $125, rental $11.50 from Contemporary/McGraw-Hill Films.

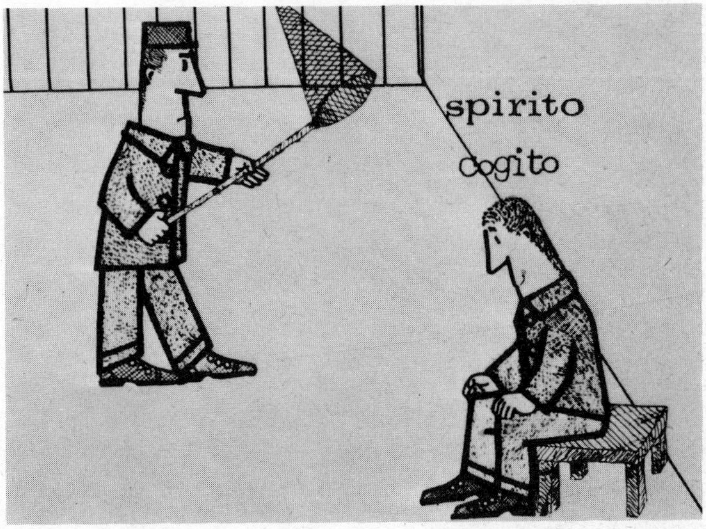

Obedience is a plainly made documentary of the experiments of Dr. Stanley Milgram at Yale about ten years ago. He set out to discover how far people would be willing to go in the name of obedience.

Volunteers were told they were to take part in an experiment about the value of punishment in teaching. The volunteer was to help a "learner" (a person secretly in on the experiment) memorize a list of words by giving him shocks each time he recited the list incorrectly. With each mistake the shocks increased in intensity. The shock machine (a dummy that the subject is led to believe actually gives shocks) has a series of levers ranging from a tiny shock to one labeled 375 volts and one marked simply "XXX -- Extreme Shock, Danger." The learner is in a different room but communicates through a speaker. As the teacher gives more and more intense shocks the learner complains of a heart condition and pleads to get out of the experiment.

The first two volunteers shown stop short of "all the way" but not without much hesitancy. The third volunteer is the film's main character as he painfully makes his way up the row of switches. "I'm not gonna kill that man in there," he says, "I refuse to take the responsibility of his getting hurt in there." The scientist simply tells him "The experiment requires that you continue," and he does. At 420 volts the man protests, "But he might be dead in there, I don't intend to be rude, but I think you should look in on him." He pulls all the levers, even the one marked with the triple X.

Before the experiment psychologists were asked to predict how many subjects would go all the way on the machine. Their composite answer was that less than one percent would. The actual results? Fifty percent pulled all the levers in spite of the learner's pleas, groans, and final silence. The overall conclusion of the experiments is that "a substantial number of people do what they are told no matter what the content of the act."

Companion films such as *Interview With My Lai Veterans, Night and Fog,* or *Hangman* would make for a powerful unit on conformity and conscience.

45 min., b&w, 1965. Sale $260, rental $25 from New York University Film Library, 26 Washington Place, N.Y. 10002. $7.75 from University of Michigan. $18 from University of California.

MINORITIES—RACE—PREJUDICE

The Conference . . . Five people arrive at a tall downtown office building for a conference. Each comes in a chauffeur-driven limousine and enters the building. The first is a well-dressed executive, but the others are no ordinary collection of businessmen. A woman in a bikini saunters in; then a Jesus figure complete with beard, sandals, and long flowing robe; next a cowboy; and finally a radical college student. They prepare solemnly for their three o'clock conference with a clown.

At the meeting, each places on the table an object signifying his identity. The round conference table begins to rotate and the screen goes blank. Shots are heard. The next scene shows the closed door outside the conference room. Slowly the participants emerge, one at a time. One does not walk away from the conference. Jesus has again been killed.

Each of the characters in the film is a symbol of a class or group of people. The film is completely allegorical. In the words of filmmaker Steve Simmons, "Each of the characters at the conference symbolically sheds his identity by placing an object on the round table. But

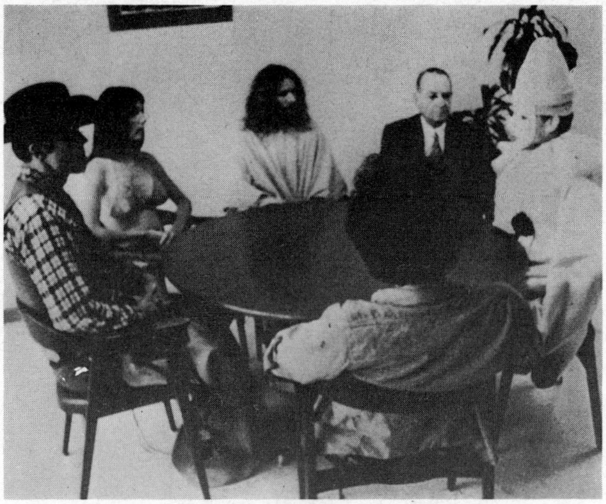

no matter how friendly the human facade may seem, once the surface has been probed and identity cracked, evil . . . . manifests itself . . . . Once in the conference room, each of the five picks up a gun and shoots Jesus Christ. The characters have changed: human psychology has not."

The film catches viewers in their own prejudices and stereotypes as they play the guessing game asking who shot who and why. Those who find the literal interpretation of the Jesus figure overstated can instead view him as one of the victimized, the object of violence committed thousands of times daily in glass and steel office buildings.

12 min., b&w, rental $15, sale $125 from Pyramid Films.

If You Label It This It Can't Be That . . . is a film about stereotypes. This film consists entirely of edited snatches of interviews with dozens of people. The people in this case are all children, and the questions are "What is a Communist?" "What is a Mexican?" Or a gypsy, patriot, bigot, old person, Indian, hard hat, or hippy. The children's answers reveal that they already have learned to apply labels to people at the drop of a question. They reveal amazing truths such as patriots are either football players or people who march in parades holding a flag, Mexicans are people who wear hats and are dumb, bigots could be either a big person or a kind of bucket, old people are clean-up ladies or dirty old men, and Indians have feathers in their head and shoot a bow and try to make people dead.

The final question asked of one little girl is "where did you find this all out?" Her revealing answer is simply "from my mother." An excellent discussion provoker on the subject of stereotypes and mental limitations.

The film is about 12 minutes, color from FilmFair Communications, 10900 Ventura Blvd., Studio City, Calif. 91604.

Bill Cosby on Prejudice . . . . is a Cosby monolog intended to make the bigot appear foolish. Cosby delivers his monolog as a man on the street who reveals he doesn't like Blacks, never liked old people, never been too tickled with kids, never cared for Jews, don't like the Irish, and on and on until he has demeaned every conceivable minority group except TV comedians.

The monolog seems improvised and too long. The film is made from a videotape transfer and has very poor color. I doubt if the entire 25 minute delivery will receive three laughs from a class. 25 min., sale $300, rental $25 from Pyramid Films,

OUR TOTEM IS THE RAVEN

As in LITTLE BIG MAN Chief Dan George plays the grandfather who guides a young man of two cultures in the ways of Indian sensitivity. Grandfather takes his teenage grandson into the wilds for a baptism into nature and an initiation ceremony. The film has many themes--man/nature unity, the death of Indian culture, tradition vs. change, baptism-initiation and death. Dan George is superb as the wise preserver of what is valuable in ancient ways. OUR TOTEM IS THE RAVEN is one of the finest "Indian films" available.

22 min., color. Inquire Holt, Rinehart & Winston.

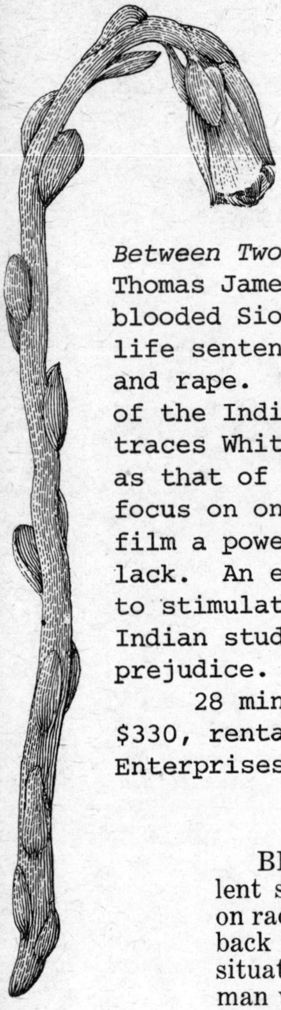

Between Two Rivers . . . A sleeper. Thomas James Whitehawk is a full-blooded Sioux Indian now serving a life sentence for robbery, murder, and rape. He is taken as symptomatic of the Indian problem. The film traces Whitehawk's background as well as that of the tribe in general. The focus on one individual gives this film a power that many documentaries lack. An emotional experience sure to stimulate much reaction. For Indian study, crime, institutions, prejudice.

28 min., color, 1969, sale $330, rental $15 from NBC Educational Enterprises.

BLACK THUMB is an excellent short film to use in a unit on racial prejudice. The film cuts back and forth between two situations. In one, a very black man works in a garden of a suburban house. The other situation is that of a suburban white liberal. He has mailed his check to an organization supporting integration and has to work out some way for his wife to have the car to attend a welfare support demonstration downtown. He leaves his home and goes to work conducting a door-to-door marketing survey. In the course of his day he finds himself at the house where our black man is working in the garden. He rings the doorbell but no one answers. As he is about to leave, he hears the sound of the hedge clipper and sees the black man. He asks, "Is the woman of the house in?" The Negro says no. He then asks, "Is the man of the house in?" The black man replies that he will go and see. He goes around the back and through the house to open the front door. "Can I help you?" he asks.

The viewer does not know that the black man is the home owner. If the viewer assumes he is a gardener, the film catches his own unconscious prejudice, just as the white liberal is caught. Some viewers will even think the film begins with what looks like a theft of garden tools—even more prejudice.

9 min., color. Holt, Rinehart & Winston. Rental $3.50 from the University of Michigan.

Ain't Gonna Eat My Mind . . . is a harrowing documentary trip down the "mean streets" of the South Bronx. Black Benjy, a member of the Ghetto Brother's, has been murdered by a rival gang and retaliation fills the neighborhood. Producer/director Tony Batten interviews Charles Milendez, Ghetto Brothers president, and walks with him in an attempt to prevent further violence. A gathering of the "families" is called and leaders of the Young Cobras, the Savage Skulls, the Nomads, The Young Sinners put aside their guns and switchblades to talk. Their "raps" are street drama of the highest order--improvised, earthy, rhythmic, tough yet deeply personal. The meeting cools things off at least for a while.

Ain't Gonna Eat My Mind continues with interviews with a junior high principal, a math teacher, youth workers and gang members. The story they tell is compelling and one that street kids in any large city can readily understand. Suburban students will find this world hard to understand, but at least they will realize that the Ghetto has

The film won a Du Pont/Columbia University Award and a 1973 N.Y. Station Emmy Award..

34 min., color, sale $400, rental apply, Carousel Films.

The Black Woman . . . This NET documentary focuses on the role of black women in relation to white society, black men, and the liberation struggle. Appearing in the film are poetess Nikki Giovanni, singer Lena Horne, Bibi Baraka (wife of LeRoi Jones), singer Roberta Flack, and dancer Lorretta Abbott. Order #CS-2184.

52 min., b&w, sale $265, rental $12.25 from Indiana University; $17 from the University of California.

POVERTY—MONEY

Banks and the Poor . . . . is the single most instructive documentary I have ever viewed. There have been thousands of films made about bank robbers, but **Banks and the Poor** is the only film in existence that shows how banks rob people. This NET film is advocate journalism at its best, carefully documenting how the poor and the middle class are victimized by banks and loan companies.

David Rockefeller, chairman of the board of Chase Manhatten Bank, compares banks to doctors taking care of people and businesses. He claims that the banking profession has paid special attention to the disadvantaged. To refute his claims the film examines the ties between banks and real estate firms and details how little has gone to finance low income housing. Banks help finance slumlords but refuse loans to the poor. Those refused at "full service banks" turn to finance companies such as Beneficial. A hidden camera at a loan company office is used to record an interview with a man who makes about $158 a week. He applies for a $800 loan and is approved. His interest rate? Twenty-five and a half percent per year. And where does the finance company get the money to loan the man? From the same bank that turned him down. Is the risk of the poor defaulting so high as to justify the astronomical interest rate? Ninety-five percent of all borrowers, even the poor, pay back loans.

The film goes on to document more ways in which banks oppress and serve the status quo. For example, the ghetto credit swindlers could be stopped by banks using their considerable financial clout.

Banks and the Poor manages to make a relatively static subject visually interesting without sacrificing thoroughness. The film is long and might be boring to many high school students, but its message is devastating and crucial.

59 min., b&w, rental $18 from the University of California and $11 from Kent State University. Rental also from Indiana University.

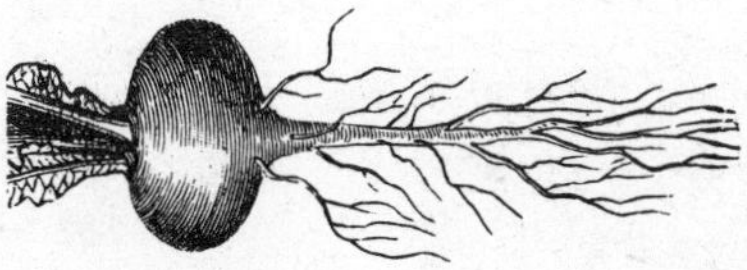

The Third World . . . . Time-Life is distributing a series of six 50-minute documentaries made for BBC-TV. **Rich Man, Poor Man** is an in-depth investigation of what has happened to "Third World" nations since post-war developers brought Western cultural values, industry and education to them. The series concludes that only the wealthier nations have benefitted while the lot of the common man in the Third World has worsened. The most important concept presented is that the standard of living in Western nations must be lowered before it can be raised in developing countries.

Filmed in Britain, Ceylon, and Ghana, each segment focuses on a different developmental process: (1) Industry, (2) Trade, (3) Food, (4) Medicine, (5) Education and (6) The State.

The film series is strong and best suited for senior high and college classes. Each film rents for $50 ($250 for the series) from Time-Life.

They Get Rich from the Poor is a 28-minute documentary on the relation of organized crime to poverty, a subject desperately in need of exposure. The film is a well-made TV documentary with the usual combination of interviews and atmosphere shots.

The film contends that the poor slums have become the "lush territory" of the syndicate with a general proposition being "You can make more money in a Harlem than a Scarsdale." Gambling has been the underground's most lucrative operation since 1920. The rich can go to Las Vegas or the lottery or the races. But the poor? They have to settle for mob-controlled numbers rackets and policy games. In one Harlem police precinct in one year over 22 million dollars is bet. So what's so bad about gambling? The money the underworld makes from the dimes and quarters of Harlem finances narcotics operations which also tear apart ghetto families. Organized crime needs slums to stay rich. One black community worker realizes "no black man brings dope into this country." In one year there were 9,500 gambling felony arrests, 32 convictions, and only one prison sentence.

Besides the dope-gambling-poverty-syndicate links the film explores government corruption, nonenforcement of laws, demoralization, and newspapers that print information useful only in the numbers game. The film might serve to awaken students who believe poverty in America is an unfortunate accident or the fault of its victims.

28 min., color, 1970, rental $15, sale $330 from NBC Educational Enterprises.

The Poor Pay More is based on the book of the same title by Columbia University sociologist David Caplovitz. The film is an exposé of the fraudulent retail practices forced upon unsuspecting ghetto consumers.

The film shows the results of investigations of furniture dealers, food chains, finance companies, and door-to-door con men -- a fair sample of those who prey on the poor and uneducated. In a furniture store, concealed cameras reveal the hidden cost system of credit; another film crew accompanies a Department of Markets Investigator on "Operation Lamb Chops," which results in the conviction of meat dealers who use rigged scales.

The retailers speak in rebuttal of the film's charges. Some rationalize and lend a touch of grim humor to the otherwise sad situation. The film concludes that the poor person is at the mercy of the local merchant who is controlled by big finance companies which in turn are controlled by respectable banking interests.

Many people believe that the poor are given as much opportunity as the rich but merely throw it away. After seeing *The Poor Pay More* students often question this belief. The film comes wound on two reels, good for dividing into two class sessions, if desired.

55 min., b&w from University of California, $14, University of Indiana, and $10 from the University of Michigan.

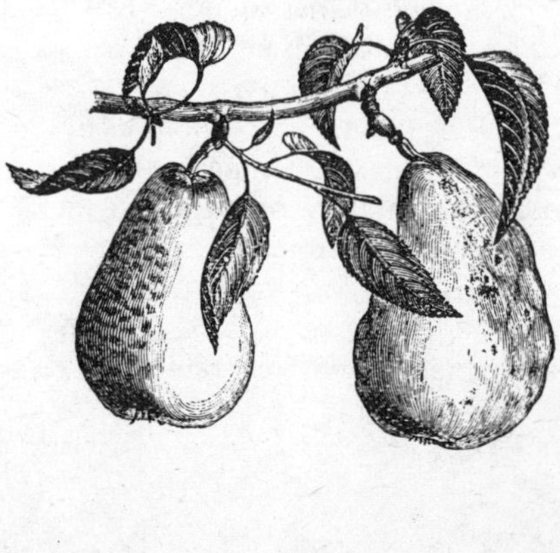

PSYCHOLOGY—FOIBLES

CRY HELP!

This NBC-TV "white paper" offers a sensitive look at two teenage girls at Napa State Mental Hospital in California. Young viewers easily identify with the girls, perhaps sensing that "mental illness" is not a unique disease but rather an extension of normal qualities within each person.

Gloria most resembles Deborah in I NEVER PROMISED YOU A ROSE GARDEN and her private fantasy world. She wears her hair so that her face is sometimes completely covered. At one point in therapy she muses "I love the Beatles...they're the only reasons I don't kill myself."

Debbie is nearly opposite in her manifestation of dis-ease. She was violent to others and herself with a case history of attempted self-mutilation.

In therapy the two highly articulate girls reveal they are more alike than different. Both seem to be filled with hate and both are victims of parents who were unable to give unselfish love that leads to self-acceptance. Abbreviated case histories are given and some of the therapy techniques are shown, including a highly charged psychodrama. NBC's angle in the telementary is to show that teens do become disturbed and that more treatment centers are needed. In classroom use the film's value lies in viewers' identification with the two girls.

81 min., color, rental a bargain $32, purchase $675 from NBC Educational Enterprises and rental $38 from the University of California.

The Mind of Man . . . This is a two-hour film directed by scientist-writer Nigel Calder and presented on NET. The film examines the operation of the human brain through interviews with scientists throughout the world and sequences of actual lab experiments. Topics included are the growth of the brain, the effects of drugs, sleep, learning, perception, language, and creativity. There are demonstrations of individuals consciously controlling the need for oxygen and lowering blood pressure. Several scientists raise the question of the role of consciousness and the "soul." The length and depth of this film make it ideal for the core of a unit on the mind, soul, human engineering, or psychology.

119 min., order #CSC-2145, purchase $785, rental around $50 or less from Indiana University, and $43 rental from the University of California.

Involuntary Control . . . What is man's potential? What inner parts of the body can be consciously controlled? *Involuntary Control* explores current research into these questions with some rather startling results.

Man has always sought control over involuntary bodily actions. Some have looked to gods, magic, or yoga with varying degrees of success. What if we look to science?

An experiment with rats is shown in which the rat is shaped through a stimulus-response pattern to increase or decrease heart rate by as much as 100 beats per minute. Another experiment shows a rat taught to blush in one ear and not in the other.

If these experiments have any application for humans the implications are profound. Already some psychologists feel that all illnesses have strong psychosomatic causes. Perhaps humans could be taught to slow down heart rate as a preventive measure against heart attacks.

The final experiment shown involves a human subject who quickly learns to control the output of alpha waves from his brain, a skill which takes Zen masters years to learn. The effect? He finds that even outside the lab he can go into an alpha state which helps to enhance concentration or to let down perceptual inhibitions. He even claims that alpha production is more powerful and rewarding than a drug-induced high.

The film is capable of holding most any audience spellbound and of opening new insights and raising new questions.

25 min., color, sale $275, rental $25 from Wiley Educational Services, 605 Third Ave., New York, N.Y. 10016.

PRINCE EUSTIS
UNEXPECTEDLY RETURNING
FROM HEIDELBERG.

The Emperor's New Armor is a parable about world and personal peace. The king in this parable is persuaded by three salesmen from Habadash Hardware Ltd. to spend $113,000 for a new innovation in kingly dress, "soft armor." What they present him looks suspiciously like the old, clanky traditional hard armor. But the king accepts the armor, pays the bill and clunks off in his new suit. When he sits down, he insists he has soft armor, even after he falls through a chair. His wife says, "I think you've been taken, dear." But the king, undaunted, orders a new chair (heavy duty for $99,000) and insists the armor is getting lighter by the minute.

It seems that the king's armor is rather pointed and has a tendency to lop off heads and to tear off the dresses of the unprotected. So all the people get fitted with the new "soft" armor to protect themselves. Even the cat has armor now.

One day, the emperor's son arrives back from college. His father greets him with a big hug, which has an effect similar to stepping on an apple with football cleats. The son dies while the king insists it's "just a little compound fracture." So the film ends. Its moral? "In a world without armor, nobody is safe."

The film has fantastic discussion possibilities. The king, like us all, adjusts the world to his own ideas. Since "I've been taken" does not fit into his world view, he adjusts the world to make it right. We all do that; the emperor merely happens to have more power. It is indeed easier to live with illusion than to change ourselves to fit reality.

Other themes in the film include the arms race, McLuhan's anti-environments, our armor of psychic defense mechanisms, power, self-image and illusion. A detailed study guide which I prepared comes with the film or can be requested free from Pyramid.

6 min., color, $100 purchase, $10 rental from Pyramid Films.

To See or Not to See. . . .is about two years old but has not gained the popularity it deserves. The National Film Board of Canada production is a humorous and satirical look at the values of seeing reality versus seeing what one wants to see. Students enjoy the film and cannot easily forget its striking visualization of the inner workings of human perception.

The evolution of a man's perception of the world is traced using a cartoon character resembling Casper the Ghost to represent his psyche. Through childhood the psyche lives at ease; reality is made to conform to the demands of fantasy and illusion. But now reality is gaining strength and the man suffers what could be called an identity crisis. Having tried drugs and alcohol to no avail he submits to a doctor's treatment --special glasses that make reality appear to conform to his illusions. All goes well until the patient encounters a steam roller whose danger the glasses minimize.

The question remains; which is more dangerous, the disease or the cure? The film asks should we strive to see things as they are and let the reality overwhelm us or should we don the glasses of illusion and suffer at the hands of the reality that is then hidden?

To See or Not to See is excellent for discussion on questions such as the soul, neurosis, perception, formation of attitudes, TA and coping with fear.

15 min., color, rental $20, sale $195 from Learning Corporation of America. Rental $14 from the University of California.

THE SEXES

Harmony. . . . is a comic animated film from Romania that questions traditional male and female roles and the integrity of the individual who plays these roles.

As the film opens a man and wife emerge from an apartment. Each assumes the conventional role society expects--the man strong and aggressive and the woman weak and passive. The two arrive at their office. He is the high-powered executive who demands complete obedience from his subordinates. His wife is a timid, terrified clerk-typist who does only menial work and quivers when she is called on the carpet by her boss-husband.

But when the two return home their roles reverse completely. She domineers and he meekly dons an apron to sweep, clean and cook. What the title ironically calls harmony is in reality a dehumanizing puppet-like existence in which both act out parts having little to do with whole human lives. Their apartment door represents the boundary line between one's public and private face.

Harmony claims that the more exaggerated and unnatural the individual's life must be outside the door, the more he or she must compensate by contrary behavior behind the door.

Excellent for a study of sex-roles, stereotypes, masculinity and femininity, the public self versus the private self, compensation, and human liberation.

8 min., color, animated by Horia Stefanescu. Sale $95, for rental or preview information inquire Wombat Films

Frankenstein in a Fishbowl. . . .is Barry Pollack's absorbing, sad and gruesome documentary about the experience of plastic surgery. The film follows two women through the pre-planning conference with the doctor, the gory surgery and the recuperation and evaluation of the process. At a recent showing to a class of high school girls one became ill, one cried for thirty minutes, and all were 100% involved.

Millie is forty-four, fat and wants a face lift. With a suave "bedside" manner her surgeon explains the face lift process that will tighten up her face and leave only small scars around the ear. Millie's $2000 face job is sad because what Millie needs is a decent diet and the will power to stick to it rather than plastic surgery that will enable her to continue to gorge candy. To improve her image she looks to doctors instead of to herself and this is her tragedy.

Pollack's cinema verite camera goes into the operating room with Millie and only those with a strong stomach will be able to watch the facial incisions and the literal lifting of the skin to stretch it taut. During the operation the doctor calmly comments on what he is doing while most of the audience will shriek, groan or simply look away from the bloody screen. Pollack doesn't seem to realize that a six foot close up of a face being cut with a scissors is more gruesome than reality.

Or perhaps he does realize and this is another of his cinematic weapons used to convince viewers plastic surgery is sad, cruel and definitely not for the sane. His use of extreme close ups, glaring lighting, his selection of shots and editing definitely convey his own disdain for the whole subject. The film, as the title hints, is both a behind the scenes look at a fascinating and rarely public subject as well as a polemic against its absurdity.

The second lady in the film receives a a nose job to smooth down the hump in her nose. The scenes of the operation are even gorier than those of Millie's.

Frankenstein. . .is a bit too long with much of the conversation between the two women in the hospital during their recovery obscured by all the bandages. But finally the bandages come off, the results at first look like both were on the losing end of a roller derby riot but finally the swelling and bruises heal. Millie looks duly plastic while the other has indeed a straight nose. Millie comments that she probably wouldn't do it again, "It's not that rewarding;" while the other already is considering smoothing off some of the point in her chin.

Frankenstein in a Fishbowl is an unfailingly engrossing film for almost any audience, excellent for values confrontation and discussion as well as to illustrate cinematic techniques of visual persuasion.

43 minutes, color, rental $45 from Time-Life Films

Anything You Want to Be . . . A feminist filmmaker explores the conflict between being a girl and being anything you want to be. The film deals with a teenage girl who settles for class secretary instead of president and whose history book turns to a cookbook in mid-sentence ("And Wilson won the election by two eggs, a cup of sugar . . ."). A medicine cabinet tells her how a woman should be, and her parents see her diploma as a preface to marriage. No answer is given.

New Day Films, 267 West Twenty-fifth St., New York, N.Y. 10001, or rent from the University of Michigan for about $4.50.

When Love Needs Care . . . The best available film about VD is Barry Pollack's *When Love Needs Care.* The film simply shows what happens when a teen visits a doctor or clinic with the suspician he or she has VD. The film's main concern is to overcome reluctance to seek help by shedding light on what happens inside the doctor's office. The idea is utterly simple and fantastically effective.

Two teens are shown going through an interview, examination, and instruction. Viewers feel they are actually in the room watching rather than watching a film about VD. *When Love Needs Care* is one of the most effective teaching films available. 13 min., color, rental $35, purchase $185 from See-Saw Films, Box 262, Palo Alto, Calif. 94302. (415) 327-4994, or rental $6.90 from the University of Michigan.

GOOD STORIES

Nudity in the classroom . . . Chekov's *The Bass Fiddle* could just as easily have been titled *What Do You Say to a Naked Lady?*

A bass fiddler, on his way to play for the prince, stops to skinny-dip in the river. While swimming he sees a dozing beautiful girl on the bank fishing. He ties a bouquet of flowers to her line and quietly swims away. When he arrives back at shore he discovers, of course, that his clothes have disappeared. And so, without a stitch, he sneaks to the bathhouse to await darkness.

Meanwhile back on the shore, the girl has awakened with her line hopelessly tangled. She undresses and plunges in after the line. (For some reason, high school boys are never bored by this film.) Naturally, upon returning she is the proud possessor of a bouquet of flowers but no clothes. She too decides to hide in the bathhouse where they both meet.

That's not the end, but need more be said? A fine adaptation of a delightful short story.

28 min., b&w, from Contemporary Films, rental $20, sale $200.

Circusz. . . . is a near masterpiece that ranks among the best short films available for classroom use. The film's strong images remain in the mind for months or even years.

A young boy carrying a violin wanders into the strange backstage caverns of a Victorian house where a circus prepares for performance. There he encounters a constant stream of the bizarre and Kafkaesque: a midget who dresses as Napoleon; a door that leads into a jungle where a seductive woman dances until snared by a black cloaked villain; a huge elevator platform that rises with a tableau of soldiers; dozens of tumblers and jugglers whose moves are tallied on a massive blackboard.

The boy finds what appears to be an audition for performers. He tells the director he wants to play an original composition on his violin, but is told that playing the violin is "by itself mere scratching." As if to show what is needed for acceptance a man approaches the director in complete silence. He kneels on a velvet cushion and

gracefully slits open his stomach. The director approves the act, "That's it, art is no idle game. Audiences want to see something."

The boy is next subjected to either sadistic torture or a severe schedule of training. He is bent nearly in two, a wagon axle is lowered onto his small arms and a strong man wipes a tear off his face with a spoon and drinks it.

Finally, he emerges from behind a curtain outfitted and made up as a jester. There is applause but mostly silence from the audience. Two eggs are placed on a mirror surface, a ladder is placed on the eggs. The boy climbs the ladder to the top where a huge die is placed on end. On top of this is placed a pole and the boy climbs the impossible configuration until he reaches the top, about 25 feet above ground. At the top he is handed his violin and plays his pitiful tune.

The Laslo Luggossy direction is awesome. There are long traveling shots that reveal various scenes so that the film is more choreographed than edited. The sound track is sparse and uses silence with shattering effect.

Circusz is based on a Kathryn Frigys short story dealing with the theme of conflict between art and the dictatorship of the audience. It is open to several interpretations and no viewer will likely exhaust the film's meanings or possible themes.

From Universal Kinetic Films for free preview with intent to purchase or for sale for $200. Write for rental information or watch MM for future distribution plans. Encourage your local library to purchase the film.

Films, Inc.

The Father is one of the best student films I've seen. The story is a 20th Century update of Chekhov's *Grief*, a tale of an old man so alone he is unable to find anyone to share the grief of his son's death. Burgess Meredith turns in a superb performance as Captain Ned, who drives a horse and buggy around New York, hiring himself for photographers and novelty rides through Central Park.

The film follows the old man on New Year's Eve, beginning as he waits while an ad agency uses the horse and carriage as background for fashion photos. No one pays him. He attempts to tell someone about his son, Stephen Patrick, but no one wants to listen to an old man talk about his son.

He picks up a fare at Lincoln Center and makes taxi driver chatter, always looking for an opportunity to tell of his grief. Near midnight a drunken party of four young people piles into his carriage and arrives at Times Square amid all its phony jubilance and ritualistic idiocy at the stroke of the new year.

A drunk at the stable after work offers no consolation. In the end only his horse listens to his feelings.

Excellent cinematography and direction. A moving film touching the edges of the fear of death, aging, loneliness, and urban alienation in any audience. Also excellent as a study in translating literature to film.

28 min. b&w, directed by Mark Fine and distributed by New Line Cinema. Rent $35 from NEFC.

The Hunt. . . .is an eerie, frightening and ambiguous film--part allegory and part horror story. The film begins in the middle of some conflict, perhaps a civil war, that is never explained to the viewer. A long haired young man, tattered and wounded, is running through a wooded area. He is chased by four or five men on horseback. Finally exhausted, the kid drops within sight of an old whitebearded frontiersman chopping wood. He takes the boy into his cabin and cares for him with almost motherly tenderness.

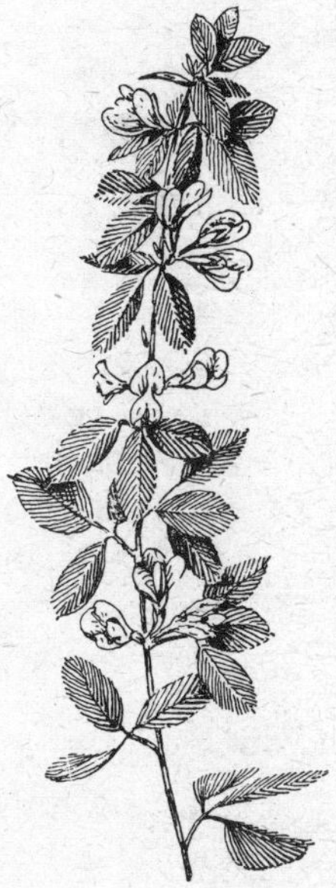

The process of healing is shown without a single word spoken in the entire film, an occasional solo flute providing the only sparse backdrop. An element of suspense keeps an audience glued to every movement the man and boy make --yet seemingly nothing happens. But the nothingness is laden with some kind of foreboding significance.

The man goes out to shoot a bird and brings it back to prepare it for eating. The boy watches, cries and walks away into the woods. The man watches through the window and soon the black clothed horsemen appear over the horizon. They ride up to the house and bring back the kid. The old man sticks a knife in his belt and steps forward. End film.

Is the film about cannibalism? About

some strange society in which there are the hunters and the hunted? About a psychological process? Based on some well known short story? I'm not sure, yet I found the film totally involving and visually rich.

The film is valuable for its understatement, its purely visual approach to story telling and its sense of strangeness. Its ultimate ambiguity might be a bit too much for most audiences but as a literary adventure it is worth a grapple.

Excellent b&w cinematography, directed by Univ. of Texas student Thomas Roberdeau, 25 min., sale $200, rental $20 from Pyramid.

The Open Window. . . . Richard Patterson set off with a $10,000 AFI grant to adapt the much studied Saki short story, **The Open Window,** to the screen. He turned out a polished short that has the look of a feature film and a slickness rarely seen in student productions.

The story concerns a man who is double-crossed into believing he has seen a ghost. The story is told in such a way that the reader or viewer is also "fooled" into believing a young girl's prank is actually an occult appearance in a house of slightly crazy people.

Patterson used professional actors including 15 year-old Cindy Eilbacher, already nominated for an Emmy for her role in an episode of the TV show **It Takes a Thief.** The story is filmed with low-key lighting in a classical style befitting the narrative. Patterson was able to shoot the film in four days with a crew of eleven. Film students might be interested to know that the warm tone of the film was achieved with the help of the fireplace. The fireplace was light whenever it was visible in a shot, but when not visible the effect of a room fireplace was created by using a filter in front of a light and adding a flicker by jiggling a twig in front of the lamp.

The somewhat eerie effect of the open window, actually French doors, was obtained by covering the doorway with a large 85N3 gell mounted on a wooden frame. Filming was in 35 mm. for theatrical distribution and scoring was done by John Green, a composer-conductor with five Academy Awards and fourteen nominations.

12 minutes, sale $160, rental $20 from Pyramid Films

Sirene. . . The plot involves a mermaid (siren) in the harbor of a surrealistic city who is charmed by a young man playing a flute. She surfaces only to be destroyed by the crane machines which surround the harbor. Cut in half by the sword of justice, she is divided between the hospital and the zoo. An innocent witness is declared guilty and hauled away. The flute player discovers that the spirit of Sirene still remains, and with it, floats off into the stars.

Don't let the plot discourage you. The animated drawings of the mechanical cranes and the prehistoric birds are absolutely frightening; the satire on the bureaucracy of the judicial process is powerful. And the whole film is steeped in the Greek myth of the sirens, told in absurd and surrealistic terms — a powerful combination. **Sirene**, by Raoul Servais, is deep in meaning, excellent for discussion, and the winner of four international film awards. It should get more.

10 min., color, available from International Film Bureau, rental $8, sale $135. Rental $10 from the University of California.

VALUES

Factory . . . Arthur Barron is best known for his direction of *Sixteenth in Webster Groves*. In *Factory* he documents the boredom and alienation of the factory worker. The workers at the wedding-ring factory are united only by a sense of futility and the weekly paycheck which enables them to survive. The film is filled with sharp irony and a sense of tragedy and frustration. Excellent for use on a "career day" or with students who are likely to find themselves faced with a "factory" in their future.

56 min., b&w, sale $225, rental $40 from Filmmakers Library, $10 from the University of Michigan.

A Wonderful Construction. . . . is a poetic eulogy to construction workers. It contrasts the reality of disgruntled hard hats working for a buck with a vision of construction workers as craftsmen capable of changing the world. Director Don Lenzer uses poetic narration, interviews with workers and the paintings and ideas of Fernand Leger for a cinematic study of reality versus the vision.

Lenzer interviews the workers at a "USA all the way" street rally. He is hopelessly out of touch with these men but presses on asking questions that the workers had never thought of: "Why do you do what you do? What are your dreams? What would you do if money were no problem?" No worker interviewed reveals any expansive hidden dreams. All work to get by and because the pay is good even though they hate the work.

Lenzer is not satisfied with their answers; he sees more. "I've learned a secret that many of you don't know. There is behind you the creative force of your work. You are craftsmen capable of changing the world." He presents the ideas and paintings of Fernand Leger who saw the entire city aflame with color and major political struggles fought over the color of a building. He saw builders as secure men who could control their own lives and manage their own work, unafraid of their neighbors and themselves; men with the courage to pursue their dreams.

But Leger died and his paintings decorate the walls of the rich and hang in museums. His vision of a gigantic circus where work and play are mixed together is yet to be born. People have stopped watching again and the buildings continue to build themselves.

A Wonderful Construction is excellent for discussion about blue collar workers, attitudes toward work, and alienation from one's labor.

15 min., color, rental $25, sale $225 from Film Images

Prometheus XX. . . . is a Bulgarian animation which changes Prometheus from the tragic hero of traditional myth into a tragi-comic anti-hero. A Chaplinesque Prometheus with a broad smile and red hair returns from the Olympians whose fire he has stolen. As he runs to present his torch to man he passes a timeless landscape which clearly places the film in both antiquity and the XX century. As he nears the city a fireman's hose douses the flame. Undaunted he again steals fire and returns; this try he is mugged. After a third theft he presents his torch to the emperor who turns out to be Nero, the world's greatest pyromaniac. As the film ends, the twentieth century Prometheus is trying again.

The torch's flame radiates various symbols: vitality, peace, unity and spirituality--the Promethean spirit. The three failures each represents a flaw in man which has prevented the potential of the flame from developing. The film poses the question: Will man's Promethean potential or his shadow side prevail?

Prometheus XX is rich in mythical allusions, symbols, levels of meaning, and comic devices. Todor Dinov's art work is fascinating and his direction faultless.

6 minutes, animated, color, sale $70. For rental info inquire from Wombat Productions

VIOLENCE—WAR—PEACE—CRIME

2 Year Machine

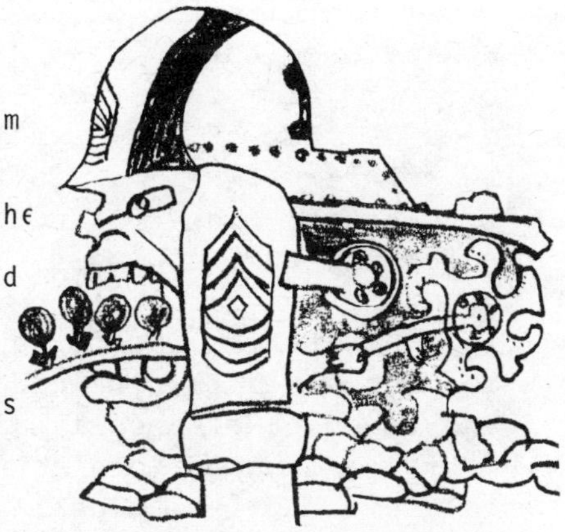

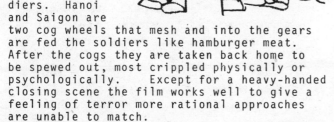

The entire film is a metaphor comparing the military and the draft to a machine (shaped rather like a toilet) that ingests young men and wheezes along changing them into soldiers. Hanoi and Saigon are two cog wheels that mesh and into the gears are fed the soldiers like hamburger meat. After the cogs they are taken back home to be spewed out, most crippled physically or psychologically. Except for a heavy-handed closing scene the film works well to give a feeling of terror more rational approaches are unable to match.

6 min., animation, rental $10, sale $90 Film Images

Among the most effective discussion-starting films available on the question of the causes of war is **The Reason Why.** The film was written by playwright Arthur Miller as an attempt to put into dramatic form "the way we're made, the impulses of the human animal toward war . . ."

The story involves two men, one the owner of a farm, the other a friend visiting from the city. As they sit outside talking, a woodchuck appears 350 yards away. The owner tells how one year he killed 42 chucks in order to protect his vegetable garden. The two compare killing animals to human warfare and the owner recounts how his "limited war" on the woodchucks developed into a real hatred until finally he realized that "what it cost to kill them I could have bought enough tomatoes for the year." The line, tossed off almost casually, hits home as the viewer recalls hearing that the money spent in Vietnam for destruction could provide every Vietnamese with enough money to retire for life.

Both men show little interest in hunting but something prompts the farm owner to get out his $65 rifle with the telescopic sight. The very presence of the woodchuck constitutes a challenge that cannot be denied. The chuck is shot in the head. The visitor asks, "Why'd you do that?" The owner replies almost as if he were a universal soldier asked why he wars, "I don't know, I probably won't anymore." But viewers know he will; there will be more dead woodchucks and more wars.

Since the film's central image is from the masculine world of hunting, the film is especially effective for use with teenage and adult men. The film never fails to spur lively discussion and thought. Maybe at that next men's group that usually sees a film about football highlights from last season?

13 min., color, rental $10 from Roa's Films, 1696 N. Astor Street, Milwaukee, Wisc. 53202. Rental $4.50 from the University of Michigan.

The Selling of the Pentagon is the controversial television program now well on its way to becoming the most noticed documentary in the country.

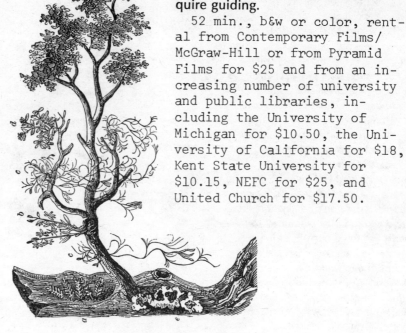

The film's central claim is that the military misuses an exorbitant public relations budget, that the horrors of an imminent invasion from Russia or China are still invoked before gullible civic groups, that even kids are subject to propaganda glorifying combat so that they yearn for the day they can trade their cereal box tanks for the real thing, and that the Pentagon prefers to use scare tactics and distortions instead of truth in order to maintain its high budget.

Discussion after this film will need no prompting, but will require guiding.

52 min., b&w or color, rental from Contemporary Films/McGraw-Hill or from Pyramid Films for $25 and from an increasing number of university and public libraries, including the University of Michigan for $10.50, the University of California for $18, Kent State University for $10.15, NEFC for $25, and United Church for $17.50.

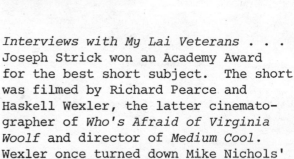

Interviews with My Lai Veterans . . . Joseph Strick won an Academy Award for the best short subject. The short was filmed by Richard Pearce and Haskell Wexler, the latter cinematographer of *Who's Afraid of Virginia Woolf* and director of *Medium Cool*. Wexler once turned down Mike Nichols' offer to film *The Graduate* on the grounds that it was "irrelevant."

Interviews . . . is far from irrelevant. The 20-minute film contains interviews with five My Lai veterans and makes for powerful viewing despite its lack of any visual content other than talking faces. The behavior of the five is very normal and matter-of-fact in contrast to their stories. The facts which emerge are that a search-and-destroy operation had been ordered which resulted in the destruction of the village and its people. According to the soldiers about 450 people were killed by about 95 Americans.

Three of the participants admit they had taken part in the massacre, but none defends the action. They are all hesitant about discussing the less-publicized rape, mutilation, and scalping which also apparently took place.

20 min., color, rental $25 from Contemporary/McGraw-Hill Films, $25 from Macmillan, $7.50 from the University of Michigan, and $8 from Kent State University.

GERM AND CHEMICAL WARFARE is a frightening and captivating CBS News Report that raises questions of ultimate concern.

The film views a simulated gas attack and explores the manufacture of the chemicals and the reasons advanced by the Pentagon for its production. One such gas is odorless, tasteless and can kill a man in seconds. It could also prove even more deadly than an atomic bomb by offsetting the globe's ecological balance for centuries. This weapon is being produced in the United States. The film asks whether it should be and concludes rather strongly that our present policy is neither safe nor effective. The announcement by President Nixon that the production of germ and biological agents should be halted does not render this film dated since the military is seeking new ways to define the same agents to continue their production and since the film's themes reach far beyond merely chemical warfare.

After viewing, consider the attitudes of the people who defended the use of the chemicals and those who objected. Consider the role of the private citizen in determining a question of such crucial concern. Discuss the question of defense against such an attack. Consider world peace and unity and the stand of the Christian on this issue.

30 min., b&w. Purchase or preview prints from Carousel Film, Inc. Rental from the University of California for $11 and from United Church for $10.

Hiroshima-Nagasaki -- August 1945 is a 16-minute b&w short consisting of film held back until recently by U.S. military authorities. The filming was done by Japanese photographers on the scene and is as powerful as *Night and Fog* in its visual impact.

An announcement is heard on Japanese radio of a "new type of bomb." Cut to makeshift hospitals and the wretched survivors accompanied by narration listing statistics of casualties and loss.

Rental $10 from New York University Film Library, 26 Washington Place, New York, N.Y. 10003. $3.25 from the University of Michigan, $9.00 from the University of California, and $8.00 from United Church.

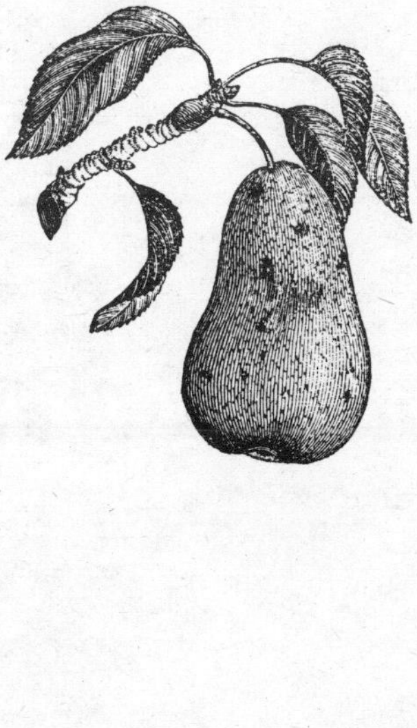

An Essay on War . . . . is a brilliant short essay by Emmy Award winner Andrew Rooney. The visuals are predominantly documentary footage with enough bombs, guns, killing and explosions to please any audience with a normal degree of bloodthirst. The combination results in a highly watchable yet memorable exploration of man's attitude toward war.

Is war like an eclipse or flood, bound to recur periodically or is it like some disease for which there might be a civilized cure? If we are really more civilized than those who have gone before, why then have we killed more than 70 million of our fellow men in this century? Perhaps it is because our killing is now done by remote control with the enemy only a statistic. The pictures of wife and children, which a soldier carries in his breast pocket, are destroyed with him.

We no longer fight for mere land or plunder. We propagandize ourself into believing that our war is for honorable and abstract reasons that even God Himself would surely bless.

We have become more proficient at killing. The scientists who invented the package of liquid fire and the engineers who designed a way to hurl it 50 miles probably love their wives and children and wouldn't hurt a butterfly. As quickly as we have learned to make something we have learned how to destroy it.

Rooney talks of the other reasons for our confusion and passion with war and about the men who fight the battles and sometimes die. **An Essay on War** must stand as one of the best written, most thought-provoking films on the subject.

23 min., b&w or color; b&w sale $135, rental $7.50; color sale $265, rental $10 from Encyclopedia Britannica Films. Rental $9.60 from the University of Michigan, $8 from Kent State University, and $17 from the University of California.

Ares Contra Atlas (8 min.), anti-war black humor, is a mini *Catch-22* with touches of *M*A*S*H*. Absurd war incidents provide an animated exercise in black humor and human futility.

Among the incidents shown are: 1 -- the survivors from a sunken ship find safety on an island only to awaken to discover that their refuge is a target for practice bombing; 2 -- an aircraft destroyed by its own bombs; and 3 -- the inhabitants of a village, attacked by bombers, scramble to the church and pray their way to salvation from destruction -- until their joy jars loose the old bell which promptly falls and kills one and all. The absurd incidents ring true (no pun intended) at a deep level. Each act of violence is ultimately self-directed; the most disastrous posture is that of security in one's own salvation.

$10 rental from Macmillan, $7.50 from United Church, $10 from the University of California.

After the First . . . A nicely made film about a 12-year-old boy's first hunting trip. The boy's sensitive reaction to the shooting of his first rabbit introduces the theme of loss of innocence. The father remarks, "After the first time it gets easier," a concept that will haunt Steven all his life, just as it has stalked mankind. The film is an excellent preface to a study of factors motivating violence and war. This film does have the power to touch deeply.

Franciscan Communication Center, 1229 So. Santee, Los Angeles, Calif. 90015. 14 min., color, sale $150, rental $14. By Nicholas Frangakis, 1971.

Un Garcon Plein d'Avenir . . . Peter Foldes is one of the most creative animators to have U.S. distribution. His images are fresh and powerful and tend to thoroughly captivate viewers, even those who are "tired" of other meaningful animated films. This film deals with war and aggression. Man is a child who devours his mother, a merciless killer before a screaming crowd in an arena, a warrior who receives medals for his killing, and still a human being who can be moved to tears by music. The ending is tragic; no simple "liberal" message is found in Foldes' work.

7 min., color, animation, from Films, Inc.

Serendipity Bomb. . .is an animated cinema paradox. Into what seems to be a ghost town wanders a traveler. The ghost town however turns out to be one very recently deserted. The town is fully furnished, even a phonograph

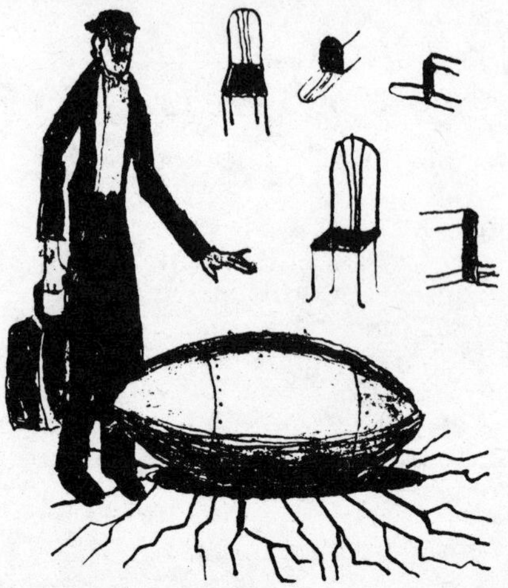

needle still sticks in the final grooves of a scratched record. The recently evacuated town becomes a playground for the traveler. He helps himself to a drink at the bar, desecrates property, ransacks a museum, contemptuously slops paint all over the hall of justice, pounds on the church organ and generally fulfills his fantasies in this emptied town.

Meanwhile on a nearby hill the town's residents watch through a telescope and try to attract the stranger's attention to warn him of danger. For in the town square lies a huge bomb, the cause of the hurried evacuation. But the stranger ignores the bomb and continues his destructive play. Finally he enters the town bank and carelessly scatters money. This is too much for the residents. They storm back into the endangered village, beat the traveler and chase him out. But the bomb explodes and the only one saved is the exiled intruder.

The animation style is superb and the story suspenseful. Its pure entertainment value is attested by the fact that **Serendipity Bomb** was shown last season on **The Great American Dream Machine.** The highly ironic plot is open to many interpretations all centering on the face that the people are destroyed in trying to save what they value while the only person who showed no sense of value was saved. The twists and ironies of the plot can be applied to themes of greed, salvation, destruction and attitudes toward material possessions.

Produced in France in 1969, directed by J.F. Laguoionie. 8 min., animated, rental $15 from Mass Media Associates.

Red Stain . . . Shades of *Yellow Submarine*, *Chromophobia*, and Tertullian! Here's a Czech animation about a fisherman and his small son who discover that their country has been invaded and an armory established near their house. The man attempts to display a notice urging peace, but is killed in the process. His blood stains the ground, and from the patch

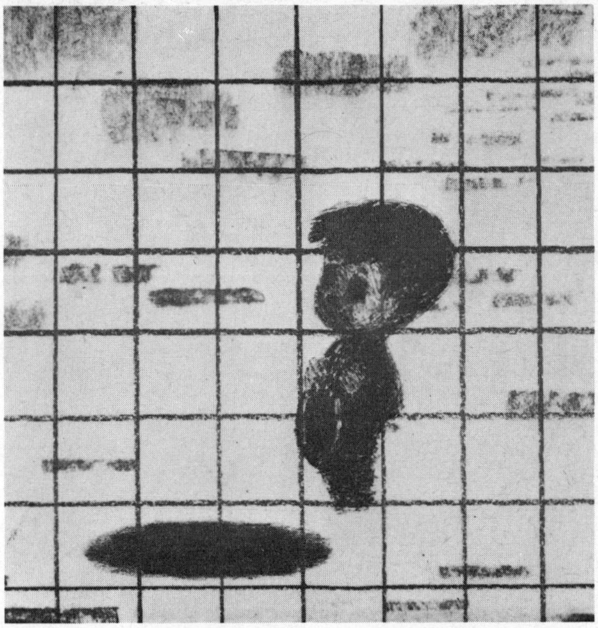

of earth emerge beautiful flowers. Military forces try to destroy them, but watched and tended by the little boy, the flowers grow and spread, eventually overcoming the powers of destruction.

The film is fine for a consideration of martyrdom (Tertullian is the one who said "the blood of martyrs is seed"), heroism, and the ancient goodness-evil struggle.

14 min., animation, color, Code 408423 from Contemporary/McGraw-Hill, sale $205, rental $20.

The Zagreb (Czech.) animation artists have mastered the difficult art of combining humor with penetrating insight. *All the Wishes of the World* tells of two friends who manage to save an enchanted fish. As a result an "enchanted secretary" (what else?) appears and agrees to grant one of them his every wish. The catch is that the other one is to have the same wishes granted but in double doses.

The two playfully exalt in their new-found power until a rivalry develops. Imagine the frustration with every wish being granted to the enemy in double measure. The catch then is to destroy the opponent without destroying oneself. What happens if one wishes for a half a bomb?

This intriguing 10-minute film is available from Contemporary for sale ($135) or rent ($12.50).

Sources for Films Described in This Section

BFA EDUCATIONAL MEDIA
2211 Michigan Avenue
Santa Monica, Calif. 90404

STEPHEN BOSUSTOW PRODUCTIONS
1610 Butler
West Los Angeles, Calif. 90025

CAROUSEL FILMS
1501 Broadway
Suite 1503
New York, N.Y. 10036
(212) 279-6734

CONTEMPORARY FILMS/McGRAW-HILL
Princeton Road
Hightstown, N.J. 08520
(609) 448-1700

828 Custer Avenue
Evanston, Ill. 60202
(312) 869-5010

1714 Stockton Street
San Francisco, Calif. 94133
(415) 362-3115

THE ECCENTRIC CIRCLE
P.O. Box 1481
Evanston, Ill. 60204
(347 Florence Avenue
(312) 864-0020

ENCYCLOPEDIA BRITANNICA
Educational Corporation
425 North Michigan Avenue
Chicago, Ill. 60611
(312) 321-6800

FILM IMAGES
17 West 60th Street
New York, N.Y. 10023
(212) 279-6653

1034 Lake Street
Oak Park, Ill. 60301
(312) 386-4826

FILMS, INC.
1144 Wilmette Avenue
Wilmette, Ill. 60091
(312) 256-4730

FILMAKERS LIBRARY
290 West End Avenue
New York, N.Y. 10023

HARTLEY PRODUCTIONS
Cat Rock Road
Cos Cob, Conn. 06807
(203) 869-1818

HOLT, RINEHART AND WINSTON, INC.
Media Department
Box 3670, Grand Central Station
New York, N.Y. 10017

INDIANA UNIVERSITY
Audio-Visual Center
Bloomington, Ind. 47401
(812) 337-8087

INTERNATIONAL FILM BUREAU
332 South Michigan Avenue
Chicago, Ill. 60604
(312) 427-4545

KENT STATE UNIVERSITY
Audio Visual Services
Kent, Ohio 44242
(216) 672-2072

LEARNING CORPORATION OF AMERICA
711 Fifth Avenue
New York, N.Y. 10022
(212) 751-4400

MACMILLAN FILMS
34 MacQuesten Parkway South
Mount Vernon, N.Y. 10550
(914) 664-5051

1619 North Cherokee
Los Angeles, Calif. 90028
(213) 463-0357

3868 Piedmont Avenue
Oakland, Calif. 94611
(415) 658-9890

8400 Brookfield Avenue
Brookfield, Ill. 60513
(312) 485-3925

8615 Directors Row
Dallas, Tex. 75247
(214) 637-2483

MASS MEDIA MINISTRIES
2116 North Charles Street
Baltimore, Md. 21218
(301) 727-3270

1720 Chouteau Avenue
St. Louis, Mo. 63103
(314) 436-0418

NBC EDUCATIONAL ENTERPRISES
30 Rockefeller Plaza
New York, N.Y. 10020
(212) 247-8300

NEFC
National Educational Film Center
Route 2
Finksburg, Md. 21048

NEW LINE CINEMA
121 University Place
New York, N.Y. 10003
(212) 674-7460

PYRAMID FILMS
Box 1048
Santa Monica, Calif. 90406
(213) 828-7577

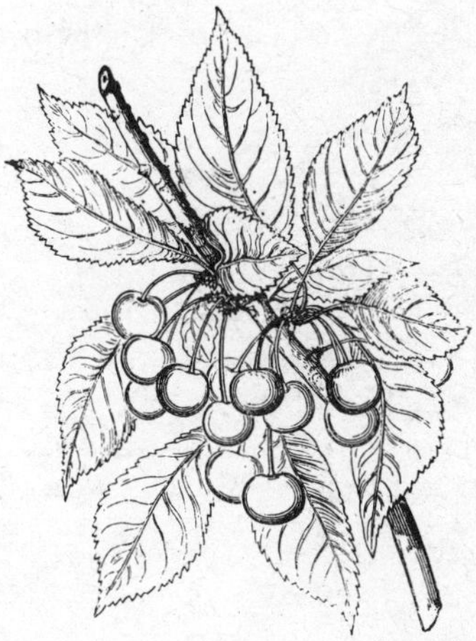

TEXTURE FILMS
1600 Broadway
New York, N.Y.
(212) 586-6960

TIME-LIFE FILMS
43 West 16th Street
New York, N.Y. 10011
(212) 691-2930

UNITED WORLD FILMS
Kinetic Division
2001 South Vermont Avenue
Los Angeles, Calif. 90007
(213) 731-2131

UNITED CHURCH OF CHRIST
Office for Audio-Visuals
1505 Race Street
Philadelphia, Pa. 19102
(215) 568-5750

UNIVERSITY OF CALIFORNIA
Extension Media Center
Berkeley, Calif. 94720
(415) 642-0460

UNIVERSITY OF MICHIGAN
Audio-Visual Education Center
416 Fourth Street
Ann Arbor, Mich. 48103
(313) 764-5350

UNIVERSITY OF SOUTHERN CALIFORNIA
Division of Cinema
Film Distribution Section
University Park
Los Angeles, Calif. 90007

WOMBAT FILMS
77 Tarrytown Road
White Plains, N.Y. 10607
(914) 428-6220

A Special List of Distributors

The following 13 film distributors all supply catalogs. Put together, these catalogs will take up a shelf a couple feet wide that will give you fingertip access to a wide range of high quality short films. This listing is carefully selected and represents the best and the largest film sources in the U.S.

Contemporary Films/McGraw-Hill is one of the largest and most popular of the commercial film libraries. Their short film catalog is 380 pages, feature film catalog is 260 pages. Write specifying the kind of film you want, and the appropriate catalog or catalogs will be sent.

CONTEMPORARY FILMS/McGRAW-HILL
1221 Avenue of the Americas
New York, N.Y. 10020

Films, Inc. One of the largest collections of both short and feature films. Old classics and experimental films, documentaries and entertainments, and just about everything in-between is available from Films, Inc. They have several catalogs, so state your category of interest when writing.

FILMS INCORPORATED
1144 Wilmette Avenue
Wilmette, Ill. 60091
(312) 256-4730

Film-Makers' Cooperative. Here is a library of personal cinema. The catalog allows the film maker to describe his or her own work. The results are fun to read but unfortunately not too helpful in trying to determine what is on the celluloid. Rental rates vary from cheap to ridiculous. Artists included are Warhol, Malanga, Robert Nelson, Carl Linder, George Kuchar, David Bienstock, Scott Bartlett, Kenneth Anger. Catalog is $2 from:

FILM-MAKERS' COOPERATIVE
175 Lexington Avenue
New York, N.Y. 10016

Other distributors for personal cinema or "underground" films include:

CENTER CINEMA CO-OP
540 North Lake Shore Dr.
Chicago, Ill. 60611

CREATIVE FILM SOCIETY
7237 Canby Avenue
Reseda, Calif. 91335
(213) 881-3887

CANYON CINEMA CO-OP
#220 Industrial Center Bldg.
Sausalito, Calif. 94965
(415) 332-1514

Indiana University. Possibly the largest film library in the U.S. The $5, 1100+ page catalog gives only brief descriptions of about 8000 short films. Indiana University rents and sells the films produced by NET and Public Broadcast Laboratory. The majority of IU's films are instructional in nature. Rentals are inexpensive and the collection makes this list because of its vastness and the presence of the PBL and NET releases.

INDIANA UNIVERSITY
Audio-Visual Center
Bloomington, Ind. 47401
(812) 337-2103

Kent State University. 7000 titles but only 7800 prints. One of the ten largest film collections in the country. Extremely inexpensive rentals. Catalog is 400 pages long and costs $3.00 from:

KENT STATE UNIVERSITY
Audio-Visual Services
Kent, Ohio 44242

Learning Corporation of America. A rapidly expanding collection of teaching films of high quality and interest as well as films of a creative and dramatic nature. Good selection of some fine National Film Board of Canada films and Zagreb and Eastern European shorts.

LEARNING CORPORATION OF AMERICA
711 Fifth Avenue
New York, N.Y. 10022

Macmillan Films is the result of mergers and various consolidations among CCM Films, Audio Brandon Films, and Fleetwood Films. The collection of both short and feature films is huge.

International Cinema catalog -- 624 pages of foreign and American feature and short films including experimental films.

Audio Brandon General Catalog -- Entertainment features and shorts such as Disney films.

CCM Educational Film Catalog -- a combination of instructional films and some from the International catalog.

MACMILLAN FILMS
34 MacQuesten Parkway South
Mount Vernon, N.Y. 10550

Mass Media Associates began as a distributor of films for religious education but has developed into one of the finest sources of value-oriented short films. About 200 short films for rental, many also for sale. Free catalog that gives quite adequate descriptions of each film from:

MASS MEDIA ASSOCIATES
2116 N. Charles St.
Baltimore, Md. 21218
(301) 727-3270

Pyramid Films distributes only short films, mostly of the highly creative and cinematic variety. They have very few "duds" in the entire collection. Among the fastest growing film distributors. Excellent film guides come with many films. A must for any film user is their free catalog.

PYRAMID FILMS
Box 1048
Santa Monica, Calif. 90406

Time-Life Films. Another rapidly expanding collection. Current strength is in documentaries, although some experimental films have been added. Many BBC-TV films are available; some good, most rather boring. A good 230-page catalog is free from:

TIME-LIFE FILMS
43 West 16th Street
New York, N.Y. 10011
(212) 691-2930

University of California Extension Media Center. One of the nation's finest university film libraries; perhaps the finest. A large selection and wide variety of films are available to organizations and "responsible individuals" anywhere in the U.S. The catalog (currently 270 pages) is free, well indexed, and nicely annotated. Periodic updates and media guides are published consistently.

UNIVERSITY OF CALIFORNIA
Extension Media Center
Berkeley, Calif. 94720

University of Michigan. A gargantuan collection of short films. Both the dry instructional films and highly creative and dramatic shorts are available from U of M. The $2 catalog runs around 600 pages, is well indexed, but only briefly annotated. Rental rates are among the lowest possible, with most films going for under $10. Periodic catalog supplements are issued detailing new acquisitions.

UNIVERSITY OF MICHIGAN
Audio-Visual Education Center
416 Fourth Street
Ann Arbor, Mich. 48103

University of Southern California. A fairly large collection of films containing many of the instructional variety (e.g., *Dividing Fractions, France and Its People, Modern Egypt,* etc.) but also many highly creative films. Especially interesting are the films made by students at USC. Most films rent for under $20, USC-produced films are for sale and rental. Catalog is $1 from:

UNIVERSITY OF SOUTHERN CALIFORNIA
Division of Cinema
Film Distribution Section
University Park
Los Angeles, Calif. 90007

Feature-Film Rental Sources

The following companies distribute (rent) feature films. A catalog from each will give you access to information on the majority of feature films currently available for rental in the U.S. Not included here are those companies which supply only entertainment films.

TWYMAN FILMS, INC.
329 Salem Avenue
Dayton, Ohio 45401
(513) 222-4014

SWANK FILMS
201 South Jefferson Avenue
St. Louis, Mo. 63166
(314) 534-6300

CONTEMPORARY FILMS/McGRAW-HILL
1221 Avenue Of the Americas
New York, N.Y. 10020

(also listed as one of the best sources of short films)

FILMS, INC.
1144 Wilmette Avenue
Wilmette, Ill. 60091
(312) 256-4730

(also listed as one of the best sources of short films)

MACMILLAN FILMS
34 MacQuesten Parkway South
Mount Vernon, N.Y. 10550

WARNER BROTHERS INC.
Non-Theatrical Division
4000 Warner Boulevard
Burbank, Calif. 91505

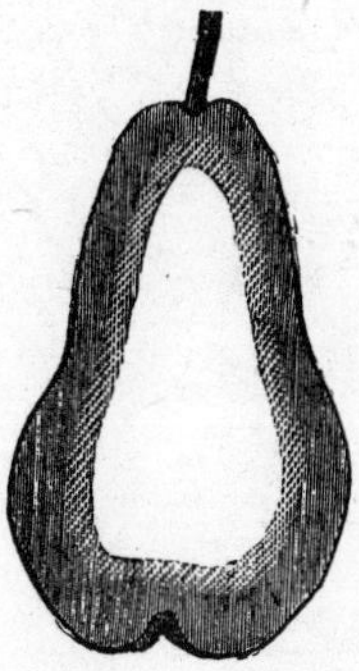

UA:16
United Artists Corporation
729 7th Avenue
New York, N.Y. 10019
(212) 245-6000

JANUS FILMS
745 Fifth Avenue
New York, N.Y.
(212) PL 3-7100

Distributors of Specialized Films

ABC MEDIA CONCEPTS
1330 Avenue of the Americas
New York, N.Y. 10019

A small selection of ABC-TV documentaries. Special emphasis on children's films. Catalog free.

ACI FILMS
35 West 45th Street
New York, N.Y. 10036

Medium-sized collection of high quality educational films. Many for children. Free catalog.

ANARGYROS FILM LIBRARY
1815 Fairburn Avenue
Los Angeles, Calif. 90025

A collection of 8-mm. film loops. Newsreel-type items in American history sell for $16 each.

ANTI-DEFAMATION LEAGUE OF B'NAI B'RITH
315 Lexington Avenue
New York, N.Y. 10016

Good collection of films about prejudice, minorities, social change. Free catalog.

APPALSHOP, INC.
P.O. Box 743
Whitesburg, Ky. 41858
(606) 633-5708

A small distributor/producer of films about Appalachia by the people of Appalachia. The workshop is more a community service organization that a commercial film distributor. Also has video tapes.
Catalog in tabloid form -- free.

BFA EDUCATIONAL MEDIA
2211 Michigan Avenue
Santa Monica, Calif. 90404

Owned by CBS, this distributor still specializes in instructional films but does rent CBS-TV documentaries. A large and quite mixed bag of films, rapidly expanding, bears watching. Free catalog.

BILLY BUDD FILMS
235 East 57th Street
New York, N.Y. 10022

Especially good for guidance or values classes on the junior high level.

BALLIS ASSOCIATES
4696 North Millbrook
Fresno, Calif. 93726

A handful of films about minority groups and social change.

BLACKHAWK FILMS
The Eastin-Phelan Corporation
Davenport, Iowa 52808

Blackhawk does not rent films. They do sell 8, super 8, and 16-mm. films, including Chaplin, Keaton, D.W. Griffith, newsreels, etc. Purchase prices range from $5 to $150. They also sell film equipment, bulbs, etc., and offer very fast service. Catalog is in the form of a periodic newspaper. $3 to be placed on the mailing list.

THE BOSTON FILM CENTER
25 Church Street
Boston, Mass. 02116

Films made by teenagers, especially ghetto residents. The films serve to illustrate what kids can do, given a camera. Enthusiasm makes up for lack of quality. Catalog free.

CAROUSEL FILMS
1501 Broadway
New York, N.Y. 10036

Sale only for this fine collection. Includes many CBS-TV productions. Catalog free.

CINEMA EIGHT
P.O. Box 245
Gracie Station
New York, N.Y. 10028

Similar to Blackhawk Films. 16-mm. films for sale include *Metropolis* for $200, *The Gold Rush* for $200, or *The Blue Angel* for $200.

DU ART FILM LABS
245 West 55th Street
New York, N.Y. 10019

For sale only are segments of Allen Funt's *Candid Camera* TV shows. 32-page catalog is free, prices range from $7.50 up (usually up).

THE ECCENTRIC CIRCLE
P.O. Box 1481
Evanston, Ill. 60204

A recent arrival to the film distribution scene and one that looks exciting. Currently a small collection of mixed quality. By all means request a catalog and follow EC's development.

ENCYCLOPEDIA BRITANNICA EDUCATIONAL CORP.
425 N. Michigan Avenue
Chicago, Ill. 60611

Watching many Encyclopedia Britannica films is about an interesting as reading an encyclopedia. Newer acquisitions have improved the collection however. Tons of films, very low rentals, free catalog.

FILM & ART
554 Lexington St.
Waltham, Mass. 02154

Value education and religious films for Eastern states only.

FILM IMAGES
17 West 60th Street
New York, N.Y. 10023

A pleasantly varied collection of quality creative films. Both features and shorts. Nice collection of films about the arts.

GAINES FILMS CO.
15207 Stagg Street
Van Nuys, Calif. 91405

Browsing through the mimeographed catalog of Gaines Sixteen Films Company is a bit like looking through a junk-filled attic. Gaines sells bits and pieces of film. For media and popular culture teachers or students their offerings could prove valuable. Some examples from a recent catalog: 450' of an NBC documentary titled *Oh Woodstock* about the Woodstock rock festival for $19.95. *On Facilitating a Group* with Carl Rogers; 800' for a purchase price of only $14.95 (these are used films).

30-minute films from the old TV series *Dr. Hudson's Secret Journal* for $12.95 each.

150' of a Beatles rehearsal.

A large selection of trailers and film clips from recent feature films.

Do not order the above, most are one-of-a kind. Instead, write for the current listing.

GILBERT'S FILMS
1509 Queen Anne Avenue North
Seattle, Wash. 98109

A new company with a small collection of films. Dick Gilbert is a professional film maker with an impressive list of credits. If you need a professionally produced film and are willing to work with the film maker contact Dick Gilbert.

GROVE PRESS FILMS
53 East 11th Street
New York, N.Y. 10003

Experimental, underground, and political shorts and features.

HAROLD MANTELL
Films for the Humanities
P.O. Box 378
Princeton, N.J. 08540

Films about literary figures such as e.e. cummings, Thornton Wilder, Ezra Pound, Lorraine Hansberry, Chekhov, Neruda, Jorge Luis Borges, Federico Fellini, Yevtushenko, and others.

HARTLEY PRODUCTIONS
Cat Rock Road
Cos Cob, Conn. 06807

Alan Watts' films on Zen, films on psychic phenomena, Islamic mysticism, and world religions. Distributes only films made by the Hartleys.

INTERNATIONAL FILM BUREAU
332 South Michigan Avenue
Chicago, Ill. 60604

A large collection of teachy films with a few creative touches in animation films from Norman McLaren and Europe.

KIT PARKER FILMS
Box 227
Carmel Valley, Calif. 93924

Kit Parker Films rents old classic features such as *The General*, *Intolerance*, *Blood of a Poet*, *Nosferatu*, *Steamboat Bill*, *Vampyr*, *Caligari*, *Birth of a Nation*, *Potemkin*, *Gold Rush*, *October*, *M*, and *The Blue Angel* for around $30 each. They also have loads of serials and shorts from back then.

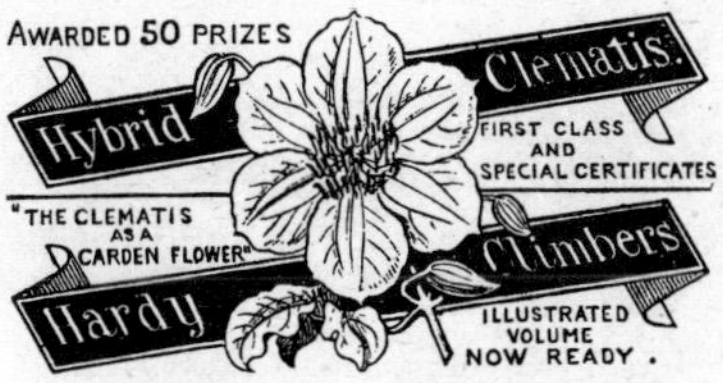

MODERN TALKING PICTURE SERVICE
2323 New Hyde Park Road
New Hyde Park, N.Y. 11040

Loads of free-loan sponsored films that no one would watch if they weren't free. A few of the films in their school catalog are good for illustrating film techniques or even methods of persuasion. Can't beat the price.

MOUNTAIN PLAINS EDUCATIONAL MEDIA COUNCIL
University of Colorado
Bureau of Audiovisual Instruction
Boulder, Colo. 80302

or
University of Nevada
Audiovisual Communication Center
Reno, Nev. 89507

or
University of Utah
Educational Media Center
Milton Bennion Hall 207
Salt Lake City, Utah 84110

or
University of Wyoming
Audiovisual Services
Laramie, Wyo. 82070

Four university film libraries have joined together to form a huge film library available at very low rentals. Films rent for from $5 - $20 west of the Mississippi and double that east of the river. 500-page catalog is currently free.

MULTI MEDIA RESOURCE CENTER
340 Jones Street, Box 439
San Francisco, Calif. 94102

A collection of sex education films that would be rated X by the MPAA. The films could be described as respectable and educational hard-core sex films.

THE MUSEUM OF MODERN ART
11 West 53 Street
New York, N.Y. 10019

The free catalog is a must for film teachers. Feature and short films that are of historical or artistic importance to the development of film as an art.

NATIONAL FILM BOARD OF CANADA
1251 Avenue of the Americas
New York, N.Y. 10020

NFBC stands as very likely the best producer of short films anywhere in the world. They do not loan out or rent their own films. They do have a sale catalog available.

NBC EDUCATIONAL ENTERPRISES
30 Rockefeller Plaza
New York, N.Y. 10020

The original source for both purchase and rental of NBC-TV documentaries. Free catalog and very reasonable prices.

NATIONAL EDUCATIONAL FILM CENTER
Route 2
Finksburg, Md. 21048

NEFC bills itself as a "one-stop film shop." NEFC rents and sells films which have proven popular for classroom use. Emphasis is on quality cinema; very few instructional films. Catalog free. Also publishes a newsletter called *Sneak Preview*.

NASA
Film Library
Washington, D.C. 20546

Some of the best space shots ever taken are here for free-loan. You won't find much criticism of America's space program, but the films are well made and often pure spectacle. Free list.

NEW DAY FILMS
267 West 25th Street
New York, N.Y. 10001

A good collection of films about women.

NEW YORK UNIVERSITY
Film Library
26 Washington Place
New York, N.Y. 10003

A small and rather expensive ($8 - $40 rentals) collection by university library standards. The film selection is excellent and offers what other university film libraries do not have. Some student and experimental films, some sale films. Catalog free.

OREGON STATE SYSTEM
OF HIGHER EDUCATION
Audiovisual Instruction
Coliseum 133
Corvallis, Oreg. 97331

An excellent collection of short films, reasonable prices, periodic catalog supplements. The fact that the films are available only in the Western states is a help in insuring dependable service but a loss to the Eastern states.

PENNSYLVANIA STATE UNIVERSITY
Audio-Visual Services
7 Willard Building
University Park, Pa. 16802

A fair-sized film library with a good selection of creative films. Specialty of this library is the "Psychological Cinema Register," an excellent collection of films about psychology. Penn State does not at this writing have a master catalog. State the subject area of interest or ask for all the catalogs and supplements. Rental prices are very low, usually under $10.

PERENNIAL EDUCATION
1825 Willow Road
Northfield, Ill. 60093

A distributor of classroom films. A mixture of the dreary and the creative. A larger than usual selection of films on "family living."

POLYMORPH FILMS
331 Newbury Street
Boston, Mass. 02115

Currently renting a package of three films about women. Good films.

ROA'S FILMS
1696 North Astor Street
Milwaukee, Wis. 53202

Shorts and features; many of the entertainment variety. Roa specializes in the religious education market and so has a fair collection of "relevant" films often used in classrooms. Free catalog.

RODALE PRESS
Film Division
Box 663
Allentown, Pa. 18105

Films about the organic lifestyle. Especially organic gardening and composting.

SEE SAW FILMS
P.O. Box 262
Palo Alto, Calif. 94302

A handful of excellent films about drug and sex education. *When Love Needs Care* is one of best films available on VD.

Film Availability Chart

	Contemporary/McGraw-Hill[1] Princeton Road Hightstown, N.J. 08520 (609) 448-1700	Kent State University Audio Visual Services Kent, Ohio 44242 (216) 672-2072 (catalog $3)	Mass Media Associates[2] 2116 N. Charles St. Baltimore, Md. 21218 (301) 727-3270	Mountain Plains Libraries[3] (Univ. of Colorado, Utah, Nevada and Wyoming)	New York Univ. Film Library 26 Washington Place New York, N.Y. 10003 (212) 598-2250	Audiovisual Instruction[4] Gill Coliseum 133 Corvallis, Oregon 97331 (503) 754-2911	Pennsylvania State Univ. Audio-Visual Services 6 Willard Building University Park, Pa. 16802 (814) 865-6314	Pyramid Films Box 1048 Santa Monica, Ca. 90406 (213) 828-7577	Roa's Films 1696 N. Astor Street Milwaukee, Wis. 53202 (414) 271-0861	National Educational Film Center Route 2 Finksburg, Mo. 21048	University of California[5] Extension Media Center 2223 Fulton Street Berkeley, Ca. 94720 (415) 642-0460	University of Michigan A-V Education Center 416 Fourth Street Ann Arbor, Mich. 48103 (313) 764-5350 (catalog $2)
Adventures of *	12.50	5.00	10.00	x		5.75	4.10		10.00	12.50	11.00	4.00
American Time Capsule		4.40				5.75	4.10	10.00			10.00	2.25
Automania 2000	12.50	5.00				5.75		12.00	12.50			
Awareness (Buddha)									25.00			7.50
Black and White: Uptight		12.35			25.00		13.30		25.00		25.00	15.00
Black History: Lost, Stolen. . .		10.15		x			10.70				19.00	10.50
Chairy Tale	10.00	3.00	10.00	x		4.50		10.00	5.00	9.00	8.00	2.50
Chickamauga	25.00	6.60						25.00			15.00	6.00
Cities in Crisis: What's Happening					18.00	7.75					17.00	7.00
Clay: Origin of the Species	10.00	3.00		x		7.75		10.00	10.00		9.00	2.50
Conformity			12.50	x			9.40				17.00	
Dead Birds	60.00	22.00		x	35.00	16.75	40.20			45.00	37.00	17.00
Death		8.50					8.30				19.00	5.75
Dream of Wild Horses	12.50	5.00		x		5.75	4.10	15.00			11.00	4.00
End of One	15.00	5.00				5.75	4.90		25.00	15.00		3.00
Eye of the Beholder			15.00	x	9.50	6.50	5.60			25.00	15.00	5.75
The Game	14.00	5.75	15.00	x	12.00	6.50					14.00	5.50
The Golden Fish	20.00					7.75	8.30	20.00	22.50	20.00		
The Hand	25.00			x				25.00				
The Hangman	15.00		15.50	x		5.75	5.10	12.00	12.50	15.00		5.00
The Hat	24.00	8.00	15.00	x	15.00	7.75	6.10		15.00	15.00	16.00	
Harvest of Shame	29.00	10.15		x	15.00	11.00	10.70	25.00			20.00	
The Hole	21.00		15.00				6.10		10.00	15.00	14.00	5.75
Holy Ghost People	35.00				35.00	11.00					24.00	10.00
Hunger in America			20.00			11.00	18.90	25.00	17.50	22.50	31.00	10.50
The Inheritance	15.00		15.00	x		8.50	11.00				16.00	9.25
Interviews With My Lai Veterans	25.00	8.00									18.00	7.50
Is it Always Right to be Right?						5.75			15.00		11.00	3.00
Invention of the Adolescent	14.00	6.60			17.50	6.50						5.60
Magic Machines									25.00			4.50
Men at Bay											19.00	8.00
Migrant						20.00	19.00	30.00			29.00	17.50
Mood of Zen							5.10					
Neighbors	12.50	5.00		x	8.00		4.60	10.00	6.00	12.50	10.00	4.00
Night and Fog	30.00	11.00				11.50	11.30	30.00		28.00	19.00	9.75
No Reason to Stay	14.00	6.60		x	10.50	6.50	6.10				12.00	
Occurrence at Owl Creek Bridge	20.00	6.60	17.50	x			?	20.00	17.50	20.00	14.00	5.50
Pas de Deux	25.00			x	9.00		3.10	15.00	25.00	22.50	12.00	3.00
The Parable			15.00		25.00			15.00	35.00	15.00	19.00	8.50
Phoebe	14.00	6.60	15.00		10.00	6.50	6.10	15.00	10.00		14.00	
The Reason Why									10.00			4.50
The Red Balloon		12.35		x	9.50	15.00	5.60		22.50		27.00	
Run			15.00			5.50						

	Contemporary/McGraw-Hill[1] Princeton Road Hightstown, N.J. 08520 (609) 448-1700	Kent State University Audio Visual Services Kent, Ohio 44242 (216) 672-2072 (catalog $3)	Mass Media Associates[2] 2116 N. Charles St. Baltimore, Md. 21218 (301) 727-3270	Mountain Plains Libraries[3] (Univ. of Colorado, Utah, Nevada and Wyoming)	New York Univ. Film Library 26 Washington Place New York, N.Y. 10003 (212) 598-2250	Audiovisual Instruction[4] Gill Coliseum 133 Corvallis, Oregon 97331 (503) 754-2911	Pennsylvania State Univ. Audio-Visual Services 6 Willard Building University Park, Pa. 16802 (814) 865-6314	Pyramid Films Box 1048 Santa Monica, Ca. 90406 (213) 828-7577	Roa's Films 1696 N. Astor Street Milwaukee, Wis. 53202 (414) 271-0861	National Educational Film Center Route 2 Finksburg, Mo. 21048	University of California[5] Extension Media Center 2223 Fulton Street Berkeley, Ca. 94720 (415) 642-0460	University of Michigan A-V Education Center 416 Fourth Street Ann Arbor, Mich. 48103 (313) 764-5350 (catalog $2)
The Searching Eye		8.00						15.00			15.00	6.50
The Selling of the Pentagon	45.00	10.15	25.00				11.90	25.00		25.00	18.00	10.50
Sixteen in Webster Grove		9.35	12.50		16.00	11.00	10.50	20.00	15.00		16.00	8.50
Stringbean	17.50		15.00			7.75	6.10	15.00	15.00	15.00		
Summer We Moved to Elm Street	17.00	11.00		x		9.50	10.30		15.00			8.50
This is Marshall McLuhan	40.00	17.00	27.50	x	38.00	13.25	18.90			30.00	35.00	
This Child is Rated X		17.00				20.00					29.00	15.00
Time for Burning	25.00	11.00		x	24.00	11.00	11.70	20.00	20.00		19.00	9.50
Time Out of War	17.50	5.75				5.50	5.10	15.00	10.00		10.00	5.00
Time Piece	17.50	5.00				5.75		15.00	15.00	15.00		4.00
Toys	12.50	5.00					4.40	12.00	12.50			
Two Men and a Wardrobe	25.00		25.00					25.00	25.00	25.00	16.00	3.50
Unicorn in the Garden	12.50				12.00			10.00	10.00			3.00
Very Nice, Very Nice	10.00	3.00				4.50	3.10	10.00			9.00	
Weapons of Gordon Parks	25.00	11.00									18.00	8.50
Why Man Creates		9.35		x		9.50	9.30	15.00			17.00	10.00
You're No Good	14.00	6.60		x	10.00	6.50	6.10					

The films listed above are among the most used quality short films of the 1970's.

Prices given are accurate as of mid 1973 but are subject to increase at the drop of a percentage point.

NOTE TO USERS: It would be misleading to present this chart as a guide to the cheapest supply of short films. University libraries are considerably more limited in the services they offer than any commercial library. Using university libraries consistently for films is likely to produce more frustrations, damaged films and no-shows than from commercial libraries. A general, but not iron clad, rule is the higher the rental price the more reliable the service. Those university libraries known to have poor service are not included in this list. Price comparisons among the various commercial distributors is valid.

Learning Corp. of America
711 Fifth Ave.
New York, N.Y. 10022
has:

THE END OF ONE	15.00
MAGIC MACHINES	20.00
PAS DE DEUX	25.00

Twyman Films
329 Salem Ave.
Dayton, Ohio 45401
has:

HUNGER IN AMERICA	52.50
MIGRANT	50.00
SELLING OF THE PENTAGON	27.50
16 IN WEBSTER GROVES	25.00
THIS CHILD IS RATED X	50.00

[1]also 828 Custer Ave.
Evanston, Ill. 60202
(312) 869-5010
or
1714 Stockton St.
San Francisco, Ca. 94133
(415) 362-3115

[2]also 1720 Chouteau Ave.
St. Louis, Mo. 63103
(314) 436-0418

[3]Write for a catalog to any one of these four universities for a single catalog. Prices are low but are doubled for any orders shipped east of the Miss. River.

[4]Western states only.

[5]Prices include special delivery postage one way.

SIM PRODUCTIONS
Weston, Conn. 06880

Small collection of animated films, mainly European.

TEXTURE FILMS
1600 Broadway
New York, N.Y. 10019

A mixed bag of educational films and creative cinema. Free catalog.

TRICONTINENTAL FILM CENTER
244 West 27th Street
New York, N.Y. 10001

Now that American Documentary Films has folded, Tricontinental is one of the best distributors of films about the Third World and radical politics.

UNITED WORLD FILMS
Kinetic Division
2001 South Vermont Avenue
Los Angeles, Calif. 90007

A small but fine collection of contemporary films exploring the fringes of experimental cinema. Also student productions of varying quality. Sale only.

Each of the following is a university film rental library offering films nationwide:

FLORIDA STATE UNIVERSITY
Media Services
Tallahassee, Fla. 32306

UNIVERSITY OF GEORGIA
Center for Continuing Education
Athens, Ga. 30601

UNIVERSITY OF KANSAS
Audio-Visual Center
6 Bailey Hall
Lawrence, Kans. 66044

UNIVERSITY OF IOWA
Audiovisual Center
Iowa City, Iowa 52240

SYRACUSE UNIVERSITY
Film Rental Center
1455 East Colvin St.
Syracuse, N.Y. 13210

VIEWFINDERS
P.O. Box 1665
Evanston, Ill. 60204

Viewfinders distributes the films of Pyramid, Centron, ACI, and others. A free catalog is available. Viewfinders also offers a free consultation service concerning the source of any film.

VISION QUEST
7115 N. Sheridan Rd.
Chicago, Ill. 60626

A small collection of short and feature documentaries. Specializing in student films and political documentaries. Includes *Monterey Pop*, *American Revolution 2*, *Asylum* and other films on R.O. Laing, and *Lord Thing*. Catalog free.

WOMBAT FILMS
77 Tarrytown Road
White Plains, N. Y. 10607

Another recent arrival on the film distribution scene and one that has an excellent but small collection of films. Especially good for junior high school use.

WOMEN'S FILM CO-OP
200 Main St.
Northampton, Mass. 01060

Small but powerful collection of films about the women's movement. Very reasonable rentals.

YOUTH FILM DISTRIBUTION CENTER
43 West 16th Street
New York, N.Y. 10011

Best collection of films made by kids.

Reviews of newly released short films (both of the obviously schoolroom variety and the personal and artistic shorts) can be found in:

MEDIA MIX NEWSLETTER
221 West Madison
Chicago, Ill. 60606
Monthly, September - May with no December issue. $5 for eight issues.

PREVIEWS
R.R. Bowker Company
1180 Avenue of the Americas
New York, N.Y. 10036
$7.50 per year.

THE BOOKLIST
American Library Association
50 East Huron Street
Chicago, Ill. 60611
Twice monthly, September - July and once in August. $15 for one year.

MEDIA REVIEW
The University of Chicago Laboratory Schools
1362 East 59th Street
Chicago, Ill. 60637
Monthly, $6 per year

FILM NEWS
250 W. 57th St.
New York, N.Y. 10019
One year is $6 for six issues.

INTERNATIONAL INDEX TO MULTI-MEDIA INFORMATION
Audio-Visual Associates
180 E. California Blvd.
Pasadena, Calif. 91105

Indexes non-book media formats including film, video audio, games, and kits. $36 per year for four issues.

A guide to drug education films that is highly recommended is the 3rd edition of *Drug Abuse Films*, an evaluative report by the National Coordinating Council on Drug Education. The 120-page report finds that of the currently available drug education aids 31% are "unacceptable" because they are inaccurate, distorted, outdated and conceptually unsound. Ironically it is these 31% that are among the most often viewed in schools. Only 16% were found to be at least scientifically and conceptually acceptable.

After much critical viewing the only films which emerged in the "recommended" category were: *Almost Everyone Does, Brain At 17, Community as the Doctor, Darkness Darkness, Flip City, For Adults Only, Glass House, Grooving, H + 2, Help, I Think, A Nice Kid Like You, Not The Giant Nor The Dwarf, Scag, Self-Awareness Film Modules, Speedscene, Up Front, Us, Weed, We Have An Addict In The House,*

What Did You Take?, and *What Do Drugs Do?*

Commended for producing consistently good materials were Guidance Associates, Wombat Productions, and Concept Films.

The entire excellent report is $5 from NCCDE, 1211 Connecticut Ave., N.W., Suite 212, Washington, D.C. 20036.

Another good drug film guide is *99+ Films on Drugs* by David Weber for $3.00 from:

EDUCATIONAL FILM LIBRARY ASSOCIATION
17 West 60th Street
New York, N.Y. 10023

Listings of educational media (films, filmstrips, audio and video tapes, records, super 8 cartridges, overheads) by subject matter, producer, and alphabetical order are found in the NICEM indexes. Prices range from $16.50 to $79.50, depending on the size of the volumes. The guides are most useful for those who need to know what is available. A multimedia "books in print." From:

NATIONAL INFORMATION CENTER FOR EDUCATIONAL MEDIA
University of Southern California
University Park, Los Angeles, Calif. 90007

National Information Center for Educational Media

Index to 16mm Educational Films (2 Vol.)
L. C. No. 76-190629
Contains 70,000 annotated entries.
Postpaid price: **$79.50** *net in the U.S. and Canada;* **$85.00** *elsewhere.*

Index to 35mm Filmstrips (2 Vol.)
L. C. No. 70-190630
Lists and describes 42,000 filmstrips.
Postpaid price: **$58.50** *net in the U.S. and Canada;* **$65.00** *elsewhere.*

Index to Educational Audio Tapes
L.C. No. 74-190631
Lists and describes the educational content of over 20,000 audio tapes.
Postpaid price: **$36.50** *net in the U.S. and Canada;* **$40.00** *elsewhere.*

Index to Educational Video Tapes
L. C. No. 79-190635
Lists and describes the educational content of over 9,000 video tapes.
Postpaid price: **$16.50** *net in the U.S. and Canada;* **$18.00** *elsewhere.*

Index to Educational Records
L. C. No. 78-190632
Lists and describes over 18,000 educational records.
Postpaid price: **$34.50** *net in the U.S. and Canada;* **$37.00** *elsewhere.*

Index to 8mm Motion Cartridges
L. C. No. 71-190633
Lists and describes over 18,000 educational 8mm motion cartridges.
Postpaid price: **$34.50** *net in the U.S. and Canada;* **$37.00** *elsewhere.*

Index to Educational Overhead Transparencies
L. C. No. 75-190634
Lists and describes over 35,000 educational transparencies.
Postpaid price: **$49.50** *net in the U.S. and Canada;* **$52.00** *elsewhere.*

Index to Psychology - Multimedia
L. C. No. 76-190637
Lists and describes over 15,000 non book titles dealing with the general and specific area of Psychology.
Postpaid price: **$22.50** *net in the U.S. and Canada;* **$25.00** *elsewhere.*

Index to Vocational and Technical Education - Multimedia
L. C. No. 72-190628
A valuable source to over 15,000 titles in seven media areas dealing with the general as well as the specific areas of vocational and technical education.
Postpaid price: **$22.50** *net in the U.S. and Canada;* **$25.00** *elsewhere.*

Index to Health and Safety Education - Multimedia
L.C. No. 70-190638
Gives the user access to over 16,000 non book titles dealing with general and very specific areas of health and safety education.
Postpaid price: **$22.50** *net in the U.S. and Canada;* **$25.00** *elsewhere.*

Index to Producers and Distributors
L. C. No. 72-190636
Lists alphabetically the names, addresses and codes for over 10,000 producers and distributors with media indicated.
Postpaid price: **$18.50** *net in the U.S. and Canada;* **$20.00** *elsewhere.*

Distributors for feature films can be found by consulting *Feature Films on 8 and 16 mm.* by James Limbacher. $13.50 from:

R.R. BOWKER CO.
1180 Avenue of the Americas
New York, N.Y. 10036

A guide to "underground" films is *Film Programmer's Guide to 16mm Film Rentals*. 164-page small type book for $5.50 to individuals and $7.50 to institutions from:

REEL RESEARCH
P.O. Box 6037
Albany, Calif.

If you're willing to wade through all the promotional films you might find a few useful and free gems in the 800-page *Educators Guide to Free Films* available for $11.75 per copy from:

EDUCATORS PROGRESS SERVICE
Randolph, Wis. 53956

The Directory of Film Libraries in North America is a 90-page booklet listing over 1300 libraries that have film collections. Compiled by the Film Library Information Council, 17 West 60th St., New York, N.Y. 10023, it is available from them for $5. Statistics on the number of films, filmstrips and records are given for many of the libraries.

Sex Education On Film is a 170-page paperback which gives brief but intelligent and critical evaluations of nearly 120 audio-visual aids that could be used in sex education classes from the primary grades through the adult level. Since most catalogs describe every film in glowing terms, a book such as this is helpful in finding and avoiding the outdated, moralistic, sterile, or just plain unreal films. Authors Laura Singer and Judith Buskin prefer films like *Phoebe* and even *Help, My Snowman's Burning Down* to the typical sex education materials. After many bleary-eyed hours of viewing films and filmstrips they found that the best films are those about people, "their feelings, their problems, and their development."

Sex Education on Film is a $3.95-paperback from Teacher's College Press, Teacher College, Columbia University, New York, N.Y. 10027.

FILM REFERENCE WORKS

Current Film Periodicals in English, a 25-page pamphlet edited by Adam Reilly, describes nearly 200 periodicals devoted entirely or partly to the cinema, ranging from the most intellectual and esoteric to the Hollywood movie magazines. In addition to a short paragraph describing the editorial content and giving subscription information, a "writer's mart" section is also included which gives each periodical's policy regarding unsolicited manuscripts. Available from the Educational Film Library Association, 17 W. 60th St., New York, N.Y. 10023, paper $2.

Take One is a Canadian film publication that ranks as one of the best available for anyone seriously interested in the art of film. Many fine features, film reviews, and news from the world of cinema. Published bimonthly and only $4.50 per year from:

TAKE ONE
Box 1778
Station B
Montreal 110
Canada

SUPER 8 FILMAKER™

Super 8 Filmaker. . .has its first issue out and so far the magazine looks like the kind that would be a standard for teachers working with the super 8 medium. The first issue is slick, attractive and contains some very interesting features including an explanation of how to shoot Cinemascope with an ordinary super 8 camera. There are also descriptions of amazing new devices coming in super 8, an article on how to make your own optical prints (all you need is a reflex super 8 camera with single frame capability and a projector with an inching knob). There is also a feature on film labs that give super 8 professional treatment complete with A&B rolls, edge numbers and optical effects.

The general tone of the first issue is a combination of how-to and consumer orientation. The magazine gives the impression that super 8 is maturing rapidly and that there will be little that can be done today in 16mm. that won't be available tomorrow in super 8.

Ask for a sample copy (or buy one for $1.50) from 342 Madison Ave., N.Y.C. 10017. Plans are for a quarterly publication at $5.00 for one year and $9 for two.

WOMEN & FILM

WOMEN & FILM is published tri-annually at 2802 Arizona Ave., Santa Monica, Ca. 90404.
Copyright ©1972 by Women & Film.
Subscription rates: $2.00 per year,
Single copy: 75¢
Issues sent free to prison addresses.
Address all correspondence to:
Women & Film, 2022 Delaware St., Berkeley, Ca. 94709 (or)
2802 Arizona Ave.,
Santa Monica, Ca. 90404

Women & Film is an 80-page magazine concerned with changing women's media image and discussing women's work in the media. It is also concerned with facilitating an exchange of resources, theories, and views among women struggling with the nature and purpose of mass media and popular art. The publication covers interviews, articles, reviews, and announcements. Past issues have dealt with women's film and video festivals, early suffragette films and contemporary women's films, erotic/pornographic films, drive-in movies, directors like Nelly Kaplan, Dorothy Arzner, Maya Deren, Godard, Sirk, Rossellini, Kubrick, etc. as well as women working in the film industry as writers, actors, editors, costumers, publicists, etc. They have supplied textbooks to a dozen universities for their courses in film and the women's movement.

WOMEN & FILM
2802 Arizona Avenue
Santa Monica, Calif. 90404
(213) 828-2778

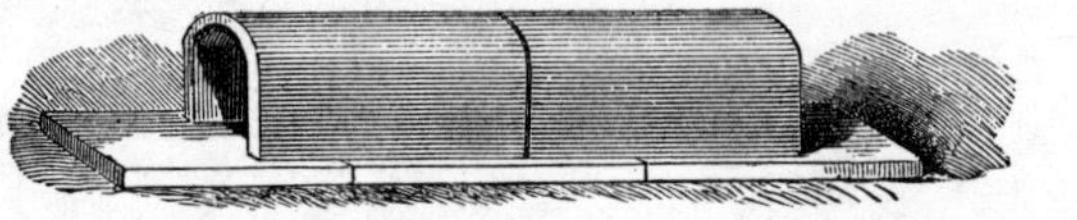

The Journal of Popular Film is another Bowling Green University publication that finds profound cosmic meanings in what ordinary human beings consider simply entertainment. The *Journal* takes a scholarly approach to films that capture the popular fancy and box office receipts in spite of the critics. Previous issues have dealt with Hollywood during World War I, detective films, monster movies of the fifties, the impact of *Birth of a Nation* on the Klan today.

Published quarterly at $4 for one year or $2 to students from:

JOURNAL OF POPULAR FILM
University Hall, 101
Bowling Green State University
Bowling Green, Ohio 43403

Man does not live on pop records alone!
Why not get some new ideas about POP MOVIES?

THE JOURNAL OF POPULAR FILM

TITLE INDEX
TO
VOLUME I OF THE JOURNAL OF POPULAR FILM

JOURNAL OF POPULAR FILM

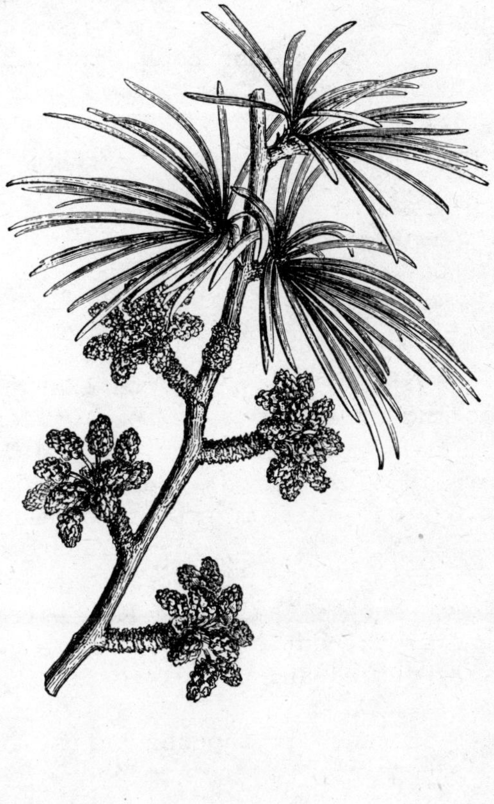

A FEW FILM PUBLICATIONS

The two best sources of books about films are:

FILMSTAKS
888 Seventh Avenue
Suite 400
New York, N.Y. 10019
15 - 27% discount on all orders to schools, libraries or institutions. 27-page catalog free.

CINEMABILIA, INC.
Film Book/Graphic Center
10 West 13th Street
New York, N.Y. 10011
Complete 264-page book catalog costs $2.50.

Making it Move by John Trojanski and Louis Rockwood is a fine book introducing students to the craft of film animation. The 150-page student book gives ideas and how-to advice on various forms of animation techniques. The teacher's handbook gives sources for animation films to use as examples as well as extra tips in making animation. The student book is $3, the teacher's manual $2, and a film illustrating the various techniques is $35 from:

PFLAUM/STANDARD
38 West Fifth Street
Dayton, Ohio 45402
(513) 224-1853

Three Major Screenplays contains the shooting scripts for *Ox-Bow Incident*, *High Noon*, and *Lilies of the Field*. There is a very brief section on film making, quotes from critics on each of the films, and typical classroom "activities." No illustrations and nothing much creative is done with the scripts, but the three films are easily rented and useful in film study.

395 pages in paperback lists at $3 or a "class price" of $2.25 from:

GLOBE BOOK COMPANY
175 Fifth Avenue
New York, N.Y. 10010

Zen and Now is an Alan Watts rap on some aspects of Eastern life-view that Westerners could use to regain their collective sanity. The visual content of the film consists entirely of nature shots from one huge garden; the idea is that one need not travel around the world to see a universe. Watts' slow, sparse narration carries the film. Some verbatim and paraphrased samples from the script:

"The great problem of civilization is to come back to your senses. People confuse what comes in by their senses with words and symbols by which they are described. The real world can never be defined; it is the "unspeakable world.' Things don't exist; the world is a multidimensional network of vibrations. As we grow up we're told what vibrations are good and what are bad. Growing up means becoming prejudiced. Even having a fever isn't necessarily dreadful. Most people in our culture would rather have money than health.

"If I talk all the time I could never hear what anyone says. If I think all the time I will have nothing to think except thought. Hence the importance of Zen meditation -- stop thinking altogether and be aware of what is. Don't name anything. Allow light and sound to play with your senses. There is no past, no future, only now."

About five minutes of the film contains no narration and allows the viewers a brief taste of non-thinking meditation. Useful in many situations from creative writing to psychology and religion. 14 min., color, rental $25, sale $150 from Hartley Productions.

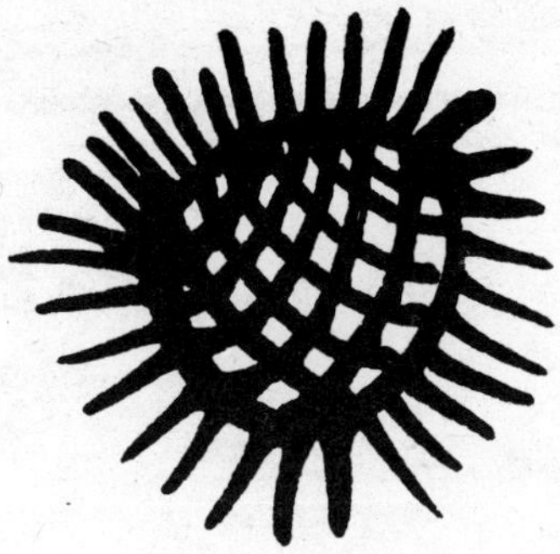

Video

LINEAR HEAT

LINEAR HEAT

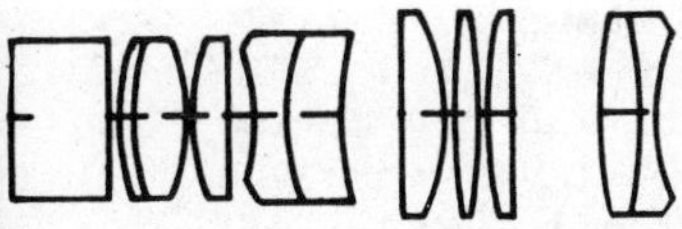

"You remember when I told you about the ideal television station. It would be alive: no canned movies, no 4-hour cold news clips. A live station, with live people, and live events.

"The whole thing would take place in a warehouse room. The camera would have been going all night: the picture transmitted would be of the camera placed in the corner of the studio-warehouse, looking out over the empty desks. Then at 6 or so, you'd see a door in the corner of the room open, and one of the news people, or secretaries, or some on-the-air person would come in: hang up his coat, start up the coffee machine, clean up his desk from the trash of the night before.

"Some more people would come in: walk around, arrange their work for the day to come. And all the time the one wide open eye the camera over in the corner would be transmitting the various acts of a television station coming to life, the staff and the soul of it coming in, stirring up the broth of a video day activities.

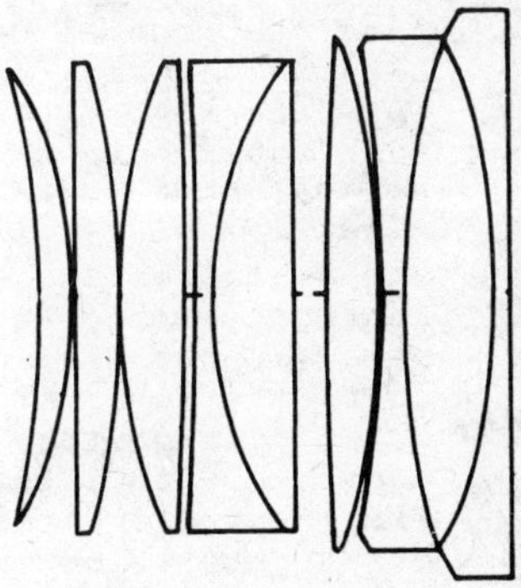

"The camera wouldn't move --- be moved --- until the first program was ready: about 7:30 or so, it would be time for the first news. So the camera, heretofore motionless, would be trollied around to the news desk, and the man there would look up and start reading out some things that had happened during the night. Then later on the camera would move over to the kitchen, or to the bandstand, or to the office: anywhere around the television warehouse where there was some activity, some life.

"At those times when there was no news, or live programming, or cook show, or someone to talk or sing or play, the camera would be left motionless: focussed on some desk, or on the technicians setting up for the next program, or the manager haggling with someone who wanted to get on the air, or the person at the front desk who took the telephone calls, or the back alley where they were bringing in some musical instruments for the late afternoon program. All people who visited the warehouse-studio-television station would be faced with themselves, being transmitted all over the community, being shown as it, the event of communication, the isness of television, were being carried to the world out there.

"And the program-non-programs would be going on all day, all evening, far into the night: the television station would make no concessions to recording, the dead art of magnetic tape: all would be live and current: and at those times when there would be 'remote programs' --- in the same way the distant cameras would carry the material live: the setting up of some meeting, the meeting, complete with intermissions, and the final desultory sweepings of the end of the operation.

"And the end of the television operation would come much as the beginning. The camera would be wheeled back to the corner of the huge room: one would see various members of the janitorial staff sweeping up, emptying the trash cans, dusting the desks, locking the door. And finally, at 2 or so, the last of the clean-up crew would go out the door, shutting it, locking it behind him: and you, the omniscient viewer, would see, across the empty room, the door clang shut, hear the lock click: and then be faced with silence, and the empty television operation, waiting there, motionless, for the next day and the next complete television act to come into being out of this silent, white, desolate room."

--- P P McFeelie: Prospectus for KTAO-TV.

American television has fulfilled its necessary promise. That is: to pacify the middle class adults as it is revolutionizing the middle class children and the entire lower class.

Since most of the literate population is antagonistic towards visual escapism --- the intelligentsia has spent (some would say misspent) their venom on the alleged banality of modern American television.

This antagonism ignores the society-change forces of video. The generation that was born in 1950 or 1955 can be truly called a visionary generation: from age 2 onwards, American children have been fed some of the most exciting, motivational, stressful visual images. For eight - twelve hours a day, an entire generation of open minded pre-adults has been subjected to two dimensional, audio-visual conceptualizing. The effect has been tremendous.

For this generation of Americans is more articulate and cynical and exciting and alive than any this country has ever produced. There are few mysteries to them. The ideals they have been presented with are all the ideals of consumption and American Standard eat-drink-smoke-play-live-feel. And like any creature exposed to 495,000 hours of such inducements, they have --- of course --- rejected all these values.

The critics and the mothers-concerned-about-effects-of-television will never understand the truth of apposition: that is, if you brainwash hard enough and long enough, the opposite will result. If you try as cleverly as American television has and does try to force consumption patterns, then the most open of receivers, the young, must follow the diametrical opposite values.

The other revolutionary force comes with the world wide distribution system of American television. There is no one in the United States who can guess the impact of I Love Lucy on the poor of Uganda, crouched eight deep before the village 12 inch television set. The message carried to the rest of the world is that of Lucy and Desi acting out their comic lives against a background of such splendor.

VANDERBILT TV NEWS ARCHIVE

VANDERBILT Television News Archive

The Vanderbilt Television News Archive, administered through the Joint University Libraries of Vanderbilt University, Peabody College, and Scarritt College, maintains a videotape collection of the evening newscasts of the three major television networks—ABC, CBS, NBC. Begun in August, 1968, this collection is added to daily as these news programs are broadcast from local stations in Nashville, Tennessee. Although network television newscasts are generally known to be the major source of national and international news for most Americans, complete videotapes of the programs are not being permanently saved elsewhere. The cost and technical problems at present are greater by far than those faced when libraries routinely maintain files of daily newspapers, but the purpose is the same: to preserve a record of today for the usefulness of that record tomorrow and later.

Characteristics of the Collection

At present, the collection consists of more than 2,000 hours of news programs, with at least seven and a half hours added each week. It is available for study, either within the Archive or through rental of the tapes for use outside the Archive. Charges depend on the extent of use and service, and on the relationship of the user to the three institutions sponsoring the Joint University Libraries.

A system of indexing and abstracting the tapes has been developed to facilitate access and reference to the collection. Work is proceeding on the abstracting of programs taped prior to November 1, 1969, and is current on programs broadcast since that date.

In March, 1972, the Archive began publication of a monthly index to television news, entitled *Television News Index and Abstracts.* The first number was for January, 1972. The index is combined with abstracts of the news programs as broadcast in Nashville, Tennessee, during a given month. It is currently being published on an experimental basis and circulated without charge to selected libraries, institutions, and individuals. After a trial period, it is the intention to continue this publication as a subscription item.

Characteristics of the Recordings

The video recordings of the programs are made in black and white, on Ampex one-inch helical-scan videotape recorders. The tapes, recorded on lo band, are playable on all Ampex one-inch helical scan video recorder/players.

Since January 1, 1971, the videotape of each program has been marked, in the recording process, with the initials of the network, the date of the program, and the Nashville time (at ten-second intervals) of the receipt of the image from the air. This information is superimposed on the program picture as the programs are recorded, greatly facilitating reference and particularizing documentation for studies based on the collection. The equipment used for making the recordings likewise has the capability of producing compiled, or subject-matter tapes. These can be made on order, subject, of course, to appropriate charges. Duplicates of programs and compiled tapes are also available in half-inch EIAJ Type I format. Audio cassettes of programs may also be rented.

Terms of Use

Within terms of Archive policies governing charges and restrictions pertaining to public showings, rebroadcast of the materials, and duplication of the tapes, the material may be rented—unaltered and as aired—either in complete programs or as compiled subject-matter tapes. No material is sold, and none can be duplicated or rebroadcast.

Basic rental charges are as follows:

$30/hr. of compiled material
$15/hr. of duplicated material
$ 5/hr. of duplicated audio-only material

with a half-hour minimum charge. Tapes rented for use elsewhere than in the Archive require deposits on the materials used. These are refunded when the tape is returned in reusable condition. Material deposits are:

$50/hr. of one-inch tape
$35/hr. of 3/4" U-Matic cassette tape
$25/hr. of half-inch tape
$ 1.50/hr. of audio tape

Viewing charges at the Archive are based on $2.00 per hour of viewing machine use.

To date, authors, graduate and undergraduate students, professors, television station personnel, and public officials have used the collection.

For access to the collection contact:

VANDERBILT TELEVISION NEWS ARCHIVE
James P. Pilkington, Administrator
Joint University Libraries
Nashville, Tenn. 37203
(615) 322-2927

Video 265

TELEVISION NEWS
INDEX
AND ABSTRACTS

Monday | November 13, 1972 | ABC

5:15:00 NAVY & RACISM

(S) Navy counsels 123 sailors who refused to return to duty aboard carrier Constellation, charging racial injustice. — HR

(San Diego, CA) Los Angeles Times editorial criticizes officers who defy integration policies of Adm. Zumwalt. [Adm. US Grant SHARP - blames permissiveness for Navy's problems.] Others think Navy moves too slow. — Dick Shoemaker

5:17:10 (COMMERCIAL)

5:19:10 DEMOS. & WESTWOOD

(S) Demo. govs. call for resignation of Mrs. Jean Westwood, McGovern's choice as Demo. ntl. chrms. — HKS

(DC) Chrm. Demo. govs. exec. cmte., AR's Dale Bumpers, calls mtg. with govs. Wendell Anderson of MN, Marvin Mandel of MD, Reubin Askew of FL, Kenneth Curtis of ME. [BUMPERS - calls for new Demo. ldr.] [ASKEW - says pty. must be reunited, & Mrs. Westwood can't do it.] — Sam Donaldson

5:21:30 (COMMERCIAL)

5:22:30 INTL. OCEAN ANTIPOLLUTION MOVE

(S) In London, England, 91 ntns. agree on new conv. to limit dumping of waste in ocean. — HR

5:22:50 GM RECALL

(S) GM recalls 155,000 1973 Oldsmobiles, Buicks, Pontiacs, & Chevrolets to install bracket on steering mechanism. — HR

5:23:20 STK. MKT. RPT.

(S) Stk. mkt. closes at all-time high; approaches 1000 mark. — HR

(NYC) 1000 level on stk. mkt. does not mean much tangible benefit to av. investor. Av. of Dow-Jones 30 blue-chip ind. corps. used as a measure for mkt. [E. F. Hutton analyst Newton ZINDER - says large cos. usually lead mkt. advances. Dow-Jones incr. could mean incr. for other stks. forthcoming.] — Gregory Jackson

5:25:30 (COMMERCIAL)

5:26:40 COMMENTARY (PENTAGON PAPERS)

(S) Pentagon Papers pub. in NY Times by Daniel Ellsberg was meant to be ultimate blow to Nixon policy, boost to peace mvt. Actually, peace mvt. almost collapsed, Nixon policy grew stronger. Pentagon Papers did not show any gross deception of Am. people by ldrs. Ntn. cannot place all blame for VN war on few scapegoats. It was a ntl. action. — HKS

5:28:30 GOOD NIGHT

GREAT PLAINS INSTRUCTIONAL LIBRARY

Great Plains National ITV Library Catalog of Recorded Visual Instruction offers nearly 150 videotape courses. The catalog offers college level courses in art, business, data processing, humanities, and psychology. There are also courses at the elementary, secondary, in-service, and adult levels. Educational institutions may preview courses at no cost except for return postage. Most courses are available on 3/4" videocassettes, although a transfer and duplication service is also provided.

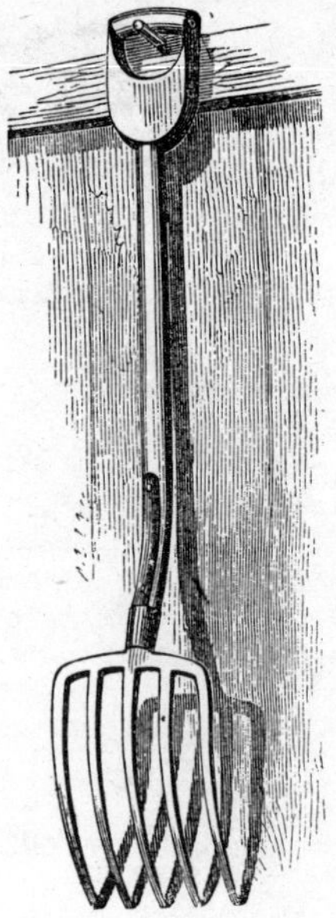

Catalog from:

GREAT PLAINS NATIONAL INSTRUCTIONAL LIBRARY
Box 80669
Lincoln, Nebr. 68501

ALTERNATE MEDIA CENTER

If you would like a free copy of the entire *Alternate Media Center* catalog, write. If you would like copies of any of the tapes in this catalog (only a small percentage of available tapes are described here), send the tape and AMC will make the transfers free of charge.

ALTERNATE MEDIA CENTER
144 Bleecker Street
New York, N.Y. 10012

The Alternate Media Center at N.Y.U. School of the Arts was funded by the John and Mary R. Markle Foundation to create working models for citizens and community participation in cable television.

Given the current technology, we chose half-inch video tape as the production tool because it is inexpensive, easy to operate, and can be plugged directly into any cable system.

Our job was to fill the gap between the rhetoric and the actuality of access—to find how people could use this new decentralized medium, cable.

This catalogue is a listing of half-inch videotapes which have been made by the Alternate Media Center and the people of the communities associated with it during its first year of operation. Most of the tapes are not finished products by over-the-air broadcast standards. They have not been made for the mass audience. They have been made for small, separate audiences, often by people who had no previous experience making television, with less and less intervention by Alternate Media Center people. Most of the tapes are attempts to see the world from the inside out rather than from the outside in, to share information rather than to impart it.

As the first year of operation comes to a close, the Alternate Media Center operates less and less as a producer of videotapes and more and more as a catalyst and resource in the information-sharing process. In the Reading, Pa. access center, for example, people have felt free to explore their own interests—consequently, the range of material appears to be infinite. The stimulation that the members of the weekly workshop meetings experience in their contact with each other provides the motivation to share ideas with the broader community. Each week new members join the workshop. The community now has a vested interest in cable.

We have tried to make this catalogue itself a process tool. From time to time, new material will be added, some of it, we hope, feedback from users of this first edition. When tapes are recycled, they will be retired from the list.

Tape #4: ***P.S. 41 kids talk about lunchtime and the lunchroom***

a) Want different food—pizza, Chinese food not welfare food—other examples—a *choice.*
b) Can't talk at lunchtime. Lunchroom is like a prison camp—examples.
d) Kids feel overdisciplined and unprotected.
d) Contradictory instructions about lunchtime activities. Kids would like a play period and conversation time just as the teachers have.
e) Kids would like to be responsible for themselves. They'd like to eat lunch in their room like the teachers do.
f) Discipline is arbitrary.

Tape #7: ***Raven School: A free high school in the community. Shot by Raven teenagers.***

a) Structure: Is the school too free? If there's no structure, can you make choices?
b) What's wrong with structure?
c) Outside people helping.
d) How we learn.
e) It's a jumble without enough structure.
f) Getting a definite idea of who we are.
g) We need a unity.
h) Liberal permissive homes / rigid schools / drugs.
i) Discipline in public school.
j) Teacher prejudice and conformity in public school.

Things we learned in Washington Heights:

- That everyone has been conditioned by the forms of broadcast TV, including us.
- That we were not able to interpret for others what they felt and saw.
- That, once we established a pattern of shooting for others, it became difficult to change the ground rules.
- That it is important for people to shoot their own tapes even if, at first, the quality is not superb.
- That each person has a different view and a different style. These differences are what create new patterns, not only in videotape but in community involvement.

Tapes 288, 604, 605: Teenagers, 3/1/72. Cabled: Teleprompter, week of March 13. Sterling, week of March 27.

A group from the Third World Teen Center came to the Council. At their center they have rap sessions, tutoring, sports. They deal with community problems in general. Presently, they have a project of visiting black colleges in the South. The kids were all black and of high school age. They expressed incredible hostility towards the older generation. They spoke about the hypocrisy of their parents in that they play the numbers, drink, some hustle and then they come down on their kids for taking drugs and having sex. The kids seemed to be very much affected by neighbors constantly reporting on them to their parents and their parents always believing the neighbors before their own children. The major area of disagreement seemed to involve sex and drugs. The kids were incredibly angry. The parents (there weren't very many there that night) were less angry than the kids, but it wasn't clear how they were reacting.

The kids were really interested in seeing themselves and other kids played back. They asked questions about the video equipment and about when the tapes would be on the cable.

Gar At The Gas Station, Oct. '71. Cabled: Mar. 6-8, '72.

This was Gar's first tape. One night, while on the all-night shift at the gas station, he brought the equipment with him and made a tape. It is a lovely self-portrait and one really gets the feel of the gas station and the people who come all night. It is very personal; and we were happy to see a tape of this nature; it alleviated our natural fear that people might imitate broadcast. I think this was a result of how video was introduced. Though the product for cable is important, the emphasis was always elsewhere.

Gar put the camera on its tiny tripod on a shelf and shot down at himself.

Tapes 527, 576, 579: Black Identity, 2/9/72. Cabled: Teleprompter, week of Feb. 21. Sterling, week of March 6.

Dr. Bill Cross, a black psychologist from Princeton University led this discussion. He talked about the fact that being black is a really important part of black peoples' lives and yet rarely do most black parents openly discuss the issue of race with their children. He feels that this isn't fair to the children, because it is not adequately preparing them for the racist society that they are going to encounter. Dr. Cross feels that "black identity" serves two kinds of functions—the first is a defensive, protective kind of function against racism, and the second is an energizing, assertive confrontation against racism. He talked about ways of instilling good feelings about being black in one's children.

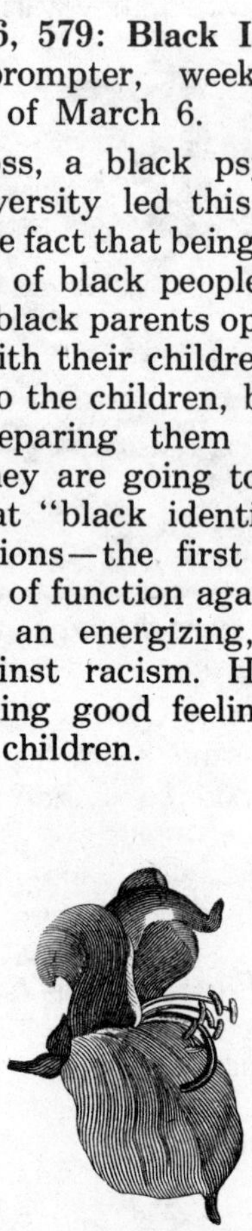

Tape #443: ***Poetry workshop,*** **12/15/71.**

John Melser leads a poetry workshop for teachers, exploring how poetry can be used with kids, how it can be used as in imaginative experience, motivating kids to get into their imaginations. John dominates the workshop. He performs for the camera and for the teachers. There were sound problems.

Tapes 715, 716: Yoga at Home.

An hour of tape shot by Peter Imber in the home of a woman who taught Yoga in Reading. She describes the philosophy of Yoga, demonstrates exercises and talks about her personal reasons for practicing Yoga.

TECHNICAL TAPES

Tape 1: Technical interview with Larry Gaines, Charleston, W.Va., 1/16/71.

A good demonstration of half-inch Sony to 1" Ampex.

Tape 258: Interview with Sy Laskewitz—engineer at Teleprompter, 9/31/71.

1) 10 minute rap about Teleprompter.
2) 10 minute rap about half-inch Sony and 3650.

Tape 304: Sterling Manhattan Cable Rap, 10/12/71.

1) Engineer Dan
2) Engineer Fern
3) John Sanfrontello.

Tape 581: Composite of Tapes 1, 258, 304.

1) Sy Laskewitz, Teleprompter: Problems in transmitting half-inch on cable.
2) John Sanfrontello, Sterling Manhattan: A word to producers of software.
3) Larry Gaines, Charlestown, W.Va.: Demonstration of editing from portapak to Ampex 1" deck.

Tape 22: Tape threading.

Correction of misthreaded tape. Correct switching of portapak. Preventing of lid shift. Head cleaning. Power. Video camera. Explanation of recording errors.

Tape 582: Signals and Correctors.

Deck to deck connections. Portapak interconnections. Transfer. Assembling of master and electronic editing. Cueing. Sound dubbing. Tail sound erase. Tape splicing.

GLOBAL VILLAGE

Global Village. . . is a video resource center pioneering in exploring the potential of videotape. They have a catalog of forty half-inch video tapes available at very low cost. Prices, including tape cost, are $14.50 for 15 minutes and $23 for up to 30 minutes. If you send blank tape to be dubbed cost is $10 for 30 minutes and $5 for another quarter-hour or any fraction thereof.

Available tapes include "Global Village Video Journal," a video magazine with a video light composition, Chinese New Year Celebration, Video/Dance, a Central Park Witch-In, massage lesson and Open Theater. The catalog also has various peoples documentaries, interviews, a report on a school district drug program and much more. This first catalog offers a greater variety of programs than a whole year of commercial TV. If you have half-inch playback capability by all means write for information to Global Village, 454 Broome St., New York, N. Y. 10012. Phone (212) 966-1515.

NATURAL SOUND WORKSHOP

PROJECT ADVISOR: John L. Reilly

ASSISTANT ADVISOR: Stefan Moore

A VIDEOTAPE BY: Ray Sundlin
and
Joe Scalzo

Natural Sound Workshop is a group of people who explore sound together. They use no instruments or extensions; the human body is the sole source of their sound. The workshop's director, composer Kirk Nurock, believes everyone can be expressive through his own personal sound. There is as much music in the world as there are people.

The tape is a look at the group in workshop activities: relaxation exercises, improvisations, compositions, and informal interviews with some of the group's members.

(B/W 15 minutes, Sony AV 5000A) New School Project

Video 271

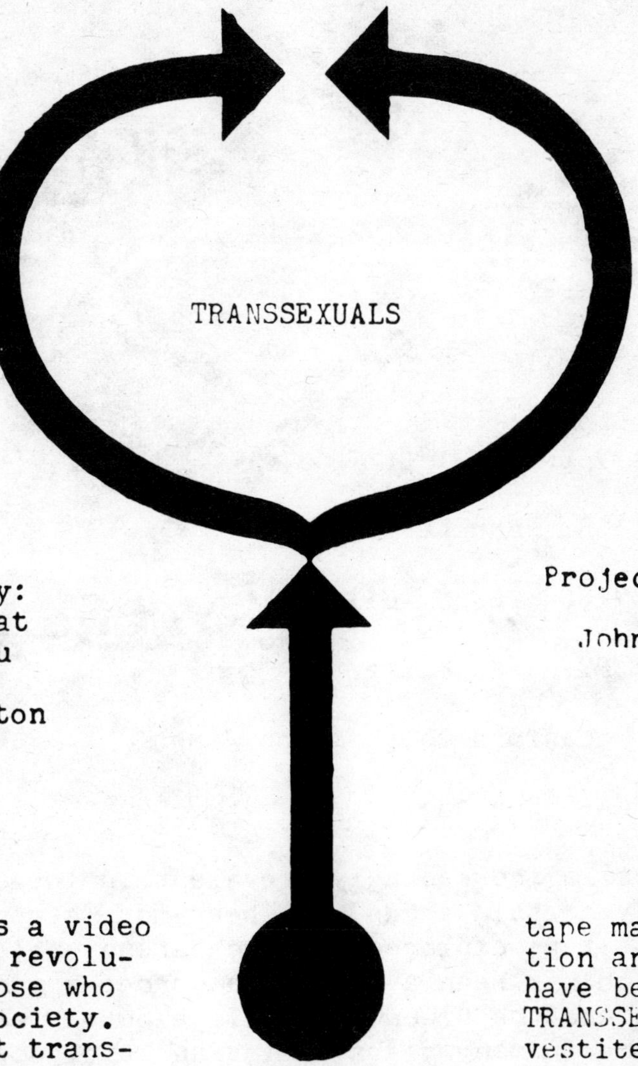

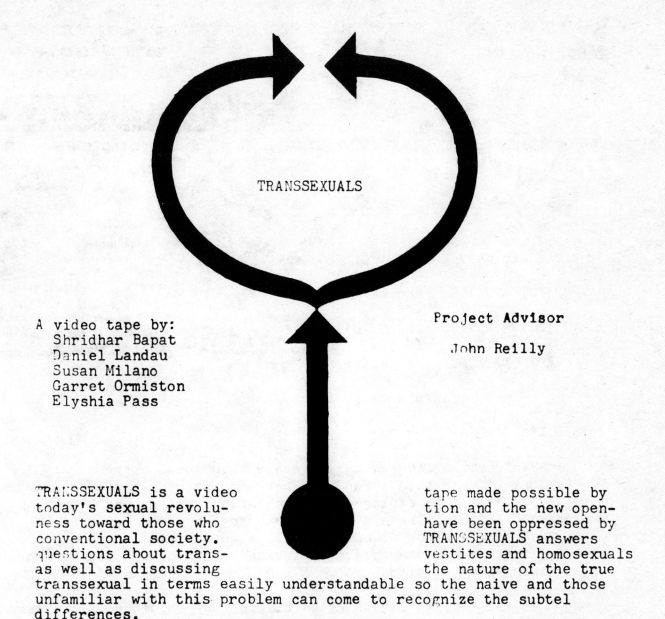

A video tape by:
Shridhar Bapat
Daniel Landau
Susan Milano
Garret Ormiston
Elyshia Pass

Project Advisor

John Reilly

TRANSSEXUALS is a video tape made possible by today's sexual revolution and the new openness toward those who have been oppressed by conventional society. TRANSSEXUALS answers questions about transvestites and homosexuals as well as discussing the nature of the true transsexual in terms easily understandable so the naive and those unfamiliar with this problem can come to recognize the subtel differences.

Just what is a sex reassignment operation? Debbie Hartman and Esther Reilly tell you about their experiences with the world famous doctor in Casablanca, the man who has performed more 'sex changes' than any other doctor in the world.

Despite the frankness of some of the scenes this tape has been cablecast by Sterling Manhattan Cable Television in New York City. The Erickson Foundation, an organization that does supportive work for post and pre-operative transsexuals, is distributing the tape to medical groups as well as to the interested general public.

* * * * * * * * *

"The best information available for those who want to really understand the transsexual and transsexualism as told by those who have been through the sex change experience."

Zelda Suplee of
The Erickson Foundation

(B/W, 22 minutes, Sony AV5000A)

272 Video

JOHN REILLY
RUDI STERN

454 BROOME ST.
N.Y.C. 10012
(212) 966-1515

Hold Glen Cove Man In Woman's Slaying

Nab Four Boys About to Fire School

VIOLENCE: CITY UNDER SIEGE

PROJECT ADVISOR: John Reilly

ASSISTANT ADVISOR: Susan Milano

A VIDEO TAPE BY: Alan Miller
and
Stanford Golob & Bob James

SPECIAL CAMERA: Ken Kohl

Violence is increasingly prevalent in large cities. Within New York City certain areas have been more strongly affected than others. This tape explores two such areas: The Baruch Housing Project, which has been averaging a murder a month for the last eight months and the Greenwich Village/SOHO areas, in which, for the first time in many years, crime and violence are becoming new and increasing problems.

Global Village investigates some of the opinions of the people in the neighborhoods involved. Sometimes their solutions are more violent than the crimes themselves! In the process the viewer will learn about attack dogs, themartial arts and community patrols.

Contrary to what one might expect the results are often filled with humor and irony. As ever, the New Yorker's adaptability to the adverse shines through.

(B/W, 23 mins., Sony AV5000A) New School Project

Child Abuse in City

New Invention Stops Burglars

GLOBAL VILLAGE VIDEO RESOURCE CENTER

Video 273

BALLAD OF A. J. WEBERMAN

A video tape by John Reilly

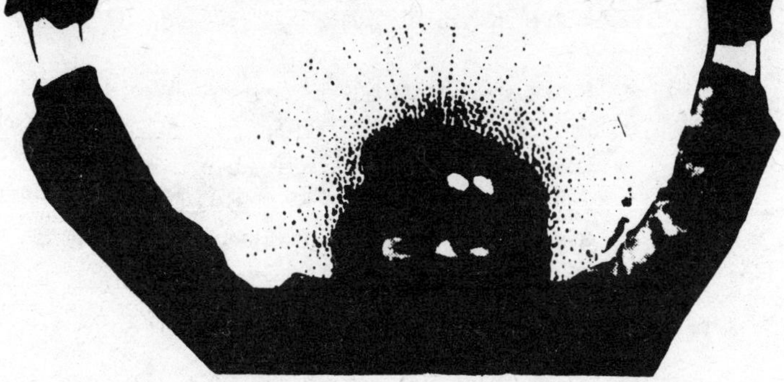

Alan Weberman is a kaleidoscope of the counter culture -- a sort of everyman's conscience. This is a video documentary about Weberman and his incredible encounters with rock star Bob Dylan and his garbage.

Weberman, as everyone should or ought to know by now, is the "world's foremost Dylanologist," nevertheless, Dylan had refused to grant Alan an interview, so the resourceful Weberman started his research and study of Dylan via his garbage can.

In this video profile we see Weberman having a wild free-for-all with Dylan's maid in front of his McDougal Street townhouse. Something of the theatre of the absurd emerges as the maid and Weberman exchange arguments about just what is Dylan's real garbage and who is the secret junkie in the Dylan household.

The tape was carried on "Free Time," WNET TV Channel 13 early in 1971, and was the cause of a brief threat from Dylan of a lawsuit.

(Color and B/W, Sony AV5000A 1/2", 23 or 15 minute versions)

TAPE #17: NEW JERSEY CAR CULTURE

A GLOBAL VILLAGE VIDEO WORKSHOP PROJECT

15 Min.,B/W

Editing Assistance: Wayne Hyde

Project Adviser: Rudi Stern

(January 1972)

A video insight into a unique subculture. Interviews with the owner, salesmen, and customers of the J. & F. Speed Shop in Saddle Brook, New Jersey are the substance of the tape. Drag racing, custom cars, cars as symbols of life-styles, and the world of Gear Heads are looked into in this class production.

ANTIOCH VIDEO

Antioch Video maintains a free-loan library of video tapes. Anyone can send them raw tape (it is preferable to send tape with information on it that might be of interest in order to maintain a fair rate of exchange) and indicate what material from the catalog is wanted and in what format. The only charge is postage.

Some of the tapes available include:

THE LAST POETS

The three black poet-musicians on the Phil Donohue Show doing their piece and responding to the audience. (60 min.)

GROUP MOTION

Concert given at Antioch in May 1971. *Group Motion* is a spectacular dance, media, happening, electronic music group which works on myth and synthesis.

LAW AND ETHICS

An unexpected struggle resulting in a shooting starts off this role-play experience for Al Denman's law and ethics class. After the staged assault, which takes place in front of the entire class, the group is broken into "witnesses" and "jury members," charged with bringing the accused to justice. (60 min.)

PENTECOSTAL FREAKOUT

Taped at a Pentecostal religious service by Hank Reisen and Tim Barrett. Includes the dramatic ritual of "speaking in tongues." (20 min.)

ELIZABETH KUBLER ROSS

Elizabeth Kubler Ross, author of *On Death and Dying*, on the Phil Donohue Show talks about her idea of death. She believes death should be respected as a natural part of living, rather than be feared. (60 min.)

BROADCAST DAY

All of the television commercials broadcast in a single 16-hour day by a Dayton, Ohio, station. A useful block for data or content analysis. (240 min.)

SEXISM IN COMMERCIAL TV

A compilation, by Gail Rebhan, of commercials and cartoons, revealing, very graphically and with a minimum of editorializing, the heavy sex-typing of male and female roles on TV, especially on children's TV. (25 min.)

THEY BECAME WHAT THEY BEHELD

From *Camera Three*, 1971, a program in which Edmund Carpenter tells about his trip to Africa with Polaroid and audiotape technology, and how people responded to it.

PRESIDENT NIXON ADDRESSES THE NATION

Various TV addresses available.

GENE YOUNGBLOOD

The author of *Expanded Cinema* speaks to the International Design Conference, 6/71, on technological futures. (120 min.)

SOFT ARCHITECTURE

The evolution of a class taught by Jerry Sirlin, at Antioch Yellow Springs, spring of 1972. The class dealt with inflatables, suspended structures, and modular spaces, and progressed from discussion to action. Tape by Bruce Finke. (50 min.)

AMERICAVIEW

A continuing chronicle of pop culture, a collage, a mosaic. The history of a decade through its popular music, public opinion formation through a TV tube. (50 min.)

According to Antioch Video's Bob Devine, "Our main operation is in doing and teaching video. We have been working with the medium since 1965, and since 1969 have developed a rather interesting curriculum in half-inch, countercultural, alternative video. Antioch offers a B.A. in video communications." They have also developed an M.A. program in media studies with a major in video in concert with Antioch Baltimore and the Center for Understanding Media. They also assist groups in the development of half-inch video programs.

ANTIOCH VIDEO
Antioch College
Yellow Springs, Ohio

VIDEOTAPES ON VIDEOTAPE

SMITH-MATTINGLY PRODUCTIONS, INC.
Box 31095
Washington, D.C. 20031
(301) 736-3742

The general disillusionment with helical scan videotape recording as an effective means of communication in education, business, government and the arts has convinced us of the need for training in the application of half-inch and one-inch VTR, and three-quarter-inch VCR (video cassette recorder). We've demonstrated our commitment to the medium by producing -- on helical scan equipment -- a series of pre-recorded videotapes which provide useful information and realistic, achieveable models for helical scan VTR/VCR productions.

Realizing that time is precious among media people, we've gone one step further and developed a course outline/syllabus incorporating our tapes, our workbook/manual INTRODUCING THE SINGLE CAMERA VTR SYSTEM, and our six years of training and production experience into a coordinated program for developing VTR competence and self-confidence among your staff, students, employees, etc. If you're considering getting into VTR or VCR, we can save you time, worry and money. If you're already there, we can help you apply this remarkable, but often mis-used, medium in cost-effective ways. Read on.

"How To" Programming

INTRODUCING CCTV/VTR

7 min. 22 sec. $30.00

Through line drawings and cartoon characters, this tape takes a brief look at the evolution of half-inch and one-inch video tape recorders. It goes on to introduce the viewer to some of the basic concepts of helical scan VTR operation. The tape is designed for the newcomer to VTR. It shows how helical scan videotape recording and closed circuit television work, and how they relate to other communication media.

VTR PRODUCTION PLANNING

28 min. $125.00

While A VIDEO ESSAY deals with one individual's approach to editing videotape, this tape takes a more typical organizational approach. The entire production planning process is documented -- from choosing and focusing a subject, through goal-setting, audience targeting, assignment of responsibilities, production conferences, actual taping, editing, evaluation, and distribution. Techniques for saving time, cutting costs, and improving overall audio and video quality are demonstrated. A "Production Planner" and critique form are included.

VTR FEEDBACK

18 min. 12 sec. $75.00

Perhaps the most significant advantage of videotape over other media of communication is its ability to synthesize, focus and feedback information -- almost instantaneously. But, after we "see ourselves on TV", what then?

The creative, meaningful use of VTR in feedback applications is not instantaneous. It requires planning, preparation, skillful execution, and proper evaluation. VTR feedback is not a spur-of-the moment activity.

This videotape describes the various uses of VTR (surveillance, feedback, and documentation), and demonstrates a variety of equipment and location setups for feedback activities. It then goes through several types of feedback situations (VTR Charades, VTR Fun and Games and Role Playing), and ends by discussing some of the problems the user may encounter in feedback activities, and ways of overcoming these problems. A closing summary condenses the "rules of the game".

SET-UP, PRODUCTION TECHNIQUES, AND PREVENTIVE MAINTENANCE FOR THE SINGLE CAMERA VTR SYSTEM

40 min. $150.00

Access to a VTR system is great -- but it's not enough. This tape shows how to hook up a basic single camera VTR system, how to adjust its controls for optimum performance in a given situation, how to accomplish production techniques like follow-thru focus and in-camera fades, and how to recognize problems when they occur -- and correct them. The goal of the tape is to assist the VTR user in achieving creative control over his equipment and production situation.

A VIDEO ESSAY -- ONE APPROACH TO EDITING VIDEOTAPE

25 min. 30 sec. $100.00

First we see a tape originally produced on a half-inch, battery-powered VTR, and then electronically edited onto one-inch tape. Through a conversation with the producer (a high school student), the planning process necessary for this kind of production is examined. One type of VTR-to-VTR editing layout is demonstrated, and the procedure for setting up and timing edits is shown. Finally, the student who produced the tape evaluates his effort, and offers suggestions for similar productions.

The tape closes with a summary of the important points and procedures necessary for planning, producing and executing an electronically-edited video essay.

INTRODUCTION TO CATV

27 min. $100.00

This tape first gives the viewer a look at the origins of cable TV. It then goes on to document an ongoing CATV operation, covering every aspect from

WELCOME TO THE WONDERFUL WORLD OF VTR

10 min. 40 sec. $35.00

Whatever our walk of life, most of us share the same concept for the use of television as a means of communication -- the commercial broadcast TV model. This tape is an attempt to show how narrow the broadcast model really is and to help VTR users break out of the artificial constraints of broadcast TV programming and into new and creative ways of using videotape recording. Common fallacies about television are exploded, and the VTR user is offered a new frame of reference for the use of television.

BASIC VTR SOUND TECHNIQUES

20 min. $75.00

Covers microphone availability, selection and application for a variety of taping situations. Automatic vs. manual audio gain, audio mixers and mixing, low vs. high impedence microphones, supplementing your basic audio track, sound editing, audio dubbing, trouble shooting your audio system and much more.

BASIC LIGHTING TECHNIQUES

20 min. $75.00

Television is the translation of light to electrical energy and back to light. VTR allows us to store light in magnetic form. Light -- or the lack of it -- is critical to the success or failure of our tapes. This program deals with "normal" lighting, cheap but effective supplemental lighting, lighting and camera point of view, simple "three-light" setups, and portable lighting. It is not, nor is it intended to be, a treatise on broadcast studio lighting.

THE PORTAPAK

30 min. $125.00

Of all the "innovations" trumpeted by the VTR manufacturers, the half-inch, battery-operated, shoulder-carried camera/VTR ensemble dubbed the "portapak" is probably the most revolutionary. Relatively easy to use, the portapak is not without its idiosyncracies. This tape covers the effective application of the portapak, from "In-The-Camera" productions to "Originating Tapes For Half-Inch and One-Inch Editing"

ENVIRONMENTAL COMMUNICATIONS

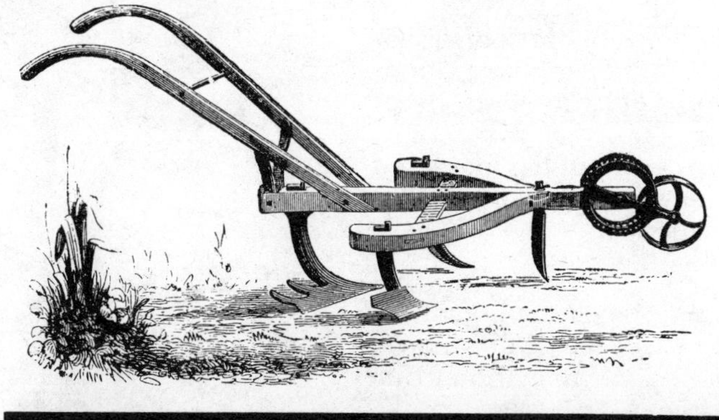

ENVIRON MENTAL COMMUN ICATIONS
62 WINDWARD VENICE

ENVIRONMENTAL COMMUNICATIONS
62 WINDWARD AVE VENICE CALIF 90291 213-392 5071

TRUCKSTOP NETWORK

A VIDEO SCRAPBOOK OF RECENT NOMADIC EXPERIENCES TRAVELING IN THE ANT FARM STAGE IV/MEDIA VAN, EQUIPPED WITH A MOBILE 1/2" VIDEO STUDIO, SELF-CONTAINED LIFE SUPPORT SYSTEM AND ICE 9 VINYL INFLATABLE. THIS TAPE DOCUMENTS A PRACTICAL DEMONSTRATION OF LIVING ON THE ROAD AND ACTING AS AN ALTERNATE COMMUNICATION NETWORK, BASED ON DECENTRALIZED TWO-WAY MEDIA EXCHANGE. FEATURES STOPS AT COLLEGE CAMPUSES, VISITS WITH PAOLO SOLERI, R. BUCKMINSTER FULLER, DAVE SELLERS (GODDARD COLLEGE). INTERVIEWS WITH PEOPLE LIVING IN TRUCKS JAZZ HERITAGE FESTIVAL IN NEW ORLEANS, PRAIRIE MOON MUSEUM, FREEWAY SURVEILLANCE OF THE HIGHWAYS OF AMERICA VIA DASH MOUNTED CAMERA, AND GREAT NEW SINGING SENSATION JOHNNY ROMANO.

AVAILABLE IN TWO 30 MINUTE VERSIONS:

ORDER NUMBER VTSN-PRIME TIME $60
ORDER NUMBER VTSN-WILD SEED $60
BOTH VERSIONS $110

GEODESIC ERECTIONS

TAPE CHRONICLES THE DESIGN AND CONSTRUCTION PROCESS OF A 30 FT. DIAMETER THREE FREQUENCY (5/8 SPHERE), ICOSA-ALTERNATE CABLE TENSED GEODESIC DOME BUILT FOR THE EXPLORATORIUM AT THE PALACE OF ARTS AND SCIENCES IN SAN FRANCISCO. BY ANT FARM, OCTOBER, 1970.

30 MINUTE VIDEO TAPE
ORDER NUMBER VTGE-30 .... $60

WHOLE EARTH DEMISE

A 20 MINUTE EDIT OF THE LAST HOURS OF THE WHOLE EARTH CATALOG. SEE CROWD DECIDE WHAT TO DO WITH $20,000 CASH; PLUS 10 MINUTES OF STEWART BRAND ON VIDEO TAPE WATCHING THE EDITED VIDEO TAPE YOU'VE JUST SEEN.

VIDEO TAPE IS A JOINT PRODUCTION OF ANT FARM, MEDIA ACCESS CENTER, AND RAINDANCE.

30 MINUTE VIDEO TAPE
ORDER NUMBER VTWED-30 .... $60

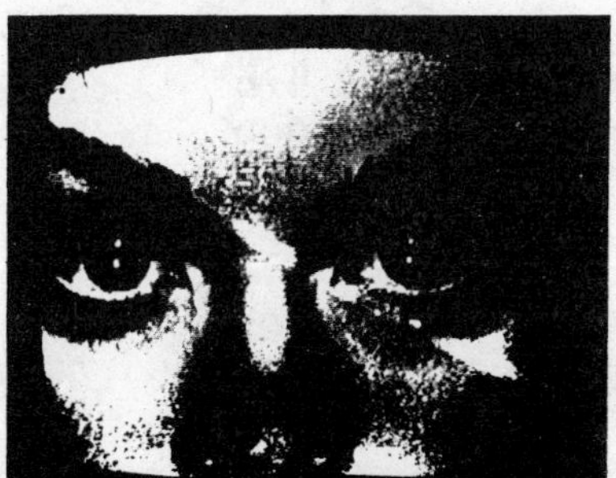

LIVING SPACE COMPOSITE

FOCUS ON ALTERNATE LIVING EXPERIMENTS AND ACCESSIBLE SHELTER MATERIALS. HOMEMADE AND HY-TECH DOME STRUCTURES, INFLATABLES, TEEPEES, RAPS WITH OWNER BUILT HOMESTEADERS, BUILDING WITH WASTE MATERIALS AND EXPERIMENTAL PLAYGROUND CONSTRUCTIONS.

SERIES DEVELOPED BY MEDIA ACCESS TAPES. FOR FURTHER INFORMATION CONCERNING ALTERNATE TV RESOURCES, GENERATING INFORMATION ACCESS, AND SOFTWARE IN 1/2" VIDEO TECHNOLOGY AND COMPATIBLE SYSTEMS, WRITE TO: MEDIA ACCESS TAPES, PORTOLA INSTITUTE, 1115 MERRILL ST. MENLO PARK, CALIFORNIA.

30 MINUTE VIDEO TAPE
ORDER NUMBER VTLSC-30 .... $60

SAM'S CAFE

THREE OAKLAND ARTISTS KNOWN AS SAM'S CAFE, RECENTLY MAILED 20,000 PHONY BILLS TO BAY AREA RESIDENTS AS A MEDIA INVERSION ART EVENT. THE PHONE NUMBERS LISTED ON THE BILLS BELONGED TO B/A, KQED TV, AND THE SAN FRANCISCO CHRONICLE. SWITCHBOARD CHAOS RESULTED FROM IRATE CITIZENS. THE SAM'S CAFE THREE WERE LATER ARRESTED AND CHARGED WITH SENDING HUMAN SHIT THROUGH THE U.S. MAIL (JARS FILLED WITH HUMAN EXCREMENT WERE SENT TO MEMBERS OF THE ESTABLISHMENT PRESS AS PART OF THE EVENT). TAPE CONSISTS OF INTERVIEWS WITH DAVE THE RED, MARK AND TERRIE (SHE ONLY EATS T.V. DINNERS), ON THE EVENING PRIOR TO THE EVENT. OFF THE AIR NEWS COVERAGE, PRESS CONFERENCE, ARREST AND TRIAL.

SUPPLEMENTAL PACKAGE CONTAINING SLIDES, NEWSPAPER DOCUMENTATION, ETC., ALSO AVAILABLE.

30 MINUTE VIDEO TAPE
VTSC-30 .... $60

INFLATABLES ILLUSTRATED

THIS VIDEO TAPE IS AN "EASY ACCESS, HOW TO DO IT" TECHNIQUE FOR BUILDING ROOM SIZE OR LARGE MEMBRANE ENVELOPES. DETAILS ON WORK WITH POLYETHYLENE FILM INCLUDE: THICKNESS, SOURCES, SEAMING METHODS, INFLATO-GEOMETRY (PATTERNS). "RULE OF THUMB" FORMULA ON FAN SIZE, AIR PRESSURES AND WIND EFFECT RELATIONSHIPS. THIS TECHNICAL INFORMATION (AUDIO) OCCURS SIMULTANEOUSLY WITH VISUAL EXAMPLES FROM TWO YEARS EXPERIENCE WITH INFLATABLES. FROM THE INFLATO-COOKBOOK BY ANT FARM.

30 MINUTE VIDEO TAPE
ORDER NUMBER VTGE-30 .... $60

INSTANT CITY

AN EXPERIMENT IN ARCHITECTURE FOR THE MOBILE YOUTH CULTURE, IN IBIZA, SPAIN, HELD SEPTEMBER 20 TO OCTOBER 20TH.

THIS TAPE DOCUMENTS THE BUILDING OF A TEMPORARY CITY IN CONJUNCTION WITH ICSID (INTERNATIONAL CONFERENCE OF THE SOCIETY OF THE INDUSTRIAL DESIGN).

30 MINUTE VIDEO TAPE
ORDER NUMBER VTIS-30 .... $60

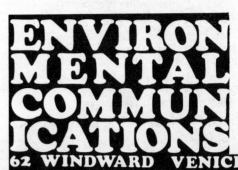

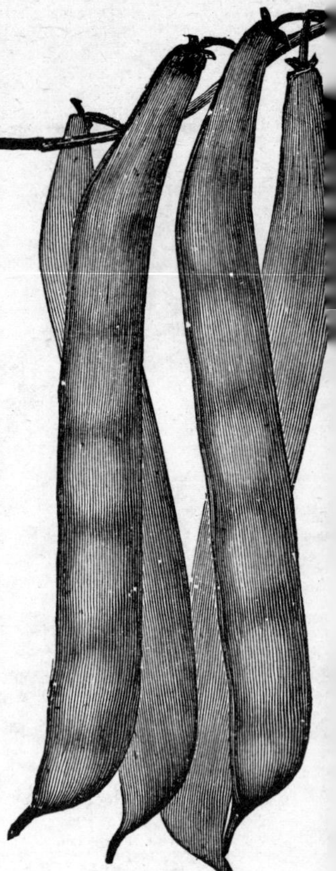

RAINDANCE VIDEO

Over the past three years we've compiled many hundreds of hours of videotape, some of it edited, much of it unedited. And we continue to make videotape, of ourselves, our environment, our friends; other environments, other cultures, other events.

During the past year the volume of videotapes we've sent out has increased substantially through both sales and exchange. Moreover, we are increasing our commitment to producing alternate video information.

Thus, we're offering three ways to get Raindance videotape:

1. *The Best of the Raindance Cultural Data Bank:* We began taping when portable video equipment first appeared almost four years ago. Our archive (cultural data bank) thus encompasses many facets of alternate television from historical events like New York's East Village at its prime in 1968, Woodstock, Altamont; through an exploration of many of the different genre of alternate television (street video, life style video, political demonstrations, documentary, and so on); to an exploration of what makes video a unique medium (feedback, time-delays, synthesized imagery).

We will sell a 10-hour package of this material for either personal or educational use as a reference library. Our price is $500 for the series, video tape included.

2. *The Raindance VideoLog.* In addition to making available tape from the past, we want to establish a regular distribution channel for our current work. *The Raindance VideoLog* will be a bi-monthly assemblage of tightly edited segments by ourselves and others offering access to up-to-date activity in alternate television. The first issue will include videotape from Vietnam, humor, life style video, and video imagery.

We will distribute this in any format a subscriber wants, including videocassettes. For a year's subscription (six issues) the price will be $250, videotape included (write for videocassete format prices as we don't yet know what the raw stock price will be). Single issues also available at $55 an hour, tape included.

3. *Videotape Exchange:* Probably the most satisfying mode of distribution we've yet found is exchanging videotapes. We're averaging about eight exchanges a month and it really seems worth it.

The offer is this: You send us some of your software, and we'll send back an equal amount ofours(for non-commercial use).

Contact: RAINDANCE VIDEO SERVICE, Post Office Box 543, Cooper Station, New York, New York 10003; or call (212) MU-7-4210.

GUERRILLA TELEVISION

THERE ARE media teachers who are very much involved in film but who consider video education as something more esoteric or less practical than film. They limit their "teaching" of TV to occasional broadsides about how puerile broadcast programming is or how advertising corrupts values. Such media teachers are comparable to the old stereotype of the English teacher working hard with *Silas Marner* while his/her cohorts swing with Fellini and Kubrick.

Television is the *only* mass media in the U.S. and film *as we know it now* has about as bright a future as Barbie dolls at Summerhill. Short and feature films are more cult phenomena than mass media. But video . . .

For those not yet ready to trade super 8's in for video porta-paks, a great way to become acquainted with the video movement is through **Guerrilla Television** by Michael Shamberg. The 140-page oversized book has two sections, a "meta-manual" and the "official manual."

The "meta-manual" is straight hip communication theory à la Fuller, Weiner, Youngblood and McLuhan as translated and expanded by an under-30 video freak. Shamberg has sections on media ecology, the epistomology of dope, survival technology, meta-service economy, info-morphology, and schools. His insights often seem near-brilliant while at other times they seem more clever than true. There are parts of this 40-page section that excited me as much as my first reading of McLuhan five years ago.

The "official manual" covers 75% of the book and is a cross between a beginners' guide to the videosphere and a utopian proposal for Media-America. Shamberg compares film to video (guess which wins?), shows how network people don't really understand television, and gives lots of practical suggestions on how to get in on the process of video, especially with kids. *Holt, Rinehart & Winston; $3.95 in paperback and $7.95 in hardcover.*

GUERRILLA TV is a manual of the hardware, software and metaphysics of alternate television
and a journal of our experiences doing it.
At bookstores from Holt, Rinehart and Winston.

Guerrilla Television

INTRODUCING THE SINGLE CAMERA VTR

INTRODUCING THE SINGLE CAMERA VTR SYSTEM is specifically designed for teachers, students, trainers, and other professionals who want to learn to communicate effectively through television. Its primary goal is to provide the user with simple but definitive information on the selection, operation and employment of a basic VTR system. More complex systems are only proliferations of the four basic components -- VTR, camera, monitor and microphone, thus self-confidence in the use of a simple system is valuable whatever the level of one's TV production happens to be.

The manual is divided into three parts, beginning with a general discussion of the use and mis-use of television, and establishing the need for certain standards in using television as a learning system. Next follows a detailed, functional description of the components of a single camera VTR system, including preventive maintenance, hook-up and shut-down procedures, and basic operating techniques. The third section comprises six exercises which supplement and reinforce the first two sections of the manual. These exercises, introduced with a chapter on production standards, are followed by a separate chapter on the shoulder-pack, battery VTR, and a discussion of the options available to supplement your basic, single camera VTR system. The manual is based on approximately nine man-years experience with commercial as well as non-commercial applications of VTR. It is in use in a wide variety of educational and training settings in the United States, Canada, Mexico, Italy, Germany, England and Latin America. 100 pages spiral bound.

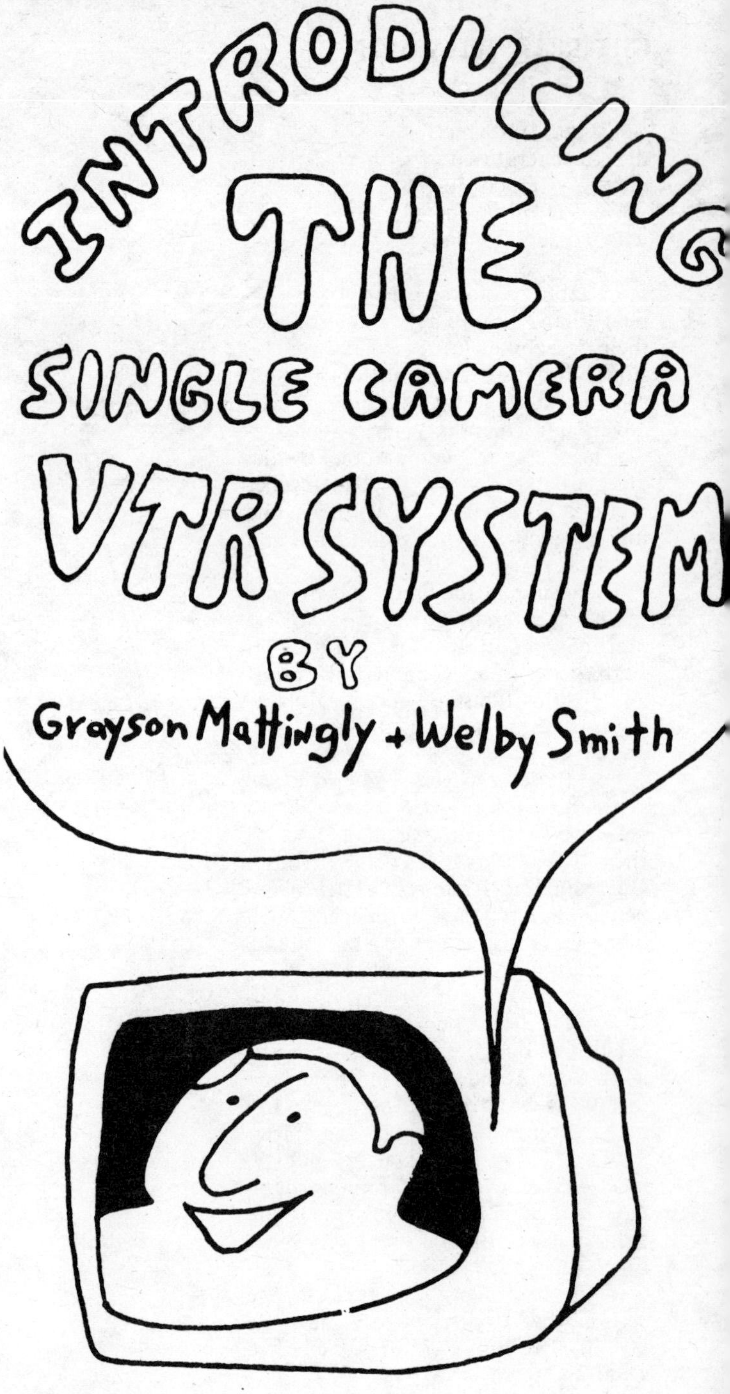


```
$8.95 from SMITH-MATTINGLY
           P.O. BOX 31095
           WASHINGTON, D.C.20031
```

VIDEOPLAYER

VideoPlayer™

INTERNATIONAL VIDEOPLAYER INDUSTRY NEWS MAGAZINE

Videoplayer is a trade journal of the videoplayer industry. Lots of press releases and publicity photos of new and forthcoming video equipment. *Videoplayer* has little value for educators unless they need to be well informed about new video equipment. The magazine does offer a fascinating glimpse into what the coming years will see in new video hardware.

Videoplayer costs $10 for one year of six issues from:

VIDEOPLAYER PUBLISHING CO.
13273 Ventura Blvd., Suite 213
Studio City, Calif. 91604

COMMUNITY ACCESS T.V.

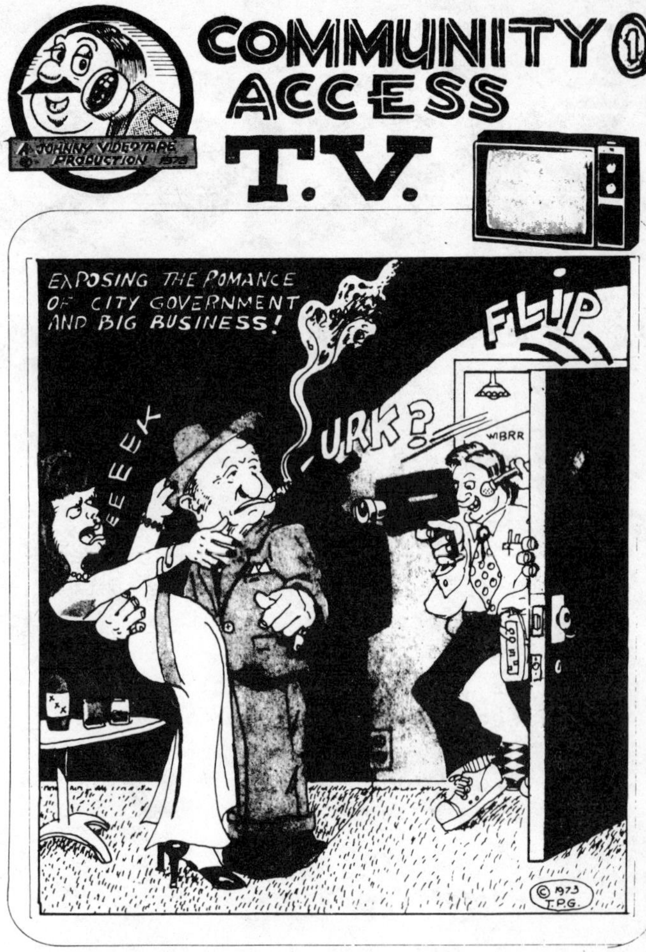

COMMUNITY ACCESS VIDEO

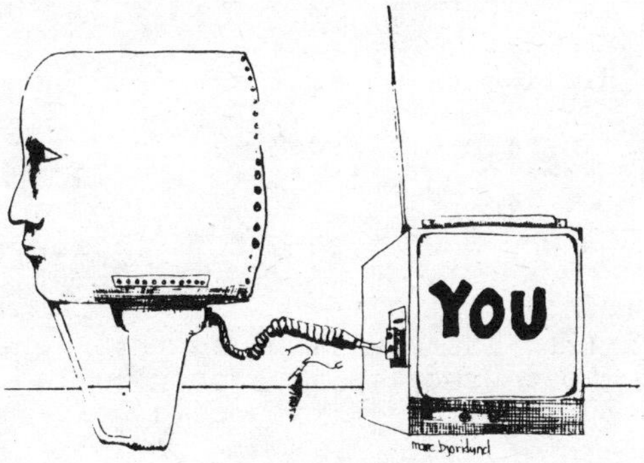

COMMUNITY ACCESS VIDEO is a tabloid newspaper-book of the format popularized by WHOLE EARTH CATALOG and BIG ROCK CANDY MOUNTAIN. The book is an extremely practical guide to the use of videotape and cable TV as a tool in building local community. The book details areas such as video hardware, sources of begging, borrowing or buying video equipment, methods of software distribution, video-to-film transfer, cable operation, economic survival and video technique and formats. One section describes exactly how to go about forming your own non-profit corporation for $20.

A bundle of solid and practical info for the video nut or school starting in video is packed into the 64 pages. COMMUNITY ACCESS VIDEO costs $3 and can be ordered through any bookstore who knows about Berkeley's BOOK PEOPLE or directly from the author:

ALLAN FREDERIKSEN
695 30th Avenue, Apt. E
Santa Cruz, Calif. 05060

CONTENTS

VIDEO MAGAZINE

AMAZE YOUR FRIENDS

BE THE FIRST ON YOUR BLOCK TO HAVE YOUR VERY OWN COPY "HUZZA"

JOHNNY VIDEOTAPE (allan frederiksen)
and
VIDEO IMAGE PRODUCTIONS (barry verdi)
announce:

We are preparing to assemble and distribute a video magazine . The first issue will be 30 minutes. Subsequent issues will be up to 60 minutes on your choice of one 60 minute or two 30 minute reels. The standard will be black and white (monochrome) EIAJ-1 or CV.

The contents will be compiled from tapes submitted to the magazine by subscribers, community, or video groups. Recommended length of tapes for initial publication may be up to 15 to 20 minutes. In addition, we will insert visual information regarding new equipment, modifications to equipment simple maintenance instructions, and special ads about video groups, tape exchanges, current trends in cable & public access, or other information submitted for publication.

Video Magazine

SUBSCRIPTION RATES WILL BE BASED ON COST:
1. ½", 64 min., 7" reel... $18.00
2. dubbing & shipping..... 5.00
TOTAL.......... $23.00
OR send your own tape and the cost is $5.00 per issue.

*** a free issue will be sent to persons whose programs are included in each publication***, (you cover tape cost)

Personal advertisements (re: your group, sale of equipment, etc.) will be inserted at $1. per minute (remember a still frame can be used for extended viewing).

DO NOT submit programs protected by copyrights.

Forward your subscription, tape and/or other information for inclusion in VIDEO MAGAZINE to:

VIDEO MAGAZINE
360-C WEST SAN CARLOS
SAN JOSE, CA

RADICAL SOFTWARE

Radical Software is a must for anyone exploring the potential of portable videotape. The contents of the magazine range from highly esoteric philosophizing by someone who has just discovered the universe to very practical nuts and bolts advice for VT users. Each issue features a "Video Directory" listing individuals and groups all over the world who are experimenting with VT. *Radical Software* soon will change its name to *Changing Channels*.

Volume I 1970-71 4 issues $10.95.
Volume II 1972-73 9 issues $12.50,
current subscription $12.50 yearly.

GORDON & BREACH
One Park Avenue
New York, N.Y. 10016
(212) 689-0360

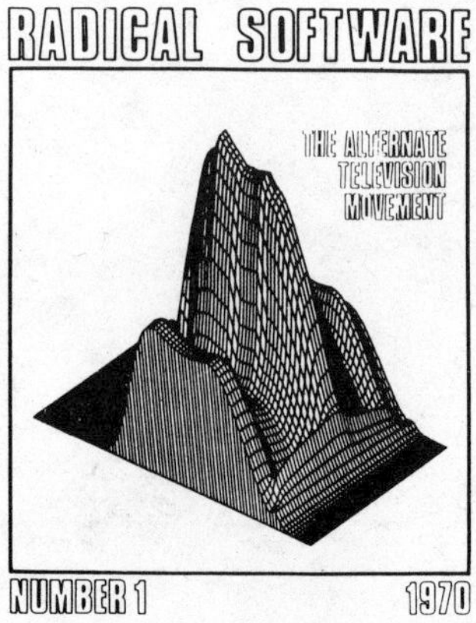

EXPLORING TELEVISION

PROBE

Why do people watch the soap operas? Possible areas for discussion. Do you agree or disagree with the following?

Soap operas always reveal the more seamy, tragic side of life. We like to watch others suffer.

Soapers give their audience a chance to experience vicariously all the things that the normal housewife-mother never actually experiences: secret romances, horrendous discoveries, great emotional challenges.

We all have an instinctive desire to gossip and listen to gossip. Soapers satisfy this desire.

Since people in soap operas are often weak willed and live in great emotional tension, we can say that we're better off than they are.

A frequent theme in the soap opera is that the mighty are brought low. Dr. A's reputation does topple when the politician goes after him. We rather enjoy seeing this.

In most TV dramas, there is the assumption that we really believe in truth, honor, fidelity. Actually most of us give lip service to these virtues, but really don't believe in them; not that much, at least. The soapers are more direct and honest in their admission that most people don't live this way.

Exploring Television . . . by William Kuhns is actually a textbook for a high school course in television (not the production end) study. The 240-page magazine-size soft-cover book is in the student workbook format and sells for $2.40 to $3.20 depending on quantity. Check out an examination copy from Loyola University Press, 3441 North Ashland Avenue, Chicago, Illinois 60657.

A SHORT COURSE IN CABLE

Cable television is currently in danger of being controlled by groups more interested in profit than in community service. Since cable TV is the single medium most likely to dominate the future of mass communications, the issue is crucial and deserves time in media classes. Cable is not simply a better quality picture for the same old programs; it can become the central nervous system for Media-America, useful not only for news but for giving the citizen access to media and even making possible a participatory democracy on a national level.

Short Course in Cable is a free booklet available from:

UNITED CHURCH OF CHRIST
Communications Office
289 Park Avenue South
New York, N. Y. 10010

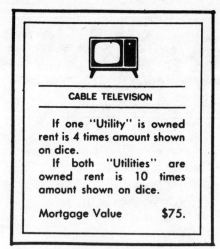

CABLE TELEVISION

If one "Utility" is owned rent is 4 times amount shown on dice.

If both "Utilities" are owned rent is 10 times amount shown on dice.

Mortgage Value $75.

source: Radical Software

EHI

EDUCATIONAL VIDEO TAPE WHOLESALE CORP.

8983 Complex Drive
San Diego, CA 92123
(714) 565-0232

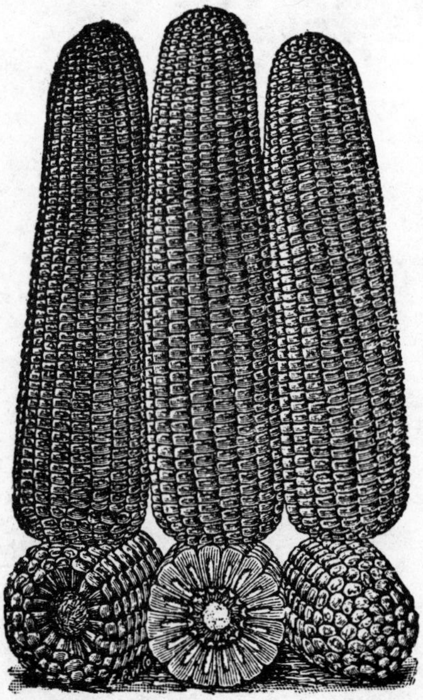

COLOR SERIES 810

backcoated video tape for
1/2" helical scan recorders

QUANTITY	60 MINUTE PLAYING TIME 2400 FEET ON 7 INCH REELS		30 MINUTE PLAYING TIME 1250 FEET ON 5 1/8 INCH REELS	
	Mfr. List	Color Series 810	Mfr. List	Color Series 810
1 - 11	$ 39.95	$ 15.95	$ 21.95	$ 9.70
12 - 49	36.75	13.95	20.19	8.95
50 - +	35.96	12.95	19.75	8.45

REELS, PLASTIC (EMPTY) - WITH BOXES, FOR 1/2 WIDE VIDEO TAPE

QUANTITY	7 INCH REELS	5 1/8 INCH REELS
1 - 9	$ 1.35	$ 1.25
10 - 24	1.15	1.05
25 - 99	0.95	0.90

NOTE - Prices and availability of all items listed above cannot be guaranteed and are subject to change without notice.

Prices shown are F O B San Diego. Shipments to all but established accounts must be prepaid. All orders not prepaid will be sent C.O.D. Shipping charges, except where included in prepayment, will be collected by carrier.

DAK

FIRST QUALITY PHILLIPS TYPE CASSETTES

We are proud of our insides

Finest cassettes made. Individually enclosed in plastic containers with tabs to prevent jamming in shipment, internal rolling guides on steel pins, anti-static moisture resistant waffer shield, MU-metal shield, lubricated wide range Polyester tape, constant pressure copper spring. Lifetime jam guarantee, all American parts.

C30-$ .95
C60-$ .90
C90-$ .85
C120-$ .75

FREE SAMPLE

FIRST QUALITY 1200′ 7″ MYLAR

Not second line but rather once used professional quality magnetic tape. Silicone lubricated high potency polished oxide, heavy duty splice free. Tape is packed in individual hinged boxes on DAK reels.

1-9-$1.25
10-23-$1.10
24-49-$ .95
50-99-$ .85
100+-$ .75

FREE SAMPLE

FIRST QUALITY 2400′ HELICAL SCAN VIDEO TAPE

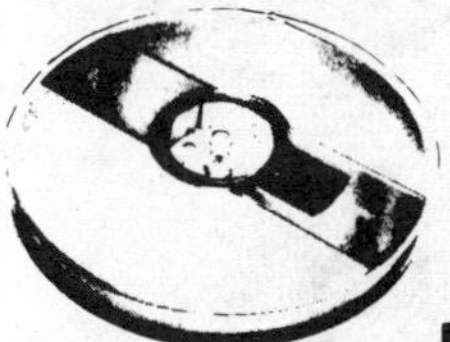

1st Quality 7″ x ½″ x 2400′ Helical-scan Video Tape for CCTV use. Silicone lubricated, and Micro polished make this an extraordinary buy. Some is new, some has been reprocessed in DAK's exclusive reprocessing center under careful 4 step Q/C operations. 1) Tape is inspected for actual physical damage and will be rejected if found. 2) Tape is removed from reel and surface cleaned and polished to remove loose oxide or binder. 3) Tape is precision center flange wound onto exclusive DAK video reel. 4) Tape is hermetically sealed in plastic canister. These operations produce virtually dropout free tape with a full new life expectancy. All tape is splice free.

$14.00

FREE SAMPLE

SEND OR CALL FOR FREE SAMPLES

DAK ENTERPRISES

10845 VANOWEN ST.
NORTH HOLLYWOOD, CALIF. 91605
984-1559 or 877-5884

For Information, Circle 200 on Post Card

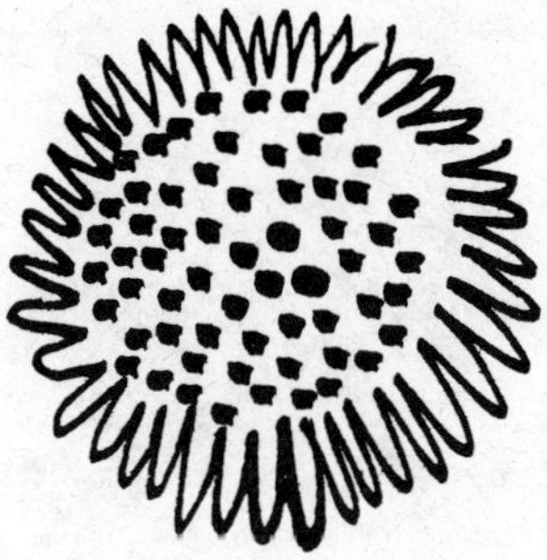

Games

SIMILE II

Simile II is one of the finest producers of learning games. *Starpower* is a classic simulation of a society in which a few people control most of the wealth and mobility is possible but limited. The game can be played using only the instruction book ($3) and some poker chips or colored paper.

Simile II has other games (including some for younger children) and a catalog is free.

SIMILE II
1150 Silverado
La Jolla, Calif. 92037
(714) 459-3719

STARPOWER

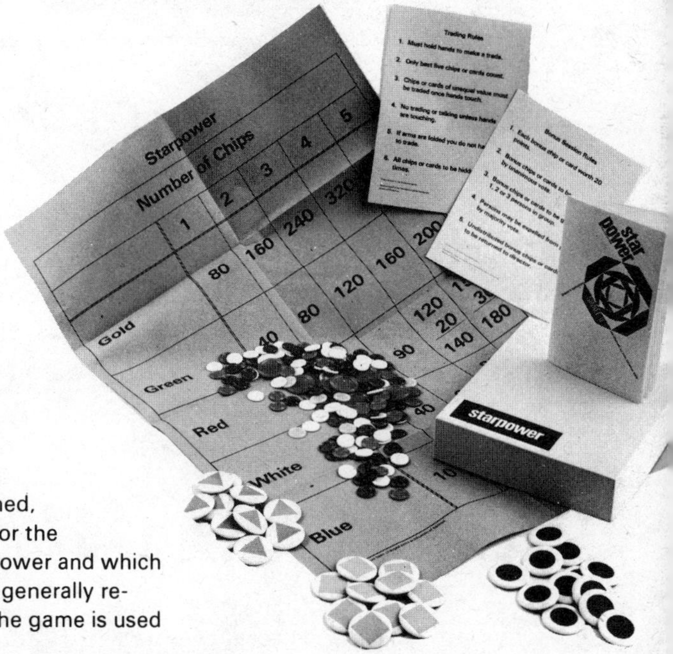

STARPOWER is our most popular game. More than half a million people have participated in the game as of June 1972 by our estimates. It is a game in which a low mobility, three-tiered society is built through the distribution of wealth in the form of chips. Participants have a chance to progress from one level of society to another by acquiring wealth through trading with other participants. Once the society is established, the group with the most wealth is given the right to make the rules for the game. The power group generally make rules which maintain their power and which those being governed consider to be racist, unfair and fascistic. This generally results in some sort of rebellion by the other members of the society. The game is used to stimulate discussions about the uses of power.
A surprising variety of people and institutions have used STARPOWER including prisons, churches, sociologists, urban planners, large and small corporations, The League of Women Voters, and management consulting firms.
STARPOWER can be played in one fifty minute period, if everything is well organized. If possible, however, it is best to plan one and a half hours for the playing of the game and an hour or more for discussion.
For younger students (fourth through sixth grades) we recommend POWDERHORN, the elementary version of STARPOWER. STARPOWER, however, is appropriate for any groups beyond the sixth grade. R. Garry Shirts, author

$3.00 ***for directions on how to make your own kit.***
$25.00 ***for an 18-35 student kit.***

CONFLICT

This is the only simulation, as far as we have been able to determine, which presents students with a specific, concrete proposal for maintaining peace in the world. Participating as national leaders in a disarmed world in the year 1999, the students test the five basic mechanisms of Arthur Waskow's disarmament model: The more consensus the more force, Gradual deterence, Minimal use of force against minimal targets, Major Power veto. Sometimes the students are able to maintain the peace, but other times the model fails and war breaks out. Whatever the outcome, the experience is an exciting way to involve students in thinking about different ways of structuring the future.

Developed by Gerald Thorpe for the World Law Fund. Appropriate for college and high school students. Accommodates 27-42 students. Played in 5-8 periods of 50 minutes each. Available approximately January 1, 1973.

Price tentatively $50.00

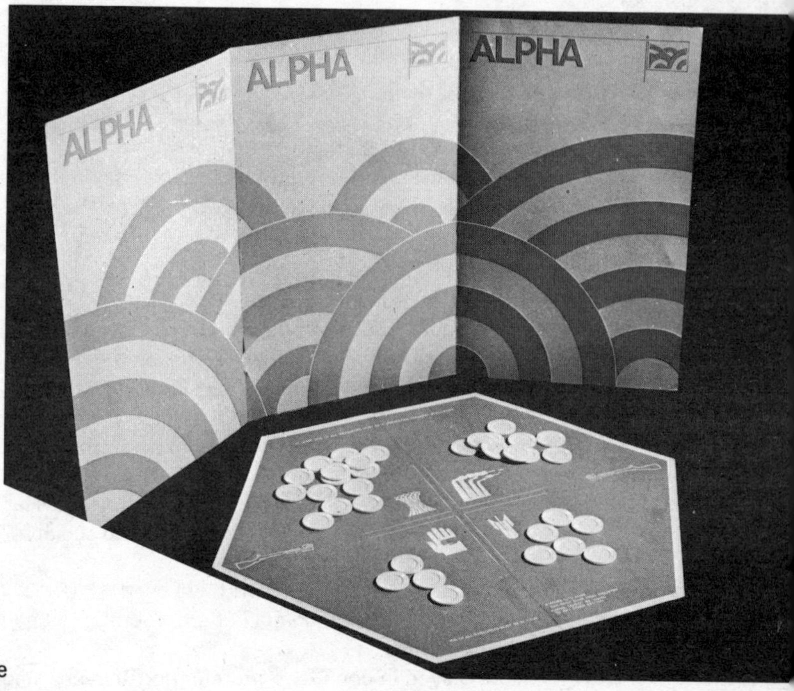

GUNS OR BUTTER

How does an arms race get started?
Is an arms race inevitable in our nation-state system?
How can the system be changed to promote peace?

These are the core issues raised by GUNS OR BUTTER. Participants serve as leaders of nations who try to increase the real wealth of their country and at the same time make sure that it is secure from attack by other nations. Participants can form common markets, trade, establish alliances, defend themselves, and attack other nations. Students get deeply involved in this simulation. It is one of our easiest games to play. Developed by William Nesbitt, author of *Teaching About War and Prevention*. Requires 18-28 students. Appropriate for 7th grade through adult. Requires 1-1/2 hours to play. Can easily be divided into two or more periods.

Price $25.00.

ATLANTIS II

n Atlantis II four families establish pre-industrial society on an island under deal conditions. In the beginning their nly problem is getting enough acreage into roduction to feed their population. Then as their echnology improves they must cope with the problems of scarce rable land, a geometrically increasing population, a surplus of echnicians and the general problems associated with environmental leterioration.

he experience helps the players understand the interrelationship of eople, food, land, and environmental deterioration. Adaptations for special nterest areas such as science, social science and mathematics are suggested. tlantis II can be played by one person or 50, by age groups from junior high onward. t is strictly a decision making game — no dice or spinners. Like chess, Atlantis II vill be played again and again. You may search for, test and prove theories regarding survival n planet earth. Teacher's instructions, ditto master of the island map and decision heets are included. Can easily be fit into almost any time periods.

'od Hodgdon and William Jarvis, authors. Available approximately January 1, 1973.

Price tentatively $10.00

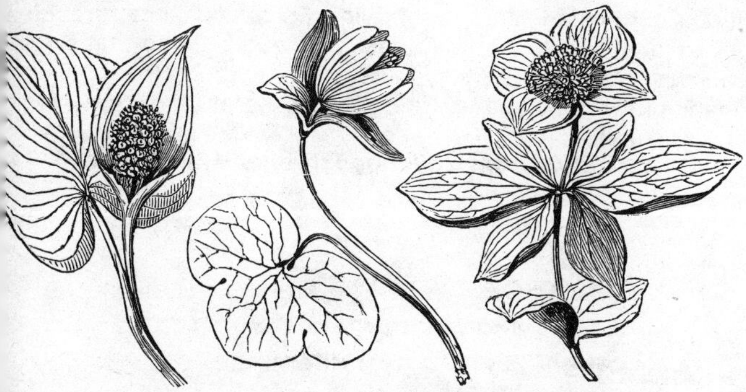

Front cover photos courtesy of: San Diego Police Department and Copley Press.

POLICE PATROL

olice Patrol is an exciting role-playing simulation de-gned to help participants explore their attitudes toward olice and authority, and to broaden their knowledge of the oliceman's job. Through a number of small group incidents they ave the chance to play roles of police, suspected criminals, citizens need of help and to observe and evaluate others. The activity encourages creased understanding of the complexities of law enforcement and the xieties, pressures and fears which affect policemen in patrol cars. Carefully thenticated cases typical of situations which occur in contemporary ban and suburban communities form the incidents around which this role aying simulation takes place. The simulation has been used successfully by teachers and police working improve student and adult understanding of police problems and responsibilities. Police Patrol requires)-35 participants and can be used with 7-12th grade students and with mixed, student-adult groups. Can be scheduled s a one, three or five day (50 minute per day) experience. Includes a teacher's manual, pre- and post-unit attitude urvey, a wall chart, police manuals and observer evaluation form. Todd Clark, of the Constitutional Rights Foundation, author.

ice $10.00.

INTERACT

Interact offers a wide selection of $10 simulation games. Each game is an elaborate unit of study requiring weeks of class time to complete. The games include thirty-five copies of a student guide and one teacher guide. The latter gives objectives, assignments, maps and charts, decision forms, bulletins, tests, bibliography, and a detailed daily sequence of teacher-student activities. Teachers have to supply their own equipment and do a considerable amount of paperwork for each unit.

Interact has games about racial problems, Vietnam, historical periods, archeology, and ecology among others. A complete catalog is free; a partial selection of *Interact* games is described here.

Contact:

INTERACT
P. O. Box 262
Lakeside, Calif. 92040
(714) 443-8762

COPE
A simulation of adapting to change and anticipating the future

This simulation of change and the future focuses attention on questions such as: What are "good" and "bad" futures? Can we "cause" the kind of future we prefer? Can we adapt quickly enough to accelerating change? First, students read and discuss an article called "Coping With Change." The classroom then becomes a think-tank called Technopolis, in which students live through five future time periods, 2000 to 2040 A.D. TIME PERIOD 1: The city is a leisurely intellectual community whose citizens research what the future will be like. TIME PERIOD 2: A complex computer called COMCON helps with information and material problems and asks citizens to provide human in-put for problems that must be solved. TIME PERIOD 3: COMCON, having assimilated all international and intergalaxic computer systems, directs all human activity and requires citizens to learn computer forms and to drastically increase their efficiency and productivity. TIME PERIOD 4: Citizens are forced to learn a new language called FUTURESPEAK and must compete with COMCON to create ever newer and more sophisticated technology. TIME PERIOD 5: COMCON has grown impatient with human inefficiency and tells citizens that human beings are apparently obsolete. COMCON asks citizens to choose between a life of uncaring bliss (COMCON would shoulder all responsibility and work) and a life of constant struggle (COMCON would continue constant change and demand increasing out-put). After this DECISION POINT the simulation ends, and students analyze their ability to adapt to the differing roles they filled during the five time periods. Debriefing centers on the implications of students' findings about change and the future. Students who have experienced the tasks COMCON has assigned them will know first-hand what "future shock" is all about.

(Science Fiction and Social Criticism)

CYCLE
An interaction unit introducing the stages of the human life cycle

Interaction activities help students learn the 8 stages of Eri Erikson's human life cycle (I-Infancy; II-Early Childhood; III-Pla Age; IV-School Age; V-Identity; VI-Young Adulthood; VII Adulthood; VIII-Mature Age). In "problems" seminar groups o stages IV through VIII, boy-girl study pairs analyze case studie of persons whom Erikson would label "healthy" or "unhealthy (e.g., in IV, School Age, a "healthy" child achieves "industry"; a "unhealthy" child experiences "inferiority"). After contactin persons living in various life cycle stages and getting thei opinions about the case studies, the study pairs join "solutions seminar groups that role-play solutions for the huma problems. Each student fills out a DECISION FORM helping hi understand how he values certain activities for persons living i differing life cycle stages. Then in a "life cycle stage" semina group, each student chooses a CONTACT PROJECT that lead him into the world to contact and analyze one person in deptl These CONTACT PROJECTS concentrate on a person' attempts to achieve Erikson's definition of "health" (e.g., "in dustry" in stage IV, "identity" in stage V, "intimacy" in stage V "generativity" in stage VII, and "integrity" in stage VIII). Afte hearing CONTACT PROJECTS reports, students evaluate othe "life patterns" persons have used to explain a human being' journey from birth to death: the Mt. Peak Pattern; the Platea and Drop-Off Pattern; the Ever-Upward Pattern; the Eve Downward Pattern; the Rollercoaster Pattern. Finally, a LIF AND DEATH SURVEY is used as a de-briefing activity to hel students understand how a person's conception of death in fluences how he lives his unique life cycle. The teacher guide in cludes a detailed literature bibliography and an approach t literary analysis keyed to stages IV through VIII so that Englis teachers can use Erikson's life cycle to help their studen meaningfully read, analyze and discuss literature either within c after this unit.

(Literature from Childhood through Mature Age)

BALANCE
A simulation of four families caught in ecological dilemmas

The first hour introduces the concept of ecosystem b simulating the last 150 years' history of an America geographical area: 15 students are animals (mountain lions beavers, jays, trout, etc); 4 are Indians who live in harmony wit their physical environment; the remainder are settlers wh dominate and kill the animals, wipe out the Indians, and subdu the wilderness while their population soars to over 100,000. Sur vivors start BALANCE with a bonus in GASPS (Goal An Satisfaction Points), the scoring system used throughout th simulation. Students are then divided into families of 4 member each living in Ecopolis, their burgeoning city with man ecological problems. Interviewing parents and adults plu reading about American air and water pollution, land usage, an population problems culminate in confrontations over whethe each problem necessitates social action. Within their clas families, students role-play 4 different identities on 4 differen occasions: father, mother, young adult, and adolescent. Eac family then fills out a Family Decision Form which tests its abilit to balance short-range economic-hedonistic goals with long range environmental goals. Before an essay evaluation end BALANCE, students conduct an ecological survey of their rea community and hold a one hour Forum in which they argu about the ecological balance of their own environmen

(Transcendentalists and/or Modern Nature Writers)

HERSTORY **A simulation of male and female roles emphasizing the American woman's circumstances, past and present**

Paired by chance, boy-girl study couples join seminar groups that study male-female role expectations. During separate 3-day cycles students examine different American marital relationships: traditional marriage, androgynous marriage, collective family, living together. Ceremonies attending such relationships are thoroughly analyzed (e.g., the religious service in traditional marriage and the written marriage contract in androgynous marriage). Students simulate aspects of marriage such as who does the domestic work and who makes key decisions. Scholarship is central to each cycle as seminar group members read and observe information substantiating or attacking HYPS (hypotheses) and then report their findings to their group. The 44 HYPS are divided into four categories on the history and position of women: manners-courtship; marriage and divorce; jobs, achievements, reform; nature-nurture. During each cycle all students also participate in and evaluate role-playing of contemporary sexual problems. Other activities include 66 SISTERS research into the contributions of American women, past and present; a two day simulation of the first women's rights convention at Seneca Falls, New York, 1848; a CONTACT PROJECT in which students examine sexual roles in the *real* world; a FUTURE FORUM in which groups discuss what they *hope* and *expect* American sexual roles will be in 2025 A.D.; pre and post MALE-FEMALE SURVEYS to chart attitude changes. HERSTORY helps young persons crystallize sexual identities during this era of change and future shock.

(Women in Literature)

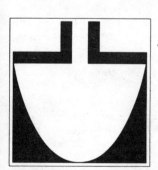

DIG

A simulation of the archeological reconstruction of a vanished civilization

DIG Divided into two competing teams with the task of secretly creating two cultures, each team in the class first writes a description of its hypothetical civilization. This description stresses the interrelationship of cultural patterns: economics, government, family, language, religion and recreation. After designing and then constructing artifacts which reflect their civilization's cultural patterns, team members carefully place these artifacts in the ground, according to the archeological principles learned during the simulation.* Then each team scientifically excavates, restores, analyzes, and reconstructs the other team's artifacts and culture. A final confrontation reveals how creatively and how perceptively each team has applied the archeological principles they have experienced. In final discussion students use what they have learned inductively about patterns of culture to analyze their own American civilization.

* If time and situation do not allow an actual archeological dig, the teacher may have students bury their artifacts in large sawdust-filled boxes in the classroom or may have students simply exchange their artifacts.

EQUALITY

A simulation of the struggle for racial equality in a typical American city

EQUALITY Students first write imaginary diaries of their lives as Uglies, slaves on the advanced planet of Fantasia. Inductively they discover what happens to free individuals' personalities when someone "owns" their bodies and therefore controls their lives. Next students draw colored ID tags (white, yellow, red, brown, or black signifying an ethnic background). These tags contain role information: age, general description, education, occupation, address. Then students move into classroom neighborhoods. Independence, their mythical city of 340,000, has 6 neighborhoods from a black ghetto to Tranquillity Estates with $75,000 homes. Students study and discuss 5 short essays on the history of black Americans. The citizens of Independence role-play certain incidents involving tension between minority groups. From daily studying and role-playing, students increase their IMPS (self-image points) and enter them on their IMPS BALANCE SHEETS. However, pressure cards are regularly handed out which give or take away IMPS. These pressure cards also act as news bulletins relating community problems that stem from racial misunderstanding. A community crisis arises over whether or not to integrate the schools. After a community meeting, each neighborhood's school board member votes for or against integration. During a final de-briefing session students discuss their own beliefs and feelings about racial problems in urban America and evaluate the simulation as a learning strategy.

"But somebody may try to close the schools."

"Should I vote YES or NO?"

EDU-GAME

$1.50 Simulation Games? . . . . A group of California high school teachers have designed a series of social studies simulation games now for sale at only $1.50 each. And they work.

Nationalism: War or Peace has students assume the roles of government officials in seven fictitious nations. In an attempt to accumulate wealth the nations are required to enter into trade agreements, and defensive and offensive alliances. Each nation is faced with the dread or temptation of war in an attempt to win the game. The actual game is described in about 10 mimeo pages. Twelve pages need to be typed and duplicated for student use. The game leaves a bit to be desired in its rendition of reality but even the discrepancies can be a valuable part of the debriefing process.

Low Income Housing Project has students play roles in the town of Middleville. The town has been given federal money to build a low income housing project for minority groups. The citizens of the town are assigned the task of deciding where the project will be built. This game requires the teacher to duplicate only three pages of material for student use. It is designed to help teach the concept of compromise, attitudes toward low income housing, and forms and effects of racial prejudice.

First Amendment Freedoms uses a mock trial set up to consider freedom of speech, religion and assembly. Actual Supreme Court cases are used as the "script" for the game and students assume the roles of courtroom personnel. Playing time of 5 class periods is a bit longer than the other games.

Other games available include: "Political Polution, Government and the Ecology Issue," "Planning an Inner-City High School," "National Priorities," "Government Reparations for Minorities," and a large selection of games relating to specific periods and incidents in American history.

Each game costs $1.50 from Edu-Game, P.O. Box 1144, Sun Valley, Calif. 91352.

UNITED STATES GOVERNMENT

PLANNING THE CITY OF GREENVILLE - A simulation activity i which the students are presented with a city planning problem. This activity illustrates the major problems in urban development and the complexities of satisfying many special interests. An open-ended activity which raises many questions and which should stimulate additional research and discussion.
(Approximate time: 2 class periods. Grade levels 7-12.)
$1.50.

POLITICAL POLLUTION - GOVERNMENT AND THE ECOLOGY ISSUE - Students assume the role of various civic and private groups in fictitious states. They are presented with a realistic ecological problem. This simulation game helps the students understand the difficulties and complexities in the attempted solution of an important issue.
(Approximate time: 5 class periods. Grade levels 7-12.)
$1.50.

CRISIS IN MIDDLETOWN - A SIMULATION IN LABOR RELATIONS - A simulation game which creates an atmosphere of labor unrest in a semi-urban community. The students assume various community roles in an attempt to solve this labor crisis. Community cooperation is emphasized but special interests and major value differences complicate the problem. Illustrates contemporary labor problems in a most dramatic way.
(Approximate time: 3-4 class periods. Grade levels 7-12.)
$1.50.

EXCHANGE - A STOCK MARKET ACTIVITY - Exchange is a simulation activity in which the operation of the stock market is analyzed. "Stock clubs" are formed which give the students a realistic appreciation of the process for buying and selling stock.
(Approximate time: 5 class periods. Grade levels 7-12.)
$1.50.

NATIONALISM: WAR OR PEACE - A simulation game in which the students assume the roles of various government officials in seven fictitious nations. In an attempt to accumulate the most wealth they are forced to enter into trade agreements, defensive alliances, and offensive alliances. They are continually faced with the choice of pursuing a policy of peace or war in an attempt to achieve their national goal.
(Approximate time: 5 class periods. Grade levels 7-12.)
$1.50.

UNITED STATES GOVERNMENT

PLANNING THE INNER-CITY HIGH SCHOOL - A simulation activity in which the students assume various roles within an inner-city community. Their purpose is to make recommendations for the development and organization of a new high school in the community. The problems of urban minorities and urban education become the subjects for exciting discussion.
(Approximate time: 2 class periods. Grade levels 7-12.)
$1.50.

LOW INCOME HOUSING PROJECT - A simulation game whereby students are given the opportunity of having an active interest in a community trying to decide the location of a low income housing project which will be occupied by minority groups.
(Approximate time: 3 class periods. Grade levels 7-12.)
$1.50.

GOVERNMENT REPARATIONS FOR MINORITY GROUPS - Through the simulation of Senate sub-committee hearings the students will investigate whether or not the government owes reparations to certain minority groups.
(Approximate time: 3-5 class periods. Grade levels 7-12.)
$1.50.

NATIONAL PRIORITIES - A simulation activity which dramatizes the diversification of public opinion on important topics of national interest. Students attempt to arrive at a consensus of opinion through negotiation.
(Approximate time: 1-2 class periods. Grade levels 7-12.)
$1.50.

FIRST AMENDMENT FREEDOMS - A simulation activity in which three important constitutional freedoms are debated in mock trial situations. Freedom of religion, speech, and assembly, are discussed from the point of view of actual Supreme Court cases. The students assume such roles as judge, defense attorney, prosecuting attorney, trial assistant, witness, and juror. The students are given an opportunity to arrive at their own decisions by analyzing the facts and interpreting the Constitution.
(Approximate time: 5 class periods. Grade levels 9-12.)
$1.50.

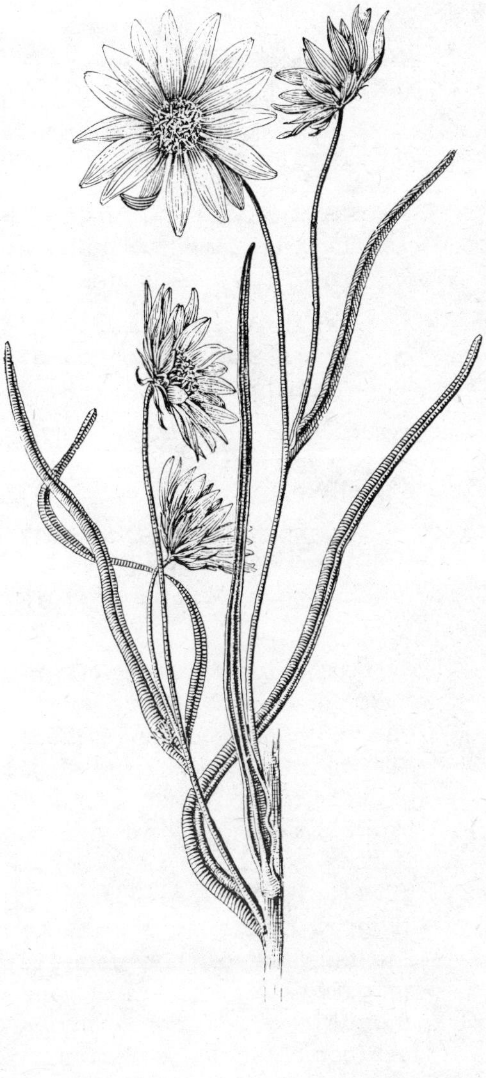

EDU-GAME

Creative Classroom Activities

P.O. Box 1144
Sun Valley, California 91352

ACADEMIC GAMES ASSOCIATES

PUBLICATIONS

Bibliographies

1. "SIMULATION, SIMULATION GAMES, GAMING: A Selected Bibliography of the Publications of Associates and Affiliates of Academic Games Associates" (Judith G. Livingston, Autumn, 1972), 8 pages, $1.00.
2. "REVIEWS, EVALUATIONS, RESEARCH STUDIES: A Selected Bibliography of Publications Based on the Simulation Games Developed by Academic Games Associates" (Judith G. Livingston, Autumn, 1972), 6 pages, $.75.

Practical Papers

1. "How to Design a Simulation Game" (Samuel A. Livingston, Revised 1972), 2 pages, $.25
2. "Six Ways to Design a Bad Simulation Game" (Samuel A. Livingston, 1972, 2 pages, $.25.
3. "Writing the Director's Manual for a Simulation Game: Some Guidelines" (Gail M. Fennessey, 1972), 9 pages, $1.25.

Payment must accompany order.

ACADEMIC GAMES ASSOCIATES, INC.
430 East Thirty-Third Street
Baltimore, Md. 21218

The Drug Debate (Karen C. Cohen, 1970) creates a structured debate in which young people present opposing viewpoints concerning legalization or prohibition of many drugs and related products in use today. Winning or losing the game is determined by relative effectiveness in changing the group's opinions about these products. The purpose of the game is to encourage informative, reasoned, and relatively unemotional discussion. A Player's Handbook, with background information on the types, use, costs, medical effects, and legal status of these drugs and products, is provided for each participant. The Coordinator's Manual, with full instructions for administering the game, and all score sheets are included. An evaluation instrument enables assessment of how effectively the issues have been debated.

Number of Players: 6 - 35
Playing Time: 45 min. per debate
Age Level: 12 - Adult
Price: $25.00 plus postage

High School simulates the process by which students allocate time and effort to various school activities in order to gain esteem from peers and parents, and ultimately to gain self-esteem. It also simulates the effect of the "social climate" of a school on students' behavior.

High School is a board game designed for approximately six players assuming roles of high school students, three rounds in each game, each round representing one year of high school. During each round, students invest their time in academic, athletic, and social activities in order to win esteem points from their parents, their peers, and themselves.

Each student is assigned a profile of his abilities for academic, athletic, and social achievement. These ability levels, together with an added component of chance, determine the rate at which the player can advance in each of the activities. Achievement in any activity is partially determined by a player's assigned ability in that activity and partially by the amount of time he chooses to spend in pursuing that activity. Achievement brings esteem from parents and peers, depending on the value placed by these reference groups on each activity. By varying the pay-off matrices for parent and peer esteem, different value climates may be simulated. Players assign their own value weightings which, strategically, should be influenced by the abilities of their student profile and the parent and peer value climates of their school. A system of friendship exchange enables players to negotiate bargains that may advance them further along the activity routes, thus maximizing their final score. The pull of team sports is simulated by an athletic team route which brings bonus esteem to all players in the game when the boys in the school invest enough time in athletics to advance the team marker to a group goal.

High School has been used with high school students, college students, and teachers. Its purpose is to increase understanding of the manner in which the social environment influences behavior. It may thus be used as a means of explicating the social system of the high school to students and teachers, and as a springboard for further study of the sociological concepts which underlie the game model.

Number of Players: 6
Playing Time: 2 hours
Age Level: 16 - Adult

Developed by:
Academic Games Associates, Inc.
(c) 1972 by James S. Coleman,
Constance J. Seidner.

GENERATION RAP

Generation Rap is a board game to be played by kids and parents. Through talking, listening, understanding, and a little bit of luck players move toward a common meeting ground. The first player who reaches that "middle ground" wins the game since that player has obviously done the most to meet the other players halfway.

Some squares instruct players to draw a card. Kids cards and parents cards present situations which have to be resolved. If a kid draws a card he must present a solution to the card. If that solution is accepted by his parents he may move forward as instructed. If the parents reject his solution they must select a parents Risk Card which usually penalizes their nonacceptance. The same procedure follows when a parent lands on a "Draw Parents' Card" square.

The purpose of the game is to stimulate family talk about values and attitudes that often are left unexamined.

$8 from:

EVI VENTURES
209 Court Street
Middletown, Conn. 06457

GENERATION RAP

KIDS CARD

YOU!

You! is a crisis resolution game set by Charles Beamer. The material in the game is a 64-page teaching guide and a series of 28 cards. Each of the cards deals with a different topic including drug use, birth control for teenage girls, long hair, pornography, tolerance, aggression and student participation in school administration. Each of the cards is similar to the popular *Squirms* role-playing sheets giving a sticky situation for role players to resolve.

The teaching guide is well developed and raises the game above simply another list of role playing situations. Teaching ideas include an explanation of how to apply value clarification techniques to the role-plays.

The cards and booklet costs $12.50 (20% off for 20 or more games ordered) from Miller Productions, 800 West Avenue, Box 5584, Austin, TX 78763.

Game 2: Birth Control Pills for Teenage Girls

Players Required: Girl (**Player A**), Parent (**Player B**), and School Assistant Principal (**Player C**).

Situation: A school nurse has found a birth control pill dispenser in **Player** A's purse. She was upset, contacted the Assistant Principal, who has called the girl and one parent in for a conference. The parent was not aware the girl was taking the pills.

Problem Statement: **Player A** wants the others to accept reality, i.e., young people indulge in sex before marriage. She emphasizes that she is not promiscuous. She is going with a boy she loves very much, but whom she cannot marry because of age and finances. She doesn't say that taking the pills is right or wrong. She says that teenagers should be human beings without worrying about unwanted pregnancies. She must make her position understood to the others.

Player B, the parent, is shocked. She says her daughter is wrong – wrong to engage in sex, wrong to take the pills. **Player B** must try to convince **Player A** she is morally wrong without putting distance between them, and without allowing a communications breakdown.

Player C believes essentially the same as B, but he is more concerned with the effect **Player A's** behavior has on the other girls. **Player C** must come to some solution of the problem that will protect the other girl students.

TELL IT LIKE IT IS — THE UNGAME

Tell it like it is!! *The Ungame* is played by 3 - 6 persons and is designed to be a sort of interpersonal ice breaker. Players draw cards while moving around the board. The cards ask questions such as "What do you most like about yourself?" or "What is the best advice you ever received?" The idea is that in answering the questions the players get to know each other on a deeper level than is ordinary in game playing. Many would object to the highly structured approach to interpersonal relations, others would find the game threatening or simply dumb; there are some situations in which a teacher might be able to use *Ungame* to some benefit.

An individual game for 3 - 6 players is $7.95, a Group Pak for up to 30 players is $37.50 from:

AU-VID
P.O. Box 964
Garden Grove, Calif. 92642

SQUIRMS

If you've heard a lot of good things about role playing lately but have been hesitant to try it yourself, what you need is a can of squirms from **Contemporary Drama Service.**

The Squirms (that's what they make the players do) are really situations printed on papers (pink for girls, blue for boys) inside a can. The role player (called in the instruction "me alone") picks one squirm and reads it to the group; one other role player is the antagonist. The situations are really squirmy. For example, "You just chickened out of a date with a boy and had your mother tell him you were ill. The next day you meet him at a tennis court." Or another, "You are asked by a friend to buy a camera which you really do want at a very cheap price. You finally find out that the camera is lifted from a big department store, but are still tempted to buy it from your friend." To make matters even more interesting, the other role player is "another person who has been shoplifting." The can of squirms comes complete with a leader's guide and discussion questions for slow starters, directions for making the role playing into a game with two teams, a scoring system, twenty squirms and a scoring pad and pencil. Price is $5 each, 2-pack for $8, 6-pack for $12.

TEENAGE SQUIRM (High School) . . . . . . BOY #5

ME ALONE: Frank, who crashes a party wishes he could stop.

SITUATION: You hear that there's a Pajama Party of girls at Ruth Anderson's house. You gather together a group of boys and crash the party with three six-packs of beer. After about an hour the party gets really wild. There is no chaperone. Ruth Anderson's parents are out of town and her older sister is out for the evening. You suddenly realize that the responsibility for this event, and its consequences, is all yours. All of the boys are feeling high on the beer and the girls are feeling silly, too. All are acting without responsibility. You try to talk sense to them but nobody will listen. What do you do?

OTHER PERSONS: Two of the wild ones at the party.

ADULT SQUIRM . . . . WOMAN #19

ME ALONE: Sue, a lonely wife in a strange town.

SITUATION: Part of Gary's (your husband) new promotion required that you move to Lakeview Heights. Gary, with his job and new people at work, is very happy. However, it is hard for you to meet new people in this strange town and you are lonely. With Gary's new job come more responsibilities, and he has to work late a good many evenings leaving you alone. There is a young man with whom you have developed a nodding acquaintance at the shopping center. Seeing you alone, he has invited you to have dinner with him. Gary will be working and you can't face another evening alone. The young man has been most polite and is quite attractive and ... you'd like to go. How do you answer him?

OTHER PERSON: The young man at the shopping center.

COLLEGE LEVEL . . . . . FEMALE STUDENT #11

ME ALONE: Janice, who discovers herself at a "pot-smoking party".

SITUATION: Your new date, Don Riddle, is a fun person, but with him apparently anything goes. He's taken you to this "groovy party" with his swinging friends and you are suddenly aware of an odd odor in the air. You suspect it is the smoke of marijuana cigarettes and you ask him. "Sure" he says, "this is a pot party. Hey, someone, pass Janice a joint." You are assured by everyone that it cannot hurt you and it is not habit-forming. Everyone is solicitous but you really don't like them and you feel no desire to "smoke pot". But you do like Don and you don't want to disappoint him. What do you do?

OTHER PERSON: Don Riddle, her date who thinks smoking marijuana is an okay kind of fun.

CONTEMPORARY DRAMA SERVICE
Arthur Meriwether, Inc.
P.O. Box 457
Downers Grove, Ill. 60515

HANG-UP

Hang-Up is a game designed to be played by teens and adults, as well as by groups that mix the two generations. In this game, you start "hung up" and move around the board, encountering a number of stress situations which may bring out your "hang ups." The game's object is to get around the board and free yourself from hang ups. Hang Ups are acted out in pantomine, charading the emotions felt in stress situations. The game is very simple to learn and even easier to teach.

Hang Up is designed to catch people in racial stereotyping and to increase empathy for the problems of prejudice. The stress situations and hang-ups bring out ordinarily dormant racism especially in people who still associate racism with slavery and the deep South while refusing to see their own prejudice.

Players are either white or black from turn to turn, depending on the dice roll. One stress situation reads "Your black friend is beginning to prefer being with other blacks." The player might have the connected hang up "To hide your low opinion of yourself, you use a false front of superiority." The player this turn is black and has to decide how this affects his assumed identity. If he views his low self-opinion as the over-riding factor, then he would be hung up. On the other hand he might believe that, being black, he would not be bothered by the situation. He explains his feelings to the others in the game and plays accordingly.

The impact of race is as inescapable in the game as in life. But in the game there is much discussion about each decision and what is hidden in real life becomes visible in playing the game. Much of the game's impact depends on the interaction among the players and their discussion of the decisions and hang-ups. The game also helps players become more aware of their real hang-ups, although this is not a stated purpose of the game.

The game is well designed, fun to play, easy to learn, and a true experience in learning. Humorous situations are built into the game as are rules protecting those who are more inhibited about acting out feelings. Postpaid in a large mailing tube for $15.75 from Synectics Education Systems, 121 Brattle St., Cambridge, Ma. 02138. Synectics also has other teaching materials dealing with developing creativity. Ask for a free catalog.

THE VALUES GAME

THE VALUES GAME is an interaction game that takes about 10 minutes to learn, costs only $6 and is a non-threatening way to introduce a group of 3-6 people to each other's values.

The game uses a spinner to advance players around the board. On each turn a card is drawn containing a topic or statement such as women's rights, the death penalty, magazines I suscribe to and why, trial marriages, how I use my leiusre time, and more. A player speaks on the card's topic for 60 seconds or is interviewed by the other players for three minutes. A player may invite challenge and has to make other value judgements on the way around the board. A player may decline to comment on any topic without penalty.

The game will not produce profound new insights in players and experienced gamers will find it simplistic but it will serve to set the stage for value education. Intended for religious education but easily adapted to local needs.

$5.95 from Orbis Books, Maryknoll, N.Y. 10545.

PERSONALYSIS

PERSONALYSIS is a simple game designed to evaluate and possibly improve self-knowledge. 3-4 can play with each game. Each person receives a card containing a list of personality traits such as energy, stability, objectivity, naturalness, sensitivity, intelligence, seriousness, etc. A particular trait is chosen by chance and each person marks a 1-5 rating. One person marks a score for himself while the others mark how he appears to them. The more agreement there is between the self-rating and the rating of others the more accurate is the player's self-image.

The game is not highly threatening and works well with the right group. An atmosphere of trust and willingness is needed in the group for the game to be educational. The traits rated could easily be revised if deemed necessary.

One set enables a number of groups to play the game, although not at the same time. $3 from Administrative Research Associates, Irvine Town Center, Box 4211, Irvine, California 92664.

WHY AM I AFRAID TO TELL YOU WHO I AM?

Why Am I Afraid to Tell You Who I Am? has been a best-selling small paperback from Argus Press. They now have made available a series of cards illustrating the various roles-people-play discussed in the book. A few activities are suggested. 40 heavy-stock cards cost $2.95 from:

ARGUS COMMUNICATIONS
7440 Natchez Avenue
Niles, Ill. 60648

SOME SUGGESTED ACTIVITIES

1. Ask two or three students each to select a card. Have them interact in a situation of their choosing, demonstrating in front of the class the characteristics of the roles selected. Discuss what communication difficulties result and why. Repeat the activity with new players.

2. Give each student a different card, and ask each student to write a story about the character he was given. Without using real names students should try to make up a story around a real person they know who is guilty of playing that role. The story can be part fiction, part true.

3. Display all the cards at once, perhaps by pinning them all on a bulletin board. Ask students to identify for themselves the roles or games they play, and explain to themselves why they think they rely on their particular roles. This should be done privately and handed in anonymously. The results should be read to the class.

4. Have each student select a card from the deck, not revealing to anyone else which role he has selected. Each should act out his

role as best he can (verbally or non-verbally) while the others guess what role he is playing. He may use props but not another person to clarify his portrayal.

5. Ask a student to select a card from the deck. Without revealing which role he has selected, he interacts with another student and demonstrates the characteristics of the role. The second student responds to the first honestly, as he would if he really encountered such a person playing this role. Discuss what reactions, responses and defenses are caused by one who plays such a role.

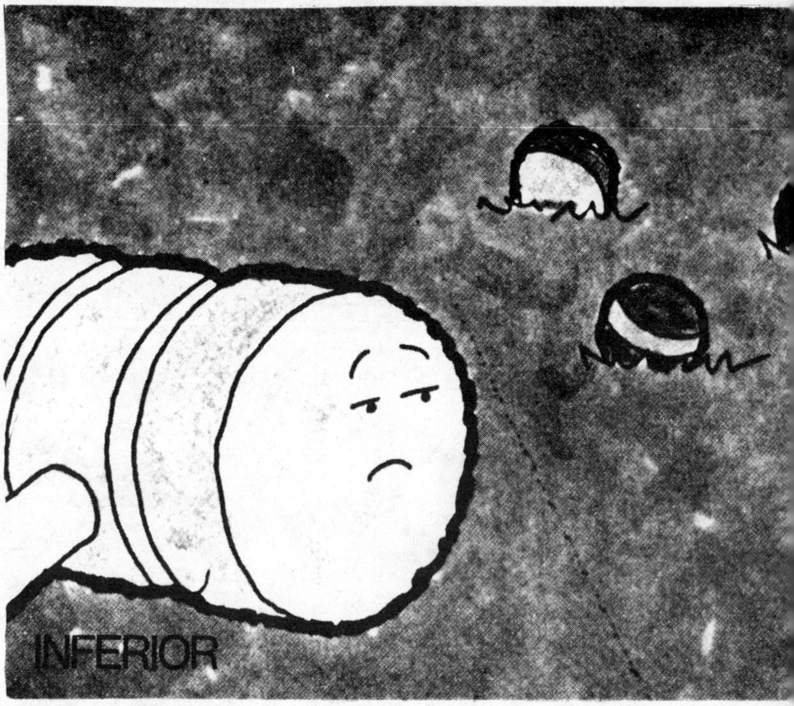

FEELIN'

Feelin' is available from:

ARGUS COMMUNICATIONS
7440 Natchez Avenue
Niles, Ill. 60648
(312) 647-7800

This game is designed to explore personal feelings and some of the variables that affect feelings. It is based on the belief that honest recognition of feelings is one of the first steps to understanding self and improving the quality of relationships.
Rarely are our feelings simple; rather, they are shades between extremes and a complex movement of many different feelings experienced at the same time.

FEELIN' consists of the following:

1. The FEELIN' Game Board
2. Deck of 30 SUBJECT CARDS
3. 36 Wooden Tokens

The number of participants should not exceed 6.

The FEELIN' Game Board consists of 16 feeling continua. These depict two opposite feelings with space in between representing intensity, gradations or shades moving from the extreme of one emotion to the extreme of its opposite. There are numerous continua because we usually experience more than one feeling at a time. The deck of 30 SUBJECT CARDS consists of topics or areas of interest common to most of us. The WILD CARD in the deck indicates that the choice of subject is open to the participants. Each player should have 6 same-color tokens.

One of the players draws a SUBJECT CARD from the deck. If any participant objects to or has a reservation about the subject drawn, then another card should be drawn. Without talking, all the players take a few moments to explore their feelings regarding the subject selected.
Then each person places his colored markers along any of the continua that apply to his feelings about the particular subject. Each places his markers on any of the locations that best represent his positions with respect to his feelings. The areas at the two ends of each continuum indicate that the feeling is especially strong. A participant should place his colored marker on this area if he feels any of the listed feelings in a strong, significant way. Or the participant may place a colored marker in the S.O.F. (Some Other Feeling) Zone if his particular feeling(s) is not included on any of the continua.
When all have put down their markers, each explains how his positions on the continua correspond to his feelings. If the level of caring and trust is high enough, participants may ask questions of each other, but the answerer is always allowed to "PASS" if he prefers not to answer.

This completes one round. To play again, draw another card and repeat the process.
Variations on this basic game are numerous

VALUING

Valuing: Exploration and Discovery is a four-unit audio-visual kit focusing on trust, value formation, and change.

The kit is for use by classes, families, or work groups. Each unit can be used for one or more sessions, depending on the wishes of the group. Each session will last approximately one and one-half hours.

Unit I - Values and Change: Basic Principles. Contains six value cards and a cassette.

Unit II - Examining Personal Values. Contains a test, spirit master, and evaluation.

Unit III - Values in Listening: An Experience in Communication. A cassette.

Unit IV - Applying Values: Three Experiences in Role-Playing and Sculpturing. Three role-play cards.

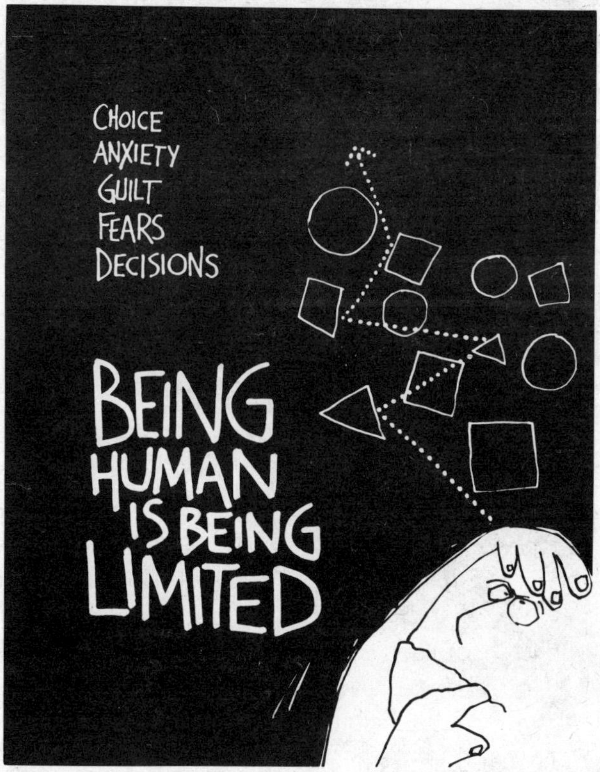

The entire kit is $17.50 from:

ARGUS COMMUNICATIONS
7440 Natchez Avenue
Niles, Ill. 60648
(312) 647-7800

Unit I

Card #3: Human Limitations

SUMMARY:

Making choices is difficult. Faced with such decisions, it is natural for us to feel anxious, guilty, afraid. We are all limited in our ability to make creative choices. Recognition of this helps us to keep these feelings in proper perspective so they do not prevent us from making responsible decisions.

SUGGESTIONS:

1. Have each person list on a sheet of paper what he or she thinks are human limitations in general — physical, mental, emotional.
2. Have each one list what he considers his own particular limitations.
3. Have each person give concrete examples of the types of choices he should *not* make, based on his personal limitations.
4. Have each one make a list of creative possibilities for his own future, based on personal limitations.
5. Ask the group to react to each one.

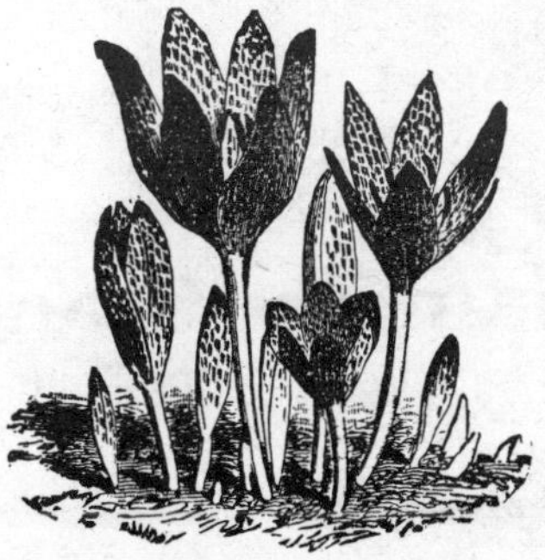

ADL HUMAN RELATIONS GAMES

Anti-Defamation League of B'nai B'rith
315 Lexington Avenue
New York, N.Y. 10016

For a Multi-Ethnic Elementary or Secondary School

Confrontation

Developed by The Far West Laboratory

The filmed confrontation episodes are each introduced by Dr. Staten Webster, University of California (Berkeley). At the end of each episode, a question mark signals the time for the leader to stop the camera and the participants to note their reactions.

The object: To raise the participants' consciousness of deeply imbedded attitudes and institutionalized procedures that can—and do—foster unhealthy human relations among members of a school community.

Part II of each of the four sound films is directed to the discussion leaders, and is geared to train them in the techniques of guiding participants through analysis, understanding, and implementation.

The Unit contains

■ One 16mm overview film (b&w; 6 mins.) called **Introduction to Human Relations.**

■ Four 16mm confrontation films (b&w; from 18-31 mins. each): **School-Community** (how procedures and attitudes of school personnel can alienate visitors); **Alienating Language** (how a teacher's words and expressions can offend, even when intended as positive); **Rules and Regulations** (how dress codes, etc. can affect teacher-student relations); **Violent Confrontation** (how dealing with civil rights issues in the classroom can result in confrontation).

■ A **Coordinator's Handbook** (64 pp. 7" x 10")

■ A **Discussion Leader's Guide** (24 pp. 7" x 10")

Unit purchase price: $410.00 (Available also for rental and/or preview.)
$50 $25

For a School That Has Become Predominantly Black

Needham: The Changing High School

Developed by Dr. Frederick P. Venditti

Lee Arnold has been created to grapple with the problems of Needham High. His/her words are printed on the screen so that all participants, regardless of sex or race, may identify. Both filmed and written incidents are included in the game, along with many opportunities for group role-play.

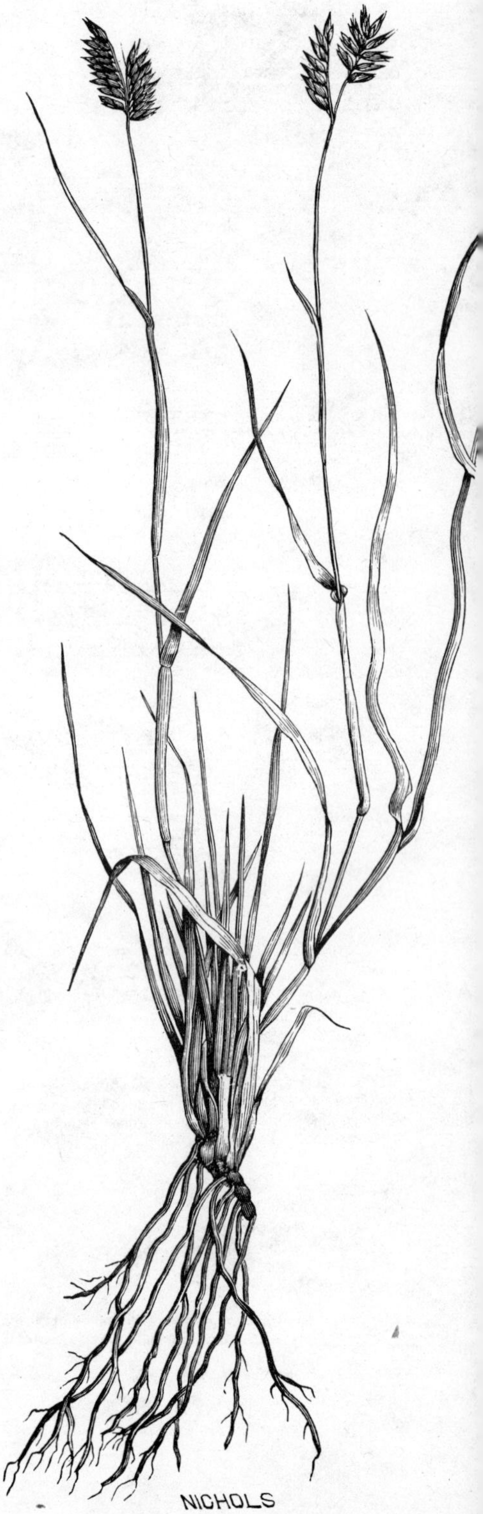

The Unit contains

■ One 16mm sound film (color; 26 mins.) with 11 problem incidents: "Is what we do in school going to help us later on?"; white teachers won't supervise after-school clubs; white teachers feel community pressure; white female teacher reacts to a black student's compliments; white teacher "at the end of her rope"; integrated faculty friction; teacher-principal relations; faculty favoritism; non-student in the building; school-community strain; rising racial tensions among students.

■ Six combination **Program Director/Group Leader Manuals** with synopses, discussion guides, and questions for all 11 filmed episodes, plus 3 written incidents; procedural outlines; background on the school and the community. 95 pp. 7" x 10".

■ Fifty **Participant's Workbooks** with background on the school and the community, incident response sheets for each of the 14 incidents. 68 pp. 7" x 10".

■ Fifty Bibliographies.

Unit purchase price: $290.00 (Available also for rental and/or preview.)
$115.00 $15.00

Helping Administrators... Teachers...Teacher-Trainees Deal With Change

For a desegregated **secondary** school

Lakemont/Solving Multi-Ethnic Problems

Developed by Dr. Frederick P. Venditti

Format identical to **Valleybrook**. This time, the teacher's name is Sandy Johnson and the confrontations depicted are more appropriate to older students.

The Unit contains

■ One 16mm sound film (color; 18 mins.) with 6 episodes: integrating an all-white school club; black pride; "How can we get our parents to care more about school?"; class does not accept a teacher's authority; Afro clothing; black father/white students.

■ A **Program Director's Manual,** as above, with 5 additional written incidents (including variations for schools with large black or Puerto Rican populations).

■ Five **Guidebooks for Leaders of Small Groups,** as above.

■ Fifty **Participant's Handbooks,** as above.

■ Fifty **Participant's Workbooks,** as above.

■ Fifty Bibliographies.

■ Five sets of role-play sheets.

Unit purchase price: $318.50 (Available also for rental and/or preview.)
$203.50 $15.00

A Word About Background and Testing . . .

Dr. Venditti is the Director of the Educational Opportunities Planning Center, University of Tennessee, and has been an innovator in education for twenty years. In developing his three simulation games, Dr. Venditti went right to the source – the classroom teacher. Every incident he used surfaced from interviews and/or questionnaires from a number of different, real schools.

The Far West Laboratory for Educational Research proceeded in a similar way to create **Confrontation.** The problem incidents were developed from actual classroom experiences in the Oakland and San Francisco school systems, and the films were extensively pre-tested for authenticity, importance, and capacity for involvement.

COMMUNITY DECISIONS GAMES

A series of activities to involve the full class as a "community" in exploring and discussing local issues—and contending with the realities of interest conflicts and value conflicts.

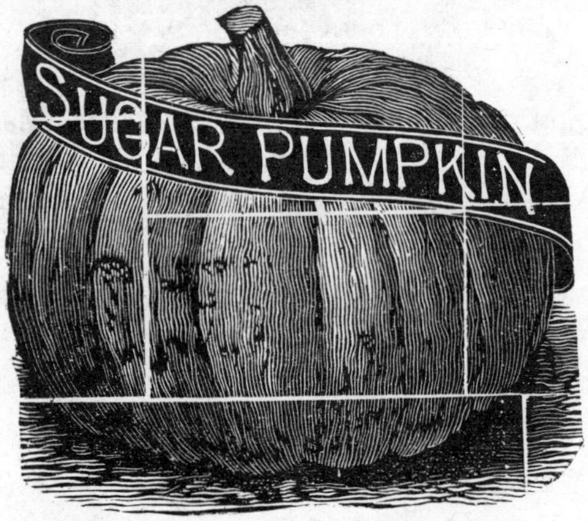

Each *Community Decisions Game* has three rounds. In each round, the class is divided into six "interest groups" of approximately equal size (public officials, manufacturers, small businessmen, and three consumer-voter groups). Each "interest group" receives an individual decision card detailing the issue at hand in the round and also circumstances which may condition the group's response in one way or the other. A large poster is used in each round to present general information (by way of maps, tables, diagrams, or words for the total "community" about the issue at hand.) After appropriate discussion, each group indicates its own decision by punching out the edge of one of five holes opposite the available decisions. A scorer (teacher or student) then collects each group's card and uses a stylus to sort the cards in McBee card fashion and thus reveal the degree to which the various groups succeeded or failed in reaching consensus (that is, all six cards will "drop" from the pack at one point if the groups have reached unanimous agreement and the highest possible score; various other scores are produced by combinations of decisions). In general, the amount of communication possible among groups and the amount of information available will grow from round to round. A four-page leader's guide describes ways in which the game can be used as stimulus for extensive research and "information campaign" activities. Each classroom unit consists of 24 large decision cards (8 x 3 rounds) and three posters. The game cards can be used as consumable items, but instructions are also given for repeated use.

New School

One of Rockland's two middle schools, the Dewey School, is badly overcrowded and in need of repair. The school board recommends that the community approve funds for a new Dewey School. Some members of a taxpayers' group, however, argue that it might be wiser to repair Dewey School and build an addition if more space is needed. Some members of the local booster club would like to see Rockland replace both of its middle schools with one big new school, complete with swimming pool and community facilities. Some parents and teachers think the community should talk about how education programs might change before deciding what kind of building it needs. The discussion climaxes with a public hearing.

EVI 3001 New Highway $4
EVI 3002 Open Space $4
EVI 3003 New School $4
EVI 3004 Budgets and Taxes $4

From:
EDUCATION VENTURES
209 Court Street
Middletown, Ct. 06457

WORLD WITHOUT WAR GAME

THE WORLD WITHOUT WAR GAME is actually a closely structured weekend experience for a group of 20-40 designed to lead to individual efforts at peace making. The "game" requires a complete weekend and includes role playing, films, readings, rap sessions, community building and soul search ing. This is not a casual board game played for fun, but an intense experience to stimulate active participation in the anti-war movement. It is ideal for a high school retreat, church group or college course that can arrange a free weekend.

The boxed game includes a 125-page instruction book, role playing cards and a few artifacts and scripts and dramas. Game organizers should be able to provide a faculty of six plus film rentals of THE WAR GAME and IS IT ALWAYS RIGHT TO BE RIGHT? or substitutes.

The leader's manual gives an hour by hour schedule and all the needed background.

The following excerpts are from a script section designed to undermine the belief that security comes from strong defenses:

"A Congressional Committee recently reported that a bomb approximately of the Hiroshima range could be put in a suitcase. We not only have the problem of new nations developing such such bombs, but also of these countries being able to plant agents in the cities of an opponent, awaiting the signal to detonate..."

(from a scenario for catalytic warfare) "..utilizing its biological agents and several submarines, South Africa causes submarines to coast along a line about 200 miles off the U.S. west coast. Without even surfacing, these subs could release an airborne plague into the onshore wind. This kind of attack could result in tens of millions of deaths in the U.S. One very likely response might be a massive retaliation by the U.S. against Russia, which would be assumed as the attacker."

The basic ingredient for the game is a group of 20-40 people who are not as fully involved as they could be in peace efforts. "I know war is bad, I don't need the game" is not a valid excuse here.

The game costs only $10 ($6 to bookstores, $9 to libraries, $8 for five or more) from World Without War Council, 1730 Grove St., Berkeley, Calif. 94709. Info also available from the Chicago office at 7245 So. Merrill, Chicago, Ill. 60649. Calif. residents add 5.5% sales tax unless exempt.

POLLUTION, POWER POLITICS

Pollution: negotiating a clean environment (a simulation exercise, complete with playing materials). Selected problems of air, water, land, and visual pollution are dealt with by participants in negotiating for a cleaner environment. The exercise permits participants to cope with the trade-offs between personal or corporate goals and environmental quality.

May be played with as few as four persons or adapted for as many as 32. Grades 7 - 12, and Adult. Materials include:

-Instructor's Manual
-Role Cards
-30 Issue and Opinion Pole Cards
-Voting Symbols
-Scoring Charts and Markers
-Overhead Transparencies

ENV 300 Exercise - $22.50

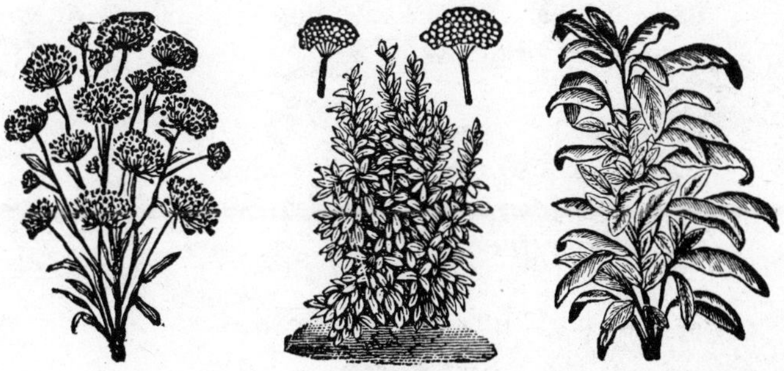

Conducting Planning Exercises: a how-to-do-it manual. Students plan and propose alternative solutions to complex social problems. Exercises are designed around issues such as student-teacher communication, drug abuse, and family life education. Activities include various combinations of debate, competition, cooperation, and simulation. Students increase problem-solving and decision-making skills and learn how to cope with divergent viewpoints, often coupled with strong emotional overtones.

The exercise accommodates from 16 to 36 students. Ideal for High School "Modern Problems" classes. Manuals include:

- -Explanation of Procedures
- -Sample Problem Statements
- -Background Information
- -Points of View
- -Bibliographies for Issues

PLN 200 Manual - $3.00.

Power Politics: a simulation exercise. An uncomplicated exercise for participants to understand the interactions between candidates in a political campaign and special interest groups. The exercise is designed around several nationally relevant issues, but can be easily adapted to include local issues.

The exercise accommodates from 20 to 40 participants. Designed for grades 9 - 12, and Adults. Materials include an Instructor's Manual. Single copies of the following may be reproduced from the resources to provide playing materials.

- -Role Cards
- -Miscellaneous Worksheets
- -Objectives List for Interest Groups
- -Glossary
- -Overhead Transparencies

PPO400 Exercise - $12.00

Future-Maker Exercises. The *Future-Maker* series of simulation and planning exercises address critical problem areas and orient students to explore crucial issues facing mankind. More exercises will be added to this series in the coming months. They are undergoing constant evaluation and will be up-dated or revised periodically. Your comments or suggestions are welcomed.

To Make a Change. Students take full responsibility for the conduct of this planning exercise. Details are given in the form of steps to follow as students take a close look at what is happening in their local area with respect to rampant technological development which holds the potential for decreasing their quality of life. Students, in the course of the exercise, identify several high-priority needs that require attention, identify resisting and encouraging forces, consider appropriate courses of action, and determine resources for carrying out the action.

The exercise is divided into two sessions so students may research problems. Guidance is given so that students commit themselves to answering specific questions between sessions, thus encouraging independent learning. Opportunities are provided for different groups to review each other's work.

The exercise requires two sessions of about two hours in length, although it may be easily adapted to meet time blocks of any length. Any number of participants may be accommodated. One *To Make a Change* booklet is required for each participant. Instructions to the coordinator are provided in the preface to the booklet. One copy of the booklet is provided from which copies may be reproduced by the teacher for classroom use.

Price: $2.00 Grades 9 - 12, and Adult.

Humanus. Students participate as "survival cell" group members, the only known survivors of a world-wide catastrophe. They are linked to the outside world, monitored and controlled by their survival computer, Humanus, which communicates to them through a "voice print-out," recorded on tape. Humanus requires that certain decisions be made by each cell if it is to survive. The cognitive goal of *Humanus* is to highlight alternative views of the future through an examination of

1. assumptions about the nature of man;
2. assumptions about man's relationship to his social and physical environment;
3. assumptions about the nature of societal change;
4. assumptions about the methods man employs to achieve change.

This uncomplicated, highly involving, and rewarding exercise takes about 1 1/2 hours to complete and is adaptable to any number of participants. A minimum of materials are required, and the exercise is easily adapted to meet different goals. A cassette recording is provided with coordinator's manual.

Price: $10.00 Grades 9 - 12, and Adult.

All six of the foregoing games are available from:

INSTRUCTIONAL DEVELOPMENT
CORPORATION
c/o Dr. Paul A. Twelker
3422 Basswood N.W.
Salem, Ore. 97304

GHETTO

simulates the pressures the urban poor live under and the choices that face them as they seek to improve their life situation.

Players learn that the condition of their neighborhood affects all of them, whether or not they are concerned. They also discover that neighborhoods can be improved through community effort.

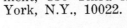

Each player is given a different personal profile describing his educational, family and economic situation, together with the number of hour-points he has available to play with in each round. There are ten rounds in the game. In each round, the player allocates his hours among several alternatives: work, school, hustling, passing time, welfare and neighborhood improvement. Hours invested in these activities yield a different number of satisfaction points; scores are computed in four areas — education, occupation, family life, and leisure time. Tables and spinners, based upon U.S. Census and other national survey data, indicate the probability of certain things happening in a person's life given his personal characteristics, past experience, and present efforts. The aim of each player is to maximize his satisfaction points.

Time for a game is 2-4 hours for 7-10 players. Any age group from junior high to adults can play. Price for the game is $20. Western Publishing Company, Inc., School and Library Department, 850 Third Avenue, New York, N.Y., 10022.

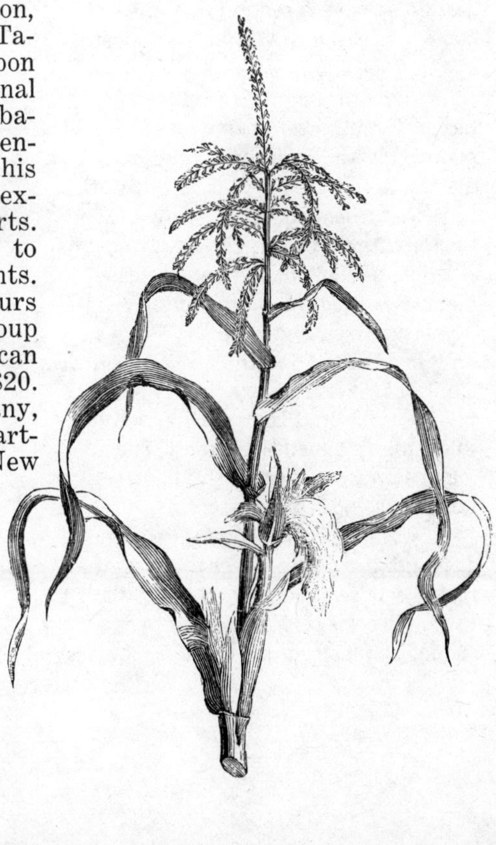

THE PROPAGANDA GAME

TECHNIQUE CARD

SECTION A: Techniques of Self-Deception

1. Prejudice
2. Academic Detachment
3. Drawing the Line
4. Not Drawing the Line
5. Conservatism, Radicalism, Moderatism
6. Rationalization
7. Wishful Thinking
8. Tabloid Thinking
9. Causal Oversimplification
10. Inconceivability

SECTION B: Techniques of Language

1. Emotional Terms
2. Metaphor and Simile
3. Emphasis
4. Quotation Out of Context
5. Abstract Terms
6. Vagueness
7. Ambiguity
8. Shift of Meaning

SECTION C: Techniques of Irrelevance

1. Appearance
2. Manner
3. Degrees and Titles
4. Numbers
5. Status
6. Repetition
7. Slogans
8. Technical Jargon
9. Sophistical Formula

SECTION D: Techniques of Exploitation

1. Appeal to Pity
2. Appeal to Flattery
3. Appeal to Ridicule
4. Appeal to Prestige
5. Appeal to Prejudice
6. Bargain Appeal
7. Folksy Appeal
8. Join the Bandwagon Appeal
9. Appeal to Practical Consequences
10. Passing from the Acceptable to the Dubious

SECTION E: Techniques of Form

1. Concurrency
2. Post Hoc
3. Selected Instances
4. Hasty Generalization
5. Faulty Analogy
6. Composition
7. Division
8. Non Sequitur

SECTION F: Techniques of Maneuver

1. Diversion
2. Disproving a Minor Point
3. Ad Hominem
4. Appeal to Ignorance
5. Leading Question
6. Complex Question
7. Inconsequent Argument
8. Attacking a Straw Man
9. Victory by Definition
10. Begging the Question

Printed in U.S.A.

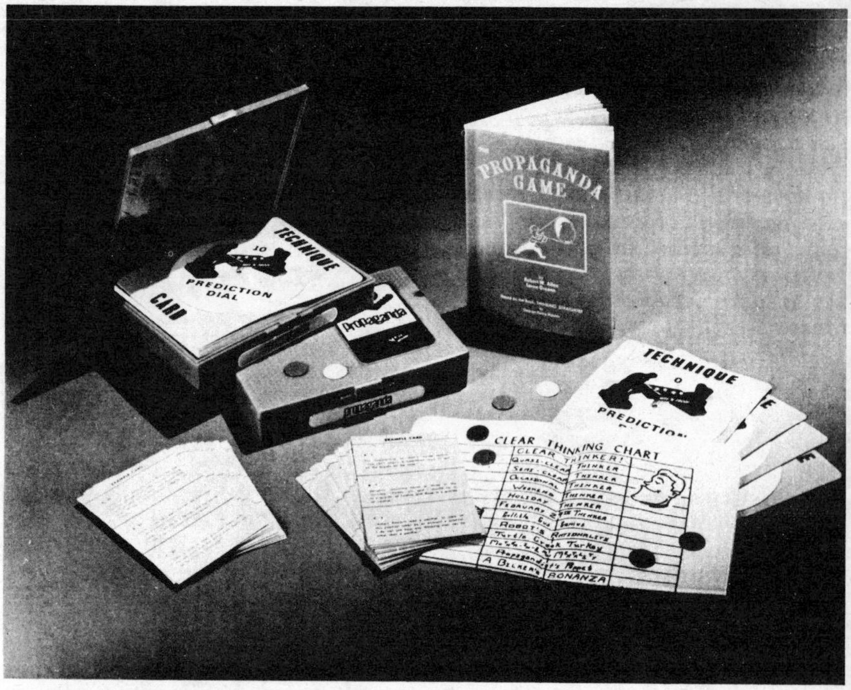

The Propaganda Game . . . . has proven itself in over seven years of use. The game teaches players to recognize techniques of persuasion and verbal manipulation. The first playing decision is to select one of the six sections as shown on the "Technique Card" reproduced on this page. A media teacher might select section D, an English teacher sections B or E, psychology or religion teacher section A, speech section F, etc. All the categories easily fit within the concerns of the English or media class.

Each of the propaganda techniques in the section being played is explained clearly from the instructor's manual before play begins. Groups of four are formed and play begins. By random draw a card is chosen giving an example of some manipulative statement. For example, from section A, "Why do we still have slums? There's only one answer. It's the greed of selfish landlords." Players next select one of the 10 techniques from section A they think the statement illustrates. The majority answer is considered correct, those agreeing score points.

To add vitality and interaction the game has provisions for challenging the majority answer and for allowing players to exercise their own brand of propaganda. The instructor's manual provides answers as a supreme court and argument settler. **The Propaganda Game** does an excellent job of teaching an awareness of manipulative techniques. The game is simple to learn and play and often produces heated discussion where involved students are really learning.

The game costs $6 plus 50¢ postage and handling from:

WFF'N PROOF
1111 Maple Street
Turtle Creek, Pa. 15145

POWER

Power

In one kit, four simulations that deepen understandings of current affairs, of uses of national power, of processes of decision making, and of actions in a crisis situation

Power presents four simulated exercises, each one based on a realistic situation in which the exercise and maintenance of *power,* or authority, depends upon the control of the communication system.

Each game is based on a different level of politics. Simulation 1 deals with international politics. In it, two subordinate nations question the authority of the dominating nation. In Simulation 2, considering national politics, a president attempts to gain support for his Supreme Court nominee. Simulation 3, about local politics, fits into any American history or American government course. The game centers around a big city mayor whose authority is being challenged by a suburban leader. In Simulation 4, about corporation management, a company president is retiring and several people are vying for his office. A total of five class periods generally is needed for one simulation.

One kit contains the materials necessary for one classroom to play all four games: background readings; player's instruction sheets; badges; money; Teacher's Manual. In addition, both the students and teacher will discover ways to use the kit's contents in "power" games of their own design.

Power is available for $13.98 from:

SCOTT, FORESMAN AND COMPANY
The School Department
1900 East Lake Avenue
Glenview, Ill. 60025

TRIAL!

TRIAL! is an interaction game in which players assume the roles of prosecution, defense, witnesses, judge, and jury and try a case developed from key bits of evidence. The game is for six to any number of players.

One team of players represents the accused and the defense lawyer; a second team represents the prosecutor and a key witness for the prosecution; and a third team represents the judge and jury. With the exception of the judge, players on the jury team can also double as witnesses for either prosecution or defense.

A game consists of an imaginary case which is developed from evidence and "tried" by the defense and prosecution. The trial can last as long as players wish it to, although typically it will run about one to two hours. At the end of the trial, members of the jury vote on the outcome. The defense wins if the accused is acquitted; the prosecution wins if the accused is found guilty; and members of the jury win if they vote the way the majority does. If there is no clear majority, there is a hung jury, and nobody wins.

In TRIAL!, the actual guilt or innocence of the accused is not determined and plays no part in the game; only whether the accused is found guilty or not.

Equipment

- Role Cards (8)
  - Accused
  - Defense Lawyer
  - Key Prosecution Witness
  - Prosecution Witness
  - Defense Witness
  - Judge
  - Jury
- Verdict Pad (1)
- Charge Cards (16 – bulls-eye symbol)
- Crime Location Cards (16 – four squares symbol)
- Crime Time Cards (8 – clock symbol)
- Incriminating Evidence Cards (24 – intertwined symbol)

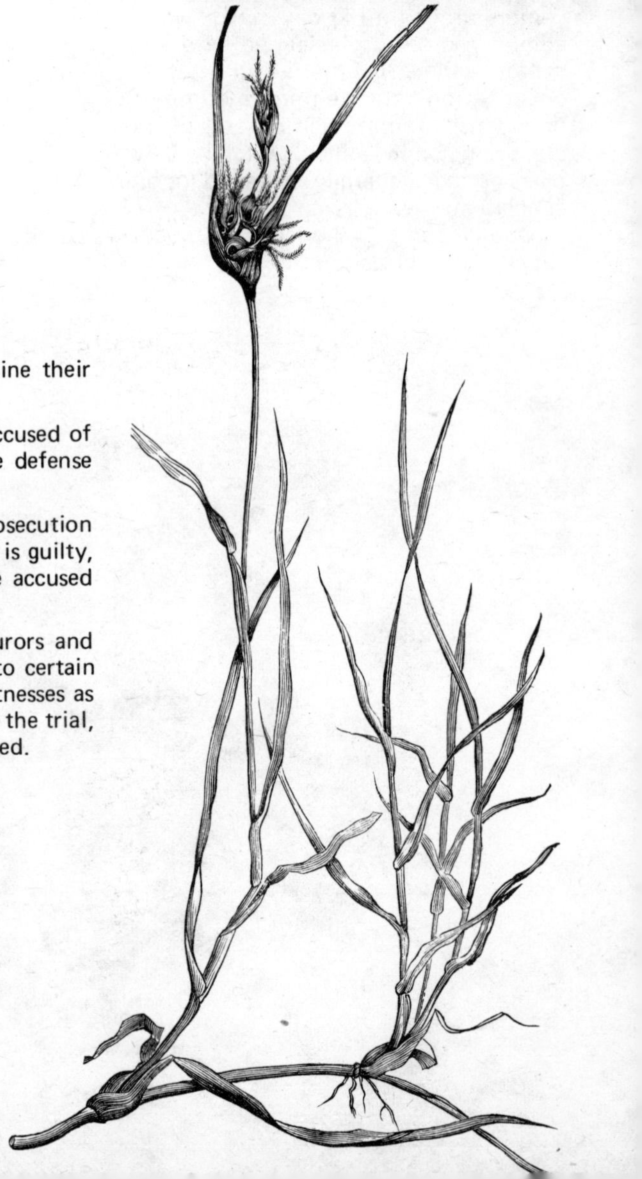

Teams

In TRIAL!, players assume various roles on teams that determine their actions for the game. The three teams are as follows:

Defense. Consists of a defense lawyer and one or more players accused of a crime. The accused will always claim he is innocent, and the defense lawyer will always act as if he is.

Prosecution. Consists of a prosecutor and one or more key prosecution witnesses. The prosecutor will always attempt to prove the accused is guilty, and the key prosecution witness will testify so as to make the accused appear guilty.

Judge and Jury. Consists of a judge and players who act as jurors and witnesses. The judge's role is to move the trial along according to certain procedures, while the other players take the roles of various witnesses as requested by the defense lawyer and the prosecutor. At the end of the trial, players on this team will vote on the guilt or innocence of the accused.

Trial! is available for $5 from:

ADULT LEISURE PRODUCTS
Locust Valley N.Y. 11560

SYSTEM

System is a game similar in concept and procedure to *Starpower*. *System* is a four-round trading game in which players find themselves in a society which:

Rewards people according to their wealth.

Allows those in control to write the rules.

Tempts people with a freedom which may or may not be enjoyable.

Sets ownership of the machines.

Some of what happens is the result of luck or circumstance, but most is directed by decisions made by the game players. The guide for *Systems* stresses the importance of and gives guidelines for a post-game discussion. A playing manual is all that is needed for the game along with 30 participants. Also available from same source is a simulation about the first year in college titled *Freshman Year* and *Atlantis Believes*, a game about the conflict between trying to develop a basic philosophical position for a Utopia and trying to deal with the political pressures in such a development.

Systems guide is $3.00 from:

UCCM GAMES
2718 University Avenue
Des Moines, Iowa 50311

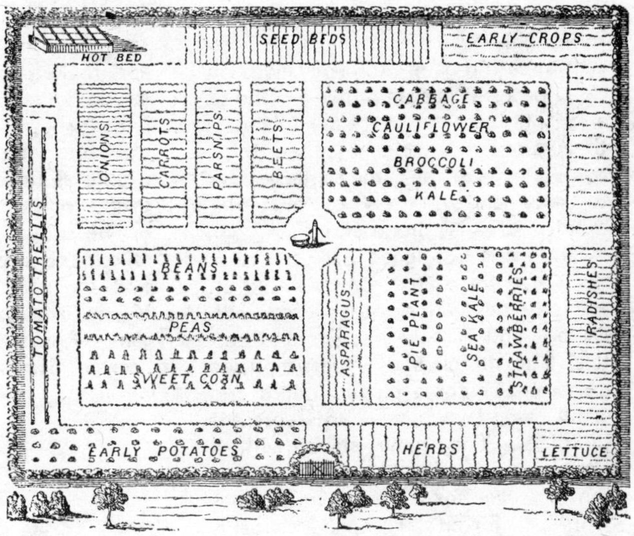

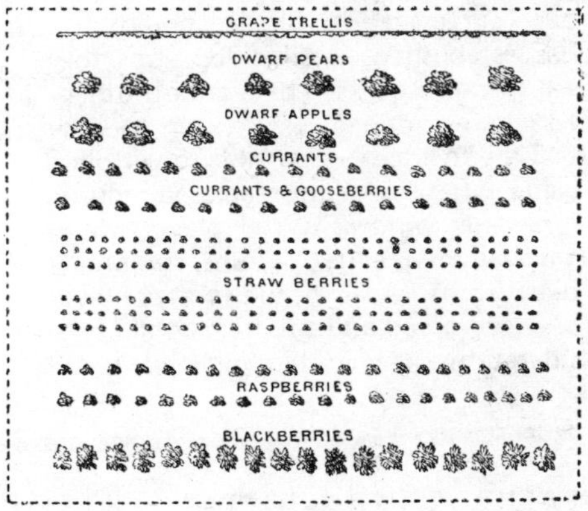

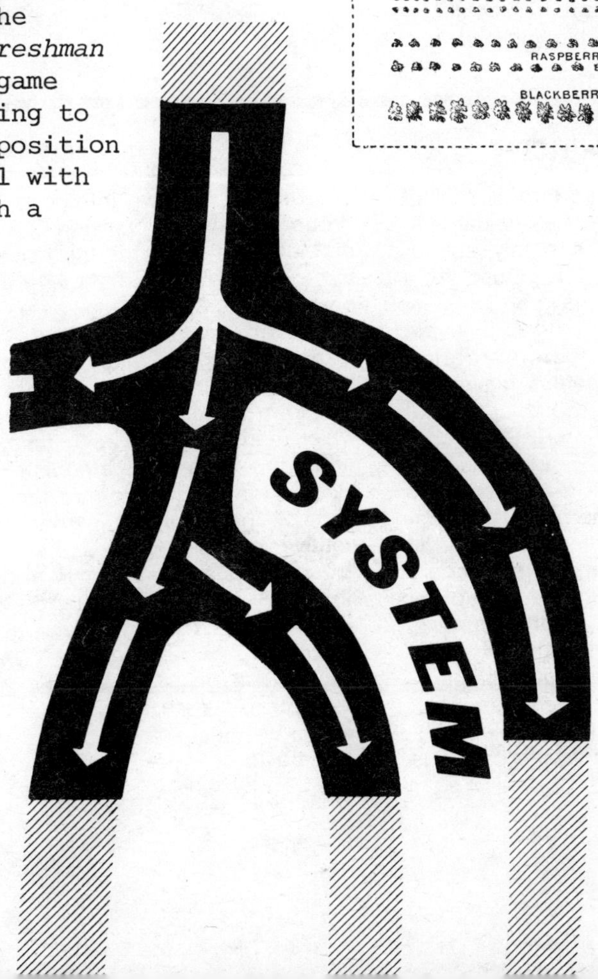

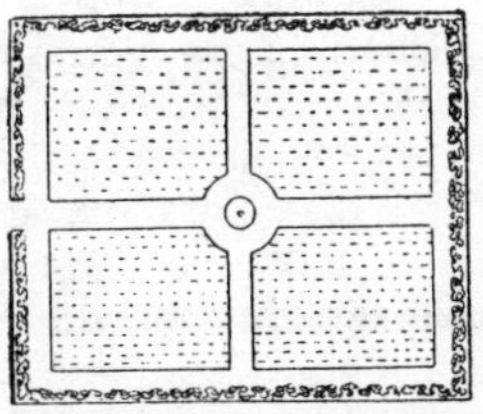

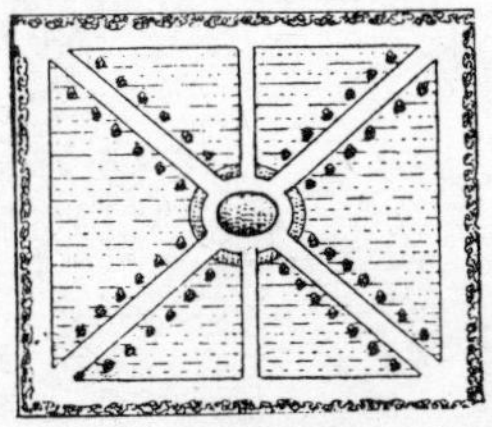

NEW TOWN

New Town is one of the most thoroughly tested and widely respected simulation games to be reviewed on these pages. It is a simplified version of a $12,000 game that city planners throughout the world have used. In its complete form the game can take days to play and progress is constantly monitored by a computer.

The game's designer, Barry Lawson, has a version of the game painted on his basement floor that uses milk cartons and various size jars and bottles. But for class use the simplified game settles for a playing board and small wooden blocks to represent buildings. The game starts with a Utopian's dream: a blank board representing space for a new town 25 miles from a major city. The players' goal is to build this new community from the ground up. The new community has been surveyed into blocks and zoning has established possible locations for schools and parks. There are no other zoning restrictions.

True to life, it is possible to win the game but build a miserable community. The winner is the player who amasses the greatest fortune, so immediately the game becomes a contest between greed and environmental considerations. Players bid for land, construct various kinds of buildings, hold town meetings, vote and discuss, trade, and make deals and compromises. In so doing students realize the forces which shape an existing community into one which most often is not as livable as it could be. There is a high degree of interaction among students.

The educational version of the game sells for $16 for the 10 student kit and $28 for the 20 student kit. A fine teacher's manual accompanies each game. From Harwell Assoc., Box 95, Convent Station, NJ 07961.

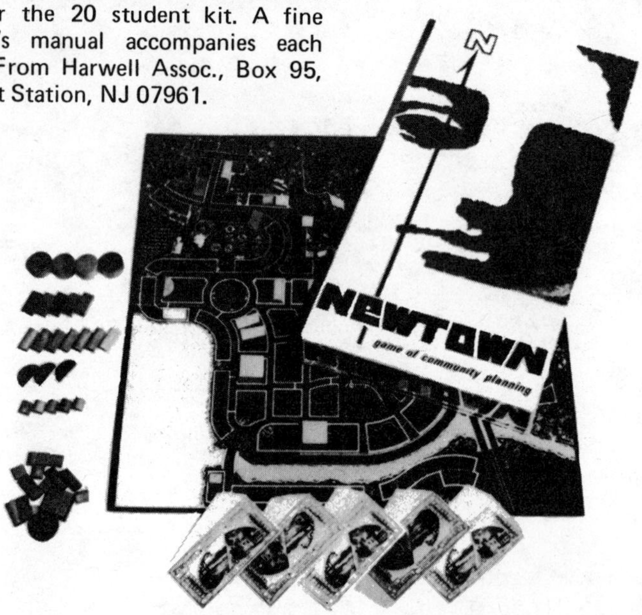

LAND USE; SACRIFICE

The Game of Sacrifice is one of the easiest of the games available to learn and teach, is highly educational and usable for groups from ten to a hundred players of almost any age. Not only does it teach about solving ecology-related problems but it enables players to experience and deal with conflicts of value, conflicts of interest and consensus.

The entire game consists of 55 cards explaining the game and containing punched holes to be used in indicating decisions. The players are assembled in ten interest groups of consumer-voters,. manufacturers, public utility executives, small businessmen and public officials. The entire group is given a series of problems to solve in which each of the ten subgroups plays its own role and defends its own interests. Each group makes a decision on the problem and indicates the decision by punching out a hole on its problem card. The ten cards are collected by the teacher-game leader and scoring takes place by inserting a "golden stylus" in each of the four punch holes and seeing which cards fall out each time.

Scoring and results are clearly explained on the master card for each round. The scoring is not competitive; rather it scores the entire group on its ability to move from indecision to decision and from thinking in terms of one's own group to thinking in terms of the whole. One of the game's purposes is to help players realize that sacrifices might be necessary and in their ultimate best interest and to experience the value and difficulties of consensus decision-making. The game takes as long as 8-10 class periods to complete, engenders much debate and productive role playing and measurably raises the players' level of awareness of the problems involved in ecology and human relations.

The game can only be played once but its cost is a low $4.95. Available from Education Ventures, 209 Court Street, Middletown, Conn. 06457.

Land Use is a real bargain. Where else could you possibly purchase 120 houses, 150 sections of highway, 10 ponds, 10 recreation areas and 100 trees for only $1.95? After playing many games with students I've found **Land Use** one of the most useful, least expensive and most educational.

The game brings out the conflict between the desire to have quality housing and the desire to preserve natural resources. Participants in **Land Use** are given a developer's delight, undeveloped land, and told to use the land according to the rules of the game. They start by simply "covering the land" but through the subtle influence of the game's scoring system are lead to discover an alternative called Cluster Zoning or Planned Unit Development. Basically this much discussed and recommended way of saving land involves grouping houses in imaginative and attractive ways in order to use up the least possible amount of land.

The game can be played in school situations, used instead of talks or films, or supplement other learning aids. It is workable with junior high through adult level groups or with groups of mixed generations. Also from Educational Ventures.

The Land Use Game

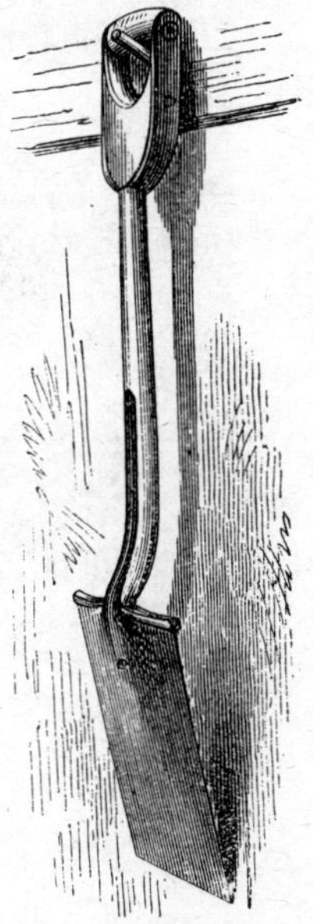

Land Use is a game for planners. Students, working in small groups and using removable, stick-on playing pieces, are given the challenge of creating a community of homes on a 10-acre site with the least possible harm to the environment. Features on the playing surface, such as trees, hillocks, and marshes, are worth various "environmental points." Whenever houses or roads are built over a prominent natural feature of the land, a corresponding number of environmental points is deducted from the original environmental worth of the site. (Players are also permitted to restore some environmental points by replacing trees, building ponds, or developing recreation areas). Groups can play and replay the game to improve their planning performance and also to test various zoning principles. A separate four-page teaching guide suggests important patterns for post-game discussion of the alternative procedures, legal questions, and value judgments brought forth during play of the game. Each game unit includes three map surfaces and ample labels for six students to play three rounds.

EVI 7002 ***The Land Use Game*** **(unit for 6 players) $2.50**
EVI 7003 ***The Game of Sacrifice*** **(ten to 100+ players) ... $4.95**

MIKE'S WORLD — YOUR WORLD

A mixed-media unit designed to help students see problems of environmental abuse in relationship to their own comforts and conveniences—and to discover more about their personal responsibilities to the world.

a look at our environment

Many, if not most, Americans still tend to see the problems of environmental abuse as a "bad guy" versus "good guy" conflict waged only at the level of big government and big industry. Few are inclined to connect their personal comforts and conveniences to the awesome dangers of waste and pollution. Yet Americans are using up resources at a rate estimated to be eight times that of the rest of the world combined. Overconsumption and/or mismanagement threaten the land, the air, and the water—the quality of our lives and perhaps life itself. *A Look at Our Environment* includes a wide variety of approaches to help students identify environmental problems and, more important, to help them see these problems in terms of their personal values and value conflicts. Multiple approaches—including exposition, role play, actual and fictional case studies, research activities, and games—are used to encourage student involvement and commitment.

75¢ per copy for student book
50¢ per copy for teaching guide

One copy free with orders for ten or more

Mike's World—Your World

This 32-page, 10 by 10-inch student text begins with a look at the world of Mike Fuller in America, 1990. It's a grim world, drastically affected by the consequences of unchecked pollution. Then the scene flashes back to Mike Fuller's world in the 1970's and a picture of how he, as an 11-year-old boy, may have helped with his family to contribute to the grimness of his future life. Besides telling about Mike's growing involvement in trying to protect the environment—and the value conflicts he faces—the text includes overview chapters on "What Our Comforts Cost" and "The Web of Life", as well as case studies and role plays about community environmental problems.

The six-page teaching guide for the text and the unit includes a pre-test, post-test designed to measure change in students' environmental attitudes, as well as a number of class projects to help students measure and document water pollution, air pollution, noise pollution, and visual pollution in their own community.

From:
EDUCATION VENTURES
209 Court Street
Middletown, Ct. 06457

ECOLOGY KITS

Kids and the young at heart like and learn from chemistry sets and microscope sets so why not produce ecology kits that would help increase environmental awareness?

Urban Research Associates (the same people who produced the SMOG and DIRTY WATER games described in the last issue) decided to do just that and have come up with five inexpensive ($5 per kit), sharply packaged ecology kits.

Kit No. 1, WHY LEAVES ARE GREEN, provides a series of experiments which can be carried out over a period of several weeks. The experiments demonstrate photosynthesis and the effect of light and oxygen on plants. The approach of the kit is inductive, encouraging basic questions like "Why am I doing this?" The kit contains peas, red seaweed, alcohol, an eyedropper, a diffraction grating and other materials needed for the experiments. The 16-page instruction booklet is excellent in this kit as in the others.

Kit No. 2 is a study of marine life titled LIFE IN THE WATER. The kit contains a "secchi disk" to measure light penetration of water, vials of algae and nutrient salts for an experiment which involves growing algae and testing their need for nutrients. A plankton net is included for use at the local stream.

Kit No. 3 is a series of three simulation games described as being able to "make anyone an expert on population growth and decline. Learn about predator-prey and competitive relationships in an ecosystem. Eat your opponent! Exhibit your skill." The games in this PREDATOR AND PREY kit take only a few hours but should be repeated until the results can be graphed. Topics treated in the kit include food chains and food webs, population sampling by the mark and recapture method, natural selection, pyramids of energy and biomass.

WHAT MOVES LIFE, Kit No. 4, is a series of projects lasting as long as six weeks. The experiments examine the reaction of shrimp (a shrimp "hatch pack" is included), beans, and peas to gravity, temperature and water. Terms such as geotropism, phototropism and stereotropism are explained.

Kit No. 5 is LIFE FROM DEATH and the most elaborate of the five. The kit contains vials of mulch, milorganite, peas, clay, nutrients, blue dye, and calcium hydroxide all used in experiments that explain and demonstrate recycling.

I would like to highly recommend these kits for age groups from sharp grade schoolers to great grandfathers. They would make excellent gifts or classroom tools. Available at some bookstores or by mail from Edmund Scientific Co., 380 Edscorp Bldg., Barrington, N.J. 08007.

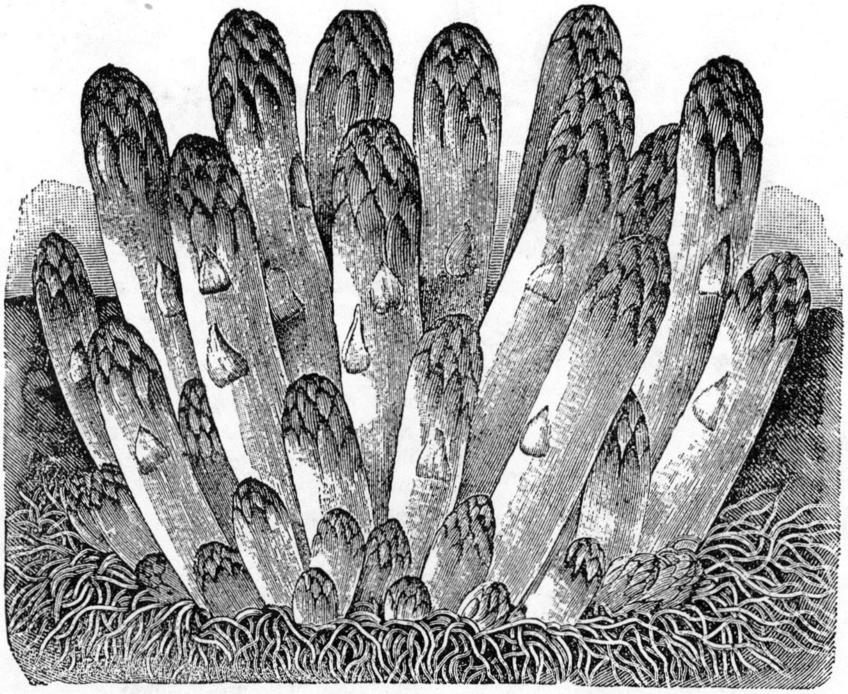

POPULATION

Population is the fourth in a series of games from Urban Systems. It edges out **Dirty Water** as my favorite so far and easily provides more fun than **Smog** or **Ecology. Population** is as glossy and classy as any board game on the market. Its dynamics resemble **Dirty Water,** and involve filling in a pyramid with just the right balance of industry, agriculture, medicine, education, and population. The pyramid has to be filled in an orderly fashion that advances through three zones of development; each zone is more difficult and complex to balance than the preceding one.

Players each represent an imaginary country whose fortunes are determined by rolls of the dice and a selection of various instruction cards. The game involves spending large sums of money (people seem to prefer games that enable them to spend thousands) and combines a mixture of chance with skillful decision making. Competition is keen and learning definitely takes place with repeated playings. My own first time through the game was a frustrating series of going back to the previous zone because of overpopulation. The second and third times I had occasional setbacks, but I generally found it easier to keep everything balanced.

A fun game for $10 at department stores, large bookstores or from Urban Systems, 1033 Massachusetts Ave., Cambridge, MA 02138.

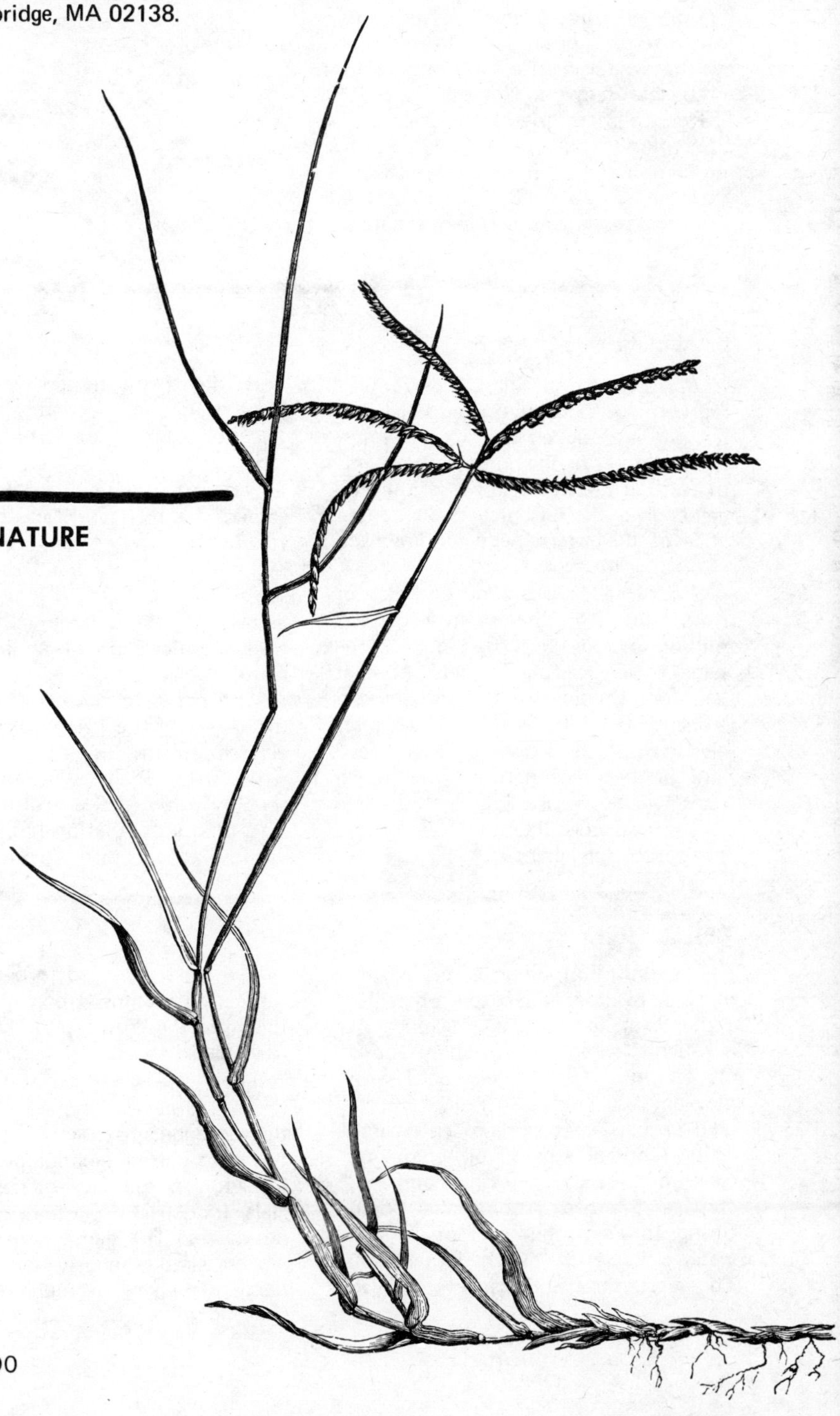

ECOLOGY: THE GAME OF MAN AND NATURE

Ecology: The Game of Man and Nature is another board game from Urban Systems, the people who brought you **Dirty Water** and **Smog.** The game involves players in achieving a balance between man's activities and the natural environment. Players advance through the four Ages of Development: Hunting, Agricultural, Industrial and Environmental. As the population grows, players compete to oc- inventions and try to maintain their supply of Ecology Points which represent environmental quality. The first player to reach the Ecology Test Square in any of the four ages with the proper balance of people, money, inventions and Ecology Points is the winner.

The game is attractively packaged but takes a fair amount of time to master its rules. In tests with high school students the players have never finished the trip around the board, always winning in the Hunting or Agricultural Age. **Dirty Water** remains the favorite of the three Urban Systems games with my students.

Distributed by Damon Corp.,
80 Wilson Way, Westwood, MA 02090

REDWOOD CONTROVERSY

The Redwood Controversy is an ingenious role-playing game in which players act as legislators, experts, and pressure groups faced with the age old choice between progress and conservation. The game is based on a real situation arising in the mid 1960's when President Johnson ordered the 90th Congress to protect the California coastal redwoods, largely owned by lumber companies. **The Redwood Controversy** simulates the heated discussion which went on in Congress to establish a Redwood National Park.

Twenty-one students are given specific roles to play and receive a briefing pamphlet explaining their position. The others (up to 30 can play) are given the more general role of senators who can lobby, argue, listen, worry about reelection and finally vote on the proposals. The resulting discussion and debate vividly point out the conflicts between ecological, financial and political interests.

A study of the redwood controversy would be rather boring if presented in lecture or print form. But given the format of this simulation game, **The Redwood Controversy** becomes a highly involving and even exciting learning experience. Suitable for high school or adult levels, the kit costs $10 ($7.50 to schools) and provides all the materials necessary for one group. From Houghton Miflin, 110 Tremont St., Boston, MA 02107.

BALDICER

Baldicer is a simulation game dealing with food production and distribution. It is designed to stimulate interest in a study of the complex problems of feeding the world's population. The game gives 10–20 players an experience of the interdependence involved in feeding the world.

Each player is a food coordinator responsible for the survival of 150 million people. In order to keep the people alive, a player must have at least one Baldicer (Balanced Diet Certificate) at all times. If a player loses all his Baldicers, his people are dead and he becomes part of the "world conscience" whose job it is to urge other food coordinators to cooperate to keep people alive.

Baldicers are earned by work performed in a 40 second work period. The work consists of writing the words "dig, sweat, push, pull" on a magic slate as often as possible. Baldicers are gained for this work and changed in value by food machines, inflation, population growth and natural and social forces. Each player keeps his own score on a large tally sheet at times reminiscent of an income tax form.

The catch to the game is that one player starts the game with 50 Baldicers, one with 35 and all the others with only 5. This is intended to roughly represent a world in which 20% of the population has 50% of the wealth. Players are not told of the unequal distribution of Baldicers. In the course of playing the game some groups learn to cooperate in order to survive while others fail.

The game needs careful preparation. Two game directors are desirable but not essential. The instruction book does contain all the needed information but not in the most organized manner. Needed to play the game is the ability to tolerate a noisy classroom, some mass confusion, and the ability to process the feelings and information gained from the game.

The game costs $25 from John Knox Press, Box 1176, Richmond, Virginia 23209, or from some bookstores.

POLLUTION

The Pollution Game is one of the simplest to play, easiest to learn games available on the subject of ecology. It is roughly based on Monopoly and is played on a large game board with moveable autos for markers. Players own properties (shopping center, pollution control board, oil company, steel mill, beach, trucking company, etc.) and move around the board trying to keep the level of air and water pollution below the lethal level. The first time the game is played students are expected to become environmental victims. Upon a second or third playing, however, they should at least begin to arrive at solutions that will enable all players to survive.

The game is designed to simulate the antagonisms and frustrations of trying to change technology and social behavior in the face of devious officials, industrial deceptions and greedy businesses. The game is meant to be played simultaneously by competing teams of players, although it will work if there is only one set and one team of players.

The game is well engineered and the rules clearly written. Cost is $12 (school price $9) per game from

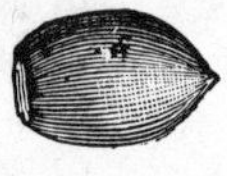

HOUGHTON MIFFLIN COMPANY
110 Tremont Street
Boston, Mass. 02107

THE PLANET MANAGEMENT GAME

The most appropriate single word to describe the **Planet Management Game** is "uncanny." I settled down to give the game a try, confident that I could manage my planet successfully. Starting with the attitude of trying to "beat the house" I ended with the realization that managing a planet, even an imaginary one, is a delicate and frustrating task.

The game begins on the planet Clarion in the year 2,000 and runs for fifty Clarion years. Actually this is a computer-designed simulation of existing conditions on planet earth. Players make decisions to improve the population, income, food and environment indices of the planet. They decide how many "bucks" to spend on each project and then feed their decisions to a cardboard computer. The computer, a deck of perforated cards, reveals the results of the decisions based on actual statistical research and historical probabilities. A graph for overhead projection is provided to note the progress or decline of the planet over the game's ten rounds. Students learn the complex interrelatedness of factors such as pollution, famine and population.

Of all the ecology games I've played so far this one impressed me most as an accurate simulation of existing conditions as well as one of the most involving and educational of the available games.

The Planet Management Game is designed for five, although even one can play as easily as an entire class. List price is $16 and school price $12 from Houghton Mifflin Company, 110 Tremont Street, Dept. M, Boston, MA 02107.

SMOG AND DIRTY WATER

SMOG AND DIRTY WATER are the much publicized board games from Urban Systems, Inc., available in book and department stores throughout the country.

DIRTY WATER is my favorite (maybe because I usually win) and by far the easier of the two to learn. Each player (2-4 may play) is the Water Pollution Commissioner of an industry-surrounded lake. He is faced with the problem of remaining economically solvent while maintaining an ecologically balanced lake. The less a player knows about ecological balance, water organisms and types of water pollution the more educational

the game becomes. The game can be enjoyed and learned by groups as diverse as grade school classes and adult education groups. The interpretation of the rules requires patience and intelligence along with a few good guesses.

Players in DIRTY WATER not only learn a few new vocabulary words (e.g., rotifers, copepods, abatement, herbicide, phosphate pollution), but also that it is neither wise nor possible to indiscriminately restrict industrial activities. They learn about the overpopulation of certain aquatic species. They learn that while it is beneficial to keep lakes and rivers stocked with various organisms, an overabundance of one kind upsets the natural balance of species. They learn to deal with the economics of pollution abatement and the problems of pollution from neighboring communities. The first player to achieve a completely stocked and balanced lake wins the game.

The Harvard and MIT urbanologists who designed the game are to be congratulated for a product that is both educational and fun.

After mastering the DIRTY WATER game I unboxed the attractively packaged SMOG game and sat down with three other adults to attempt a contest. After ten minutes I was forced to give up in the face of the complexities of the rules and the ambiguity of the rulebook. Having since spent a lot more time deciphering the 12-page booklet, I think I can now play the game.

The purpose of SMOG is to acquaint players with some of the complexities with which a local administrator must deal in controlling the quality of air over his town. The most important sources of air pollution in the game are automobiles and the industries which burn sulfur-containing fuels, but players learn that they cannot simply restrict industry or abolish autos and still win. Instead they learn suitable abatement—air pollution control—techniques and plan for transportation and solid waste management systems which efficiently reduce air pollution levels. The players also learn that they must have the support of the townspeople and must remain economically stable.

Each player assumes the position of the air pollution control manager in a growing town and moves along a "Decision Tree" making decisions which affect his financial status, popularity, and growth of his town, as well as the air quality. "Outrageous Fortune" cards and changeable wind direction (determined by a roll of the die) represent the very real elements of chance. A player wins the game by accumulating 2000 "Management Credits."

I found the game less educational and more complicated than DIRTY WATER. The two games could also be used in school situations if the teacher understands the rules completely and if the games are followed with further instruction.

Both games can be purchased in stores or mail ordered from:

URBAN SYSTEMS, INC.
1033 Massachusetts Avenue
Cambridge, Mass. 02138

TRIPPLES

Tripples is a board game that takes only a minute to learn and yet can be as simple as checkers or nearly as complex as chess.

A sample game board is reproduced on this page. To play, each player must move his marker (use paper squares or any small marker) from ■ to □ or from ● to ○ . Play is one tile at a time, alternating moves. You may move only in the direction of one of the three vector arrows under your opponent's game piece. Each move decides your opponent's alternatives. Blank spaces are out of bounds.

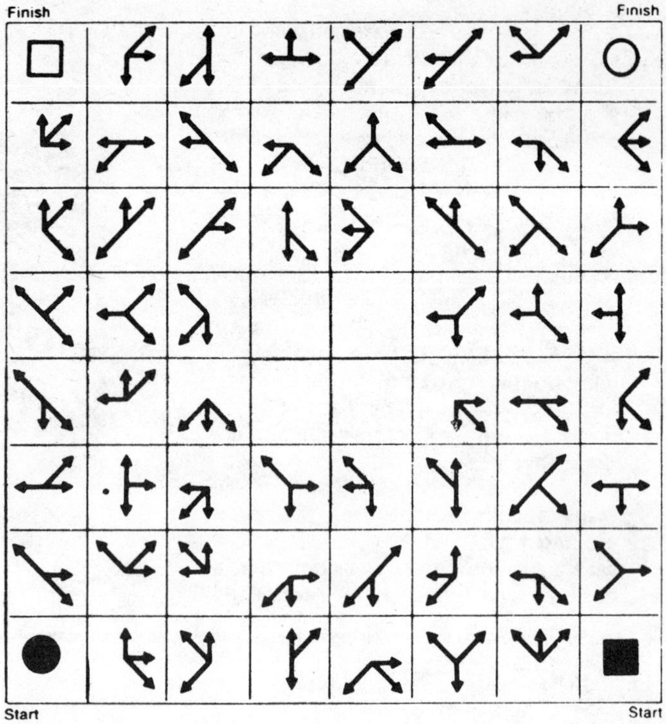

A plastic game board for *Tripples* is available at many toy and game departments or for $5.85 each from:

ASK YOUR FATHER TOY SHOP
120 South Street
Pittsfield, Mass. 01201

GAMES & PUZZLES MAGAZINE

Games & Puzzles is a periodical for individuals who enjoy playing board games. Poker, chess, Scrabble, Go, crossword puzzles, mazes, mathematic puzzles, etc., are the scope of *Games & Puzzles*. Note that this publication is not about classroom-type simulation games. Each issue contains puzzles to solve, games reviews, articles on the strategy of game playing, and a contest . Published monthly for $9.00 by surface mail or $16.50 by air mail from:

GAMES & PUZZLES
19 Broadlands Road
P.O. Box 4
London N6 4DF
England

(Material on this page is copyrighted and reprinted by permission of *Games & Puzzles*.)

GOTCHA

Don't get caught by failing to solve this maze in less than ten minutes.

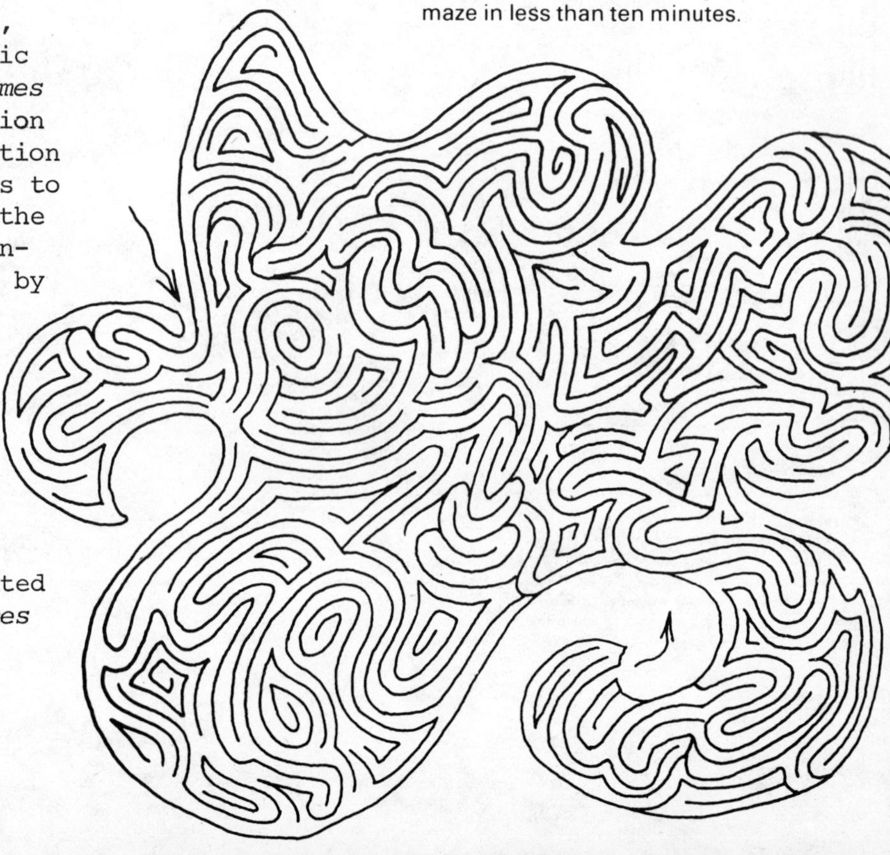

Reproduced from *Mazes*

SCRABBLE TEASER No. 14

WIN £15

Here is the Scrabble board at a crucial point in an exciting game. Yours is the next move and you must do the best you can to score the most points in your move. Use standard GAMES & PUZZLES rules on page 34.

Cut out the letters provided and paste them onto the board in the positions of your choice. Send the board and your scores to GAMES & PUZZLES. Or, if you would prefer not to cut the magazine, just send your word or words and your score to GAMES & PUZZLES. Only words appearing in the latest edition of Chambers Twentieth Century Dictionary and simple derivatives (that is, verb tenses and plurals) of such words will be allowed. The judges' decision on any interpretation will be final. If two or more entrants score the same number of points, the prize money will be divided equally among the winners.

This competition is sponsored by J. W. Spears & Sons Ltd., Enfield, Middlesex, the manufacturers of Scrabble®.

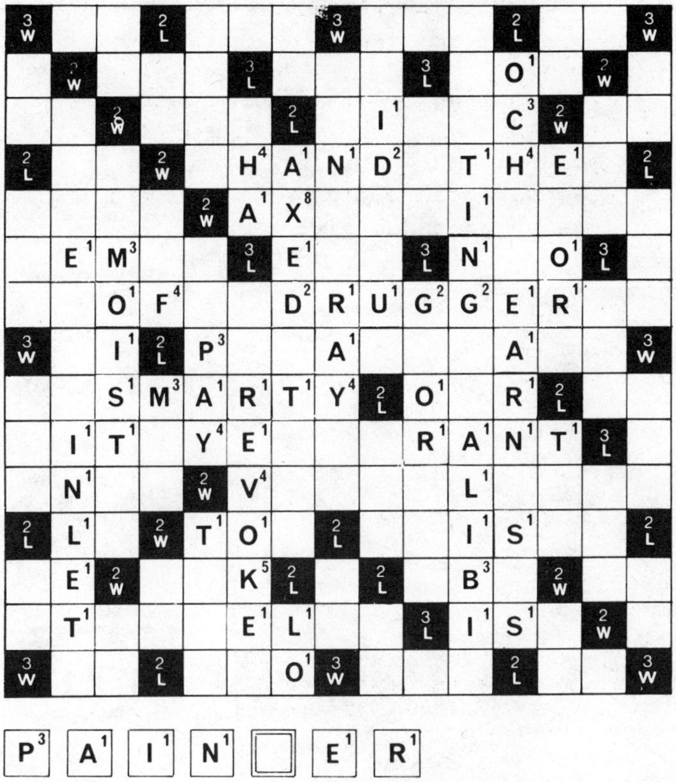

THE LABYRINTHINE MAZE

The fourth in GAMES & PUZZLES' series of tricky mazes is the Labyrinthine Maze. If you can travel through the maze in under a quarter of an hour, you can congratulate yourself.

Reproduced from Mazes, published by Pan Books Limited.

WORDS OUT OF LETTERS

Using the letters below, each once and only once, see how many seven-letter words you can make.

Feel free to use proper names. You may use words from any dictionaries that you wish.

We have found over a dozen words. See if you can find more than that. Perhaps we have missed some of the words that you will find. If so, write and let us know.

PSYCHOLOGY TODAY

Psychology Today offers a series of games that have been widely used in classrooms. The games originally appeared in the magazine. Shipping and handling charge is 75¢ per order.

Buy three games and receive a *Feel Wheel* free from:

PSYCHOLOGY TODAY READER SERVICE
P.O. Box 700
Del Mar, Calif. 92014

Games of fun, action and expanding Self-knowledge

BLACKS & WHITES

How much can a white person understand about the black struggle for economic opportunity and political equality? When you play *Blacks & Whites*, you get the insider's view of economic and emotional frustration most blacks know as a sad fact of life. Why is the ghetto both a place and a state of mind? Why is welfare money doled out in amounts that are sufficient to keep you alive... but not enough to really let you live? You'll gain new insights into these and other vital issues of racial equality in the U.S. when you play *Blacks & Whites*.
$6.95 (plus shipping and handling)

SOCIETY TODAY

As in life itself, the object of every player of *Society Today* is "making it." Taking advantage of your opportunities to the fullest, trying to stay clear of the pitfalls, and in the end getting what you want out of life. What counts in this game is: your knowledge of people and events, confidence in yourself, your skills and your luck. You'll learn about the forces at work in our society, and the many (often subtle) ways they are affecting your life as you play *Society Today*.
$7.95 (plus shipping and handling)

BODY TALK

In this country, we are rarely taught to use our bodies as effective, conscious communicators. *Body Talk* is designed to help remedy this situation—and it's plenty of fun, too! *Body Talk* teaches how to express and receive emotions successfully without using words. A Deck of 52 cards with suits labeled Hand, Head, Whole Body and Interpersonal has 13 different emotions cards, so no combination of emotion and means of expression repeats. The object is to get rid of your cards by expressing the designated emotion.
$5.95 (plus shipping and handling)

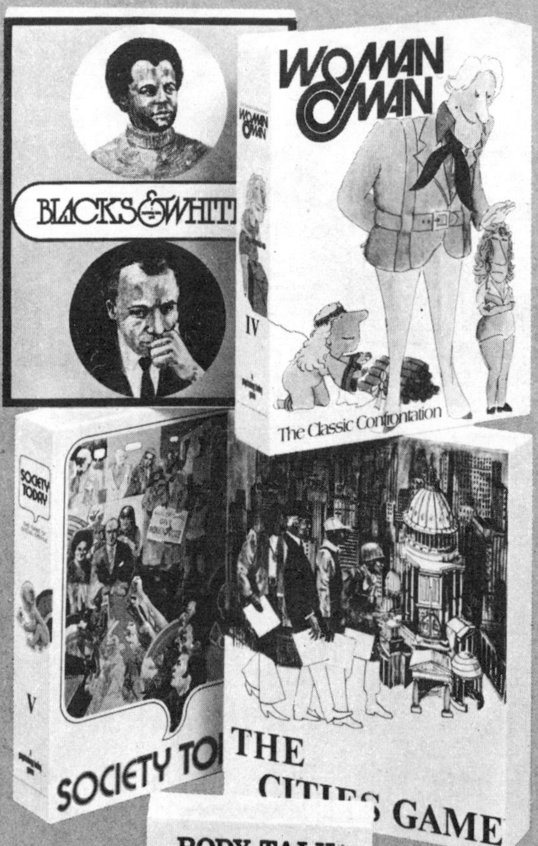

WOMAN & MAN

As you play *Woman & Man* you're likely to discover a good part of your present "understanding" of the other sex is based on false assumptions and attitudes subtly imposed by society. *Woman & Man* is a game of both Women's and Men's Liberation—designed to help you sweep away the stereotypes of traditional male and female roles... paving the way for more direct and meaningful contact with members of the opposite sex.
$7.95 (plus shipping and handling)

THE CITIES GAME

Why are cities falling apart? Why is transportation so bad? Why is the air almost unbreathable and the streets littered with refuse? What can be done about it? *The Cities Game* gives you an insight into the reasons for urban collapse... and the ways effective corrective action can be taken. What are the political pitfalls? Can you play a dirty game and still win idealistic victories? Play *The Cities Game* and find out.
$6.95 (plus shipping and handling)

★★★★★★★★★★★★★★★★★★

FREE FEEL WHEEL

The *Feel Wheel* is more than a game; it's a device developed by psychologists to bring out the feeling sides of human experience. And we've discovered that using the *Feel Wheel* while playing the other Psychology Today Games makes the play even more fun, more involving. So we are making you this special offer: If you order any three Psychology Today Games at the regular price, we will send you a FREE *Feel Wheel!* **Available individually for $7.95 (plus shipping and handling).**

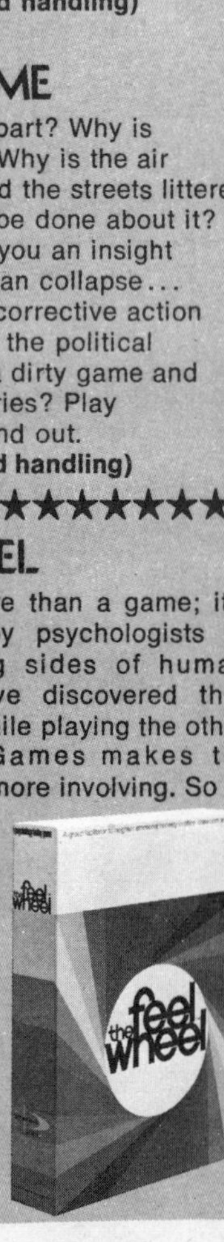

SIMULATION SHARING SERVICE

The Simulation Games Center is involved in two major projects. One is to gather together as many simulations as possible, review them, and, if possible, run them in informal or classroom settings. After this has been done, then the Center attempts to make suggestions to individuals and groups who contact the Center requesting specific simulations for specific programs or courses.

The second project of the Center is to write up as many game reviews as possible that are based on actual game experience. Once this review has been written it is placed in the newsletter, *Simulation Sharing Service*. A booklet of all the reviews is now being prepared and will be released late in 1973.

The *Simulation Games Center* is not directly involved in designing simulations for specific events. There have been a number of occasions where existing simulations have been adapted for a program. The Center also conducts workshops and seminars for individuals and groups that wish to be trained in simulation administration and to provide exposure to the broad range of games available on the market today.

A final project is to assemble the names of people around the country who would like to share their simulations with others and/or to work with them on new simulations by "play testing" to determine use and suitability.

If you have any questions about the *Simulation Games Center* or *Simulation Sharing Service*, address your inquiry to:

SIMULATION GAMES CENTER
221 Willey Street
Morgantown, West Va. 26505
Attn: George M. McFarland

The Red and Blue Game. This is a simple little exercise that is suitable for any group of eight or more people from high school age on up. By the time it is completed (about one hour) you will have exposed the participants to the following concepts:

1. That people, in every situation, exert influence on others or they are influenced by others.

2. That people do not really like to think of themselves as followers.

3. That many people feel guilty or uncomfortable about leadership.

4. That it is possible to enter a social situation with the idea that everyone can win rather than have winners and losers.

5. That it is very difficult to create trust -- even in simple situations with few variables.

There are a lot of other things people learn from this exercise -- but the above they always learn. Just be sure, once the game is over, to allow for some time to talk about what happened. This is when the real learning takes place.

Step #1: Ask your people to pair up (male-female or strangers or any other combination). After they are paired, have them do a hand dancing exercise nonverbally. Hand dancing is when they stand facing each other with their hands outstretched and palms open. They then place their open palms close to their partner's palms and proceed to move their hands and arms without touching while acting as a mirror of their partner. It is sometimes called a hand-mirroring exercise. (3 minutes)

Step #2: Instruct participants to decide who led the hand dance and who followed. (1 minute)

Step #3: Divide the group into leaders and followers. Have the groups separate as far as possible (different rooms) and discuss the following questions.

1. What do you think about being in this group -- personally?

2. What do you think about the other group?

3. What do you think the other group thinks about you? (10 minutes)

Step #4: Optional -- have them come back and share. (10 - 15 minutes)

Step #5: Have them pick one or two people from their group to go to the other group and be accepted. People will go from each group and seek admission to the other group. If they do not get a unanimous acceptance -- then they are not allowed entry and must return to their old group. Remember -- the people are selected on the basis of their ability to get into the other group. (10 minutes)

Step #6: Play Red and Blue -- Indicate that the name of the game is Win As Much As You Can. It is played in a series of 10 three-minute rounds. Put up the chart printed below.

Allow no conversation between teams at any time. Allow one or two negotiators from each team to confer for three minutes between rounds 2 and 3, 5 and 6, and 8 and 9. Point out that the scores will be multiplied by three in round 3, 5 in round 6, and 10 in round 9. Each round the team must finally decide what color to choose without consulting with the other team.

After the game is over, point out that they were to win as much as they could (which would have been 50 points total or 25 for each team). They could only get that much if they had chosen blue each round. (40 minutes limit)

Step #7: Discuss the entire exercise. (30 minutes to one hour)

Possible questions for discussion:

1. Who were the real leaders and followers?

2. Did you always agree with the majority of your group?

3. Was it difficult to trust the other group? Why?

4. Why did your group pick red? Did you see that the game was a trap to lure you into a winner and making someone else a loser?

5. Did you ever misread the nonverbal communication of the other group?

Notes:

There is nothing magic about time limits or suggestions. Feel free to be flexible with them. The times given have been proposed on the basis that if the experience is going to maintain a lively, interesting pace then these are the maximum times to be allowed.

(From an issue of *SSS Newsletter*.)

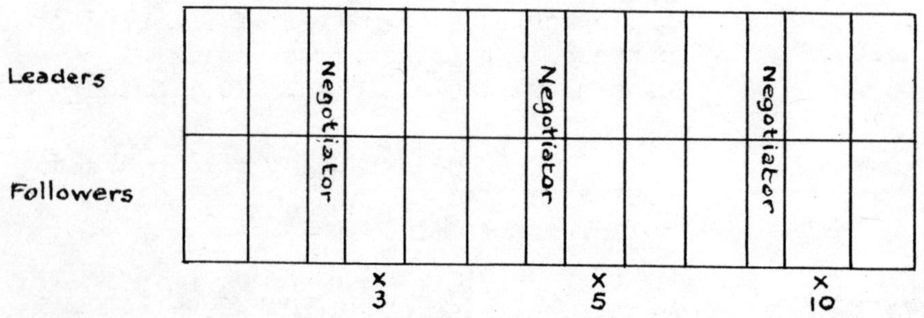

2 Reds = -1 for each team

1 Red & 1 Blue = +1 for choosing Red

= -1 for choosing Blue

2 Blues = +1 for each team

GUIDE TO SIMULATION GAMES

Guide to Simulations/Games For Education and Training . . . . by David Zuckerman and Robert Horn has been revised and greatly expanded. This second edition describes over 600 simulation games in 500 pages and also has chapters on "Getting into Simulation Games" and "How Students Can Make Their Own Simulations." The basic format of the 2nd Edition is the same as the first, each game is described but no critical evaluation is provided. Prices and sources are given for each game. The book is a basic reference source for curriculum centers and libraries who need up-to-date information on simulation games. Still $15 from Information Resources Inc., P.O. Box 417, Lexington, MA 02173.

Economics

The Community

Erwin Rausch c. 1968

Playing Data

Age Level:
- High School
- College
- Management/Administrative

Number of Players: Minimum 3, no maximum

Playing Time: 2 to 5 hours in 30 minute periods

Preparation Time: 1 hour at first only

Materials

Components:
- Players' manuals
- Administrator's manual
- Worksheets

Supplementary Material: A Guide to Teaching

Comment

THE COMMUNITY is the only game we've encountered which gives students a chance to experience the problems of the local, tax-supported economic systems in which they live. The problems of limited funds and competing priorities with which it deals lie close to the root of our national turmoil; I'd like to see every student playing the game from time to time. THE COMMUNITY is an interactive game, and calls for cooperation as well as competition and conflict; too many economics games-and business games as well-ignore the cooperative aspects of man's admittedly self-oriented interactions. Further, I think that of all economics games THE COMMUNITY makes the most significant use of role playing to increase learning. Game events are deterministic, with quantitative (zero sum) outcomes. Play is by teams, and calls for rapid thinking, coalition formation, bargaining and decision making. Results of outside evaluation are available from Didactic Systems, but not from SRA. (D.Z.)

Summary Description

Roles:
- The players represent in turn the taxpayers of the community, the employers and employees,the elected officials

Objectives:
- To earn point credits for acievements and avoid demerits and losses: to build the "best" community

Decisions:
- Determining wage rates
- Determining tax rates and allocation of public revenues to public needs
- Deciding which improvements to approve

Purposes:
- The game is intended to acquaint students with the public sector of the economy
- It illustrates the basic problems of selecting and financing public services

Cost: (1) $1.25, $1.50 for teacher's guide
(2) $1.87 for six players, minimum order $10.00 must include teacher's guide

Producer: (1) Science Research Associates, Inc.
259 East Erie Street
Chicago, Illinois 60611
(2) Didactic Systems, Inc.
Box 500, Westbury, New York 11590

Skill Development: Various

Quiet on the Set—Take One

Patrick A. Mardney

Playing Data

Age Level:
. High School
. College
. Continuing education
. personnel entering an advertising or audio-visual communication firm

Number of Players: 1 to 6

Playing Time: Unknown

Preparation Time: Unknown

Materials:
. dice
. board
. administrator's manual
. pawns
. pegs
. playing decks
. terminology cards
. de-briefing cards

Comment

. non-interactive
. probabilistic: play is influenced by minor random events
. free form role play
. qualitative outcomes
. individual play, calling for skill and decision making (D.Z.)

Summary Description

Roles: . The director of an automotive photographic shooting situation on a stage

Objectives: . To overcome production problems and produce the film

Decisions:
. Which equipment to use
. How to place equipment
. How to overcome production problems

Purposes: . The game may be used to teach stage terminology, types of production problems, and how to use stage equipment, personnel and locations

Cost: Unknown

Producer: Entelek Incorporated
43 Pleasant Street
Newburyport, Massachusetts 01950

Social Studies

The Dynasty Game

Paul Carlos Huang
Dynasty International, Inc. c. 1969

Playing Data

Age Level:
. Junior High
. High School

Number of Players: Minimum 4, no maximum in 4 to 8 teams

Playing Time: Minimum 2 hours in 45 minute periods, maximum variable

Preparation Time: 2 to 3 hours

Materials:
. Board
. Cards
. Players' manuals
. Team manuals
. Administrator's manual
. 47 wooden pieces
. Canvas playing board
. Metal container for the game
. Highly durable packaging

Comment

. interactive, with elements of both conflict and cooperation
. probabilistic
. assigned role positions
. qualitative outcomes
. individual and team play
. play involves decision making, strategic thinking, bargaining, and coalition formation (D.Z.)

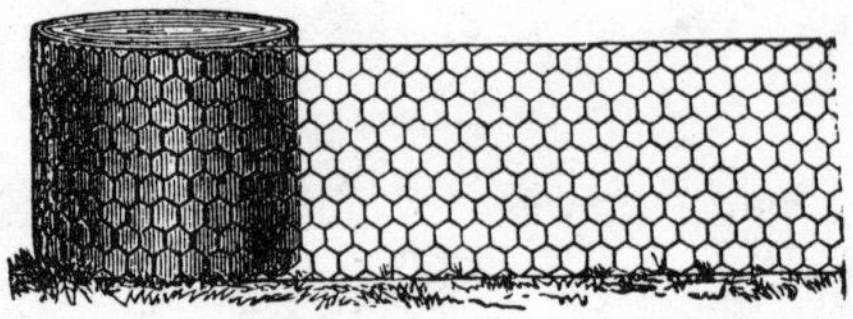

Summary Description

Roles:
. Players represent social positions within an agricultural society
. Players or teams are the Emperor, the upper class positions and the lower class positions

Objectives: . With the exception of the Emperor, all players or teams should move up the social ladder

Decisions: . How does one solve the social-political-economic problems of rural society, such as: the population problem; the building of the public works; how much to tax the public; should players revolt if taxes are too high? etc.

Purposes: . To aquaint students with the real problems of the world. Problems which must be faced by everyone: the population problem, social welfare systems, taxation and what it means, revolution and its problems, the cost of public works, the value of law and order, and the problems created by disorder (the bandit)

Cost: $15.00, commercial set
$30.00, educational set

Producer: Dynasty International, Inc.
815 Park Avenue, New York, N.Y. 10021

SIMULATION/GAMING/NEWS

Simulation/Gaming/News is a tabloid newspaper about learning games. The paper is aimed at the person interested in teaching with games but with a limited formal training in simulations.

The paper reviews games and even occasionally prints a do-it-yourself simulation device ready for use. The subject matter of the games ranges from business to religion. *SGN* is currently the only periodical to treat gaming on a refreshingly clear and simple level.

$5.00 for four issues (published every other month during the school year) from:

SIMULATION/GAMING/NEWS
Academic Games Associates
Box 3039 University Station
Moscow, ID 83843

6 Ways to Design a Bad Simulation Game

By Samuel A. Livingston
The Johns Hopkins University

The following comments refer to a particular type of game (social simulation games) intended for a particular purpose: to increase the players' understanding of the behavior of people in the situation simulated. "Understanding" behavior, in this context, means knowing the reasons for it and the probable consequences of it.

1. Write a scenario for a role-playing exercise and pass it off as a simulation game. Don't make any attempt to reproduce the incentives that guide the behavior of people in the real situation that the so-called simulation game represents. Don't try to determine what resources each person has that he can use to influence the actions of the others. Just write profile sheets for the players that say things like: "You're an idealistic young sociology professor. Now go to the faculty meeting and act like an idealistic young sociology professor."

Of course, the role descriptions can be much more elaborate. The crucial point in keeping the exercise from being a real simulation game is to make sure that the players have no objective standard for judging the quality of their decisions. One way to accomplish this is to avoid having the players make any decisions, so that the whole exercise consists of players expressing their simulated feelings.

2. Begin designing your game by designing the materials. Don't worry about constructing a model. Don't spend a lot of time trying to figure out the reasons for people's decisions in the real-world situation. Instead, spend your time on artwork, graphics, and layout. Make a big, beautiful game board, decorate the cards with realistic pictures, and so on. Then, after you have made all the materials, try to think of something for the players to do with them.

3. Have the players spend most of their time doing things that have nothing to do with the things that concern the real people that the players represent. One way to accomplish this is to have the players spend all their time manipulating the game materials—rolling dice, moving tokens, sorting cards, and so on.

A good way to focus the players' attention on these game features that have nothing to do with the real world is to base the game on Monopoly or Parcheesi; have the players roll dice to see how far they can move their tokens along a path.

4. Have most of the players spend most of their time doing nothing at all. Although you can never reach the ideal state of having none of the players doing anything, you can come close to it. One way is to design a game for a large group in such a way that only one player at a time can do anything active. Then each player will spend most of his time waiting for his turn. Another way is to include as players in the game a lot of people who have very few decisions to make in the real-life situation. Then these players can sit there trying to look interested while the other players make all the decisions.

5. Have the players' success or failure in the game determined almost entirely by chance. There are at least two ways to make your simulation a game of chance. One way is to have a roll of the dice or a spin of a spinner determine the actions that a player is permitted to take. The other way is to include a step in which the players draw a chance card with results that will overwhelm the results of their plans and strategy.

Often just adding a deck of chance cards can turn a good simulation game into a bad one. For example, if the object of the game is to make money, and if by skillful play, clever strategy, and careful planning a good player can earn two or three hundred dollars more than a poor player, the chance cards can provide random bonuses or penalties of four or five hundred dollars.

6. Try to include in the game every aspect of the real-life situation. Your game will then be so complex as to be unplayable. If you want to make doubly sure the game will be unplayable, confront the players with several pages of rules that they have to learn before they can begin to play. And of course, don't construct a simplified version for beginners. Make the players begin with the game in its most complete and complex version.

* * *

("Six Ways to Design a Bad Simulation Game" is adapted from a presentation to the 11th Annual Symposium of the National Gaming Council in October, 1972. Additional copies are available from Academic Games Associates Inc., 430 E. 33rd St., Baltimore, Md. 21218 for 25c each.)

DEVIATE: TRY PLAYING THE PICTURE GAME

By Karin Merrill

Get, before beginning:

Four sets of felt pens, drawing pencils, or other drawing materials, drawing paper, tape to fasten pictures on a blackboard or wall.

Then, begin:

Tape four blocks on the classroom floor to help players in the formulation of groups. Also tape four sections on the blackboard or wall for use during the voting sequence of the game. THE PICTURE GAME is divided up into a series of rounds, each having a different time limit imposed upon the players; total playing time is approximately 45 minutes. Rules are given only for the round then under way!

Round One:

The game leader has the class divide itself into four groups, leaving the membership and size distribution of each group up to the class. Players will be informed at this time that they have two minutes to select a group spokesperson. Each of these group leaders will then come forward and collect sufficient paper and crayons for everyone in the group.

Round Two:

The game coordinator informs the class that from now on, only group spokespersons will be allowed to communicate directly with the coordinator. Then the following announcement is made to the groups:

Every person in the class will now draw a visual representation of himself/herself, or something you feel best describes your identity to the other groups. There is a time limit imposed.

(An authoritative tone of voice in reading this announcement is desirable!)

The time limit, which is obviously flexible to allow for adjustment to different age groups, should be determined by the game leader. Ten minutes is usually sufficient. The game leader should also insist that all questions be asked only by the group leaders. A **very limited** number of questions is desirable.

Round Three:

The game leader instructs players to put their group "symbol" on their drawings. No questions should be answered regarding the "symbol." The game leader now asks all group spokespeople to tape their group's drawings on the designated (blocked) area of the wall or blackboard. Then the following is read to the class:

Each group will have five minutes to collectively decide on the value and credibility of each picture on the board. You do not vote on your own picture. A zero to 5 point scale will be used, with 5 as the highest score a picture can receive. Spokespersons will publicly announce their group's decision at the end of the time period.

The game leader should, again, allow a limited number of questions, and those from group spokespersons only. The game leader should refuse to elaborate on the criteria used in voting, other than reading the announcement again. No questions **must** be answered by the game leader at any time during the game—arbitrariness is encouraged!

Round Four:

The game leader now writes above each picture the score allotted to it from the participating groups. After each single picture is voted upon, the total number of group points are determined by combining the scores.

After all the pictures are evaluated, the game leader should ask the class who won the game, and then offer this suggestion: In terms of community standards, high- and low-scoring groups (those with highest and lowest total group points) would be considered deviant sub-cultures, while the middle groups would represent prevailing community standards.

* * *

Notes on THE PICTURE GAME

The first immediately striking aspect of "The Picture Game" is that uneven membership of groups in a game based on an individual point system is a frequent occurrence, and in fact, is desirable. Just as larger and smaller deviant sub-cultures exist in society, an uneven distribution of power and membership is a necessary and important factor in a sociological discussion of deviance.

The groups who have a larger membership than others represent the large body of society which tends to stigmatize smaller deviant sub-cultures (who are represented by the smaller groups in the game). The smaller groups must necessarily compete for points, too, or survival through power in the community. However, all groups alternate both community and deviant roles, or judging and being judged themselves.

Perhaps the most interesting feature of the game involves group interaction. At no time is personal discussion or group intermingling forbidden to any of the players. Thus, it is possible in the context of the game for two or more groups to form a coalition of power to gain the maximum number of points. The physical realities of the game—that is, a number of people sitting closely together on the floor—are conducive to this occurring. However, since the game leader does not specifically encourage the alignment, game players usually will not deviate from the authoritarian structure of the game.

The assumption that the game leader is completely controlling the situation (heightened by his/her tone and attitude) is a good example of an unconscious obedience to authority, a unique product of our socialization

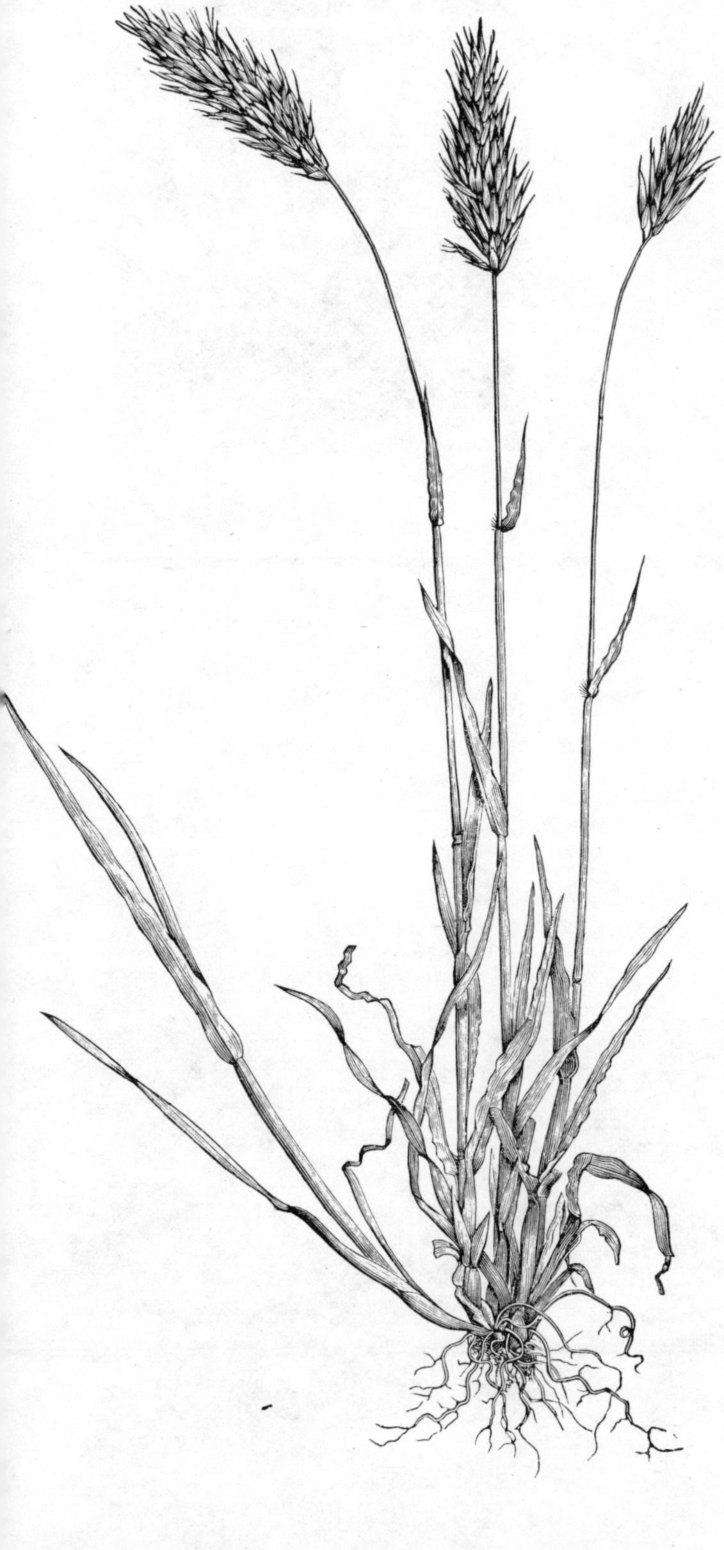

process. This reluctance to rebel or even openly question the rules of the game obviously symbolizes the un-thinking trust and confidence in the "rules" of society, which, in this case, perpetuate the status quo in the stigmatization and socialization processes concerning deviance. **As in simulated form in real life, two deviant sub-cultures rarely merge to form a more effective and beneficial coalition for survival.**

The vague and ambiguous instructions given to the groups as standards for judging pictures fundamentally represent the stigmata associated with having (or not having) certain qualities which are arbitrarily decided upon by the community interpretation. Thus all players feel a solidarity with their own group, and at the same time, must consider their own individual efforts.

Hopefully, those players who receive relatively low scores on their picture will gain a better perspective on the stigmatization process of a deviant: judgment based on very abstract and relative standards, leading to social disapproval. And those who receive a high score will understand the reverse role-model: acceptance and membership in the community.

The scoring process is based on the theory that every member who participates in a "judgment" will have a different perspective of an artistic success. The group decision will enable players to understand more clearly the embodiment of community standards, although individual analysis still occurs. The basic premise of the voting procedure is to suggest that deviance, as well as beauty, is in the eye of the beholder.

* * *

(Karin Merrill can be contacted at 407 First St., No. 1, San Rafael, Ca. 94901, and would be pleased to have reports of experience with THE PICTURE GAME.)

GAMES FOR GROWTH

Games for Growth: Educational Games in the Classroom. . . is a non-technical 200-page paperback explaining the reasons behind simulation gaming, the role of the teacher, the design and adaption of games and the problem of evaluation. Includes 40 pages of games with emphasis on the elementary level but also includes games for junior and senior high. Also has a fine bibliography and a series of practical appendices. By Alice Kaplan Gordon, from Science Research Associates, the Palo Alto Center, 165 University Avenue, Palo Alto, Ca. 94301. The book sells for $4.25 or $3.50 for schools.

GROWTH GAMES

Growth Games . . . is subtitled "How To Tune in Yourself, Your Family, Your Friends." Authors Howard R. Lewis and Dr. Harold S. Streitfeld describe 200 techniques of the Human Potential Movement. There are "growth games" on meditation, non-verbal communication, fantasy trips, muscular tensions, the creative family, breaking through blocks, letting go, and the unconscious. There is some theory in the book but it remains superficial. The authors get carried away with their ideas at times but the book should provide ideas if you pick and choose carefully. $7.50 for the 290-page hardcover from Harcourt Brace, Jovanovich, 757 Third Avenue, N.Y. 10017.

Multi-Media

INTRODUCTION

This section is titled "Multi-media" simply because filmstrips have such a bad reputation -- deservedly. The word "filmstrip" conjures images of boring class sessions in a darkened room, listening to a lecture while inane pictures designed to keep the audience awake are flashed on the screen.

After viewing hundreds of strips, I've come to the conclusion that they proliferate because producers find them a source of high profit margin and teachers find them fine for pacifying bored kids. When the lights are out no one notices how many eyes are closed.

Most filmstrips are made backwards. In communication as in architecture "form follows function." First the message and then the most effective medium. But filmstrips are produced the other way around; a filmstrip producer won't make a film or write a book. The fact that a particular topic lends itself to the filmstrip medium as well as Marcel Marceau to a radio show matters not at all.

Take any filmstrip and look at the pictures alone. What do they communicate? On 90 percent of the strips I've previewed they add absolutely nothing. They do serve the purpose of providing something for the eye so the natives don't become too restless. A true multi-media production uses its multitude of media to communicate. Filmstrips use sound to communicate and visuals as a control agent. A well-conceived filmstrip should be educational for an entire audience of people half of whom are blind and the other half deaf.

Such disguised lectures still provide the norm for filmstrips, but there are exceptions. A handful of filmstrip producers are making creative and high quality sound filmstrips that are of interest to almost any informed audience. The filmstrip is a still-to-be-discovered art form with unlimited potential.

In this section I've listed a few of the filmstrip producers who have come to my attention whose work is more likely to excite than to bore. I hope that future editions of this catalog can include more. Filmstrip descriptions are sometimes taken directly from those submitted by the producer because they are judged to be an accurate reflection of the film-strip. Also in this section are a few suppliers of slides with many uses.

SCHLOAT PRODUCTIONS

Alienation

An examination of alienation in modern society; its causes, its effects.

Part One: Discussion of the meaning of alienation; forms of alienation, causes of it; alienation as a healthy response; the alienated as hero, rebel, underdog, cynic, revolutionary, innovator; universality of alienation; results of alienation; self alienation; Christ as alienated individual; observations from Kenneth Kenniston, Erich Fromm, the *Bible*.

Part Two: Nature as a refuge; Freud's view: civilized man's growing industrialization and urbanization as a cause of alienation; rapid change as a cause of alienation; decreasing influence of family, community, religion; the individual's feeling of powerlessness in mass society; hope for the future; observations by Henry David Thoreau, Philip Slater, Erich Fromm, Michael Harrington, Albert Camus, Vance Packard, Emile Durkheim, Johann Huizinga.

Two Color Sound Filmstrips, Program Guide
Release Date: April, 1973

Catalogue Number 329/N	
Sound on Discs	$40.00
Sound on Cassettes	$46.00

Sometimes it seems there are far too few alienated people.

The Visual City

Writer-photographer Fran Hosken here establishes a connection between the visual expression and the urban functions of a city.

WHAT IS A CITY?

Good question. Here pictures from all over the world show the functions of a city and how people "use" it.

Monoliths.

SPACE AND SCALE

This segment explores the visual criteria of a city. Space and scale are difficult to define in words — but not in pictures. Here we see how avenues, courts, columns, fountains, bridges, parks and buildings combine to give a city its special look.

COLOR, TEXTURE AND PATTERN

The surface qualities of the materials used to build the urban environment are observed with the purpose of making the audience look with new eyes at what surrounds them every day.

FORM AND MOVEMENT

The success of a city or urban space can be measured in the interaction of people.

This filmstrip is the climax of the presentation and establishes the connection between people, their activities, and the physical arrangements of the city. Location photography from around the world emphasizes the excitement and variety of city happenings.

4 Color Sound Filmstrips, Program Guide
Part One: 81 Frames, 8 Minutes
Part Two: 83 Frames, 9 Minutes
Part Three: 80 Frames, 8 Minutes
Part Four: 80 Frames, 7 Minutes
Release Date: October, 1972

Catalogue Number 468/N	
Sound on Discs	$66.00
Sound on Cassettes	$78.00

Poetry: Commitment and Alienation

A program designed to shorten the distance between poetry and students by visually interpreting poems and themes to which they can respond intellectually.

Escape?

The question of identity is an immediate question with most people on the conscious level and a lifetime quest for everyone. How do we see ourselves? How do others see us? Can we have different identities for different people and situations? Poets and adolescents seek their identity in much the same way — by speculating about values and beliefs and commitments. The period of alienation most people experience can be painful and frustrating. These are the ideas explored in this program: Commitment and Alienation.

Part One: the poets' quest for identity in a classic religious sense — in reference to God. Quotations from the *Bible,* Yeats, Ginsberg, Auden, Hopkins, Donne, Thomas.

Part Two: the poet's search for meaning in other forms of commitment — to other people, to the sensual nature of the world, to social or political involvement, to mortality. Quotations from cummings, Arnold, Spender, Stevens, Moore.

Two Color Sound Filmstrips, Program Guide
Part One: 116 Frames, 13 Minutes
Part Two: 76 Frames, 9 Minutes
Release Date: January, 1973

Catalogue Number 740/N	
Sound on Discs	$40.00
Sound on Cassettes	$46.00

Free Will and Utopias

What is man? How should he live in society?

The two sound filmstrip approach facilitates analysis of basic questions — enabling students to see distinct topics and play with their interconnections.

IS MAN FREE?

Using examples ranging from Lt. Calley to *The Brothers Karamazov*, this sound filmstrip looks at man as he is. Concepts discussed include: free will, determinism, dignity, conscience, freedom, environment, operant conditioning and the Horatio Alger myth.

The program explores the ideas of B. F. Skinner, Reinhold Niebuhr, Jean Paul Sartre and Sigmund Freud.

UTOPIAS

We are all at least partly defined by the societies in which we live. Like people in all ages, we imagine a better condition than our own. This is the germ of utopia.

Utopias discusses state, society, order, control, individuality, technology, equality, justice, wealth and democracy. It examines ideas contained in More's *Utopia,* Plato's *Republic,* Bacon's *New Atlantis,* Morris' *News From Nowhere,* Zamiatin's *We,* Thoreau's *Walden,* Skinner's *Walden Two* and Huxley's *Brave New World.* It also includes comments from the work of Buckminster Fuller, Paolo Soleri, John Lobell, John Donne and Friedrich Nietszche.

Two Color Sound Filmstrips, Program Guide
Part One: 66 Frames, 14 Minutes
Part Two: 68 Frames, 15 Minutes
Release Date: December, 1972

Catalogue Number 611/N	
Sound on Discs	$40.00
Sound on Cassettes	$46.00

Is there such a thing as Free Will?
What is a Utopia?

Teach a deeper understanding of China through her poetry.

Chinese Poetry

An exploration of Chinese literature and culture.
Poetic expression provides us with a reflection of the thoughts and feelings of a people. For the Chinese this is especially true since they have been recording their thoughts in a living, written language for more than 25 centuries, longer than any other people. It is for this reason that the poetry of China is offered to students in America — that through the study of her literature we will learn about her as a people, we will dig beyond those iron curtains and commune walls. We will become more tolerant, more understanding, more appreciative.

Part One: Folk song origins of Chinese poetry, recurrent themes and devices, excerpts from *East Gate Willows, Spirit of the Mountain, Book of Songs,* Selections from works of Li Shang-yin, Tu Fu, Wang Wei, Li Po, Li Ch'ing-chao, Pai Chui.

Part Two: Western discovery of China, parallels between literary and social revolution. Selections from work of Dr. Hu Shih, Hus Chih-mo, Kuo Mo-Jo, Mao-Tse-tung, Ai-ching, Yu Kwang-chung.

Note: This set complements a soon to be released program, *Chinese Art,* described elsewhere in this brochure.

Two Color Sound Filmstrips, Program Guide.
Part One: 91 Frames, 12 Minutes
Part Two: 100 Frames, 15 Minutes
Release Date: February, 1973

Catalogue Number 241/N	
Sound on Discs	$40.00
Sound on Cassettes	$46.00

Complete catalog free from:

SCHLOAT PRODUCTIONS
150 White Plains Road
Tarrytown, N.Y. 10591

ARGUS

What man values tells us who he is and what he is in the process of becoming. These filmstrips explore human values. They probe the ways in which values affect our lives and shape our destiny. Unique combinations of sights and sounds take viewers on journeys into the real world where values are often confused, abstract, obscure, or in conflict. The filmstrips probe, cajole, challenge, and amuse. They create enjoyable as well as enlightening experiences. They touch on the "gut" issues of today's world, particularly the world of youth. But they never preach; they never judge. These thought-provoking filmstrips encourage viewers to reflect and discover their own attitudes toward life and other people. (Appropriate for young adults, parents, teachers, and other study groups.)

The filmstrips from Argus Communications are brief, fast moving, and stunningly photographed. Preview reading scripts are available upon request from:

ARGUS COMMUNICATIONS
7440 Natchez Avenue
Niles, Ill. 60648

WHY AM I AFRAID TO TELL YOU WHO I AM?

"I am afraid to tell you who I am because if I tell you who I am, you may not like who I am and that is all I have." This is an exploration of the games and masks we use to avoid honest communication. Based on John Powell's popular paperback, this two-part filmstrip explores basic psychological principles involved in interpersonal relationships and growth in self-awareness. The games and masks show our tendencies to make others react to us in the way we *want* them to react. We must recognize this reliance on mechanical and manipulative patterns before we can mature as persons. The viewer is given an opportunity to compare his patterned reactions with his real potential for authentic growth. Which of these games do I play? Thirty-six roles are introduced, including such notable types as: "always right", "the body beautiful", "the clown", "the dominator", "the flirt" and "the worrier". Photo and cartoon characterizations round out this most extraordinary presentation. (Two filmstrips, record or cassette and guide.) Approx. 210 frames, approx. 20 minutes.

Record F-64 **$35.00**
Cassette F-65 **$35.00**

CONSUMERLAND: HOW HIGH THE MOUNTAIN?

Via satirical and humorous cartoon illustrations, viewers take a unique tour of a fictitious country called CONSUMERLAND. In this land, discovered long ago by the explorer Christopher Consumer, all citizens enjoy the right, indeed the responsibility, to accumulate as many possessions as possible in their relentless pursuit of happiness. The underlying philosophy in this land is known as "happiness galore" and is based on two historic documents: The Declaration of Dependence and The Right to Bills. Sure this filmstrip is humorous. But it is provocative, too. It poses open-ended questions that involve viewers in discussion of their part in the consumer syndrome. Approx. 120 frames, approx. 10 minutes.

Record F-60 **$17.50**
Cassette F-61 **$17.50**

THE WONDER OF IT ALL

If there is a single characteristic shared by all children, it is the capacity to wonder. To delight in the simple, ordinary things that are all around. Too often this ability to perceive reality with wonderment and joy is lost in the process of growing up. The world connives to take away the wonder and leave only boredom. This filmstrip serves as a catalyst to help restore the viewer's sense of wonder that may have been lost in the routine of daily existence. Here is a delightful invitation to re-encounter the wonder of the world and the wonder that is us. Return to the joy-filled times of childhood fantasy. A poetic and picturesque invitation to rediscover life. Approx. 100 frames; approx. 10 minutes.

Record F-68 **$17.50**
Cassette F-69 **$17.50**

YOU HAVE TO WANT SOMETHING

All of us experience times of confusion and indecision. Young people particularly grope for identity and direction. Failure to find it results in apathy and even a loss of interest in life itself. It isn't enough to be "against", either. It is important to know what we are "for" and why. Values determine choices and behavior. This filmstrip looks at some traditional American values that are now questioned by many people. Short vignettes of contrasts are intended to provoke the viewer to think in terms of what he really values. The objective is to challenge vascillating or apathetic behavior, to encourage the viewer to identify, clarify and choose his own values. The accent is on the positive. Approx. 100 frames; approx. 10 minutes.

Record F-62 **$17.50**
Cassette F-63 **$17.50**

TECHNOLOGY: MASTER OR SLAVE?

Throughout history man has had slaves in one form or another. Modern man, however, finds himself in a unique and extremely challenging position. As his competence in technology advances at an unbelievable rate, his society and his earth are being threatened. Vast forces are put into play with little or no thought given to the consequences. Radical changes are made with no knowledge of what final effect they will have on man and society. Will science and technology — creations of man's own ingenuity — enslave him or will he master their power and potential to improve the quality of human life? This filmstrip is an ironic and provocative treatment of one of the most important issues of our times. Approx. 100 frames; approx. 10 minutes.

Record F-66 **$17.50**
Cassette F-67 **$17.50**

PERCEPTION

"A spirited narration delivered against the ever increasing beat of a drum urges awareness of line, shape, texture, color, and pattern in one's surroundings." (*The Booklist*, April 1, 1971.) Considers such questions as "Do you see what I see?" while exploring both perception and creative expression. The guide includes sensory exercises designed to heighten individual perception. (Revised 1971) 85 frames; 8:45. F-74 **$17.50**

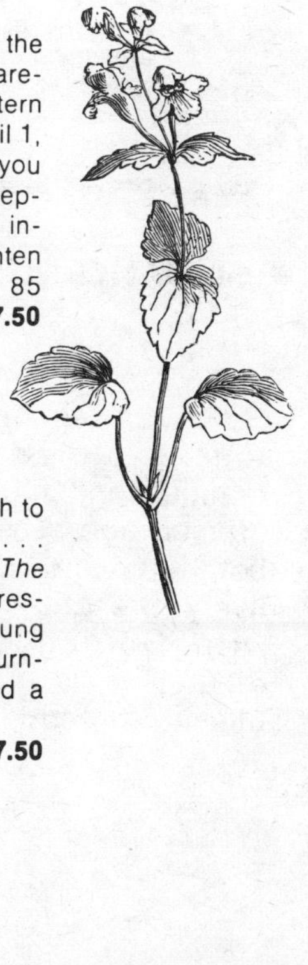

POLLUTION

". . . provocative and imaginative approach to the problems of the modern environment . . . an intense and realistic presentation." (*The Booklist*, April 1, 1971.) Here is an impressive discussion-starter for adult and young adult groups. The accompanying guide furnishes questions, statistics, resources, and a daily pollution chart. 90 frames; 8:30.

F-70 **$17.50**

WAR OR PEACE

". . . excellent stimulus for discussion in history, social sciences, humanities, and current events classes . . ." *(The Booklist,* March 1, 1971.) Song, poetry, scripture and philosophy combine in this multi-media exploration of the forces that have shaped war, aggression and peace. The accompanying guide contains arms statistics as well as resource materials. 54 frames; 11:40. F-75 **$17.50**

ECOLOGY

Our natural world operates on an ecosystem of recycling, balance and conservation that man must learn to respect. Sound and visuals thoughtfully keyed to contemporary concerns. All generations until now have selfishly exploited the earth's resources with no consideration of the consequences. Will ours be the first generation to plan a future and care for the earth? Or will there be any future at all? (Revised 1971) 113 frames; 10:40. F-71 **$17.50**

BUILDING THE EARTH

Priest, poet and scientist Pierre Teilhard de Chardin probes for answers to the questions of the meaning of life. Penetrating the mysteries of the basic composition of the universe to the beginning of reflective thought and through the socialization of man, Teilhard gives us vital and optimistic insights. Ideal for provocative philosophical, scientific, and religious inquiry. With discussion guide. (Revised 1971) 108 frames, 11:00. F-72 **$17.50**

LIGHT SHOW

Light and form, color and shape blend and separate in visual after visual. The non-linear progression encourages use with your choice of sound as a discovery medium for interpretation in art, literature, and drama classes. No sound or guide. 76 frames. F-73 **$17.50**

MAN THE MAN

We took a young girl's moving and sensitive poetic interpretation of man and set it to music, dramatic narration and photographic interpretation. If your group is language arts, religion or adult education we know you will want to look several times at this penetrating exploration of the meaning of man. Perfect use of the medium. 104 frames; 9:55. F-78 **$17.50**

FACES OF MAN

This filmstrip explores the diversity and beauty of faces. In expressions, in features, in crowds, alone. Sense the beauty in diversity. Do you create stories behind each face that you see? Deepen your awareness of what there is to see in a face and the risk involved in communicating. A fascinating study for any youth or adult group. With accompanying guide. 78 frames; 6:00. F-76 **$17.50**

ROLES & GOALS

Which comes first — role or goal? Young people are searching for new answers to the old quandry. Many feel a contradiction between the two, especially when roles and goals are imposed on them by others. Excellent for youth and adults and a good generation gap bridger. 77 frames; 6:00. F-77 **$17.50**

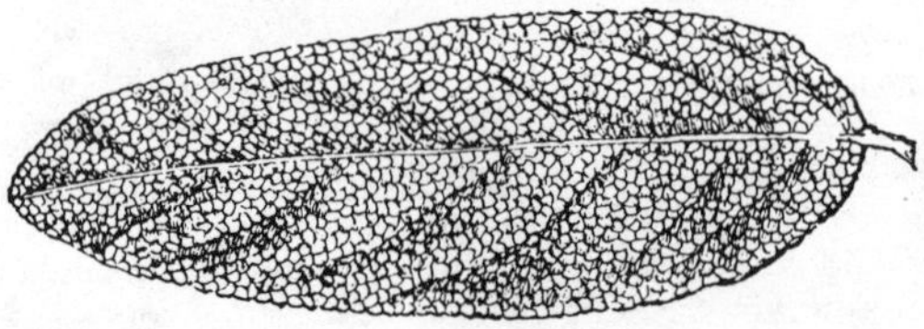

PREVIEW INFORMATION
Reading scripts and generous full color samplings of the filmstrip visuals available in bound edition for preview purposes. Requests for additional preview materials will be honored only if accompanied by a purchase order and signature of the potential buyer. Ten day preview basis only.

GUIDANCE ASSOCIATES

What is Marriage? is a two part Guidance Associates filmstrip that explores the present realities and future possibilities of marriage. The filmstrip uses both interview and narration in a lively presentation in keeping with Guidance Associates' reputation as one of the finest filmstrip producers.

The strip approaches marriage not as a religious union but as a social phenomenon. Marriage is presented as an almost inevitable adult experience; 95% of the population marries and most at a rather young age.

A bachelor is interviewed and tells of the various pressures placed on him by family, friends and employer to be married. A successfully married couple tells why they think they have enjoyed marriage. Dr. Margaret Mead questions adolescent dating patterns and proposes a need for alternative forms of marriage as well as alternatives to marriage itself. Occasional pauses are provided in the narration for discussion.

Part II deals with possibilities for the future of marriage—living arrangements between unmarried people, staying single, group marriages and even homosexual marriages. The filmstrip concludes with the recognition of certain common elements needed for any successful relationship.

The filmstrip is a provocative stimulus for discussion and value education. Two filmstrips with records or cassettes and discussion guide cost about $40 from Guidance Associates, Pleasantville, N.Y. 10570.

Mass Media: Impact on a Nation. . . is a two part Guidance Associates production. Part I begins with a brief history of media and then focuses on television through comments by Nicholas Johnson and Erik Barnouw. Part II begins with the 1968 Chicago Convention and Spiro Agnew's remarks about the media to examine restraints on media.

The filmstrip is a bit dated but still serves nicely as an introduction to a unit or course on the effects of mass media.

Freedom of the Press--Today is also from Guidance Associates with the help of the Associated Press. The two part filmstrips examines the crucial topic of freedom of the press versus the need for government secrecy. An excellent introductory unit that features comments by Herb Klein, J. R. Wiggins (former editor of the **Washington Post**), and two Pulitzer Prize Winning correspondents--Horst Faas and Peter Arnett.

Cost of each filmstrip is about $35 from Guidance Associates

MASCULINITY and FEMININITY is a fine filmstrip. Part one points out the male and female stereotypes and explains that these stereotypes are taught from childhood and not a matter of anatomy determining destiny. It points out that if a man feels secure in his masculinity, he does not have to reinforce his male image. The filmstrip encourages more flexible attitudes towards sexual roles. This is a rare and valuable teaching aid about **sexuality** instead of the more limited concept of **sex.** It examines the sex roles in other cultures to substantiate the concept that sex roles are learned and can be a deadening limitation on personal freedom and development. $40 for the two filmstrips and records from Guidance Associates.

THE PEOPLE PROBLEM is a set of two sound filmstrips from Guidance Associates and the Associated Press. Part I defines the scope of the world population explosion and outlines its consequences. Dr. Bernard Berelson, President of the Population Council, explains how the population problem is more one of the quality of life than its quantity. The uneven distribution of population and resources, the skyrocketing rate of population growth on the world level, and the problem of the greatest growth being where it can be least afforded, are pointed out. The cause of the problem is pinpointed in the medical advances which have prolonged life and decreased the death rate; death control was never challenged on ethical grounds while birth control lagged behind, considered immoral by many. Problems of overcrowding and violence, war, crime and the slums are related to excessive population growth.

Part II of the filmstrip tackles the question of how to deal with these problems. It comes to a very affirmative stance for birth control, freely chosen.

Discussion guide, two color filmstrips and two lp records for $35 from Guidance Associates

VENEREAL DISEASE: A PRESENT DANGER is a Guidance Associates Filmstrip which succeeds admirably in presenting the facts young people should know about America's number one communicable disease. The filmstrip does not intend, and does not attempt, to treat the moral aspects of the problem nor the Christian viewpoint on the matter. It is, however, the best presentation of the medical and social facets of VD.

Part one presents a brief summary of the history of VD pointing out that both gonorrhea and syphilis are impossible to have except with close physical contact with another and can be easily cured but only by a doctor. It then focuses on gonorrhea which is ten times more common than syphilis and is actually epidemic in the U.S. It points out that gonorrhea is a painful disease, often causes sterility, cripples and can effect later pregnancies. The male and female symtoms are examined and the treatment explained.

Part two looks at syphilis, a disease contracted by 80,000 Americans yearly. The symptoms disappear without treatment but the disease can resurface any number of times up to twenty years from the time of contraction causing severe brain or heart damage. Because of this, syphilis is perhaps the more dangerous of the two as it leaves the impression of just a passing rash. Treatment and prevention of the disease are examined and the usual questions answered.

Two filmstrips, two 12" lp records, $40 from Guidance Associates, Harcourt, Brace & World leaders discuss their religion, sense of values and humor, land ownership, and the "Red Power" movement for freedom and self-determination. *Produced in cooperation with The Associated Press.*

Part I: 113 frames/16 minutes
Part II: 97 frames/13 minutes
2 filmstrips; 2 12" LPs/$35.00/7D-400 406
2 filmstrips; 2 cassettes/$39.00/7D-400 414
Discussion Guide

"This filmstrip program presents a balanced and realistic view of a very real situation with fair and accurate facts." THE CATECHIST

The Exploited Generation

Program helps students understand the economic and cultural role of mass advertising in our society. In Part I, students see how advertisers and manufacturers view them as a market; how industry researches youth tastes and interests. Young people discuss their own buying habits and motivations; analyze factors which distinguish wise from unwise buying; comment on use of status, personal insecurity and conformism as selling tactics. Part II focuses on ways young people can become more effective consumers. Experts discuss dealing with sales personnel, credit buying, banking, consumer education. Features exclusive interviews with former Presidential Adviser Betty Furness, disc jockey Gary Stevens, George Johnson of *Seventeen* Magazine, and Samuel Grafton, publisher of *Youth Report.*

Part I: 107 frames/14 minutes
Part II: 105 frames/14 minutes
2 filmstrips; 2 12" LPs/$35.00/7D-101 251
2 filmstrips; 2 cassettes/$39.00/7D-101 277
Discussion Guide

Dare to Be Different

Program discusses the powerful forces representing tradition and conformity in American society, and students probe valid and false expressions of individuality — total personal nonconformity, rebellion for its own sake, willingness to sacrifice for strongly held beliefs. Program stimulates discussion of criteria for conforming to group standards, social norms, family direction, particularly when choices involve conflicting values and loyalties. Program emphasizes the individual's responsibility for his actions and stresses the importance of distinctions between reflex rejection and creative evaluation of ideas and customs we live by.

Part I: 97 frames/15 minutes
Part II: 113 frames/15 minutes
2 filmstrips; 2 12" LPs/$40.00/7D-100 956
2 filmstrips; 2 cassettes/$44.00/7D-100 949
Discussion Guide

The American Poor: A Self-Portrait

Composed entirely of on-location photography and the words of people candidly discussing their own situations and problems, program focuses on similarities *and* distinctions between urban and rural poverty today. Part I examines dietary, medical, transportation and housing problems of poor people in Patten, Maine (population 1300). Program examines the area's depressed timber and farming economy, aid available to the poor, the reluctant exodus of young people seeking better employment and living standards. Part II portrays attitudes and facts of life among the poor of Pittsburgh, Pennsylvania; considers crime and drugs as complications of urban poverty; proximity with more affluent groups; the humiliation of being forced onto welfare for lack of work; strong general resentment and desire to permanently escape poverty neighborhoods.

Part I: 89 frames/12 minutes
Part II: 71 frames/12 minutes
2 filmstrips; 2 12" LPs/$35.00/7D-417 509
2 filmstrips; 2 cassettes/$39.00/7D-417 517
Discussion Guide

The Literature of Protest

Program develops insights into social dissent through an analysis of past and present protest literature. Part I excerpts and discusses selections from Aristophanes, the *New Testament,* 9th-century China, 18th and 19th-century England and America. Part II focuses on the 20th century through works by muckrakers Lincoln Steffens and Upton Sinclair, anti-war poet Wilfred Owen, Sinclair Lewis, the political protest literature of H. L. Mencken and John Dos Passos, post-World War II protest against nuclear warfare and totalitarianism. Part III begins with "Beat Generation" writers Allen Ginsberg and Lawrence Ferlinghetti. Students compare early 60's protest by Rachel Carson and Michael Harrington with recent works concerning the anti-war movement, black militance, campus radicalism, consumerism and ecology.

Color and b/w.

Part I: 71 frames/13 minutes
Part II: 80 frames/14 minutes
Part III: 74 frames/14 minutes
3 filmstrips; 3 12" LPs/$49.50/7D-517 001
3 filmstrips; 3 cassettes/$55.50/7D-517 019
Discussion Guide

"This is excellent for high school and adult audiences, to put the civil disobedience movement into its historic context and to spark discussion." FILM NEWS

American Film Festival Blue Ribbon Award

Civil Disobedience

Examines origins of social, political and racial protest in the United States; pro and con arguments on violent and nonviolent protest. Students explore issues including civil rights, Vietnam, labor strikes, campus unrest; consider the contributions of Thoreau, Ghandi and Martin Luther King in developing the philosophy of nonviolence. Program analyzes official resistance to protest and the "law and order" issue; features exclusive interviews with William Sloane Coffin of Yale, Floyd McKissick, Reverend Andrew Young of the S.C.L.C. and Dean Robert McKay of New York University Law School. *Produced in cooperation with The Associated Press.*

Part I: 103 frames/19 minutes
Part II: 86 frames/15 minutes
2 filmstrips: 2 12" LPs/$35.00/7D-403 707
2 filmstrips; 2 cassettes/$39.00/7D-403 723
Discussion Guide

DENOYER-GEPPERT

Denoyer-Geppert Audio-Visuals has a conservative image and is commonly thought of as the maps-and-globes people. They have now released some fine filmstrips that deserve at least a 30 day review.

WOMEN: THE FORGOTTEN MAJORITY is an edited version of a Gloria Steinham talk. The visuals are almost incidental to the talk (as is the case in most filmstrips) but they do give the eyeball something to do. Ms. Steinham's talk is not her best but is concise, easily understandable and sure to provoke plenty of discussion. There are two strips and a record, total playing time is 28 min. Frames change every 16 seconds on the average. Gloria Steinham, even at her worst, is better than 99% of most other filmstrip scripts.

THE RESPONSIBLE EXERCISE OF STUDENT RIGHTS provokes the kind of discussion about school conditions that is productive but that can easily be obtained without the filmstrip. Why listen to other kids talk about their school when you could be listening to your own students? Do you need to spend $34 and 35 minutes merely to "provoke discussion?"

IS DEMOCRACY ALIVE AND WELL? is an excellent "heavy" filmstrip featuring interviews with Paul Goodman, Barry Goldwater, Richard Ottinger, Allard Lowenstein, Julian Bond and Michael Harrington. The contrasting opinions on American Democracy give plenty of room for choice and debate on a crucial topic. Two filmstrips, two records, total playing time 32 minutes.

Others in production include ON BEING BLACK by William Grier, POWER OF MY SPIRIT: THE AMERICAN INDIAN with commentary by Buffy Ste. Marie, CLEARWATER: A DREAM FOR A RIVER as told by Pete Seeger, and others that sound equally interesting.

Each filmstrip costs $34 and all are available for 30 day free preview from Denoyer-Geppert

Lifestyle 2000: Inquiry into the Future
. . . . Schools are only beginning to recognize that a study of the future is a valid part of the curriculum. In response to this recognition a few companies are producing media material about the future. One of the best to come along so far is the Denoyer-Geppert filmstrip **Lifestyle 2000.** The sound filmstrip is in four parts, each about 80-frames in 10 minutes. Each consists of an interview with a futurist--Hugh Downs, Paolo Soleri, Herman Kahn and Ray Bradbury. The four segments, however, are economically placed on two rolls of film. The Hugh Downs segment provides a gentle and general introduction to the study of the future paving the way for the mind-blowing ideas of Paolo Soleri. Soleri works mostly with young people in Arizona building his city of the future--a gigantic single building that serves as a total environment. Herman Kahn talks of knowledge and the ability to control the future and Ray Bradbury delivers a kind of pep talk encouraging optimism.

$30.60 from Denoyer-Geppert, 5235 Ravenswood Ave., Chicago, IL 60640. Also ask for their rapidly growing catalog of filmstrips.

A full documentation of the recent San Francisco oil spill—a tragic event that has since been repeated on countless other shorelines. The program explores the nature of responsibility—where did the responsibility lie? Who accepted responsibility? Who denied it? Students see for themselves the effects of a man-made disaster in terms of ecology and politics. They will follow the activities of the volunteers who responded to calls for help to save birds and clean beaches. See *ad hoc* groups labor hour after hour in an attempt to save thousands of birds coated in oil; grasp the full implication of the disaster as they watch two people spend two hours cleaning a single sea bird.

The concerned parties were all interviewed on the site—the Coast Guard, the Sierra Club, city officials, oil company executives—all give their views on the cause and effect of the massive oil spill. The program proceeds to examine the far reaching political, social, ecological consequences to San Francisco and the surrounding communities, focusing on the complex inter-relationships of groups within nature and groups within human society.

Two parts $34.00 *Cat. #69715*

Viva La Causa: The Migrant Labor Movement

Through a series of interviews with migrant workers and union organizers, this program traces the rise of Cesar Chavez's farm workers union. More than anything else it is a study in patience—an outstanding example of the successful use of non-violence to achieve social and economic reforms. The Mexican-American migrant workers of California, under Chavez's dynamic leadership have used the establishment's processes to fight for their cause—law suits, strikes, protest marches, letters to Congressmen, boycotts. Slowly and painfully through every legitimate means of protest these disenfranchised workers have begun to attain the means with which to change their lives. Aft decades of low wages, seasonal emplo ment, substandard housing, lack of ed cation and medical care, a new begi ning has been made for America's la unprotected workers.

Personal interviews reveal the dep of individual and collective patience men and women face trial, jail, pr longed appeals, waiting until justice done in the courts. The Mexican-Ame icans have accepted society's judgme because they believe in the justice their cause—the right to a living wag a decent home, education for their chi dren, medicine for their sick. Wea from the long struggle, they rema hopeful that their first gains are by r means their last. This program is ideal suited for classes in American histor current affairs, economics and civics.

Two parts $34.00 *Cat. #697*

MULTI-MEDIA PRODUCTIONS

P.O. BOX 5097
STANFORD, CA. 94305

DARWINISM AND ECONOMIC LIFE

What lesson can we learn in our economic life from the principles of Charles Darwin? Why does saturation lead to depletion? Why is infinitely prolonged growth not possible? What are the advantages of specialization? An examination of the national economy from the viewpoint of Darwin's principles, showing the relationship between the principles of ecology and those of economics. Two filmstrips.

Cat. No. 7-07042R (Record) $14.95
Cat. No. 7-07042C (Cassette) $16.95

THE CULT OF TRUE WOMANHOOD

Is the typical male attitude toward women really only a continuation of pre-Victorian attitudes that evolved in the New World? What were the four cardinal virtues demanded of women then – and do they differ much from what men expect today? Why did the Cult of True Womanhood die down – but the concepts linger on for a century? The program traces the evolution of True Womanhood from its birth in 1800 to its demise at the end of the Civil War. Illustrations from contemporary magazines. Two filmstrips.

Cat. No. 7-07053R (Record) $14.95
Cat. No. 7-07053C (Cassette) $16.95

FEMINISM AS A RADICAL MOVEMENT

Is the radical nature of Woman's Liberation today just a reflection of other radicalism or in the true tradition of Feminism? Why have women been forced in the past to disguise their goals in order to win acceptance? Is there really anything to be gained by trying to convince people that change is really an expression of conservatism? This program reviews the Woman's Movement, the struggle for the vote, the disillusionment that followed, and the new direction of feminism. It provides a needed background to understanding today's events. Two filmstrips.

Cat. No. 7-07063R (Record) $14.95
Cat. No. 7-07063C (Cassette) $16.95

LEGAL AND ILLEGAL – THE DISPOSSESSION OF THE INDIANS

Why do men feel the need for a legal cloak to the most heinous deeds? Why does so much of society's actions seem directed toward some form of legal justification for everyting? Are legality and morality synonomous? The various justifications, some moral, some legal, most illegal that were erected by the settlers to dispossess the Indians from their lands are examined. The student is encouraged to try to develop a mental framework in terms of the context of the times to understand the past. Two filmstrips.

Cat. No. 7-07055R (Record) $14.95
Cat. No. 7-07055C (Cassette) $16.95

WHAT WAS AND IS FASCISM?

The political, economic, and social philosophy of fascism, from historical theory to practice. Evaluations of fascism in Germany, Italy, and Spain, as well as the minor nations, from contemporary sources. Fascism today.

50 slides. Cat. No. 8-07016 $32.50

WILL THE REAL JOHN F. KENNEDY PLEASE STAND UP?

What were President Kennedy's beliefs on the major issues facing the nation? Was he a statesman or merely a seeker for power? The myth and the realities. An exercise in problem solving.

50 slides. Cat. No. 8-07017 $32.50

THE SUPREME COURT – INTERPRETER OR LAWMAKER?

How did the founding fathers see the Supreme Court? How have the justices seen it? How has the president seen it? How has the congress seen it? What does "strict constitutionalist" mean to various people? A basis for a mock trial.

50 slides. Cat. No. 8-07018 $32.50

THE ELECTORAL COLLEGE – A FRAUD OR PRESERVER OF THE RIGHT OF THE MINORITY?

How did the founding fathers view the electoral college? What have been the views of politicians and statesmen through history? Proposals for "reform". The arguments against "reform". A basis for a mock debate.

50 slides. Cat. No. 8-07019 $32.50

GUN CONTROL – OR PRESCRIPTION FOR DICTATORSHIP?

The views of the founding fathers on the right to bear arms. Opposing views throughout history on that right. Modern views on gun control. Evaluations of gun control laws. Proposed solutions and positions against such solutions. A basis for a debate.

50 slides. Cat. No. 8-07020 $32.50

O-IT-YOURSELF AUDIO-VISUAL KITS

ese unique kits enable you and your class to develop their own audio-visual presentation in a true inquiry mode. The facts and gamut of inions are included in a memory bank in pamphlet form, and the tools to develop a presentation are included, as well as how-to-do-it ormation. You and your class determine the directions in which you wish to proceed, the extent of involvement, and the themes and rusts.

ch kit consists of the following:

a. Five copies of a student handbook which includes:
   - Background on the subject
   - Summarization of existing opinions, without conclusions
   - Quotes from divergent sources, not paraphrased
   - Chronology, where applicable
   - Dramatis Personnae, where applicable

b. A set of slides in plastic envelopes.

c. A handbook on how to develop and produce audio-visual materials.

d. A teacher's manual, including means of involving the class, as well as some suggested themes and thrusts.

e kits may be used in just about any way you or the class decide – individual, group, or class projects – exposition, persuasion, briefing ckgrounder, debate, trial, light and sound show – either based on the suggested themes and thrusts or anything that seems relevant to e class.

ch kit is self-contained. We've eliminated the need for library research so students can concentrate on the materials. The quotes and urce materials reflect a wide divergence of opinions, many of which may be new to the students. We want to give the students a balanced ew, but still don't want to give them an encyclopaedic presentation. In many ways, it's little different from an ordinary library signment, except that the emphasis is on operation, rather than research.

WHAT WAS THE BASIS OF MODERN AMERICAN FOREIGN POLICY?

The intervention in Mexico in 1913, the reasoning of Woodrow Wilson about the U.S. role in the world, the defense of freedom and democracy as the cornerstone of foreign policy, the reaction of the American people, the genesis of our interventions in World Wars I and II, Korea, Viet Nam.

50 slides. Cat. No. 8-07001 $32.50

WILL THE REAL GEORGE WASHINGTON PLEASE STAND UP?

The separation of the man from the legend. What was he really like? What did he think of the basic problems that all peoples as well as nations face? What can we learn from him about the issues that divide us today?

50 slides. Cat. No. 8-07002 $32.50

MY COUNTRY, RIGHT OR WRONG?

What is patriotism? The three basic approaches as articulated by Washington, Lee, and Wilson, their application to modern life, the views of others through the ages, definitions of "country," "right," and "wrong".

50 slides. Cat. No. 8-07003 $32.50

SHALL WE DISARM?

A history of disarmament in modern times. The contrasting opinions of the nuclear powers, and the non-nuclear powers, total versus limited disarmament, the need for security.

50 slides. Cat. No. 8-07004 $32.50

FREEDOM OF THE PRESS, OR LICENSE TO LIBEL?

A history of the evolution of freedom of the press since the 16th century, the opinions of the founding fathers, the supreme courts, those on the right, those on the left. The limitations of freedom of actions. The meaning of the Bill of Rights.

50 slides. Cat. No. 8-07005 $32.50

WHAT'S BEEN HAPPENING TO OUR FOOD?

The balance between the need for improved yield and the use of chemicals, anti-biotics, and additives, and the need for purity. Views of industry, agriculture, government, and lay people, as well as the medical profession. Basis for a mock trial.

60 slides. Cat. No. 8-07006 $38.50

HOW CAN WE IMPROVE POLICE-COMMUNITY RELATIONS?

The attitudes of urban dwellers toward police, and the attitudes of police toward civilians. The problems of law enforcement. Demands for law and order. Demands for community control of police. An exercise in problem solving.

50 slides. Cat. No. 8-07007 $32.50

WHAT IS A CONSERVATIVE?

The conservative political philosophy as expounded by conservatives. The individual versus society, in all respects. The conservative view of freedom and social responsibility. Both from an historical as well as a contemporary view.

50 slides. Cat. No. 8-07008 $32.50

WHAT IS A LIBERAL?

The liberal political philosophy as expounded by liberals. The individual versus society, in all respects. The liberal view of freedom and social responsibility. Both from an historical as well as a contemporary view.

50 slides. Cat. No. 8-07009 $32.50

WHAT IS A RADICAL?

The radical approaches to political and social problems. The spectrum of radical views. The changing nature of radicalism. The radical movements of today and their views of freedom and social responsibility. Both from an historical as well as a contemporary view.

50 slides. Cat. No. 8-07010 $32.50

THE RISE OF THE WORKING CLASSES.

The working classes in pre and industrial revolution times. The response to the factory system. The impact on the workers. The labor movement. Liberalism and conservatism, and their impact on the working classes. An historical perspective with meaning as we enter the post-industrial age.

50 slides. Cat. No. 8-07011 $32.50

WHAT IS COLONIALISM?

The rationale for imperialism. The white man's burden. Colonialism by non-white societies. Economic versus political imperialism. Ideological versus political imperialism. Is colonialism dead or has it taken new forms?

50 slides. Cat. No. 8-07013 $32.50

WHAT CAN BE DONE IN THE MIDDLE EAST?

The historical background. The growth of Zionism. The role of the big powers. The political, social, and economic problems. Proposals for solutions.

60 slides. Cat. No. 8-07014 $38.50

SHOULD THE CIVIL WAR HAVE BEEN FOUGHT?

Northern and southern views on the nature of the Union. Peaceful solutions advocated for the ending of slavery. Views on the legality of the war. Centralism versus federalism. Basis for a mock trial.

50 slides. Cat. No. 8-07015 $32.50

CURRENT AFFAIRS

Current Affairs

Color sound filmstrips, records, cassettes and multimedia for secondary education.

CURRENT AFFAIRS
24 DANBURY RD.,
WILTON, CONN. 06897

Zero Population Growth: Hope for Future Generations?

Sanctity of Life, World Population Explosion and Human Progress

FULL COLOR SOUND FILMSTRIP

Projections call for the world population to exceed six billion by the year two thousand, with the greatest increase occurring in the underdeveloped countries. Yet even today, most people in the developing nations live in abject poverty. Since there are insufficient resources even today to improve their material well-being in a meaningful way, what prospects are there once their number has doubled? Using the interview technique, the filmstrip delves into the moral and pragmatic aspects of zero population growth, Proponents and opponents of abortion and other methods for regulating the population growth present their views and recommendations. A section of the filmstrip assesses the impact of population slowdown in America on business and government, shifts in lifestyles and spending patterns.

PRICE: $17.50 with record; $19.50 with cassette

Mass Media and the Freedom to Communicate

The Public's "Right to Know," National Interest, Truth in News

FULL COLOR SOUND FILMSTRIP

The mass media have opened up new horizons in world communications. Deep-seated, fundamental issues, however, have also emerged. The filmstrip traces the rapid evolution of mass communications, examines the validity of the public's "right to know" in the light of the trend toward "advocacy journalism," and assesses the impact that a genuine free flow of ideas could or would have on the family of nations and the individual. Also examined are the problems of the freedom of the press and other media against the background of fresh attempts by an increasing number of governments to evoke the issue of the national interest in justifying overt or covert censorship.

PRICE: $17.50 with record; $19.50 with cassette

Must the World Go Hungry?

POVERTY, OVERPOPULATION, UNEQUAL DISTRIBUTION OF WEALTH
FULL COLOR SOUND FILMSTRIP/1973 (No. 360)

An estimated two-thirds of the world's population live at, or below, subsistence levels. Even the U.S. offers a contrast of poverty amid prosperity. The filmstrip examines the staggering task of feeding the world's rapidly rising population, evaluates the prospects for finding new sources of foods and foodstuffs, such as the seas, and assesses the relative merits of the "zero population" concept in the light of religious beliefs, humanitarian considerations, and widespread ignorance. Is hunger inevitable in a world of unequal living standards, unequal distribution of wealth and national resources?

PRICE: $17.50 with record; $19.50 with cassette

CONSUMER EDUCATION

PRODUCED IN COOPERATION
WITH
THE COUNCIL OF BETTER BUSINESS BUREAUS, INC

Frauds and Deceptions

FULL COLOR SOUND FILMSTRIP / RECORD OR CASSETTE / ADDITIONAL 30 MINUTE RECORDED INTERVIEW, AND TEACHER'S GUIDE (1972) (No. 381)

Fraud and deception has existed in every society since ancient times. For example, in our own society, in the 19th century, deceptive advertising, fake medicines, and worthless land and stock sales were notorious. Today, the public is both better informed and better protected by law against fraud. But fraud and deception have hardly disappeared from the market place. In many cases, they have simply become more sophisticated. This program shows how to recognize and avoid being taken in by various frauds and deceptions.

PRICE: $25.00 with records; $30.00 with cassettes

FULL COLOR SOUND FILMSTRIP / RECORD OR CASSETTE / ADDITIONAL 30 MINUTE RECORDED INTERVIEW, AND TEACHER'S GUIDE (1972)
(No. 380)

Advertising is a force in modern day living. Whether it is consumer-oriented or institutional, the various media — TV, radio, and print — are used to help the consumer in making his choice. Advertising gives useful information, but also plays upon desires and fears. Whereas advertising today can be helpful to the consumer, some feel the need for more regulation by the advertiser himself, the government, or private agencies to counteract deceptive practices.
PRICE: $25.00 with records; $30.00 with cassettes

FULL COLOR SOUND FILMSTRIP / RECORD OR CASSETTE / ADDITIONAL 30 MINUTE RECORDED INTERVIEW, AND TEACHER'S GUIDE (1972)
(No. 382)

This program discusses whose responsibility it is to see that consumer interests are protected. "Consumer power" is represented by government spokesmen, independent consumer groups, and organizations at the community and neighborhood level. The work of Ralph Nader, the consumer advocate, and other spokesmen for the consumer movement are presented. The methods for consumer protection today are many: publicity; lobbying for consumer-oriented legislation; boycotts and organized complaints at the local level; and consumer cooperatives. The future possibilities of "consumer power" are presented for discussion as well as its challenge to today's society.
PRICE: $25.00 with records; $30.00 with cassettes

Each multi-media unit contains one color sound filmstrip with record or cassette plus an additional 30 minute recorded interview with notable authorities in the consumer movement.

SPECIAL OFFER: Six titles - $135.00 with records; $162.00 with cassettes

---

PERSPECTIVES ON AGING

Concept Media, in association with leading gerontologists and health care professionals, has created a stimulating and unique audio-visual series entitled PERSPECTIVES ON AGING. This series explores and explodes the myths of the aging process and provides an extensive program for those involved in caring for the aged. It dispels, among others, the myth that old age is a period of intellectual deterioration, and is synonymous with illness. The series' basic premise is that "the aged" are not actually a homogeneous group at all in terms of interests, needs, and lifestyle. It is as illogical to group 65-year-olds with 95-year-olds as to group 5-year-olds with 35-year-olds!

The contemporary audio-visual format maximizes the impact on the learner, while increasing involvement and discussion. Its multidisciplinary approach affords a comprehensive overview of the aged — physiological, psychological, and sociological.

Designed, primarily, for health care personnel, the materials in this series make up a comprehensive study of the elderly and their problems, and provide innovative, in-depth solutions. These materials may be purchased as a complete unit, or separately, for specialized classes. When purchased individually, each program comes with its own instructor's manual.

FILMSTRIP 1. Myths and Realities — Presents common misconceptions about the aged, and realistically explores financial resources, health, housing, transportation, retirement and social roles

FILMSTRIP 2. Physical Changes and Their Implications — Examines the physical changes that accompany aging and the manner in which the body systems and functions are affected by them.

FILMSTRIP 3. Implications for Teaching — Surveys the physiological, sociological, and psychological factors which influence the elderly and affect their learning, and presents specific teaching techniques which are effective with the elderly.

FILMSTRIP 4. The Confused Person: Approaches to Reorientation — This program focuses on the difficulties of caring for the aged, confused person. It differentiates between functional and organic disorders, and between reversible and irreversible brain syndromes.

FILMSTRIP 5. "Old People's Home" — A Poetic Essay On Aging — Intended for the broadest of audiences, this emotional impact program may be used separately for many varied classes. It is a dramatic photographic essay of W. H. Auden's poem, "Old People's Home," and brings into question our growing cultural practice of putting the aged away into "homes" where, often, they are unseen and forgotten.

PERSPECTIVES ON DYING

Concept Media, in association with some of the field's leading authorities, has designed an audio-visual series titled, Perspectives on Dying. This series teaches how to confront and cope with the feelings that often erupt and inundate those in the dying situation. The day-to-day experiences dealt with are universal ones faced by nurses, social workers, spiritual advisers, and the families of dying patients. The approach is sensitive, yet sensible – progressive, yet practical. The materials are innovative and stimulating, as effective as the student's and instructor's personal involvement.

The series consists of the following:

FILMSTRIP 1. American Attitudes toward Death and Dying — Presents the situation of interaction with the dying person and shows how denial of death creates difficulty. Examines in depth three cultural factors behind denial: urbanization, advances in medical science, and secularization. Traces how denial of death is reflected and reinforced in day-to-day living.

FILMSTRIP 2. Psychological Reactions of the Dying Person — Focuses on the dying person's response to his fatal illness in terms of personal characteristics, interpersonal relationships, and the nature of his illness, with the resultant complex interplay of feelings. Discusses the coping mechanisms of denial, regression, and intellectualization, plus the emotional reactions and circumstances that determine the dying person's final state of mind.

FILMSTRIP 3. Hazards and Challenges in Providing care — Presents two dying situations: (1) A patient begins to die unexpectedly, and (2) The patient is terminally ill and the situation essentially involves comfort care. Examines the nurse's interaction with the patient and her involvement where controversy exists. Discusses the factors making interaction with the dying patient especially difficult.

FILMSTRIP 4. Guidelines for Interacting with the Dying Person — Discusses how the care-giver can meet the three basic psychological needs of a dying person: to maintain a feeling of personal dignity; a sense of security; and some element of hope. Discusses the importance of encouraging self-expression, and listening with sensitivity and concern. Suggests how to establish reassurance and structure a hopeful environment.

FILMSTRIP 5. Viewpoint: The Dying Patient, and FILMSTRIP 6. Viewpoint: The Nurse — Personal accounts of dying patients and of nurses who care for them. The programs utilize open-ended formats to help viewers become aware of and express their personal feelings.

Instructor's Manual — A guide book containing presentation guidelines, script narrations, study questions and a selected bibliography.

Role-Playing Cards — Sets of cards which provide role-playing experiences. Each situation presents an interaction problem related to dying. The student tries out his responses to determine their effectiveness.

Personal Questionnaire — A set of provocative questions aimed at helping each student to greater awareness of his own perspectives on dying. A packet of 20 is included.

Supplementary Text — "Confrontations of Death," developed at the Oregon Center for Gerontology, includes evocative, thought-provoking prose and poetry.

SEMANTICS: LANGUAGE AND BEHAVIOR

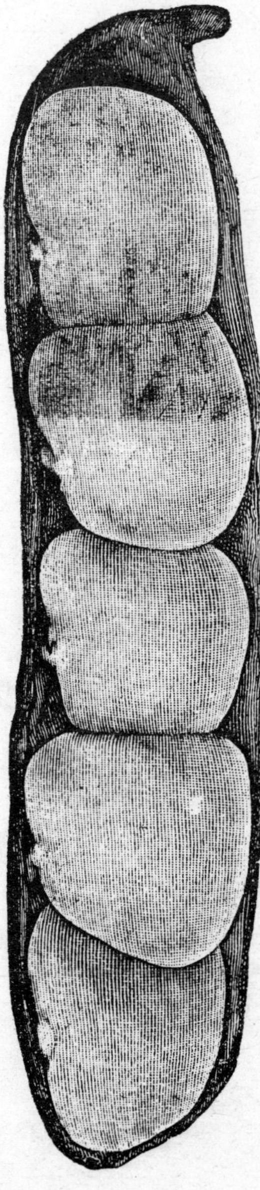

Semantics: Language and Behavior . . . . comes in the kind of box any ten year old would love to have as a Christmas gift container. Inside are six sound filmstrips, an instructor's manual, a huge photo, a student booklet plus five cellophane-wrapped simulation games. The price for the entire set is $150. The pricing and design follow a basic rule of multi-media resources:" a $100 item is preferable to a $10 item even if the same ideas could be taught just as effectively for the lower price."

The program is set up in six units each including a filmstrip, exercises from the student workbook and a game designed to allow students to practice the semantic principles taught in the filmstrip. The six units teach the concepts of body language, stereotypes, inferences, abstraction, connotation, and slanting.

Each filmstrip deals with only one or two very specific ideas. Filmstrip # 2, for example, makes only one statement, "Words are not the same as the things they describe." Occasionally the filmstrips and discussion questions slip into a condescending tone. One question asks if Martin Luther King and Adolf Hitler "are the same". Filmstrip #2 sputters into the final frame with the comment that words are important because they are "what we have to reach out to one another across the barriers of time and space and help end our loneliness." In spite of these lapses and some pedagogical fluff, the program does have a collection of good ideas about a topic that students can easily grasp as important.

The most valuable part of the program are the five role-playing games. One has students in small groups attempting to achieve goals verbally. ("You have been caught cheating on a test. Confess. Get the teacher to forgive you and give you another chance.") In the process players must use a certain number of fallacies. Other students in the group try to spot the fallacies.

"Manipulation" has students design an advertising campaign, name brands and models, design packaging and present their products to investors for acceptance.

In another role-play game, **Eden II**, a group must select six people to start a new society on a recently discovered planet. The six are to be selected from a list of twelve. Other students act as observers and note inferences, judgments or stereotypes.

A free Semantics Overview will be sent if you wish more information. Contact Concept Media, 1500 Adams Ave., Costa Mesa, Calif. 92626.

WOMEN ON WORDS AND IMAGES

WOMEN ON WORDS AND IMAGES has prepared a slide show based on the material in DICK AND JANE AS VICTIMS, Sex Stereotyping in Children's Readers. Representative slides have been chosen from a total of 150 readers and have been organized to heighten their impact on audiences. The points made in this study are dramatic and are made immediately understandable by the slide show which crystalizes the research themes of DICK AND JANE AS VICTIMS.

Educators, librarians, teachers, parents, community resource people, indeed any person involved with children, will find this slide show an enlightening experience. Although school readers are more biased than reality, in their exaggeration they clarify as well as magnify the reality. Thus the harmfulness of sex role stereotyping is exposed to be seen clearly, regardless of how innocent the original intent. This slide show examines sex role stereotyping as it exists today in all instructional materials and in society itself.

This presentation consists of 140 slides which are arranged in one carrousel tray and a tape which contains narrating comments; the length is approximately 20 minutes. The cost of renting them is $35 plus $5 for postage and handling. Due to the great demand for this presentation, please allow several weeks in requesting a date, with an alternative date listed if possible. To reserve it, write to WOMEN ON WORDS AND IMAGES, P. O. Box 2163, Princeton, N.J. 08540.

The slide show, tape narration and script may be purchased from WOMEN ON WORDS AND IMAGES for $500. Please allow four weeks for delivery.

THE DISTORTED IMAGE

Sometimes John and Selma Appel don't laugh when they see a cartoon. They say they don't see any humor in cartoons with ethnic stereotyping.

Appel, professor of American thought and language, and his wife have been collecting depictions of immigrants and ethnic groups in American popular graphics for the past 10 years.

The collection which started as a hobby, now includes more than 1,500 slides and approximately 300 actual original and reproduction of prints. But Appel saw the educational value in his collection, and he has used it in the classroom while studying American civilization.

Appel says he believes he and his wife are the only private collectors who specialize in ethnic caricatures.

"Many think that the subject is not worth scholarly attention," he says. But he contends that "popular art confirms the experience of the majority, and it reflects the attitudes and concerns of the people for whom it is produces."

IN ADDITION to its cartoons, Appel's collection contains illustrated almanacs, book illustrations, dime novels, comic valentines and postcards, trade cards and advertising novelties, wall posters and billboard cards, illustrated songsheet covers, and brochures for home study correspondence school courses.

"The collection is basically from the period of the 1820's to the 1920's and it was during this time that it was popular to make fun of the immigrants," Appel says.

He says that what were considered cartoons at that time, "is now considered degradation."

APPEL HAS BEEN assisted throughout the project by his wife, Selma. She has served as co-researcher and took most of the photographs for the slides.

She says that they have found most of the graphics at the Smithsonian Institute in and the Library of Congress in Washington. Others have come from searches of libraries' rare book rooms, and flea markets and antique shows.

The Appels spent a year at the Smithsonian as visiting scholars. Most of their slides from the Smithsonian collection were produced under grants from the Kettering Foundation.

A grant from the New World Foundation and several MSU research grants have helped defray expenses of the Appels' project.

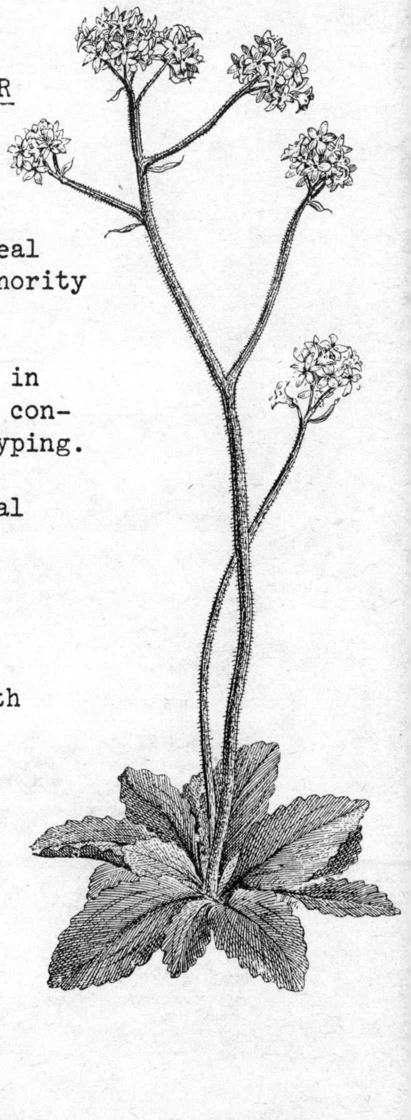

THE DISTORTED IMAGE: STEREOTYPE AND CARICATURE IN AMERICAN POPULAR GRAPHICS, 1850-1922.

60 slides/color/cassette/manual/$35.00.

Cartoons and illustrations from large-circulation magazines reveal the extent and nature of stereotyping which has affected all minority groups in the United States.

This presentation is designed for advanced high school students in history, sociology and psychology classes. The detailed manual contains a suggested two-day lesson plan on the subject of stereotyping.

(Also available with record or reel-to-reel tape at an additional $5 charge, on special request.)

PUBLICATIONS DEPARTMENT
Anti-Defamation League of B'nai B'rith
315 Lexington Avenue
New York, N.Y. 10016

ENVIRONMENTAL COMMUNICATIONS

Environmental Communications began in 1969 as a matrix for the production and distribution of audio visual media designed to express relationships in man's environment. We explore and document the physical and cultural surroundings through the use of still photography, film, sound and video tape.

We not only distribute works of our own, but also those of other artists, designers, photographers, psychologists, historians, architects, ecologists and educators working creatively in the field of environmental communications.

Although nature has been generous in creating harmonious environments on this planet, for the most part man has miserably failed to live according to this standard. Instead he has made environments that tend to inhibit his freedom of options and belittle his creative potential. As a reaction to these intolerable circumstances Environmental Communications began to investigate expanded systems for seeing and being in the environment, and searching for a redefinition of education that encompasses all of human growth and includes all of life's experiences.

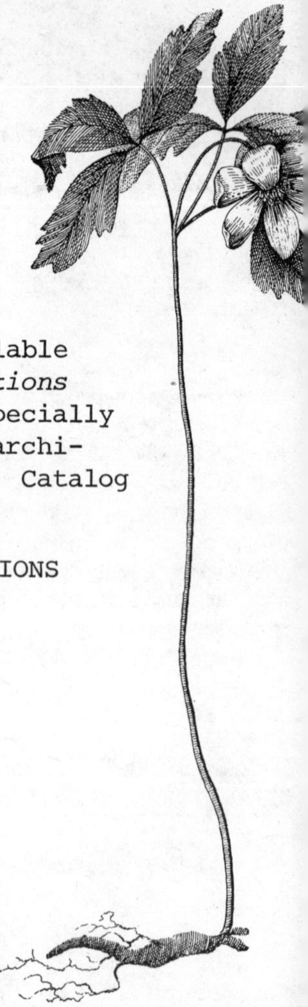

A catalog of the slides available from *Environmental Communications* is a must for a school -- especially one teaching urban studies, architecture, or popular culture. Catalog from:

ENVIRONMENTAL COMMUNICATIONS
62 Windward
Venice, Calif. 90291
(213) 392-4964

METAPHORS: ARCHITECTURE AND OTHER THINGS

Metaphor at its root means "carry-over." Basically, whenever two or more things are compared by a brain, certain characteristics called "similarities" are perceived to be shared between them. For example, a canary and a lemon are both yellow; beeswax and snow crystals are both hexagonal. This seemingly simple process is the basis of all design: architectural, environmental, industrial, artistic, etc. Series attempts to trace the significance of metaphor throughout history, and in the present, as it relates to architecture and design. Conceived and documented by David MacDermott.
Set of 43 color slides, booklet.
Order Number ASM-43 . . . .$45
A book entitled "Metaphors: Architecture and Other Things," by David MacDermott will be available in Summer, 1973.

HARDCORE L.A. (DING-BATS ETC.)

Series documents low cost minimal "ding-bat" housing. These rectangular buildings dominate whole sections of Southern California. Also included are other members of the "ding-bat" family—franchise hamburger stands, car washes, etc.—the meat and potatoes of Los Angeles building.
Set of 40 color slides.
Order Number ESHC-40 . . . .$40

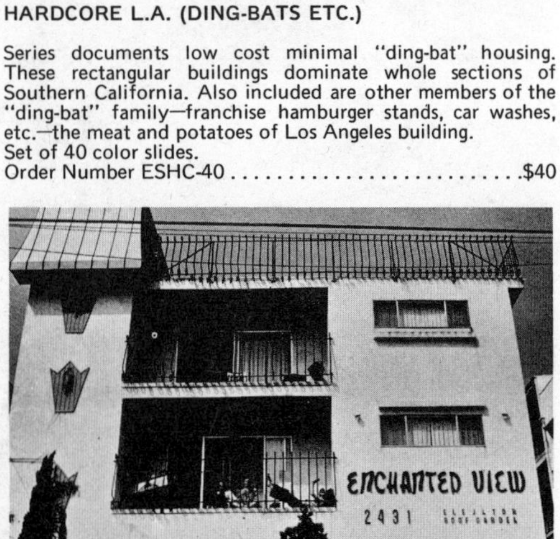

LAS VEGAS: CITY OF ILLUSION

A visual "trip" through the Las Vegas environment. The series illustrates growth and development trends, and sociological functions of fantasy in a pop art city, extended from Los Angeles' influences. Includes visual study of light and neon used to create an atmosphere of this "adult Disneyland."
Set of 50 color slides.
Order Number ESLA-50 . . . .$50

Multi-Media 349

THEMATIC SLIDES MARK IV

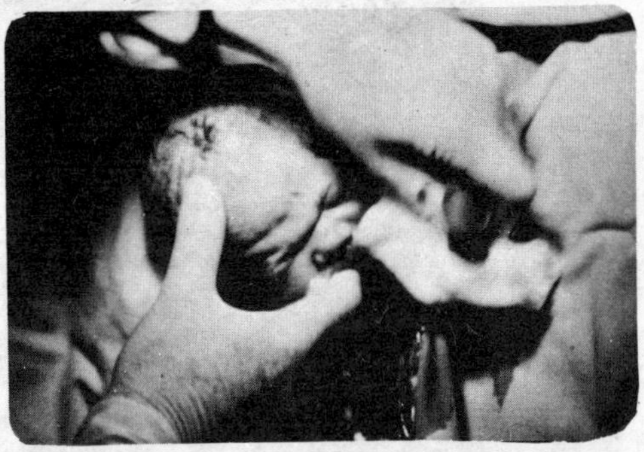

THEMATIC SLIDES

Mark IV's Thematic Slides are well known for their fine photographic quality and versatility. They serve to expand the viewer's sensitivity to current values, nature and the human condition, and are thus suitable for use in the classroom, workshops, discussion groups and worship services. Each series is packaged in clear plastic folios within a vinyl loose-leaf binder. Also included is a booklet containing topic introductions, discussion questions, and suggestions for multi-media presentations combining slides with pop/rock music. To further facilitate multi-media use of these slides Mark IV offers a free cross-reference guide.

THEMATIC SLIDES

Series I contains 200 slides - 20 slides on each of the following topics: Beauty, Happiness, Drugs, Loneliness, Pollution, Poverty, Technology, Race Relations, War, and Youth.
Price: $70.00 #S200

Series II contains 200 slides - 20 slides on each of the following topics: Nature, Family, Death, Female, Male, Open and Shut, Reconciliation, New Life and Hope, Prison, Signs For Our Time.
Price: $70.00 #S400

Slide Folios: Clear plastic slide folios for storing your own slides are available at 30¢ each.

Mark IV Presentations, La Sallette Center,
Attleboro, MA 02703

SLIDEAS

Slideas is a collection of nicely photographed slides arranged by general topics. Each set has twenty slides and sells for $9.00. Sets are titled: Wonder, Alone, Together, Faces and Feelings, Metropolis, Seasons, Searching, and Sharing. Each set comes in a vinyl folder, from:

LOYOLA UNIVERSITY PRESS
3441 North Ashland Avenue
Chicago, Ill. 60657

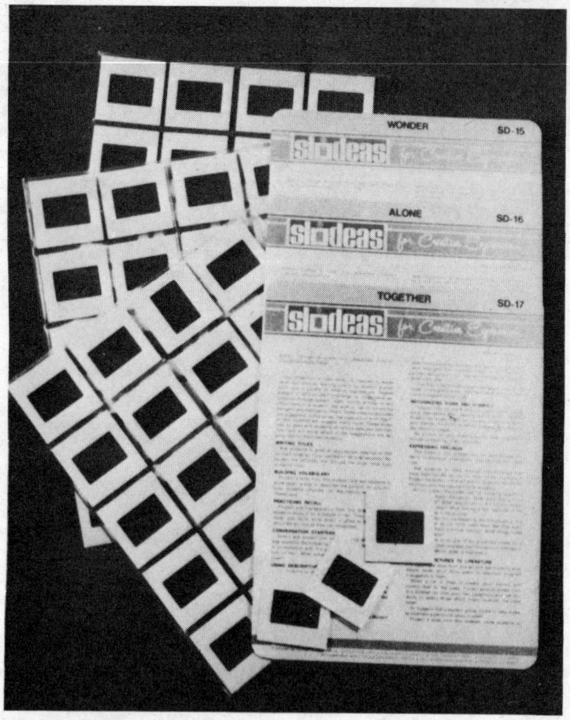

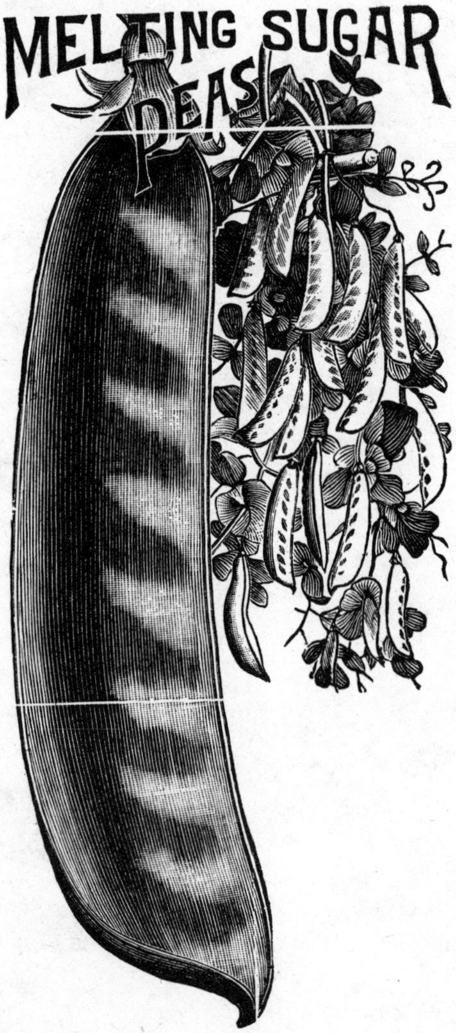

Devices

WOMEN'S GRAPHICS COLLECTIVE

The posters from *Women's Graphics Collective* are not the sort usually found in schoolrooms, but they are more provocative and undeniable than most. Posters cost $1 - $2 each. Catalog from:

WOMEN'S GRAPHICS COLLECTIVE
852 West Belmont
Chicago, Ill. 60657

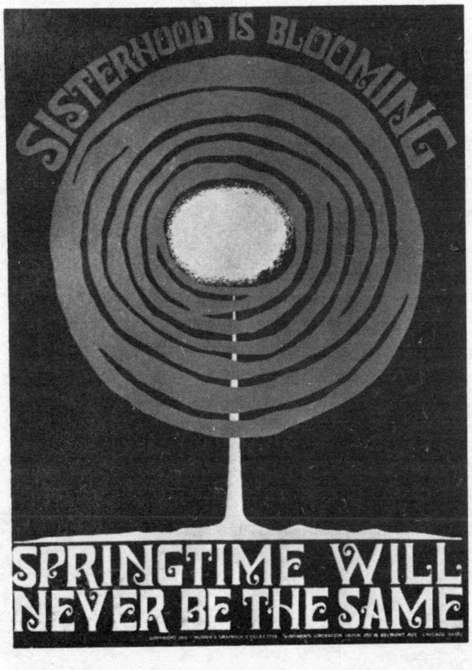

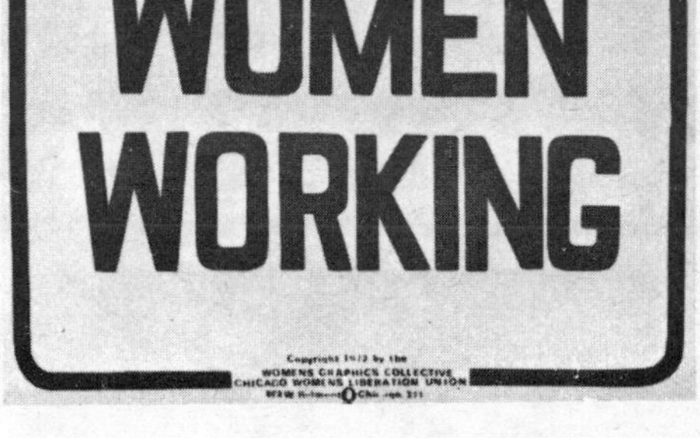

ARGUS POSTERS

Argus Communications is probably the most popular supplier of posters for classrooms. Their printing quality is top notch and the selection vast. Catalog free from:

ARGUS COMMUNICATIONS
7440 Natchez Avenue
Niles, Ill. 60648

#287 We have nowhere else to go . . . this is all we have.
Margaret Mead

#254 As long as there's an apple tree there'll be apple time.
Hal David

#220 I am waiting for a rebirth of wonder. I am waiting for someone to really discover America.
L. Ferlinghetti

#286 Some things become so completely our own that we forget them.
Antonio Porchia

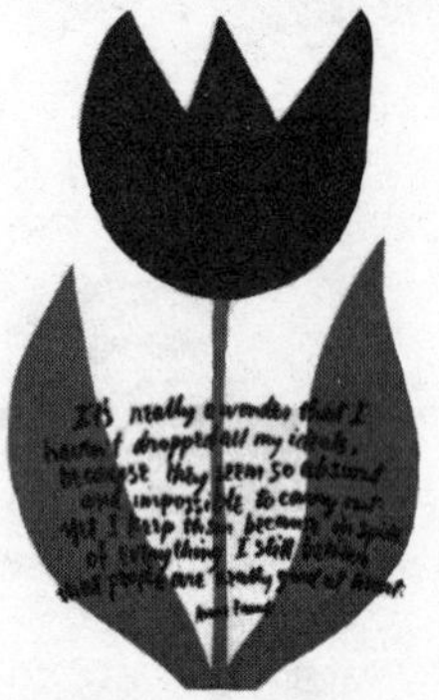

#201 It's really a wonder that I haven't dropped all my ideals, because they seem so absurd *
Anne Frank

#126 Hunger doesn't go away when you take a picture of it.

COMPUTER ART

OCTAL CRYSTAL — 20" x 20" — one color

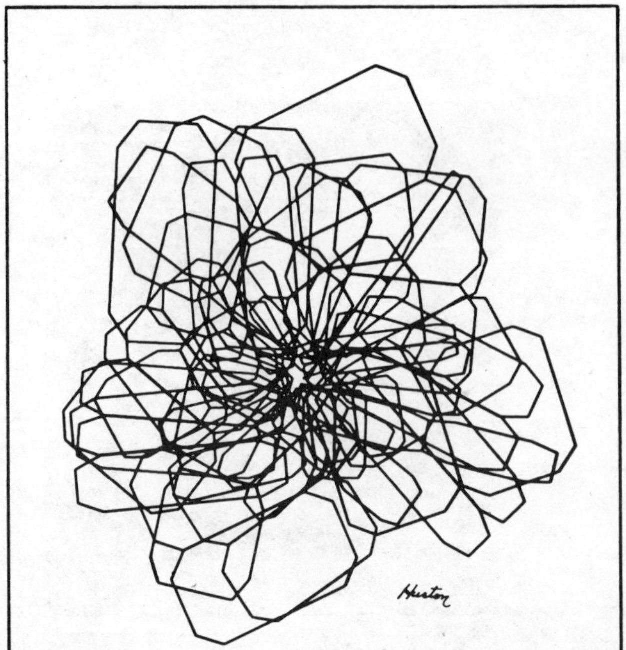

Computer art is a creative process of interaction between the artist and the computer. The artist controls originality and composition through input parameters and the skillful execution of each drawing. This control allows each computer art "original" to become literally one of a kind. In other words, each art program is a model and each "original" is one of an infinite number of different simulations of the original idea. Thus, computer art combines the rare qualities of logic, precision, and human value.

In computer art, each drawing begins with an idea that must then be analyzed for geometry, form, and aesthetic value. An idea of value is then logicized into a workable computer program. Through programmed control the computer becomes a highly versatile drawing instrument able to produce graphic art displays. However, in the final analysis, each display must be evaluated subjectively by the individual.

For a free catalog of beautiful, reasonably priced computer graphics, write to COMPUTRA. Mention EDU.

Thomas J. Huston
COMPUTRA
Box 608
Upland, Indiana 46989

EDU

No person or school system considering the educational possibilities of a computer should miss *Edu*, a newsletter published 5 times a year for $2 by:

DIGITAL EQUIPMENT CORPORATION
Educational Products Group
146 Main Street
Maynard, Mass. 01754

THIS ISSUE OF EDU FEATURES CREATIVITY

General Articles:
- Exploring Creativity
- What is Creativity?
- A Creative View

Creative Applications For You To Try:
- Computer Designed Dinnerwear
- Games For Motivation
- Going Around in Circles

Creative Applications of Computers:
- Social Sciences and the Computer
- Students Run the Show in Delaware
- Millsaps Gets New Science Teacher
- Ripon College Uses Timeshared-8
- The Minicomputer and Student Response
- CAI Goes to Medical School

Opinion:
- Bringing Computers to the People

PEOPLE'S COMPUTER COMPANY

is a newspaper. . .

about having fun with computers

and learning how to use computers

and how to buy a minicomputer for yourself or your school

and books. . .and films. . . and tools of the future.

Teletypewriters are the Volkswagens of computer terminals ... rugged, dependable, inexpensive, ugly and noisy!

TTY COST SAVING TIPS

Definition: *ASR 33, is a Model 33 TTY with paper tape reader/punch*

KSR 33, same but without paper tape.

Nothing can beat an ASR 33 TTY for price, performance and reliability, but buying them is a gas. One way to save lots of dollars is to buy your TTY from a different supplier than your computer vendor (DEC and HP now encourage this). This requires that your school business office prepare two bid forms, one for the computer and one for the TTY.

The reason for this is simple. TTY bought from Teletype Corporation only cost about $800 (though you may have to wait 6 to 8 months for delivery). From a computer supplier, the same TTY may run as high as $1600. In most metropolitan areas you can find 3 or 4 independent sources of TTY that will sell you a new ASR 33 for $1200 or less. They'll make any modifications necessary to make your computer and TTY compatible. Rebuilt like new models are selling today for less than $900 from these same sources. You can lease a TTY for $50 to $60 per month, including maintenance if you'd care to go that route.

Think twice before you buy KSR models. They'll save you a few dollars but at some point you'll discover you need the paper tape capability.

MAINTENANCE CONTRACTS. TTY maintenance contracts are absurdly expensive ($20 to $25 per month) and of questionable necessity. There's bound to be someone in your area who will come out on call for around $10 per hour or so. Your TTY will take a big beating but not big enough to justify the charge by vendors for monthly maintenance contracts.

TTY PAPER. By the roll, your local office supply dealer charges as much as $2.00 for average quality TTY paper. At that price the poor house beckons for you! Buy in case lot quantities and save a fortune. Our recent experience dropped the price to $0.98/roll for a case of 12 rolls. When we bought 6 cases (72 rolls), the price dropped to $0.73 per roll. The paper is not fancy but more than adequate for classroom use. This experience was with the brand PERFECTION, stock number 6210. Have your district office supply store order this brand for you.

PUNCH PAPER TAPE. Ditto with paper tape. $1.25 was the going price until we bought a case of 28 rolls. That brought the price down to $0.52/roll or $12.88 for the case. Brand: PERFECTION again, stock number 8219.

TTY RIBBONS. Ribbons cost about $1.00 each and constantly need replacement. One way to save money is to simply flip your used ribbon over (the print mechanism only uses the top half of the ribbon). That will double the life of the ribbon. To save BIG money go to your school business education department and ask them for any old (unused) ribbons they still have in stock for machines they no longer have. We found some Underwood ribbons that had been around for years. We had to respool them onto teletype spools (a pain) but it saved us money.

If you're buying terminals with acoustic couplers, I suggest you do NOT buy the built in couplers. Rather, buy a separate coupler that you will have to locate on the floor. The built-in couplers are too easy for some smarty to disconnect accidentally or on purpose. Separate couplers are also accessible for repair, etc.

If you have some hints for cost savings or if you can recommend a TTY supplier in your area, let us know and we'll include it in future issues.

In the San Francisco Bay Area, a source for TTY purchase, lease and/or maintenance is:

Data Terminals & Communications
P.O. Box 5583
San Jose, California 95150
(408) 378-1112

June 1972 price list tells us:

ASR 33	$49/mo. year lease	$1100 purchase
Acoustic Coupler	$14/mo.	298 purchase

They also have used and rebuilt materials at considerable savings and an excellent, cheap acoustical enclosure (an acoustical closure cuts the volume of sound down to something less than a rock band). We've had excellent experience with these people.

For those of you out there in the big, wide, wonderful world, you can always lease TTY from Western Union. Call their toll free number (800-631-7050) for more information. Model 33 ASR with acoustic coupler is $65/month.

GETTING STARTED IN BASIC

experiment

Strings? Numerical expressions?

```
PRINT "MY HUMAN UNDERSTANDS ME"
```

This is a string. It is enclosed in quotation marks.

with " "	**without** " "
`PRINT "7 + 5"`	`PRINT 7 + 5`
This is a string. It is enclosed in quotation marks.	This is not a string. It is a numerical expression.

If a PRINT statement contains more than one item. (string or expression), the items must be separated by commas or semicolons.

Your turn again. Try these.

```
SCR

10 PRINT "7 + 5=" , 7 + 5
20 END
RUN
```

Note the comma.

```
7 + 5=        12
```

comma spacing

```
10 PRINT "7 + 5=" ; 7 + 5
20 END
RUN
```

Note the semicolon.

```
7 + 5= 12
```

semicolon spacing

Good luck!

remember... to get a copy of the program in the computer's memory, type LIST and press RETURN.

BOXES

Deep down inside the computer there are 26 little boxes.

Box	Content	Box	Content	Box	Content	Box	Content
A	7	H		O		V	
B	5	I		P		W	
C		J	4	Q		X	2.5
D		K		R		Y	
E		L		S	-6	Z	
F	2	M		T			
G		N		U			

Each box can contain one number at any one time. We have already stored numbers in some of the boxes.

7 IS IN BOX A
5 IS IN BOX B

What number is in box F? _____ *In J?* _____

–6 is in box _______ *and 2.5 is in box* _______

O.K., using a *pencil*, put 8 into C. In other words, write the numeral "8" in the box labelled "C." Then do the following, carefully!

FIRST – *Put 12 into N.*

SECOND – *Put 27 into N. But wait! A box can hold only one number at a time . . . before you can enter 27 into N, you must first erase the 12 that you had previously entered.*

When the computer puts a number into a box, it *automatically* erases the previous content of the box.

Tell it to the computer.

```
10 LET A = 7      ←—— PUT 7 INTO BOX A.
20 PRINT A        ←—— PRINT THE CONTENT OF BOX A.
99 END
RUN

 7
```

Another example.

```
10 LET A = 7
20 LET B = 5
30 PRINT A+B, A-B, A*B, A/B
99 END
RUN

 12            2             35            1.4
```

More practice? O.K.

```
10 LET A = 2
20 LET B = 3
30 LET C = 4
40 LET D = 5
50 PRINT A+B+C+D, A*B*C*D, A*(B+C), (A+B)/(C+D)
```

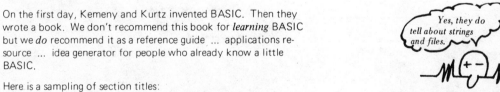

REMEMBER

A program is a set of statements. Each statement tells the computer to do some specific thing. So far, we have used only two types of statements, **PRINT** and **END**.

A statement begins with a line number. The computer obeys statements in line number order.

BASIC PROGRAMMING   Kemeny and Kurtz

On the first day, Kemeny and Kurtz invented BASIC. Then they wrote a book. We don't recommend this book for *learning* BASIC but we *do* recommend it as a reference guide ... applications resource ... idea generator for people who already know a little BASIC.

Here is a sampling of section titles:

What is BASIC? What is Timesharing? **String Variables** Eternal Calendar **Roots of Equations** Curve Plotting **Prime Numbers** Random Numbers **Dealing a Bridge Hand** Knight's Tour **Tictactoe – A heuristic Approach** Tax Depreciation **Critical Path Analysis** String Files **Linear Regression** Electrical Networks **Markov Chains** Polynomials **Marriage Rules in a Primitive Society** A Mode from Ecology **Harmony in Music.**

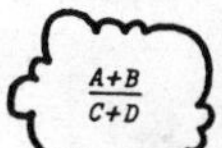

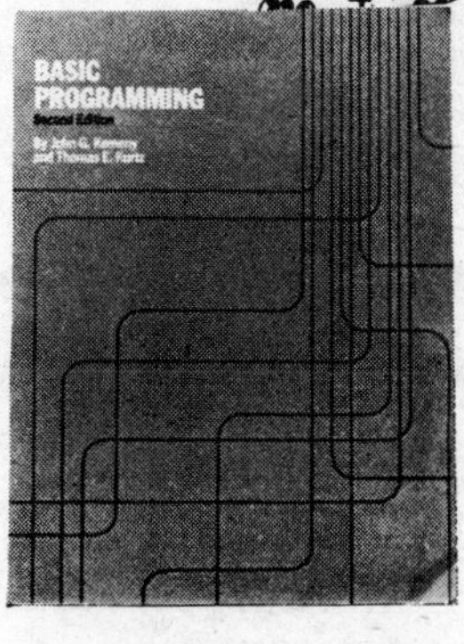

BASIC Programming *(2nd Ed.)*
by John G. Kemeny
and Thomas E. Kurtz

from: *John Wiley and Sons, Inc.*
605 Third Avenue
New York, NY 10016

price: *$6.25*

1967, 1971; 150 pages

with a little help from MY COMPUTER LIKES ME *when I speak in BASIC*

MY COMPUTER LIKES ME available from:
Dymax - People's Computer Center
P.O. Box 310
Menlo Park, California 94025
$1.19 (plus tax for California residents)

BEWA...

The problem presented was: How can I get the money for hardware or how can I get more money to increase the system we have? The situation is the same and therefore my response is the same to each question. YOU HAVE TO GET THE ENTIRE SCHOOL INVOLVED IN YOUR COMPUTER EDUCATION PROGRAM! *If you set up a program that is limited to math students or you set up all sorts of fancy prerequisites so that only a limited number of students use your computer, then you cannot expect support or more money from anyone but the few people who use the system. Even if every math student in school uses the computer at some time during the year, only you and he know it and he can't do you much good when it comes to promoting more money.*

You have to get out of the math problem-solving syndrome (that's what I call it) and try to get as many other people involved with your computer as possible. The science department is the first logical choice. The Huntington Project computer programs (see page 3) make it easy for any science teacher to get involved with a computer. These programs cover a wide range of science topics and are available, ready to run on most educational computer systems. The business department is the next logical user. I'm a business teacher and I'm not convinced that you'll find much support there, but look anyway for the one person who is teaching data processing or is interested in teaching it. Social studies teachers have an inherent disdain for computers but you can probably find one who is into gaming or simulations who would enjoy having his students do a simple economic simulation or simply play a computer game. The resources are available from HP and DEC. All you need to do is get them and use them.

Some schools have done some far out things like scouting football games for the athletic department using the computer. Some have done work in English on a very basic level. There are even things that can be done with home economics and art. One easy thing to do for anyone, is the tabulation of surveys or correcting tests, if you want to get into that.

The important thing is you have to get others involved. You'll break your fanny doing it, but if you want to get more than a one terminal minimum system you are going to have to substantiate your need. You can't substantiate a need if only the math department is using the computer.

INTERRUPT: COMPUTER PEOPLE FOR PEACE

NEWSLETTER OF
COMPUTER PEOPLE FOR PEACE

Published by:
Computer People for Peace
291 Sterling Place
Brooklyn, New York 11238

CPP, now in existence for almost five years, is the only organization in the computer field that stands for peace, equality and civil liberties for all people--and for the use of computers and technology to help achieve these goals.

WHERE THE MONEY GOES:

To publish INTERRUPT. This issue cost over $500 to print and to mail to our members and friends in the U.S. and abroad.

To hold "SANER" conferences for members and friends.

To publicize and hold public meetings on computer uses and misuses.

To research and print in-depth booklets on computer technology in war, data banks, and health.

To aid and cooperate with nationwide movements against war and oppression.

To get together members to form new CPP collectives, which may share the responsibility for publishing INTERRUPT.

In order to actively face the next four years, CPP needs you! Won't you pay your 1973 dues now? In accordance with the wage/price freeze, help is still voluntary and dues are still only $10!

☐ I'd like to join. Here's my $10. (Booklets free if you join now.)

☐ Please put me on the mailing list.

Please send me the CPP booklets:

___copies of Data Banks, Privacy and Repression @50¢

___copies of Health: Big Business for Computers @50¢

___copies of Technological Warlords @$1

All 3 for $1.50 ☐

NAME_______________

STREET_______________

CITY,STATE,ZIP_______________

Interrupt is probably the best source of information on the problems that socially conscious persons working in computer-related jobs in industry encounter. It is therefore invaluable to students who are considering becoming computer professionals, as well as concerned people in general. Controversial issues are discussed, and various conferences where computer people gather are covered from a point of view similar to PCC's "Use computers for people, not against them."

POPULAR COMPUTING

Popular Computing claims to be "the only publication designed for those who are interested in computing for its own sake. A must for the computing hobbyist -- undergraduate student -- teacher of computing and dedicated professional."

Popular Computing is published monthly for $15 yearly (or $12 if payment accompanies order). Undergraduate students may subscribe at half price.

POPULAR COMPUTING
Box 272
Calabasas, Calif. 91302

COMPUTER CONVINCER KIT

COMPUTERS ARE OLD STUFF!

Computers aren't new anymore.

But lots of people still don't see it that way.

Computers aren't revolutionary—they're used in schools all over the country.

If you believe that you (or your school) need a computer to teach more effectively...

If you are already convinced, but others aren't so sure...

How about getting your hands on a Convincer Kit?

Hundreds of teachers, administrators, and school board members have bought them to help get EduSystems into their schools. The Convincer Kit is a collection of brochures, essays, ideas and arguments(?). And many of the elements of the kit can be used after you get your EduSystem, too.

It includes:

Presentation Materials
- Presentation Guidelines and Overhead Projector Transparencies (for convincing)
- Common Questions and Answers about Educational Computers.

Curriculum Materials
- Teach Yourself BASIC I
- BASIC Application Programs
- Problems for Computer Mathematics
- Educational Program Index

Software and Manuals
- BASIC Demonstration Programs and Tape
- EduSystem 10 User's Guide
- Introduction to Programming Handbook
- Programming Languages Handbook

The kit costs $15.00—far less than the actual value! And it includes Discount and Bonus Certificates, too!

Fill out this form and order your Convincer Kit today. There's still time to get your EduSystem for the next school year!!

Computer Convincer Kit available for $15 from:

DIGITAL EQUIPMENT CORPORATION
Educational Products Group
146 Main Street
Maynard, Mass. 01754

FOR COMPUTER CONSUMERS

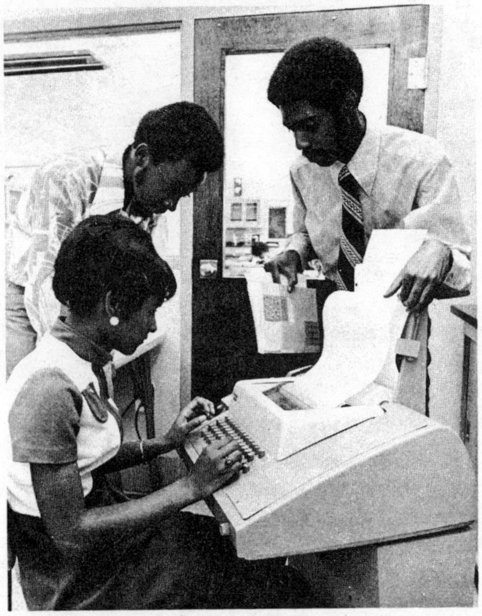

FOR COMPUTER CONSUMERS...

Still in the thinking stage about buying or leasing a computer? Maybe the final decision is close at hand—or maybe it's still just an idea. Whatever the case, we'd like to recommend that *before* you decide or go *one* step further—get your hands on a recent study entitled "Development of Specifications for a Low Cost Computer System for Secondary Schools", by George Kleiner of Stevens Institute of Technology.

This report is the result of research which was subsidized by a U. S. Office of Education Grant. Mr. Kleiner discusses Time-Sharing Services, Minicomputers and selected observations on education computer systems.

For your copy write to:

George Kleiner
Sci-Tronic Systems
Box 947
New York, NY 10008

This makes an ideal companion report to the two previous NSF and OE sponsored studies recommended on these pages:

Nevison, John M. and Kurtz, Thomas E., *The Computer as Pupil: The Dartmouth Secondary School Project.* Final Report, Oct. 1970. Kiewit Computation Center, Dartmouth College, Hanover, N.H. 03775.

Darby, C. A., Jr., Korotkin, A. L., Romashko, T., *Survey of Computing Activities in Secondary Schools.* Oct. 1970. American Institutes for Research, 8555 Sixteenth Street, Silver Spring, Maryland 20910.

And while we're at it, let us recommend another booklet intended for people who are concerned with the planning of computer courses for in-service or formal training of teachers. The title is "Computer Education for Teachers in Secondary Schools. An Outline Guide." It's available for 75 cents from:

AFIPS Headquarters
210 Summit Avenue
Montvale, N.J. 07645

Reprinted from
Digital Equipment's EDU Newsletter

EDMUND SCIENTIFIC COMPANY

Most science teachers know about *Edmund Scientific Corp* as a supplier of all sorts of low-cost educational devices. But Edmund also has materials of interest to those working with psychology, photography, computers, or even special lighting effects for dances or dramatic productions. Catalog is free from:

EDMUND SCIENTIFIC CORPORATION
555 Edscorp Building
Barrington, N.J. 08007
(609) 547-3488

Behavioral Science Lab From "Psychology Today"

Learn important insights into human behavior—how we perceive, learn, forget, think. Study stimulus control, latent learning, mirror image effects, color mixing; train insects to respond to certain stimuli, run mazes, and much more. Designed by psychologists for home use, sophisticated apparatus has been ingeniously simplified for your use. Kit includes 18 experiments (plus suggestions for many more). 30-page manual (5¼ x 8¼"); fish tank; insect maze; human maze; tachistoscope; perception discs and goggles. An excellent kit for teachers, students, experimental psychologists, and Science Fair participants. **No. 71,584 $13.75 Ppd.**

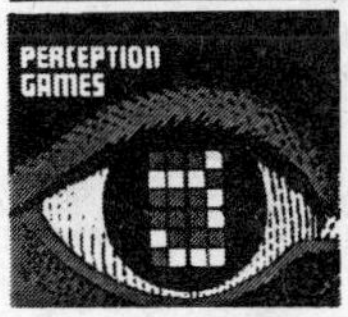

15 Perception Games

How good are you at seeing the overall view of things? These games improve your ability by making you think. Incl. 36 Perception cards, 6 ESP cards, 40 chips. **No. 71,162 $3.50 Ppd.**

360 Devices

Available Again! Now in Stock!

Holograms are true 3-D pictures taken by splitting a laser beam into two parts. One part is reflected from a mirror onto a high-resolution, photographic recording plate; the other is reflected from the subject onto the plate. Interference between the wavefronts of the two creates an image which shows incredible characteristics. When the recorded image is reconstructed, the subject is suspended in mid-air beyond or in front of the hologram and appears in true 3-D perspective. You can look around, over the top and under the subject and see all the details! The entire scene is recorded everywhere on the plate, while at no spot exclusively. Cut off a few areas of the plate, each piece will still contain the full scene. This can be done repeatedly.

Very Easy To See And Demonstrate

Reconstruct these holograms with light from a laser, 35mm projector, or high-intensity desk lamp and our included monochromatic filter. (Note: Reflection holograms do not require a filter and can even be viewed with a penlight.) When you look through the hologram the image appears in 3-D against a dark background. Change your angle of view by moving your head and the image also changes its perspective against the background. Instr. incl. for building viewing box and using 35mm projector as light source.

4 Types Available . . . 1/3 Off Regular Prices

Transmission Type (pictured) produces chessmen scene beyond the hologram.

Projected Image Type. Dinosaur scene is projected in front of the hologram.

Double Scene Type. 2 scenes; dinosaurs and geometric shapes recorded on same film. View them separately by rotating hologram 180°.

Reflection Type. Place light source in front of hologram (even penlight works). Scene of geometric shapes is reflected beyond hologram. Filter not required.

Type	Approx. size	Stock No.	Price Ppd.
Transmission-film	2½ x 4"	**41,090**	**$ 3.00**
Transmission-film	4 x 5"	**40,969**	**7.50**
Transmission-glass	4 x 5"	**40,984**	**20.00**
Transmission-film	8 x 10"	**60,687**	**30.00**
Proj. Image-film	2½ x 4"	**41,092**	**5.00**
Proj. Image-film	4 x 5"	**41,095**	**10.00**
Dbl. Scene-film	2½ x 4"	**41,091**	**5.00**
Dbl. Scene-film	4 x 5"	**41,094**	**10.00**
Reflection-glass	4 x 5"	**41,093**	**20.00**

Precision Mirrors For Making Holograms

Aluminized optical flats with guaranteed accuracies of .000005" (1/5 wave) and .000002" (1/10 wave) or better. Also use in telescopes, siderostats, coelostats, etc. Individually cased. Instr. incl.

Dia.	Thick. ±	Wave	Stock No.	Price, Ppd
2"	1/2"	1/10	**1920**	**$42.00**
3	5/8	1/10	**1921**	**66.00**
2	1/2	1/5	**1923**	**24.00**
3	5/8	1/5	**1924**	**42.00**

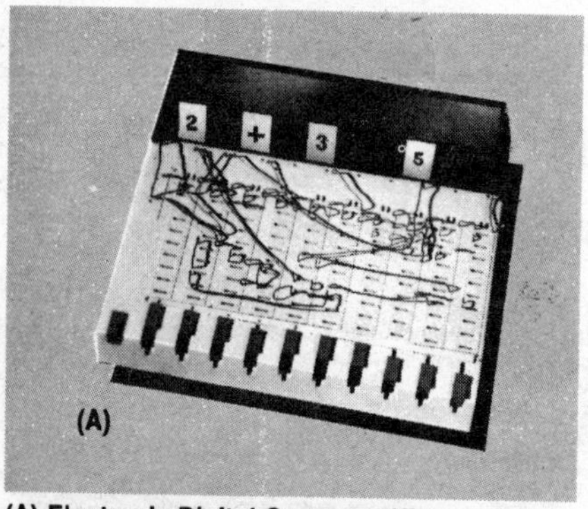

(A)

(A) Electronic Digital Computer Kit

You build it; program it; learn from it! Perform 39 fascinating experiments—play computer casino, predict weather, diagnose illness symptoms, solve mysteries, test intelligence, try to "outwit" it, even play miniature chess with it. Readout from illuminated control panel. Includes everything needed except 2 "D" size batteries. 11 x 12½ x 4". Informative instruction book leads you step-by-step. For ages 10 and up.

No. 71,434 $31.50 Ppd.

Make Positive Transparencies From Negatives In Less Than 2 Minutes . . .

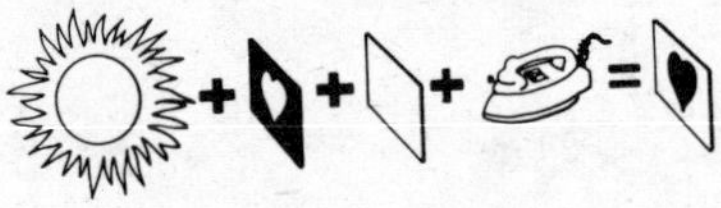

No messy chemicals, special equipment, darkroom or complicated procedures. All you need is a sunny day, warm iron, and Kalvar® heat-developing film to turn your negatives into positives with resolution as high as 400 lines/mm. You can get top quality b&w positives from b&w or color negatives. Great for examining negative contrast, discerning images in color negatives, making special-effect transparencies (multiple exposures are easy), fast and inexpensive duplicating of positives, rough intermediate b&w negatives from color transparencies. Using the sun (500w projector takes a few seconds longer), expose the film through your negative (a positive transparency will produce a negative which in turn produces another positive). Exposure time about 1 minute. Then simply press an iron (set at "synthetic") over film (or dip film in boiling water). Develops in about 2 seconds. Available in sheet and roll form. Instr. Incl. **Two 59" long x 35mm-wide rolls** (unperforated; enough for 72 35 mm frames total)

No. P-41,348 $3.75 Ppd.

2 pkgs., 24 sheets ea. (2¼" sq.) **No. P-41,349 $3.75 Ppd.**

12 Quality Hardwood Puzzles

Here is a brainteasing assortment of wood puzzles tha will provide hours and hours of pleasure. Included ar 12 different puzzles . . . animals and geometric form to take apart and reassemble. Special design gives th whole family a chance to test their skill, patience, an most important of all, their ability to think and reaso while having fun. Excellent amusement for recuperatin youngsters. **No. 70,205 $6.75 Ppd**

Set of 6 of above puzzles. **No. P-71,515 $4.10 Ppd**

Bio-Feedback Training Instruments

For Monitoring Signals Coming From The Brain, Heart, and Sympathetic Nervous System.

What is Bio-Feedback?—*This is the exciting new field based upon the use of sensitive electronic instruments allowing us to observe what goes on within our complex bodies.*

How do we measure the feedback?—*Many electrochemical activities occur in the body and can be detected by using certain devices. In the brain, many wave forms have been recorded and classified into specific shapes and rhythms. The most common are Alpha waves (found when you are totally relaxed) and Theta waves (occurring most during creative moods).*

Why would we want to measure these waves?—*It is now known that states of organs in the body, previously believed to be self-regulating, are subject to voluntary control by the individual when monitored through external equipment. By measuring and through training, some voluntary control can be obtained in varying alpha and theta brain waves. Many believe control of these waves can lead to total relaxation, improved memory, and concentration. These units which we have selected after much research, are great for laboratory, classroom, or just plain fun. All are completely safe and simply receive signals without implanting electrodes in the body. Regardless of your desire, we assure you many pleasant, interesting, and safe experiences with these fine instruments.*

Bio-Feedback Trainer — This lightweight instrument combines brain wave, heart rate, and skin resistance feedback in one package. Head electrodes hooked to a high gain amplifier allow brain waves to be filtered, signaling an audible beep for each Alpha or Theta wave passed. Most can learn to control Alpha rhythm in 10 to 12 hours. Wrist and finger contact electrodes pick up heartbeat and skin response which is reproduced as an audible tone. Complete with head, wrist, and finger electrodes. threshold control, and conducting solution. Size: 6¼ x 3¾ x 2". Wt. 2 lb.

No. 71,606 $120.00 Ppd.

EMOTION METER . . . TELLS ALL

Lie Detector Type Device Really Works!

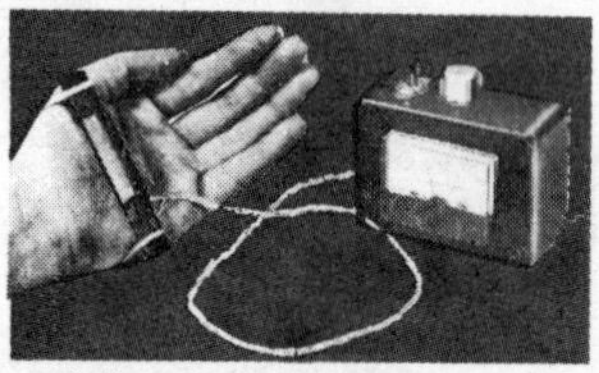

Test your friends, relatives, co-workers, or classmates . . . find out what their hidden likes or dislikes are! The Emotion Meter (a transistorized electronic device) measures changes in body resistance caused by changes in a person's emotional state. It indicates these changes on an easy-to-read 50-microampere meter. The needle movement only indicates an emotional response, not whether it is favorable or unfavorable. Easy to use, this amazing instrument is both sensitive and accurate, but its effectiveness depends upon the questions asked and the interpretation of the meter response by the user. This unusual item is perfect for entertainment and educational purposes. Great for parties, science projects, psychological experiments, and tests on the reactions of plants and animals to various stimuli. Plastic case: 2-7/8 x 4 x 1¾" overall, with: on/off switch; sensitivity control; "skin contact" bar; 1½-ft. bar cord; and instructions with suggested uses and games. Includes long-lasting 9v battery. Wt.: 10 oz. It's a fine product that provides plenty of fun and insight.

No. 41,422 $17.75 Ppd.

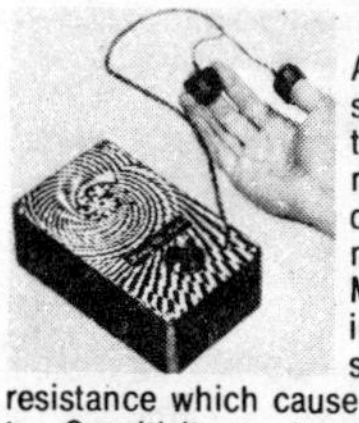

Hang Up Meter . . . Audio

A high pitched tone gives your secrets away every time! Similar to scientific "psychogalvanometers" used for years by psychologists to learn about the nervous system, The "Hang Up" Meter audibly measures changes in skin resistance. Changes in stimuli mean changes in skin resistance which cause changes in pitch from the meter. Sensitivity can be adjusted for a wide range of individual differences in skin resistance. 12-pg. booklet contains 10 different psychological experiments incl. word association, lie detector tests, and self awareness and control. Plastic case (2-1/8 x 3¾ x 6¼") with sensitivity control: 2 "finger-contact" pieces; and 2½-ft. cord.

No. 71,738 $29.75 Ppd.

U-FILM

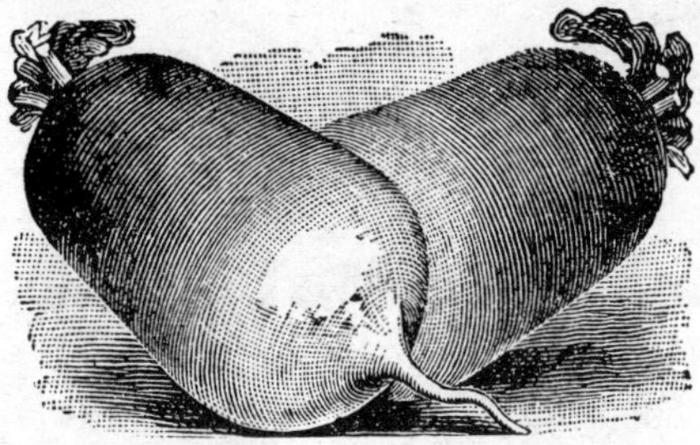

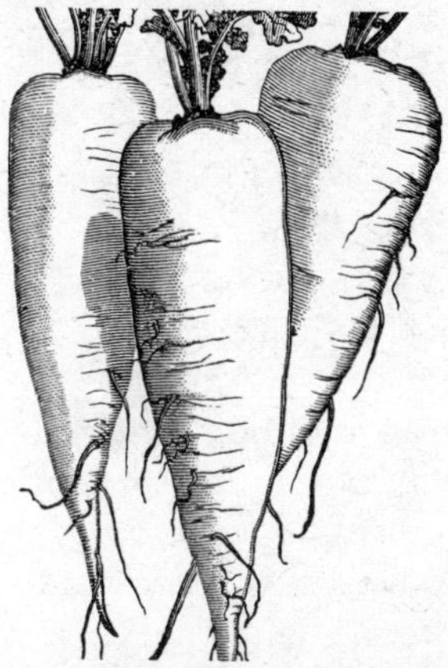

WRITE! TYPE! DRAW YOUR OWN FILMSTRIPS WITH "U" FILM.

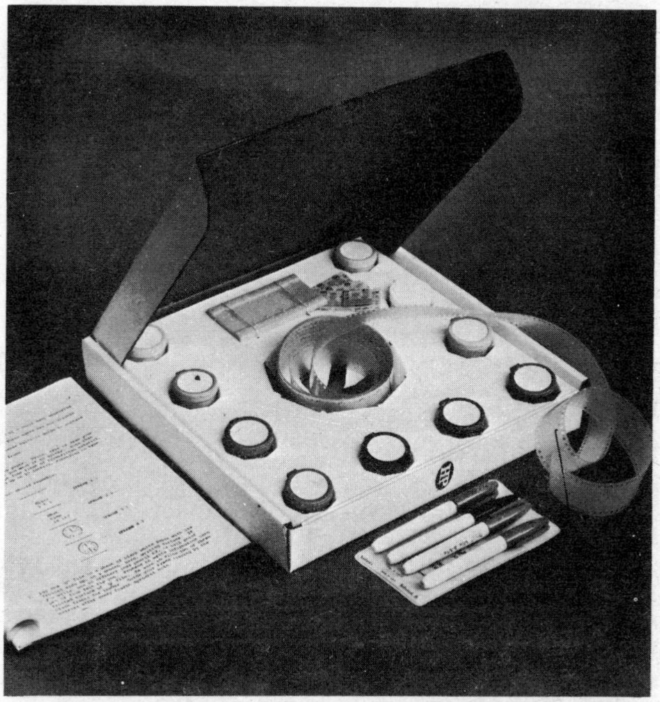

The "U" Film* Kit enables anyone to create his own filmstrip quickly, easily and without any special equipment. The uses are endless: teaching, in-service training, presentations. They can be made to meet specific needs in language arts, science, math, art; or to suit any teaching or training situation.

"U" Film can be used to add specific information to existing filmstrips. How often have you wished that there were a few more frames that would make your point or include your reinforcement material.

"U" Film can be used for greater student involvement by having them create their own filmstrips. It encourages self-expression after a particular activity or in making reports. It can involve the gifted child and the difficult child equally in the dimension of a new medium.

"U" Film is standard 35mm filmstrip material that has a specially treated blank surface on which you can write, draw or type as you would on paper. If a change is necessary or you make a mistake, you can erase what you've done and reuse the same area.

"U" Film is inexpensive (a 32 frame filmstrip costs less than 60¢), easy to use and works with any filmstrip projector.

"U" Film* Kit (Stock No. 9901) .... User Net $13.00

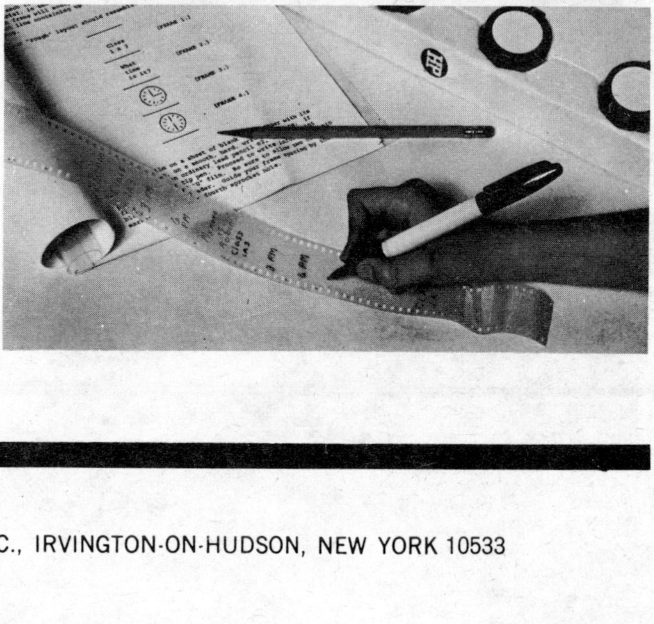

Consists of:

- 25-foot roll of "U" Film (there are 16 frames per foot of film).
- Colored Marker
- 10 Plastic Storage Cans
- 10 Blank Can Labels
- One Quik Splice* Filmstrip Splicer Block and Splicing Tapes (for joining "U" Film to your existing filmstrips)
- One complete Applications Manual

Large rolls of "U" Film* are available in:

25 foot roll (Stock No. 9902) only $ 6.60 user net
100 foot roll (Stock No. 9906) only $19.80 user net
1000 foot roll (Stock No. 9905) only $98.00 user net

INEXPENSIVE CAMERAS FOR GROUP OR CLASS USE

Imperial Camera Corporation has a *Model 900* camera with fixed focus. The camera uses Kodak 126 film cartridges that take 12 black-and-white or color prints or 20 color slides. The camera does use a flashcube, and batteries are required. In a minimum order of 48 cameras the cost is only $3.50 per camera. Imperial has other inexpensive cameras from $5 - $20 each in quantities.

IMPERIAL CAMERA CORPORATION
421 North Western Avenue
Chicago, Ill. 60612
(312) 829-2424

900 CAMERA

An easy-to-use camera designed for mass sales. Features drop-in cartridge film loading, fixed focus (no lens settings), uses flashcube for indoor shots. Cannot double expose. Simplicity of operation creates many snapshooters regardless of age. Uses Kodak 126 film that takes 12 black-and-white or color prints, or 20 color slides. The ideal camera to generate sales on film, flashcubes, batteries, processing.

STOCK NO. 900 — Suggested List Price **$7.50*** (LESS CUBE)

The *Diana Camera* has been used successfully by many schools even with very young children. The camera has an "instant" and "bulb" shutter speed, 3 f-stop settings, and three focus settings. Minimum order is a carton of 72 cameras for $47.52 (plus freight), which works out to 66¢ per camera. Flash attachments are $46.08 for a case of 144 (or 32¢ each). A carton of 100 rolls of #120 film is only $35.

POWER SALES COMPANY
Box 113
Willow Grove, Pa. 19090

Visual Motivations distributes the *Snapshooter* camera to schools. The *Snapshooter* has only one control and no flash capacity. The advantage here is that Visual Motivations has a film club, provides cheap film and processing, and gives tips to teachers on teaching methods with the camera. Of the three companies listed here Visual Motivations is the one most aware of the educational potential of the cameras they sell.

VISUAL MOTIVATIONS COMPANY
44 Mary Watersford Road
Bala-Cynwyd, Pa. 19004
(215) 934-6777

Made in U.S.A.

ꞏKAGE NO. SP
ludes Camera, Wrist Strap,
126 Snapshooter Black-and-
te Film Cartridge.
t: Quantity Less Than 25,
$2.00 Each. 25 or Over @
$1.50 Each.

PACKAGE NO. SPB
"BUILD-YOUR-OWN" CAMERA KIT—Includes Camera Parts Unassembled, Easy-To-Follow Instructions, and 126 Snapshooter Black-and-White Film Cartridge.
Cost: Quantity Less Than 25, $2.00 Each. 25 or Over @ $1.50 Each.

Just snap any 126 Film Cartridge onto back of camera and get clear, sharp pictures. Snapshooter is made here in the U.S.A. and takes color, slide film, and black-and-white.

126 Black and White Film Cartridges. Minimum Quantity — 30 Cartridges @ .40 Cents Each.

126 Color Negative (Print) Film Cartridges. Minimum Quantity — 10 Cartridges @ .80 Cents Each.

SNAPSHOOTER FILM is Kodak Compatible and can be processed anywhere.

KAGE NO. CMBS
Contained Package Consists
ne SP Kit, One SPB Kit and
(4) - 126 B/W Film Car-
es.
Students Can Work on Three
rent Projects or Six Students
Work on One Project Each.
for Economy Minded Edu-
s. Cost: $5.00 (No Minimum
tity Required).

PACKAGE NO. SFPM
For your students Slide and Film Presentations. FUJI-126—20 Exposure Color Slide Film with Processing Included @ $2.49 Each. (Minimum Quantity 6 Cartridges.) Just shoot and mail to nearest city listed on pre-paid mailer.

364 Devices

Visual Motivations Company

44 Mary Watersford Road • Bala-Cynwyd, Pennsylvania 19004 1–(215)–934–6777

SIX (6) EXCITING NEW PACKAGES FROM SNAPSHOOTER

ECONOMICALLY PRICED FOR THE EDUCATOR WHO DOES NOT HAVE DARKROOM EQUIPMENT OR WHO WISHES TO USE COLOR PRINT & SLIDE FILMS.

1. CAMERA AND BLACK & WHITE FILM WITH DEVELOPING & PRINTING INCLUDED (1 PRINT EACH) # SPFP - $ 3.00 EA.

2. "BUILD-IT-YOURSELF" CAMERA AND BLACK & WHITE FILM WITH DEVELOPING AND PRINTING INCLUDED (1 PRINT EACH) # SPBFP - $ 3.00 EA.

3. CAMERA AND FUJI COLOR PRINT FILM WITH DEVELOPING AND PRINTING INCLUDED (1 PRINT EACH) # SPCFP - $ 3.95 EA.

4. "BUILD-IT-YOURSELF" CAMERA AND FUJI COLOR PRINT FILM WITH DEVELOPING & PRINTING INCLUDED (1 PRINT EACH) # SPBCFP - $ 3.95 EA.

5. 126 BLACK & WHITE FILM - 12 EXPOSURE - WITH DEVELOPING & PRINTING INCLUDED (1 PRINT EACH) MINIMUM ORDER 10 # BWFP - $ 1.50 EA.

6. 12 EXPOSURE FUJI COLOR PRINT FILM WITH DEVELOPING & PRINTING INCLUDED (1 PRINT EACH) # 126 MINIMUM ORDER 10 # CPFP - $ 2.79 EA.

PLUS - 20 EXPOSURE FUJI 126 COLOR SLIDE FILM WITH PROCESSING INCLUDED MINIMUM ORDER 6 # SFPM - $ 2.49 EA.

CASH WITH ORDER - SHIPPED PREPAID
BILLING ON OPEN ACCOUNT - SHIPPED FOB PHILA.

AT A MINIMUM OF EXPENSE YOU CAN SUPPLEMENT YOUR VISUAL LITERACY PROGRAM. HAVE YOUR YOUNGSTERS TAKE THE PICTURES AND LEAVE THE PROCESSING TO US.

IN-PLANT PROCESSING TIME IS 48 TO 72 HOURS. ALL FILM RECEIVED IN A GROUP PACKAGE WILL BE PROCESSED AND RETURNED VIA UPS OR PP SPEC DEL.. ALL INDIVIDUAL FILM PROCESSING ORDERS WILL BE RETURNED VIA 3RD CLASS MAIL.

VISUAL MOTIVATIONS COMPANY IS DEDICATED TO --

"BETTER LEARNING THROUGH PHOTOGRAPHY"

EMOTIONOMETER

Emotionometer. . . .In psychology, guidance or even in the study of responses to literature an understanding of the nature of emotions and feelings is essential. A memorable way to demonstrate that emotions are physical events that are both observable and measurable is to bring to class a galvanic skin response detector. A GSR meter measures the change in the body's ability to conduct electricity caused by chemical changes that accompany emotions.

With a GSR meter experiments can be conducted to show that attempts to lie, loud noises and emotion charged words produce a real physical change. One convincing experiment is to attach the meter to a volunteer and use it to register responses to a list of words. The needle on the meter will invariably jump at the mention of words that are important to the volunteer and will remain steady in the presence of meaningless words. The GSR is one of the primary responses measured by a lie detector.

Even the best meter will work only sometimes--the more trials the more accurate the findings. Probably the best on the market is sold by BRS Foringer, 5451 Holland Drive, Beltsville, Md. 20705 for around $60. I have used the BRS Foringer GSR monitor and have found it satisfactory in operation and of great interest to students.

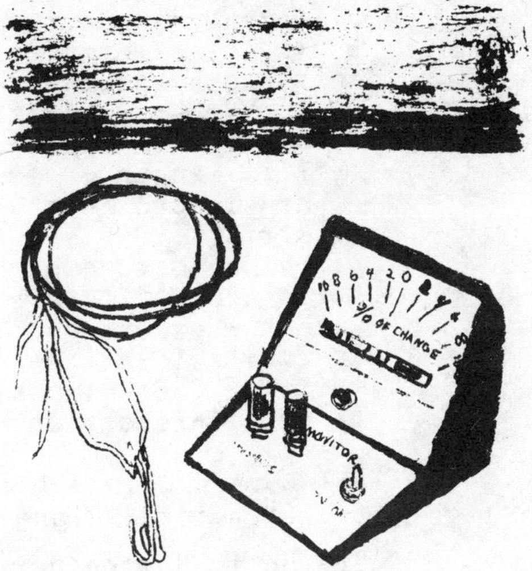

Edmund Scientific has one for $17.75 postpaid (catalog number 41,422- - they call it an emotion meter). Another untested model sells for $29.95 (called a "Lie Detector") from Sonic Devices, Inc., 69-29 Queens Blvd., Woodside, NY 11377.

BURTON HARPSICHORD KIT

The Burton Harpsichord is a finely crafted do-it-yourself kit very reasonably priced between $200 and $650. Information from:

HERBERT WM BURTON HARPSICHORDS
Box 80222
Lincoln, Nebr. 68501
(402) 477-1001

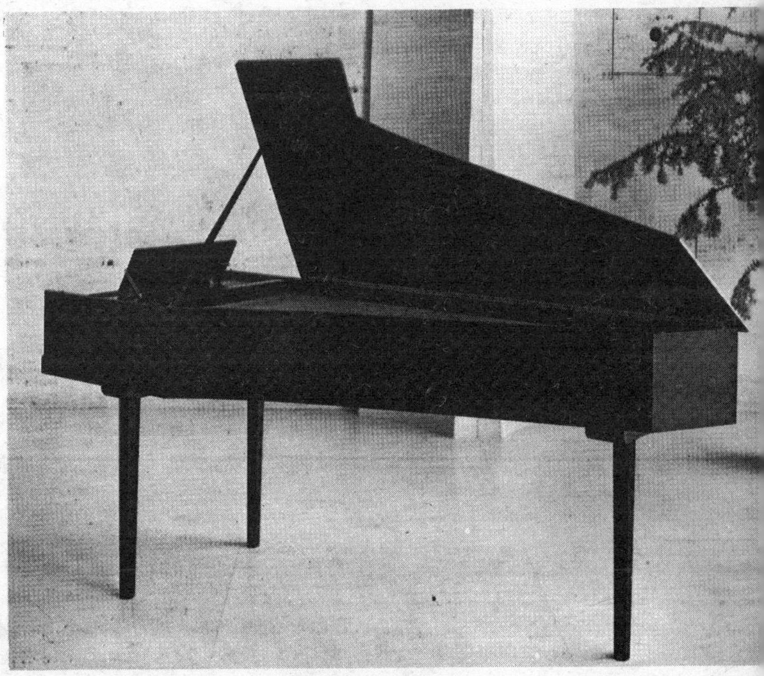

SOME GENERAL INFORMATION

The Burton Harpsichord Kits are available in three different dispositions: the 8', the 8'x8', and the 8'x4'. (The terms 8', 8'x4', etc., does not mean that the harpsichord is eight feet long or four feet wide. Rather, that the instrument has a pitch corresponding to a pipe organ whose pipes are eight feet in length or four feet in length. For example, a harpsichord in the 8'x4' disposition has two sets of strings. One set sounds 8' pitch, the other 4' pitch, an octave higher than the 8'). All Burton Harpsichord Kits are designed with an Angled side, with the exception of our 8'x4' harpsichord, which is available with either Angled or Bent side. Details of each disposition follows this section of general information.

All Burton Harpsichord Kit models are available in two forms: BASIC and COMPLETE.

The Basic Burton Harpsichord Kits are for the person with a good knowledge of woodworking. Included in Burton Basic Harpsichord Kits, are all parts not easily obtained locally... keyboard, strings, soundboard, tuning pins, etc. The woods for the case of the harpsichord must be selected and cut by the builder according to the detailed plans and specifications included in the Basic Kit Instruction Manuals. Common nails and screws found in all hardware stores must also be purchased by the Basic Kit builder.

Complete Burton Harpsichord Kits include everything needed to complete a Burton Harpsichord Kit (except a few common tools and liquid finishing materials). In addition to the wooden case parts, which have been precisely cut and fitted by the cabinet makers of Burton Harpsichords (working in our shop--absolutely no work is "farmed" out of our shop, allowing for rigid quality control), such items as an x-acto knife, emery boards, glue, sandpaper, etc., are also included.

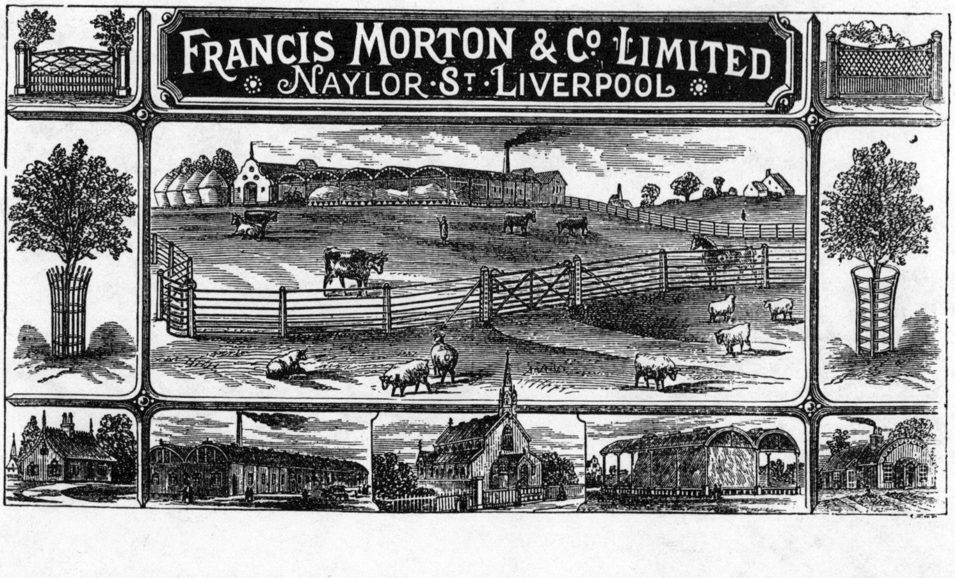

DOME EAST

me *Kit 1* is a Bucky Fuller version
plastic Tinker Toys. With the
me Kit you can construct over 15
dels illustrating geodesic concepts.
e Kit contains the 20-page *Dome*
scovery handbook, plastic hubs, and
oden struts.

In addition to the *Dome Kit 1*,
me East also has for sale a Green-
me (advertised as "the perfect green-
use), and various other domes that
n be used for storage, covering a
imming pool, or even for a shelter.

Dome Kit 1 is $4.75 each. Other
mes range up to over $10,000. For
formation write:

DOME EAST CORPORATION
325 Duffy Avenue
Hicksville, N.Y. 11801
(516) 938-0500

A beautiful, fully erected Greendome geodesic greenhouse is ready and waiting for you to start enjoying your gardening in complete comfort and protection in any season.

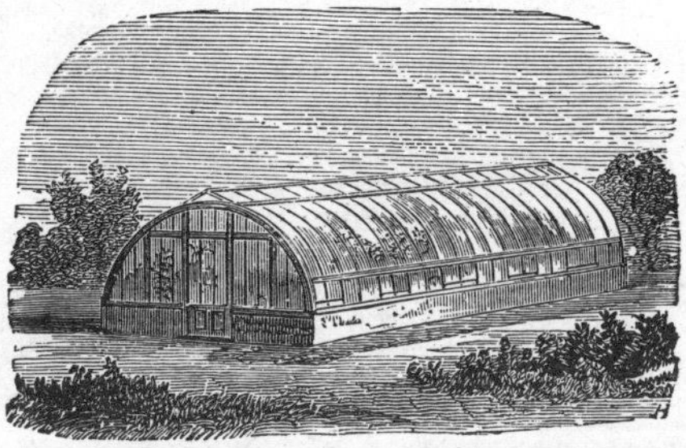

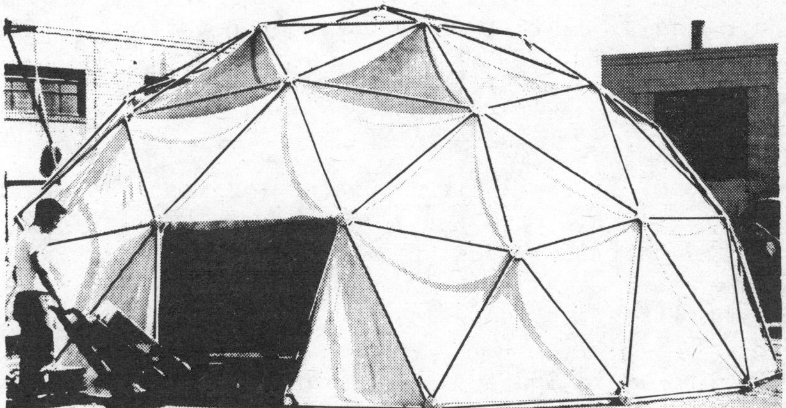

SHELTERDOME 30 warehouse is a quick addition to your expanding storage needs.

SPECIFICATION OF SHELTERDOME 45

DOME EAST corporation

DIAMETER: 45 feet

HEIGHT: 17 feet at center

VOLUME: 20,000 cubic feet

WEIGHT: under 1500 lbs.

MATERIALS: 190 struts of aluminum pipe, 400 yards of vinyl, dacron material

COST: Less than $10,000 which includes heating, lighting and ventilating systems.

The New York Botanical Gardens, in their new expansion and modernization program, found they needed additional classroom space in a hurry. DOME EAST'S SHELTERDOME series of geodesic domes provided just the structure needed at a price in line with their budget. Mr. John Reed, Director of Educational Services, at the N.Y. Botanical Gardens has discovered that the 45 foot SHELTERDOME is ideally suited to their education program. "The dome has no pillars or posts to hinder movement or sight. The high arching ceiling and translucent walls give a pleasant feeling of openess while we conduct classes and growing experiments." Some of the classes conducted in the dome include: "Indoor Plantscaping", "Horticulture for industrial Arts", "Terrariums, Bottle and Dish Gardens", "Fundamentals of Ferning", "How to Grow House Plants".

The New York Botanical Gardens has already ordered two additional SHELTERDOMES to be used as exhibit areas during renovation of existing facilities. These domes will be relocated later and used as greenhouses.

ABOUT THE NASA STUDY: One of the features which makes SHELTERDOME timely and different is that it is designed through the utilization of a computer program which was first written for geodesic dome enclosures on the moon: "Advanced Structural Design Concepts of Future Space Missions" (March 1970 NASA Contract 14-008-002). The structural analysis of this classroom-dome was generated through the use of the ICES STRUDL II computer program, developed at Massachusetts Institute of Technology. (ICES/STRUDL II = Integrated Civil Engineering System Structural Design Language)

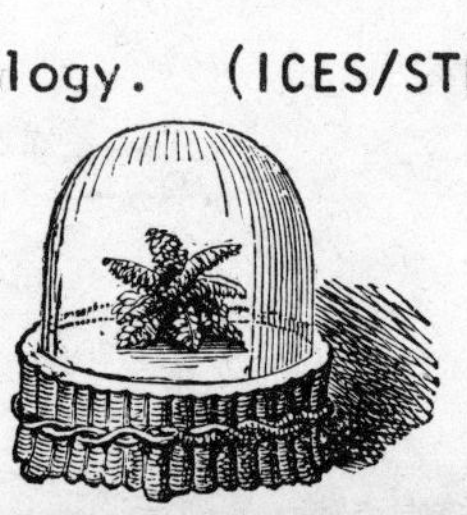

ZOMETOY — ZOMEWORKS

ZOMETOY

zomeworks corporation
p.o. box 712
albuquerque, new mexico 87103
(505) 242-5354

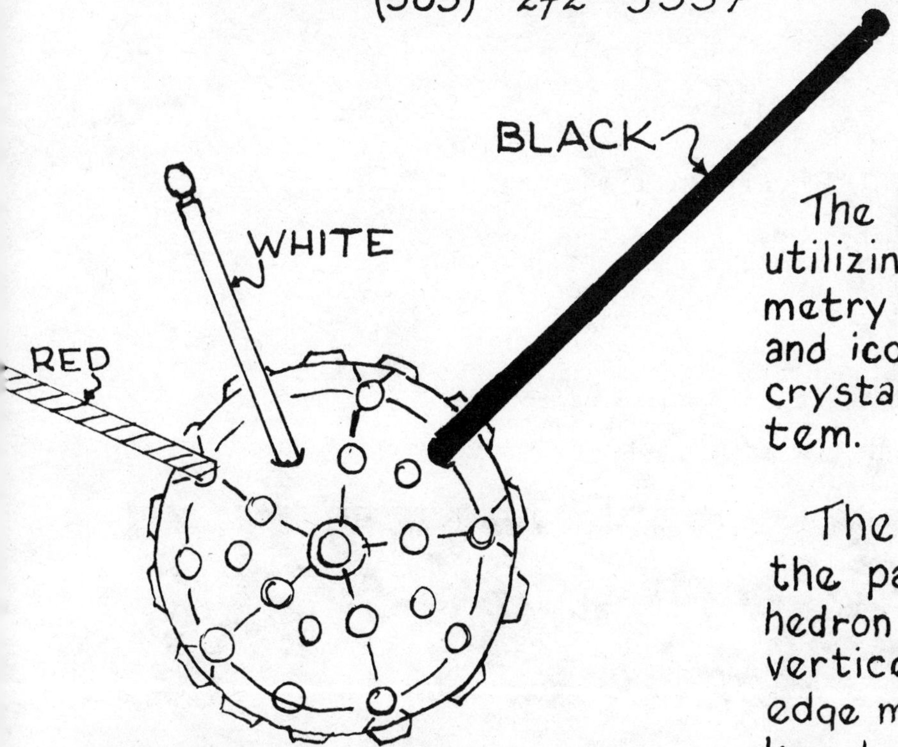

u.s. patent no. 3722153

RED sticks pop in vertices
BLACK sticks along lines (edge midpoints)
WHITE sticks in centers

Sticks of the same color are in the divine portion (which means that with three different length sticks in the series, the long one will be equal in length to the sum of the middle and short one.)

The ZOMETOY involves utilizing the five-fold symmetry of the dodecahedron and icosahedron for a novel crystal-like structural system.

The connector follows the pattern of the icosahedron, with holes at the vertices, face midpoints and edge midpoints. This is the key to the structural system.

TRIANGLES ARE NECESSARY FOR STABILITY.

POSSIBLE ANGLES ARE DISCUSSED IN ZOME PRIMER

DETAILS OF STRUCTURAL SYSTEM EXPLAINED AND ILLUSTRATED IN ZOME PRIMER.

PRICE LIST AND ORDER FORM

#101 - ZOMETOY SAMPLER KIT - includes; instruction sheet .... $ 15.00
15 connectors
71 #3 sticks (red, white, black)
35 #2 sticks (red, white, black)

#103 - LARGE ZOMETOY KIT*- includes; Zome Primer, ... 100.00
all sizes of sticks in all
three colors, hand made wooden
carrying case. 901 pcs.

#107 - DOUBLE ZOMETOY KIT*- includes; same as #103, 1801 pcs.... 150.00

#111 - EXTRA PLASTIC CONNECTORS - package of 10 .... 3.50

#113 - EXTRA #4 STICKS (longest stick) 3.50
15 black sticks
10 red sticks
10 white sticks

#117 - EXTRA #3 STICKS - includes; same numbers as #113 .... 3.50

#119 - EXTRA #2 STICKS - includes; same numbers as #113 .... 3.50

#123 - EXTRA #1 STICKS (shortest stick) includes; 3.50
same numbers as #113.

#127 - ZOME PRIMER - An elementary explanation of the 3.00
geometry of zonohedra and the 31
zone star on which the ZOMETOY is
based.

Index

The letter preceding page numbers in this index denotes the section in which the reference will be found and in most cases the kind of medium it is. For example, "America: f/205" indicates a film entitled America found on page 205.

Key:

b = Publication section
o = Organizations
p = Periodicals
a = Audio
f = Films
v = Video
g = Games
m = Multi-Media
d = Devices